Books by Perla Meyers

Perla Meyers' From Market to Kitchen Cookbook

The Peasant Kitchen

The Seasonal Kitchen

Perla Meyers'
From Market to Kitchen
Cookbook

Perla Meyers'
From Market
to Kitchen
Cookbook

Harper & Row, Publishers

NEW YORK

Cambridge
Hagerstown
Philadelphia
San Francisco

1817

London
Sydney
São Paulo
Mexico City

Design and Photography: Pentagram

**Library of Congress Cataloging in
Publication Data**
Meyers, Perla.
Perla Meyers' from market to kitchen
cookbook.
1. Cookery. 2. Marketing (Home economics)
I. Title. II. Title: Market-to-kitchen
cookbook.
TX715.M626   1979   641.3
78–20178
ISBN 0–06–013033–4

80 81 82 83 10 9 8 7 6 5 4 3 2

**To Bob,
Claude, and my mother
for their love,
support, and encouragement**

Contents

Acknowledgments

Although sincere thanks are owed to many people, in particular the many marvelous chefs who contributed their skills and knowledge to the making of this book, certain people deserve particular mention: *Janet Schlesinger* and *Michael di Benedetto,* for their spirited and painstaking thoroughness in testing the recipes; *Paula Singer* and *Sally Placksen,* for editorial support; and *Colin Forbes* and *Dan Friedman,* for their imaginative and practical design of the book. I would especially like to thank *Roger Straus* for his invaluable support.

Many thanks are also owed to the many wonderful shops and markets throughout the country who helped me with the shopping information—in particular, Mr. Nicholas D'Agostino of D'Agostino Supermarkets; Macy's Marketplace; Oscar Bell of the Empire Produce Market; Mr. Friedmann of the Akron Butcher Shop; Mr. Robert Newman of the Rosedale Fish Market; Raffetto's Pasta Shop; and Dean and Deluca.

Introduction

One day several years ago, I asked a group of my students to go out and buy the ingredients for that day's class. We had decided on a fall menu: a simple velouté soup made with a seasonal vegetable, a sauté of chicken, and poached pears for dessert. The marketing list was fairly simple, and contained nothing very exotic. But when the class returned and unpacked their purchases, I discovered—much to my surprise—that even the simplest shopping list calls for knowledge and a discerning eye. They had brought back vegetables that were past their prime, limp celery, pears that were both underripe and bruised, chicken that had already been cut up in the market; as for the basics, they had selected salted butter and oil labeled simply "salad oil." I quickly realized that my students—all of whom were interested in food and had taken several cooking classes already—lacked basic shopping know-how. They were willing to settle for the convenience of getting everything in one market rather than take the time to explore and search for the perfect ingredient in another shop. I quickly backtracked, explaining that proper shopping is the first and most crucial step in learning how to cook well. To this day, in addition to teaching the techniques and preparation of certain dishes, I find myself spending much of my time introducing students to the how-to's and where-to's of buying basic quality ingredients.

To my mind, knowledge of one's ingredients is really the basic factor that determines a good cook. No matter how creative a cook you are, you will always be handicapped in the kitchen by mediocre ingredients. Since I am involved in the preparation of food all the time, I am naturally more selective than many people, and spend a great deal of time shopping for the right ingredient. I try to let every market inspire me, whether it is a corner supermarket, a roadside farmer's stand, or an exciting and unusual specialty shop. (By specialty shop, I am not referring to the chic, overpriced gourmet store, cheese shop, or bakery, but a small store that specializes in good meat, fish, produce, coffees, spices, or ethnic foods.) I refuse to consider marketing "just going out to get some groceries." I am a firm believer that being a "food person" means loving every aspect of the food experience, from the moment you enter the supermarket to the time you choose the right cheese, fruit, or wine.

There is always so much involved in creating the *total* food picture. No matter how you look at it, cooking requires time and effort. Despite what many cookbooks tell you, there is no room for gimmickry in the preparation of a first-rate dish. Gaining an understanding of what quality is all about, and learning to savor and appreciate every ingredient—simple or exotic—will bring you that much closer to preparing a truly wonderful meal.

The quest for quality ingredients is exactly what this cookbook is about. My first two books, *The Seasonal Kitchen* and *The Peasant Kitchen,* were based on my belief that fresh foods and in-season ingredients are essential to the success of good cooking, and both books focused on how to work with them in the kitchen. Because marketing has always been such a natural part of my own life, I assumed that everyone who cared about food knew how to buy it properly. But my students' shopping experience made me realize that when I talked about each dish, I had to start at the *beginning*—and at the beginning, there is the market. I decided to write this book in order to help people who love and care about food to find the best ingredients, and to show them that marketing can be a rich, wonderful, and exciting experience, not just another item on a long list of chores.

Although the art of buying food carefully is familiar to most Europeans, particularly in the countries where real markets still thrive, selective marketing is simply not a part of the American shopping tradition today. As I observe people here filling their shopping carts with processed and frozen foods, I am always chagrined at the lack of knowledge and appreciation that characterizes the marketing habits of many Americans. All cooks will, of course, in time develop their own marketing habits, based on how much time they have, how much they care, and the local availability of good, fresh ingredients. But before settling into a shopping routine and making one store a habit, it is essential for you to consider and learn the basics of proper marketing. Once these are mastered, you can then determine where you consistently get the best meat, fish, dairy products, fresh produce, and

staples to stock your pantry. I cannot challenge the convenience of the supermarket one-stop shop, particularly for working women who have large families to feed and may be pressed for time. But I still believe a distinction should be made (as it is in Europe) between what I consider supermarket "staples" and other items such as fresh meat, fish, and produce, which I feel it is advisable to buy in smaller specialty shops.

It may seem tedious and time-consuming to take so much care in selecting the raw materials for a meal. I am often asked, "What is it about food that you find so exciting?" I have never really examined my feelings about food in depth, because I have always been naturally delighted by the different colors, textures, tastes, regional origins, seasons, and versatility of food. I love the endless combinations, the variations on different cuisines of the world. I look forward to going to my favorite butcher shop, fish market, and produce stand each week, anticipating the seasonal offerings: paintbrush-thin asparagus, local strawberries, salmon, and shad in the spring; the bonanza of fresh fruits and vegetables in summer; firm, crisp apples and decorous squash in the fall; winter's prime citrus fruits, tiny sweet bay scallops, and mussels. I feel that I will never be able to learn all there is to know about food. There is always something new to invent, and cooking keeps me creative as I continue to experiment with new combinations of textures and flavors.

I suppose this lifelong interest in food really began when I was growing up in Spain. While my mother was an astute and careful shopper who scanned the entire market before settling down to buy anything, it was my father who really *loved* food, and thrived in the extraordinary bustle and vitality of the market. Every Saturday morning, the two of us would set out with a warning from my mother not to buy too much. I can still remember my father winking at me and the sense of excitement we shared in discovering an unusual fruit, a new cheese, or pastry. He always reminded me that markets were *special,* and so were the people who cared about food. He had a wonderful relationship with many of the local shopkeepers, who were always on the lookout for us, waiting to greet us warmly and urging us to sample their cheeses, sausages, or fruits. They were generous and full of good humor, and we were eager to chat and taste their delicious morsels. It was the kind of mutual respect that exists only between the small shopkeeper and an appreciative customer.

After the inevitable "gourmand" shopping spree, my father and I would settle down at a sidewalk café right at the entrance of Barcelona's Boqueria Market and nibble shiny black olives and the usual assortment of *tapas,* the Spanish hors d'oeuvres served on small, oval plates—chewy marinated baby squid, some pickled sardines, and slices of spicy chorizo sausage. This was an equally important part of the marketing ritual, after which we made our last two stops—one at the flower stand, and last but

not least at the pastry shop. Spanish pastries have never been known for their quality and were certainly not too distinctive, but my father, with his Viennese sweet tooth, liked them nevertheless. He loved the glacéed fruits, particularly the glacéed chestnuts, which we would always sample right in the shop. By the time we came home, we unpacked an assortment of foods that never really made much sense, but would often force my father into the kitchen to come up with a spur-of-the-moment preparation for the whole basket of wild mushrooms or black currants we had not been able to resist buying that day. Many of the best meals at our house were those impromptu ones, and so much good humor was involved that when, inevitably, I was put to work shelling either peas or the first seasonal batch of fresh fava beans, it did not seem to be a chore.

Looking back on my childhood, I consider myself very lucky, for it was in this environment, surrounded by these respectful attitudes toward food, that I was taught to appreciate the simplest fare, whether it was a ripe peach, a steaming bowl of mussels, or a crisp spring radish simply dipped in butter and sprinkled with salt. It all contributed to my food education. The simple way of life exposed me to nearly every aspect of food, its cultivation, and preparation, and gave me a natural awareness and curiosity when it came to buying and preparing all kinds of ingredients and concoctions. Marketing was woven into the pattern of my life at an early age, and to this day I continue to explore every market, wherever I may be.

During my college days in Geneva, I again eagerly awaited Saturday mornings, anticipating a visit to the wonderful outdoor market that takes place twice a week in the old, picturesque part of town. Although the feeling of this spotless, picture-postcard market was so different from the one in Barcelona, it was the highlight of my week. My friends and I would meet at a small square that overlooked the steep, winding cobblestone streets, and we would savor all the wonderful sights and smells. As the sun rose, it revealed an army of neat farmers bustling to and from their small vans, which overflowed with local produce. The small tables set up for the day were crowded and piled high with pungent mountain cheeses, baskets of fresh eggs, country hams, and gutsy homemade terrines. Tiny mounds of fresh goat cheese at various stages of ripeness had a distinct and wonderful aroma that combined with the smokiness of the superb Swiss mountain sausages.

As we strolled past the stalls filled with brightly colored fruits, vegetables, and flowers, the narrow streets of the old town echoed with the sounds of people and animals and was as festive as a carnival. It was a feast for *all* the senses, not just the palate. We looked at everything but stopped only occasionally, to buy a tiny, steaming hot cheese tart, a piece of fruit, or a slice of pâté. Part of my Saturday ritual was (as it always has been) to buy three or four fresh flowers for the small vase in my room. Then, at noon, it was suddenly over. The vans and trucks were reloaded, went along their way, and the old town resumed its peaceful character. Market day was at an end. My friends and I would fall into the chairs of one of the student cafés, where we unwrapped our treasures, ordered coffee and some wine, and started to nibble on cheese, sweets, a slice of pâté, in no particular order.

Last year, almost twenty years later, I was back in Geneva with my husband. It was a Saturday morning. When I realized the day, I suddenly felt the same rush of excitement and anticipation I had experienced as a student. I *had* to return to the marketplace to see if anything had changed. Once again, I fell entirely under its spell. Though we went not intending to shop, I found myself unable to resist. We left with loaves of bread under our arms, pears, cheese, and sausages wrapped in paper for a picnic lunch. Little, in fact, had changed since my student days: the tiny turnips still glowed with freshness, and the new radishes looked like bunches of bright rubies.

When I first came to America, understandably I found it very difficult to get used to the way people marketed here. But it wasn't long before I became adventurous and started to search out the best of what my new setting had to offer. I stopped trying to duplicate the flavor of the Mediterranean market, and came to appreciate the wide range of ingredients in

American markets for their own distinctive tastes and excitement, using my instinctive knowledge and traditional background to guide me.

What we have in the United States works for us in a different way from what I was used to in Europe. Here we have a mélange of everything from small specialty shops to open-air markets to giant supermarket complexes that seem almost like futuristic cities unto themselves. Thus we have a wide and wonderful range of shopping possibilities, if only we use them wisely. In a city like New York, for instance, there is a unique vibrancy and energy. A totally Italian market district rubs shoulders with the exotic and aromatic fish shops and produce stalls of Chinatown. Each cuisine has a vastly different style and philosophy, yet within a few-block range ingredients for both can be gotten. In the Italian groceries one can buy various kinds of mozzarella cheese, slabs of Parmesan, fresh spicy or sweet sausages, special pasta flour, and fruity olive oils. Then walk to Chinatown for special greens, fresh coriander, the best fresh ducks and the superb Oriental dried mushrooms. Second generation immigrants of many nationalities, in fact, have been inspired to open specialty food stores catering to their fellow countrymen's love of ethnic culinary tradition. Recently these stores have become known and patronized, not only by the ethnic population to which they cater, but by all people who enjoy cooking with foreign foods. In American cities more than anywhere else in the world,

you can find not only shops that serve one particular tradition, but stores where several cuisines are featured under one roof—such as a combination of Greek, Mediterranean, and Middle Eastern foods.

Of course, this great availability of ethnic specialty shops does not exist all over the country. But I have always found that all markets, wherever they may be around the United States, do make a personal statement about their environment and the people who live in the region. I remember vividly a farmer's market in a small Texas town. Trucks slowly pulled up in the faint light of dawn, and farmers dressed in overalls and huge ten-gallon hats ceremoniously opened up the backs of their vans to display their cargo—bushel baskets brimming with rosy peaches, tomatoes, and okra. Or the extraordinary Pike Market in Seattle. Here I found vendors displaying a spectacular array of crustaceans and shiny fresh salmon, along with the crispest vegetables, brilliant green and white leeks and baskets of jewel-red tomatoes. I walked along munching a warm, crusty loaf of sourdough bread, taking in the wonderful vitality of this great American market. I am continually amazed at the number of cities that still have markets, even where you least expect them. No matter where I am, when I approach a local resident asking, "Can you direct me to the market?" I find that they are always happy to show me, because I am interested in a source of local pride and pleasure. A market still thrives in their town!

It wasn't always this way. Only recently have markets in America undergone a new burst of life. The renaissance of simpler, traditional lifestyles, characterized by bread-baking, tending vegetable gardens, canning, and preserving, has led to a renewed interest in and greater patronage of open-air and specialty markets. In the midst of an increasingly technological society, people are seeking the solace of old traditions and are making an effort to preserve some of these elements in their daily twentieth-century lives. I also feel that with the increased interest in cooking—particularly ethnic cooking—people are returning to the markets so they can enjoy a more direct sense of the raw materials they are going to use. They are looking for excellence, and are willing to spend more time shopping for a variety of quality ingredients. Happily, because of this the existing small butcher shops, fish markets, and farmer's markets are growing stronger. They are being treated with new respect, admiration, and appreciation. Even people who have been supermarket oriented for years are venturing into these markets and specialty stores, both because of their atmosphere and their better quality.

When it comes to the small specialty shop, I believe that for every technological step society has made, that there are still those of us who will hang onto certain traditional amenities of life that make shopping a pleasure rather than a chore. At the butcher shop, fish market, cheese shop, or local produce stand, for example, it is possible to find character, individuality, and personalized attention. This special attention, showered on you by the people behind the counter (plus the superior quality of their foods) is what has made the specialty shop exist and retain its distinctive charm and flavor. How pleasant to enjoy a conversation with your butcher as he cuts your meat exactly the way you like it! And if you shop there, or at any other small shops regularly, proprietors will learn your tastes and soon be able to recommend or advise you based on their personal knowledge of *you*, their most important customer.

I am always surprised to hear how many people are actually intimidated by the idea of shopping in a small store. They prefer the anonymity of a supermarket. Perhaps they feel that they will be expected to buy something if they walk into a small shop, or that they will be scrutinized by the shopkeeper. Possibly, they are embarrassed to admit that they really don't understand what determines quality and are afraid to ask. But more than likely, the small storekeeper will respect you for asking questions and valuing quality, and more often than not will be flattered by the fact that you have acknowledged and tapped his expertise.

In America, however, the fact is that one is raised to think that the supermarket is less expensive and just as good, if not better than, the small market. To some extent, it is true that the supermarket can offer savings in time and money, and does offer the hurried shopper a quick overview of the basics available for cooking. But supermarket shopping also carries with it certain distinct shortcomings, and these must be understood, and a smart shopping routine worked out in order to make the best use of what the supermarket has to offer.

Not long ago, small markets were the only place to shop in this country. What is this strange animal called the supermarket? Where did it come from? Actually, the supermarket originated during the depression, when a handful of clever businessmen began buying food in large quantities at a discount, and sold it at reduced prices to consumers. Mass merchandising was remarkably successful, and supermarkets flourished, buying more food for less money, and selling it cheaper than the grocery stores. Skeptics predicted that with the passing of hard times the supermarket fad would fade. But as American society recovered and grew more affluent, supermarkets followed suit, expanding their selection of items, upgrading the quality of merchandise on the shelves, and improving their services and appearance. Today the average supermarket stocks an impressive array of about 12,000 different items. But if you know how to scan the miles of shelves in the supermarket's spacious aisles, you won't be overwhelmed.

First, you must realize that one doesn't need half of what one buys. The supermarket is notorious for inducing people to buy impulsively, straying from their carefully thought-out shopping list to bring home everything from new junk foods to the latest health food. As you wheel your cart up and down the aisles, you must ask yourself, "Do I really need this in my kitchen pantry? What's my marketing philosophy?" Everyone has one—it's as personal as the style of clothes you wear. Overlook the time-savers—frozen, processed, prepared, and "fun" foods. Search for well-priced, high-quality foods. The same rules apply to the supermarket as to the specialty store: No matter where you shop, do it with a discerning eye. If you're in the supermarket, be aware that there's a world outside. If you can't find *exactly* what you're after, step outside and search for it!

The greatest advantage of using the supermarket properly is that many of the basics are on hand at more reasonable prices than they would be in a small country store or corner grocery. And supermarkets, with their constant sales, do offer savings to the price-conscious consumer. Dairy products are without a doubt a good supermarket buy, as are rice, legumes, basic baking ingredients, flour, nuts, chocolate, and the all-season vegetables. But watch your step the minute you venture into purchasing any fresh foods —meat, fish, cheese, vegetables, and fruits.

Interestingly, even in Europe, the supermarket has become a growing phenomenon in recent years, and the little markets in southern France, Spain, and Italy have started to disappear. But despite the supermarket's increasing popularity, it is still not as firmly entrenched in the European lifestyle as it is here. Europeans are still rooted in tradition, and have not succumbed to the lure of the one-stop shop. They do not expect the supermarket to provide them with everything. While they use it for basics and for some produce, they will still go to their favorite butcher shop or fish stand when it comes to meat and fish, not allowing themselves to forfeit quality for the sake of convenience. You will rarely find a French or Spanish housewife buying bread or cheese at the supermarket.

While I am the first to admit that ideally it would be wonderful to shop exclusively in small specialty markets if one had the time and money, the reality of today's world is that the widespread availability of the supermarket and its convenience have made drastic changes in our style of eating and shopping. If you adjust to it properly, understand its shortcomings, and use it carefully, the supermarket can work to your advantage. And if you are aware of its assets and its limitations, you should be able to use it without losing your sensibility as a cook.

You must remember too, that supermarkets vary, and some are better than others. Outstanding among supermarkets is the Gelson Market in Century City, Los Angeles, where produce displays are truly extraordinary. The meat department excels in magnificent presentation, and the wonderful open butcher shop gives the customer easy access to any one of the staff, all of whom are ready and willing to answer questions. The Byerly Market in Minneapolis is another example of how exciting, distinctive, and thrilling the supermarket experience can be when there is a real philosophy behind the store and shoppers are handled with care. In this market, not only can customers ask questions, but they have access to a whole library of cookbooks. In general, however, the quality of the supermarket often depends on the community it caters to, and within a certain chain there are often great differences in quality, particularly in the produce and meat areas. Ultimately, supermarkets are run by people, and some managers take more pride in their work than others.

Personally, I have always been fascinated with the supermarket. It has its own special pace and vibrancy, not unlike the excitement of the open-air market, and can serve you well—if you have the right criteria in mind. Because I am always challenged to use the supermarket as creatively as I can, I have used as many supermarket staples in these recipes as I could.

For me, food is a way of life. If *you* are a "food person" or are becoming one, then naturally you will find yourself becoming increasingly critical of the quality and substance of a dish. If this is the case, it is essential to understand what, how, and where to buy. The next step is back into the kitchen. There you can begin to create, combining the quality, textures, and tastes of good, fresh ingredients and basic supermarket staples to come up with a myriad of wonderful dishes. In the pages that follow, you have all the basics to take you from market to kitchen. The last step—and in some ways perhaps the best of all—is from the kitchen to your table, with countless beautiful meals to be shared by family and friends.

Perla Meyer

From Market to Kitchen Cookbook

Supermarket
milk
butter
salt
olives
peanut oil
tomato paste
2 chickens

Angelo's Market
italian rice
½ lb. Parmesan
1 french bread
clove honey

Angelo's Market
italian rice
½ lb. Parmesan
french bread
honey

The Essential Kitchen: The Kitchen Pantry

Whenever I discuss cooking with any of my students I soon find that one of the most difficult and time-consuming aspects of good cooking is marketing. For the everyday cook especially it can be a tedious and frustrating experience, particularly when the menu is decided ahead of time. Often you find yourself chasing around looking for a specific ingredient essential to your meal—a perfect avocado or a particular Middle Eastern spice. By the time you have stopped at the various produce stands, supermarket, butcher shop, and specialty store naturally you are exhausted, and your entire creative energy has been drained before you ever set foot in your kitchen.

As much as I would like to romanticize and embellish the marketing art, it *is* both time-consuming and frustrating when you are looking for quality in every ingredient. However admittedly it is a great deal easier to prepare spur-of-the-moment meals, or even carefully planned ones, when you have on hand the basics essential to the everyday kitchen. The foods I discuss in this chapter represent a highly "personal" shopping list and are usually related to my particular style of cooking. I do not include any prepared foods, salad dressings, or frozen foods other than the ones I would use myself in the preparation of a specific dish in this book (or in either of my other books, to which I sometimes refer.) I do not list cookies, crackers, cereals, soft drinks, or ice cream. While I realize that most people buy these foods, I do not consider them to be "basic" cooking items. Nor do I list the

variety of processed cheeses and cold cuts. Again, these are items that many people keep on hand for sandwiches or quick lunches, but personally I never use them, either on their own or for cooking.

Specialty items such as canned imported chestnuts, lumpfish caviar, imported crackers, green peppercorns, and virgin olive oil are now becoming increasingly available in the gourmet sections of many supermarkets. However many important ingredients—Italian rice, Italian dried mushrooms, sherry wine vinegar, and a number of others—still require a stop at a specialty store.

As with most things we do routinely, marketing involves a certain amount of habit. Most people are accustomed to certain foods and to certain brands. When they are inspired to try new things it is usually a result of a strong advertising campaign or a new, eye-catching package. This is true of my own shopping habits (although my Mediterannean background has made me naturally skeptical of any highly advertised food item). But I am the first to admit that I often automatically reach for a certain type of pasta on the supermarket shelf without trying every brand. In working on this book, however, I did try various brands when it came to certain basic items that should be on everybody's shopping list. I found that canned tomatoes, for example, varied greatly in quality, with some domestic brands giving better results than the imported ones. I found differing quality in many dairy products, as well as other regionally distributed foods such as pasta. In addition to confirming—or in some cases changing—some of my shopping customs, it showed me once again how important it is for the knowledgeable shopper to experiment with different brands before settling for just any brand because of convenience, packaging, familiarity, or advertising.

When I shop for items other than staples I go to more than one supermarket. I find it challenging to look for good produce or the specialty items that are now appearing more and more on supermarket shelves. In one sense these items and the others that make up the list in this chapter are only a beginning—a guideline. Admittedly the list is somewhat biased, since I am still the kind of shopper who loves to seek out the specialty store for certain foods.

Furthermore, if the list strikes you as limited (when you think of all the things available in the supermarket), this is because I would rather spend my food budget on a good piece of cheese, a fine olive oil, a special vinegar, or a box of beautifully ripe raspberries.

I strongly believe that it is possible to cook well and creatively with the ingredients mentioned here, most of which are available in good supermarkets. I also believe that once marketing with good food in mind becomes a matter of habit, you will soon discover that there, in the aisles of your supermarket, local butcher shop, or greengrocer, is where good food really begins. With a little bit of extra attention and shopping flair your meals will automatically reflect the quality of your marketing expertise!

Meats

Beef

Avoid beef that is too red in color and has excessive moisture. This is usually an indication that the meat is too fresh and has not been aged. Also avoid any beef with a two-tone coloration and coarse texture.

Steaks (Pan-Frying and Grilling Cuts)

The most popular and most available cut is the *porterhouse* or *T-bone* steak. This cut comes from the short loin and has a good portion of the tenderloin attached. Personally, I only like this cut for outdoor grilling.

The *shell steak* is my favorite cut for pan frying. It has both texture and good flavor. The cut is also called *New York strip* or just *strip* in some parts of the country. Some markets sell it boned, which removes much of the juiciness of the steak. Look for shell steaks with the bone in and buy them at least ½ to ¾ inch thick.

Although the *club or Delmonico* steak is considered excellent for pan frying, I personally find it a less interesting cut. It is usually somewhat less expensive than the shell steak. Be sure that when you order club steaks you get them. Some butchers and supermarkets try to pass rib steaks for club. These will be tough and dry when pan fried.

The *sirloin steak* is a popular cut for outdoor grilling, although many people like to oven-broil it (a method I never use). Sirloins vary in shape and bone size.

Personally, I find them wonderful for outdoor grilling only.

I have never liked the tenderloin, or *filet mignon,* considered the most elegant of all beef cuts, and find it a gummy, uninteresting piece of meat. It is, however, often a good buy, since you can buy the entire tenderloin and use it in a variety of preparations. Pan sautéed and served in a green-peppercorn or mustard sauce, this cut can give delicious and flavorful results.

Braising Cuts

Lesser beef cuts can be used successfully in braising with excellent results. I particularly like to use the *rump pot roast,* the *brisket* and the *chuck pot roast.* More expensive cuts such as the *eye round* and *sirloin tip* are usually dry and less flavorful.

Stewing Cuts

Personally, I find lean chuck to be an excellent choice of meat for stewing. I usually have the butcher at the supermarket cut up the chuck for me into 1½- to 2-inch pieces. Another good choice is the rump pot roast. Avoid the sirloin tip, the top round and bottom round. These cuts are usually dry and less flavorful. Special cuts such as oxtails and beef shinbones are inexpensive but rarely available in supermarkets. They are extremely flavorful and useful in many interesting preparations. They are well worth the additional stop at a butcher shop.

Ground Beef

Again I find fresh-ground chuck to be the

most flavorful meat. Ground sirloin is far more expensive, more lean but also very good, and ground round is even leaner and less flavorful. The key to buying ground beef at the supermarket is not to buy it already ground but to choose a whole cut and ask the butcher to grind it for you. Avoid all packages that read ground beef or hamburger. These unspecified cuts contain a great deal of fat and are usually watery as well.

Lamb

Lamb is rated Prime, Choice, and Good, but Choice lamb is actually better than Prime because it is less fatty. When buying lamb in a supermarket, watch out for freshness. In many regions where there is not a large turnover in lamb, the cuts are often left in the cases too long and the meat develops a distinct heavy flavor. When buying lamb, look for bright-red color. (The lamb carried in supermarkets is 6 to 8 months old and the meat is redder than that of beef.) Fat should be waxy white without any brown or dark edges. Packages of lamb chops should look fresh, and none of the meat should be discolored.

Chops

Both rib and loin chops are popular cuts and usually available in good quality in every supermarket. While I prefer loin chops for pan sautéing, I usually use the rib chops for outdoor grilling. Loin roasts and rack of lamb are both glamorous and expensive cuts. The whole loin contains the tenderloin and makes an elegant juicy roast. The rack is less meaty but equally delicious,

and personally I prefer it. Prepare it simply roasted with a final topping of bread crumbs, parsley, and garlic as in the Rack of Lamb l'Orientale in *The Seasonal Kitchen*. Both cuts can easily be special-ordered from a good supermarket butcher, but are rarely found in the meat case.

Leg

The leg is my favorite roasting cut. The roasting method is discussed in detail on page 136. It can also be boned, tied, and casserole roasted. Because the full leg has become an increasingly expensive cut, it is now found in most supermarkets cut into two roasts, the shank half and the sirloin. The shank half is meatier and usually more expensive. Personally, I prefer to buy the whole leg, which stays juicier and more flavorful. Only buy a leg of lamb at a supermarket that has a large turnover and where you are assured of complete freshness. A leg of lamb should never weigh more than 6 to 6½ pounds, trimmed; otherwise it has a distinct lamby flavor and is basically already a mutton leg. Baby leg of lamb, weighing 3 pounds, is a delicacy well worth looking for. It requires knowing a top-quality butcher, who can usually get it for you particularly around Easter.

Shoulder

Lamb shoulder chops are often available in supermarkets but boned shoulder of lamb, which I consider to be the best stewing cut, requires an additional stop at a quality butcher. You can, however, ask the supermarket butcher to cut up the unboned shoulder chops into 2-inch pieces and use it successfully for braising and ragoûts.

Breast
Breast of lamb is often available in supermarkets. Boned breast is an excellent, inexpensive cut that should be stuffed, rolled, and roasted. Supermarket butchers seldom bone this flavorful cut, so you may have to shop for it at your butcher.

Shanks
Lamb shanks are a meaty and inexpensive cut that is both flavorful and extremely versatile. They are good for roasting and braising, and can be used in ragoûts or soups, such as the Russian Lamb Soup on page 107. Whenever I see lamb shanks in the supermarket, I buy them and work out my menu around them.

Ground Lamb
Though expensive, ground shoulder of lamb, used extensively in Middle Eastern cooking, is excellent in many preparations. It should be well seasoned. Combined with spices and herbs (cumin, oregano, parsley, and thyme), mashed garlic, and finely minced onions, it can be sautéed and then braised together with vegetables, as in the Middle Eastern Vegetable-and-Lamb Casserole on page 207. Avoid supermarket ground lamb patties and either grind the lamb yourself or buy it ground at a good butcher shop.

Pork
Most of the pork available in the United States goes into the processing of hams, bacon, sausage meat, and cold cuts. This leaves little choice of fresh pork cuts, with even a more limited variety available in supermarkets. When buying pork, look for whitish-pink flesh and firm, white fat. Some marbling is an indication of maturity and a more tender cut. The key to pork, however, is its absolute freshness, and all packaged pork should have no discoloration or any accumulation of liquid in the package.

Center-Cut Rib or Loin
This cut is the most popular one, and is available in every supermarket either cut into chops or as a roast. Personally, I find it dry and nowhere as flavorful as some of the lesser cuts. If you are planning to use either of them, buy the roast from the shoulder end, which is more tender and far juicier.

Shoulder Chops
The shoulder chops are less expensive than either the center cut of the rib or loin. They can be found in many supermarkets and are excellent for braising and pan frying.

Pork Shoulder Butt
A wonderfully juicy and rather inexpensive cut, the shoulder butt can be used whole for roasting, cubed, for stewing, and ground in stuffings. It is rarely available in supermarkets and may require an additional stop at a good butcher shop.

Ground Pork
Essential to all meat stuffings and pâtés, ground pork can rarely be purchased at supermarkets anywhere; it usually requires

an additional stop at a butcher shop. With the growing popularity of the food processor, however, a small amount of pork can easily be ground at home. You will often only need ½ to 1 pound in any given meat stuffing.

Bacon
Only slab bacon is useful in cooking. Unfortunately, it is not always available in supermarkets and may require an additional stop at a butcher shop.

Smoked Jowl
This pork cut is smoked and sold as slab bacon in many supermarkets. It is a good, meaty, and inexpensive substitute, and I often use it. Blanch it for three minutes in boiling water and dry thoroughly on paper towels and use it in preparations calling for bacon.

Salt Pork
Good, meaty salt pork is rarely available in supermarkets any more and may require an additional stop at your butcher shop. It can, however, be frozen successfully. Avoid salt pork that has no meat in it whatsoever. This is basically lard and would not do in dishes calling for salt pork. Look for lean salt pork and blanch it for 3 to 5 minutes in boiling water before using it in any given preparation.

Fresh Ham
The fresh ham comes from the hip and leg of the pork. It is a large cut usually weighing anywhere from 12 to 14 pounds. It is often cut in half and sold in supermarkets as shank half and butt half. The shank end is somewhat cheaper. Fresh hams are usually carried in supermarkets only during the holiday season. At other times of the year they are usually available precooked and require only a short roasting time in the oven.

Spare Ribs
Spare ribs, a popular barbecuing cut, are available in every supermarket. Personally, I much prefer the country ribs, which are meatier and delicious when braised with sauerkraut or roasted and served either with red cabbage or a white-bean casserole. Country ribs can be cut into serving pieces and used in a tasty and simple Paella, such as the one in *The Peasant Kitchen*.

Veal
Very little milk-fed veal is ever available in supermarkets anywhere, and this superb, delicate meat requires an additional stop at a top-quality butcher shop. Grass-fed veal has a deep pink color and can actually be labeled *young beef*. While veal is graded, that is not a criterion for quality, since milk-fed veal is baby calf that should not have any marbling. When buying veal, look for pale pink flesh with firm, waxy white fat; it should be free of any discoloration whatsoever.

Scaloppine
These lean, thin boneless veal cutlet that are so popular in Italian cooking should be cut from the leg only. You can now find veal scaloppine in some New York supermarkets, but even if they look good

and fresh I do not recommend buying them, since they are rarely cut properly. Have a good butcher cut scaloppine for you as described on page 131 and use them the same day of purchase.

Chops (Loin and Rib)
Both loin and rib chops are now available in some supermarkets and when properly cooked can give excellent results. Be sure to look for chops that look fresh, free of discoloration (light tan spots) and for packages that are free of accumulated liquid.

Rib and Loin Roasts
If the supermarket carries the chops, you can usually special-order the entire center rib or loin cut. This is an expensive cut and the veal can be somewhat dry. For best results, casserole-roast this cut on a bed of aromatic vegetables and baste it every 10 minutes with Brown Chicken Stock (page 531) as described in the veal introduction on pages 132–133. Grass-fed older veal can give excellent results when prepared this way.

Shoulder Roasts
This is a less expensive cut that I like to use both for roasting and stewing (cut up in pieces for a ragoût). If you see it in the market, buy it and work your menu around it. Most of the time this cut requires an additional stop at your butcher.

Breast
The breast of veal is a very bony cut that is usually prepared with a pocket ready for stuffing. Use either a sausage or a bread stuffing for it and roast it as you would any other veal roast. Since the cut is quite dry, it should be basted with stock every 10 minutes. It is then delicious served either hot or cold. Any supermarket that carries veal usually carries the breast at areasonable price, and at some good markets it can be special ordered.

Ground Veal
Just as with pork, ground veal is essential in making stuffings and pâtés. You will not be able to find ground veal at a supermarket and may have to grind it yourself or have the butcher do it for you. Avoid veal patties. These are ground from scraps of veal and are usually stringy and watery.

Poultry

Chicken

Chicken is by far the best supermarket buy today. Because of the large turnover in chickens everywhere, they are usually fresh and inexpensive. Depending on the region, chickens come into the market either with a distinctly yellowish skin or a whitish-blue color. This depends largely on the feed but has nothing to do with the taste of the bird. Personally, I find yellow chickens too fatty, but in certain parts of the country there is simply no choice any more, and essentially freshness is the key to a good chicken. When buying chickens look for clear, bright color with little or no liquid in the package. The fat should look fresh and the chickens must be free of bruises.

Small Fryers and Broilers

A 2½- to 3-pound chicken is excellent for broiling, roasting, and spit roasting as well. I also cut it up and use it for braising.

Roasters

A 3½- to 4½-pound roasting chicken is usually the best buy. It can be stuffed with the stuffing of your choice; I like a well-flavored sausage stuffing or a spinach-and-bread stuffing. It should be roasted on a bed of finely diced aromatic vegetables and basted with stock every 10 minutes according to the directions in the introduction to the chicken chapter on page 227.

Legs

I highly recommend buying chickens whole and cutting them up yourself. You will, however, find several recipes in this book that call for chicken legs—in which case it is more economical to buy the legs only. These are always legs with their thighs attached. They are naturally more expensive than a cut up chicken, but are especially good for tomato-based sauces and brown sauces. Look for chicken legs that have been properly cut up, with as much skin as possible covering the flesh. The skin protects the meat from drying up during cooking and is also far more attractive looking in the finished dish.

Breasts

Chicken breasts usually come boned or unboned. It is extremely easy to bone chicken breasts, and they are usually less expensive this way than the already boned, skinned ones. Keep the bones for a stock as described on page 94, and use the chicken breasts within a day of purchase. When buying chicken breasts at a supermarket look for a pale rosy clear color. There must be no liquid in the package and no discoloration in the flesh whatsoever.

Wings, Giblets, and Necks

If you find wings, necks, and giblets in the supermarket, buy them and use them for both a basic Chicken Stock or the Brown Chicken Stock on page 531. If you don't plan to make the stock right away, freeze the giblets for later use.

Chicken Livers

Personally, I rarely buy chicken livers in the supermarket unless I'm completely assured of freshness. Avoid frozen livers, and look for containers that have large, rather light-colored livers. Look for containers that have the minimum accumulation of blood. Use chicken livers within a day of purchase.

Duck

Duck is described in detail on pages 230–32.

Turkey

Turkeys are described in detail on pages 229–30. Note the following special cuts:

Breasts

Many supermarkets now carry fresh turkey breasts. These can be cut into thin slices and used in many preparations calling for either veal scaloppine or chicken breasts.

Legs

Whenever I see fresh turkey legs in the supermarket, I buy them and use them together with cabbage, turnips, carrots and potatoes for a full flavored one-dish meal soup.

Following is a list of seasonal fruits and vegetables carried in most supermarkets. Many of them—such as apples and oranges, or spinach, mushrooms, and broccoli—have a long season. But *all* produce is at its best when at the very height of its season, and this is when it should be a part of your shopping list. (At the times of its peak season, in fact, supermarkets will usually carry produce at a more reasonable price than the specialty store.)

No matter where or when you shop for produce, be aware of quality, and know what you are looking for. Whenever possible, avoid supermarkets where produce is prepackaged. While an eggplant may look perfectly fresh in a cellophane wrapping, when you get it out of its container it may have a large bruise and wrinkled skin on its other side. Bagged produce, such as turnips or baking potatoes, may appear from the outside to be of uniform size—but when you get it home, you may find a variety of sizes. Certain fruits and vegetables—Brussels sprouts, for example, and all varieties of berries—are almost invariably prepacked. This is unfortunate. The only way you can test for ripeness and freshness with them is to peek at the bottom of the container to see if all the berries appear fresh. Even if prepackaging does not *necessarily* mean inferior quality or uneven sizing, it does mean that you cannot select your fruits and vegetables yourself. It also forces you to buy quantities you may not need or want.

Often the key to supermarket produce shopping is knowing the department manager in the hopes of getting some special attention. This, of course, is easier in a specialty store, where quality merchandise has been selected beforehand, but the supermarket produce manager often takes great pride in his work, and can be most helpful, particularly if he recognizes the fact that you are a knowledgeable shopper. He may bring out a fresh bunch of parsley for you, a bag of crisp spinach, or a ripe melon. If, however, the manager doesn't come to the rescue, or if there is simply no more of a certain item in stock, avoid any fruits or vegetables that look bruised or picked over, even if you don't have the time to make an additional stop at a specialty shop.

In learning to select certain fruits and vegetables, experience is the best teacher. With much produce, however, crispness and freshness are obvious, and you can quickly learn to tell the difference between good and bad. You should also learn which particular fruit or vegetable to buy for various cooking purposes. A baking potato, for example, cooks differently from a new or all-purpose potato, and is used in different preparations; a red delicious apple will not hold up when baked in a tart, while a golden delicious will; and certain pears are good for eating, while others are good for poaching.

All the information on how to shop for and use produce is in the market-to-kitchen chapter of *The Seasonal Kitchen*. However,

I have included here a list, of the produce, first of fruits and then of vegetables, most knowledgeable cooks should be familiar with. (Certain regional produce is not mentioned here; it should, however, of course be included in the repertoires of creative cooks in the particular areas of the country where these fruits or vegetables are available.)

No matter how convenient the supermarket one-stop shop may be, I cannot stress enough the importance of knowing your produce and shopping for it with great care and special attention.

Apples

To me apples are synonymous with fall. Although apples are now available year round in every supermarket, the pleasure of buying a basket of crisp apples at a New England roadside stand cannot be duplicated. What's more, the average market only carries two to three varieties of apples at any time, while many of the best apples are the lesser known varieties picked locally and sold at roadside stands and farmers' markets. It is essential, however, for every knowledgeable cook to be familiar with the basic supermarket varieties and to use the right apple for a specific preparation.

Red Delicious
The red delicious is a beautiful apple but it is strictly an eating apple and a good addition to the fruit salad bowl. Always look for large bruise-free apples and avoid those that are small, imma-

ture looking, and with a greenish
tint.

Golden Delicious
The golden delicious is an excellent baking
apple and is particularly good for tarts, as it
does not fall apart in cooking and each
slice retains its shape. It is also my favorite
apple for sautéing and using as an
accompaniment to roast pork or duck.
Avoid green, underripe apples or those that
are large and deeply yellow, as they are
usually mealy and lacking in flavor.

Mcintosh and Cortland
Both mcintosh and cortlands are wonderful
eating and cooking apples. The "mac" is
the best apple for an apple sauce since it
disintegrates into a rich juicy pulp. Both the
cortland and mcintosh are at their best
during the fall months, at which time you
can find them inexpensively priced at many
roadside stands. I usually make large
quantities of apple sauce with either apple
variety and keep it for later use.

Rome Beauty
The rome beauty appears in supermarkets
in late fall and early winter. It is a perfect
baking apple to be used whole, cored, and
filled with butter, cinnamon, and sugar,
then baked in a slow oven for 1 hour or
until tender. Serve the baked apple at room
temperature accompanied by a rum custard
or a sugared Crème Fraîche.

Apricots
Apricots are one of the best early summer
fruits worth looking for. Unfortunately they
are rarely available in supermarkets outside
the West Coast. Since apricots are
extremely perishable they are rarely
available ripe, even at their peak season. In
addition, apricots will not ripen properly off
the tree. And if slightly bruised an apricot
will not ripen properly either, making it
even harder for anyone to enjoy this
wonderful fruit at its best. Underripe
apricots can be used successfully, however,
in a compote by poaching them in a sugar
syrup flavored with cinnamon and vanilla.
When buying apricots choose the light to
deep orange fruit that yields slightly to the
touch. Avoid green or bruised apricots.

Avocados
The avocado, with its rather bland flavor
but buttery interesting texture, has gained
popularity in recent years both here and in
Europe. Although more than 200 types of
avocados are grown only two or three are
available commercially year-round in
supermarkets throughout the country. You
will find, depending on the seasons, large
to medium-sized green, smooth-skinned
avocados or smaller, rough-skinned ones
that turn black when ripe. All avocados
have a buttery green flesh that turns dark as
soon as it is exposed to air. This darkening
can be avoided if you rub the exposed
flesh with the cut side of a lemon. At their
peak during the winter and spring months,
ripe and inexpensive avocados can be
found in markets in Florida, Arizona, and on
the West Coast. On the East Coast and in
the Midwest avocados are more expensive
and rarely available ripe, which means that
if you plan to serve an avocado at its best

you have to think about it two to three days ahead of time. To ripen place the avocado (it must be free of bruises) in a brown paper bag. It should be ripe and ready to serve within two to three days, at which point it will yield to slight pressure. A ripe avocado should be refrigerated where it will keep for another two to three days.

Bananas

Bananas are one of the great year-round fruits, found in every supermarket at a good price. What's more, it is the only fruit I can think of that develops better flavor when ripened off the vine or tree. Bananas will ripen well in the market or at room temperature in a corner of your kitchen. I find bananas to be a staple in the everyday kitchen since they are wonderfully versatile and lend themselves to many preparations. Bananas are a good addition to a fruit salad and they also combine well with apples and oranges. They can be served hot either baked or sautéed in sweet butter, brown sugar, and orange juice (as in the Flambéed Bananas in *The Seasonal Kitchen*) or they can be made into delicious fritters. Sautéed bananas are a delicious topping to ice creams or they can be used as a filling for crêpes, as in the Banana Crêpes on page 497. Overripe bananas can be put to good use in a banana bread, a crêpe, or banana pancakes served for breakfast. When buying bananas look for ones that are not fully ripe but are free of bruises and brown spots. Avoid bananas that are too green, however, and those that have soft spots. Even a light tan spot in a banana will turn dark and mushy when the banana is ripe.

Keep unripened bananas at room temperature and when ripe use them as soon as possible. You can refrigerate ripe bananas for two to three days. Their skins will turn dark but this will not effect their flavor.

Berries

Although many varieties of delicious berries grow wild in many regions of the United States only strawberries, blueberries, raspberries, and cranberries are cultivated for commercial purposes. These can be found during their peak season in every supermarket and in many specialty greengrocers. Other berries like black and red currants are cultivated for preserving purposes and unfortunately rarely appear in the markets, but you may find them sometimes at roadside stands and farmers' markets.

Strawberries

The most popular berry in the country—strawberry—is synonymous with spring and early summer cooking. Strawberries start appearing in markets as early as January, at which time they are usually imported from Mexico and are extremely expensive. I find strawberries to be at their best and most flavorful, as well as at their least expensive, during the peak season in late spring and early summer. Unfortunately strawberries are always sold in one-pint containers, where you will find several less-than-perfect berries at the bottom. When buying strawberries do not go by size. A small ripe berry is usually sweeter and richer in flavor than the giant mealy strawberry. Look for full red-colored berries and avoid bruised, discolored, and underripe fruit. Be sure to check the container carefully and transfer the berries to a bowl as soon as possible. Remove any moldly spots and discard any damaged berries. Serve the strawberries within a day or two of purchase.

Blueberries

Of all the berries the blueberry is the one that has lost most of its flavor owing to commercial cultivation. You can now find blueberries as early as May and in their peak season they are often large, but often tasteless. Blueberries, however, combine well with other fresh fruits and their lack of flavor can be adjusted by topping them with a sherry zabaglione or a lemon mousse (see the recipe for Blueberries in Lemon Mousse in *The Seasonal Kitchen*). They are also good served sugared and accompanied by a bowl of crème fraîche that has been sugared and flavored with blackberry or currant liqueur. When buying blueberries look for a silvery bloom, which is a natural protective wax coating. The fruit should be plump, firm, and uniform in size. Small berries can be as good as large ones. (In fact, the small locally picked wild blueberries found in the season in many farmers' markets and roadside stands are far more flavorful than the large cultivated ones.) Wild blueberries vary a great deal in size and unfortunately are never sold in supermarkets.

Raspberries

Raspberries are the most expensive of all berries, since they are extremely perishable and hard to ship. Because of their high cost raspberries are usually only carried by top-quality supermarkets and they often require an additional stop at a specialty greengrocer. However, they are well worth the effort and to me they are the most elegant of berries requiring a minimum of adornment. Simply sugared or accompanied by sugared Crème Fraîche they add the finishing touch to a spring or early fall meal.

When buying raspberries look for plump, ripe berries in dry, unstained cartons. Transfer raspberries to a bowl as soon as you can and discard any moldy ones. Do not wash them.

Cranberries

Cranberries are synonymous with fall and holiday cooking. During their peak season —September through January—cranberries can be found in every supermarket where they are sold in one-pound bags. The cranberry is a hard berry that cannot be used uncooked. Cooked with plenty of sugar, fresh orange juice, raisins, diced apples, and flavored with cinnamon and nutmeg they will reduce to a thick, somewhat tart yet delicious pulp. Refrigerate the cranberry preserve and it will keep well for 2 to 3 months in a well-sealed jar. It is an excellent accompaniment to roast pork, duck, turkey, or game and can also be used successfully as a filling for crêpes.

Blackberries

Blackberries are being cultivated in larger

quantities nowadays and can be found in many good markets during the summer months. The blackberry is most perishable and should be used as soon possible after purchase. Blackberries usually have an extremely tart flavor and I prefer to cook them together with sugar to a thick purée. I use the blackberry purée as a filling for crêpes or in combination with a pastry cream as a filling or topping for tarts.

Cherries
There are a great many varieties of cherries grown in this country but only two reach the average market. During their peak season—May through August—cherries are an essential part of my shopping list. Besides the simple pleasure of nibbling from a bowl of sweet, crisp, tangy cherries I like to cook them in a sugar or wine syrup with a cinnamon stick and a few cloves. The cherry compote will keep refrigerated for several weeks and can be served as a dessert accompanied by sugared Crème Fraîche or as a topping for ice cream. When buying cherries look for bright red to deep red, dark firm cherries with bright glossy surfaces. Avoid buying cherries that had been pre-packaged in cellophane containers or those that are overripe and bruised. As soon as you have purchased the cherries pick them over carefully and discard any moldy ones. Chill the cherries and rinse quickly only minutes before serving.

Figs
A superb fruit, figs are unfortunately not available fresh in many parts of the country because they are extremely perishable and do not ship well. On the East Coast figs are carried only by fine greengrocers and are prohibitively expensive. On the West Coast, however, both green and black figs can be found in many good supermarkets quite inexpensively. Fresh figs can be served either peeled or unpeeled together with prosciutto or finely sliced smoked ham as an appetizer. As a dessert, figs can be served simply chilled or as in the Fresh Figs in Raspberry Soured Cream on page 509. This is one of my favorite ways to serve this very special fruit.

When buying figs look for those that are somewhat soft to the touch but not mushy. Avoid unripe figs; they will never ripen properly once they are off the tree and will have a mealy, uninteresting flavor. Once refrigerated figs should be used within a day or two of purchase.

Dried figs are available year-round in every supermarket. They do not compare to the fresh fruit and can only be used in cakes or as a snack.

Grapefruit
Grapefruits are now a year-round fruit available in every supermarket. However, they are at their best and least expensive from January through May. Grapefruits are often thick-skinned and not as juicy as they should be. When buying grapefruit look for quality rather than size. Buy firm, compact heavy fruit with thin skins. The color may vary from a light pink to a deep yellow and has nothing to do with the taste of the fruit.

Avoid grapefruits that are pointed at the stem and those that are ridged and rough skinned—all indications of a pulpy grapefruit.

Texas Ruby Red Grapefruit
This grapefruit is a treat and, next to a good orange, the best winter fruit I know. Unfortunately this juicy, thin-skinned grapefruit does not travel well and is not sold in most parts of the country.

Grapes
Since there are now so many varieties of grapes available you can find one or two in every supermarket year-round. Because grapes will not ripen once they are off the vine be sure to taste one before buying the bunch. My favorite varieties are thompson seedless grapes and Muscadet. Both are green and are at their best when they have turned to a pale green, almost straw color. When buying grapes, either red or green, choose those that are plump, free of wrinkles or bruises, and firmly attached to the stem in compact, fresh-looking bunches. Avoid buying grapes packaged in cellophane-covered boxes.

Kiwi Fruit
The kiwi fruit has been gaining popularity in this country as well as in Europe. As with all exotic fruits it is now used by many of the *nouvelle cuisine* chefs either as an accompaniment to veal or duck or as part of a fresh fruit salad and as a garnish. The dark brown, fuzzy skin of the kiwi conceals a brilliant green pulp that when ripe is quite delicious and unique in flavor.

Imported from New Zealand, kiwis are usually sold only at quality greengrocers and fine supermarkets. Their peak season is March through November. When buying kiwis look for fruit that yields to the touch. Avoid any that have shriveled or bruised skins. Unripe kiwis will ripen in a brown paper bag within one to two days at room temperature.

Kumquats
Kumquats belong to the citrus family and are sold in one-pint containers in many supermarkets in Florida, Arizona, and on the West Coast during the winter and early spring months. There they are an inexpensive fruit that can be used creatively in many dishes. They are less common in the East. Kumquats are an unusual fruit inasmuch as the skin of the fruit is sweet and the flesh tart. Thinly sliced they can be dipped into hot caramel and served as a garnish to a roast pork or sautéed calves' liver. Look for plump, deep, and firm fruit with crisp, fresh-looking stems and leaves.

Lemons
The lemon is an indispensable fruit and a must in every kitchen. I keep lemons on hand at all times and use them in innumerable preparations, from a simple salad dressing to a more elaborate Lemon Crêpes on page 500. Fortunately lemons are available year-round in every market but they vary in quality, size, and cost depending on the region. When buying lemons avoid large, rough, thick-skinned lemons that feel light to the touch and usually lack juice. Look for medium-sized

elongated, smooth, somewhat-shiny lemons and keep them refrigerated in a dry vegetable bin.

Limes

Limes belong to the citrus family and look like green lemons. The only type available in supermarkets outside Florida and some parts of the West Coast is the large, smooth green lime. Personally I find that the taste of this lime lacks the characteristic and unique flavor of the Mexican and the Florida key lime, which is small, extremely juicy and, when ripe, almost yellow in color. When buying limes look for thin-skinned fruit that yield slightly to pressure. Store limes in a dry vegetable bin as you would lemons.

Mangoes

A tropical fruit native to the Caribbean islands, mangoes are becoming increasingly popular and can now be found in many good supermarkets or specialty greengrocers during the late spring and early summer months. In Florida, where some mangoes are now being cultivated, this interesting fruit is relatively inexpensive. I find it the most flavorful of all tropical fruits, and I serve it often sliced, sugared, and sprinkled with Cointreau as an accompaniment to a bowl of vanilla ice cream. It is also excellent combined with sugared Crème Fraîche or quickly heated in butter and brown sugar with a sprinkling of rum. When buying mangoes look for fruit that is yellowish-red rather than green and that yields lightly to pressure. Avoid any bruised fruit. An unripe mango can be left

at room temperature for two to three days and will develop flavor; however they are never as good as tree-ripened fruit and often develop decay before ever reaching the right degree of ripeness. A ripe mango should be served as soon as possible after purchase. It can be refrigerated for a day or two before serving.

Melons

Melons are a superb summer fruit that can be served creatively at any meal. A lovely and refreshing breakfast starter, a chilled slice of ripe melon is also an excellent classic accompaniment to the thinly sliced prosciuitto or smoked ham served as an appetizer. Melons can also be cubed, sugared, and tossed in a little lemon or lime juice and served as a simple but delicious ending to a meal. Although there are about eight types of melons cultivated, only two to three reach the average supermarket other than markets on the West Coast. On the West Coast and in the southern states there is a better selection of melons and prices are far more reasonable than in the Northeast and Midwest. The basic supermarket varieties are the cantaloupe, honeydew, and watermelon, while great and succulent melons like the casaba, cranshaw, and Spanish and Persian melons can only be found in specialty greengrocers and at farmers' markets during the summer.

Finding a ripe cantaloupe or honeydew at a supermarket is not an easy task and requires a trained eye. When selecting a melon look for a roundish shape, free from flat surfaces (an indication that the melon was left to lie on the ground in the same position for a great length of time). The melon should yield slightly to pressure at the blossom end and have a pleasant, distinctive aroma. With the exception of the honeydew, melons do not ripen off the vine although the cantaloupe becomes somewhat juicier when left at room temperature for two to three days. It is best to use all your senses in selecting a properly ripe melon. As for casabas and cranshaws, these superb, rather large melons have a distinctive aroma when ripe; there should be a slight rattling of seeds when the melon is shaken. Avoid those that sound watery and where the blossom ends are too soft. This is a sure sign of its being overmature and having a fermented flavor.

Nectarines
Nectarines are available in every supermarket during the summer months. They look like a smooth-skinned peach but, because most nectarines are picked before they are mature and shipped large distances, they are rarely juicy and often have a distinct mealy, bland flavor. This is not the case with nectarines bought on the West Coast where the ripe fruit is carried in many supermarkets. Select nectarines that have a rich yellow color or those that are mixed with bright red. Avoid bruised or hard nectarines. Most nectarines that are shipped underripe will never ripen properly but will get softer and somewhat juicier. Leave them at room temperature for two to three days before serving. Nectarines can be used in preparations calling for peaches. They are an excellent poaching fruit; I use

them either in a sugar- or white-wine syrup or simply sliced, sugared, and served in a strawberry purée.

Oranges
Oranges can now be found in most supermarkets year-round. However, apart from an occasional juice orange, I buy them only during the winter and early spring months at which time they are extremely juicy and less expensive. Oranges are a most versatile fruit. They lend themselves to many simple preparations. Sliced oranges sprinkled with Cointreau and topped with strawberry purée make an excellent and refreshing dessert. A sliced orange-and-sweet onion salad is a lovely accompaniment to a roast pork or duck. In southern states such as Florida and Louisiana and on the West Coast, oranges are far less expensive than in the Northeast and Midwest. Oranges should be used in many interesting preparations and not limited to the basic fruit salad or breakfast table. The best eating orange by far is the California navel. It is an almost seedless orange that peels easily and separates neatly into segments. When buying oranges choose firm, heavy oranges. Avoid lightweight oranges and those with rough, thick skins which indicate a pulpy unjuicy orange.

Papayas
A tropical fruit, papayas are becoming increasingly popular and can be found in many supermarkets both in Florida and on the West Coast during the winter and spring months. (In the Northeast and

Midwest papayas are carried only by specialty greengrocers.) This somewhat pear-shaped fruit has smooth skin with color ranging from bright green to yellow. Because the fruit bruises easily it is rarely available ripe and will require ripening in a brown paper bag for two to three days. Look for papayas that are more than half yellowish and yield lightly to pressure. A ripe papaya can be refrigerated but should be used within two to three days of purchase. Papayas should be served lightly chilled and sprinkled with lime juice, either by themselves or as an accompaniment to smoked ham or prosciutto. They make an interesting addition to the fruit salad bowl.

Peaches

A superb summer fruit when properly ripe, the peach can often be disappointing. Peaches are extremely perishable and are bruised easily. They are rarely available ripe in supermarkets even during their peak season June through August. During the summer months you will find wonderful locally grown peaches at roadside stands and farmers' market in most regions of the country. I find it well worth the additional stop to get a locally grown peach; I find them the most exciting of the summer fruits and serve them in many interesting ways. When buying peaches select fruit that is firm but that will yield slightly to pressure. The color of the peach depends largely on the variety. Freestone peaches are yellowish when ripe while the cling type turn a deep orange or a light orange with a reddish blush. A ripe peach has a distinct aroma and should never be bought packaged.

Avoid buying underripe, overly firm peaches with a distinct green color. Peaches will not ripen properly off the tree and even if they get soft they never develop their natural juices.

California peaches that are shipped to the Northwest and Midwest usually result in a pulpy, uninteresting fruit that rarely develops full flavor. Do not buy bruised peaches because as the peach ripens even light tan spots turn into large dark bruises. Ripe peaches should be used within a day or two of purchase. Refrigerated they may keep for an additional two to three days. Bring them back to room temperature before serving.

Pears

Pears, like apples, are now available in every supermarket year-round. They are one of my very favorite fruits. The pear has a lovely shape and a delightful aroma. A ripe pear is a superb dessert but unfortunately like peaches, pears are mostly shipped too green, which often prevents them from developing their full sweet taste. Again, as with apples, it is essential for any knowledgeable cook to understand the characteristics of the many types of pears and use them accordingly.

Bartlett

The first pear to appear in late August is the bartlett (called Williams pear in Europe). This is a wonderful juicy thin-skinned pear that turns a bright yellow when ripe. It is a good all-purpose pear but I particularly like to use bartletts for poaching in a sugar syrup or in a white or red wine syrup flavored with cinnamon cloves and vanilla.

Bosc

The bosc pear is an elongated, brown-skinned pear that in my opinion is the best eating pear when ripe. It is at its best during the fall and winter months but I have rarely found a good bosc pear in a supermarket, where these pears are usually rather small and underripe. A top-quality bosc is usually found only in specialty greengrocers and may require an additional stop.

Anjou

The anjou is a late winter pear that when ripe turns a yellowish green. It can be used in all preparations calling for bartlett pears. In most supermarkets the anjou pears are sold completely green and underripe. Avoid buying these pears since they never develop full flavor and even when poached remain rather tasteless and uninteresting.

Comice

Many people consider the comice pear the finest eating pear. It is rarely available in supermarkets and may require an additional stop at a quality greengrocer, depending on the region. When ripe the comice is a large, almost-round pear with a lovely rather thick, greenish-yellow skin and a wonderfully buttery texture. Serve the comice as a dessert pear accompanied by a soft French cheese such as brie, triple crème, or a blue cheese such as Roquefort

or Pipo Crèm', a milder and creamier blue cheese.

Persimmons

The persimmon is one of my favorite fall and early winter fruits. It has a brilliant orange, smooth skin and a unique sweet yet somewhat spicy flavor and an interesting texture. Until recently it was impossible to find a persimmon in markets outside some southern states, Arizona, and the West Coast. Even now most persimmons sold in the Northeast and the Midwest are carried only by quality greengrocers. Because the fruit bruises easily and is extremely perishable, many of the persimmons shipped to the Northeast arrive at the market underripe and hard. While a partially ripe fruit can be left at room temperature for two to three days to ripen, the underripe fruit turns black and decays before ever reaching the right stage of maturity. A persimmon should be served by itself. It is not a good addition to the salad bowl, where its somewhat soft texture and unique flavor competes with other fruits. Slice it and sprinkle it with sugar and a touch of lime juice or a few drops of Cointreau or peach brandy; the Persimmon Parfait on page 518 is another simple yet delicious way to serve this superb fruit.

When buying persimmons, look for plump, glossy, deep orange fruit that yields lightly to the touch. Avoid any bruised fruits or those that are extremely hard with brownish green areas near the stem end. Once ripe, use a persimmon as soon as possible or refrigerate it. It will keep for two to three days.

Overripe persimmons make a delicious bread, baked like a zucchini or banana bread with the addition of raisins, spices (cinnamon, nutmeg, mace, and cloves) and 2 to 3 tablespoons of good brandy or dark rum. I serve this persimmon bread as a cake, often accompanied by a rum-flavored custard or a hard sauce.

Pineapples
Of all tropical fruits a good pineapple is by far the most interesting. A dead-ripe pineapple is a marvelous fruit, but when served unripe it is woody and almost tasteless. For years, particularly in Europe, fresh pineapple was considered the caviar of the fruit world. Now good pineapples are available at reasonable prices in most supermarkets, particularly during their peak season—March through June. The two most popular types of pineapple—those that most people are familiar with—are the sugar loaf and the dole. Until recently a dole pineapple was automatically associated with Hawaii which is where most pineapples come from. However, a large number of dole pineapples are now grown in Honduras and Costa Rica and are less expensive than those coming from Hawaii. Unfortunately pineapples are often picked before they reach their peak of ripeness and their flavor never develops to its fullest. When buying pineapple look for one that has a slight orange to yellowish tint and where there is a distinct and fragrant aroma. It should also yield to slight pressure and the top should be green and fresh looking. (Contrary to what most people believe the ease which with you can pull out a leaf of a pineapple has little to do with the ripeness of the fruit.) Avoid pineapples that are small and hard with greenish spots and those completely lacking in aroma.

Plums and Prunes
Plums start appearing in many markets as early as May, but their natural peak season is July through September, at which time good, ripe plums can be bought in many supermarkets everywhere. Unfortunately, supermarket varieties are usually confined to the standard bright red and dark red plums. The wonderful greengage, with its greenish-yellow skin and juicy yellow flesh, and the small damson plum are carried mostly by specialty greengrocers and farmer's markets during the season.

All plums should be almost ripe when bought, with a distinct, juicy, sweet flavor. Choose plums that are firm but yield lightly to pressure. Unripe plums will never ripen once off the tree and will simply get soft and mealy. Avoid buying packaged plums or those that are even slightly bruised; also avoid soft, overripe plums.

Prune Plums
The prune plum, also called Italian plum, is a superb fall fruit that lends its wonderful taste to tarts and compotes. When ripe, this juicy purple plum can easily be cut in half and the pit removed. It is delicious eaten raw or poached in a white- or red-wine

sugar syrup. Italian plums are usually available in all markets, particularly in those catering to Italian and Mediterranean communities. When buying Italian plums, look for fruit that is almost ripe and yields lightly to pressure. Underripe plums never develop full flavor and will only get soft and mealy.

Avoid bruised or shriveled plums or those that are overripe and too soft.

Artichokes

A winter and spring vegetable, the artichoke is plentiful in California and Arizona. In those states it is available in all supermarkets at a reasonable price. In other regions it is more of a specialty item and is carried in supermarkets only at the height of the season. Served hot or cold, it is one of the best and most interesting vegetables, with a nutty, unique flavor. When buying artichokes, select compact, tightly closed artichokes of good green color. In winter you will often find brownish streaks on the outer leaves due to frost damage. This does not effect the flavor of the artichoke.

The globe artichoke is best poached and served with a garlic- or herb-flavored mayonnaise or the Garlic-and-Anchovy Sauce on page 61. The artichoke bottom or heart is a delicacy, and is one of the best morsels in the vegetable world. Directions on how to prepare it are on page 408.

Three to four cooked artichoke bottoms add a superb taste to a ragoût of veal or a sauté of chicken. They can also be served as an appetizer topped with a spoonful of an Herb-Flavored Hollandaise (page 541). Personally, I much prefer the small, compact artichoke, which can be used in many interesting preparations, but unfortunately is only available in California supermarkets. This basically Mediterranean vegetable is delicious when braised in olive oil, parsley, lemon juice, and garlic, or cooked and combined with eggs in an open-faced omelette. On the East Coast, the small artichokes are available in many good specialty greengrocers' catering to Mediterranean or ethnic cooks.

Asparagus

The asparagus is without a doubt the best of our spring vegetables. In recent years it has begun appearing in specialty markets as early as late January. The peak season, however, is April through June, and at that time asparagus is available at all supermarkets at a reasonable price. Aside from the basic cooked and buttered asparagus, there are innumerable ways to use this splendid vegetable. It can be puréed in soups, served cold in salads and even pan fried with a sprinkling of sugar and dry sherry. Avoid buying prepacked asparagus, and try to purchase it loose or tied into bundles of uniform-sized stalks. Look for tightly closed tips and a bright-green color. Avoid asparagus with large white markings and woody bottoms. The stalk of early asparagus is usually thin and often stringy. Large flat asparagus mark the height of the season and are more tender and flavorful. Although asparagus can be refrigerated for several days in a plastic bag, they quickly lose their flavor. It is best to serve them within a day or two of purchase.

Beets

Beets are one of my favorite vegetables, and I wish they were available year round. In California, I have seen beets in many markets during the winter months, but their natural peak season is June through October. At that time they are an inexpensive vegetable that can be used in many exciting preparations. The Cold Summer Beet Soup on page 101 is one of my favorite spring and summer soups. Creamed beets make a delicious accompaniment to chicken or veal dishes, and cold beets make superb appetizers and hors d'oeuvre salads.

Look for firm, round beets with deep red color and crisp tops. Most beets come tied in uneven bundles. Try to select small to medium beets and avoid the very large ones, as they tend to be woody. Beet tops are often sold separately in the summer both in supermarkets as well as farmer's markets. They are wonderful vegetables simply braised in a little olive oil and garlic, or cooked in butter and treated like spinach.

Broccoli

Broccoli is considered a new vegetable, as it has gained in popularity only in the last twenty years. It is a close relative to the cauliflower and can be used in many of the same preparations. Many supermarkets carry broccoli throughout the year, but I consider it a fall and winter vegetable, since it is at its best and least expensive from October through May. Even the most amateur cook has recognized the ease with which this versatile vegetable can be cooked, and fresh broccoli seems to be one of the best-selling vegetables during the winter months. It can be served either hot or cold, puréed in soups, or cooked, diced, and combined with rice in a saffron-flavored risotto.

When buying broccoli look for firm, compact, dark-green flower clusters. The leaves should be small and crisp, and the stems not too thick or woody. To keep broccoli fresh, it should be cleaned and stored in a plastic bag. Use within a day or two of purchase.

Brussels Sprouts

Miniature members of the cabbage family, Brussels sprouts become a supermarket item during the winter months. Unfortunately, they're almost always sold in 1-quart containers, which makes it impossible to select even-sized sprouts. Look for firm, compact, dark-green sprouts and discard those with yellowish outer leaves and soft, open heads. Properly cooked, Brussels sprouts do not have a cabbagy aroma, as some people tend to think. It is important to blanch them first for 8 to 10 minutes. Then drain them and they are ready to be braised in butter, alone or together with bacon and onions as in the Fricassée of Brussels Sprouts à la Campagnarde on page

416, a wonderful dish that does justice to this gutsy winter vegetable.

Cabbage

Considered a winter vegetable in Europe, cabbage is available here in every supermarket at all times of the year. This is probably due to the ever-constant popularity of cole slaw. But cabbage's year-round versatility and its affinity to so many other superb vegetables makes it good in soups, braised as an accompaniment to roast pork or duck, and particularly delicious when stuffed and braised in a tomato sauce. Most supermarkets only carry the smooth-leaf cabbage and the red cabbage, yet I much prefer the curly-leaved savoy cabbage, which is more delicate and flavorful. Savoy cabbage is carried by many supermarkets in the Northwest during the winter months, while in the Northeast it can only be found at specialty greengrocers'. It is, however, well worth the extra effort to find. (The Cabbage Soup à la Paysanne in *The Peasant Kitchen,* in which a whole head of stuffed cabbage is braised in a full-bodied meat stock is still one of my winter favorites.) Of all vegetables, the inexpensive red and white cabbage should be a staple in everyone's kitchen.

Carrots

Packaged carrots are carried by every supermarket. They are an all-season staple that should be on everyone's shopping list. An essential ingredient in stocks, they should be used creatively as a vegetable as well. In California supermarkets, as well as some Northeast markets, carrots are available with their green tops attached. These are far fresher than packaged carrots and are worth looking for.

When buying carrots by the bunch, look for those that are well formed, smooth, well colored and firm. If you do not plan to use them immediately, remove their feathery tops and store in a plastic bag. Young carrots are best when braised in a little water together with a lump of butter and a large pinch of sugar. Tossed with some parsley, dill, mint, chives, and a touch of cream, they are one of the most delicious yet inexpensive vegetables and go well with innumerable meat dishes.

Cauliflower

Cauliflower is one of the best and most versatile late summer and fall vegetables. In peak season you will find snowy white cauliflower, their heads cocked among crisp green leaves. By the time cauliflower is sold in the supermarket, most of the green leaf has been trimmed and the vegetable is wrapped in clear cellophane. Look for firm, compact, creamy-white heads. Avoid yellowish cauliflower and those with loose, open flower clusters. Cauliflower is a wonderful vegetable both hot and cold. Use it in a creamy soup or as a cooked vegetable tossed in a brown caper-and-lemon butter. As a salad, toss it in a mustard-flavored vinaigrette.

Celery

Celery is another kitchen staple. Together with carrots and onions, it is a must in the everyday kitchen. Celery is essential in flavoring stocks and many other vegetable soups. But it can also be used creatively on its own. The Celery Soup à la Francaise in *The Seasonal Kitchen* is a year-round favorite, and braised celery hearts are a delicious accompaniment to many meat dishes. (Celery hearts are sold in packages of two in most supermarkets.) When buying celery, look for fresh, crisp stalks of good green color and use the leafy tops as part of a Bouquet Garni (page 546). Store celery in a plastic bag. It will keep well for at least two weeks.

Corn
To anyone living in the Midwest and the Northeast, fresh corn is automatically associated with summer and early fall cooking. The best corn is always to be found at roadside stands. At the height of the season many supermarkets carry excellent corn, but since the key is absolute freshness, supermarket corn can never be quite the same as farmer's market corn, which is picked several times a day. When buying corn, look for fresh green husks with silky ends that are free of any brownish decay. Whenever possible, pull back the corn husks and choose the ones with small to medium-sized plumped kernels. Use corn on the day of purchase. Simply cooked and buttered, the delicious flavor of corn is unsurpassable, even by the most elaborate preparation.

Cucumbers
A basic staple on my shopping list, cucumbers are available year round in every supermarket. Although they often come packaged, you can better judge their freshness if you choose them yourself. Soft spots and shriveled ends usually indicate a bitter flavor. Cucumbers are one of the least expensive summer vegetables, and during that season should be used in both hot and cold preparations. A chilled cucumber soup is one of summer's best starters, and sautéed cucumbers are an excellent and flavorful garnish to roast chicken or poached and grilled fish. The hothouse or gourmet cucumbers are usually only carried by specialty greengrocers. Particularly in winter, I find them far superior to the average cucumber, since they are crisper, more flavorful, and less seedy. They are somewhat more expensive, but their crisp texture lends itself particularly well to sautéing.

Eggplant
Originally from Asia, the eggplant can be considered a Mediterranean vegetable. Every Mediterranean country uses this delicious vegetable creatively, both by itself and in combination with other vegetables. Most supermarkets carry eggplant at the peak season, August through September. Although you can find eggplants year round at every good greengrocer's, they are rarely good in winter months.

When buying eggplant, look for a firm, shiny fruit. Avoid cellophane-wrapped eggplants, since you will be unable to tell whether the skin is wrinkled or bruised. A good eggplant will be light. Heaviness, particularly in winter months, is an indication of large seeds and often bitter flavor. Use the vegetable within a day or two of purchase.

Garlic

Most garlic sold in supermarkets comes in small boxes, in which it is packaged two to a box. Avoid buying garlic this way and look for the large, crackly, firm white heads, which are fresher and whose individual clove is large and easy to peel. Fresh garlic is at the top of my shopping list. I'm extremely partial to it and love its characteristic flavor in many dishes as well as in salad dressings. Garlic bulbs will keep for several weeks stored in a dry vegetable bin.

Leeks

Unfortunately, leeks are still a specialty item in many regions, and although the demand for them is growing, many supermarkets seem to ignore this splendid vegetable. For me cooking would be incomplete without leeks. I use them in innumerable preparations, either in cream soups or as a flavoring for stocks. As a vegetable, poached leeks have an interesting, rather mild flavor. Cold they can be dressed in a mustard vinaigrette and served as an appetizer. Braised leeks are excellent combined with eggs in an open faced omelet or a quiche. In Seattle and San Francisco I saw lovely leeks in many supermarkets. However, in most regions they require a special stop at the greengrocer's.

When buying leeks, look for bunches with medium-sized bulbs. They should have crisp, dark-green tops. Although available year round, leeks are at their best and least expensive from October to May. If not using immediately, remove all but 2 inches of the leek's greens. Carefully rinse leeks, removing all sand and grit. Dry and store in a plastic bag. Leeks will keep from a week to 10 days.

Lettuce.

See under Salad Greens, pages 29–30.

Mushrooms

The only mushroom available commercially both in supermarkets and at greengrocers' is the cultivated white mushroom. Sometimes available loose, most mushrooms come packed in ½-pound or 1-pound cellophane-covered boxes. Look for creamy-white tops with caps that are tightly closed around the stem. Avoid mushrooms with wide-open caps and dark gills or spongy texture. Refrigerated in a brown paper bag, mushrooms will keep for 2 to 3 days. Do not wash them. Clean by gently rubbing the tops with a damp paper towel and use either raw in a salad or sautéed in butter as an accompaniment to roasts or sautéed meats and poultry. Mushrooms are used in many recipes in this book, in combination with other vegetables and in preparations such as a ragoût of veal.

Onions

One of the most important staples in the everyday kitchen, onions can be used creatively in innumerable dishes, many of them easy and inexpensive. You will usually find 2 to 3 varieties of onions in every supermarket. The all-purpose onion is the globe onion, and I use this only for cooking.

Red Onions
Red onions cannot be used in cooking but are excellent in salads, especially tomato or roasted pepper salads. Look for small onions with a dry, crackling skin.

Bermuda Onions
Bermuda onions are often available in supermarkets and have a much sweeter taste than the globe onion, though both serve basically the same purpose. Bermuda onions are particularly good for onion soup or braised in an onion quiche.

White Onions
I have only seen the tiny white (pearl) onions in supermarkets on the West Coast, but I have heard that they are sometimes available in supermarkets in the East. These are wonderful in innumerable dishes and especially as an accompaniment to roasts or in combination with other vegetables such as carrots, peas, and Brussels sprouts. If you see them in the market, buy them and plan your menu or vegetable dish around them. You will find many uses for them in this book.

Parsley
Just as my kitchen is never without fresh garlic, neither is it ever without parsley. Since parsley is available fresh in every supermarket year round, I see no reason to buy it dried and bottled, particularly since dried parsley flakes are no substitute for this delicate herb. Look for fresh, crisp parsley with deep green color. Avoid, if you can, cellophane-packaged parsley or parsley that is wilted or yellowish. Do not wash parsley until you are ready to use it. Simply store it in a plastic bag in the vegetable bin. It will keep up to 10 days.

Italian Parsley
While curly parsley is often used for decorative purposes, Italian flat leaf parsley is strictly a cooking herb. It is stronger in flavor than the curly variety and is an important flavoring for tomato sauces and stocks. It is usually only carried by specialty greengrocers, but I have seen it in many supermarkets both on the West Coast and the New York area.

Parsnips
Sold in packages the way carrots are, parsnips are a year-round vegetable available in most supermarkets. They are at their best in winter months, at which time they are a sweet, delicious and inexpensive vegetable. I keep them on hand at all times, just as I do carrots and onions. They are a good addition to all stocks, and when combined with carrots can be used for a spur-of-the-moment cream soup or vegetable purée. When buying parsnips, look for small to medium-sized firm, well-shaped spears. If you buy them loose, store in a plastic bag. They will keep for 10 days to 2 weeks.

Peas
Together with asparagus, fresh peas are a sure sign of spring. Unfortunately, outside of California they are not always available

in every supermarket, even during their peak season. This is a pity, because frozen or canned peas cannot compare in texture or flavor to fresh ones. Personally, I find it well worth the effort to stop at a specialty greengrocer's for fresh peas, and when I see them in the supermarket I always plan my menu around them. When buying peas look for young pods; break one open and taste the peas. They should be small to medium in size and very sweet. Avoid large or yellowish heavy pods, which indicate overmaturity and lack of freshness.

Peppers

Green peppers are a year-round vegetable carried by every supermarket. In addition to having a natural afinity to other summer vegetables such as tomatoes, cucumbers, and radishes, they can also be stuffed with a variety of inexpensive staples such as rice, tuna, and ground meat. All Mediterranean cuisines have made great use of the green pepper, and I have included many of my favorite preparations in *The Seasonal Kitchen* and *The Peasant Kitchen,* as well as here. The red bell pepper (basically the mature green pepper) can now be found in many supermarkets during the fall and sometimes even year round. Personally, I consider the red pepper one of the most exciting vegetables and buy them whenever I can. Roasted Red Peppers (see page 545) have a unique smoky flavor that is both mild and extremely interesting. I use them in many preparations throughout this book, hot in combination with meat and vegetables, or cold in salads or as an appetizer.

Select peppers that are firm, well shaped, thick skinned, and glossy. Avoid peppers that seem wilted and flabby or have punctured skins. In the summer, their natural peak season, peppers have the crispest texture and best flavor.

Potatoes

Together with onions, carrots, and celery, potatoes play a major part in the everyday kitchen. Unfortunately they are often used without much imagination and served simply baked, mashed, or fried. There are innumerable exciting ways to use this versatile vegetable, both hot and cold. The average supermarket carries 3 types of potatoes year round: the baking potato, the all-purpose potato, and the new potato (also called red potato). These cannot be used interchangeably and every knowledgeable cook should be familiar with the characteristics of each types. Baking potatoes are good for frying and for gratins (in which they are baked with grated cheese, butter, and cream or a meat sauce.) The all-purpose potato is good mashed and in puréed soups. The new potato is excellent for potato salads, and great for sautéing or for use in vegetable soups where the potato should retain its shape.

Select potatoes that are well shaped, firm, and unsprouted. Personally, I prefer buying potatoes loose rather than in bags, but most supermarkets do not give you the choice. The red new potatoes can either be brown-skinned or red. The best are the ones grown locally. They can usually be found at farmer's markets and roadside stands during spring and summer, their peak season. However, this varies according to the region. A bowl of small new potatoes simply cooked, buttered, and parslied is one of the great inexpensive and delicious dishes that reminds me year after year what freshness and taste is all about.

Radishes

Packaged radishes are avialable in every supermarket year round. The best radishes, however, are the ones that come with their greens attached. These are much fresher and far more flavorful. Radishes add their crisp, tangy flavor to many salads—particularly cucumber and green bean salads—and are good combined with romaine lettuce or watercress. A radish and cucumber salad tossed with fresh dill and garlic is a great, inexpensive year-round appetizer.

Although the tops indicate freshness, remove them as soon as you can and store the radishes in a plastic bag. They will keep for 10 days to 2 weeks.

Rutabaga

The rutabaga is known to many cooks by the name *turnip*. Actually, this large yellow-looking turnip has a much stronger taste than the white turnip, and I personally am not too fond of it. However, it is an inexpensive vegetable that is available in every supermarket during the winter months. When cooked, puréed, and enriched with butter and cream, the rutabaga is tasty, easy to prepare, and a

good accompaniment to roast pork, chicken, or duck.

Salad Greens

One of the most versatile part of the meal is the salad course. It has gained enormous popularity in recent years, and not just as the traditional accompaniment to the main course. Salads are now served either as starters or as simple and refreshing lunches or even supper meals. Personally, I much prefer serving a crisp salad together with a variety of well selected cheeses at the end of the meal, and I like to vary the greens and dressings according to the seasons. The first step towards making a good salad is knowing how to select your greens and their compatibility with each other and other vegetables. It is essential to remember that the salad bowl is not a catch-all, and that although extremely simple to make, a good salad requires some technique—particularly that demanded in putting together a well-balanced homemade salad dressing—and as much care as any well-prepared dish.

Belgian Endive

The Belgian endive does not belong to the salad green family only, but should be considered a vegetable as well. However, I am including it here because it is so often used in salads either in combination with lettuce or by itself. The Belgian endive is to the salad world what the raspberry is to the fruit world. A wonderfully versatile, unique, and exciting vegetable, endive are imported from Belgium, and they are expensive even in the height of their season, winter through spring. In the Northeast Belgian endive are carried by most supermarkets. I have also seen them in markets on the West Coast and in the Midwest. In other regions, buying endive may require an additional stop at a fine greengrocer's.

The endive is a compact, cone-shaped vegetable. Its color is creamy white, with some pale-yellow outer leaves. Wrapped in tissue, it is imported in boxes, but is often then carried in supermarkets in cellophane-wrapped packages (two to three in a package). When buying endive, look for very firm, well-bleached stalks four to six inches long. Avoid washing them. Simply wipe them with damp paper towels and remove any wilted outer leaves. If you must wash them, rinse them quickly under cold water but never let them soak, or else they will get excessively bitter. Endive will keep well refrigerated in a plastic bag for several days. Aside from serving them raw, endives can be served as a vegetable, as in the Braised Endives à la Provençale *(The Seasonal Kitchen)* or in a soup, as in the Cream of Endive Soup on page 103.

Bibb Lettuce
By far the most elegant lettuce, bibb is usually expensive and only available at top-quality supermarkets and specialty greengrocers'. A bibb, endive, and watercress salad adds an elegant finishing touch to a meal. Bibb resembles Boston lettuce but is much smaller and more compact, with crisper leaves and a more definite piquant flavor.

Boston Lettuce
The Boston lettuce is a delicate buttery green that lends its pretty leaves to many platter decorations. It is quite fragile and should not be combined with other greens in the salad bowl. Boston lettuce is available in most supermarkets everywhere and together with romaine I find it a wonderful basic lettuce that takes particularly well to a dressing like Claude's Lemon Vinaigrette on page 462. When buying Boston, look for fresh, crisp leaves and a tight core. Rinse the lettuce gently, then pat dry carefully with paper towels. Combine the lettuce with a dressing just before serving.

Curly Endive or Chicory and Escarole
Both the curly endive and the escarole are considered acid or character greens. They have a tangy, definite, somewhat mustardy flavor that combines well with other greens and takes well to a dressing such as the Vinaigrette Provençale on page 461. These lettuces should be served always with a full-bodied dressing made out of sherry wine vinegar and fruity virgin olive oil. Both greens are available at most supermarkets everywhere. Escarole can be braised like spinach in a little fruity olive oil and a few sliced cloves of garlic and served as a vegetable. It can be substituted for the Belgian endive in the Cream of Endive Soup on page 103.

Iceberg Lettuce
A crisp but uninteresting lettuce, the iceberg is a most popular lettuce in this country and is therefore available year

round everywhere. It is less perishable than any other lettuce and can be handled without much care. It does not absorb dressings well, and its crispness does not make up for its total lack of flavor. Personally, I never use it other than in certain sandwiches.

Leaf Lettuce (Field Lettuce)
Leaf lettuce is becoming increasingly popular and can now be found in many good supermarkets, particularly on the West Coast. The leaves are long and curly and do not form a head. They are either pale green or red-tipped in color. The leaf lettuce is a buttery, delicate green that does not combine well with other salad greens (with the exception of watercress) but has a personality all of its own. Look for crisp, fresh-looking lettuce. Rinse and dry carefully and use the same day as purchase.

Romaine Lettuce
By far my favorite lettuce, the romaine combines all of the essential qualities of a good, flavorful green. Available in all supermarkets year round, the romaine combines well with other greens, particularly fresh spinach, Belgian endive, and watercress, and takes well to a variety of dressings. It is also the only lettuce that can be added successfully to a mixed summer salad of tomatoes, cucumbers, peppers, and radishes. When buying romaine, avoid buying it in cellophane-covered packages. Look for crisp, long, bright leaves free of dark spots or decay. The outer leaves are often coarse and should be discarded. The inner leaves

have a lovely, pale-green color with a tangy, slightly bitter flavor. Once rinsed and dried, romaine can be stored in a plastic bag in the vegetable bin. It will keep for several days.

Watercress
The watercress is a member of the mustard family, which accounts for its peppery tangy flavor. Watercress is cultivated for commercial use in large quantities and is available in many good supermarkets. In some regions however, watercress is still considered a specialty item and requires an additional stop at a quality greengrocer's. Aside from its decorative purposes, watercress is a wonderful green that combines well with every other lettuce and is a marvelous addition to a mayonnaise and several soups. Watercress is usually sold in bunches and left packed in ice. Look for fresh, bright, deep-green watercress with crisp stems. Avoid limp watercress that has yellowish leaves. Store the watercress bunches in a bowl with ice cubes and cover loosely with a plastic bag. Use within a day or two of purchase.

Scallions
Also called *green onions,* scallions have a somewhat sharper flavor than chives. They are available in every supermarket. I use them for flavoring omelettes and in many salads, such as tuna, egg, sausage, cucumber, or mixed summer salads.

Shallots
One of the most important kitchen staples, the shallot is still a specialty item in many

areas. This is unfortunate, since the interest in cooking in general should have convinced supermarket chains by now that there is a demand for this important ingredient. The shallot is a cross between the onion and garlic, but it has a sweeter, more subtle flavor than either of them, that combines particularly well with wine and is essential in many sauces and fish preparations. Shallots can be kept for weeks in a plastic bag in a dry area of your refrigerator.

Snowpeas
For some mysterious reason in many markets it is now easier to find snowpeas than it is to find fresh peas of the regular variety. Although rarely available in supermarkets, many specialty greengrocers carry this crunchy and delicious vegetable practically year round. Its natural peak season, however, is from spring through September. Snowpeas are widely used in Oriental cooking, but cannot be substituted in recipes calling for fresh peas. They are one of the quickest and most delicious vegetables to prepare—quickly sauté or stir fry in a little vegetable oil with a touch of salt, sugar, and a little dry sherry.

When buying snowpeas, look for crisp, bright-green pods and avoid any yellowish wilted ones. Store the snowpeas in a plastic bag and they will keep for several days.

Sorrel
Sorrel is one of the great spring vegetables which I use extensively throughout this book, and I feel it has an important place in the everyday kitchen. Sorrel leaves can also be simply cooked down; they "melt" into a thick purée which freezes well. Together with leeks, shallots, Belgian endive, and fennel, sorrel is still considered a specialty item and requires an additional stop at a quality greengrocer's. Sorrel looks and cooks like spinach, but its somewhat sour flavor adds a tangy, interesting touch to many dishes.

When buying sorrel, look for young, slender, pale-green leaves and avoid those that are large, heavy, and dark green. These indicate maturity and usually result in an extremely sour and stringy texture. Use sorrel within a day or two of purchase.

Spinach
Spinach is by far the best and most versatile winter vegetable available to us. Many supermarkets carry spinach in 10-ounce cellophane bags. Other markets, particularly on the West Coast and in the Northwest, carry leaf spinach in bunches. Packaged spinach is cleaner (it is also called New Zealand spinach, and while it does belong to the spinach family, it lacks the flavor of real leaf spinach).

When buying spinach look for clean bags of crisp leaves and avoid any that show wet or yellowish spots. Loose spinach should be crisp, with dark, shiny leaves. After thoroughly cleaning spinach and rinsing it in several changes of cold water, remove the stems and cook as soon as possible. (Spinach can be cooked in a casserole without adding water. The water that clings to the leaves is sufficient.) Once cooked, spinach will keep for 3 to 4 days in a covered bowl.

Squash (Summer and Winter)

Summer Squash
Two types of summer squash are usually carried in supermarkets—the *zucchini* and the *yellow squash*. While both are at their best during the summer, zucchini are now available year round. Select zucchini that are firm, small, and well shaped, with glossy, dark-green skin. Avoid large zucchini (these are usually too seedy), or those that are pale green. Also avoid shriveled zucchini with soft tips. Zucchini will keep for 3 to 4 days and are one of the quickest vegetables to prepare. They can be simply sautéed in a fruity olive oil or braised in lemon butter. They're wonderful when combine with other vegetables, particularly roasted peppers, onions, tomatoes, and eggplant.

Winter Squash
Both the *acorn* and *butternut squash* are supermarket staples from fall through spring. I find acorn squash by far the most flavorful of all winter squash. Baked, puréed, and combined with butter and brown sugar, it is a delicious accompaniment to roast duck, roast pork, or turkey.

String Beans
String beans are now available in many regions year round, but they are better, tastier, and less expensive from June through August, the height of their natural peak season. In some regions, you will only find the flat green bean during the winter months. Personally, I much prefer the round, thin string bean, but both are excellent when cooked properly. When buying string beans, select clean, crisp, ripe beans that snap easily when bent. They should be crunchy and not too big; the smaller they are the better. Avoid beans packed in cellophane boxes, since it is hard to tell how crisp or fresh they are.

Wax Beans
The yellow wax bean is rarely available in supermarkets, probably because it is less popular. In the summer however it is to be found in many farmer's markets. Wax beans are cooked exactly as green beans, and are lovely when combined in a cold salad.

Tomatoes
Because of the incredible popularity of the tomato, this vegetable can be found in every supermarket year round and seems to be part of everyone's all-season shopping list. No matter how much is said in praise of the really ripe summer tomato, many people still buy the tasteless pink hothouse variety. Personally, I find them useless and prefer to wait for their natural season before buying them. The natural season, however, depends largely on regional availability. In Florida, Arizona, and California, good tomatoes can be bought in many supermarkets during the winter months. In those places they should be an important part of the essential shopping list. For those of us living in the

Northeast or the Midwest, delicious tomatoes are usually found only at farmers' stands, and the season is unfortunately limited to three short months. During that time, I consider the tomato the most important vegetable in the everyday kitchen.

When buying tomatoes, select firm, plump tomatoes that have the distinct aroma of the vine ripened fruit. Avoid pink hothouse tomatoes or those packaged in cellophane. To ripen a tomato, place in a brown paper bag and leave at room temperature until ripe. Chill until ready to serve, but always bring tomatoes back to room temperature before serving.

Turnips

In Europe, the tiny purplish-white turnip is a sure sign of spring. Here turnips are available in supermarkets year round. In California and the Northwest you can buy them with their greens attached, and you can tell more easily how fresh they are by the crispness of their tops. (Turnip greens are also a wonderful vegetable, one that can be cooked just like spinach or beet tops. Turnips are an inexpensive vegetable that works particularly well with carrots and potatoes. They're also an excellent addition to a hearty cabbage soup, white bean soup, or a creamy leek-and-potato soup.

In the Northeast turnips are mostly sold in bags during the winter and spring months. Since turnips are one of my favorite vegetables, I am always willing to make an additional stop at a greengrocer's, where I can usually pick small, even-sized turnips. When buying turnips with their tops, remove immediately and store the turnips in a plastic bag. They will keep for 4 to 6 days.

Dairy Products

Butter

I use only unsalted butter in cooking. The label on the package is often misleading. It will read "sweet butter" and then, in small print, "lightly salted butter." In supermarkets that have a small turnover, sweet unsalted butter is usually frozen. Since unsalted butter does not have the long shelf life of salted butter it has to be sold fresh. Once butter has been frozen it tends to be more watery and is more apt to burn. However, in cooking it is still better to use this than the salted kind.

Buttermilk

For anyone who has ever had a glass of buttermilk in Austria or Switzerland, ours simply cannot compare. However, it is a must in making Crème Fraîche. I usually use the leftover for buttermilk pancakes or Irish soda bread, which are both quick and fun to make.

Cheeses

Aside from the basic cooking cheeses such as ricotta, mozzarella, cream cheese, and Swiss cheese, good cheeses are rarely available in supermarkets unless the market has a deli counter where the turnover is large enough, and where a knowledgeable salesperson can assist you.

Parmesan and Romano

An important cooking cheese such as Parmesan is only good when bought by the piece or when grated at a good specialty shop. Avoid any canned or bottled Parmesan as well as Romano. Also avoid domestic Camemberts and any processed cheeses. Good Parmesan is expensive but well worth the additional cost. Specialty shops often sell both Parmesan and Romano, either grated (which is somewhat cheaper) or in bulk. Bulk Parmesan is the best way to buy this excellent cheese; it keeps for several months in the refrigerator. I usually prefer grating it myself in small quantities as I need it.

Cream Cheese

Unfortunately, we don't have much choice as far as cream cheese is concerned. All supermarket cream cheese is of the same quality. Personally, I prefer whipped cream cheese, since it is less gummy than the packaged variety. I keep cream cheese on hand at all times for quick fillings for tomatoes, cucumber balls, or mushrooms. Combined with a little sour cream, minced scallions, fresh dill, or sautéed mushrooms, a cream cheese filling is both inexpensive and quickly prepared.

Ricotta

Ricotta cheese is now a supermarket staple and is usually made by a regional dairy. This means that there are one or two brands available in every region. The only way to find a brand to your liking is to try various kinds. In heavily populated Italian areas, you will often find fresh ricotta available in an Italian or specialty grocery store. It is worth looking for, since this is a wonderful, mild cheese that can be used in many fillings, such as the Sausage Crêpes with Tomato Sauce on page 395, and in innumerable desserts, such as the Poached Pears in Ricotta-and-Orange Cream on page 517.

Mozzarella
This cheese is usually made by the same company that makes ricotta, and the quality can vary greatly. Fresh mozzarella is usually only available in Italian grocery stores. It is a wonderfully bland-textured cheese that is always automatically associated with pizza. Yet it can and should be used in many other preparations. Grilled red peppers alternating with finely sliced mozzarella and dressed in a garlic vinaigrette is one of my favorite summer appetizers. The Crostini alla Romano in *The Peasant Kitchen* is both a simple and inexpensive starter to a meal and can also be served as an easy supper dish. Here fine slices of mozzarella are sandwiched between thin slices of Italian bread and deep fried. They are then served in a garlic and anchovy butter.

Swiss Cheese
I only buy Swiss cheese by the piece, never sliced or grated. While supermarket Swiss cheese is bland and almost tasteless, it is useful to have on hand if you cannot get the imported Swiss, Appenzeller, or Gruyère cheese. Imported Swiss cheese usually comes from Argentina and is particularly useful in a gratin of potatoes or as a topping for sautéed breaded veal scaloppini.

Cream

Heavy Cream
Unfortunately, pure heavy cream is getting harder and harder to find. More and more supermarkets only carry ultrapasteurized cream. This cannot be used in making Crème Fraîche, nor does it whip as well as the non-ultrapasteurized heavy cream. Look for heavy whipping cream, and if it is not available ask for it at your supermarket. You can usually still find it in small grocery stores that carry dairy products from local dairies.

Sour Cream
Sour cream, like ricotta, is usually produced by a regional company, and the quality varies greatly from region to region. Personally, I prefer using Crème Fraîche (page 544), which is easy to make and far better than commercial sour cream. Crème Fraîche is made in Pennsylvania and shipped to many good specialty shopsacross the country. While it is very good, it is unreasonably expensive and I use it only when I need Crème Fraîche on the spur of the moment.

Eggs

Eggs are dated and are usually good when bought in a supermarket with a large turnover. Do not buy eggs by the size marked on the carton; rather, open the box and decide for yourself if the egg is really the size you want. It is also a good idea to make sure that none of the eggs are broken. Personally, I prefer brown eggs, since the shell is somewhat harder. Avoid buying eggs at farmers' markets unless you are sure their supply is local and fresh. These eggs are sold without being dated and are often not as fresh as the ones sold in supermarkets.

Frozen
Foods

Milk
The key to milk is freshness. If I have milk around for more than 3 to 4 days, I usually use it for a custard or a rice pudding.

Frozen Berries
Frozen strawberries and raspberries are both good to have on hand for a spur-of-the-moment dessert. Both can be puréed and used successfully as a topping for ice cream or sliced oranges, or to bind a fresh winter fruit salad.

Frozen Peas
Rather than a vegetable, frozen peas serve in the winter months as a garnish for some rice dishes, such as a paella or for a cream-of-vegetable soup. They provide texture and color rather than taste. Cooked, puréed, and buttered, however, they can be quite flavorful and I often use the purée as a bed for poached eggs or sautéed veal scaloppine.

Frozen Spinach
Frozen spinach is only useful for its color. You can use frozen spinach for the Spinach Crêpes on page 390 or as an addition to the stuffing in the boned and stuffed chicken on page 233.

Canned
Goods

Anchovies.
I keep both flat and rolled anchovies on hand at all times. I use the flat variety finely minced as a flavoring for butter sauces, salad dressings, and mayonnaise, as well as for some Mediterranean dishes. The rolled anchovies are usually used only as a garnish.

Anchovy paste
Anchovy paste is good to have on hand when you need small quantities of anchovies.

Bouillons
The use of canned bouillons as a substitute for stock is described in detail on page 94. All brands need bolstering with aromatic vegetables and possibly some meaty bones and chicken giblets. However, they are good to have on hand for a last-minute soup.

Caviar
I prefer the lumpfish caviar, and like both the red and the black varieties. They are inexpensive and very useful in a variety of fillings and sauces. I use them in many recipes throughout the book. Lumpfish caviar can be kept refrigerated for several months and is good to have on hand to garnish hard-boiled eggs or mix into a dill-flavored mayonnaise.

Legumes
White Beans, Kidney Beans, and Chick Peas
These canned legumes can be rinsed off and added for texture (rather than flavor) to various soups.

Peas
I find canned peas to be a vegetable in themselves. These have little to do (besides the shape) with real fresh peas, but I find them useful in a variety of dishes.

Roasted Peppers (Pimientos)
Although I would much rather roast my own peppers (see page 545), when using those already prepared, I prefer the jarred or canned variety of roasted peppers to pimientos. Although both are made from red peppers, pimientos have a strong, vinegary taste and come only in jars. The roasted peppers often come in cans and are somewhat less expensive. They have a pleasant smoky flavor, which is similar to the home-roasted peppers, but since the texture is different, I still much prefer making my own. Both roasted peppers and pimientos can be used interchangeably in many preparations throughout this book.

Sardines
I find sardines to be a wonderful kitchen staple, since they can be used for quick hors d'oeuvres or as a garnish to an egg salad. They're also delicious when simply served in a lemon and dill dressing. Buy only sardines packed in pure olive oil. Most people prefer them boneless and skinless. However, the ones with skins and bones are much more flavorful. Avoid canned oysters, canned mussels, canned shrimp, as well as canned crab meat and salmon. These items are usually expensive and have an artificial taste that does not compare to the fresh seafood.

Tomatoes

Since good fresh tomatoes are limited to a relatively short season in most parts of the country, canned tomatoes are an important part of the everyday kitchen. The quality of canned tomatoes varies greatly. Many brands are often sour and very watery. There are two to three good domestic brands and several imported ones available in specialty stores. Avoid chopped or diced tomatoes or those packed in heavy purée.

Tomato Paste

Tomato paste is extremely useful in the preparation of many dishes. Tomato paste adds color and sweetness to many tomato-based dishes. You can find tomato paste packed in tubes imported from Italy in many specialty stores. I usually search for this kind of tomato paste since it keeps well and you can use a teaspoon or two any time you need it without having to open an entire can, as is the case with commercial tomato paste.

Tuna

The best canned tuna is the one labeled *light tuna,* which is essentially dark tuna. It is more moist and somewhat less expensive than white tuna, and has a much betterflavor. Tuna packed in olive oil is by far the best. (Progresso tuna in olive oil is the only American brand I know, and I find it extremely moist and flavorful.)

Fruits

Dark raisins, golden raisins, currants, and prunes are important items in the everyday kitchen. Other dried fruits such as apricots and dates are good in many desserts but I find them less essential. All dried fruits should be sun ripened without any preservatives added to them. Most supermarket brands are satisfactory when properly stored (in well-sealed containers). and will keep for several months without drying out. Personally I prefer unpitted dates to the pitted variety since the texture and flavor is far superior. Most domestic dates are coated with corn syrup, which adds an unpleasant sweet flavor. During the holidays, however, many supermarkets carry sun-ripened dates in the produce section of the market. The best brands are Calavo and Dromedary. Dried apricots are a wonderful fruit but supermarket brands are never as good as the ones found in health food stores or specialty stores featuring nuts.

Herbs

Most supermarkets carry two to three brands of dried herbs. Personally, I find Spice Islands to be the best domestic brand. Because it is also the most expensive, it is not always available in every supermarket other than those on the West Coast, Arizona, and the Northwest. If you cannot get Spice Islands, look for bottled dried herbs that are coarsely ground and have a good, fresh color. Herbs and spices play a major role in every cuisine, but whereas spices are the basis of Indian, North African, and Middle Eastern cooking, herbs are more important in the cuisines of Europe in general, particularly France and the Mediterranean countries. The spice shelf has become an essential part of everyone's kitchen, and most cooks are now feeling more comfortable using herbs and spices. Unfortunately, most people, aside from not even knowing the difference between herbs and spices, use too many of both and use them often, arbitrarily, and indiscriminately.

Spices are made out of the more fragrant pungent roots, bark, buds, stems, and leaves of tropical and subtropical plants. Dried herbs are made out of the leaves of the fragrant, usually annual plants that grow in temperate climates. The everyday kitchen requires only six to seven dried herbs at any time. These should be kept in tightly closed jars, since their fragrant aroma evaporates rather quickly. Replace dried herbs every four to six months, and always rub the herb into a given dish between the palms of your hand to extract all the aromatic oils. A good, freshly dried herb will have a distinct and interesting aroma, while the one that has been sitting on your spice shelf for too long will lack any, and will not add any interest to your dish.

The six major dried herbs are thyme, oregano, rosemary, tarragon, bay leaves, and majoram. Sage, which is also a good herb when dried, is, however, more interesting and far more delicate when used fresh. It is excellent with pork and some lamb preparations, but is an acquired taste and can easily overpower a given dish. Other herbs, such as parsley,

dill, chives, garlic, chervil, and coriander are only good fresh. Avoid buying garlic powder or salt as well as onion salt or powder. These, more than any dried herb, change the flavor of foods, and would never be used by any serious, knowledgeable cook.

Hot Chili Peppers

Many recipes throughout this book call for dried hot chili peppers. These are the small red, hot chilies that are available dry in every supermarket in Texas and the West Coast but are only available in specialty shops and Oriental grocery stores in the Northeast and the Midwest. Since chili peppers keep indefinitely in a well-sealed jar, they are well worth looking for. If you cannot find them at all, use hot pepper flakes instead, but you must remember that the result will not be quite the same.

Mushrooms

Several recipes in this book refer to dried mushrooms. These are wild mushrooms that have been dried but cannot be used as a fresh vegetable any more. The best dried mushrooms are imported from Italy or Central Europe and can be found in many good specialty stores. These mushrooms have a unique smoky aroma and flavor that cannot be duplicated by fresh mushrooms. They add their marvelous taste to many sauces, risottos, veal, and chicken dishes. Dried mushrooms will keep in a well-sealed jar for as long as a year, and I find them an important kitchen staple.

Legumes

White beans, split peas, red kidney beans, lentils are the beans used most often. All these legumes are good to have on hand in your kitchen pantry. They are inexpensive and extremely nutritious. All legumes can be used in a variety of soups and salads. The white beans braised with onions, bacon, and cream in *The Seasonal Kitchen* is a wonderful accompaniment to many roasts, and cooked red kidney beans are a hearty and flavorful addition to a variety of ragoûts. Domestic brands of beans do not compare to those of Italy, France, or Spain. But imported legumes can only be found in Italian or Greek specialty shops. They are well worth the slight additional cost if you can findthem.

Pasta

Every supermarket carries a wide variety of dried pasta shapes. Personally I keep only spaghetti and spaghettini (thin spaghetti) on hand at all times unless I need a special shape for a specific dish. The quality of domestic dried pasta is discussed in detail in the introduction to the rice and pasta chapter on page 323. Although the ingredients on the box of imported dried pasta from Italy read the same as those of domestic, I find a great difference in texture between them. There is a great difference also among the domestic brands, and for those cooks who care about the consistency of their cooked pasta they should try the different brands as well as the imported ones. (I consider De Cecco to be the best imported dried pasta available in this country.) As a general guideline it is best to use thicker pasta such as spaghetti and flat noodles for heavier tomato or meat sauces and oil-based sauces or light cream sauces. Dishes that requires fresh pasta such as fettucine or ravioli cannot be made with any supermarket brand of dried pasta. Avoid frozen or prepared pasta dishes such as stuffed manicotti or baked lasagna.

When it comes to breads in the supermarkets it is indeed a sad tale. The only bread I can personally recommend buying in the supermarket is a unsliced home-style white bread. When sliced and sautéed in butter, it can be topped with avariety of braised vegetables; it is also used to prepare appetizers. When it comes to special breads—such as pita, rye, or black bread—these can be found in supermarkets catering to ethnic groups. There you may find good rye bread and Italian or French breads that are baked locally and delivered fresh to the supermarket every day. Avoid prepared breads such as garlic-flavored loafs or frozen herb-flavored breads. If you don't bake your own bread it is well worth the additional stop at a good bakery. You can freeze the breads for later use.

Flour
All-purpose, unbleached flour is a basic kitchen item. When making the Basic Tart Shell (page 483) in a food processor I prefer using Wondra instant flour, since it has a lower gluten content and produces a fine-textured crust. When making the dough by hand, however, use the all-purpose unbleached flour. A fine pastry flour is far better than any commercial flour in making puff pastry but obtaining it requires an additional stop at a specialty store. Semolina flour (made from durum wheat) is the only kind to use when making fresh pasta. It is not available in supermarkets but is carried by many specialty shops. It is well worth looking for, since the quality of the pasta is far superior when made with this flour.

Thickening Agents
Cornstarch, arrowroot, and potato flour are other essentials for the well-stocked kitchen. Cornstarch is useful for thickening sauces, generally red sauces. I often also use it for making pastry cream. Both arrowroot and potato flour are also useful for thickening sauces. Personally I prefer them to cornstarch, since they do not give food that glossy artificial appearance.

Cornmeal (Yellow)
Yellow cornmeal can be used in preparations that call for semolina, which is widely used in the making of the Italian dish polenta flavored with butter and Parmesan cheese. This is an excellent accompaniment to roast or grilled meats. I also like to serve it as an accompaniment to certain hearty ragoûts.

Rice

Rice is by far one of the most important kitchen staples, and any knowledgeable cook should have more than one type of rice on hand.

Regular Rice

Converted (parboiled) rice or long-grain rice are both long grain, but converted rice requires somewhat more liquid and takes a little more time to cook. It is also more expensive. Short-grained rice is only available in supermarkets catering to Spanish or Oriental communities. I like having this rice on hand at all times since it is far less expensive than long-grain rice and is excellent in many preparations. I use it in the curried ragoût of vegetables as well as in all rice desserts, such as the Lemon Caramel Rice Pudding on page 521.

Italian Rice

Italian rice is available only in specialty shops and is more expensive than any other cultivated rice since it is imported. It is, however, essential for making a true risotto and is well worth the additional cost. Long-grain rice can be substituted for Italian rice when necessary but it requires a different method of cooking and the result cannot be compared to the real risotto. Directions for how to make a true risotto are on page 327.

Brown Rice

Many health food advocates prefer brown rice to any other rice, and they are willing to spend the additional cooking time to prepare it. I prefer working with either long-grain, short-grain, or Italian rice since I find that these types lend themselves to many more preparations than brown rice.

Wild Rice

Wild rice is a luxury item that is more expensive than any other rice and is usually sold by only top-quality supermarkets. It has an interesting taste and texture that goes particularly well with roast duck, pork, turkey, or game.

Baking
and
Dessert Needs

Candied Fruits
Supermarket varieties of candied fruits are useful in many desserts. Because usually they are not as good as the ones found in specialty stores they usually need marinating in a liqueur beforehand to give them additional flavor.

Chocolate
Domestic chocolate does not compare to either Swiss or French chocolate but can be used successfully in most preparations. Always buy semisweet chocolate, which is higher in cocoa content. While I keep a basic good domestic brand such as Baker's semisweet chocolate at hand at all times, I will usually buy either Lindt semisweet or extra-bittersweet chocolate or the French Lanvin baking chocolate for special chocolate preparations. These can now be found in many specialty shops and in some top-quality supermarkets, as well as in many candy shops that carry imported chocolates.

Cocoa
The best cocoa (in my opinion the only cocoa to use) is the unsweetened Droeste cocoa imported from Holland. It is available in the gourmet section of almost every supermarket.

Coffee
Instant coffee is often used to flavor desserts and chocolate sauces. Whenever I have to use it I prefer using instant espresso coffee, as the taste is slightly stronger. Often recipes call for prepared coffee; for these I use good brewed coffee. Although buying coffee at the supermarket is more

convenient than stopping for it at a specialty shop, it is not much less expensive and the difference in quality, choice, and taste is enormous. People who care about the complete meal will naturally seek out coffee beans in a specialty store with a good variety of types and blends. Fortunately, a growing variety of coffees are now offered, not only in gourmet shops but also in the fine food sections of department stores. Many good coffees may be purchased unblended and then you can grind and blend them to your own satisfaction. This allows you to create a blend that is suitable to your own taste.

Gelatin
A staple in everyone's kitchen, unflavored gelatin should be used carefully; too much can result in desserts that taste and look like glue. Used carefully gelatin is an important addition to many mousses and Bavarian creams.

Leavening Agents
Both baking soda and baking powder are essentials that every cook needs to have on hand to prepare many cakes and desserts.

Nuts
When buying nuts it is best to look for those sold in vacuum-packed cans where you are more assured of freshness.

Almonds
Usually whole almonds are less expensive than the slivered variety. The freshest almonds are whole unpeeled ones, but for most recipes they will have to be blanched,

and for some recipes they also have to be
toasted. To blanch place the almonds in
boiling water for 1 minute then peel. To
toast place the blanched almonds on a
cookie sheet in a 200-degree oven for
5 minutes, or until dry and lightly
toasted.

Hazelnuts (Filberts)
Unfortunately hazelnuts are not available in
the average supermarket and require a
special trip to aspecialty store. They are
extremely important, however, in the
preparation of many desserts. While walnuts
and pecans are often interchangeable,
hazelnuts have a unique and interesting
flavor that cannot be substituted for by
either walnuts or almonds.

Pine nuts (Pignolias)
These are a specialty item but seem to be
increasingly available in good supermarkets
throughout the country. They come either
jarred or in cellophane packages. The
packages are usually less expensive than
the jarred variety, but you should be
careful, since their freshness depends
largely on the supermarkets' turnover. Pine
nuts are excellent in many stuffings,
desserts, rice dishes, and some
Mediterranean sauces.

Sugar
The basic kitchen needs four types of sugar:
granulated, very fine or superfine, dark
brown, and confectioners' sugar. I use the
superfine sugar when making chocolate
sauces and meringues because it dissolves
more quickly. Brown sugar is excellent

when melted with butter for sautéing fruit
such as apples, pears, or bananas.

Unless you are cooking one or another type of ethnic food, such as Indian or Northern African, that requires a great deal of spices, buy spices in small quantities and store in well-sealed jars no longer than 4 to 6 months. Some spices are best kept refrigerated, such as paprika, ground cumin and chili powder. Aside from the basic ground spices (cinnamon, ginger, nutmeg, ground cloves, caraway seeds, ground cumin, curry powder, ground allspice, tumeric, and saffron), you will also need cinnamon sticks and vanilla beans. (Along with vanilla extract, the vanilla bean is an essential ingredient in every kitchen. Use the bean for sugar syrups and flavoring milk, since the extract will discolor the food and add a bitter flavor if cooked; it should only be used to flavor finished dishes.) Many spices (cloves, nutmeg, cumin seeds, coriander seeds, and allspice) are far more flavorful when bought whole and ground as needed. Some can be ground with a mortar and pestle, others in a pepper or spice mill. Nutmeg should be grated; nutmeg graters are an essential gadget available in every cookware shop.

Extracts

Pure vanilla (the best brand is made by Park Davis and is sold in most drugstores), pure almond, and pure orange extracts are essential in the everyday kitchen. Avoid any artificial extracts. Pure lemon extract is good to have on hand for acidulating water. A few drops in a large bowl of water will keep apples, pears, or artichokes from turning dark.

Mustard

In my opinion, the best mustard on supermarket shelves is the Grey Poupon Dijon-style mustard, which is made in this country according to a Dijon formula. Some supermarkets carry imported Dijon mustards; however I find them more expensive and rarely of better quality than the domestic variety. For specialty mustards such as Pommery and herb-flavored mustards, it is best to buy these at a specialty store. These mustards are considered condiments rather than cooking mustards. Other good cooking mustards are Diablo and Colman's. Traditionally Colman's only came in dry form but now is also available as prepared mustard. (When reconstituted, dry mustard is extremely strong and very good as an addition to many sauces or as an accompaniment to poached fish and shellfish dishes.) Be sure to reconstitute dry mustard in a little water and let it develop flavor for 30 minutes to 1 hour before using.

Salt

The best cooking salt is coarse salt, often called kosher salt. When buying table salt avoid the iodized kind; personally I find thischanges the flavor of foods.

Soy Sauce
I much prefer buying soy sauce in an Oriental specialty store, where there is a choice of both dark and light soy sauce and where the quality is far superior. However, when such a shop is not available to you, supermarket soy sauce will do.

Tabasco and Worcestershire Sauce
Both of these are essential basics for flavoring certain hot and cold sauces. One bottle of each will usually last you for about a year.

Vinegar

Cider Vinegar
Cider vinegar is the all-purpose golden brown vinegar made from apples. It is good to have on hand for certain salads, such as cucumbers, red cabbage, and beet salads.

Distilled White Vinegar
This vinegar is used mostly for pickling. I usually keep it on hand during the summer when I pickle my surplus garden vegetables such as green beans, peppers, or cucumbers.

Wine Vinegars
Both red and white wine vinegars are essential to a good salad dressing and are an extremely important basic to have on hand. Good red wine vinegar is rarely available in supermarkets although Spice Island and Four Monks are the best

domestic brands. In recent years a French vinegar called Dessaux Fils, an imported French vinegar from Orléans, has become available in many good supermarkets. Many excellent French and Spanish wine vinegars can be found in specialty stores and cook stores throughout the country. They are well worth their higher cost since their flavor is so important in many dishes. Be sure to keep vinegars in a cool, dry place or they will mold and produce a sediment.

Specialty Foods

Honey

Most supermarket brands of honey are neither interesting nor exceptionally flavorful. However there are marvelous, interesting types of honey available at all good specialty stores. Excellent honeys such as Swedish or English heather or clover honey are delicious when added to whipped cream together with some scotch or a flavored liqueur. Honey is a wonderful topping for a cup of freshly made espresso coffee or as an accompaniment to a chocolate mousse.

Jams and Jellies

Jams have lately become a gourmet item and the available variety has grown in supermarkets everywhere. The best jams, however, are still the ones carried in specialty stores. For cooking purposes, both apricot preserves and currant jellies are the most used in the kitchen. These can be bought in every supermarket, even under store brands.

Olives

Black Olives

Avoid canned black olives; they simply have no taste whatsoever. You can now find bottled or cured olives in many good supermarkets. (These have wrinkled skins and are similar to the niçoise olive from the south of France.) Greek olives are large oil-cured olives that areusually available in the dairy department of large supermarkets and are good in many salads and as a garnish.

Green Olives

These can be bought in every market. Some come stuffed with pimientos, others with anchovies. I prefer the whole unpitted green olives or the cracked green olives found in Italian specialty stores.

Oils

The quality of oil used in the basic kitchen is of great importance. As a cooking oil I use peanut or safflower oil. Good olive oil is essential in salad dressings and for sautéing vegetables or for the many Mediterranean dishes in this book. Avoid buying "imported olive oil" or any olive oil under a supermarket label. A label marked "imported olive oil" does not indicate where that oil comes from and is usually bottled with a mixture of mediocre oils with a rancid, unpleasant flavor. Pure Italian olive oils (either Berio or Bertolli) are now available in most supermarkets. The extra virgin olive oils (made from the first pressing of the olives) are usually imported from France and are only carried in good specialty stores. Fine Italian virgin olive oils are harder to find even in these specialty shops. Both, however, are well worth looking for and also worth the additional cost. The unique flavor of a fine olive oil is hard to duplicate and it is often essential to the success of many preparations.

Pickles

The only pickles that I find useful in many preparations are the dill gherkins, which are mild-flavored and have a crisp texture. They can be diced and included in sausage, rice, tuna, or other cold salads.

Teas

Quality teas are now sold in the gourmet
sections of most supermarkets. Twinings
Teas imported from England are sold both
bagged and loose. Again as with coffee, tea
buffs should seek the unusual teas at
gourmet and specialty shops.

Appetizers

When I think of appetizers, the word conjures up images of Northern European and Mediterranean cuisines and the leisurely eating and drinking in those countries that always initiate a fabulous meal. To me this course represents the important, relaxing transition from the chores and cares of the day to the pleasures of the dining table. Like magnificent scenery on a stage when the curtain has just risen, the appetizer must hint at the action to follow, teasing the palate and whetting the appetite without giving away too much or reflecting too specifically the things to come. It must be *just right*—carefully planned and in perfect balance with the menu in general. Obviously you would not serve a country pâté to be followed by a hearty beef stew, or two dishes both in a tomato sauce. Use common sense and try to select an appetizer that will make an interesting contrast with the main course.

For many people the word *appetizer* brings to mind little tidbits of food. The English use the word *starters*, which to my mind is really more appropriate. A starter or hors d'oeuvre can be anything at all, and with just a little imagination and creativity an immense variety of foods can come into the picture. For an informal occasion it can be something as simple as a hard-boiled egg topped with a dollop of mustard-flavored mayonnaise or a raw mushroom salad delicately tossed with a homemade vinaigrette. At an important dinner party a more elaborate choice might take center stage: a salmon mousse, spinach crêpes filled with a velouté of seafood, pâté en croute, or any of the appetizers of *haute cuisine*.

Most of the time, however, the appetizer should be something simple and light. The peasant cook's way of creating a menu has always held a special fascination for me. If you examine any ethnic cuisine you will find that the appetizers are usually made from the most basic ingredients available, and they always reflect the season and the climate. As the peasant cooks know so well, often we too can turn to nature for the perfect inspiration. The Mediterranean kitchen has always had a special flair for presenting vegetables ingeniously. All through that region cooks set vegetables apart from the rest of the meal, giving them the importance they deserve. Following their native instincts they turn almost any vegetable dish into a wonderful appetizer. The Basque way of serving roasted red peppers with sliced onions and an anchovy-and-garlic cream is one of my favorite fall appetizers. In the winter, I often start a meal with a hearty vegetable ragoût such as the Fricassée of Brussels Sprouts à la Campagnarde (page 416). A Greek raw vegetable salad is a perfect beginning to any summer meal. The combination of ripe tomatoes, cucumbers, peppers, onions, and fresh crumbled feta cheese dressed simply in olive oil and vinegar is a glorious yet simple starter. Asparagus is a superb spring appetizer served either hot or cold and dressed with a vinaigrette, Hollandaise, mustard sauce, or simply lemon butter. In fact, almost every cooked vegetable in season, when treated with understanding, imagination, and respect, can become the delicious opener of a meal.

Central European cuisines make great use of soups as starters, from the many varieties of gutsy winter legume soups to the light and lovely summer fruit soups. In some areas, such as Alsace in France or regions of Austria, Germany, and Hungary, where sausages and hams are an important part of the region's cooking, you will always find tasty sausages, country pâtés, tangy sausage-and-potato salads, or even a simple slice of ham set out on the table to precede the main dish.

When it comes to using fish as starters, no one can rival the Scandinavians. Because of a profusion of herring and other small fish, these countries have created an incredible array of fish salads. When these fish dishes are added to the already wide selection of Scandinavian appetizers, they make the Swedish smörgåsbord one of the most brilliant and unforgettable appetizer tables anywhere in the world. Denmark is another country that has proved its ingenuity when it comes to appetizers. The Danes have mastered the art of the open sandwich, using the simplest of ingredients to turn each into a tiny masterpiece. A slice of hard-boiled egg, a radish, a slice of cucumber, and a lovely sprig of fresh parsley mounted on a small square of dark bread is all that is needed to create a beautiful, simple morsel that is a perfect starter to a meal. For those who think that the word *appetizer* is synonymous with

"fingerfood," here is fingerfood elevated to its highest aesthetic level.

What the smörgåsbord is to Scandinavia, the antipasto is to Italy. Beautifully arranged and one of the great visual joys of the table, it is a colorful spread of raw vegetables, salads, various salami, prosciutto, marinated fish and shellfish, and a variety of olives. Since most Italians would consider a meal incomplete without some kind of pasta, almost invariably that comes next—perhaps some fresh gnocchi (marvelous potato dumplings) or a small portion of fettucine tossed in a sauce. While Americans think of their meals in terms of a meat dish, vegetables, a starch, and possibly a salad served all at once, the Italian cook astutely separates the elements. Following the antipasto or pasta is either a meat, fish, or poultry dish, usually served simply with crusty bread and a vegetable. This logical and well-balanced meal concludes with a salad and simple fruit dessert. It is to my mind just as simple (if not simpler) for the cook to prepare than a meal that requires juggling three or four dishes at once.

In Spain it is the egg that is considered a multifaceted mainstay of the daily menu. The Spanish have an inspired way with this simple, basic food. The open-faced omelet flavored with spinach, onions, or potatoes and served in pie wedges is a classic in Catalan cooking. Fried eggs placed on a bed of stewed tomatoes with peas and chorizo sausage is a favorite in the south. Years ago, some kind of fish was as essential to the appetizer spread as was the egg; a Spanish cook would not have considered a meal complete without it. Unfortunately today few people can afford the luxury of fresh fish and now it is reserved for use as a special appetizer and main course, often served only on Friday. Shellfish, however, remain a highly popular part of the "tapas"—the Spanish version of hors d'oeuvres. Mussels in a spicy tomato sauce and tiny clams stewed in garlic and olive oil are two of my favorites; they are still to be enjoyed in most restaurants and in many Spanish homes. Vegetables too are used creatively as starters in Spanish cooking. One of the reasons I have always loved cooking them as much as I do is that I can remember the care with which I always saw them being prepared. In our house they were served almost daily as appetizers, and I still find myself serving them this way today.

From the Spanish tapas to the Italian antipasto, the international or ethnic array of appetizers is varied, delicious, and tantalizing. In this country we have all the ingredients available to us to create nearly all the great ethnic starters. If we want to give an Italian, Indian, or Middle Eastern theme to an appetizer course, or even to a meal itself, all we need to do is explore some of the good specialty shops that can now be found in most major cities.

For the everyday cook, however, appetizers can most easily be made from the staples of the kitchen and supermarket. Most often that is where the working person has to turn when he or she wants to prepare an easy yet attractive and tasty starter to a meal. I always keep my pantry stocked with the ingredients that will allow me to prepare an appetizer without much fuss: tuna, anchovies, eggs, pimientos, a good fruity olive oil, and vinegar. These are the beginnings of any number of unpretentious and delicious appetizers: hard-boiled eggs cut in half and garnished with a parsley- or curry-flavored homemade mayonnaise; tomato halves or cucumber boats stuffed with a quickly made, spicy tuna salad; or seasonal supermarket staples such as broccoli, mushrooms, or carrots dressed in oil and vinegar. Even a cheese soufflé can be made in a matter of minutes with such market staples. And now with the food processor, a French country pâté—generally considered by most housewives as a gourmet treat that would have to come from a specialty shop—can become one of the simplest and least expensive appetizers you can make at home.

Of all courses, appetizers are one of the most challenging to the inventive cook. Leftovers can be used ingeniously in devising new and exciting appetizers. Creating something special and unique from an ordinary staple—an egg or canned tuna—demonstrates a cook's inventiveness and knowledge of food. I remember how impressed and delighted I was last year during a visit to the home of an excellent cook in Sweden. Here was the elegant smoked salmon presented in a completely new way. This hostess served a mound of buttery braised spinach placed on individual slices of sautéed bread, which were topped with the lovely salmon cut into thin julienne strips.

In most kitchens cold roast beef can be diced and used together with some diced cooked potatoes to make an interesting appetizer salad. So can cold tongue, roast turkey, and many vegetables. Any cold meat, served at room temperature rather than straight from the refrigerator, can become the basis of an appetizer when dressed with a caper sauce or anchovy mayonnaise; even leftover rice and cooked potatoes can be transformed into delicious starters.

In this country we are especially fond of raw vegetables. Yet I am always surprised and disappointed to find that carrot sticks and celery stalks seem to be the most popular—often the *only*—items that go on the crudité platter. Cucumbers, radishes, broccoli, cauliflower, red and green peppers, and fennel will add color and character to the raw vegetable platter and will certainly make it a far more attractive spread. A cream-of-anchovy sauce is the perfect accompaniment to crudités, as it is for nearly every kind of dip. In fact a versatile range of dips can be made using homemade mayonnaise or yogurt as a base. These are infinitely more exciting than the prepared ones you can buy in the store.

Admittedly it is hard to surpass the classic marriage of sweet sliced prosciutto and a ripe piece of melon, or the instant elegance of a beautifully sliced smoked salmon, so

reminiscent of the appetizer cart in most elegant restaurants. While I agree that these expensive starters certainly have a place on the formal menu (particularly for the cook who is pressed for time or is organizing a last-minute dinner party), essentially these do not require any imagination or talent. If you are going to serve something like this, with more exotic fruits often available nowadays, why not serve the prosciutto with sliced mangoes, kiwis, or—as the Romans do—with figs? I am delighted every time a cook adds a new twist or gives a personal "signature" to the simplest of ingredients. When I think of smoked salmon, it is not the restaurant hors d'oeuvre cart that I remember with such pleasure, but the lovely appetizer served by the inventive Swedish cook.

At home I may serve appetizers in the living room with pre-dinner drinks, at the table, or, on occasion, even as a major part of an informal meal accompanied by soup and dessert. But whether I am eating in a Spanish *taverna,* a French *bistro,* or in my own home or someone else's, an innovative, inviting appetizer always represents a particularly gracious beginning to the meal. It offers a sense of anticipation and well-being unmatched by any other course.

Artichokes
in
Piquant Hollandaise

Serves: **6**
Preparation time: **15 minutes**
Cooking time: **25 minutes**
Type of recipe: **elementary**
Cost: **moderate**

Ingredients
6 large artichokes
1 lemon, halved

Sauce:
4 large egg yolks
2 teaspoons white wine vinegar
1 Tablespoon ice water
1 cup hot melted butter
2 Tablespoons well-drained tiny capers
1 small dill gherkin, finely minced
3 to 4 anchovy fillets, finely minced
1 Tablespoon finely minced shallots or scallions
Salt and freshly ground black pepper

Garnish:
Sprigs of fresh parsley

Preparation
1.
Cut the stems off the artichokes. With a sharp knife cut the tips off the leaves. Immediately rub the cut parts with 1 lemon half.
2.
In a large enamel casserole bring salted water to a boil. Add the artichokes and cook for 20 to 25 minutes, or until tender. Test by piercing the bottoms with the tip of a sharp knife.
3.
While the artichokes are cooking, make the sauce. In a heavy enamel cast-iron saucepan combine the yolks, vinegar, and ice water. Whisk the mixture until well blended. Place the saucepan over the lowest possible heat and cook, whisking constantly, until the mixture starts to

thicken. Add the melted butter a few drops at a time as if you were making a mayonnaise. The mixture will thicken. If it shows any signs of curdling immediately remove from the heat and add 1 tablespoon ice water. Continue whisking until the sauce is thick and smooth and all the butter has been incorporated.
4.
Remove the sauce from the heat. Add the capers, gherkin, anchovies, and shallots or scallions and blend well. Taste and correct the seasoning, adding salt and a large dash of pepper. Set the sauce aside.
5.
Drain the artichokes and carefully spread the leaves out from the center. Scoop out the fuzzy choke with a grapefruit spoon and fill each artichoke with a little sauce. Place on a serving platter and garnish with sprigs of parsley; serve the remaining sauce on the side.

Remarks
This piquant Hollandaise is equally good with other vegetables such as broccoli or asparagus. It is also an excellent accompaniment to poached bass or salmon steaks.

Artichokes
in
Lemon-and-Garlic Sauce

Serves: **4 to 6**
Preparation time: **10 minutes**
Cooking time: **20 minutes**
Type of recipe: **elementary**
Cost: **moderate**

Here is a delicious, cool spring hors d'oeuvre. Tiny artichokes are available in most California markets. In late spring they can also be found in many Italian markets throughout the northeast.

Ingredients
12 to 16 small artichokes
Juice of ½ lemon
1 large lemon, cut in quarters
6 to 8 Tablespoons fruity olive oil
8 peppercorns
3 large cloves garlic, peeled and crushed
1 large sprig fresh thyme, or 1 teaspoon dried
1 bay leaf
Salt

Garnish:
Finely minced fresh parsley

Preparation
1.
Remove several layers of artichoke leaves until only the light green tender cones are left. Trim the bases and cut 1 inch off the tops. Quarter the artichokes and drop into a large bowl of water. Add the lemon juice. This will keep the artichokes from turning dark.
2.
In a 10-inch enamel skillet combine the quartered lemon, olive oil, peppercorns, garlic, thyme, and bay leaf. Add the artichokes and enough water to barely cover. Season with salt, then bring to a boil. Reduce the heat and simmer partially covered for 15 to 20 minutes, or until tender but not falling apart.
3.
Transfer to a serving bowl, discard the quartered lemons, cool, and serve sprinkled with parsley.

Cold
Asparagus
Tivoli

Serves:	**4 to 6**
Preparation time:	**15 minutes, plus overnight to chill sauce**
Cooking time:	**10 minutes**
Type of recipe:	**elementary**
Cost:	**inexpensive**

Ingredients

1½ cups Crème Fraîche (page 544) or sour cream
3 Tablespoons sauerkraut juice
2 teaspoons grated onion
2 to 3 Tablespoons minced fresh chives
3 Tablespoons finely minced fresh dill
Salt and freshly ground black pepper
2 pounds fresh asparagus
Juice of ½ lemon
2 Tablespoons olive oil

Optional:

½ cup finely diced, freshly cooked and peeled shrimp

Preparation

1.
A day ahead, combine the Crème Fraîche or sour cream in a bowl with the sauerkraut juice, onion, chives, and dill. Season the mixture with salt and pepper, then add the optional shrimp. Chill the mixture overnight.

2.
The next day peel the asparagus with a vegetable peeler and cut off the tough ends of each stalk. Tie the asparagus into equal bundles, leaving 1 stalk loose for testing.

3.
Bring salted water to a boil in a large pot. Add the asparagus bundles and cook them uncovered over high heat for 10 minutes, starting to test for doneness after 8 minutes. Cook until just tender, then drain and rinse under cold water to stop any further cooking. Put on a double layer of paper towels and, when drained well, place on a serving platter.

4.
Sprinkle the asparagus with lemon juice, olive oil, and a large grinding of black pepper. Lightly chill and serve with the sauce in a dish on the side, accompanied by thinly sliced black bread and a bowl of sweet butter.

Remarks

The sauerkraut juice adds an interesting pungency to the sauce. If you cannot find sauerkraut juice, drain a small can of sauerkraut, which will render about ½ cup juice. You may add more juice if you like. The sauce is equally good with hot asparagus, with 3 tablespoons melted butter instead of the lemon juice and oil.

Avocado-Stuffed
Tomatoes

Serves: **6**
Preparation time: **35 minutes, plus 2 to 4 hours to marinate**
Cooking time: **none**
Type of recipe: **elementary**
Cost: **inexpensive**

Ingredients

12 small shrimp, cooked and peeled
½ cup Vinaigrette Provençale (page 461)
6 ounces cream cheese
2 large cloves garlic, peeled and crushed
Salt and freshly ground black pepper
1 large ripe avocado, peeled and cubed
2 Tablespoons finely minced fresh parsley
2 Tablespoons finely minced fresh chives
6 medium ripe tomatoes

Garnish:
Sprigs of fresh parsley

Optional:
2 tablespoons sour cream

Preparation

1.
Place the shrimp in a small bowl. Add a little vinaigrette, toss, and chill for 2 to 4 hours.

2.
In a blender or food processor combine the cream cheese, garlic, salt, pepper, and avocado. Purée the mixture until smooth. When using a blender you may need 1 to 2 tablespoons sour cream.

3.
Transfer the mixture to a bowl and season with salt and pepper, then add the parsley, chives, and remaining vinaigrette. Blend the mixture. Taste and correct the seasoning, then cover and chill.

4.
Cut ¼ inch off the tomato tops, then carefully scoop out the pulp and seeds. (Reserve the pulp for soups and stocks.)

5.
Sprinkle the tomatoes with salt and let them drain upside down on a double layer of paper towels for 20 minutes.

6.
Fill the tomatoes with the avocado mixture. Top each with a sprig of parsley and garnish each tomato with 2 of the marinated shrimp. Serve chilled as an appetizer.

Remarks

The avocado-and-cream-cheese mixture can also be served as a dip for all vegetables. If you serve it this way, add another ¼ cup vinaigrette to the dip. You may also vary this simple appetizer by dicing the shrimp and adding them to the avocado mixture, serving the tomatoes on a bed of Boston lettuce.

Eggplant Sandwiches
à la Genovese

Serves: **6 to 8**
Preparation time: **30 minutes**
Cooking time: **1 hour**
Type of recipe: **elementary**
Cost: **inexpensive**

Ingredients

3 to 4 large eggplants, cut into ½-inch slices
Salt
Ice water
1 cup fresh basil leaves, rinsed and dried
6 Tablespoons fruity olive oil
½ to ¾ cup vegetable oil, for sautéing
2 Bermuda onions, cut in half and thinly sliced
2 large cloves garlic, peeled and finely mashed
Freshly ground black pepper
1 Tablespoon tomato paste
4 to 5 large ripe tomatoes, peeled, seeded, and chopped, or 1 can (35 ounces) Italian plum tomatoes, well drained and chopped
Large pinch of dried oregano
1 teaspoon dried thyme
8 to 12 thin slices mozzarella cheese

Garnish:
Finely minced fresh parsley
Pimiento strips
Greek black olives

Optional:
Rolled anchovy fillets

Preparation

1.
Do not peel the eggplant. Drop the slices into a large bowl of salted ice water and let the eggplants soak for at least 30 minutes. Drain the eggplant slices thoroughly on a double layer of paper towels.

2.
While the eggplant is soaking, place the basil leaves in a blender and add enough olive oil to make a smooth paste. Reserve the basil paste.

3.
Heat the vegetable oil in 2 large skillets. Add the eggplant slices and sauté until nicely browned on both sides. Transfer the eggplant slices to a double layer of paper towels and set aside.

4.
In a heavy 10-inch skillet heat the remaining olive oil. Add the onions and garlic and cook the mixture for 10 minutes over medium heat. Partially cover the skillet and continue cooking the onion mixture for 35 to 40 minutes, or until very soft and nicely browned.

5.
Season with salt and pepper. Add the tomato paste and tomatoes. Add oregano, thyme, and half the basil paste. Bring to a boil and cook the mixture until the tomato water has evaporated and the mixture is thick. Whisk in the remaining basil paste. Taste the mixture and correct the seasoning. Let it cool.

6.
Place single rounds of eggplant on a serving platter. Top each with a slice of mozzarella and then with a little of the

Serves:	**6**
Preparation time:	**15 minutes**
Cooking time:	**none**
Type of recipe:	**elementary**
Cost:	**inexpensive**

onion-tomato mixture. Cover with the remaining slices of eggplant.

7.
Sprinkle each eggplant sandwich with a little minced parsley. Garnish with rolled strips of pimientos and black olives, or use rolled anchovy fillets instead of the black olives. Serve the eggplant sandwiches at room temperature as an appetizer or as an accompaniment to roast or grilled lamb or a barbecued steak.

Remarks
The eggplant sandwiches can be made hours ahead and left at room temperature. For variation you could add finely minced anchovy fillets to the tomato mixture.

Some sliced ripe tomatoes, alternated with thinly sliced mozzarella and dressed in a basil vinaigrette, are one of summer's most refreshing appetizers. Come fall, try a switch to red peppers and an anchovy-flavored dressing. The result is an equally delicious and colorful fall appetizer.

Ingredients
8 to 10 large Roasted Red Peppers (page 545)
1 package (14 ounces) whole milk mozzarella cheese, thinly sliced
6 Tablespoons fruity olive oil
3 Tablespoons red wine vinegar
1 large clove garlic, crushed
1 to 2 teaspoons anchovy paste
1 small red onion, peeled and thinly sliced
2 Tablespoons finely minced fresh parsley

Garnish:
8 to 10 Greek black olives

Grilled Peppers
with
Garlic-and-Anchovy Sauce

Serves:	**4 to 6**
Preparation time:	**10 minutes**
Cooking time:	**10 minutes**
Type of recipe:	**elementary**
Cost:	**inexpensive**

Preparation

1.

Prepare the peppers according to the directions on page 545. Cut in half lengthwise.

2.

Place the peppers on a rectangular serving platter alternating them with mozzarella slices.

3.

Combine the oil, vinegar, garlic, and 1 teaspoon anchovy paste in a small jar. Cover and shake the dressing until smooth and well blended. Taste and correct the seasoning. You may want a stronger taste of anchovies; if so, add the remaining teaspoon and blend thoroughly into the dressing.

4.

Spoon the dressing over the platter with peppers and cheese and sprinkle with onion rounds and parsley. Garnish with black olives and serve at room temperature as an appetizer accompanied by crusty French bread.

The wonderful red bell pepper can now be found in many markets almost year round. To be at its best, it should be grilled, peeled, and served at room temperature. Here it is served with a warm cream sauce perfumed with garlic and anchovies. Serve with plenty of crusty bread.

Ingredients

8 to 12 large Roasted Red Peppers (page 545)
3 Tablespoons butter
1 teaspoon crushed garlic
4 to 6 anchovy fillets, finely minced
½ teaspoon flour
1½ cups heavy cream
2 Tablespoons well-drained tiny capers
Freshly ground black pepper

Garnish:
Sprigs of fresh parsley

Stuffed Peppers Palermo

Serves:	**6 to 8**
Preparation time:	**30 minutes**
Cooking time:	**1 hour, 15 minutes**
Type of recipe:	**elementary**
Cost:	**inexpensive**

Peppers lend themselves to innumerable stuffings, anything from cold leftover rice salad, scrambled eggs, or a vegetable mixture. Serve the peppers at room temperature or lightly chilled.

Ingredients

8 small green peppers
6 Tablespoons fruity olive oil
3 Tablespoons finely minced fresh parsley
3 large cloves garlic, finely minced
1 can (10 ounces) tuna, packed in olive oil
3 to 4 anchovy fillets, finely minced
1 cup finely chopped tomatoes (3 to 4 ripe tomatoes, peeled, seeded, and chopped)
½ cup unflavored bread crumbs
2 hard-boiled eggs, finely minced
¼ cup well-drained capers
Salt and freshly ground black pepper
1 teaspoon dried oregano

Preparation

1.
Prepare the peppers following the directions on page 545.

2.
In a heavy 2-quart enamel saucepan melt the butter but do not let it brown. Add the garlic and anchovies and cook for 2 to 3 minutes, stirring constantly, until the anchovies have melted to a paste.

3.
Add the flour and whisk the mixture for 1 to 2 minutes without letting it brown.

4.
Add the cream, bring to a boil, and stir until slightly reduced and the sauce is thick. Add the capers, then taste and correct the seasoning, adding a large grinding of black pepper. Keep the sauce warm.

5.
To serve, place 2 peppers on each serving plate. Spoon 2 tablespoons of the sauce onto each plate and garnish with sprigs of parsley. Serve the remaining sauce on the side, accompanied by crusty French bread, which each guest can dip into the hot sauce.

Remarks

The peppers can be grilled 1 to 2 days ahead and refrigerated. Bring them back to room temperature before serving. The sauce can be made several hours ahead and slowly reheated on top of the stove. It should, however, not be made the day before since the garlic may turn and give the sauce a bitter aftertaste.

Spinach and Tuna Loaf

Serves:	**6 to 8**
Preparation time:	**10 minutes**
Cooking time:	**1 hour, 10 minutes**
Type of recipe:	**elementary**
Cost:	**inexpensive**

Preparation

1.
Preheat the oven to 350 degrees.

2.
Core the peppers and rinse them under cold running water. Set aside.

3.
In a large heavy skillet heat 3 tablespoons oil. Add the parsley and garlic and cook for 2 to 3 minutes. Add the tuna, anchovies, and tomatoes. Stir the mixture and cook for 3 to 4 minutes, or until most of the tomato water has evaporated.

4.
Add the bread crumbs, hard-boiled eggs, capers, salt, pepper, and oregano. Cook the mixture for another 3 minutes, or until thick, then taste and correct the seasoning.

5.
Stuff the peppers with the mixture. Place them in a well-oiled heavy baking dish and drizzle with the remaining olive oil.

6.
Bake for 1 hour, spooning the oil over the peppers every 10 minutes. Remove the dish from the oven and let the peppers cool to room temperature. Serve as an appetizer or as part of an hors d'oeuvre table.

Remarks
If you can get red bell peppers, use half green, half red peppers. For variation, sauté 6 to 8 small, shelled shrimp in the oil, then dice and add them to the stuffing.

Here is an excellent spinach pâté that can be served as an appetizer for a spring supper or as part of an hors d'oeuvre table. The loaf can also be served hot, accompanied by a well-flavored tomato sauce.

Ingredients
2 packages (10 ounces) fresh spinach
3 large eggs
¾ cup heavy cream
4 ounce flaked tuna, packed in olive oil (1 small can)
4 to 6 anchovy fillets
½ cup minced scallions (both white and green parts)
⅓ cup bread crumbs
Salt and freshly ground black pepper

Garnish:
2 lemons, quartered
Sprigs of fresh parsley

Preparation

1.
Preheat the oven to 375 degrees.

2.
Remove the stems from the spinach, wash thoroughly under cold running water, and drain in a colander.

3.
Place the spinach in a large saucepan and cook over medium heat until the spinach leaves are completely wilted, or for about 4 to 5 minutes. Drain the spinach and chop finely. Set aside.

4.
In a blender or food processor combine the eggs, cream, tuna, anchovy fillets, and

Spinach Ramekins à la Bernoise

Serves:	**6 to 8**
Preparation time:	**40 minutes**
Cooking time:	**30 minutes**
Type of recipe:	**elementary**
Cost:	**inexpensive**

scallions. Blend the mixture for 30 seconds, or until smooth.

5.
Combine the spinach, bread crumbs, and egg mixture in a bowl and blend thoroughly. Season with salt and pepper.

6.
Butter a loaf pan, then cover the bottom with a piece of waxed paper. Butter the paper, then pour the spinach mixture into the pan. Cover the pan with foil.

7.
Place the loaf pan inside a roasting pan and pour boiling water around it. The water should come halfway up the sides of the loaf pan.

8.
Bake the spinach loaf for 1 hour, or until the tip of a knife comes out clean.

9.
Cool and unmold the spinach loaf. Cut into ½-inch slices and overlap them on a rectangular serving platter.

10.
Garnish the platter with quartered lemons and sprigs of parsley. Serve lightly chilled or at room temperature.

Remarks
The spinach loaf can be made 2 to 3 days ahead, wrapped in foil and refrigerated. It can also be served accompanied by an anchovy-flavored vinaigrette (Vinaigrette Niçoise, page 460).

Ingredients
2 packages (10 ounces) fresh spinach, well rinsed and drained
3 Tablespoons butter
4 Tablespoons finely minced scallions (both green and white parts)
Salt and freshly ground black pepper
Freshly grated nutmeg
¼ cup homemade bread crumbs
2 whole eggs, plus 2 yolks
1 cup light cream
3 Tablespoons freshly grated Parmesan cheese

Sauce:
2 Tablespoons butter
½ pound fresh mushrooms, stems removed and caps quartered
Salt and freshly ground black pepper
1 to 1½ cups heavy cream
1 Beurre Manié (page 000)

Garnish:
Sprigs of fresh parsley

Preparation

1.

Preheat the oven to 350 degrees.

2.

In a large casserole bring salted water to a boil. Add the spinach and cook for 5 minutes. Drain the spinach thoroughly in a colander, pressing down with your hand to extract all the moisture. Transfer the spinach to a chopping board and mince finely. Set aside.

3.

Next prepare the sauce. In a heavy skillet heat the butter. Add the mushrooms and sauté over high heat for 2 to 3 minutes, or until the mushrooms are nicely browned. Toss the mushrooms back and forth in the pan to cook them evenly. Season with salt and pepper, then add 1 cup cream. Bring to a boil and whisk in bits of Beurre Manié, stirring the sauce constantly until it heavily coats a spoon. Set aside.

4.

In a heavy 10-inch skillet heat the remaining butter. Add the scallions and cook for 2 minutes without browning. Add the minced spinach and season with salt, pepper, and a grinding of nutmeg and cook for 5 minutes over low heat.

5.

Transfer the spinach mixture to a mixing bowl. Add the bread crumbs and blend well.

6.

In another bowl combine the egg yolks, whole eggs, cream, and Parmesan cheese. Whisk the mixture and season with salt and pepper. Fold this into the spinach mixture.

7.

Butter 6 to 8 six-ounce porcelain ramekins. Cut circles of waxed paper to fit inside the ramekins and then butter the paper.

8.

Spoon the spinach mixture into the ramekins. Place them in a baking pan and add boiling water to the pan; the water should come halfway up the sides of the ramekins.

9.

Place the baking pan in the oven and bake the spinach ramekins for 15 minutes, or until the tip of a sharp knife comes out clean.

10.

Remove baking pan from the oven. Run a knife along the side of each ramekin and unmold onto an ovenproof serving platter. Cover with foil and keep warm.

11.

Reheat the mushroom sauce over low heat, adding a little more cream if the sauce has thickened too much.

12.

Spoon the sauce around the spinach cakes. Garnish each with a sprig of parsley and serve hot as an appetizer or as an accompaniment to roast or grilled meats.

Remarks:

The spinach ramekins can be baked several hours ahead. The cakes can be unmolded, covered with foil, and reheated in a 200-degree oven. The sauce can also be prepared several hours ahead and reheated over low heat.

Stuffed Tomatoes
à la Basquaise

Serves: **6**
Preparation time: **15 minutes**
Cooking time: **15 minutes**
Type of recipe: **elementary**
Cost: **inexpensive**

Like peppers, tomatoes lend themselves to many delicious stuffings, both hot and cold. Here they are filled with a vegetable mixture that can be varied by seasoning it with a touch of curry and cumin

Ingredients
6 medium ripe tomatoes
Salt
1 can (7½ ounces) tuna packed in olive oil, flaked
4 to 6 anchovy fillets, finely minced
5 Tablespoons finely minced fresh parsley
2 large Roasted Green Peppers (page 545), finely diced
½ cup roasted Italian peppers, finely diced, or ½ cup pimientos, finely diced
2 Tablespoons finely minced green olives
1 Tablespoon well-drained tiny capers
¾ cup bread crumbs
Freshly ground black pepper
1 teaspoon finely minced garlic, plus 1 large clove, peeled and crushed
3 Tablespoons fruity olive oil

Preparation
1.
Preheat the oven to 375 degrees.
2.
Cut the top ¼ inch off the tomatoes and scoop out most of the pulp without breaking the skin. Season the tomatoes with salt and place them upside down on a double layer of paper towels.
3.
Place the tomato pulp in a sieve. Sprinkle with salt and let it drain for 30 minutes.

4.
In a bowl combine the tuna, anchovies, 3 tablespoons parsley, green peppers, Italian peppers or pimientos, olives, capers, and tomato pulp. Work the mixture with a wooden spoon until well blended. Add ½ cup bread crumbs. Season with salt, pepper, and the crushed garlic clove. Taste the mixture and correct the seasoning. Fill the tomatoes with the tuna mixture and reserve.
5.
In a small bowl combine the remaining bread crumbs with the remaining parsley and the minced garlic. Sprinkle each tomato with a little of the bread-crumb mixture and place in a well-oiled baking dish.
6.
Drizzle the olive oil over each tomato and place the baking dish in the center of the oven.
7.
Bake the tomatoes for 10 to 12 minutes, or until they are well heated through and slightly tender. Do not overcook.
8.
Serve the tomatoes at room temperature or slightly chilled as an appetizer or as an accompaniment to grilled lamb chops or steak.

Cold Stuffed Tomatoes Genovese

Serves:	**6 to 8**
Preparation time:	**30 minutes, plus 4 to 6 hours ahead to prepare rice**
Cooking time:	**20 minutes**
Type of recipe:	**elementary**
Cost:	**inexpensive**

Ingredients

½ cup long-grain rice
Salt
6 to 8 small ripe tomatoes
2 Tablespoons finely minced scallions (both green and white parts)
2 Tablespoons finely minced fresh parsley
2 Tablespoons finely minced green pepper
2 Tablespoons finely minced pimientos
4 flat anchovy fillets, finely minced
1 Tablespoon basil paste (¾ to 1 cup tightly packed fresh basil leaves and 1 to 2 Tablespoons olive oil, puréed to a fine paste)
Freshly ground black pepper
1 teaspoon Dijon mustard
⅓ cup heavy cream, whipped

Garlic Vinaigrette:

6 Tablespoons olive oil
2 Tablespoons red wine vinegar
1 teaspoon Dijon mustard
1 large clove garlic, peeled and crushed
Salt and freshly ground black pepper

Garnish:

Sprigs of fresh parsley
Tiny black olives

Preparation

1.
About 4 to 6 hours ahead, prepare the rice. In a small saucepan bring 1 cup salted water to a boil and add the rice. Reduce the heat and simmer covered for 20 minutes, or until tender. Cool the rice completely.

2.
Cut a ¼-inch slice off the top of each tomato. With a small sharp knife carefully loosen and remove the pulp. Discard the seeds, then mince the pulp and reserve. Sprinkle the tomatoes with salt and place them upside down on a double layer of paper towels.

3.
Make the vinaigrette by combining all the ingredients together in a blender. Blend thoroughly and set aside.

4.
Transfer the rice to a bowl. Add the scallions, parsley, green pepper, pimientos, anchovies, and minced tomato pulp. Add a little vinaigrette and the basil paste. Blend the mixture thoroughly. Season with salt and pepper and reserve.

5.
In a bowl combine the Dijon mustard and whipped cream. Blend thoroughly and add to the rice mixture. Stir the mixture until well blended and reserve.

6.
Place the tomatoes on a serving platter. Drizzle with the remaining vinaigrette and fill the tomatoes with the rice salad. Garnish each with a sprig of parsley and a black olive and serve the tomatoes at room temperature or slightly chilled.

Pasta Salad
Jardinière

Serves: **4**
Preparation time: **20 minutes**
Cooking time: **5 minutes**
Type of recipe: **elementary**
Cost: **inexpensive**

Cold pasta salads are becoming increasingly popular. They are wonderful for summer lunches and simple warm-weather suppers. For a variation, combine the noodles with cold leftover Eggplants à la Bohémienne (page 423).

Ingredients
2 cups broccoli florets
7 Tablespoons fruity olive oil
¾ pound green fettucine (long flat noodles)
2 Tablespoons red wine vinegar
2 large cloves garlic, peeled and crushed
1 can (7½ ounces) flaked tuna, packed in oil
3 Tablespoons finely minced fresh parsley
1 small red onion, peeled and thinly sliced
1 cup finely diced mozzarella cheese
½ cup small black oil-cured olives
1 large Roasted Red Pepper (page 545), thinly sliced
Salt and freshly ground black pepper

Garnish:
8 to 12 ripe cherry tomatoes

Optional:
1 small ripe avocado, peeled, seeded, and thinly sliced

Preparation
1.
In a medium-sized saucepan bring salted water to a boil. Add the broccoli and cook for 3 to 4 minutes, or until just tender. Drain and cool. Set aside.

2.
In a large casserole bring salted water to a boil and add 1 tablespoon olive oil. Add the noodles and cook them for 9 minutes, or until just tender; do not overcook. When done immediately add 3 cups cold water to the casserole to stop the noodles from cooking further. Let the noodles cool completely in their cooking water.

3.
Combine the vinegar, remaining fruity olive oil, and garlic in a small jar. Shake the dressing until it is well blended. Set aside.

4.
Drain the noodles and transfer to a large salad bowl. Add the flaked tuna, parsley, onion, mozzarella, olives, and red pepper. Season with salt and a large grinding of black pepper.

5.
Pour the dressing on the salad and toss lightly. Taste and correct the seasoning. Top the pasta salad with broccoli florets, and toss lightly again.

6.
Garnish the pasta salad with tomatoes and optional slices of avocado. Serve at room temperature.

Remarks
When making the pasta salad in the summer omit the the broccoli florets and instead add 2 to 3 tablespoons finely slivered fresh basil leaves to the salad bowl. You may also add 1 small zucchini, diced and quickly sautéed in 2 tablespoons of olive oil, to the salad bowl.

Hard-Boiled Eggs
in
Sauce Nîmoise

Serves: **4**
Preparation time: **10 minutes**
Cooking time: **10 minutes**
Type of recipe: **elementary**
Cost: **inexpensive**

Ingredients
10 large cloves garlic, peeled
5 large hard-boiled eggs, plus 1 large raw egg
3 to 5 Tablespoons fruity olive oil
3 to 4 anchovy fillets
1 Tablespoon finely minced fresh parsley
1 Tablespoon diced onion
1 Tablespoon tarragon vinegar
Salt and freshly ground black pepper

Garnish:
2 Tablespoons well-drained tiny capers
Sprigs of fresh parsley
Leaves of Boston lettuce

Preparation
1.
In a saucepan combine the garlic with water to cover. Bring to a boil, reduce the heat, and cook the garlic until very tender. Drain and place in a food processor or blender.
2.
Cut one hard-boiled egg in half, remove the yolk, and add it, together with the raw egg, to the food processor or blender.
3.
Blend the mixture until smooth, then start adding the oil by droplets until the sauce becomes thick and smooth.
4.
Add the anchovies, parsley, diced onion, and vinegar. Blend the sauce again until very smooth. Taste and correct the seasoning; you may want to add a little more vinegar.

5.
Season the sauce carefully with salt and pepper, then place a large leaf of lettuce on each serving plate. Peel the remaining eggs and cut them in half. Place them cut-side down on each plate and spoon the sauce over them.
6.
Garnish with sprigs of parsley and sprinkle each egg half with a few capers. Serve lightly chilled as an appetizer, accompanied by buttered black bread.

Remarks
This sauce is also an excellent accompaniment to cooked artichokes, both hot and cold. You can make the sauce 2 to 3 days ahead and refrigerate it covered. It can also be served as a dip for a platter of raw vegetables.

Eggs
in
Green Sauce
à la Monégasque

Serves:	**6 to 8**
Preparation time:	**10 minutes**
Cooking time:	**10 minutes**
Type of recipe:	**elementary**
Cost:	**inexpensive**

Hard-boiled eggs are one of the most versatile of foods. They are excellent as part of a hors d'oeuvre table, as an appetizer, or in simple supper dishes. They can be used with many sauces and vegetables; here they are combined with a piquant sauce from northern Italy.

Ingredients
6 to 8 large eggs
¼ cup homemade bread crumbs
1 cup fresh parsley
1 cup pimiento-stuffed green olives
4 to 6 flat anchovy fillets
2 large cloves garlic, peeled and chopped
2 Tablespoons red wine vinegar
½ cup fruity olive oil
2 Tablespoons well-drained tiny capers
Salt and freshly ground black pepper

Garnish:
Whole radishes
Rounds of green and red pepper

Preparation
1.
In a saucepan combine the eggs with water to cover. Bring to a boil, reduce the heat, and simmer the eggs for 8 minutes, shaking the pan back and forth to center the yolks.
2.
Drain the eggs, peel, and cut in half lengthwise. Remove the yolks and mince all but 2 yolks. Reserve the whites.
3.
In a blender or food processor, combine the bread crumbs, parsley, olives, anchovies, garlic, 2 whole yolks, and wine vinegar. Blend the mixture at top speed, adding the olive oil in a slow stream. When the mixture is smooth and well blended pour it into a bowl. Add the capers, then season with salt and pepper.
4.
Place the egg halfs on a round serving platter. Fill the cavities with a spoonful of the sauce and sprinkle with the remaining minced yolks. Garnish the platter with whole radishes and rounds of green and red peppers and serve slightly chilled.

Tart
Avignonnaise

Serves: **6**
Preparation time: **25 minutes**
Cooking time: **1 hour**
Type of recipe: **elementary**
Cost: **moderate**

Ingredients

**1 nine-inch unbaked Basic Tart Shell
(page 483)**
2 Tablespoons fruity olive oil
2 Tablespoons finely minced shallots
**1 can (35 ounces) Italian plum tomatoes,
well drained and finely chopped**
Salt and freshly ground black pepper
1 teaspoon dried thyme
½ teaspoon dried oregano
1 Tablespoon Dijon mustard
**¼ pound smoked or baked ham, thinly
sliced**
**8 to 10 slices Italian or Swedish fontina
cheese, cut 1 inch by 4 inches and ⅛
inch thick**
**3 Tablespoons freshly grated Parmesan
cheese**
3 to 4 thin slices prosciutto, 2 inches long
6 to 8 thin slices mozzarella cheese

Optional:

1 Tablespoon finely minced fresh basil
2 large cloves garlic, peeled and crushed

Preparation

1.
Preheat the oven to 350 degrees.
2.
Prepare the pastry for baking, following the
directions on page 483.
3.
In a heavy 2-quart saucepan heat the oil.
Add the shallots and cook for 1 minute, or
until just soft but not browned.
4.
Add the tomatoes, then season with salt,
pepper, thyme, oregano, and the optional
basil. Cover the saucepan and simmer the
tomato mixture for 25 to 30 minutes, stirring
every 10 minutes to prevent the tomatoes
from scorching. Add the optional garlic
cloves. Taste the mixture and correct the
seasoning, then set aside.
5.
While the tomato mixture is cooking,
partially bake the tart shell according to the
directions on page 484. Remove the shell
from the oven.
6.
Spread a thin layer of mustard on the shell.
Cut the ham slices into thin triangles, as if
you were slicing a pie. Place the triangles
in a thin layer in the tart shell.
7.
Top the slices with the fontina, covering the
ham entirely.
8.
Spread a layer of the tomato mixture over
the cheese. Sprinkle lightly with the
Parmesan cheese and top with the slices of
prosciutto. Cover the prosciutto with the
slices of mozzarella cheese, again covering
the entire tart shell. Sprinkle with the

Serves:	**4 to 6**
Preparation time:	**15 minutes**
Cooking time:	**20 minutes**
Type of recipe:	**elementary**
Cost:	**inexpensive**

remaining Parmesan and place the shell on a baking sheet.

9.
Bake for 25 to 30 minutes, or until the cheeses have melted and the tart is very hot. Unmold the tart onto a serving platter and serve warm as an appetizer, cut into pie-shaped pieces and accompanied by a well-seasoned salad.

Remarks
For variation you can substitute 1 cup well-seasoned ratatouille for the tomato fondue or 1 medium eggplant, peeled, thinly sliced, and sautéed in fruity olive oil. If you cannot get good quality prosciutto, substitute with another layer of thinly sliced smoked ham.

Ingredients
2 cups milk
3 cups water
Pinch of salt
4 peppercorns
1 bay leaf
1 to 1½ pounds smoked haddock (finnan haddie)

Sauce:
1 hard-boiled egg
1 whole raw egg
1 Tablespoon Dijon mustard
1½ teaspoons white wine vinegar
1 teaspoon granulated sugar
Salt and freshly ground black pepper
½ to ¾ cup olive oil
2 Tablespoons finely minced fresh dill

Garnish:
Sprigs of fresh dill

Optional:
Slices of avocado, sprinkled with salt and lemon juice

Cold Mackerel
in
Saffron Sauce

Serves:	**4 to 6**
Preparation time:	**25 minutes, plus 24 hours to chill**
Cooking time:	**25 minutes**
Type of recipe:	**elementary**
Cost:	**inexpensive**

Preparation

1.
Combine the milk with 3 cups water in a medium-sized enamel casserole. Season lightly with salt and add the peppercorns and bay leaf. Add the smoked haddock. (If the fish is not covered by the liquid add enough water to cover.)

2.
Bring to a boil slowly on top of the stove. Immediately reduce the heat and poach the fish for 12 to 15 minutes. Do not overcook.

3.
Remove the fish from the poaching liquid. Cool and wrap in foil to prevent it from drying. Set aside at room temperature and make the sauce.

4.
Slice in half and separate the hard-boiled egg. Set aside the white for another purpose, then mash the yolk together with the whole egg in the bowl. Add the Dijon mustard, vinegar, sugar, salt, and pepper. Beat the mixture with a small electric beater until smooth. Slowly add the oil and continue beating until the sauce is thick and smooth. Add the dill, taste, and correct the seasoning. Chill the sauce until serving.

5.
Unwrap the fish and cut it crosswise into thin slices. Place 3 slices on each serving plate. Spoon a little sauce over each slice and garnish with sprigs of dill and the optional avocado slices. Serve as an appetizer accompanied by buttered pumpernickel bread.

I always look forward to going to the Boston fish market in early spring to find the first mackerel of the season. Unfortunately the season for the Boston mackerel, which is less oily and much more delicate than the Spanish mackerel, seems all too short. It is also unfortunate that it is rarely available outside the northeast. If you cannot get it, use smelts or mullets in this recipe.

Ingredients

6 to 8 mackerel, each weighing ¾ to 1 pound, cleaned
Salt and freshly ground black pepper
1 teaspoon ground cumin
Flour for dredging
6 Tablespoons olive oil
1 cup finely minced onions
2 cloves garlic, finely minced
½ teaspoon dried thyme
1 bay leaf
¼ teaspoon fennel seeds
1 can (35 ounces) Italian plum tomatoes, drained, and chopped, or 6 ripe tomatoes, peeled, seeded, and chopped
½ cup tomato purée
1 Tablespoon tomato paste
1 cup dry white wine
1 teaspoon saffron threads

Garnish:
1 lemon, thinly sliced
Finely minced fresh parsley

Preparation

1.
Preheat the oven to 350 degrees.

2.
Season the mackerel with salt, pepper, and cumin. Dredge lightly with flour, shaking off the excess. Set aside.

3.
Heat 3 tablespoons oil in a large heavy skillet. Sauté the mackerel until nicely browned. Turn them once carefully with a large spatula. Transfer the mackerel to a deep baking dish.

4.
Discard the fat in the pan if it has burned and wipe the pan with paper towels. Add the remaining oil to the skillet. Add the onion and garlic and cook the mixture until soft but not browned. Add the herbs, tomatoes, tomato purée, and tomato paste and cook for 3 to 4 minutes over high heat.

5.
Add the white wine. Season with salt and pepper and add saffron. Bring to a boil and cook the mixture over low heat for 10 minutes, or until most of the tomato water has evaporated and the sauce is quite thick. Taste the sauce and correct the seasoning.

6.
Strain the tomato sauce over the mackerel through a fine sieve, pressing down to extract all the juices. Cover the baking dish with foil and place in the center part of the oven. Bake for 10 to 12 minutes.

7.
Remove the dish from the oven. Cool and then chill covered for 24 hours.

8.
About 30 minutes before serving, bring the fish back to room temperature. Garnish the dish with lemon slices, arranging them flat-side down along the sides of the dish. Sprinkle with parsley and serve as an appetizer accompanied by a bowl of sweet butter and crusty French bread.

Remarks
This is also an excellent supper dish. Serve it accompanied by boiled tiny new potatoes.

Cold Smelts
in
Cider Vinegar Sauce

Serves: **6**
Preparation time: **10 minutes, plus 24 hours to marinate**
Cooking time: **15 minutes**
Type of recipe: **elementary**
Cost: **inexpensive**

Ingredients

12 to 14 small smelts, cleaned but left whole
Salt and freshly ground black pepper
Flour for dredging
3 Tablespoons peanut oil
1 cup cider vinegar
½ cup water
2 small onions, peeled and thinly sliced
1 small carrot, scraped and thinly sliced
1 teaspoon pickling spices
1 dried hot chili pepper
1 teaspoon mustard seeds
6 to 8 peppercorns
2 bay leaves
2 large sprigs fresh dill

Garnish:

1 cup finely diced cooked beets
2 to 3 tablespoons finely minced fresh dill

Preparation

1.
Season the smelts with salt and pepper. Dredge lightly with flour, shaking off the excess. Set aside.

2.
In a large heavy skillet heat the oil. Add the smelts and cook over medium heat until nicely browned, turning them once carefully with a wide spatula.

3.
Place the smelts in a glass serving dish and set aside.

4.
In an enamel saucepan combine the vinegar, water, onions, carrots, pickling spices, chili pepper, mustard seeds, peppercorns, and bay leaves. Bring to a boil then reduce the heat and simmer for 5 minutes.

5.
Cool the marinade and pour it over the smelts. Bury the dill sprigs among the smelts. Cover and chill for 24 hours.

6.
Bring the smelts back to room temperature, then remove the bay leaves and the sprigs of dill and garnish the smelts with the diced beets and minced fresh dill.

7.
Serve the smelts as an appetizer accompanied by thinly sliced, buttered black bread.

Fish Mousse
in
Romaine Lettuce
Packages

Serves: **6**
Preparation time: **40 minutes**
Cooking time: **30 minutes**
Type of recipe: **intermediate**
Cost: **moderate**

A lovely and light appetizer, these little bundles of fish mousse wrapped in lettuce leaves are both delicious and wholesome. They are served hot here, but are equally delicious cold accompanied by a bowl of Crème Fraîche seasoned with a little lime juice and finely minced chives or dill.

Ingredients

¾ to 1 pound whiting fillets, cut into small pieces
2 large egg whites
1 teaspoon grated onion
1 cup cold heavy cream
Salt and freshly ground white pepper
12 to 24 outer leaves romaine lettuce
2 cups Vegetable Stock (page 539)

Sauce:

3 large egg yolks
1 cup Crème Fraîche (page 544)
1 Tablespoon minced shallots
¼ cup white wine vinegar
¼ teaspoon dried tarragon
6 to 8 Tablespoons butter
Salt and freshly ground white pepper

Preparation

1.
In a food processor combine the fish fillets, egg whites, and grated onion. Grind the mixture until smooth. With the motor running, gradually add the cream in a slow stream. When all the cream has been added, the mixture should be thick and smooth. Season the mixture with salt and pepper.

2.
In a casserole bring salted water to a boil. Add the lettuce leaves, 2 at a time, and blanch for 10 seconds. Remove the lettuce leaves and dry on a double layer of paper towels.

3.
Remove the center ribs from each leaf. Place a heaping tablespoon of the fish mixture on each leaf (if the leaves are small you may need 2 leaves for each package), then fold the sides over the filling and roll up.

4.
Place the lettuce packages seam-side down in a buttered heavy baking dish. Add the Vegetable Stock; it should not cover the packages but should come up three quarters of the way. Cover the dish with buttered waxed paper and set aside.

5.
Preheat the oven to 325 degrees.

6.
Make the sauce. In a bowl combine the egg yolks and Crème Fraîche. Whisk the mixture until smooth and reserve.

7.
In a heavy saucepan combine the shallots, vinegar, and tarragon. Cook the mixture until the vinegar has evaporated.

Pâté of Fish
with
Asparagus

Serves:	**6 to 8**
Preparation time:	**30 minutes**
Cooking time:	**1 hour, 45 minutes**
Type of recipe:	**intermediate**
Cost:	**inexpensive**

8.

Remove the saucepan from the heat and add the egg mixture. Place the saucepan over the lowest possible heat and whisk the mixture until it starts to thicken. Start adding the butter, 1 tablespoon at a time, and keep whisking the sauce until it is thick and smooth. If the sauce can absorb 8 tablespoons of butter, use it; if it seems to be quite thick you may only need 6 tablespoons of butter. Do not let the sauce come to a boil at anytime or it may curdle. (If the sauce should show any signs of curdling, immediately remove the saucepan from the heat and add 1 tablespoon cold heavy cream, whisking the sauce again until smooth.) Season the sauce with salt and pepper, then strain through a fine sieve into another saucepan. Keep warm over a pan of warm, but not hot, water.

9.

Place the baking dish in the oven and bake for 20 minutes. Remove the dish from the oven. Transfer the lettuce packages to individual serving plates. With paper towels wipe away any juices that may have accumulated on the plates. Spoon a little of the sauce around each lettuce package and serve immediately.

Remarks

The sauce can be made well in advance and kept warm over a pan of warm water. Just be sure to whisk it every 15 or 20 minutes to prevent it from curdling. The lettuce packages can be prepared several hours ahead and baked at the last moment.

Ingredients

6 to 8 thin fresh asparagus spears (6 to 8 inches long)
1 pound whiting fillets, cut into small pieces
2 egg whites
1 teaspoon grated onion
1½ cups cold heavy cream
Salt and freshly ground white pepper
Dash of cayenne pepper

Sauce:

1 cup tightly packed fresh watercress, well rinsed and stemmed
4 egg yolks
1 Tablespoon lemon juice
1 Tablespoon ice water
1 cup hot melted butter
Ice cubes, if necessary
Salt and freshly ground white pepper

Optional:

1 pound fresh asparagus, cooked and buttered

Garnish:

Sprigs of fresh watercress

Preparation

1.
Scrape the asparagus spears, removing 1 or 2 inches at the bottom of each spear. They should be of even length, about 6 to 8 inches long. Set aside.

2.
In a large saucepan bring salted water to a boil. Add the asparagus and cook over high heat for 7 to 8 minutes, or until tender; do not overcook. Drain thoroughly on a double layer of paper towels and set aside.

3.
Preheat the oven to 350 degrees.

4.
Place the fish fillets together with the egg whites and onion in a food processor. Add the cream slowly and blend the mixture at high speed until it is smooth and all the cream has been incorporated. The mixture must be very smooth. (If you are using a blender you may have to do this in small batches.) Transfer to a bowl and season with salt, pepper, and a dash of cayenne. Taste and correct the seasoning.

5.
Butter a loaf pan and then pour half the fish mousse into the pan, smoothing it with a spatula.

6.
Place the cooked asparagus on top of the mousse in a layer, starting ½ inch from the edges of the pan. Top the asparagus with the remaining mousse, smoothing it again with a spatula. Cover with buttered waxed paper.

7.
Set the loaf pan into a larger baking dish. Pour boiling water into the larger dish; it should come halfway up the side of the loaf pan. Bake for 1 hour, 30 minutes, or until a knife comes out clean. Remove the pâté from the oven but keep it warm in the hot-water bath while you make the sauce.

8.
In a small saucepan bring salted water to a boil. Add the watercress leaves and cook for 2 to 3 minutes. Drain and, when cool enough to handle, mince the watercress leaves and set aside.

9.
Combine the yolks, lemon juice, and ice water in a heavy-bottomed enamel saucepan. Whisk the mixture over low heat until it starts to thicken. Be extremely careful, since the eggs must not cook or they will curdle.

10.
Add the hot melted butter by droplets, whisking constantly until the mixture is thick and smooth. (If at any time it shows signs of curdling, immediately remove the saucepan from the heat and add a small ice cube, whisking constantly until the sauce is smooth again.)

11.
Season the sauce with salt and pepper, then transfer it to a blender and add the watercress leaves. Blend the sauce until smooth and transfer to the top of a double boiler. Keep the sauce warm over hot, but not boiling, water.

12.
Cook the remaining optional asparagus in salted boiling water until barely tender. Drain on a double layer of paper towels and set aside.

Cold
Fish and Asparagus Pâté
with
Emerald Sauce

Serves:	**6 to 8**
Preparation time:	**15 minutes**
Cooking time:	**5 minutes**
Type of recipe:	**intermediate**
Cost:	**inexpensive**

13.
Run a sharp knife along the sides of the pâté and unmold onto a rectangular platter. Using paper towels wipe away any liquid that has accumulated around the pâté. Spoon the watercress sauce over the pâté and garnish it with the optional cooked asparagus and the sprigs of fresh watercress. Serve immediately as an appetizer accompanied by crusty French bread.

Remarks
The entire pâté can be made a day ahead and reheated in a 200-degree oven. Wrap the pâté tightly in foil and place in a hot-water bath for 1 hour, or until thoroughly heated. The sauce can be made several hours ahead and kept warm over a pan of hot water. Whisk it every 10 to 15 minutes to be sure it does not curdle. If it shows any signs of curdling, immediately add 1 tablespoon ice water and whisk until the sauce is smooth again. You may omit the asparagus garnish and simply serve the pâté garnished with fresh sprigs of watercress.

The preceding pâté is equally delicious served lightly chilled. If you prefer it cold, serve it with the following sauce, accompanied by thinly sliced and buttered black bread.

Emerald Sauce:
1 bunch fresh watercress leaves, well rinsed and stemmed
2 large eggs
1½ teaspoons tarragon vinegar
1½ teaspoons Dijon mustard
Salt and freshly ground white pepper
¾ to 1 cup vegetable oil
2 Tablespoons finely minced fresh parsley
2 Tablespoons finely minced fresh chives
1 Tablespoon finely minced fresh tarragon or dill
1 Tablespoon finely minced fresh chervil

Garnish:
Sprigs of fresh watercress
1 lemon, quartered

Steamed Mussels
in
Parsley-and-Sorrel Sauce

Serves: **4 to 5**
Preparation time: **25 minutes**
Cooking time: **15 minutes**
Type of recipe: **elementary**
Cost: **inexpensive**

Preparation

1.
Drop the watercress leaves into rapidly boiling salted water for 2 minutes. Drain and place on a double layer of paper towels. Set aside.

2.
Combine the eggs, vinegar, and mustard in a blender and season the mixture with salt and pepper. Blend at high speed until smooth, then start adding the oil by droplets, blending the mixture until it is thick and smooth.

3.
Add the parsley and watercress and blend the mixture thoroughly at high speed.

4.
Transfer the sauce to a serving bowl. Add the finely minced fresh herbs. Taste and correct the seasoning. Spoon the sauce over the pâté, covering it completely. Garnish with sprigs of watercress and lemon quarters and serve the pâté lightly chilled but not cold.

Remarks

The sauce can be made several days ahead and kept in a covered jar in the refrigerator. The sauce can also be served as a topping for cold poached eggs or hard-boiled eggs, or as an accompaniment to poached fish.

Good fresh mussels need little adornment. To my mind, they are a wonderfully distinctive shellfish that can be served in many simple and elegant ways. Here is one of my springtime favorites.

Ingredients

2 Tablespoons butter
2 Tablespoons finely minced shallots
5 to 6 pounds fresh mussels, well scrubbed
½ cup dry white wine
1 Bouquet Garni (page 546)
1 cup Crème Fraîche (page 544)
1 Beurre Manié (page 544)
3 Tablespoons finely minced fresh parsley
2 cups fresh sorrel leaves, cleaned, stemmed, and leaves cut into thin julienne strips
2 Tablespoons finely minced fresh chives
2 to 4 Tablespoons cold butter, for enrichment
Freshly ground black pepper

Preparation

1.
In a large heavy casserole melt 2 tablespoons butter over low heat. Add the shallots and cook for 1 or 2 minutes, or until soft; do not brown.

2.
Add the mussels, wine, and Bouquet Garni and bring to a boil. Partially cover the casserole and cook until all the mussels open, shaking the casserole back and forth to ensure that the mussels cook evenly.

3.
As soon as the mussels are done use a

Mussel Soufflé

Serves: **4**
Preparation time: **30 minutes**
Cooking time: **35 minutes**
Type of recipe: **intermediate**
Cost: **inexpensive**

slotted spoon to transfer them to a bowl; set aside.

4.
Discard the bouquet, bring the poaching liquid to a boil, and add the Crème Fraîche and cook the sauce until reduced by half. Be sure to taste often, since as the liquid reduces it also becomes saltier. As soon as it has reached the right flavor, whisk in bits of the Beurre Manié; use just enough to thicken the sauce.

5.
Reduce the heat and add the parsley and sorrel. Simmer for 2 to 3 minutes, or until the sorrel has melted into the sauce. Remove the sauce from the heat.

6.
Add the chives and whisk in the cold butter, then set the sauce aside. Taste and correct the seasoning.

7.
Remove and discard the top shell of each mussel, then place the mussels in the lower halves on individual serving plates. Spoon a little sauce over each and serve immediately.

Remarks

If you cannot get fresh sorrel you can make the dish and vary it by using a bunch of fresh watercress leaves. When using watercress leaves, remove the stems and poach the leaves in boiling salted water for 2 to 3 minutes. Mince the leaves and add them, together with a little lemon juice and a teaspoon of Dijon mustard, to the sauce.

Ingredients

2 Tablespoons finely minced shallots
1 cup Fish Stock (page 536)
1 teaspoon dried thyme
1 sprig fresh parsley
1 bay leaf
2 pounds fresh small mussels, well scrubbed
3 Tablespoons butter
3 Tablespoons flour
4 large egg yolks
Salt and freshly ground black pepper
6 egg whites

Preparation

1.
Preheat the oven to 375 degrees.

2.
In a large casserole combine the shallots, fish stock, thyme, parsley, and bay leaf. Add the mussels and cook covered over high heat until the mussels have opened.

3.
Remove the mussels with a slotted spoon to a side dish. Discard any mussels that have not opened.

4.
Strain the stock through a fine sieve into a saucepan. Bring the stock to a boil and reduce over high heat to 1 cup. Reserve.

5.
Reserve 4 to 6 mussels in their shells for the garnish. Remove the remainder of the mussels from their shells and discard the mussel shells. Remove the black rim around the mussels and set aside for the soufflé.

6.
In a heavy 2-quart saucepan melt the butter. Add the flour and cook the mixture for 2 to 3 minutes without letting it brown.

7.
Remove the saucepan from the heat. Add the hot mussel stock all at once and whisk until the mixture is well blended.

8.
Return the saucepan to the heat and cook the mixture until thick and smooth.

9.
Add the egg yolks and cook for 1 to 2 minutes, whisking constantly. Do not let the mixture come to a boil or the yolks may curdle.

10.
Add the mussels, season with salt and pepper, and set aside.

11.
Beat the whites in a stainless steel bowl, adding a pinch of salt, until they form stiff peaks. Fold a little of the whites into the mussel mixture to loosen it, then fold the remaining mixture into the whites.

12.
Butter a 6-cup soufflé mold and pour the mixture into the dish. Set in the oven and bake for 25 minutes.

13.
When done, remove the soufflé from the oven and garnish with the whole unshelled mussels. Serve immediately.

Remarks
The soufflé mixture can be prepared as much as 40 minutes ahead. If you want to make the soufflé for a large group of people, double the recipe and turn the mixture into an oval *au gratin* dish. The soufflé will only rise a little, but the texture and taste will be the same and the dish can be prepared up to the baking point well in advance and refrigerated. The mussels can be poached and shelled a day or so ahead of time and left in their cooking liquid.

Marinated Scallops
in
Mushroom Sauce

Serves: **5 to 6**
Preparation time: **15 minutes, plus 5–6 hours to marinate and chill**
Cooking time: **5 minutes**
Type of recipe: **elementary**
Cost: **moderate**

Ingredients

3 cups Vegetable Stock (page 539)
1 pound fresh tiny bay scallops
3 cups finely sliced fresh mushrooms, stems removed
Salt and freshly ground black pepper
3 Tablespoons olive oil
2 Tablespoon white wine vinegar
1 teaspoon Dijon mustard
1 to 1½ cups Mayonnaise (page 540)
2 Tablespoons chili sauce
1 large clove garlic, peeled and crushed
3 Tablespoons finely minced scallions (white part only)

Garnish:
Boston lettuce leaves
Sprigs of fresh parsley

Optional:
Slices of ripe avocado, sprinkled with lemon juice and seasoned with salt and pepper

Preparation

1.
In a saucepan heat the Vegetable Stock. Add the scallops and cook for 2 to 3 minutes, or until the scallops turn an opaque white. Do not let the stock return to a boil. Remove from the heat and let the scallops cool completely in the stock.

2.
Place the mushrooms in a bowl and sprinkle with salt and pepper. Set aside.

3.
Combine the oil, vinegar, and mustard in a small bowl and whisk until smooth. Spoon the dressing over the mushrooms and toss them. Allow to marinate for 30 to 40 minutes.

4.
In a bowl combine 1 cup Mayonnaise with the chili sauce, garlic, and scallions. Blend thoroughly and season with salt and pepper. Set aside.

5.
Drain the scallops and place them in a serving bowl. Remove the mushrooms from their marinade and drain thoroughly. Add them to the scallops.

6.
Add the seasoned mayonnaise and toss the salad lightly. There should be just enough mayonnaise to bind the ingredients, but you may need a little more.

7.
Chill the salad 4 to 6 hours before serving as an appetizer. Garnish with sprigs of parsley and serve on the lettuce leaves. Or you could serve the salad accompanied by the optional avocado slices.

Watercress and Scallop Salad

Serves: **4**
Preparation time: **15 minutes, plus additional time to chill**
Cooking time: **5 minutes**
Type of recipe: **elementary**
Cost: **moderate**

The new cuisine has brought with it a wave of unusual and often pretentious concoctions. However some of the simpler dishes, such as this delicious salad, are worth trying. The walnut oil gives a distinct flavor to the salad and combines extremely well with the tangy flavor of the watercress. If you cannot get bay scallops use sea scallops, dicing them after they have been chilled.

Ingredients
2 bunches fresh watercress
2 cups Vegetable Stock (page 539)
½ pound fresh tiny bay scallops
4 tablespoons Crème Fraîche (page 544)
2 teaspoons Dijon mustard
4 Tablespoons walnut oil
2 Tablespoons red wine vinegar
Salt and freshly ground black pepper
2 Tablespoons minced fresh chives or scallions (both white and green parts)

Preparation
1.
Trim the watercress, discarding some of the heavier stems. Wash the leaves quickly under cold water and dry gently in a kitchen towel. Transfer the watercress to a salad bowl and chill until serving.
2.
In an enamel saucepan heat the Vegetable Stock. Add the scallops and poach without letting the stock come to a boil for 3 minutes, or until the scallops turn an opaque white. Do not overcook or they will be tough and rubbery.
3.
Chill the scallops in their cooking liquid for 30 minutes, or until you are ready to serve the salad.
4.
In a bowl combine the Crème Fraîche, mustard, walnut oil, and vinegar. Whisk the mixture until smooth and season with salt and pepper. Add the chives or scallions and correct the seasoning.
5.
When ready to serve drain the scallops thoroughly. Add them to the watercress in the salad bowl and top with the dressing. Toss lightly, adding a large grinding of black pepper, and serve immediately as an appetizer accompanied by crusty French bread.

Feuilletés of Scallops
with
Leeks

Serves: **4 to 6**
Preparation time: **15 minutes**
Cooking time: **20 minutes**
Type of recipe: **Difficult**
Cost: **Expensive**

Here is an appetizer that is most elegant and delicious. The steamed scallops are bound in a light mustard hollandaise and are flavored with braised leeks. The puff pastry gives the dish an elegant touch.

Ingredients

4 to 6 Feuilletés (page 548)
1 egg, beaten with 1 tablespoon water
4 medium leeks, well rinsed and with all but 2 inches of the greens removed
10 Tablespoons cold sweet butter
Salt and freshly ground black pepper
2 cups Vegetable Stock (page 539)
¾ pound fresh small bay scallops
2 large egg yolks
2 Tablespoons cream
1 teaspoon Dijon mustard
Juice of ½ lemon

Preparation

1.
Preheat the oven to 450 degrees.

2.
Rinse a baking sheet with cold water, then place the Feuilletés on the sheet. Brush with the egg wash and place the baking sheet in the center of the oven. Bake for 15 to 20 minutes, or until the Feuilletés have risen and are nicely browned. Remove from the oven and set aside.

3.
Cut the leeks into 2-inch julienne strips and set aside.

4.
In a heavy small skillet heat 2 tablespoons butter. Add the leeks, together with 2 tablespoons water and season with salt and pepper. Cover the skillet and simmer the leeks for 5 minutes, or until just tender. Set the skillet aside.

5.
In a 2-quart saucepan heat the Vegetable Stock. Place a vegetable steamer in the saucepan and put the scallops in 1 layer in the steamer. Season lightly with salt and pepper. Cover the saucepan and steam the scallops over the aromatic broth for 3 to 4 minutes, or until they turn an opaque white. Remove the saucepan from the heat and reserve.

6.
In a heavy 10-inch skillet heat 3 to 4 cups water and keep warm.

7.
In a heavy 1½-quart saucepan combine the egg yolks, cream, mustard, and lemon juice. Stir the mixture until it is well blended. Place the saucepan inside the skillet and

Shrimp Salad
à la Paysanne

Serves:	**6**
Preparation time:	**20 minutes**
Cooking time:	**25 minutes**
Type of recipe:	**elementary**
Cost:	**moderate**

whisk the mixture until it starts to thicken. (Do not let the water in the skillet come to a boil.)

8.
Whisk in 1 tablespoon at a time of the remaining butter, whisking constantly until all the butter has been absorbed and the mixture is thick and smooth. Season with salt and pepper, then taste and correct the seasoning, adding more lemon juice or mustard if necessary. Remove the sauce from the heat and add the scallops and leeks to the sauce. Fold gently, then set aside.

9.
Cut the Feuilletés in half crosswise. Place the bottom halves on the individual serving plates and top each with the scallop-and-leek mixture. (The mixture does not have to fit exactly into the pastry squares.) Top each with the other half of the pastry and serve immediately.

Remarks
The Feuilletés can be baked several hours ahead of time and reheated in a slow oven. The entire dish can be prepared 2 to 3 hours ahead of time and kept warm over a pan of warm but not hot water. For a simpler variation of this dish substitute slices of white bread (crust removed and sautéed in clarified butter) for the puff pastry. Use only 1 slice of sautéed bread for each serving and sprinkle the scallop-and-leek mixture with minced parsley.

Ingredients
1 pound fresh shrimp
4 to 6 small new potatoes
1 cup Mayonnaise (page 540)
2 Tablespoons chili sauce
Juice of 1 lemon
1 Tablespoon Dijon mustard
1 large clove garlic, peeled and crushed
1 cup cooked peas
3 Tablespoons finely minced scallions (both white and green parts)
3 dill gherkins, finely minced
3 Tablespoons diced pimientos
Salt and freshly ground black pepper

Garnish:
6 to 8 cherry tomatoes
2 Tablespoons finely minced fresh parsley

Shrimp and Avocado Salad

Serves:	**6**
Preparation time:	**15 minutes, plus 2 hours to marinate**
Cooking time:	**5 minutes**
Type of recipe:	**elementary**
Cost:	**moderate**

While avocados are a basically bland vegetable, their wonderful texture adds interest to many salads. Here they are combined with shrimp in a light garlic-flavored mayonnaise. It is a simple yet delicious year-round appetizer.

Preparation

1.

In a large saucepan bring salted water to a boil. Add the shrimp, return to a boil, and cook for 3 minutes. Drain the shrimp and, when cool enough to handle, peel and cube. Set aside.

2.

Cook the potatoes in salted water until barely tender. Drain. Cool completely, then peel and cube. Set aside.

3.

In a bowl combine the Mayonnaise with the chili sauce, lemon juice, mustard, and garlic. Blend thoroughly and set aside.

4.

Combine the shrimp, potatoes, peas, scallions, dill gherkins, and pimientos in a serving bowl.

5.

Add the mayonnaise and toss lightly. Season with salt and pepper.

6.

Garnish with cherry tomatoes and parsley. Serve lightly chilled, accompanied by thinly sliced, buttered pumpernickel bread.

Remarks

You can substitute a cubed ripe avocado for the peas and garnish the salad with sieved hard-boiled eggs.

Ingredients

1 pound fresh shrimp
2 Tablespoons white wine vinegar
3 Tablespoons olive oil
1 teaspoon Dijon mustard
1 cup Mayonnaise (page 540)
1 large clove garlic, peeled and crushed
2 Tablespoons chili sauce
Dash of Tabasco sauce
Salt and freshly ground black pepper
1 large ripe avocado, peeled and seeded
Juice of ½ lemon
3 Tablespoons finely minced scallions or fresh chives

Optional:
2 Tablespoons minced fresh dill

Garnish:
Sprigs of fresh parsley or dill
Lemon wedges
6 slices avocado

Preparation

1.

In a large saucepan bring salted water to a boil. Add the shrimp. Return the water to a boil and cook the shrimp for 1 minute, or just until they turn a bright pink. Drain the shrimp and, when cool enough to handle, peel and discard the shells.

Serves:	**6**
Preparation time:	**25 minutes**
Cooking time:	**30 minutes**
Type of recipe:	**elementary**
Cost:	**inexpensive**

Here is an elegant appetizer that can also be served as a luncheon main course. Because of the rich sauce it is sufficient to serve 1 crêpe per person. Although this dish may sound elaborate, it is really quite simple. The crêpes should be prepared 1 or 2 days ahead, covered, and refrigerated. The fish mousse takes only minutes to do and the sauce can be made while the crêpes are being heated in the oven. The sauce can also be made a day in advance and reheated in the top of a double boiler over warm water.

Ingredients

½ pound whiting fillets, cut into serving pieces
½ teaspoon grated onion
1 large egg white
¾ cup cold heavy cream
Salt and freshly ground white pepper
6 Entrée Crêpes (page 388)
2 Tablespoons melted butter

Optional:
1 tablespoon finely minced fresh dill

Sauce:
1 Tablespoon finely minced shallots
¼ cup white wine vinegar
3 large egg yolks
1 cup Crème Fraîche (page 544)
8 to 12 Tablespoons cold butter
Salt and freshly ground black pepper

Optional:
1 tablespoon finely minced fresh dill or chives

2.
Cube the shrimp and place it in a mixing bowl. Set aside.

3.
In a small mixing bowl combine the vinegar, olive oil, and mustard and whisk the dressing until well blended. Pour the dressing over the shrimp, toss and then marinate for 2 hours.

4.
While the shrimp is marinating combine the Mayonnaise, garlic, and chili sauce and season with a dash of Tabasco sauce and salt and pepper. Whisk the mixture until smooth and set aside.

5.
Cube the avocado and sprinkle it with lemon juice. Set aside.

6.
Drain the shrimp and combine with the avocado, scallions, and optional dill in a serving bowl. Add the mayonnaise and fold lightly into the shrimp-and-avocado mixture.

7.
Taste and correct the seasoning. Chill the salad until serving.

8.
Serve the salad on individual plates. Garnish with sprigs of dill, lemon wedges, and additional slices of avocado. Serve accompanied by thinly sliced, buttered black bread.

Garnish:
Sprigs of fresh parsley or dill

Preparation
1.
Preheat the oven to 325 degrees.
2.
In a food processor combine the whiting pieces, grated onion, and egg white. Grind the mixture, adding the heavy cream in a slow stream. When all the cream has been absorbed the mixture should be smooth and fluffy. Season the mousse with salt and pepper and add the optional dill. Taste the mousse and correct the seasoning. Set aside.
3.
Place a heaping tablespoon of mousse on each crêpe and roll them up. Butter a large *au gratin* dish and place the crêpes seam-side down in the dish. Drizzle with the melted butter. Cover the dish with foil and place in the oven. Bake the crêpes for 20 minutes.
4.
While the crêpes are in the oven make the sauce. In a heavy 2-quart enamel saucepan combine the shallots and vinegar. Cook the mixture until the vinegar has evaporated, then remove the saucepan from the heat and set aside.
5.
In a bowl combine the yolks and Crème Fraîche and whisk until smooth. Add the egg-yolk mixture to the saucepan.
6.
Place the saucepan over the lowest possible heat and whisk the mixture constantly until it starts to thicken. Add the cold butter in small pieces, whisking constantly. If the sauce absorbs the 8 tablespoons of butter easily, add the remaining 4 tablespoons. Season the sauce with salt and pepper and add the optional dill or chives. Taste the sauce and correct the seasoning. Keep the sauce warm by putting the saucepan into a larger pan of warm water, whisking every 2 to 3 minutes.
7.
When the crêpes are done, transfer them to individual serving plates. Spoon a little of the warm sauce over each crêpe, covering it completely. Garnish with a sprig of fresh parsley or dill and serve immediately.

Remarks
If the sauce gets too thick, thin it out with a little heavy cream and a few drops of lemon juice.

Soups

When I was growing up homemade soups were an important part of our meals. The large iron pot was a reassuring presence in the kitchen, cooking away as our cook and my mother prepared the vegetables or attended to some other aspect of the meal. Shopping with soup in mind was an essential part of the daily marketing. One never knew before reaching the busy, bustling market which produce would be the most attractive that day or what surprises the stands would have. Soup came into your mind the minute you entered the market, since there were several stands that carried only soup greens tied in bundles. Here were carrots, celery tops, parsley root, leeks, and brilliant, bright orange pumpkins which would add wonderful flavoring to our stocks. After purchasing these essential aromatic vegetables we would look for what was plentiful and fresh. Depending on the season, there would be mounds of tiny white turnips, lovely cabbage, or, in the summer, heaps of fresh, somewhat overripe tomatoes perfect for the soup pot. The greens would always catch your eye—a basket of sorrel, watercress, or crisp bright green spinach. Making our way through the crowded market, we would add to the basket some fresh fish, a chicken, or some meaty beef bones, keeping in mind as we did so the rich and fragrant stocks the bones and trimmings would make.

Nowadays soups are always the first thing I teach my beginning students. Soups call for simple, basic techniques of cooking, and they offer a marvelous introduction to many fundamentals of good, creative marketing.

Soups combine the best of all possible worlds in one simmering pot—a rich stock, fresh vegetables, meat, or poultry, or fish. Well-prepared and well-seasoned, there is no such thing as a soup that doesn't work.

Because of my Mediterranean background I have a special love for soup. I cannot think of a single part of the world where it is not a featured item in the local cuisine. Its appeal has always been universal, and traditional recipes have lasted through the centuries. What a range we have to choose from! There is a soup for every season, climate, and occasion. I am particularly fond of the traditional regional soups of both Central and Mediterranean Europe. The robust "family" soups of these regions —the French garbure, the Italian minestrone, the Catalan gutsy cabbage soup —offer the character and straightforwardness that are the most satisfying qualities a soup can possess. Like Japan's simple broth served as the customary starter to a meal or like South America's hearty black bean soup, these are essentially reflections of the common sense and ingenuity of everyday cooks. Theirs was the cooking that really depended (and still does) on the imaginative use of basic ingredients: the produce, meat, poultry, or fish most readily available in the local markets.

Part of the great appeal of soups stems from the fact that they are basically good-natured. In comparison with the gutsy, delicious one-dish meals they make, they demand relatively little time or culinary talent. They can easily be made in advance and, because they can be made in large quantities and frozen for future use, they are a cheap, economical way to feed a large family. While soup was once an important mainstay for the peasant farmer's wife who both helped out in the fields and cooked the meals, so it ought to be today for the working person who comes home after a long day and still has to feed the family. There is nothing quite as comforting as the knowledge that there is a hearty, nourishing soup to fall back on, whether it has been simmering away on the stove all afternoon or stocked in the freezer, ready to be heated in a matter of minutes.

For the American cook, whose shopping is so easy because of the supermarket, soups should be the staple of the family meal. We have access to such a wealth of varied, good-quality ingredients, and many ethnic soups can be duplicated easily. Surprising as it may seem, these soups are often better and more flavorful here than they are in the countries of their origin. On a recent trip to Russia I searched in vain for a good Ukrainian borscht; in Austria, I sampled many versions of goulash soup, only to find nowadays that they are mostly served watery and lack the gutsiness and flavor required. But despite the fact that America is a rich composite of countless cultures and ethnic heritages, and that we are fortunate in having an availability of ingredients almost unparalleled anywhere in the world, ns have fared poorly here. Many ns have grown so used to the of opening a can (or more

recently, reconstitiong a dehydrated packet) that they are unaware of how much they can actually do with just a few supermarket staples and all-season vegetables.

I have noticed a great rise in the popularity of soups in recent years. New "potageries" as well as many soup-bread-and-salad restaurants have opened, and in regular restaurants soups appear on the menus in greater numbers than ever before. Yet while many more people enjoy soups when they dine out, I think few seem to realize how easy they are to make at home. At my dinner table nothing can equal the essence of a full-bodied broth laced with a seasonal vegetable, or the velvety texture of a carefully seasoned cream-of-asparagus or sorrel soup. To me these soups mean spring! When summer comes, what is more refreshing than a chilled tomato soup flavored with fresh basil or coriander leaves? Or the gutsy *Soupe Menton,* the French version of the Italian minestrone flavored with basil that combines the best and freshest of the garden in one aromatic soup. In the fall and winter months, soups rise to the top of my cooking repertoire. Warm and wintry soups range from a creamy potato-and-vegetable soup to a hearty cabbage, turnip, and dried bean soup. A country broccoli-and-pasta soup is another of my favorite cold-weather meals. It is good to have in your repertoire at least two soup recipes for each season that will let you take advantage of the most flavorful, plentiful, and inexpensive vegetables available fresh at the local markets.

Whenever possible I let the market's best offerings inspire my menu, and at our house at least once a week dinner consists of a hearty soup, salad, an omelet or frittata, some good bread, fresh sweet butter, and a simple fruit dessert. This is the "friendliest" kind of meal I can imagine.

It is to the *cuisine des pauvres*, and the steaming marmite of bygone days that we must return to discover the simple secret of all the great European soups: begin with the freshest basic ingredients you can find. This means you must be on the lookout for the all-season staples of the supermarket. Carrots, potatoes, onions, leeks, turnips, salt pork or bacon, and beef bones all add flavor and character to soups. So do the legumes—chick peas, split peas, lentils, and dried beans. With a little inspiration you can make a variety of satisfying, filling, and highly nourishing spur-of-the-moment soups.

Fresh produce is the most important ingredient in any soup. I find that there is little difference in the appearance of the produce area of the supermarket from one month to the next. However there are growing numbers of small vegetable markets everywhere, and since these give prominent display to seasonal specialties, one glance at the bins is an instant indication of the time of year. Summer is of course a bonanza for produce. In addition to the supermarkets and greengroceries, there are roadside stands and, if you garden, the treat of your own homegrown vegetables. In the summer it is often a good idea to watch the supermarkets for

height-of-the-season specials on usually higher priced produce. At these times they are likely to be less expensive there than in the smaller markets. In other seasons if you plan to make a soup you might find yourself more limited in the choice of fresh vegetables in your supermarket. Try to work with fresh staples rather than canned varieties. One of the great advantages of soups is that they can be simplified and altered creatively.

Fresh herbs too abound in summer, and they can lend wonderful new dimensions to a familiar soup. Basil, coriander, fennel leaves, and mint, for instance, lend a special touch to a chilled tomato soup. The herbs, whether parsley or dill or the stronger herbs, must be added to the soup before serving. They should never be cooked, as this will cause them to lose their aromatic flavor.

In making good soups it is essential to use both common sense and experience in realizing which ingredients work well together. Undoubtedly, these were two of the greatest assets possessed by the cooks who long ago created these classic soups. Soups are no different from salads; they should be made with care. The soup pot should never be treated as a haphazard catchall for whatever you have around the kitchen. Try to respect the character of each vegetable: some are delicate, others strong. Observe the correct cooking time for each, and learn which flavors and textures complement the others. Developing your instincts is part of the adventure of good cooking. Season and taste often as you cook and, when in doubt, remember that it is better to use too little liquid than too much. A good, strong concentrated soup can always be thinned out, but a too-thin soup is nearly impossible to correct. Most soups are better the day after they have been made because they have had a chance to develop flavor.

The essence of any homemade soup is its base. The three basic homemade stocks— chicken, beef, and fish—are easy to prepare. A good stock will transform even the simplest soup ingredients into a memorable dish. While beef stock requires long hours of slow simmering, chicken stock can be ready in one to two hours. A fish stock is finished in only thirty minutes. Because of the importance of these stocks, always watch for specials in your supermarket. Buy chicken wings and giblets whenever possible, and freeze them if you are not going to make the stock right away. I always bone my own chicken since the backbone, giblets, and wings are essential to a good stock. Many people buy boned chicken breasts; in that case, if you are dealing with a butcher, ask him for the bones and use them for your stock. Once it is made, you can use the stock for other preparations, such as basting a roast chicken or making a sauce. If the fish market has trimmings, get them that day and, as with the chicken parts, freeze them if you don't have the time to make the stock. They are most often inexpensive, sometimes even free.

Vegetable soups are usually made with a base of onions, minced garlic, parsley, and possibly tomatoes stewed gently in butter before adding the vegetable of your choice. While most vegetable soups generally call for celery, I use it in moderation since it has a tendency to overwhelm other, more subtle ingredients. On its own however it makes the wonderful cream soup that is one of my all-season favorites (sometimes thickened with potatoes; other times with a cream base).

A beef stock is best reserved for soups such as cabbage, onion, and legume, since it is too strong for mild vegetables such as carrots, spinach, and mushrooms. You may also combine some inexpensive beef bones with chicken giblets to make your stock, and use it with the hearty, all-season vegetables. All soups made with dried legumes are enhanced by adding a piece of smoked pork butt or ham hock, which gives the soup a marvelous, smoky flavor. They do tend to oversalt the broth, however, and must be used carefully.

Although I rarely use any canned products, I find myself having to use canned tomatoes or chick peas for certain soups, particularly in the winter months. Canned broth can be used for certain vegetables that have great flavor and character—cabbage, split peas, and lentils. I find that College Inn is a good brand, but no matter what canned broth you use, it should still be bolstered with some aromatic vegetables, such as a carrot, an onion, a stalk of celery, and a bay leaf. Let it simmer for an hour before making the soup. Often a doctored-up stock is better than a homemade one for soups that are to be served cold, since they will not cause the soups to gel.

With the great popularity of food processors, many cooks have become enamored of cream soups. While a lovely, creamy soup is quick and often delicious, the lack of texture often detracts greatly from its character. It is often hard to distinguish a watercress from a spinach soup. This is partly because our produce lacks the rich flavor of yesteryear, but it is also because texture is important to soups. When making a cream soup, I always remove some of the cooked vegetables prior to puréeing, adding them later to the puréed soup and heating through without overcooking. Tiny bits of raw vegetables, such as sliced leeks, fresh peas, or diced zucchini, also make a lovely addition to certain puréed soups. They cook quickly and give the soup a welcome, unexpected personality. When it comes to hot soups, I like to enrich them with cream; a good lump of butter added to the individual soup bowl just before serving is, of course, the most flavorful enrichment of all.

In addition to carrying all the basics necessary for good homemade soups, the supermarket shelves are also filled with canned soups and instant mixes. No matter how many "natural" ingredients have gone into the making of these soups, I find they still have a canned, unnatural flavor. As for flavor enhancers and preservatives, such as the much-used monosodium glutamate and

large quantities of salt, these are used by manufacturers as much to mask the *absence* of flavor as they are to "preserve" whatever flavor there is. I also find that it takes more time and effort to improve a canned soup than it does to make a homemade one. While there are some acceptable canned soups (like Progresso Lentil Soup, on which the ingredients read like real food and not a chemistry lab manual), a serious cook would never consider using them. Aside from offending taste and texture, they don't really make economic sense. Since the less expensive homemade soups are so easily frozen, it just isn't worth the trouble or expense of fixing up small quantities of the canned varieties.

I am also discouraged by the influx of dry mixes, since their growing presence in the supermarket indicates that people are using them. Like most of the canned soups, these have chemical additives in the separate spice packets. If you choose to eliminate these ingredients and substitute your own, you are left with the actual purchase of little more than bouillon and some dehydrated vegetables. These simply aren't worth the time, trouble, or expense— not when you can so easily come up with a really fabulous soup of your own.

I love soups, and I find them easy and fun to make. They are a way of life. There is hardly a day when I don't serve some kind of soup, either to my family or friends at a dinner party. And whenever I eat a good homemade soup at someone else's house, it

never fails to confirm my belief that any
cook who understands the fundamentals can
be creative when it comes to the
preparation of soups.

Red Bean
Soup
à la Cubana

Serves: **6 to 8**
Preparation time: **20 minutes, plus overnight to soak beans**
Cooking time: **2 hours, 5 minutes**
Type of recipe: **elementary**
Cost: **moderate**

Ingredients
1½ cups dried red kidney beans
3 Tablespoons olive oil
1 large onion, finely diced
1 cup diced celery
2 cloves garlic, crushed
Salt
1 bay leaf
1 large sprig fresh parsley
1 pound smoked pork butt
Freshly ground black pepper
Dash of cayenne pepper

Optional:
2 smoked frankfurters
½ cup cooked white rice
1 cup chicken or beef bouillon

Garnish:
Finely minced fresh parsley

Preparation

1.
A day ahead place the beans in a large bowl and cover with 2 inches cold water. Soak the beans overnight.

2.
The next day drain the beans and set aside.

3.
In a large heavy casserole heat the oil. Add the onion, celery, and garlic and cook the mixture for 3 to 4 minutes, or until soft but not browned.

4.
Add the beans, then add enough water to cover beans by 2 inches. Season lightly with salt, then add the bay leaf, parsley, and smoked pork butt. Bring to a boil, reduce the heat, and simmer for 2 hours, or until the beans are very tender.

5.
Cool the soup and discard the bay leaf and parsley sprig. With a slotted spoon remove half the beans and purée them in blender. Return the bean purée to the soup.

6.
Remove the smoked pork butt and dice, then return it to the soup, together with the optional smoked frankfurters and rice.

7.
Reheat the soup. Taste and correct the seasoning, adding a large grinding of black pepper and a pinch of cayenne pepper. If the soup is too thick add the additional chicken or beef bouillon. Garnish with minced parsley and serve the soup hot as a main course to a light supper.

White Bean and Cabbage Soup Toulousaine

Serves:	**8**
Preparation time:	**20 minutes, plus overnight to soak beans**
Cooking time:	**2 hours**
Type of recipe:	**elementary**
Cost:	**moderate**

Here is a hearty, inexpensive one-dish meal I often serve for Sunday supper or informal entertaining during the fall and winter months. The beef shin is a deliciously tender piece of meat that adds great flavor to this kind of soup. You may, however, substitute a meaty piece of salt pork and some meaty beef bones.

Ingredients

1½ cups dried Great Northern beans
8 to 10 cups beef bouillon or water
1 pound beef shin bones
1 pound smoked shoulder butt
2 onions, peeled and each stuck with a clove
4 large cloves garlic, unpeeled
2 carrots, scraped and quartered
3 stalks celery, scraped and cut in half
3 ripe tomatoes, quartered
Salt
6 to 8 black peppercorns
1 large cabbage (about 1½ pounds), cut into large chunks
4 medium potatoes, peeled and quartered

Preparation

1.
A day ahead place the beans in a large bowl. Cover with 2 inches cold water and soak overnight. The next day drain the beans.

2.
Preheat the oven to 325 degrees.

3.
Place the beans in a large casserole and cover with bouillon or water. Add the meat and/or bones, smoked butt, onions stuck with cloves, garlic, carrots, celery, and tomatoes. Bring the mixture to a boil on top of the stove and season with salt, then add the peppercorns. If the bouillon does not cover the vegetables and meat mixture by 2 inches, add additional water.

4.
Cover the casserole and place it in the oven. Cook for 1 hour, 15 minutes to 1 hour, 30 minutes, or until the beans and meat are both very tender.

5.
Remove the casserole from the oven and place over moderate heat on top of the stove. Add the cabbage and potatoes and simmer for another 30 minutes. Taste the soup and correct the seasoning.

6.
Remove the meat and bones from the casserole and cut the meat into serving pieces, then return to the casserole.

7.
Serve the soup in deep individual soup bowls accompanied by slices of black bread and a bowl of sweet butter.

Remarks:
The soup can be prepared 1 or 2 days ahead and reheated. It is best to separate the meat from the liquid for refrigeration and then reheat it together just before serving.

White Bean
and Sorrel
Soup

Serves: **6**
Preparation time: **20 minutes, plus overnight to soak beans**
Cooking time: **2 hours, 25 minutes**
Type of recipe: **elementary**
Cost: **inexpensive**

Ingredients

1 cup dried Great Northern beans
Salt and freshly ground black pepper
1 onion, stuck with a clove
1 bay leaf
3 Tablespoons butter
2 large leeks, well rinsed and finely minced
5 to 6 cups Light Chicken Stock (page 531)
1 pound fresh sorrel, rinsed and with stems removed
1 cup heavy cream

Preparation

1.
A day ahead, place beans in a large bowl and cover with 2 inches cold water. Soak the beans overnight. The next day drain the beans.

2.
Preheat the oven to 325 degrees.

3.
Place the beans in a casserole and cover with 2 inches fresh water. Season with salt and pepper, then add the onion stuck with clove and bay leaf. Cover the casserole, place in the oven, and cook the beans for 2 hours, or until very tender.

4.
Drain the beans, reserving the cooking liquid.

5.
In a large heavy saucepan heat the butter. Add the leeks and cook covered for 10 minutes, or until very soft; do not let the leeks brown. Add the beans and the chicken stock and simmer for 10 minutes.

6.
Purée the mixture in a blender or food processor until smooth. Season with salt and pepper, return the mixture to the saucepan, and keep it warm.

7.
Place the sorrel in a casserole and cook over low heat until it is reduced to a purée. The water that clings to the leaves after washing is enough to cook the sorrel. Drain the sorrel in a fine sieve.

8.
Transfer the sorrel to a chopping board and mince finely. Add the sorrel to the bean soup, together with the cream, and reheat the soup for 5 minutes. Taste and correct the seasoning, adding a large grinding of black pepper. If the soup is too thick add a little more stock or some of the bean cooking liquid. Serve the soup hot, accompanied by crusty French bread.

Remarks

The sorrel can be replaced with fresh spinach or a combination of spinach and watercress. Add a little lemon juice to the soup in order to obtain some of the tartness that sorrel gives to the soup.

Serbian
Bean
Soup

Serves: **6**
Preparation time: **15 minutes, plus overnight to soak beans**
Cooking time: **2 hours, 15 minutes**
Type of recipe: **elementary**
Cost: **inexpensive**

Ingredients

½ pound dried Great Northern beans
6 to 7 cups beef bouillon
1 onion, peeled and stuck with a clove
1 bay leaf
1 large sprig fresh parsley
1 stalk celery with leaves
1 carrot, scraped and cut in half crosswise
Salt
6 peppercorns
2 Tablespoons butter or chicken fat
1 teaspoon oil
2 cups finely minced onions
2 cloves garlic, peeled and crushed
Freshly ground black pepper
1 teaspoon dried marjoram
2 teaspoons imported paprika
3 Tablespoons tomato paste
1 cup sour cream
Large pinch cayenne pepper
1 to 2 cups thinly sliced frankfurters or garlic sausage

Garnish:
Finely minced fresh parsley

Preparation

1.
A day ahead place the beans in a bowl and cover with 2 inches cold water. Soak overnight.

2.
The next day preheat the oven to 325 degrees.

3.
Drain the beans and place them in a casserole. Add enough bouillon to cover by 2 inches. Add the onion stuck with clove, bay leaf, parsley sprig, celery stalk, and carrot. Season lightly with salt. (Too much salt will toughen the beans.) Add the peppercorns and bring to a boil on top of the stove, cover, then place the casserole in the oven. Cook the beans for 1 hour, 30 minutes to 2 hours, or until they are very tender.

4.
When the beans are done remove the casserole from the oven and discard the vegetables. With a slotted spoon transfer 2 cups beans to a bowl and set aside.

5.
Purée the remaining beans, together with the cooking stock, in a blender or food processor. Transfer the puréed mixture to a bowl and set aside.

6.
In a large heavy casserole melt the butter or chicken fat with the oil, then add the onions and garlic. Season with salt, pepper, and marjoram and cook the mixture partially covered for 10 to 15 minutes, or until very soft and lightly browned.

Perla Meyers' From Market to Kitchen Cookbook

Cold
Summer Beet
Soup

Serves:	**6 to 8**
Preparation time:	**15 minutes, plus overnight to chill**
Cooking time:	**45 minutes**
Type of recipe:	**elementary**
Cost:	**inexpensive**

7.
Add the paprika and tomato paste and stir until well blended. Immediately add the bean purée and bring to a boil. Reduce the heat, cover, and simmer the soup for 25 to 30 minutes.

8.
While still hot whisk in the sour cream. Taste the soup and correct the seasoning, adding the cayenne pepper. (The soup should be somewhat spicy.) If the soup is too thick thin it out with a little more bouillon.

9.
Add the reserved beans and the frankfurters or garlic sausages and heat through. Sprinkle with parsley and serve in individual bowls, accompanied by slices of black bread and a bowl of sweet butter.

Remarks
This soup is best when prepared 1 to 2 days ahead, which gives it a chance to develop flavor. You may add a piece of smoked pork butt to the beans while they are cooking. This will give the soup an additional delicious flavor.

Here is a simple, uncooked summer soup that gets better and better each day. So make it 1 to 2 days ahead and serve it as an appetizer or as part of a luncheon menu.

Ingredients
3 medium to large beets, well scrubbed but not peeled
1 quart buttermilk
2 cups sour cream
¼ cup lemon juice
½ cup finely minced scallions (both white and green part)
2 large cloves garlic, peeled and crushed
½ cup finely minced fresh dill
Salt and freshly ground black pepper

Garnish:
Sprigs of fresh dill
1 lime, thinly sliced

Country Broccoli Soup

Serves: **6**
Preparation time: **20 minutes**
Cooking time: **50 minutes**
Type of recipe: **elementary**
Cost: **inexpensive**

Preparation

1.
A day earlier, bring salted water to a boil in a large saucepan. Add the beets and cook over medium heat for 45 minutes, or until the beets are very tender.

2.
Drain the beets and when they are cool enough to handle peel them. The skin will slip off easily. Cube the beets fine, reserving 1 cup for garnish.

3.
Purée the remaining beets in a food processor, adding a little buttermilk until the mixture is completely smooth. Set aside.

4.
In a large bowl combine the remaining buttermilk, sour cream, lemon juice, scallions, garlic, and dill. Add the beet purée and whisk the soup until well blended. Season with salt and pepper. Add the remaining cubed beets and chill the soup overnight.

5.
The next day taste the soup again. It may need a little more lemon juice; correct the seasoning.

6.
Serve the soup chilled but not cold in individual soup bowls. Garnish each with a slice of lime and a sprig of dill. Served accompanied by thin slices of buttered pumpernickel.

Ingredients

1½ to 2 pounds fresh broccoli
3 Tablespoons butter
3 large leeks, well rinsed and sliced (2 inches of the greens removed)
2 all-purpose potatoes, peeled and cubed
6 to 8 cups Chicken Stock (page 530)
Salt and freshly ground black pepper
1 cup heavy cream or Crème Fraîche (page 544)
3 to 4 slices stale white bread, crusts removed
2 cloves garlic, peeled and cut in half
3 Tablespoons olive oil

Garnish:
Freshly grated Parmesan cheese

Preparation

1.
Peel the broccoli stalks with a vegetable peeler. Remove the leaves and cut the stalks into ¾-inch cubes. Reserve 2 cups of the cubed broccoli and coarsely chop the remaining broccoli. Set both aside.

2.
In a large casserole heat 2 tablespoons butter. Add the leeks and cook covered over low heat for 2 to 3 minutes without browning.

3.
Add the potatoes and chopped broccoli, then add the stock and bring to a boil. Reduce the heat and season with salt and pepper. Simmer for 30 minutes, or until the vegetables are very tender.

Cream of Endive Soup

Serves: **6**
Preparation time: **10 minutes**
Cooking time: **25 minutes**
Type of recipe: **elementary**
Cost: **expensive**

4.
Cool the soup and purée in a blender or food processor.

5.
Return the soup to the casserole. Add the reserved cubed broccoli and cook over low heat for 15 minutes, or until the broccoli is tender.

6.
Add the cream, then taste and correct the seasoning. Keep the soup covered.

7.
Rub the bread slices with the cut side of the garlic cloves. Cut into ½-inch cubes and reserve.

8.
Heat the oil and remaining butter in a heavy skillet. Add the bread cubes and sauté over medium heat until nicely browned on all sides, tossing the cubes in the pan to brown them evenly. Set the bread cubes aside until completely cool; the croûtons will get crisp as they cool.

9.
Serve the soup in individual bowls, topped with a few croûtons and accompanied by a side bowl of freshly grated Parmesan cheese.

Remarks
This soup can be made several days ahead and refrigerated. It can also be frozen for 1 or 2 months. You may also garnish the soup with finely cubed sautéed bacon.

Most soups are only as good as the stock they are made with. The Belgian endive is a delicious, slightly mild vegetable that demands a well-flavored stock to give the soup the texture it needs.

Ingredients
6 large Belgian endive
4 Tablespoons butter
Salt and freshly ground white pepper
Large pinch granulated sugar
5 cups full-bodied Chicken Stock (page 530)
3 Tablespoons flour
¾ to 1 cup heavy cream

Garnish:
1 to 2 tablespoons finely minced fresh parsley, dill, or fennel greens

Cream
of Fennel
Soup

Serves:	**6**
Preparation time:	**10 minutes**
Cooking time:	**1 hour**
Type of recipe:	**elementary**
Cost:	**inexpensive**

Fennel, one of the great fall-winter vegetables, is just starting to become popular. Here it is used in a simple yet delicious cream soup.

Ingredients

5 Tablespoons butter
2 large fennel bulbs, tops removed and bulbs halved, then thinly sliced
2 to 3 leeks, well rinsed and thinly sliced
Salt and freshly ground black pepper
6½ cups Chicken Stock (page 530)
2 all-purpose potatoes, peeled
1 cup heavy cream

Garnish:

2 Tablespoons finely minced fennel tops or fresh parsley

Preparation

1.
Remove any wilted outer leaves from the endive. With the tip of a sharp knife remove the hard base. Slice the endive crosswise into ½-inch slices and set aside.

2.
In a large heavy saucepan melt the butter. Add most of the endive, reserving 1 to 1½ cups. Season with salt, pepper, and a large pinch of sugar. Add 2 to 3 tablespoons stock. Cover the saucepan and simmer the endive over low heat for 10 to 15 minutes, or until tender.

3.
Add the flour and cook for 1 to 2 minutes, stirring constantly. Add the reserved stock and bring to a boil, whisking constantly, until the soup is smooth and thick. Remove from the heat and cool.

4.
Purée the soup in a blender or food processor and return it to the saucepan.

5.
Reheat the soup over low heat. Add the remaining sliced endive and simmer the soup for another 5 minutes, or until the endive are tender. Add ¾ cup cream. Correct the seasoning and simmer the soup until it is well heated. (If the soup seems too thick add the remaining ¼ cup cream.)

6.
Garnish the soup with the parsley, dill, or fennel greens and serve hot.

Remarks
The soup can be made a day ahead and reheated slowly on top of the stove.

Middle Eastern
Lamb and Bean
Soup

Serves:	**8**
Preparation time:	**30 minutes, plus overnight to chill**
Cooking time:	**2 hours, 35 minutes**
Type of recipe:	**elementary**
Cost:	**moderate**

Preparation

1.

In a small heavy skillet heat 2 tablespoons butter. Add 1 cup fennel and 1 cup leeks. Season with salt and pepper and add ½ cup stock. Cover tightly and simmer the vegetables until they are tender but not browned. If the stock has evaporated add a little more. Set aside.

2.

Melt the remaining butter in a heavy casserole. Add the remaining leeks, fennel, and potatoes and cook for 3 to 4 minutes. Season with salt and pepper. Add 6 cups remaining stock and bring to a boil. Reduce the heat and simmer covered for 25 to 30 minutes, or until the vegetables are very tender.

3.

Cool the soup completely and then purée in a blender until smooth.

4.

Return the soup to the casserole, whisk in the cream and the leek-and-fennel mixture, and reheat the soup. Taste and correct the seasoning.

5.

Garnish with fennel tops or parsley and serve the soup hot, accompanied by crusty French bread.

One of the most satisfying winter meals is a one-dish soup that combines meat and vegetables. It can be prepared well in advance and varied according to what is available fresh at the market.

Ingredients

½ pound slab bacon, in 1 piece
2 pounds lamb shoulder, cut into 2-inch cubes
2 to 3 pounds lamb bones
4 carrots, scraped
4 stalks celery, well rinsed
2 large onions, peeled
1 parsnip, scraped, or 1 parsley root, scraped
10 to 12 whole cloves garlic, unpeeled and crushed
1 hot chili pepper
Salt
6 to 8 peppercorns
1 large cabbage (about 1½ pounds), cut into chunks
3 cups cooked white beans (page 99)

Garnish:
Finely minced fresh parsley

Optional:
Slices of stale French bread, fried in olive oil

Preparation

1.

A day ahead, bring water to a boil in a saucepan, add the bacon, and cook for 5 minutes. Drain and set aside.

2.

In a large casserole combine the cubed lamb, lamb bones, bacon, 2 carrots, 2 stalks celery, onions, parsnip or parsley root, garlic cloves and chili pepper. Add water to cover. Season with salt and peppercorns and bring to a boil, then reduce the heat. Remove with a slotted spoon the scum that rises to the surface and simmer the mixture covered for 1 hour, 30 minutes to 2 hours, or until the meat is tender but not falling apart.

3.

Cool the soup. Discard the vegetables and lamb bones and refrigerate overnight.

4.

The next day degrease the soup completely. Bring to a boil, then reduce the heat and simmer for 10 to 15 minutes.

5.

While the soup is simmering dice the remaining carrots and celery stalks and add to the soup, together with the cabbage. Cook for 10 to 15 minutes, or until the vegetables are tender.

6.

Remove the bacon and cube it. Return it to the soup, add the white beans, and heat through. Taste the soup and correct the seasoning. The soup should be somewhat spicy.

7.

If desired place 1 or 2 slices of optional bread into deep soup bowls and add a large ladle of the soup, meat, and bacon. Sprinkle with parsley and serve hot.

Remarks:

You can add peeled, diced potatoes to the soup instead of the white beans. You could also add turnips and 2 cups fresh green beans, cut into 1-inch pieces.

Russian Lamb Soup

Serves: **8**
Preparation time: **30 minutes, plus a day ahead to prepare stock**
Cooking time: **5 hours**
Type of recipe: **elementary**
Cost: **moderate**

Ingredients
Stock, as given below
2 Tablespoons olive oil
1 Tablespoon butter
2 onions, peeled and minced
2 leeks, well rinsed and thinly sliced (both green and white parts)
3 cloves garlic, peeled and minced
1 can (35 ounces) Italian plum tomatoes, well drained and chopped
1 Tablespoon tomato paste
1 hot chili pepper
1 bay leaf
½ teaspoon dried oregano
Salt and freshly ground black pepper
2 lamb shanks
2 cups peeled and cubed potatoes
2 parsnips, scraped and cubed

Stock:
3 pounds lamb bones
2 carrots, scraped and cut in half
2 stalks celery
1 large onion, peeled and stuck with a clove
1 large sprig of fresh parsley
Salt
6 to 8 peppercorns

Garnish:
2 Tablespoons finely minced fresh parsley
Sour cream

Preparation
1.
Start by making the stock; this is best done a day ahead. In a 6-quart casserole combine the bones, vegetables, and parsley.

Add water to cover and season with salt and peppercorns. Slowly bring to a boil, then reduce the heat and simmer partially covered for 2 to 3 hours, carefully skimming the stock several times during cooking. Let the stock cool. Strain into a large bowl and refrigerate.

2.
The next day degrease the stock thoroughly and reserve.

3.
In a large heavy casserole heat the oil and butter. Add the onions, leeks, and garlic and cook the mixture covered over low heat until soft but not brown.

4.
Add the tomatoes, tomato paste, chili pepper, bay leaf, oregano, salt, and pepper and cook the mixture for 10 minutes, stirring several times until the tomato water has evaporated and the mixture is thick.

5.
Add the lamb shanks and reserved stock and bring to a boil. Reduce the heat and simmer partially covered for 1 hour, 30 minutes, or until the lamb shanks are very tender.

6.
Add the potatoes and parsnips and continue cooking until the vegetables are tender. Taste the soup and correct the seasoning. Remove the meat from the bones, dice, and return to the soup.

7.
Ladle the soup into large soup bowls. Garnish with parsley and add a dollop of sour cream to each bowl. Serve hot as a main course to a family supper.

Mediterranean Lentil Soup

Serves:	**6**
Preparation time:	**20 minutes**
Cooking time:	**1 hour, 30 minutes**
Type of recipe:	**elementary**
Cost:	**inexpensive**

Ingredients

3 Tablespoons olive oil
1 large onion, finely minced
2 large cloves garlic, minced
1 stalk celery, finely minced
1 Tablespoon tomato paste
4 large ripe tomatoes, peeled and coarsely chopped
Salt and freshly ground black pepper
½ teaspoon dried thyme
1½ cups lentils, soaked in cold water for 2 hours
6 to 8 cups beef bouillon
1 large sprig fresh parsley
2 bay leaves

Vinaigrette:

3 to 4 Tablespoons red wine vinegar
½ cup olive oil
2 Tablespoons minced fresh parsley
1 cup tightly packed fresh basil leaves
1 small ripe tomato, cubed

Preparation

1.
In a large heavy casserole heat the oil, add the onion, garlic, and celery. Cook the mixture over medium heat until soft but not brown. Add the tomato paste and tomatoes. Season with salt, pepper, and thyme, then bring to a boil. Reduce the heat and simmer for 3 to 4 minutes.

2.
Drain the lentils and add to the casserole together with the bouillon, parsley sprig, and bay leaves. Bring to a boil, reduce the heat, and simmer partially covered for 1 hour to 1 hour, 15 minutes, or until the lentils are very tender.

3.
While the soup is simmering, prepare the vinaigrette. Combine the vinegar, olive oil, parsley, and basil leaves in a blender or food processor. Blend at high speed until smooth and set aside.

4.
When the soup is done add the vinaigrette and cubed tomato. Taste and correct the seasoning.

5.
Serve the soup at room temperature or lightly chilled accompanied by crusty French bread.

Remarks

For a sharper taste, start by using 3 tablespoons vinegar and add more according to your preference.

Cream of Mussel and Saffron Soup Provençale

Serves: **6**
Preparation time: **30 minutes**
Cooking time: **45 minutes**
Type of recipe: **elementary**
Cost: **moderate**

Ingredients
1 onion, finely minced
1 Bouquet Garni (page 546)
¾ cup white wine
4 pounds fresh mussels, well scrubbed and cleaned
2 Tablespoons fruity olive oil
2 Tablespoons finely minced shallots
1 can (14 ounces) plum tomatoes, well drained and diced
Salt and freshly ground black pepper
1 teaspoon dried thyme
½ teaspoon dried oregano
2 Tablespoons flour
2 cups Fish Stock (page 536)
¼ teaspoon saffron powder
1 large clove garlic, crushed.
Large pinch of cayenne pepper
1 large Roasted Red Pepper (page 545), diced
½ to ¾ cup heavy cream or Crème Fraîche (page 544)

Garnish:
2 Tablespoons finely minced fresh parsley

Preparation
1.
In a large heavy casserole combine the onion, bouquet, wine, and mussels. Bring to a boil, cover, and cook the mussels until they open. Shake the casserole several times to insure all the mussels are cooking evenly. Discard any that have not opened.
2.
Transfer the mussels to a colander and strain the liquid through a double layer of cheese cloth. Set liquid aside.

3.
Shell the mussels and discard the shells. Remove the black rim around each mussel and reserve the smallest mussels for the soup (about 1 to 1½ cups), setting the others aside for another purpose.
4.
In a large heavy saucepan, heat the oil over low heat. Add the shallots and cook for 2 minutes without browning. Add the tomatoes and season with salt, pepper, thyme, and oregano. Cover the saucepan and cook for 10 to 15 minutes.
5.
Uncover the saucepan and add the flour, whisking the mixture until well blended.
6.
Add the reserved mussel stock, Fish Stock, and saffron powder. Bring to a boil, then reduce the heat and simmer for 20 minutes.
7.
Cool the soup and purée in a food processor or blender, then return it to the saucepan. Season with salt and pepper and add the garlic and a dash of cayenne powder. Add the reserved mussels and the roasted pepper cubes and heat the soup over low heat.
8.
Add ½ cup cream or Crème Fraîche and heat again. (If the soup is too thick add the remaining ¼ cup cream.
9.
Garnish with parsley and serve hot, accompanied by thin slices of French bread sautéed in olive oil.

Potage
Bernoise

Serves:	**6 to 8**
Preparation time:	**20 minutes**
Cooking time:	**5 minutes**
Type of recipe:	**elementary**
Cost:	**inexpensive**

Until recently, fresh mushrooms were not a summer vegetable. Now with the availability of fresh mushrooms practically year round this soup is a delicious and refreshing addition to a summer menu. Since the soup freezes well it can be made in the spring in areas where fresh mushrooms are not available in the summer.

Ingredients
2 large bunches scallions
4 Tablespoons butter
2 Tablespoons flour
5 cups warm Light Chicken Stock (page 531)
1½ pounds fresh mushrooms, finely chopped (stems included)
1 cup heavy cream or Crème Fraîche (page 544)
Salt and freshly ground black pepper

Garnish:
1 cup thinly sliced fresh mushrooms
2 Tablespoons finely minced fresh parsley
1 Tablespoon finely minced fresh chives

Preparation
1.
Trim the scallions. Remove 1 inch of the greens and finely chop the remainder. Set aside.
2.
In a large heavy casserole heat the butter over low heat. Add the scallions and cook covered for 2 to 3 minutes without letting them brown.
3.
Add the flour and cook for 1 to 2 minutes,

stirring constantly. Add the stock all at once and whisk until the soup is smooth and comes to a boil. Add the mushrooms and immediately remove the casserole from the heat. Let the mushrooms warm up in the soup until the soup is cool.
4.
Purée the soup in a blender or food processor, then transfer to a bowl and whisk in the cream or Crème Fraîche. Season with salt and pepper and chill until ready to serve.
5.
An hour before serving bring the soup back to room temperature and garnish with mushroom slices, parsley, and chives. Taste and correct the seasoning. Serve the soup accompanied by crusty French bread or thin slices of buttered flat bread.

Remarks
For variation garnish the soup with finely minced fresh dill instead of parsley and enrich it with Crème Fraîche instead of heavy cream. This will give the soup an interesting and different flavor. If the soup gets too thick thin it out with another cup of stock and a little more cream.

Onion
Soup
Bretonne

Serves: **6 to 8**
Preparation time: **30 minutes**
Cooking time: **1 hour**
Type of recipe: **elementary**
Cost: **inexpensive**

Ingredients
3 Tablespoons butter
1 Tablespoon oil
3 medium Bermuda onions, peeled and thinly sliced
Salt and freshly ground black pepper
8 cups rich Beef Stock (page 533)
3 carrots, scraped and cut into thin julienne (⅛ inch thick and 2 inches long)
6 to 8 slices day-old French bread, cut ¾ inch thick
½ pound ripe Camembert cheese

Preparation
1.
In a large heavy saucepan heat the butter and oil and add the onions. Season with salt and pepper, then cook for 2 to 3 minutes over moderate-to-high heat, stirring constantly. Reduce the heat and simmer the onions partially covered for 45 minutes, or until soft and a deep golden brown.
2.
Preheat the oven to 325 degrees.
3.
Add the stock to the saucepan and bring to a boil. Reduce the heat and cook for 15 minutes. Add the carrots and continue simmering the soup until the carrots are tender. Taste and correct the seasoning. Keep the soup warm.
4.
Place the bread slices on a baking sheet and toast in the oven until golden brown. Remove from the oven and reserve.
5.
Remove the rind from the Camembert and cut into 6 to 8 cubes.
6.
Place a slice of toast in each individual soup bowl, then top with a Camembert cube. Spoon the hot soup into the bowls and serve hot.

Remarks
The soup can be made several days ahead and reheated. It can also be frozen successfully. For a variation you may use another type of cheese such as Gorgonzola or another blue cheese.

Mediterranean
Onion
Soup

Serves: **6 to 8**
Preparation time: **20 minutes**
Cooking time: **2 hours**
Type or recipe: **elementary**
Cost: **inexpensive**

The classic onion soup is a gutsy one-dish meal that allows great room for interesting variations. Here is one from the southwest part of France that I particularly like to make in the summer when good fresh tomatoes are plentiful.

Ingredients

3 Tablespoons fruity olive oil
4 to 5 cups thinly sliced onions
Salt and freshly ground black pepper
1 teaspoon granulated sugar
1 teaspoon dried thyme
3 cloves garlic, peeled and crushed
1 bay leaf
½ teaspoon dried oregano
1 large sprig fresh parsley
2 tablespoons flour
1 tablespoon tomato paste
8 large ripe tomatoes, peeled, seeded, and chopped (3 pounds), or 1 can (35 ounces) Italian plum tomatoes, drained and chopped
6 to 8 cups Chicken Stock (page 530) or bouillon
½ cup tiny pasta (tubetini)

Garnish:

Finely minced fresh parsley or a mixture of well combined fresh parsley and basil

Preparation

1.
In a heavy-bottom casserole heat 2 tablespoons oil and add the onions. Season with salt and pepper and add the sugar. Cook the onions over medium heat for 15 minutes, or until lightly browned. Add the thyme, garlic, bay leaf, oregano, and parsley. Partially cover the casserole and continue cooking the onions over low heat for 30 to 40 minutes, or until they are very soft and nicely browned. Stir the mixture from time to time to prevent the onions from burning.

2.
Add the flour and stir to blend thoroughly with the onions.

3.
Add the tomato paste, tomatoes, and stock and bring to a boil. Reduce the heat and simmer the soup partially covered for 30 to 40 minutes. Taste the soup and correct the seasoning. Add the pasta and continue simmering the soup until the pasta is soft.

4.
Garnish the soup with parsley or a mixture of parsley and basil and serve the soup hot.

Remarks

This soup is at its best when prepared a day ahead and reheated. It may also be served cold. For a variation add 1 finely diced zucchini and 1 cup finely cubed fresh green beans to the soup 15 minutes before it is done. You may serve the soup with a side bowl of freshly grated Parmesan cheese.

Onion Soup Soubise

Serves: **6**
Preparation time: **15 minutes**
Cooking time: **1 hour, 10 minutes**
Type of recipe: **elementary**
Cost: **inexpensive**

Ingredients

2 Tablespoons butter
1 Tablespoon oil
5 to 6 cups onions, peeled and chopped
Salt and freshly ground black pepper
1 teaspoon granulated sugar
2 cloves garlic, peeled and crushed
3 Tablespoons flour
6 to 7 cups Beef Stock (page 533) or beef bouillon
1 cup heavy cream

Garnish:
2 Tablespoons finely minced fresh parsley

Preparation

1.
In a heavy-bottomed 3-quart casserole heat the butter and oil and add the onions. Sprinkle with salt, pepper, and sugar. Cook the onions over medium heat for 15 minutes or until they are lightly browned.

2.
Partially cover the casserole, lower the heat, and continue cooking the onions for 40 to 50 minutes, or until they are soft and nicely browned. Add the garlic and cook for 1 to 2 minutes.

3.
Add the flour and stir to blend it thoroughly with the onions.

4.
Add 6 cups stock all at once and stir the soup until it comes to a boil and the mixture is smooth. Cover and simmer the soup for 20 minutes.

5.
Cool the soup and purée in a blender.

6.
Return the soup to the casserole. Add the cream, then season with salt and pepper and heat through. Taste and correct the seasoning.

7.
Pour the soup into individual bowls and garnish with parsley.

Remarks
The soup can be made a day ahead and refrigerated and reheated the next day. It can be also be frozen for several weeks.

Split Pea
Soup
Jardinière

Serves: **6**
Preparation time: **20 minutes**
Cooking time: **2 hours, 15 minutes**
Type of recipe: **elementary**
Cost: **inexpensive**

Ingredients

2 Tablespoons butter
1 cup finely diced salt pork
2 carrots, scraped and diced
2 leeks, well rinsed and diced
2 large stalks celery, diced
1 cup split peas, covered with water and soaked overnight
4 to 6 cups Chicken Stock (page 530)
1 Bouquet Garni (page 546)
Salt and freshly ground black pepper
2 Tablespoons oil
2 Tablespoons flour
1 cup heavy cream

Garnish:

2 Tablespoons finely minced fresh parsley, mint, or coriander

Preparation

1.
In a large heavy casserole heat the butter, add the salt pork, and cook over low heat until nicely brown. Add the carrots, leeks, and celery and cook for another 3 to 4 minutes.

2.
Drain the split peas and add to the casserole together with the stock and bouquet. Season with salt and pepper and simmer the soup for 2 hours. Discard the bouquet.

3.
In a small skillet heat the oil, add the flour and cook, stirring constantly, until the mixture turns a hazelnut-brown. Add the mixture to the soup and whisk until well blended.

4.
Add the cream and simmer the soup for another 10 minutes. Taste and correct the seasoning.

5.
Just before serving, sprinkle with parsley, mint, or coriander and serve hot, accompanied by French bread and a bowl of sweet butter.

Potato and Celery Root Purée

Cream of Saffron Soup

Serves: **6**
Preparation time: **15 minutes**
Cooking time: **35 minutes**
Type of recipe: **elementary**
Cost: **inexpensive**

Serves: **6**
Preparation time: **15 minutes**
Cooking time: **20 minutes**
Type of recipe: **elementary**
Cost: **inexpensive**

Ingredients

2 medium celery knobs, scraped and quartered
1 Tablespoon flour
4 to 6 medium all-purpose potatoes, peeled and quartered
2 to 4 Tablespoons butter
Salt and freshly ground black pepper
⅓ to ½ cup heavy cream

Preparation

1.
Combine the celery knobs in salted water to cover, then whisk in the flour. Bring to a boil and cook the celery root for 25 minutes, or until very tender. (The flour will prevent the celery root from turning dark.) Drain well and set aside.

2.
Cook the potatoes in salted water to cover until very tender.

3.
Drain the potatoes and combine with celery root in a food processor. Add the butter and season with salt and pepper. Add some cream and purée with quick on-and-off motions until the purée is smooth and well blended. You may need a little more cream if mixture is stiff. Taste and correct the seasoning.

4.
Keep the purée warm in the top part of a double boiler until ready to serve. When ready to serve, transfer to a deep dish and serve hot.

Remarks

For a stronger celery-root taste use 3 celery knobs instead of 2, cutting down on the number of potatoes.

Ingredients

¾ cup heavy cream
2 large egg yolks
5½ cups Chicken Stock (page 530)
½ teaspoon powdered saffron
3 Tablespoons butter
1 onion, peeled and finely minced
1 Tablespoon tomato paste
2 large ripe tomatoes, finely cubed (seeded but not peeled)
3 Tablespoons flour
¼ cup long-grain rice
Salt and freshly ground black pepper
1 cup finely diced green pepper
1 cup finely diced red pepper

Garnish:

2 Tablespoons finely minced fresh parsley

Optional:

½ cup cooked fresh peas

Preparation

1.
In a small bowl combine the heavy cream with the egg yolks. Whisk the mixture until well blended and set aside.

2.
Heat the stock with the saffron in a saucepan and keep hot.

3.
Melt the butter in a heavy casserole, add the onion, and cook over low heat for 3 to 4 minutes, or until the onion is soft but not brown.

4.
Add the tomato paste and tomatoes to the

Spring Soup

Serves: **6**
Preparation time: **25 minutes**
Cooking time: **20 minutes**
Type of recipe: **elementary**
Cost: **inexpensive**

casserole. Bring to a boil and cook until the tomato water has evaporated.

5.
Add the flour to the tomatoes and cook, whisking constantly, for 2 minutes.

6.
Add the stock all at once. Bring to a boil and whisk the soup until smooth.

7.
Strain the soup through a sieve and return it to the saucepan. Add the rice and cook, covered, until soft. Season the soup with salt and pepper.

8.
Add the green and red pepper and simmer the soup until the peppers are just tender. They should still be slightly crunchy. Add the cream-and-egg yolk mixture and heat the soup without letting it come to a boil or the yolks will curdle.

9.
Sprinkle the soup with parsley and add the optional green peas. Taste and correct the seasoning, and serve the soup hot accompanied by crusty French bread.

Remarks
The soup can be made 2 to 3 days ahead and reheated. Be sure not to let the soup come to a boil so as not to curdle the yolks. You may freeze the soup if you omit the cream-and-egg yolk mixture, adding it after the soup has been defrosted and reheated. The soup is equally delicious served cold. If you serve it cold use 2 tablespoons flour in the mixture instead of 3.

Ingredients
6 cups Chicken Stock (page 530)
1 package (10 ounces) fresh spinach, well rinsed and stems removed
4 Tablespoons butter
½ cup diced smoked ham
1 cup finely minced scallions (both green and white parts)
3 Tablespoons flour
1 cup cooked peas (preferably fresh)
6 small fresh mushrooms, stems removed and caps thinly sliced
Salt and freshly ground black pepper
½ to ¾ cup Crème Fraîche (page 544)

Garnish:
2 Tablespoons finely minced fresh parsley or a mixture of finely minced fresh parsley and chives

Preparation
1.
In a large saucepan heat 2 cups stock. Add the spinach and cook for 3 to 4 minutes, or until the spinach leaves are wilted. Remove from the heat and cool.

2.
Purée the spinach–stock mixture in a blender or food processor until smooth. Pour into a saucepan, add the remaining stock, and heat over low heat. Set aside.

3.
In a heavy 3-quart saucepan melt the butter. Add the ham, cover, and cook for 2 to 3 minutes over low heat.

4.
Add the scallions, again cover the saucepan, and simmer for another 3 to 4

Spinach Crêpe
Soup
Printanier

Serves:	**6**
Preparation time:	**30 minutes, plus 2 hours to chill**
Cooking time:	**2 hours, 40 minutes**
Type of recipe:	**elementary**
Cost:	**moderate**

minutes, or until the scallions are soft but not brown.

5.

Add the flour and stir the mixture with a wooden spoon until the flour is thoroughly incorporated into the scallion–ham mixture.

6.

Remove the saucepan from the heat and add the spinach–stock mixture all at once. Whisk the soup until it is smooth and well blended.

7.

Return the saucepan to the heat and bring the mixture to a boil. Reduce the heat and simmer for 5 minutes.

8.

Add the peas and mushrooms and season with salt and pepper. Heat the soup again without bringing it back to a boil; the mushrooms should stay crisp and crunchy.

9.

Fold ½ cup Crème Fraîche into the soup, then taste and correct the seasoning. (If the soup seems too thick add additional Crème Fraîche to thin it out.)

10.

Garnish the soup with parsley or a mixture of parsley and chives and serve hot.

Remarks

Soup can be made 1 or 2 days ahead and reheated on top of the stove. Do not let the soup come to a boil, for the mushrooms must still retain their crispness.

Ingredients

1 three-and-one-half-pound chicken, quartered
8 to 12 chicken wings
3 carrots, scraped and cut in half
3 stalks celery, cut in half and with greens attached
3 leeks, well rinsed, with all but 2 inches of greens removed
1 parsnip, scraped
1 parsley root, scraped, or 1 small bunch small fresh parsley
1 Bouquet Garni (page 546)
Coarse salt
6 peppercorns
Salt and freshly ground black pepper
1 cup fresh peas, shelled
1 cup fresh asparagus tips
10 to 12 Spinach Crêpes (page 390)
1 cup shredded fresh spinach leaves

Garnish:
3 Tablespoons finely minced fresh parsley
Freshly grated Parmesan cheese

Preparation

1.

In a large 6- to 7-quart casserole combine the chicken, chicken wings, carrots, celery stalks, leeks, parsnip, and parsley root. Season with the Bouquet Garni, coarse salt, and peppercorns. Add 8 to 10 cups cold water, or enough to cover the ingredients by 1 to 2 inches.

2.

Place over high heat and bring the stock to a boil. Reduce the heat and simmer the stock partially covered for 2 to 2½ hours,

Country
Turkey
Soup

Serves:	**6 to 8**
Preparation time:	**30 minutes**
Cooking time:	**2 hours, 45 minutes**
Type of recipe:	**elementary**
Cost:	**moderate**

skimming off any scum that rises to the surface.

3.
When the stock is done strain it through a fine sieve into a large bowl. Chill the stock for 2 hours, or until completely set.

4.
Thoroughly degrease the chicken stock and return to a casserole. Bring to a boil and season carefully with additional salt or pepper if necessary. Add the peas and asparagus tips and cook for 3 to 4 minutes, or until just tender. Keep the soup warm.

5.
Cut the Spinach Crêpes into ¼-inch strips and add to the soup. Heat the soup until the crêpe strips are well heated through. Add the shredded spinach leaves and cook for another 2 minutes, or until they are just wilted.

6.
Spoon the soup into individual serving bowls. Garnish with parsley and serve accompanied by a bowl of Parmesan cheese and crusty French bread.

Remarks
For variation, add an egg to each bowl of soup to have a version of the famous *zuppa pavese.* Break each egg into a saucer and slide it into each soup bowl. Preheat the oven to 325 degrees and place the individual soup bowls in the oven. Heat for 5 minutes, or just long enough for the yolk to set. Serve at once, adding a large grinding of black pepper. The creamy texture of the egg will add an unusual dimension to this interesting spring soup.

One of the most delicious soups can be made from turkey or chicken wings. The soup is actually a one-dish meal perfectly suited to family suppers or informal entertaining.

Ingredients
4 Tablespoons chicken fat or butter
1 Tablespoon oil
2 large turkey wings, cut in half, or 8 to 10 whole chicken wings
Salt and freshly ground black pepper
2 large onions, finely minced
2 carrots, scraped and finely minced
2 stalks celery, finely minced
3 Tablespoons flour
½ cup dry white wine
8 cups hot Chicken Stock (page 530)
1 Bouquet Garni (page 546)

Livers:
6 to 8 large chicken livers
2 Tablespoons butter
1 teaspoon oil
Salt and freshly ground black pepper
1 large onion, thinly sliced

Garlic Croûtons:
3 cloves garlic
6 to 8 thin slices French bread
4 Tablespoons olive oil

Garnish:
2 Tablespoons finely minced fresh parsley

Preparation

1.
In a large heavy casserole heat 2
tablespoons chicken fat or butter and the
oil. Add the turkey or chicken wings and
brown them over high heat on all sides.
Season with salt and pepper, then remove
wings and set aside.

2.
Add a little more fat or butter to the
casserole and add the vegetables and cook
over moderate heat until nicely brown,
scraping well the bottom of the pan. Cook
the vegetables for about 15 minutes, being
sure the onions do not burn. Season with
salt and pepper.

3.
Add the flour, blend, and cook for 1 to 2
minutes without browning.

4.
Add the wine, bring to a boil, and reduce
by one-half.

5.
Add the hot stock and return the soup to a
boil.

6.
Place the turkey or chicken wings in the
casserole. Add the bouquet, partially cover
the casserole, and simmer the soup for 2
hours.

7.
While the soup is simmering, prepare the
chicken livers. Clean the livers thoroughly,
removing any green spots. Cut the livers in
half.

8.
Heat the butter and oil in a heavy 10-inch
skillet and add the livers. Season with salt
and pepper and cook over high heat until

nicely brown on all sides. With a slotted
spoon remove the livers to a side dish.

9.
Add the onion to the pan and sauté until
nicely brown. Return the chicken livers to
the skillet and cook with onion over low
heat for another 2 to 3 minutes. Cool the
liver-onion mixture and then dice. Set aside.

10.
Prepare the garlic croûtons. Crush the
garlic cloves to a paste using a garlic press.
Smear each bread slice with a little of the
crushed garlic paste.

11.
Heat the olive oil in a large skillet and
saute the bread slices until lightly brown on
both sides. Set aside.

12.
When the soup is done discard the bouquet.
Remove the meat from the wings, sliver it
finely, and return it to the soup. Add the
chicken liver mixture and heat through.

13.
Ladle the soup into large individual soup
bowls and float a garlic croûton in each.
Sprinkle with parsley and serve hot.

Remarks
When using chicken wings you do not have
to take the meat off the wings; simply place
1 or 2 wings in each soup bowl. The soup
can be made 2 to 3 days ahead and
reheated. The chicken liver mixture and
croûtons, however, should be made at the
last moment and added to the soup just
before serving.

Tomato and Leek
Soup

Serves:	**6 to 8**
Preparation time:	**20 minutes**
Cooking time:	**1 hour**
Type of recipe:	**elementary**
Cost:	**inexpensive**

It is often said that the simplest foods are the most delicious. This is true of this late-summer soup that combines crisp fresh leeks with ripe tomatoes. The soup can also be served cold and it freezes beautifully.

Ingredients

2 Tablespoons olive oil
2 Tablespoons butter
3 to 4 leeks, well rinsed and thinly sliced
6 cups Chicken Stock (page 530) or bouillon
Salt and freshly ground black pepper
1 large sprig fresh thyme
1 large sprig fresh marjoram
1 large sprig fresh parsley
2 cloves garlic, peeled and crushed
3 pounds ripe tomatoes, peeled, seeded, and coarsely chopped
1 bay leaf or 1 teaspoon dried oregano and ½ teaspoon dried thyme
½ to ¾ cup cooked rice
1 cup Crème Fraîche (page 544), or 1 cup sour cream

Preparation

1.
In a large heavy casserole heat the oil and butter. Add the leeks and ½ cup stock. Season with salt and pepper.

2.
Cover the casserole and cook the leeks over low heat for 10 minutes or until very soft.

3.
Tie the thyme, marjoram, and parsley sprigs together to make a bouquet garni.

4.
Add the garlic, tomatoes, remaining stock, bouquet garni, bay leaf or dried herbs, salt, and pepper. Bring to a boil and cook the mixture for 40 to 50 minutes. Cool.

5.
Purée the soup in a blender or food processor and return it to the casserole. Add the cooked rice. If the soup seems too thin (this depends on the quality of the tomatoes) add more rice. Set aside.

6.
When ready to serve, reheat the soup and whisk in the Crème Fraîche or sour cream. Taste and correct the seasoning, adding a large grinding of black pepper. Serve hot accompanied by crusty French bread.

Remarks

For a more interesting texture braise 1 additional leek and then reserve 1 cup of the braised leeks. Add this to the soup later, together with the cooked rice.

Spring Vegetable Soup

Serves: **6**
Preparation time: **25 minutes**
Cooking time: **30 minutes**
Type of recipe: **elementary**
Cost: **inexpensive**

Ingredients

4 Tablespoons butter
3 Tablespoons flour
6 cups hot Chicken Stock (page 530)
2 to 3 small turnips, peeled and cubed
2 leeks, well rinsed and thinly sliced
(some of the greens included)
1 cup shelled fresh peas
2 cups fresh asparagus, finely cubed
2 cups fresh spinach leaves, well rinsed
1 small head Boston lettuce (about 2 cups)
1 cup heavy cream
Salt and freshly ground black pepper

Preparation

1.
In a large heavy casserole heat the butter. Add the flour and whisk for 1 or 2 minutes without browning.

2.
Remove the casserole from the heat and add the hot stock all at once. Whisk until the mixture is smooth.

3.
Return the casserole to the heat. Bring to a boil, whisking constantly, and cook until the soup is thick and smooth.

4.
Add the turnips, leeks, and peas. Simmer the soup until the vegetables are almost tender.

5.
Add the asparagus and cook for another 5 minutes, or until just tender.

6.
Add the spinach and lettuce and cook until just wilted.

7.
Add the cream and season with salt and pepper. Taste the soup, correct the seasoning, and serve hot accompanied by crusty French bread.

Remarks

This is a good-natured soup that allows you to vary the vegetables according to what is available at the market. The all-season vegetables such as carrots, potatoes, and celery can be added or substituted for some of the other vegetables in the soup.

Potage
Aurore

Serves: **6 to 8**
Preparation time: **25 minutes, plus 2 to 4 hours to chill**
Cooking time: **1 hour**
Type of recipe: **elementary**
Cost: **inexpensive**

The problem with cold vegetable soups is that it is often hard to retain the essence and taste of the vegetables once the soup has been chilled. Here is a gutsy summer soup reminiscent of the famous vichyssoise. It is flavored with a garlicky tomato fondue and is equally good served hot on a cool evening.

Ingredients

5 Tablespoons butter
2 Tablespoons olive oil
4 large leeks, well rinsed and thinly sliced
3 medium all-purpose potatoes, peeled and cubed
Salt and freshly ground black pepper
6 cups Light Chicken Stock (page 531) or bouillon
2 Tablespoons finely minced shallots
3 large ripe tomatoes, peeled, seeded, and chopped
1 Tablespoon tomato paste
1 cup heavy cream
2 cloves garlic, peeled and crushed
Pinch of cayenne pepper

Garnish:
3 Tablespoons finely minced fresh chives

Preparation

1.
In a large casserole heat 3 tablespoons butter and 1 tablespoon oil, then add the leeks and potatoes. Season with salt and pepper and toss the mixture in the butter and oil for 2 minutes.

2.
Add the stock to the casserole and bring to a boil. Reduce the heat and simmer the soup covered for 1 hour, or until the vegetables are very tender.

3.
While the soup is cooking heat the remaining butter and oil in a small heavy skillet. Add the shallots, tomatoes, and tomato paste and cook the mixture over high heat until it is thick and the tomato water has evaporated. Season with salt and pepper and set aside to cool.

4.
Cool the soup, then purée in a blender or food processor and return it to the casserole.

5.
Add the tomato–shallot mixture, heavy cream, and garlic and whisk until well blended. Season with a dash of cayenne pepper, taste, and correct the seasoning. Chill for 2 to 4 hours before serving.

6.
Just before serving sprinkle with chives and serve accompanied by crusty French bread and a bowl of sweet butter.

Remarks
When serving the soup hot, garnish with finely minced parsley instead of chives. If the soup is too thick, thin it out with a little light cream or milk. This soup freezes beautifully. Do not, however, add the garlic to the soup or it will turn bitter. In the summer add to the soup 2 tablespoons of fresh basil leaves that have been shredded.

Soupe
Fermière

Serves: **6**
Preparation time: **20 minutes**
Cooking time: **1 hour**
Type of recipe: **elementary**
Cost: **inexpensive**

Ingredients

5 Tablespoons butter
2 cups thinly sliced leeks (2 large leeks with some of the greens included)
Salt and freshly ground black pepper
2 cups all-purpose potatoes, peeled and diced
2 cups scraped and cubed carrots
2 cups scraped and cubed turnips
6 to 7 cups Chicken Stock (page 530)
1 cup heavy cream

Garnish:

Finely minced fresh parsley, or a mixture of finely minced fresh parsley and fresh chives

Preparation

1.
In a large heavy saucepan heat 2 tablespoons butter. Add the leeks. Season with salt and pepper and cook covered over low heat for 5 to 6 minutes without browning.

2.
Add the remaining vegetables and stock. Season again with salt and pepper and bring to a boil. Reduce the heat and simmer covered for 45 minutes, or until the vegetables are very tender. Cool the soup.

3.
With a slotted spoon remove 2 cups diced vegetables and reserve.

4.
Purée the remaining liquid and vegetables in a blender or food processor. Return to the saucepan and bring to a boil. Reduce the heat.

5.
Add the cream and the reserved vegetables and heat through. Taste and correct the seasoning. If the soup seems too thick add another cup of stock.

6.
Just before serving whisk in the remaining 3 tablespoons of butter, sprinkle with parsley or parsley and chives and serve the soup hot, accompanied by crusty French bread.

Remarks
The soup can be made 2 to 3 days ahead and reheated. If the soup is to be frozen do not add the cream. Freeze the soup and when reheating add the cream then.

Zucchini and Pasta
Soup
Milanaise

Serves: **4 to 5**
Preparation time: **15 minutes**
Cooking time: **30 minutes**
Type of recipe: **elementary**
Cost: **inexpensive**

Ingredients
1 Tablespoon butter
2 Tablespoons fruity olive oil
1 cup finely minced onion
2 cups finely diced zucchini
Salt and freshly ground black pepper
6 cups Chicken Stock (page 530)
¼ pound spaghettini (thin spaghetti)

Garnish:
Finely minced fresh parsley
1 cup freshly grated Parmesan cheese

Preparation

1.
In a large heavy saucepan heat the butter and oil. Add the onion and zucchini and season with salt and pepper. Cover the pan and cook the mixture for 10 to 15 minutes, stirring 2 or 3 times.

2.
Add the stock and bring to a boil. Reduce the heat and simmer the broth for 15 minutes.

3.
While the soup is simmering, bring salted water to a boil in a large casserole. Add the spaghettini and cook for 7 to 8 minutes, or until barely tender; do not overcook.

4.
Drain the spaghettini and add it to the broth. Cook the soup for another 2 minutes, then taste and correct the seasoning, adding a large grinding of black pepper.

5.
Sprinkle with parsley and serve the soup in deep individual bowls, with a side dish of freshly grated Parmesan cheese.

Remarks
For a variation you can combine finely diced fresh green beans and zucchini as well as 1 small carrot, finely diced. Cook the vegetables together in the oil and butter for 10 or 15 minutes before adding them to the stock.

Meats

Beef

I still remember the first meal I had when I arrived in this country. My friends took me to an all-American steak house and I was faced with a giant steak, a baked potato, and a huge salad. The steak was a wonderfully tender, a superb piece of meat the likes of which I had never had before. But what I found most shocking was its *size*. I wasn't sure that it was all for me. Certainly there was enough meat on my plate to serve two people!

I have since adjusted to the quantity of meat people consume in this country and now, more often than not, I follow the example, often serving a large roast as the main part of a meal. For a European this is an unheard-of luxury. I remember watching housewives buying meat—particularly beef —in markets of Spain, France, or Italy. Beef would be sliced paper thin, the cautious shopper carefully watching both butcher and scale. Often I heard the worried question, "Is this going to be enough for four?" The frugality of the European cook is understandable. Beef, more than any other meat, is extremely expensive and in many cases is considered a luxury. Because of this the European cook has had to be more creative than the American in balancing a meal. She will complement the small quantity of meat with interesting vegetable dishes, soups, and grains. In America meat and potato consumption is a well-established habit, and *meat* usually means *beef*. In spite of increasingly high prices, the American family consumes more beef than any other family in the world.

While it is true that our product is far superior to that of any European country, it is hard to believe that, with all the recent reports on nutrition and health, beef is still the meat most desired and most accepted by many. Trying to break Americans of their meat-and-potatoes habit would be as foolish as trying to stop the Chinese from eating rice or the Italians from eating pasta. When it comes to creative cooking, however, I really feel that the serious cook should explore other types of meat, particularly poultry and fish.

One of the reasons that beef is so popular is that it requires practically no cooking talent. The ingredients are simple: a good piece of beef and a decent broiler. Presto, you have a good automatic meal. How often do you hear a hurried cook say to herself, "I'll just throw a steak in the broiler and make a salad. . . ." It never occurs to many cooks that there are interesting and delicious alternatives that take just as little time and make for healthier, far more creative meals; for example some sautéed boneless chicken breasts or a few scaloppine of veal sautéed and sprinkled with parsley and lemon juice. Furthermore, beef and particularly a steak often lets you down, for the simpler the preparation, the more important the quality of the meat. More often than not that simple but expensive meal can turn into a fiasco.

I am the first to admit that I love a good steak; I also appreciate a tender, well-seasoned roast beef. When I use these expensive cuts I take the opportunity to experiment with other components of the meal. A lovely gratin of potatoes, a ragoût of fennel, and an endive or watercress salad tossed with diced walnuts and Roquefort can all work in perfect harmony around the simple steak. Getting that wonderful piece of beef has become more and more difficult, unless you are willing to pay a premium price for a Prime cut of beef at a good butcher shop. Most Americans buy their meat at the supermarket. The average supermarket carries only the Choice cuts of beef, and their quality depends on how the chain buys its beef, how they age it, and what the turnover is. The butcher in the supermarket is only a meatcutter. While the private butcher personally supervises his buying and carefully selects the sides of beef for his clientele, the supermarket chain buys by price with no quality control outside of the FDA inspection. This means that what may be an excellent piece of meat one day may be mediocre the next, depending on what the current price of beef is and what the chain has been able to buy at the most advantageous price. This makes shopping in the supermarket both chancy and frustrating, since appearance often has little to do with quality. Bright red, fresh-looking cuts of beef are often tough and full of water, owing to a lack of proper aging. It is aging that makes for the major and most significant difference between supermarket and butcher-shop beef. While the independent butcher will age his beef for three to six weeks, the supermarket will only hang its uncut sides for two days. The vacuum-packaged meats are aged somewhat longer, but they still cannot compare to the aging in a good butcher shop.

Another difference between the supermarket and the private butcher is the range of meats and cuts available. While your private butcher will carry specialty cuts—oxtails, fresh tongue, shin bones (so wonderful in soups), sweetbreads, and calves' liver—the supermarket choice is far more limited for the creative cook. Certain cuts of meat have become established as the most popular. Outside of these, few unusual cuts are available in the supermarket. Among the inexpensive popular cuts, I find chuck (shoulder roast) and bottom round the most popular and best cuts for stewing or braising. (The eye round is attractive, but always somewhat dry.) The top round, rolled and tied, and silver tip (the corner of the sirloin) are also popular for roasting. For steaks the chuck cut with the bone in, about two to three inches thick, is the most popular and least expensive. More expensive cuts, even in the supermarket, are the porterhouse, shell, club, and delmonico steaks, and, of course, the most appreciated tenderloin (filet mignon). Still the most elegant and sought after cut for roasting is the tender and extremely flavorful rib roast or "standing rib," the ends of which (short ribs) are juicy and good for braising or soups. In the hands of a good cook many of these cuts graded choice can give excellent results. I have always found that supermarket butchers are extremely helpful and are willing to give special attention when they feel you know what you want.

In order to compensate for the lack of flavor in so much of supermarket beef, I usually turn to the French sauces or herb-flavored butters to enhance and complement these lesser quality cuts. These sauces do not need to be elaborate. Many of the chefs now experimenting with the voguish *nouvelle cuisine* have turned their backs on the heavy, elaborate sauces once associated with beef prepared in the Franch manner. Now you will find a light touch of vinegar or green peppercorns added to the natural pan juices of a pan-fried steak. This is a wonderful way to serve good beef. The emphasis is on a good meat stock, which is used to deglaze the pan to achieve a concentrated, full-bodied sauce.

In Mediterranean cooking there are few dishes made with beef, mainly because there is little beef available in that part of the world. Most beef preparation in Italy and provincial France use thin slices of beef that are then stuffed with an inexpensive sausage stuffing or rolled around a piece of bacon and a light but well-seasoned bread stuffing. The beef rolls are braised for a long time, either in a tomato-based sauce or one made of onions and a good beef stock. This is a brilliant way to make a little beef go a long way.

Beef stews are more popular in Central Europe than in Mediterranean countries, although both Italy and France have gutsy beef stews simmered slowly in full-bodied red wine. Central European stews are rarely made with wine, but are heavily flavored with onions, often spiced with paprika and flavored with wild mushrooms or peppers. These robust and hearty stews are delicious cold-weather food; they are filling and can be made from inexpensive supermarket cuts of beef. I prefer to make stews or ragoûts from pork or veal shoulder. Besides requiring a shorter cooking time, they are as flavorful as the beef stews and much lighter. I also find that these meats usually blend better with a greater variety of seasonal vegetables that can be added to the ragoût at the last moment. Unfortunately these simple cuts of pork or veal are not as common in the average supermarket as is beef. However many of the ragoûts in the pork section of this chapter that call for pork butt can be made successfully with lean chuck, which requires two more hours of slow braising but makes a delicious, full-bodied stew that can be prepared easily several days in advance and reheated.

Because I am not fond of beef tenderloin, I have not included many preparations for this cut in this chapter. The Fillet of Beef en Casserole in *The Seasonal Kitchen* remains one of my favorite ways to prepare this otherwise bland and unexciting piece of meat.

A fillet steak has a certain instant elegence about it and makes a great-tasting dish if you quickly sauté in hot butter, then deglaze the pan juices with a touch of Scotch or Madeira and add some brown stock and a spoonful of shallots. Because this is basically a simple and quick preparation, it leaves plenty of room for a variety of vegetable dishes, such as the Spinach Ramekins à la Bernoise (page 64) or the Green Beans à la Crème (page 411).

After many tries I have concluded that broiling in a home oven usually doesn't give good results. The meat "cooks" and loses its juices. The French method of pan-broiling a steak, however, is wonderful and I use it all the time for cooking small cuts of beef. While admittedly the best cuts of beef are the club steak or shell steak, you can also pan-fry lesser cuts with excellent results. Be sure to use a heavy, well-seasoned cast-iron pan, or two if you are going to make more than two steaks. Heat a little butter and oil to the smoking point (rendered pork, duck, or chicken fat is much better and will brown the meat more quickly.) Sear the steaks, sautéing them for 2 to 3 minutes on each side, or until they reach the right degree of doneness (a medium rare steak will be somewhat resistant to the touch.) Season the steak with coarse salt and a large grinding of freshly ground pepper, and sauté for another minute on each side. Remove the steak to a serving platter and deglaze the pan juices with ½ cup good brown stock. Reduce the stock until it has cooked down to 2 tablespoons of concentrated juices, then spoon the sauce over the steak. The French *maître d'hôtel* butter (flavored with minced parsley, garlic, and a touch of shallots) is still one of my favorite accompaniments to a good steak. Other flavored butters, such as mustard butter or anchovy-and-herb butter, are also delicious toppings and will add both flavor and enrichment to a pan-fried steak.

The average cook buys ground meat at a supermarket, often without questioning the quality. Ground beef should be of the utmost freshness, and should be used soon after it has been chopped. The best way to be assured of freshness is to choose a lean piece of chuck steak and have the butcher grind it for you while you wait. Ground beef can be prepared in many ways other than the simple broiled all-American hamburger. One of my favorite dishes is a Basque method of braising meatballs in a rich, somewhat spicy tomato sauce flavored with red and green peppers, truly one of the great ways of using ground beef. Freshly ground hamburgers are equally good, however, simply pan-fried with a flavored butter just like a pan-fried steak. Because of the little time involved in making a hamburger, the creative cook should take the time to prepare an interesting vegetable garniture to serve an imaginative, well-balanced yet inexpensive meal.

Veal
In recent years I have found that I can be far more creative with other cuts of meat than beef. Rather than try to make something from a poor-quality beef cut, I have turned to pork, lamb, and veal as well as to poultry for a more imaginative and varied cooking repertoire. If beef ranks high on some cooks' lists because it is inexpensive and relatively easy to prepare, veal is without a doubt at the top of every

serious cook's list because of its fine, delicate flavor. When I stop to think about meats and am looking for a certain preparation to experiment with, I always turn to veal. In spite of its high price and scarcity, it is by far the most wonderful meat to work with—solid, without any fat or waste.

Although the French and Swiss use veal in large quantities, it is the Italian cook who has been the most inventive with this versatile meat. Veal lends itself to so many preparations, flavorings, and sauces. Because of the "lightness" of most veal dishes, you can also turn your creativity and attention to a myriad of starchy accompaniments, from potatoes to simple buttered fettucine.

For the American cook veal is unfortunately a source of constant frustration because there is little "real" veal available; what is available is usually extremely expensive. Top-quality veal comes from a calf that is fed only on powdered milk and eggs. It is slaughtered at three to four months and has a smooth, firm, pale pink flesh with snowy white fat. The difference between a milk-fed calf and a grass-fed animal is immediately evident to the knowledgeable shopper. While one is pale pink, the other has a deep pink to light red flesh which is already somewhat marbled with fat. While this older calf can be used successfully for stewing and casserole roasting, its taste does not in any way resemble the incredibly delicate and "elegant" meat so sought by every serious and educated cook.

Although some quality butchers claim that the demand for veal has grown tremendously in recent years, I sincerely doubt that this is true across the country. The cost of growing top-quality veal is so high that all but two growers shy away from it. Most veal found in supermarkets, as well as in most butcher shops nationwide, is grass-fed which in reality is young beef. In New York and some of the other major cities where the demand for veal by both restaurants and serious cooks is growing, some supermarkets are making an attempt to bring in top-quality veal. I was recently told by the president of one of New York's best supermarket chains that they are extremely successful in selling various cuts of top-quality veal at top prices.

With the increasing popularity of Italian cooking, particularly Northern Italian, the veal scaloppine has become the most popular (and least expensive) cut. Because one pound of these small, thin scallops will serve four people, this cut is more economical than most beef or other meat cuts. The perfect scaloppine should be cut across the grain either from the top round (which is the very best cut), the eye, bottom round, or the sirloin. The best scaloppine are cut from a solid piece of meat without any muscle separations. This unfortunately is not customary here and you must be very explicit with your butcher who—for a price —will cut veal properly for you. When scaloppine are cut with the muscle or are "butterflied" they will contract during cooking and become tough and dry. The scaloppine should be cut less than ½ inch thick and then flattened between two pieces of waxed paper to a thickness of ⅛ inch. The great popularity of scaloppine is easy to understand. Just as with chicken, there is no limit to the number of wonderful ways they can be served. They are delicious simply sautéed in butter with a touch of lemon and parsley or great with other herbs such as dill, chervil, chives, and tarragon. Additional ingredients like thin slices of smoked ham, Swiss cheese, or heavy cream all lend their flavor to this delicate cut. Vegetables such as a purée of peas or braised spinach go wonderfully with scaloppine as either a topping or a "bed."

Most recipes call for the veal scaloppine to be seasoned with salt and pepper, lightly floured, and quickly sautéed for two to three minutes on each side. The pan juices are then deglazed with a little stock or cream that is reduced and spooned over the veal. An Italian friend has recently taught me a different method which is excellent and especially good for lesser-quality veal. Here the veal scallops are seasoned, floured, and sautéed in a very hot buttered baking dish. The pan juices are deglazed with a few spoonfuls of concentrated stock and poured over the veal. The dish is covered tightly and placed in a preheated 325-degree oven for 25 minutes. I find that this method produces a more buttery and far more flavorful scaloppine.

For the supermarket shopper who cannot get good veal scaloppine, the next best choices are rib or loin chops. These can be prepared simply as chops, but I often bone them (reserving the bones for a brown stock) and prepare the "medallions" in the above manner. The veal medallion should be nicely browned on both sides before placing it in the oven with the deglazed pan juices. Because of the somewhat more robust flavor of the veal chop or "medallion," these lend themselves well to gutsy preparations and ingredients. I often sauté them together with a large sprig of fresh tarragon or rosemary, or add a few spoonfuls of the Provençale Tomato Fondue (page 542) to the pan juices. Flavorful cheeses and hams such as Italian fontina, Gruyère, prosciutto, or smoked ham are excellent toppings for these cuts. A garnish of roasted red and green peppers, thinly sliced and added to the reduced pan juices, makes this a superb, highly flavored but simple dish.

While good scaloppine should come from a milk-fed calf, you can use the darker-fleshed supermarket veal for roasting. The older veal should still be extremely lean and it is at its best when casserole roasted. Choose a 3½- to 4-pound boneless roast preferably cut from the shoulder. This is an less expensive, juicy cut of meat, but it does tend to fall apart when sliced. A more expensive cut is the boned loin, which I find too dry but which is often more obtainable. Season the roast carefully with a paste made from salt, pepper, sweet paprika, thyme, and some Dijon mustard. If you like add 1 large crushed clove of garlic and rub the roast thoroughly with the mixture. Using a heavy casserole, brown on all sides in a combination of butter and oil.

Add 2 to 3 peeled and chopped onions to the casserole together with ½ cup brown stock. Cover tightly and place in a preheated 325-degree oven. Baste the roast every 10 minutes with the pan juices. A 4-pound roast will be done in 1 hour, 45 minutes. This method produces a juicy roast with delicious, full-bodied pan juices. My favorite way to serve it is accompanied by Italian dried wild mushrooms. Simmer 1 ounce of the mushrooms in 1 cup of good stock until tender, then slice and add together with the cooking liquid to the roasting pan juices. The unique, fragrant, and somewhat smoky flavor of these wild mushrooms is in perfect balance with the delicate flavor of the veal.

For stews and ragoûts my favorite cut is the shoulder. The gelatinous quality of this cut produces the most wonderful sauce, and I often combine the ragoût with a variety of seasonal vegetables such as fresh peas, sautéed mushrooms, tiny onions, or three quartered artichoke hearts. The Ragoût of Veal Provençale (page 168) is just one of the many elegant ragoûts made possible by this incredibly versatile meat. You may vary it by adding tiny turnip balls or a julienne of leeks and carrots. The sauce of any ragoût can also be reduced and flavored with an "accent" herb such as chervil, dill, or chives and some Crème Fraîche.

Pork

Pork is one of the most misunderstood meats in this country. A number of religions have strict taboos against it and even until recently undercooked pork did present real dangers to one's health. Today many people still approach this meat with a wariness that is no longer deserved. I am always surprised to find it popular both with the serious, creative cook and with those who seek to feed a family inexpensively. In Europe and Scandinavia, where pork is the most popular everyday meat, every part of it is used imaginatively. Although it is usually associated with cold weather and considered a "heavy" food, it is also used extensively in Mediterranean countries, particularly Spain and Italy. There roast suckling pig is a delicacy. Pork is also ground and used to stuff numerous vegetables and inexpensive cuts of meat.

Because so much of the pork goes into making cold cuts, bacon, and frozen sausages, a shopper's choice at the supermarket is limited to two or three cuts. Almost invariably you will find loin or rib chops and sometimes shoulder chops. When I asked several supermarket meat managers why it is so difficult to find pork butt—an inexpensive and juicy cut good for both roasting and stewing—they answered simply, "Demand." There is no demand for it and therefore the average supermarket does not carry it. Many cooks have been led to believe that the center loin cut is the most elegant and flavorful for roasting. Unless they have had the opportunity to taste other cuts they will continue to accept the limited supermarket selection. This is particularly frustrating for the serious cook, who has to go to a specialty butcher for a cut as basic as the shoulder butt. Ground pork, so essential for sausage stuffings and pâtés, cannot usually be bought at a supermarket either, since it is against the law for the market to grind pork on any machine that has been used for other meats.

In general buying pork at a supermarket demands an experienced and cautious eye. Unlike beef, whose flavor is enhanced by weeks of dry aging, pork is at its best when very fresh. Pork is not graded by the government, so when you buy you really must rely on freshness alone. Be sure to find out from the meat department manager where the pork comes from. (In the Northeast the best pork comes from the Midwest.) Ask about delivery days. As with chickens, buy the pork on the days when it is going to be put out fresh. Look for rosy pink, clear meat with white, firm fat. Avoid pork with dark spots and yellowish fat. Watch for the tenderloin; it is usually a shade darker than the rest of the chop and a real delicacy. In Europe it is as much appreciated as the fillet mignon. When I can get it here, I cut it into ½-inch medallions and serve them quickly sautéed in a green peppercorn or mustard sauce. Because of the old stigma of pork's being hazardous to one's health many cooks still believe in roasting the meat until it is so well done it is overcooked. Then they complain about its toughness. Today however pigs are raised and fed by modern, hygienic methods, compared to the days when they were fed on kitchen refuse, and there is really no danger now in eating pork slightly pink. Roasted and basted with a simple chicken stock it can be a deliciously tender piece of meat that

produces the best pan juices I know. Like duck, it has a wonderful affinity to many fruits. Sautéed apples, pears, prunes, and raisins are all delicious and add an interesting touch. Many of the basic vegetables—braised red cabbage, Brussels sprouts, onions, or glazed carrots—are excellent accompaniments to this gutsy, tasty meat. Although it is somewhat harder to serve, a pork roast will remain much juicier when left on the bone. Many cooks feel that the boneless roast is both easier to carve and more elegant to serve. If you use the boned roast I find it best to braise it in a covered casserole on a bed of onions and some Brown Chicken Stock (as in the Braised Pork in Onion Sauce on page 180.)

Aside from roasts, ragoûts are my favorite way to serve pork. Here the cubed meat is browned and braised in some stock and aromatic vegetables for 1 hour, 30 minutes. The result is a delicious, full-bodied, tender, and flavorful stew. It is far less expensive than beef, takes less time to cook, and can be prepared several days ahead and reheated. The ragoût can be combined with a variety of seasonal vegetables and easily frozen for later use. A Ragoût of Pork Ticino (page 187) can be as elegant as any beef dish, while the Viennese Ragoût of Pork (page 188) is a hearty, easily prepared dish perfect for family suppers.

I also like the Viennese way of using pork cutlets. The loin pork chops are cut about ½ inch thick, boned, and flattened between 2 pieces of waxed paper like veal scaloppine. Seasoned with salt, pepper, a touch of paprika, marjoram, and caraway seeds, they are dredged lightly with flour and sautéed in hot butter until they are nicely browned on both sides. The pan juices are then deglazed with either a little white wine or lemon juice and a few spoonfuls of brown stock. The pan is covered and the cutlets partly braised for 10 minutes. Since pork has a great affinity to the "character" herbs, I often add a sprig of fresh oregano, sage, or rosemary to the pan. The result is a simple, inexpensive, and flavorful dish that takes 15 minutes to prepare and can be served beautifully with any of the seasonal vegetables, mashed potato dishes, or a pilaf of rice.

Pork, like chicken, is a challenge to the knowledgeable shopper and cook, since it is usually a very good supermarket buy. With the addition of some basic all-season fruits or vegetables and an imaginative touch, you can be more creative with pork than with beef.

Lamb

On a recent trip to Paris my husband and I spent ten gastronomic days enjoying the city's many superb restaurants. After a few days of sheer gluttony neither of us could face another rich menu. We decided to go back to Chez l'Ami Louis, a small, unpretentious restaurant that specializes in two great dishes: homemade foie gras and roast spring lamb. After we managed to consume a large portion of foie gras with crusty country bread, we were greeted with roast lamb accompanied by sautéed potatoes heavily perfumed with freshly

minced garlic and parsley. Though it was simple, it was also sublime, and was the most memorable meal I have had in Paris in years.

Whenever one hears about lamb, "spring lamb" is always used to describe the very best you can get. Because the natural cycle of lamb is to be born in the spring, genuine spring lamb is usually on the market only in April and May. Anyone lucky enough to visit Provence in late spring should not miss the baby leg of lamb roasted and flavored with fresh mountain herbs. Once you have tasted this delicate meat at its best, eating lamb will never be the same. Unfortunately though, in this country, even in springtime, it is never available in supermarkets and must be ordered from a top-quality butcher. (It may also be found at some Greek or Italian markets, since spring lamb is a traditional Easter feast.) At this time of year, this pale and rose-colored meat is delicate and mild flavored. Fall lamb is still excellent, but by late winter the lamb is much older and the meat darker, sometimes already marbled with fat; the heavy "mutton" flavor is more developed. The difference between this and the tender spring lamb is comparable to the difference between beef and superb veal.

Although lamb is graded and many butchers proudly claim that they carry Prime lamb, I find good Choice lamb less fatty and prefer it to Prime. Lamb should be eaten fresh. Because of the delicacy and tenderness of the young animal, it should not be hung for more than a week. We have wonderful lamb in Texas and the Midwest, yet most of the lamb eaten in this country is consumed in the Northeast, particularly in the New York metropolitan area where there is a heavier ethnic population. People with Mediterranean backgrounds especially love cooking with lamb and have a rich repertoire of creative preparations.

Although the basic grilled lamb chop by far out sells every other cut in the supermarket, other cuts for some of the more ethnic preparations are becoming increasingly popular. Lamb shish kebabs in which the meat is cubed and marinated in lemon juice, olive oil, and herbs are a favorite summer barbecue dish; the lamb curries that can be made easily with inexpensive cuts such as the breast are also increasingly in evidence. Many more quality restaurants feature a roast leg of lamb on their menu, and with people becoming increasingly sophisticated in their lamb-eating habits, you can now even get it served medium rare.

A properly seasoned roast leg of lamb is without doubt one of the greatest dishes ever conceived. In addition to the classic French garnish of cooked flageolets or white beans, lamb also works beautifully with every Mediterranean vegetable. The Ratatouille Basquaise in *The Peasant Kitchen* or the Curried Cold Vegetable Ragoût (page 441) are both wonderful with it. When preparing a leg of lamb for roasting be sure to season it carefully 2 to 3 hours ahead. Since garlic is especially good

with lamb, I insert bits of garlic paste all along the bottom of the leg. I also insert bits of mashed anchovies and some fresh rosemary leaves. The anchovies season the meat but do not give it a fishy flavor. I then season the leg with a paste much the same as the one used for roast chicken on page 227 and roast it on a bed of quartered onions, basting it with brown stock or a lamb stock every 10 to 15 minutes. For a medium rare leg of lamb, count 12 minutes per pound and let the meat "rest" for 15 minutes before carving. Two years ago I came upon an interesting variation that I have since found excellent for more mature lamb. In the Braised Leg of Lamb Arlésienne (page 193) the leg is boned and rolled, then braised with 50 large garlic cloves for 3 to 4 hours in a covered casserole. The addition of a large bouquet of fresh herbs and some good stock results in an extraordinarily tender piece of meat with concentrated and wonderfully flavorful pan juices. The lamb is juicy and can be eaten with a spoon.

Many of the classic lamb dishes are in the form of ragoûts or stews. Irish lamb stew can be superb when well prepared, and the Navarin of Lamb Printanière is basically a peasant preparation that evolved into a classic spring dish. The lamb is cubed and braised with tomatoes and onions and combined with a garniture of spring vegetables. All lamb stews are best when made with the shoulder of lamb, which has become increasingly expensive and is rarely available in the supermarket. An excellent and easily obtainable alternative is to get shoulder chops and have the butcher cube them for you. This will give a rich stew with the bones still in. It is somewhat more difficult to eat, but it is also extremely flavorful since the bones add a great deal of body to the sauce. (Many of the bones fall out once the meat is cooked, and can easily be removed.)

I prefer using lamb to prepare a "blanquette"—a stew in which the lamb, like a chicken, is poached with aromatic vegetables and then combined in a sauce made from butter, flour, and stock. I find that lamb lends a more interesting flavor to the dish, traditionally made with veal, and that the relatively inexpensive lamb shanks available in most supermarkets are excellent for this preparation. One of my favorite "white" ragoûts is the Lamb in Dill Sauce in *The Seasonal Kitchen* and the Ragoût of Lamb with Leeks on page 202.

Rack of lamb is considered to be the most elegant way of all to serve lamb. (It is probably the cut most used in quality restaurants.) The rack consists of seven or eight rib chops and can be ordered in advance from most supermarkets. Although this is an expensive cut, it makes superb dinner party fare. Since it only needs twenty minutes of roasting, it also allows the cook time to spend on imaginative vegetable dishes. The Eggplant Sandwiches à la Genovese on page 59, or the Braised Belgian Endive in Cream (page 427), are just some of my favorite accompaniments.

With new methods of breeding and feeding, lamb comes to us now with less fat, more protein, and fewer calories. Yet for some reason we just are not accustomed to consuming large quantities of this meat. This is too bad. Even though delicious lamb is available all year now, many people still think of it only in connection with the Easter holiday, just as others only serve turkey at Thanksgiving and Christmas. Many claim that lamb demands an "acquired" taste. Having grown up in the Mediterranean region, where exciting lamb dishes are prepared with such great creativity and flair, and having enjoyed the tender spring lamb of Provence as well as the mature lamb of England, I can only say that once the taste for this fine and tender meat has been "acquired," it is sure to become a must.

Specialty Cuts
There are a variety of specialty items, most of which must be bought from a good butcher since they are rarely available at the supermarket. Some, like the elegant and tender sweetbreads, are considered delicacies while others, like oxtail, are used in more ordinary dishes. Calves' liver and sweetbreads are two of the great specialty items I most love to use. The *nouvelle cuisine* chefs use both these variety meats with great creativity. I include several of my favorite preparations of these cuts here. When you buy calves' liver make sure it is very light in color and firm textured. Sweetbreads should never be bought frozen. They are basically bland but lend themselves to many wonderful preparations.

Their unique texture is appreciated by every great chef, and there is hardly a good restaurant these days that does not feature either a calves' liver or a sweetbread dish.

Grilled Steaks
in
Herb Butter

Serves: **4**
Preparation time: **10 minutes**
Cooking time: **20 minutes**
Type of recipe: **elementary**
Cost: **expensive**

Ingredients
4 Tablespoons salted butter, at room temperature
2 Tablespoons finely minced shallots
2 Tablespoons finely minced fresh parsley
2 Tablespoons Clarified Butter (page 545)
2 1¾-inch-thick club or shell steaks
Coarse salt
Freshly ground black pepper

Garnish:
Sprigs of fresh parsley

Preparation
1.
In a small bowl combine the softened butter, shallots, and parsley. Cream the mixture to a smooth paste with a fork and set aside.
2.
In a heavy 2-quart saucepan bring water to a boil. Reduce the heat until the water is barely at a simmer. Place a heavy dinner plate on top of the saucepan, then place half the herb butter on the plate. Reserve the rest of the butter.
3.
In a heavy 10-inch skillet heat the Clarified Butter until it is almost smoking. Add the steaks but do not crowd the pan. The steaks must be at least 1 inch apart. Sauté the steaks over high heat for 3 to 4 minutes, then reduce the heat and cook for another 7 minutes.
4.
Turn the steaks, sprinkle with coarse salt and freshly ground pepper, and sauté for

another 5 to 6 minutes. The steaks are done when little drops of the red juices begin to ooze from the surface. Don't overcook; the steaks must remain quite rare.
5.
Transfer the steaks to the warmed plate and top with the remaining herb butter. Cover the entire plate tightly with foil and let the steaks absorb the butter for 3 to 4 minutes.
6.
Place the steaks on a cutting board and slice crosswise into thin slices.
7.
Transfer the slices to a serving platter and spoon the herb butter over the steaks. Add a large grinding of black pepper, garnish with sprigs of parsley, and serve with tiny sautéed potatoes.

Remarks
For variation you can add a mixture of fresh herbs such as thyme, chervil, or tarragon to the herb butter. A large barbecued sirloin steak can also be served the same way by placing the still-rare steaks on a large platter. Place the herb butter on top and let the steaks absorb the butter for several minutes. This gives a barbecued steak an additional delicious flavor.

Sautéed Steaks
in
Mustard Sauce

Serves: **4**
Preparation time: **10 minutes**
Cooking time: **15 minutes**
Type of recipe: **elementary**
Cost: **expensive**

The method of pan-frying steaks is used both in France and Northern Italy. It is an excellent method for cooking small rib roasts as well. None of the juices are lost and the steaks become crisp yet perfectly juicy and tender. The pan-frying method also allows you to create a short sauce such as this mustard sauce or a green peppercorn sauce.

Ingredients

1 teaspoon dry English mustard
3 Tablespoon Clarified Butter (page 545)
2 shell steaks, each cut 1½ inches thick
Salt and freshly ground black pepper
1 Tablespoon butter
2 Tablespoon finely minced shallots
¼ cup Scotch whisky
¾ cup Brown Chicken Stock (page 531)
1 to 1½ Tablespoons Dijon mustard

Garnish:
Sprigs of fresh watercress

Preparation

1.
In a small bowl combine the dry mustard with a little water and let the mixture develop flavor for 30 minutes.

2.
In a cast-iron skillet (large enough to hold the steaks without crowding) heat the Clarified Butter and, when the butter is very hot, add the steaks. Sauté the steaks over moderate-to-high heat for 3 to 4 minutes. Reduce the heat and continue sautéing for another 3 to 4 minutes.

3.
Turn the steaks and sauté them on the other side for 4 to 5 minutes, or until little drops of red juices begin to ooze from the surface of the steaks. Regulate the heat so that the fat is always very hot but not burning.

4.
When the steaks are done, season them with salt and pepper. Transfer to a carving board and set aside.

5.
Discard all but 1 tablespoon of fat from the pan. Add the tablespoon of unclarified butter and, when melted, add the shallots and cook until soft, scraping well the bottom of the pan with a wooden spoon. Do not let the shallots burn.

6.
Add the Scotch, bring to a boil, and reduce to a glaze.

7.
Add the stock, bring to a boil, and cook until the sauce is reduced to 3 tablespoons. Whisk in the dissolved mustard as well as 1 tablespoon Dijon mustard, blending it well with the pan juices. Taste the sauce, and

Fillets of Beef
à la Portugaise

Serves: **6**
Preparation time: **30 minutes**
Cooking time: **15 minutes**
Type of recipe: **elementary**
Cost: **expensive**

correct the seasoning. Add the remaining ½ tablespoon mustard if you wish. Set the sauce aside.

8.
Slice the steak crosswise into thin slices.

9.
Place the steak slices slightly overlapping on individual serving plates and spoon some of the mustard sauce on each portion. Garnish each plate with a sprig of fresh watercress and serve accompanied by a gratin of potatoes.

Remarks
Although this dish requires last-minute cooking it is a delicious and elegant supper dish for 4 persons. A 1½-inch steak cooked for 12 to 14 minutes will be medium rare. For a rare steak reduce the cooking time by 2 to 3 minutes.

Ingredients
4 Tablespoons butter
2 Tablespoons finely minced shallots
2 large ripe tomatoes, peeled, seeded, and finely chopped
1 Tablespoon tomato paste
Salt and freshly ground black pepper
2½ pounds beef tenderloin, trimmed of all fat
1 Tablespoon oil
¼ cup Scotch whisky
1 teaspoon meat glaze
¾ cup concentrated Brown Chicken Stock (page 531)
1 cup Crème Fraîche (page 544)
1 Beurre Manié (page 544)

Garnish:
Sprigs of fresh watercress

Preparation
1.
In a small heavy skillet heat 2 tablespoons butter, add the shallots, and cook for 2 minutes without browning. Add the tomatoes and tomato paste and cook the mixture until the tomato juices have evaporated and the mixture is thick. Season with salt and pepper and reserve.

2.
Cut the fillets into ½-inch slices and set aside.

3.
In a 10-inch cast-iron skillet heat the remaining butter and the oil. When the butter is very hot and starts to turn brown, add the fillets 2 to 3 at a time. Do not crowd the pan; the steaks should not touch each another. Cook over high heat for 2 to

Braised Beef Birds Hongroise

Serves: **4 to 6**
Preparation time: **15 minutes**
Cooking time: **1 hour**
Type of recipe: **elementary**
Cost: **moderate**

3 minutes on each side, or until nicely browned. Season the steaks with salt and pepper and transfer to a side dish. Continue sautéing until all the steaks are done.

4.
Discard all but 2 tablespoons of fat from the pan. (If the fat has burned, discard it and add 2 tablespoons butter to the skillet.) Add the Scotch, bring to a boil over high heat, and reduce to 1 tablespoon.

5.
Add the meat glaze and stock. Bring to a boil and cook over high heat, scraping the bottom of the pan well to loosen any particles. Cook until reduced to ¼ cup.

6.
Add the Crème Fraîche and season with salt and pepper. Bring to a boil and cook until reduced by one third. Add the tomato mixture, heat through, then whisk in bits of Beurre Manié, cooking the sauce until it heavily coats a spoon. Taste and correct the seasoning, then reduce the heat to a simmer.

7.
Return the steaks to the skillet, pouring back any juices that have accumulated in the plate.

8.
Spoon the sauce over the steaks and simmer for another minute. The steaks should not cook.

9.
Transfer the steaks to a serving platter and again spoon the sauce over them. Garnish with sprigs of fresh watercress and serve immediately.

Ingredients

12 strips slab bacon, cut ½ inch by 2½ inches
6 to 8 beef slices, cut from the top round (4 inches by 8 inches and ½ inch thick)
Salt and freshly ground black pepper
1½ teaspoons dried marjoram
2 Tablespoons Dijon mustard
1 to 1½ teaspoons imported paprika
12 one-half-inch strips green peppers, cut 2½ inches long
12 thin strips Italian roasted peppers or pimientos, cut 2½ inches long
12 thin strips dill gherkins, cut 2½ inches long
2 Tablespoons butter
2 Tablespoons oil
2 Tablespoons finely minced shallots, or 1 cup finely minced onions
1 large clove garlic, peeled and crushed
1 Tablespoon tomato paste
1 to 1½ cups Brown Chicken Stock (page 531)
1 teaspoon cornstarch, mixed with a little stock

Garnish:
Sprigs of fresh parsley

Preparation

1.
In a small saucepan bring water to a boil and add the bacon strips. Cook for 2 to 3 minutes, then drain and dry thoroughly on paper towels. Set aside.

2.
Season each slice of beef with salt, pepper, and marjoram. Spread each with a thin layer of mustard and sprinkle with paprika.

Roast Beef in Onion Sauce

Serves:	**6**
Preparation time:	**15 minutes**
Cooking time:	**1 hour, 50 minutes**
Type of recipe:	**elementary**
Cost:	**expensive**

3.
Place a strip each of green pepper, roasted pepper or pimiento, dill gherkin, and bacon in the center of each beef slice. Roll up the beef slices and secure with toothpicks or tie at both ends with kitchen string.

4.
Heat the butter and oil in a large heavy skillet. Add the beef rolls but do not crowd the pan. Sauté the rolls over high heat until nicely browned on all sides. Season with salt and pepper and remove from the pan to a side dish. Reserve.

5.
Remove all but 2 tablespoons of fat from the pan. Add the shallots or onions and garlic. Cook until nicely browned, then stir in the tomato paste and ½ cup stock. Return the rolls to the pan and simmer over low heat for 45 minutes, or until the beef rolls are tender. Check every 10 minutes; if the pan juices are too reduced add a little more stock.

6.
When the rolls are done transfer them to a serving platter.

7.
Whisk a little of the cornstarch mixture into the pan juices; use just enough to thicken the juices. Spoon the pan juices over the beef rolls. Garnish the platter with sprigs of parsley and serve immediately accompanied by a gratin of potatoes.

Ingredients
1 five-pound rib roast, preferably first cut
Salt and freshly ground black pepper
2 teaspoons imported paprika
1½ teaspoons dried thyme
2 Tablespoons butter
1 Tablespoon oil
2 onions, peeled and quartered
1 to 1½ cups hot beef bouillon

Sauce:
2 Tablespoons butter
1 Tablespoon oil
2 large Spanish onions, peeled and thinly sliced
Pinch of granulated sugar
Salt and freshly ground black pepper
¼ teaspoon dried thyme
½ cup dry white wine
1 cup Brown Chicken Stock (page 531)
1 Beurre Manié (page 544)
1 Tablespoon Dijon mustard

Garnish:
Sprigs of fresh watercress

Preparation

1.

Preheat the oven to 500 degrees.

2.

Rub the roast well with salt and pepper, paprika, and thyme and set aside.

3.

In a 12-inch cast-iron skillet heat the butter and oil. Place the roast in the skillet and brown over moderate-to-high heat on both sides. Then place the roast topside down in the pan and continue cooking until the fat is well browned and crisp.

4.

Spoon off and discard all but 2 tablespoons of the accumulated fat from the skillet. Put the onions around the roast and add a little bouillon. Place the skillet with the roast in the oven. Reduce the heat to 375 degrees.

5.

Cook the roast for 1 hour, 40 minutes (or 18 minutes per pound for a medium-rare roast), basting it every 10 minutes with a little more bouillon and removing the accumulated fat.

6.

While the roast is in the oven make the onion sauce. In a 10-inch cast-iron skillet heat the butter and oil. Add the onions and cook over moderate-to-high heat for 10 minutes, or until they start to brown. Stir them several times to make sure they are not burning.

7.

Sprinkle the onions with a pinch of sugar and season with salt and pepper. Lower the heat and cover the skillet, simmering the onions for 30 to 40 minutes, or until they

are very soft and have a deep, rich brown color.

8.

Uncover the skillet, raise the heat, add the thyme and wine, and cook until the wine is reduced to a glaze.

9.

Add the Brown Stock, bring to a boil, and whisk in bits of Beurre Manié until the sauce heavily coats a spoon. Whisk in the mustard, taste the sauce, and correct the seasoning. Set the sauce aside.

10.

When the roast is done transfer to a carving board. Carefully degrease the pan juices and discard the onions. (This is best done by transferring the pan juices to a defatter.) Add the well-degreased pan juices to the onion sauce and heat the sauce without bringing it to a boil again.

11.

Transfer the sauce to a serving bowl. Garnish the roast with sprigs of fresh watercress and serve the sauce on the side.

Remarks

The sauce can be prepared several hours ahead and reheated.

Ragoût of Beef
à la Viennoise

Serves: **6**
Preparation time: **20 minutes**
Cooking time: **2 hours**
Type of recipe: **elementary**
Cost: **inexpensive**

Ingredients

1 ounce imported dried mushrooms (Italian or cèpes)
2 cups concentrated Beef Stock (page 533) or bouillon
4 pounds boneless chuck, cut into 1½-inch cubes
2 Tablespoons pork fat or butter
1 Tablespoon oil
Salt and freshly ground black pepper
3 cups finely minced onions
2 teaspoons tomato paste
1 teaspoon imported paprika
1 teaspoon dried marjoram
1 Tablespoon caraway seeds
1 cup sour cream
3 Tablespoons finely minced fresh dill

Optional:
1 Beurre Manié (page 544)

Garnish:
½ pound fresh mushrooms, stems removed and caps sautéed in butter and oil
Finely minced fresh parsley

Preparation

1.
Rinse the dried mushrooms thoroughly under cold water. Place them in a saucepan and add the stock, bringing to a boil. Reduce the heat, cover, and simmer the mushrooms for 20 to 30 minutes, or until tender. Drain the mushrooms and dice them, then return to the stock and set aside.

2.
Preheat the oven to 375 degrees.

3.
Dry the meat thoroughly with paper towels.

4.
In a large heavy skillet heat 2 tablespoons fat and the oil. When the fat is very hot add the meat a few pieces at a time. Do not crowd the pan or the meat will not brown evenly. Sauté the meat on all sides until nicely browned. Season with salt and pepper and transfer to a heavy casserole as the pieces are cooked. Continue sautéing the meat, adding a little more butter or oil if needed.

5.
When the meat has been browned add the onions to the skillet. Sauté over medium heat, scraping well the bottom of the pan to loosen particles and cooking the onions until they are soft and nicely browned.

6.
Add the tomato paste, paprika, marjoram, and caraway seeds and stir the mixture for 1 to 2 minutes. Season with salt and pepper and add the mushroom stock. Bring to a boil and transfer to the casserole with the meat. Cover tightly and place in the center of the oven.

Boulettes
à la Paysanne

Serves: **4 to 5**
Preparation time: **35 minutes**
Cooking time: **20 minutes**
Type of recipe: **elementary**
Cost: **inexpensive**

7.
Braise the meat for 1 hour, 30 minutes, or until tender but not falling apart. When the meat is done remove the casserole from the oven. With a slotted spoon transfer the meat to a side dish and reserve.

8.
Bring the pan juices to a boil on top of the stove and whisk in half the optional Beurre Manié; add just enough to thicken the sauce. Taste and correct the seasoning.

9.
Whisk in the sour cream and dill. Return the meat to the casserole, cover, and simmer until the ragoût is heated through.

10.
Transfer the meat and sauce to a serving dish, top with the sautéed mushrooms, and sprinkle with parsley. Serve accompanied by freshly cooked, buttered noodles or a potato purée.

Remarks
The ragoût can be prepared a day in advance and reheated on top of the stove or in a slow oven. It can also be frozen. There are 2 types of imported dried mushrooms available in good supermarkets. Avoid the thinly sliced white variety and look for the other, which is dark and large and has an intense smoky aroma.

Ingredients
2 pounds ground beef, such as top sirloin
1 small onion, peeled and grated
2 cloves garlic, peeled and crushed
2 Tablespoons fresh parsley, finely minced
1 teaspoon dried thyme
Salt and freshly ground black pepper
¼ cup white bread crumbs (unflavored)
Flour for dredging

Vegetable Garnish:
1 cup finely cubed slab bacon
3 medium baking potatoes, peeled and cut into 1-inch cubes
4 Tablespoons butter
2 Tablespoons oil
Salt and freshly ground black pepper
¾ pound small fresh mushrooms
¾ to 1 cup Brown Chicken Stock (page 531)
2 Tablespoons minced fresh parsley
1 teaspoon finely minced garlic

Garnish:
Sprigs of fresh parsley

Preparation
1.
In a large bowl combine the ground meat, onion, garlic, parsley, and thyme. Season the mixture with salt and pepper. Add the bread crumbs and work the mixture with your hands until smooth and well blended. Add 4 tablespoons of water and work the mixture again with your hands until well blended. If the mixture seems heavy add 2 more tablespoons water. Work the mixture

into oval meatballs, dredge them lightly with flour, and set aside.

2.
Prepare the vegetable garnish. In a large saucepan bring salted water to a boil. Add the bacon and cook for 3 minutes, then drain the bacon in a colander. Place the bacon on a double layer of paper towels and set aside.

3.
In another saucepan bring salted water to a boil and add the potatoes. Bring to a boil and cook for 3 to 4 minutes, then drain on a double layer of paper towels and set aside.

4.
In a large heavy skillet heat 2 tablespoons butter and the oil. When the butter is very hot and the foam starts to subside add the meatballs and cook on all sides until nicely browned. Regulate the heat so that the fat is not burning in the pan. Cook the meat until it reaches the degree of doneness that you like. It should, however, still be quite pink. Test a meatball with the tip of a sharp knife; the juices should still run quite pink.

5.
When the meatballs are done remove them from the skillet and place them on a side dish. Reserve.

6.
Add the remaining butter to the skillet. Add the bacon and cook until it is almost crisp. Transfer the bacon cubes with a slotted spoon to a side plate and reserve.

7.
Again add more oil, if necessary, to the pan. Add the potato cubes and cook over moderate heat for 5 minutes, or until the

cubes are nicely browned. Shake the pan back and forth to brown the potatoes evenly. Season with salt and pepper and transfer with a slotted spoon to a side dish.

8.
Add the mushrooms to the skillet. Sauté for 2 to 3 minutes until nicely browned. Transfer the mushrooms to a side dish.

9.
Lower the heat, add ¾ cup stock, and bring to a boil. Reduce the stock by one third.

10.
Return the bacon, potatoes, and mushrooms to the skillet and toss until well coated with the pan juices.

11.
Return the meat to the skillet, covering it with the vegetable mixture. If the sauce has reduced too much add the remaining ¼ cup stock. Add the parsley and garlic and cover the pan. Simmer over the lowest possible heat for 2 to 3 minutes; do not overcook or the meat will be dry.

12.
Transfer the meatballs and vegetable garnish to a serving platter. Garnish with additional sprigs of parsley and serve immediately.

Remarks
You may prepare the entire garnish well in advance and reheat it in the skillet just before serving. The vegetable garnish is equally good with thinly sliced London broil or any other beef that has been either sautéed in the skillet or cooked over a charcoal fire.

Boulettes
à la Viennoise

Serves: **4 to 5**
Preparation time: **35 minutes**
Cooking time: **2 hours**
Type of recipe: **elementary**
Cost: **inexpensive**

*Meatballs play major roles in many
European cuisines from Scandinavia to the
Middle East. They are sometimes made from
pork, veal, or lamb and they are often
sauced and interestingly spiced. This
Viennese version, in which the meatballs are
braised in a sweet-and-sour sauce, can be
served either as a simple supper dish or for
Sunday supper accompanied by a
well-seasoned green salad.*

Ingredients

2 pounds ground lean chuck beef
**2 Tablespoons finely minced fresh
parsley**
1½ cups finely minced onions
¼ cup fresh white bread crumbs
8 Tablespoons water
Salt and freshly ground black pepper
Flour for dredging
2 Tablespoons butter
1 Tablespoon oil

Sauce:

2 Tablespoons butter
3 cups finely chopped onions
4 Tablespoon granulated sugar
2 Tablespoons water
**3 cups hot Beef Stock (page 533) or
bouillon**
Juice of 1 large lemon
Salt and freshly ground black pepper
**1 Tablespoon cornstarch, mixed with a
little stock**

Preparation

1.
In a bowl combine the ground meat,
parsley, and onions. Work the mixture with
your hands until well blended. Add the
bread crumbs and water and blend again
thoroughly. Season with salt and pepper
and shape into round meatballs. Dredge
lightly with flour, shaking off the excess.

2.
In a large heavy skillet heat 2 tablespoons
butter and a little of the oil. Add the
meatballs; do not crowd the skillet. Sauté
the meatballs over moderate-to-high heat
until nicely browned on both sides. As they
are done, transfer the meatballs to a heavy
casserole and set aside. Add more oil as
necessary to sauté remaining meatballs.

3.
When the meatballs are done discard all
but 1 tablespoon fat from the skillet in
order to prepare the sauce. Add the butter
and, when the butter is hot, add the 3 cups
onions. Cook the onions until they are
nicely browned, scraping well the bottom of
the skillet. Transfer the onions to the
casserole and wipe the skillet with paper
towels.

4.
Add the sugar and water to the skillet and
stir until well blended. Cook the sugar over
high heat until it turns a hazel nut-brown.

5.
Add 1 cup hot stock, being careful to avoid
spattering, and bring to a boil.

6.
Add the caramelized stock to the casserole,
together with the remaining stock, and
season with salt and pepper. Cover the

Tunisian
Gratin of Meat
and Potatoes

Serves:	**6 to 8**
Preparation time:	**35 to 40 minutes**
Cooking time:	**1 hour and 45 minutes**
Type of recipe:	**elementary**
Cost:	**inexpensive**

casserole and simmer the meat for 1 hour, 30 minutes.

7.
Add the lemon juice and simmer the meatballs for another 15 minutes. Taste and correct the seasoning. Remove the meatballs to a serving dish and reserve.

8.
Carefully degrease the sauce. Whisk in a little of the cornstarch mixture; add just enough to thicken the sauce.

9.
Spoon the sauce over the meatballs and serve hot, accompanied by sautéed turnips or a potato purée.

Remarks
The meatballs are best when prepared a day in advance and refrigerated. The next day carefully degrease the sauce. Reheat the meatballs on top of the stove over low heat and then whisk in the cornstarch mixture.

Ingredients
3 Tablespoons olive oil
1½ cups finely minced onions
1 teaspoon finely minced garlic
1½ pounds ground pork
½ pound ground beef
2 teaspoons chili powder
1 teaspoon hot pepper flakes
½ teaspoon ground cumin
1 teaspoon dried thyme
1 teaspoon dried oregano
1 teaspoon dried marjoram
1 Tablespoon tomato paste
1 can (35 ounces) Italian plum tomatoes, well drained and chopped
Salt and freshly ground black pepper
2 large eggs
4 large baking potatoes, peeled and thinly sliced

Sauce:
5 Tablespoons butter
5 Tablespoons flour
3 cups hot milk
2 egg yolks
Pinch of freshly grated nutmeg
½ cup grated Parmesan cheese
Salt and freshly ground black pepper

Optional:
1 package (10 ounces) fresh spinach, cooked and finely minced

Preparation

1.

Preheat the oven to 350 degrees.

2.

In a large cast-iron skillet heat the oil. Add the onions and garlic and cook over medium heat until the onions are limp and lightly browned. Add the meats and cook, breaking up the mixture with a fork until it loses its pink color and is lightly browned. Add the chili powder, pepper flakes, cumin, and herbs and continue cooking for another 2 to 3 minutes.

3.

Add the tomato paste and tomatoes, season with salt and pepper, and bring to a boil. Reduce the heat and simmer the mixture covered for 15 minutes.

4.

Cool and add the eggs, blending them thoroughly into the mixture. Add the optional spinach and taste and correct the seasoning; the mixture should be highly seasoned. Set aside.

5.

Prepare the sauce. In a heavy enamel saucepan heat the butter. Add the flour and cook over medium heat for 2 minutes, stirring constantly without letting it brown. Remove the saucepan from the heat and add the hot milk all at once. Stir until the mixture is smooth and well blended, then return the saucepan to medium heat and cook the sauce, whisking constantly until it is thick and smooth. Remove from the heat. Add the yolks, nutmeg, and Parmesan cheese and blend thoroughly. Season with salt and pepper set aside.

6.

Dry the potatoes thoroughly with paper towels. Make a layer of potatoes in a rectangular baking dish, overlapping them lightly. Season with salt and pepper. Place a layer of the meat mixture on top. Make another layer of potatoes and season with salt and pepper. Continue with another layer of meat, then finish with a layer of potatoes. Season with salt and pepper and top with the sauce.

7.

Place the baking dish on a cookie sheet (to catch the drippings) and set in the preheated oven. Bake for 1 hour, 30 minutes. If the top of the gratin has browned cover it loosely with foil for the last 30 minutes.

8.

Serve hot, directly from the dish, accompanied by a well-seasoned green salad.

Remarks

This dish can be made several hours in advance and reheated in a 200-degree oven.

Gratin of Meat
and
Polenta

Serves: **6 to 8**
Preparation time: **15 minutes**
Cooking time: **1 hour, 35 minutes**
Type of recipe: **elementary**
Cost: **inexpensive**

Ingredients

3 to 4 Tablespoons fruity olive oil
1½ cups finely minced onions
1 teaspoon finely minced garlic
1½ pounds ground meat
1½ cups Tomato Sauce (page 543)
1 teaspoon dried thyme
½ teaspoon dried oregano
2 Tablespoons finely minced fresh parsley
Salt and freshly ground black pepper
½ pound fresh mushrooms, stems removed and caps thinly sliced
2 large eggs
⅓ cup homemade bread crumbs

Polenta:

3 cups water
1½ teaspoons salt
¾ cup yellow cornmeal
2 Tablespoons butter
3½ Tablespoons freshly grated Parmesan cheese
Salt and freshly ground black pepper

Topping:

2 Tablespoons melted butter
2 Tablespoons freshly grated Parmesan cheese

Preparation

1.
Prepare the meat mixture first. In a large heavy skillet heat 2 tablespoons olive oil over moderate-to-high heat. Add the onions and garlic and cook the mixture until it is soft but not browned.

2.
Add the ground meat, breaking it into tiny pieces with a fork, and sauté for 5 minutes, or until lightly browned. Add the Tomato Sauce, thyme, oregano, and parsley. Season with salt and pepper to taste. Reduce the heat and simmer the mixture partially covered for 35 to 40 minutes. Set aside.

3.
In a separate skillet heat the remaining olive oil over high heat and sauté the mushrooms until they are nicely browned, or for 2 to 3 minutes, then season with salt and pepper. Add the mushrooms to the meat mixture and transfer the entire mixture to a mixing bowl. Add the eggs and bread crumbs and blend thoroughly. Set aside.

4.
Preheat the oven to 350 degrees.

5.
Make the polenta. In a heavy 2-quart saucepan bring 2 cups water to a boil and add the salt, then add the cornmeal in a slow stream, stirring the mixture constantly to avoid lumping. Reduce the heat to low and cook until the cornmeal mixture comes away from the side of the pan, or for about 10 to 15 minutes. Remove the saucepan from the heat and add the butter and Parmesan cheese. Stir until well blended and season with salt and pepper.

Sautéed Veal Chops
in
Avocado Sauce

Serves:	**4 to 6**
Preparation time:	**15 minutes**
Cooking time:	**30 minutes**
Type of recipe:	**elementary**
Cost:	**expensive**

6.
Butter a rectangular baking dish. Spread half the polenta mixture in the dish. Top the polenta with the meat mixture, smoothing it with a spatula. Finish with the other half of the polenta, again smoothing it with a spatula.

7.
Add the topping. Dribble the melted butter over the polenta and sprinkle with the Parmesan cheese.

8.
Cover the baking dish loosely with foil and place in the center of the oven. Bake for 35 minutes. Five minutes before the gratin is done uncover it to brown the top.

9.
When done, remove the polenta gratin from the oven and let it sit for 30 minutes before serving. Serve accompanied by a well-seasoned green salad and some crusty French bread.

Remarks
The entire dish can be prepared several hours ahead and baked just prior to serving.

Ingredients
1 cup ripe avocado pulp
2 Tablespoons heavy cream
Lemon juice
4 to 6 veal rib chops, cut 1 inch thick
Salt and freshly ground white pepper
Flour for dredging
3 Tablespoons butter
1 Tablespoon oil
1 onion, peeled and cut in quarters
3 large cloves garlic, peeled and cut in half lengthwise
½ cup concentrated Brown Chicken Stock (page 531)
1 cup Crème Fraîche (page 544)

Optional:
Bits of Beurre Manié (page 544)

Garnish:
Slices of avocado
Lemon juice
Sprigs of fresh parsley

Preparation

1.
In a blender combine the avocado pulp and heavy cream and purée the mixture until smooth. Add a few drops lemon juice to keep the avocado from turning dark. Set aside.

2.
Season the veal chops with salt and pepper. Dredge lightly with flour, shaking off the excess. Set aside.

3.
In a large cast-iron skillet heat 2 tablespoons butter and 1 tablespoon oil. When the fat is very hot and the foam starts to subside add the chops but do not crowd the pan. Add the onion and garlic cloves and sauté the chops for 2 to 3 minutes on each side, or until they are nicely browned.

4.
Reduce the heat. Add 2 tablespoons stock and bring to a boil. Cover the skillet and braise the chops over the lowest possible heat for 10 to 12 minutes, adding a little stock every few minutes and turning the chops once.

5.
When the chops are done they should be nicely browned and glazed. Transfer them to a serving platter, cover, and keep warm.

6.
Discard the garlic cloves and the onions and increase the heat. Add any remaining stock to the pan and reduce the pan juices to a glaze. There should be no more than 1 to 2 tablespoons pan juices left.

7.
Add the Crème Fraîche and bring to a boil. Season with salt and pepper and cook until the cream is reduced and heavily coats a spoon. (Add little bits of Beurre Manié if you want to stretch the sauce; however, this sauce should be short and concentrated.)

8.
Remove the pan from the heat and whisk in the avocado purée and remaining butter. Taste the sauce and correct the seasoning.

9.
Place the chops on a platter and spoon the avocado sauce over them. Garnish each chop with an additional slice of avocado. Drizzle a little lemon juice over them and sprinkle with salt and pepper. Garnish the platter with parsley and serve immediately.

Remarks
The chops may be sautéed in advance and braised in a 325-degree oven just before serving. Once the avocado purée has been added to the sauce it must not be cooked any further.

Braised Veal Chops
in
Tarragon Sauce

Serves:	**4 to 6**
Preparation time:	**25 minutes**
Cooking time:	**35 minutes**
Type of recipe:	**elementary**
Cost:	**expensive**

While good veal scallops often hard to find at the average supermarket, veal chops are more readily available in many good markets. I use veal chops in many preparations that call for scaloppine. Their advantage is that you can cook them somewhat in advance since they can be reheated in a slow oven for 20 minutes.

Ingredients

4 to 6 rib veal chops, cut ¾ inch thick
Salt and freshly ground white pepper
Flour for dredging
2 Tablespoons butter
1 Tablespoon oil
2 Tablespoons finely minced shallots
3 Tablespoons cognac or brandy
2 large ripe tomatoes, peeled, seeded, and finely chopped
3 Tablespoons finely minced fresh tarragon
¾ cup Brown Chicken Stock (page 531)
¾ cup Crème Fraîche (page 544) or heavy cream
1 Beurre Manié (page 544)

Garnish:
Sprigs of fresh parsley

Preparation

1.
Season the veal chops with salt and pepper and dredge lightly with flour, shaking off the excess.

2.
Heat the butter and oil in a 12-inch cast-iron skillet and add the chops; do not crowd the pan. Sauté the chops over moderate-to-high heat until nicely browned. Turn and sauté on the other side, being careful not to let the fat in the pan burn. Remove the chops to a side dish and reserve.

3.
Remove all but 2 tablespoons fat from the skillet. (If the fat has burned, discard it and replace it with 2 tablespoons fresh butter.) Add the shallots and cook for 1 to 2 minutes until soft but not browned.

4.
Add the cognac or brandy. Bring to a boil and reduce over high heat to a glaze.

5.
Add the tomatoes, 1 tablespoon tarragon, salt, and pepper and cook over high heat until the tomato juices have evaporated.

6.
Reduce the heat and return the chops to the skillet. Add ⅓ cup of stock and cover. Simmer for 20 minutes, adding a little more stock to the skillet every 10 minutes. Turn the chops once during their cooking time. When the chops are done transfer them to a serving platter and keep warm.

7.
Add the remaining tarragon and the cream to the skillet. Bring the sauce to a boil and cook over high heat, whisking in bits of the

Sautéed Veal Chops
in
Roquefort Sauce

Serves:	**4**
Preparation time:	**15 minutes**
Cooking time:	**10 minutes**
Type of recipe:	**elementary**
Cost:	**expensive**

butter paste until the sauce thickens and heavily coats a spoon. Taste and correct the seasoning, adding a little more tarragon if you wish.

8.
Spoon the sauce over the chops and garnish with parsley. Serve immediately accompanied by braised rice or buttered noodles.

Remarks
You may brown the chops several hours ahead. If you finish the dish entirely, cover with foil and place in a 200-degree oven. The chops can be kept warm for 20 to 30 minutes.

Ingredients
2 Tablespoons imported Roquefort cheese
4 Tablespoons butter
4 veal rib chops, cut ¾ inch thick
Salt and freshly ground white pepper
Flour for dredging
1 Tablespoon oil
¼ cup dry vermouth
¾ cup Brown Chicken Stock (page 531)
1 cup heavy cream

Optional:
1 Beurre Manié (page 544)
4 sautéed and buttered Artichoke Bottoms (page 408)

Garnish:
Sprigs of fresh watercress

Preparation
1.
In a bowl, mash the cheese with 2 tablespoons butter until it is a smooth paste. Set aside.
2.
Season the veal chops with salt and pepper. Dredge lightly with flour, shaking off the excess. Set aside.
3.
In a 10-inch cast-iron skillet heat the remaining butter and the oil. When the fat is very hot add the veal chops and brown over high heat on both sides.
4.
Reduce the heat and add 2 tablespoons of the vermouth. Continue cooking until it evaporates completely.

Veal Scaloppine in Butter, Anchovy, and Lemon Sauce

Serves: **4**
Preparation time: **15 minutes, plus 30 minutes to chill meat**
Cooking time: **30 minutes**
Type of recipe: **elementary**
Cost: **expensive**

5.
Add 3 to 4 tablespoons stock. Turn the chops and simmer for another 2 to 3 minutes, or until the stock has almost completely evaporated and the chops are nicely glazed. Transfer the chops to a side dish and keep warm.

6.
Increase the heat and add the remaining vermouth to the skillet. Cook until reduced to a glaze, then add the remaining stock. Bring to a boil and reduce the stock to 2 tablespoons.

7.
Add the cream and bring again to a boil. Continue cooking, whisking in bits of optional Beurre Manié until the sauce heavily coats a spoon.

8.
Add the cheese-butter paste and heat the sauce through without letting it return to a boil.

9.
Remove the skillet from the heat, taste, and correct the seasoning. Place the veal chops on individual serving plates.

10.
Spoon some of the sauce around each chop and garnish each plate with watercress. If desired place an optional buttered Artichoke Bottom on each plate and serve immediately.

Remarks
When glazing the chops as they are cooking be careful not to overcook them or they will be dry. It is important to sauté the chops over very high heat so as to brown them quickly.

Ingredients
8 small veal scaloppine
Salt and freshly ground white pepper
Flour for dredging
2 large eggs, lightly beaten
2 cups fresh white bread crumbs
2 Tablespoons butter
2 to 3 Tablespoons oil

Sauce:
6 Tablespoons butter
Juice of 1 large lemon
4 flat anchovy fillets, finely minced
1 large clove garlic, peeled and crushed
2 Tablespoons well-drained small capers

Garnish:
Thin slices lemon
Finely minced fresh parsley

Preparation
1.
Season the veal scallops with salt and pepper. Dredge them lightly with flour, shaking off the excess. Dip them into the beaten eggs, turning them to coat properly, and then dip them into the bread crumbs, coating them evenly. Place the veal scallops on a large plate, cover with waxed paper, and refrigerate 30 minutes.

2.
In a large cast-iron skillet, heat the butter and oil. When the butter starts to foam add the veal scallops a few at a time; do not crowd the pan.

3.
Sauté the meat over medium heat until it is nicely browned on both sides. Transfer the scallops to a well-buttered baking dish,

Veal Scaloppine
in
Orange-and-Port Sauce

Serves: **4**
Preparation time: **20 minutes**
Cooking time: **10 minutes**
Type of recipe: **elementary**
Cost: **expensive**

overlapping them slightly. Set aside. Continue sautéing until all the veal scallops are done. You will probably need 1 to 2 tablespoons additional oil.

4.

Prepare the sauce. In a small saucepan melt the butter over low heat. Add the lemon juice, anchovies, garlic, and capers. Heat until the anchovies have blended with the butter. Spoon the butter sauce over the veal scallops. Cover the dish tightly with foil and set aside.

5.

40 minutes before serving preheat the oven to 325 degrees. Place the baking dish in the oven and bake for 20 or 30 minutes, or until the veal scallops are well heated.

6.

Uncover the baking dish, garnish each veal scallop with a lemon slice and sprinkle with parsley. Serve right out of the baking dish.

Remarks

The veal scallops can be sautéed 1 to 2 hours ahead and heated in the sauce just before serving. Do not refrigerate the sautéed meat or it will dry.

Ingredients

1 navel orange
3 Tablespoons Grand Marnier
8 small veal scaloppine
Salt and freshly ground white pepper
Flour for dredging
2 Tablespoons chicken fat
1 Tablespoon oil
⅓ cup port wine
½ cup Brown Chicken Stock (page 531)
1½ Tablespoons apricot jam
Lemon juice

Garnish:

Sprigs of fresh watercress

Preparation

1.

With a vegetable peeler remove the orange peel, being careful not to include the white part. Cut the peel into thin strips 2 inches long and about ⅛ inch wide.

2.

Place the orange strips in a small saucepan and cover with water. Bring to a boil and simmer for 3 to 4 minutes, or until tender. Drain the oranges strips, transfer to a bowl, add the Grand Marnier, and marinate for 15 to 20 minutes.

3.

Meanwhile with a sharp knife peel the orange, removing all the white membrane and exposing the orange flesh. Slice the orange crosswise into 8 thin slices. Discard the pits and set the orange aside.

4.

Dry the veal scaloppine thoroughly with paper towels and season with salt and

Veal Scaloppine
in
Parsley Sauce

Serves:	**4 to 5**
Preparation time:	**10 minutes**
Cooking time:	**30 minutes**
Type of recipe:	**elementary**
Cost:	**expensive**

pepper. Dredge lightly with flour, shaking off the excess.

5.
In a large cast-iron skillet heat the fat and oil. Add the scaloppine and sauté quickly over moderate-to-high heat for 2 minutes on each side, or until nicely browned. Do not crowd the pan and do not overcook the veal. Transfer the scaloppine to a serving platter and keep warm.

6.
Add the port to the skillet. Bring to a boil and cook until it is reduced to 1 tablespoon, then add the stock. Bring to a boil and continue cooking until the stock is reduced by one third. Whisk the apricot jam into the sauce and continue cooking until the jam is melted. Add the orange peel, the Grand Marnier, and lemon juice to taste. Continue simmering the sauce for another 2 to 3 minutes, or until it heavily coats a spoon. Taste the sauce and correct the seasoning; it should have a somewhat sweet-tart flavor.

7.
Transfer the veal to a serving platter. Dip the orange slices in the sauce and then place 1 slice on each scaloppine. Spoon a little of the sauce over each scaloppine, garnish with sprigs of fresh watercress, and serve immediately.

Ingredients
8 to 10 small veal scaloppine
Salt and freshly ground white pepper
Flour for dredging
2 Tablespoons rendered chicken fat, or 3 Tablespoons butter
1 Tablespoon peanut oil
1 onion, peeled and cut in half crosswise
¾ cup Brown Chicken Stock (page 531)
1 cup heavy cream
1 Beurre Manié (page 544)
3 Tablespoons finely minced fresh parsley
1½ Tablespoons finely minced fresh chives
1 large clove garlic, peeled and crushed

Garnish:
2 small carrots, scraped and cut into thin julienne matchsticks (2 inches long and ⅛ inch wide)

Preparation
1.
Preheat the oven to 325 degrees.
2.
Dry the veal thoroughly with paper towels. Season with salt and pepper, then dredge lightly with flour, shaking off the excess. Set aside.
3.
In a large cast-iron skillet heat the fat or a mixture of 2 tablespoons butter and oil. Add the veal and onion; do not crowd the pan. Sauté the veal quickly over moderate-to-high heat until nicely browned on both sides, or for about 1 minute on each side. Transfer the veal to a buttered baking dish and reserve.

Veal Scaloppine Primavera

Serves: **4 to 6**
Preparation time: **35 minutes**
Cooking time: **35 minutes**
Type of recipe: **elementary**
Cost: **expensive**

4.
Add the stock to the skillet, bring to a boil and reduce by half. Add the cream and season with salt and pepper. Bring to a boil and cook until the cream is reduced by one third.

5.
Discard the onion. Whisk in bits of the Beurre Manié; add just enough until the sauce lightly coats a spoon.

6.
Add the parsley, chives, and garlic. Taste the sauce and correct the seasoning.

7.
Spoon the parsley sauce over the veal, cover the baking dish with foil, and place in the oven. Bake the veal for 20 to 25 minutes.

8.
While the veal is in the oven bring salted water to a boil in a small saucepan. Add the carrots and cook for 3 minutes, or until barely tender; Do not overcook. Drain the carrots and set aside.

9.
In a small heavy skillet heat the remaining tablespoon butter. Add the carrots and sauté over moderate-to-high heat for 1 to 2 minutes, or until they are lightly browned. Set aside.

10.
Remove the baking dish from the oven and uncover. Garnish each scaloppine with a few carrot strips. Serve the veal immediately from the baking dish, accompanied by Mushroom Risotto Piémontaise (page 320) or crusty French bread and a well-seasoned green salad.

Although veal scaloppine is an expensive cut of meat this is not an extravagant dish since a little veal goes a long way in this type of preparation. Here the scaloppine are combined with fresh peas and asparagus for a deliciously simple spring meal.

Ingredients
12 to 14 asparagus stalks
¾ cup fresh shelled peas
8 to 10 veal scaloppine (each 5 to 6 inches long)
Salt and freshly ground white pepper
Flour for dredging
6 Tablespoons butter
2 Tablespoons oil
1 cup concentrated Chicken Stock (page 530) or Brown Chicken Stock (page 531)
1 cup heavy cream
1 Beurre Manié (page 544)

Garnish:
Finely minced fresh parsley

Preparation

1.

Preheat the oven to 325 degrees.

2.

Scrape the asparagus stalks and discard the woody bottoms. Cut 3-inch long spears off the stalks and slice the stalks into ¾-inch cubes. Reserve the spears.

3.

In a saucepan bring salted water to a boil. Add the asparagus cubes and the peas and cook for 2 to 5 minutes, or until just tender. Drain in a colander and reserve.

4.

Season the veal with salt and pepper, then dredge lightly with flour, shaking off the excess.

5.

In a large heavy skillet heat 2 tablespoons butter and 1 tablespoon oil, then add the veal, 2 or 3 pieces at a time; do not crowd the pan. Sauté the veal over moderate-to-high heat for 2 minutes. It should be lightly browned on both sides.

6.

Transfer the veal to a baking dish. Add another 2 tablespoons butter and 1 tablespoon of oil and continue sautéing until all the meat is done. You may need a little more butter and oil.

7.

When all the meat is done add the chicken stock to the pan. Bring to a boil and reduce over high heat to ¼ cup.

8.

Add the cream and season with salt and pepper, then bring to a boil. Reduce the heat and whisk in bits of Beurre Manié until the sauce is lightly thickened. Taste and correct the seasoning.

9.

Add the reserved asparagus and peas to the sauce and spoon the sauce-and-vegetable mixture over the veal. Cover with foil and set in the oven.

10.

Bake for 20 minutes.

11.

While the scaloppine are in the oven bring salted water to a boil. Add the asparagus spears and cook for 5 minutes, then drain and reserve.

12.

In a small heavy skillet heat remaining 2 tablespoons butter. Add the asparagus spears and sauté over low heat for 2 minutes. Set aside.

13.

When the veal is done remove the dish from the oven. Garnish with the sautéed asparagus spears and the parsley. Serve the veal scaloppine from the baking dish, accompanied by braised rice and a well-seasoned green salad.

Veal Scaloppine
Zingara

Serves: **4**
Preparation time: **25 minutes**
Cooking time: **45 minutes**
Type of recipe: **elementary**
Cost: **expensive**

Ingredients
3 Tablespoons olive oil
3 Tablespoons butter
½ pound fresh mushrooms, stems removed and caps thinly sliced
Salt and freshly ground black pepper
3 Tablespoons finely minced shallots
2 cloves garlic, finely minced
1 teaspoon tomato paste
3 large ripe tomatoes, peeled, seeded, and finely chopped
2 Roasted Green Peppers (page 545), sliced in thin strips
2 Roasted Red Peppers (page 545), sliced in thin strips
2 Tablespoons thinly sliced pimiento-stuffed olives
8 to 12 small veal scaloppine
Flour for dredging
¼ cup dry white wine

Optional:
1 Tablespoon well-drained tiny capers

Garnish:
Finely minced fresh parsley

Preparation
1.
In a small skillet heat 1 tablespoon oil and 1 tablespoon butter. Add the mushrooms and cook over high heat until nicely browned. Season with salt and pepper. Transfer the sautéed mushrooms to a side dish and reserve.
2.
Add another tablespoon each of oil and butter to the pan. Add the shallots and garlic and cook for 2 minutes without letting the mixture brown. Add the tomato paste and tomatoes. Bring to a boil and cook the mixture until the tomato water has evaporated.
3.
Add the pepper strips, olives, optional capers, and mushrooms. Season the mixture with salt and pepper and reserve.
4.
Preheat the oven to 325 degrees.
5.
Season the veal with salt and pepper and dredge lightly with flour, shaking off the excess.
6.
In a large cast-iron skillet heat the remaining butter and oil. Add the veal a few scaloppine at a time; do not crowd the pan. Sauté the veal for 2 to 3 minutes on each side, or until lightly browned. Do not overcook.
7.
Transfer the veal to a buttered baking dish. Continue to sauté remaining scaloppine. When all the veal has been sautéed, add the wine to the skillet. Bring to a boil and reduce to 1 tablespoon.
8.
Add the prepared tomato-and-pepper mixture to the skillet and cook for 1 or 2 minutes. Spoon the tomato mixture over the veal, cover with foil, and bake for 25 minutes.
9.
When the veal is done sprinkle with parsley and serve directly from the baking dish, accompanied by a pilaf of rice, crusty French bread, and a well-seasoned green salad.

Scaloppine Tropical

Serves: **4**
Preparation time: **10 minutes**
Cooking time: **25 minutes**
Type of recipe: **elementary**
Cost: **expensive**

With the growing fad of new cuisine dishes we are now faced with a variety of unusual concoctions using unfamiliar fruits or vegetables and new (often unsuccessful) combinations. Braised salmon is served with fresh raspberries, leeks are combined with caviar or sautéed calves' liver—these new combinations are all part of this wave of French cooking laced with the exotic. Some dishes, however, manage to make it and this simply cooked veal cutlet, topped with a slice of kiwi fruit, happens to be one of them. It is an amusing and somewhat unusual-looking dish.

Ingredients

8 small veal scaloppine
Salt and freshly ground white pepper
Flour for dredging
2 to 3 Tablespoons butter
1 teaspoon oil
¼ cup port wine
1 to 1½ cups Brown Chicken Stock (page 531)
1½ to 2 Tablespoons apricot preserves
Few drops lemon juice
1 Beurre Manié (page 544)
1 ripe kiwi fruit, peeled and thinly sliced

Garnish:

Sprigs of fresh watercress
1 kiwi, peeled and sliced

Preparation

1.
Preheat the oven to 325 degrees. Butter a rectangular flameproof baking dish and set aside.

2.
Dry the veal thoroughly with paper towels. Season with salt and pepper and dredge lightly with flour, shaking off the excess.

3.
In a large cast-iron skillet heat 2 tablespoons butter and the oil. When the butter is very hot and the foams starts to subside add the veal a few scaloppine at a time; do not crowd the pan. Sauté the veal over moderate-to-high heat for 1 to 2 minutes on each side, or until the scaloppine are lightly browned. Remove the veal scaloppine and place slightly them overlapping in the baking dish. Continue to sauté remaining veal.

4.
Add remaining tablespoon butter to the skillet and when the butter is very hot add the port wine. Bring to a boil and reduce to a glaze.

5.
Add the stock and bring again to a boil.

6.
Strain the apricot preserves into the skillet and cook the mixture until it is reduced by one third.

7.
Whisk in bits of Beurre Manié; use just enough to thicken the sauce. It should not be too thick. Taste the sauce and correct the seasoning, adding a few drops of lemon juice. (The sauce should have a somewhat sweet-tart flavor.)

Veal Rolls
Italienne

Serves:	**6**
Preparation time:	**25 minutes**
Cooking time:	**50 minutes**
Type of recipe:	**elementary**
Cost:	**expensive**

8.
Spoon a little sauce over each veal scaloppine. Cover the baking dish tightly and place in the center of the oven. Braise for 20 minutes.

9.
Remove the dish from the oven and transfer the veal to a serving platter.

10.
Place the baking dish over low heat on top of stove. (If the sauce has reduced too much add a little more stock.) Taste the sauce and correct the seasoning; you may want to add a little more of the apricot preserves. Add the kiwi slices and heat them gently in the sauce for 1 minute or less.

11.
Place a kiwi slice on each veal scaloppine and spoon the sauce over the entire dish. Garnish with sprigs of fresh watercress and additional kiwi slices and serve immediately.

Ingredients

1 pound ground pork, or a mixture of ½ pork and ½ veal
1 Tablespoon grated onion
¾ cup finely minced cooked spinach
½ teaspoon dried thyme
2 Tablespoons freshly grated Parmesan cheese
1 egg, lightly beaten
2 Tablespoons bread crumbs
Salt and freshly ground white pepper
12 to 14 veal scaloppine
Flour
3 Tablespoons butter
2 Tablespoons oil
12 tiny white onions, peeled
1 teaspoon meat glaze
2 teaspoons tomato paste
1½ cups Brown Chicken Stock (page 531)

Garnish:
Sprigs of fresh parsley
Broccoli purée

Optional:
1 Beurre Manié (page 544)

Preparation

1.
In a bowl combine the ground meat, onion, spinach, thyme, Parmesan cheese, egg, and bread crumbs. Season with salt and pepper. Work the mixture with a wooden spoon until smooth and well blended. Sauté a small spoonful of the mixture, then taste and correct the seasoning.

2.
Season the veal scaloppine with salt and

Paupiettes of Veal
with
Carrots and Onions

Serves: **4 to 6**
Preparation time: **40 minutes**
Cooking time: **30 minutes**
Type of recipe: **intermediate**
Cost: **expensive**

pepper on both sides. Place a little of the meat mixture on each scaloppine, then roll up the scallops and tie them on both ends with kitchen string. Dip in flour, shaking off the excess. Set aside.

3.
Preheat the oven to 325 degrees.

4.
In a large cast-iron skillet heat the butter and oil. Add the veal rolls and cook until nicely browned on all sides. Transfer to a side dish and reserve.

5.
Discard all but 2 tablespoons fat from the pan. Add the onions and cook for 2 to 3 minutes. Roll the onions back and forth in the pan until they are nicely browned. They will not brown evenly.

6.
Add the meat glaze, tomato paste, and stock to the pan. Bring to a boil, scraping well the bottom of the pan. Cook the stock until it is reduced by one third.

7.
Return the veal rolls to the pan and cover and place in the oven. Bake for 20 minutes.

8.
Transfer the veal rolls and onions to a serving platter. If the sauce seems too thin, place the pan over high heat and whisk in bits of Beurre Manié, cooking the sauce until it heavily coats the spoon. Taste, correct the seasoning, and spoon the sauce over the veal rolls. Garnish with sprigs of parsley and a purée of broccoli.

Veal birds are a very good way of braising veal of lesser quality since the stuffing keeps the meat moist. Many vegetable garnishes can be served with this delicious dish. Carrots and onions go particularly well and are my favorite all-season accompaniment.

Ingredients
8 to 12 veal scaloppine
Salt and freshly ground black pepper
1 teaspoon dried thyme
Flour for dredging
5 Tablespoons butter
1 Tablespoons oil
¼ cup dry white wine
1½ cups Brown Chicken Stock (page 531)
1 Bouquet Garni (page 546)
1 cup finely cubed slab bacon
16 small white onions, peeled
Large pinch of granulated sugar
1 pound young carrots, peeled and cut into 1-inch cubes

Stuffing:
½ pound ground veal
1 egg white
¾ cup cold heavy cream
1 large clove garlic, crushed
1 Tablespoon finely minced shallots
Salt and freshly ground black pepper

Optional:
2 teaspoons potato flour or arrowroot, mixed with a little stock

Garnish:
Finely minced fresh parsley

Preparation

1.

Begin by making the stuffing. In a stainless steel bowl that has been chilled for 30 minutes, combine the ground veal and egg white. Start beating the mixture with a small electric beater, adding the cream in a slow stream. Beat the mixture until all the cream has been incorporated into the meat. Add the garlic and shallots and fold them into the mixture. Season with salt and pepper. Set aside.

2.

Season the veal with salt, pepper, and thyme. Place a spoonful of the stuffing on each of the scaloppine. Roll them up and tie the rolls on both ends with kitchen string.

3.

Dredge the rolls lightly with flour, shaking off the excess. Set aside.

4.

Preheat the oven to 325 degrees.

5.

In a large heavy casserole heat 2 tablespoons butter and 1 tablespoon oil. When the butter is very hot and the foam starts to subside add the veal rolls and brown them evenly on all sides. Remove the rolls from the pan. Set aside.

6.

Discard all but 2 tablespoons of fat from the pan and add the wine. Bring to a boil and reduce to 1 tablespoon.

7.

Add ¾ cup stock to the pan and bring to a boil. Season with salt and pepper, then return the veal rolls to the skillet. Add the Bouquet Garni, cover tightly, and place in the oven. Braise the veal rolls for 25 minutes.

8.

While the veal is braising prepare the vegetables. In a small saucepan bring water to a boil, add the bacon cubes, and cook for 2 to 3 minutes. Drain the bacon cubes on a double layer of paper towels, drying them thoroughly.

9.

In a heavy skillet heat the remaining butter and add the bacon cubes. Sauté for 2 minutes, or until they are almost crisp. Remove with a slotted spoon to a side dish and reserve.

10.

Add the onions to the skillet, sprinkle with a pinch of sugar, and season with salt and pepper. Cook the onions for 2 to 3 minutes, tossing them in the butter until they are lightly browned. Add the carrots and the remaining stock. Cover the skillet tightly and cook the vegetables over low heat for 15 to 20 minutes, or until tender. Check the vegetables every 10 minutes to be sure that the stock has not evaporated completely. You may need 2 to 3 tablespoons more stock. Return the bacon cubes to the skillet to heat through. Set aside.

11.

When the veal is done remove it from the oven and transfer the rolls to a serving dish. Add the vegetable-and-bacon mixture to the casserole in which the veal has been cooked. Bring to a boil on top of the stove and whisk in a little of the optional flour mixture if the juices are not thick and

Éminance of Veal
Printanier

Serves:	**4**
Preparation time:	**15 minutes**
Cooking time:	**15 minutes**
Type of recipe:	**elementary**
Cost:	**moderate**

concentrated. Cook until the sauce heavily coats the spoon. Taste and correct the seasoning.

12.
Spoon the vegetable-and-bacon mixture around the veal rolls. Garnish with parsley and serve immediately, accompanied by crusty French bread or sautéed potatoes.

Ingredients

2 leeks
1 carrot, scraped
5 Tablespoons butter
Salt and freshly ground white pepper
4 Tablespoons water
1 pound veal cutlets, pounded thin and cut into thin julienne strips
2 teaspoons oil
2 Tablespoons finely minced shallots
½ cup dry white wine
½ cup concentrated Brown Chicken Stock (page 531)
1 cup heavy cream
1 Beurre Manié (page 544)

Preparation

1.
Remove all but 2 inches of green on the leeks. Rinse the leeks thoroughly under cold water.

2.
Cut both the leeks and carrots into matchsticks 2 inches long and ⅛ inch thick.

3.
In a cast-iron skillet heat 2 tablespoons butter and add the leeks and carrots. Season with salt and pepper and add water. Cover the skillet and simmer the vegetable mixture over low heat for 5 to 6 minutes, or until the vegetables are just tender; do not overcook. Set the pan aside.

4.
Season the veal with salt and pepper. In a large heavy skillet heat 2 tablespoons butter and the oil. When the butter is very hot and the foam starts to subside, add the veal. Do not crowd the pan or the meat will steam and render a great deal of juice. Sauté over high heat for 2 minutes, shaking the pan back and forth to cook the strips evenly. Remove the pan from the heat and transfer the veal to a side dish.

5.
Add the remaining butter to the skillet, then add the shallots and cook for 1 or 2 minutes, or until they are soft and lightly browned.

6.
Add the wine and bring to a boil. Cook until it is reduced to a glaze.

7.
Add the stock to the pan and continue cooking until it is reduced to 2 tablespoons.

8.
Add the cream and bring again to a boil. Season with salt and pepper and cook until the cream is reduced by one third.

9.
Whisk in bits of Beurre Manié; you will only need about a third. The sauce should heavily coat the spoon. Taste the sauce and correct the seasoning.

10.
Remove the skillet from the heat. Return the veal and sautéed vegetables to the sauce and toss lightly. Place the skillet over very low heat and cook until the veal and vegetables are just heated through. Taste again and correct the seasoning, adding a large grinding of white pepper.

11.
Place the veal and vegetables on a serving platter and spoon the sauce over them. Serve immediately accompanied by a gratin of potatoes and a well-seasoned endive salad.

Remarks
For variation you can add 4 to 6 fresh mushrooms, stems removed, and caps cut into thin julienne strips. These should be sautéed separately in 2 tablespoons butter until lightly browned. The mushrooms should be added to the sauce together with the leeks and carrots.

Ragoût of Veal
Provençale

Serves: **4 to 6**
Preparation time: **35 minutes**
Cooking time: **2 hours**
Type of recipe: **elementary**
Cost: **moderate**

Ingredients

3 tablespoons butter
¾ cup olive oil
3 pounds boneless veal shoulder, cut into 1½-inch cubes
Salt and freshly ground black pepper
Flour
2 medium onions, finely minced
6 large cloves garlic, finely minced
4 to 6 ripe tomatoes, peeled, seeded, and chopped, or 1 can (35 ounces) Italian plum tomatoes, drained
1 teaspoon dried thyme
1 teaspoon dried oregano
1 bay leaf
1 large sprig fresh parsley
¾ cup dry white wine
2 cups Chicken Stock (page 530) or bouillon
3 egg yolks
1 Tablespoon lemon juice
1 Tablespoon cornstarch, mixed with a little stock
10 to 12 black olives

Garnish:
2 Tablespoons finely minced fresh parsley

Preparation

1.
Preheat the oven to 350 degrees.

2.
In a cast-iron skillet heat the butter and 1 tablespoon oil. Add the meat; do not crowd the pan. Sauté until nicely browned on all sides, then season with salt and pepper, sprinkle lightly with flour, and toss the meat in the pan until it is evenly coated and lightly glazed. Transfer the meat to a casserole and reserve.

3.
To the fat remaining in the pan add the onions and 2 cloves garlic. Cook the mixture over medium heat until lightly browned, scraping well the bottom of the pan.

4.
Add the tomatoes, herbs, and salt and pepper. Bring to a boil, add the wine, and cook until reduced by half.

5.
Add the stock, bring to a boil, and pour the mixture over the meat. Cover the casserole and set in the oven. Braise the meat for 1 hour, 30 minutes to 1 hour, 45 minutes, or until the meat is tender but not falling apart.

6.
While the meat is braising, combine the remaining garlic and the yolks in a blender. Blend at high speed until smooth, then slowly add the remaining oil by droplets, continuing to blend until the mixture is thick and smooth. Season with salt, pepper, and lemon juice. Set aside.

7.
When the meat is done, remove with a slotted spoon to a side dish. Discard the bay

Ragoût of Veal
with
Rosemary

Serves:	**4 to 5**
Preparation time:	**20 minutes**
Cooking time:	**2 hours**
Type of recipe:	**elementary**
Cost:	**moderate**

leaf and parsley. Bring the pan juices to a boil over high heat and reduce the sauce by one third. Whisk in the cornstarch mixture until the sauce heavily coats the spoon.

8.
Return the meat to the casserole and heat through. Add the garlic sauce, taste, and correct the seasoning. Do not let the sauce return to a boil.

9.
Just before serving add the black olives and heat in the sauce.

10.
Transfer the ragoût to a serving dish, garnish with parsley, and serve accompanied by French bread and a well-seasoned salad.

Remarks
The ragoût can be made 1 or 2 days ahead but do not add the garlic mixture until the last minute. Do not let the sauce come to a boil once the garlic sauce has been added or it will curdle.

The fresh herbs are essential to this simple ragoût. Rosemary is one of the simplest herbs to grow both indoors and outdoors. It does well either potted or planted outdoors in a sunny, dry location. For variation add 1 medium zucchini, cubed and sautéed in 2 tablespoons fruity olive oil, and ½ cup small Niçoise black olives to the ragoût. These will give a distinct provençale flavor to this dish.

Ingredients
3 pounds boneless veal shoulder, cut into 1½-inch cubes
Salt and freshly ground black pepper
4 Tablespoons butter
2 Tablespoons oil
Flour
Pinch of granulated sugar
2 cups finely minced onions
2 large cloves garlic, peeled and finely minced
⅔ cup dry white wine
1 Tablespoon tomato paste
3 large tomatoes, peeled, seeded, and finely chopped
1 large sprig fresh parsley
1 bay leaf
1 large sprig fresh rosemary
1 large sprig fresh thyme
1½ cups Brown Chicken Stock (page 531)
1 Tablespoon potato flour, or arrowroot, mixed with a little stock

Garnish:
2 Tablespoons finely minced fresh parsley

Preparation

1.

Preheat the oven to 350 degrees.

2.

Season the veal with salt and pepper and set aside.

3.

Heat 3 tablespoons butter and 1 tablespoon oil in a large cast-iron skillet. Add the veal a few cubes at a time; do not crowd the pan. Sauté the veal over medium heat until it is nicely browned on all sides. Remove from the pan and reserve. Continue sautéing until all the meat is done.

4.

Return the veal to the skillet. Sprinkle with flour and sugar and toss the meat in the fat until it is well coated with flour and nicely glazed. Transfer the veal to a casserole and set aside.

5.

Add a little more butter and oil to the skillet. Add the onions and garlic and cook the mixture, scraping well the bottom of the pan, until the mixture is nicely browned.

6.

Add the wine, bring to a boil, and reduce to ¼ cup. Set aside.

7.

In a small saucepan put the tomato paste and tomatoes. Bring to a boil and cook for 3 to 4 minutes, or until some of the tomato water has evaporated. Season with salt and pepper, then add the tomato mixture to the veal in the casserole. Bury the parsley sprig, bay leaf, rosemary, and thyme sprigs in the casserole. Add enough of the stock to barely cover the veal.

8.

Cover the casserole and set in the center of the oven. Braise for 1 hour, 15 minutes to 1 hour, 30 minutes, or until the meat is just tender; do not overcook.

9.

With a slotted spoon remove the veal to a side dish and reserve. Strain the pan juices into a bowl, pressing down on the vegetables to extract all the juices. Return the pan juices to the casserole and bring to a boil over high heat, reducing the sauce by one third.

10.

Taste and correct the seasoning. Whisk in a little of the potato flour or arrowroot mixture; add just enough until the sauce is thick and coats a spoon. (The sauce should have a distinct rosemary flavor; if it doesn't add 1 to 2 teaspoons finely minced fresh rosemary to the sauce.)

11.

Return the veal to the casserole and simmer over low heat until heated through. Transfer the ragoût to a serving dish.

12.

Garnish with parsley and serve hot accompanied by a dry Mushroom Risotto Piémontaise (page 328).

Remarks

The entire ragoût can be prepared several days ahead and reheated in a low oven for 35 to 40 minutes, or until heated through. The ragoût can also be frozen successfully for 4 to 6 weeks.

Sauté of Veal
with
Artichokes

Serves:	**4**
Preparation time:	**30 minutes**
Cooking time:	**2 hours**
Type of recipe:	**elementary**
Cost:	**moderate**

Ingredients

3 pounds boneless veal shoulder, cut into 1½-inch cubes
Salt and freshly ground black pepper
3 Tablespoons butter
1 Tablespoon olive oil
2 Tablespoons finely minced shallots
½ cup dry white wine
Flour for dredging
2 large cloves garlic, peeled and crushed
1½ cups Brown Chicken Stock (page 531)
3 medium artichokes
1 lemon, cut in half

Optional:

1 Beurre Manié (page 544)

Garnish:

2 Tablespoons finely minced fresh parsley

Preparation

1.
Preheat the oven to 325 degrees.

2.
Season the meat with salt and pepper. In a 10-inch cast-iron skillet heat 2 tablespoons butter with a little oil. Add the meat a few cubes at a time; do not crowd the pan. Sauté the veal on all sides until it is nicely browned.

3.
Remove the meat from the skillet and continue browning until all the meat is done. Set aside.

4.
Add a little more butter and oil to the pan. Add the shallots and cook until they are nicely browned, scraping well the bottom of the pan. Add 2 tablespoons wine, bring to a boil, and reduce to a glaze.

5.
Return the veal to the skillet, sprinkle lightly with flour, and shake the pan back and forth to evenly coat and glaze the meat with the flour. Add the remaining wine together with the garlic. Bring to a boil and add a few tablespoons stock. Cover the pan tightly and set in the center of the oven. Add 3 to 4 tablespoons stock every 15 minutes until you have added 1 cup stock.

6.
While the veal is braising prepare the artichokes. Remove the outer leaves from the artichokes until they are cone shaped and pale green. With a sharp knife cut off the leaves at the base and rub the artichokes with the cut part of the lemon. Drop into a bowl of water and set aside.

Braised Pork
in
Brown Onion Sauce

Serves:	**6**
Preparation time:	**20 minutes, plus 2 to 4 hours to marinate**
Cooking time:	**2 hours, 35 minutes**
Type of recipe:	**elementary**
Cost:	**moderate**

7.
In a large enamel saucepan bring salted water to a boil. Add the artichokes and cook for 10 to 15 minutes, or until just tender. Drain and, with the tip of a sharp knife, remove the choke and trim the outer part. Cut each into 1-inch cubes and set aside.

8.
Thirty minutes before the veal is done add the artichoke cubes to the skillet, cover, and finish cooking the meat. When done transfer the veal and artichokes with a slotted spoon to a serving dish.

9.
Add the remaining ½ cup stock to the skillet. Bring to a boil and whisk in bits of optional Beurre Manié until the sauce heavily coats the spoon. Taste the sauce and correct the seasoning.

10.
Spoon the sauce over the veal and garnish with parsley. Serve accompanied by a well-seasoned salad and crusty French bread.

Remarks
This is a ragoût cooked in very little liquid, giving it a delicious, very concentrated sauce.

Ingredients
2 Tablespoons soy sauce
1½ Tablespoons Dijon mustard
4 large cloves garlic, peeled and crushed
1 teaspoon dried thyme
1 large sprig fresh rosemary, or 1 teaspoon dried
1 teaspoon finely minced fresh gingerroot
3 Tablespoons olive oil
Freshly ground black pepper
1 three-pound boned and rolled loin of pork, preferably cut from the shoulder end
2 Tablespoons butter
12 to 14 medium white onions, peeled
Salt
2 Tablespoons brown sugar
½ cup dry white wine or dry sherry
1½ cups beef bouillon
1 Bouquet Garni (page 546)
1 Tablespoon cornstarch, mixed with a little stock

Garnish:
Sprigs of fresh watercress

Preparation

1.

Several hours ahead combine in a small bowl the soy sauce, mustard, 2 garlic cloves, thyme, rosemary, and gingerroot. Add 2 tablespoons oil and a large grinding of black pepper. Rub the roast with the mixture. Make tiny slits along the bottom of the roast and insert the remaining 2 garlic cloves. Let the meat marinate for 2 to 4 hours in a cool place or overnight in the refrigerator.

2.

When ready, preheat the oven to 350 degrees.

3.

In a large heavy casserole heat the butter and 1 tablespoon oil. When the butter is very hot and the foam starts to subside add the roast and brown over medium heat until nicely browned on all sides. Be sure to regulate the heat so as not to burn the roast. Transfer the meat to a side dish and reserve.

4.

Discard all but 2 tablespoons of fat from the casserole, then add the onions and season with salt and pepper. Cook the onions, tossing them in the fat until they are nicely browned on all sides. (The onions will not brown evenly.)

5.

Add the sugar and continue cooking the onions until they are well glazed and nicely browned.

6.

Add the wine or sherry and bring to a boil. Reduce to 1 tablespoon.

7.

Add 1 cup bouillon and Bouquet Garni. Remove the casserole from the heat and add the roast. Cover and set in the center of the oven. Braise the roast for 2 hours, 15 minutes, basting it every 15 minutes with the pan juices. When the meat is done, transfer to a cutting board and reserve.

8.

Thoroughly degrease the pan juices and discard the bouquet.

9.

Add the remaining bouillon to the casserole. Set over medium heat and whisk in a little of the cornstarch mixture; add just enough for the sauce to heavily coat a spoon. Taste and correct the seasoning.

10.

Thinly slice the roast and place overlapping slices on a serving platter. Spoon the onion sauce over or around the roast and garnish with sprigs of watercress. Serve immediately, accompanied by a pilaf of rice or a gratin of potatoes.

Casserole-Roasted Pork
Aixoise

Serves: **6**
Preparation time: **30 minutes**
Cooking time: **2 hours, 30 minutes**
Type of recipe: **elementary**
Cost: **moderate**

Ingredients

1 three-pound boned loin of pork, cut from the shoulder end
Salt and freshly ground black pepper
1 teaspoon dried thyme
1 teaspoon dried marjoram
1 teaspoon imported paprika
2 to 3 cloves garlic, peeled and crushed to a paste
1 Tablespoon butter
2 Tablespoons fruity olive oil
2 onions, peeled and cut in eighths
1 Bouquet Garni (page 546)
⅓ cup dry white wine
1 cup Brown Chicken Stock (page 531)
2 teaspoons cornstarch, mixed with a little stock
2 Tablespoons finely minced fresh parsley
1 large clove garlic, peeled and crushed

Vegetable Garnish:

1 cup unpeeled cubed eggplant
1 small zucchini, unpeeled and finely cubed
Salt
6 to 8 Tablespoons fruity olive oil
1 Tablespoon finely minced shallots
2 large fresh tomatoes, peeled, seeded, and chopped
1 to 2 teaspoons tomato paste
1 large Roasted Red Pepper (page 545), thinly sliced, or ½ cup jarred roasted peppers, thinly sliced
½ cup small black oil-cured olives
Freshly ground black pepper

Preparation

1.
For the garnish, sprinkle the eggplant and zucchini cubes with salt and let the vegetables drain separately on a double layer of paper towels.
2.
Preheat the oven to 375 degrees.
3.
Season the roast with salt and pepper, thyme, marjoram, and paprika. Make tiny slits in the roast and insert bits of the garlic paste.
4.
In a large casserole heat the butter and oil. Add the roast and cook over moderate heat until nicely browned on all sides. Add the onions, Bouquet Garni, and wine, and bring to a boil. Cook until the wine is reduced by half.
5.
After the wine is reduced, add ½ cup stock. Cover the casserole and place in the oven. Roast for 2 hours, 15 minutes, basting the pork every 15 minutes with the pan juices.
6.
While the roast is in the oven prepare the vegetable garnish. Dry the zucchini and eggplant cubes thoroughly with paper towels. In a cast-iron skillet heat a little olive oil. Add the eggplant cubes and brown over moderate heat on all sides. Remove with a slotted spoon to a side dish and reserve.
7.
Add a little more oil to the skillet, add the zucchini cubes, and cook for 2 to 3

minutes, or until nicely browned. Remove
from the skillet and reserve.

8.
Add remaining oil to the skillet and add the
shallots. Cook for 1 or 2 minutes, or until
soft but not browned. Add the tomatoes and
a teaspoon tomato paste. Bring to a boil and
cook the mixture until the tomato water has
evaporated and the mixture is thick. Taste
the tomato mixture; if it's slightly acidic,
add the second teaspoon tomato paste and
blend well.

9.
Return the eggplant and zucchini to the
skillet together with the peppers and olives.
Heat the mixture through, season with salt
and pepper, and set aside.

10.
When the roast is done transfer it to a
cutting board and reserve. Discard the
bouquet but leave the onions in the
casserole. Thoroughly degrease the pan
juices.

11.
Place the casserole on top of the stove.
Bring the pan juices to a boil and add the
remaining stock together with the vegetable
garnish. Whisk in a little of the cornstarch
mixture, add just enough to thicken the
sauce if necessary.

12.
Add the parsley and garlic to the sauce.
Taste and correct the seasoning.

13.
Slice the roast, placing the overlapping
slices on a serving platter. Spoon the sauce
along both sides of the roast and serve
immediately with crusty French bread and a

pilaf of rice, or serve with an
accompaniment of cooked white beans
seasoned with a little lemon juice and fruity
olive oil.

Remarks
The roast may be kept warm in a preheated
and then turned-off oven for 30 to 40
minutes. Do not slice the roast until ready to
serve or it may dry out.

Braised Roast Pork
à la Valencienne

Serves: **6**
Preparation time: **15 minutes**
Cooking time: **2 hours, 25 minutes**
Type of recipe: **elementary**
Cost: **moderate**

Ingredients

**1 three-pound boned, rolled roast loin of
pork, preferably cut from the shoulder
end**
Coarse salt
Freshly ground black pepper
1 teaspoon dried thyme
½ teaspoon dried marjoram
1 teaspoon imported paprika
**2 cloves garlic, peeled and crushed to a
paste**
2 Tablespoons butter
1 Tablespoon oil
**1 large onion, peeled and coarsely
chopped**
½ cup scraped and cubed carrots
½ cup dry white wine
1 cup Brown Chicken Stock (page 531)
1 Bouquet Garni (page 546)
2 Tablespoons cognac or brandy
1 cup heavy cream
1 Beurre Manié (page 544)
**1 Roasted Red Pepper (page 545) or ½
cup diced roasted peppers**
1 teaspoon green peppercorns, crushed

Garnish:
Sprigs of fresh watercress

Preparation

1.
Preheat the oven to 350 degrees.
2.
Season the pork roast with coarse salt,
pepper, thyme, marjoram, and paprika,
rubbing it well with the mixture. Make tiny
slits along the bottom of the roast and insert
bits of the garlic paste.
3.
In a large heavy skillet heat the butter and
oil. Add the pork roast and brown it over
low heat on all sides. Be sure to regulate
the heat so as not to burn the fat.
4.
When the meat is nicely browned, transfer
it to a casserole. (If the fat has burned,
discard and replace it with 1 tablespoon
fresh butter.)
5.
Add the onion and carrots to the pan and
cook for 2 to 3 minutes, or until lightly
browned. Add the wine and bring to a boil.
Cook until the wine is reduced by half, then
transfer the onion-and-carrot mixture to the
casserole.
6.
Add ¼ cup stock to the casserole. Add the
Bouquet Garni, cover, and place in the
oven. Braise the roast for 2 hours, basting
every 10 to 15 minutes with the pan juices.
When done, transfer the meat to a carving
board and reserve.
6.
Remove the bouquet and thoroughly
degrease the pan juices. (You must not
leave any fat at all; it is best to degrease
the pan juices by using a defatter.) Return
the pan juices to the casserole and place

Roast Pork Landaise

Serves: **6**
Preparation time: **30 minutes**
Cooking time: **3 hours**
Type of recipe: **elementary**
Cost: **moderate**

the casserole over moderate heat. Reduce the pan juices by half, then add the cognac. Bring to a boil and cook for 2 to 3 minutes, or until the alcohol has evaporated. Add the remaining stock, bring to a boil, and cook over high heat until reduced by half. Whisk in the cream and continue cooking until the cream is reduced by half.

8.
Strain the sauce through a fine sieve into a saucepan. Whisk in bits of Beurre Manié; add just enough until the sauce heavily coats a spoon. Add the diced red pepper and green peppercorns and simmer the sauce covered for another 3 to 4 minutes. Taste the sauce and correct the seasoning.

9.
Carve the roast and place the slices overlapping on a serving platter. Spoon the sauce over the slices, garnish with sprigs of fresh watercress, and serve.

Remarks
The entire dish can be prepared 1 hour ahead. Place the roast on a dish and cover with foil. Place the dish over a pan of hot, but not boiling, water and set aside. Keep the sauce warm until serving.

Ingredients
1 four-pound boned loin of pork
Salt and freshly ground white pepper
1½ teaspoons dried thyme
2 large cloves garlic, peeled and crushed to a paste
2 Tablespoons butter
1 Tablespoon oil
1½ cups hot beef bouillon
2 onions, peeled and cut in eighths

Sauce:
18 to 24 pitted prunes
½ cup port wine
¼ cup granulated sugar
¼ cup red wine vinegar
1½ cups hot Brown Chicken Stock (page 531)
1 Tablespoon arrowroot, mixed with a little cold stock

Optional:
2 to 4 Tablespoons cold butter

Garnish:
Rounds of orange slices
Sprigs of watercress

Preparation

1.
Preheat the oven to 375 degrees.

2.
Soak the prunes for the sauce. Combine the prunes with water to cover in a medium saucepan, bring to a boil, reduce the heat, and simmer for 5 to 7 minutes. Drain the prunes and combine with the port wine in a bowl. Set aside.

3.
Season the roast with salt, pepper, and thyme. Make tiny slits in the meat and insert little pieces of the garlic paste into each slit.

4.
In a large heavy roasting pan heat the butter and oil over medium heat. Place the roast topside down in the pan and brown for 3 to 4 minutes. Do not let the fat burn in the pan. Turn the roast and add ⅓ cup bouillon to the pan together with the onions and set in the oven.

5.
Roast the meat for 2 hours, 45 minutes, basting it every 10 to 15 minutes with a little bouillon. The pan juices must not dry out or the onions will burn. In the last 30 minutes of roasting cover the meat loosely with a sheet of aluminum foil.

6.
While the pork is roasting make the sauce. In a 2-quart saucepan combine the sugar and vinegar. Cook the mixture over high heat until it caramelizes and turns to a thick brown syrup.

7.
Add the stock, being careful to avoid spattering, bring to a boil, and immediately remove from the heat. Set aside.

8.
When the roast is done transfer it to a cutting board.

9.
Strain the prunes, reserving the port.

10.
Carefully degrease the pan juices, then set the roasting pan over moderate heat. Add the port and the caramelized stock and bring to a boil, scraping well the bottom of the pan.

11.
Whisk in a little of the arrowroot mixture and cook the sauce until it is thick and smooth.

12.
Strain the sauce into a heavy saucepan and whisk in the optional cold butter.

13.
Slice the roast, overlapping the slices on a platter. Pour the sauce over the meat and garnish with orange slices and sprigs of watercress. Serve with the spiced carrot and raisin rice on page 337.

Roast Pork
in
Green Peppercorn Sauce

Serves: **4 to 6**
Preparation time: **15 minutes**
Cooking time: **2 hours, 30 minutes**
Type of recipe: **elementary**
Cost: **moderate**

Ingredients

1 four-pound pork loin roast, preferably cut from the shoulder end, bone in
Salt and freshly ground black pepper
½ teaspoon dried thyme
½ teaspoon dried marjoram
½ teaspoon imported paprika
1 large clove garlic, crushed
Flour
2 Tablespoons butter
1 Tablespoon oil
½ cup dry white wine
2 onions, peeled and cut in half
1½ cups Brown Chicken Stock (page 531)
1 Tablespoon crushed green peppercorns
2 teaspoons cornstarch, mixed with a little stock

Garnish:
Sprigs of fresh watercress

Preparation

1.
Preheat the oven to 350 degrees.

2.
Season the roast with salt, pepper, thyme, marjoram, and paprika. With the tip of a sharp knife make tiny incisions and insert the pieces of garlic. Sprinkle the roast lightly with flour.

3.
In a large flameproof baking pan, heat the butter and oil. Add the roast, fat-side down, and sauté over low heat until nicely browned. Turn the roast over and sauté for another 3 to 4 minutes. Add the wine to the pan, bring to a boil, and add the onions. Place the pan in the oven and roast for 2 hours, 30 minutes, adding 3 to 4 tablespoons stock every 15 minutes and basting the roast with the pan juices.

4.
When the roast is done transfer it to a serving platter, slice thinly, and keep warm.

5.
Carefully degrease the pan juices. Place the baking pan over high heat, bring the pan juices to a boil, add the peppercorns, and whisk in a little of the cornstarch paste until the sauce heavily coats a spoon.

6.
Taste and correct the seasoning. Spoon the sauce over the pork, garnish with sprigs of watercress, and serve accompanied by braised rice, buttered noodles, or a potato purée.

Roast Pork
in
Onion Sauce

Serves: **6**
Preparation time: **35 minutes**
Cooking time: **3 hours**
Type of recipe: **elementary**
Cost: **moderate**

Ingredients

1 four-pound boned loin of pork
Salt and freshly ground black
pepper
1 teaspoon dried marjoram
1 teaspoon dried thyme
1 teaspoon dried rosemary
1 teaspoon imported paprika
3 cloves garlic, peeled and crushed with
a little salt to a paste
4 Tablespoons butter
1 Tablespoon olive oil
1½ to 2 cups Brown Chicken Stock
(page 531) or beef bouillon
½ cup dry white wine
16 to 18 small white onions
2 Tablespoons brown sugar
¼ teaspoon ground cinnamon
1 Tablespoon cornstarch, mixed with a
little stock

Garnish:
Sprigs of fresh watercress

Preparation

1.
Preheat the oven to 375 degrees.

2.
Season the pork with salt and pepper. Rub with marjoram, thyme, rosemary, and paprika. Make small slits in the roast and insert a little of the garlic paste into each slit. Set aside.

3.
In a large oval or rectangular baking dish heat 2 tablespoons butter and 1 teaspoon oil over medium heat. Place the roast top-side down and brown on all sides for 2 to 3 minutes.

4.
Transfer the baking dish to the oven. Add 2 to 3 tablespoons stock or bouillon to the pan and baste the roast with it. When the liquid has evaporated add ¼ cup wine and continue roasting until the wine has evaporated.

5.
Add the remaining wine and again roast until the wine has evaporated, basting the roast 2 to 3 times with the pan juices.

6.
Add a little more stock to the pan. You will need 2 to 3 tablespoons every 10 to 15 minutes. Roast the pork for a total of 2 hours, 45 minutes, basting with the pan juices.

7.
While the roast is in the oven drop the onions into boiling water for 1 minute. Drain the onions and peel without slicing off the root ends. Cut a small cross about ½ inch deep in the root end of each onion. This will keep them from bursting later.

8.
In a 10-inch cast-iron skillet heat the remaining butter and oil. Add the onions and sauté until they are browned on all sides, shaking the pan back and forth to cook them evenly.

9.
Add the brown sugar, cinnamon, salt, and pepper and sauté the onions for another 2 to 3 minutes, or until well coated with the sugar.

10.
Add a little stock. Cover the pan and braise the onions over the lowest possible heat for 15 to 20 minutes, or until tender. Check the

Viennese
Roast Pork

Serves:	**4 to 6**
Preparation time:	**35 minutes, place 2 hours to soak prunes**
Cooking time:	**2 hours, 30 minutes**
Type of recipe:	**elementary**
Cost:	**moderate**

onions several times to make sure that the sugar is not burning in the pan; you may need a little more stock. Set the onions aside.

11.
When the roast is done transfer it to a cutting board and slice thinly. Place the slices overlapping on a serving platter and keep warm.

12.
Carefully degrease the pan juices. Place the roasting pan over direct heat. Add the onions and any remaining stock to the pan. Bring to a boil and whisk in a little bit of the cornstarch mixture; add just enough until the sauce heavily coats a spoon.

13.
Spoon the sauce and the onions over the roast and garnish the platter with sprigs of fresh watercress. Serve immediately.

Remarks
You can add sautéed cubed turnips to the sauce just before serving. The Potato and Turnip Purée (page 439) is another delicious accompaniment to this dish.

Ingredients
1 package (1 pound) pitted prunes
½ cup dry white wine
1 four-pound loin of pork, bone in
Salt and freshly ground black pepper
1 teaspoon dried thyme
1 teaspoon dried marjoram
3 Tablespoons oil
1 large carrot, scraped and coarsely chopped
1 large onion, peeled and chopped
2 stalks celery, peeled and chopped
1½ cups hot beef bouillon or Brown Chicken Stock (page 531)
¾ cup heavy cream
1 Tablespoon cornstarch, mixed with a little bouillon

Preparation
1.
Combine the prunes and wine in an enamel saucepan. Heat slowly without letting the wine come to a boil. Set aside for 2 hours.

2.
Preheat the oven to 350 degrees.

3.
Season the roast with salt, pepper, thyme, and marjoram.

4.
Heat the oil in a large flameproof baking dish. Place the roast fat-side down first and then brown on both sides over medium heat.

5.
Transfer the roast to a side dish. Add the vegetables to the pan and cook for 3 to 4 minutes. Return the roast to the baking dish. Set in the center of the oven and bake for 2

Braised Pork Chops Aosta

Serves:	**4 to 6**
Preparation time:	**40 minutes**
Cooking time:	**40 minutes**
Type of recipe:	**elementary**
Cost:	**moderate**

hours to 2 hours, 15 minutes, basting several times with the hot bouillon or stock.

6.
When done transfer the roast to a platter and keep warm in a turned-off oven.

7.
Place the baking dish over direct heat. Drain the prunes and reserve. Pour the wine into the dish and cook until the wine and pan juices are reduced by ½.

8.
Strain the pan juices into a heavy 1-quart saucepan, pressing down on the vegetables to extract all the juices.

9.
Add the cream. Bring the sauce to a boil, stirring constantly until it is reduced by ⅓. Add the prunes, then whisk in a little of the cornstarch mixture until the sauce heavily coats the spoon. Season with salt and pepper and reserve.

10.
Slice the roast. Place the slices on a serving platter and spoon the sauce over it. Serve accompanied by braised rice and Sautéed Apples (page 546).

Ingredients
1 pound fresh chestnuts
4 Tablespoons butter
2 teaspoons oil
12 to 16 small white onions, peeled
Sprinkling of granulated sugar
Salt and freshly ground black pepper
1 to 1½ cups Brown Chicken Stock (page 531)
4 to 6 pork chops, cut ¾ inch thick, preferably from the shoulder end
Flour for dredging
¼ cup dry white wine
2 large cloves garlic, peeled and crushed
1 Bouquet Garni, of 1 large sprig fresh thyme or 1 teaspoon dried, 1 large sprig fresh parsley, and 1 bay leaf
1 teaspoon cornstarch, mixed with a little stock

Garnish:
Sprigs of fresh watercress

Preparation

1.

Cut a sharp slit on the flat side of the chestnuts with the tip of a sharp knife. Drop the chestnuts into rapidly boiling water and cook for 3 to 5 minutes. Leaving the rest of the chestnuts in the hot water, remove 2 to 3 at a time and peel with a sharp knife, discarding the brown inner skin. Reserve the peeled chestnuts.

2.

Heat 2 tablespoons butter and a little oil in a 10-inch skillet. Add the onions and sprinkle with sugar and a pinch of salt and pepper. Roll the onions in the butter until they are lightly browned and slightly caramelized. The onions will not brown evenly.

3.

Add the chestnuts and ¾ cup stock. Bring to a boil, reduce the heat, cover the skillet, and simmer the onion-and-chestnut mixture for 15 minutes, or until the vegetables are tender. If the chestnuts are still tough remove the onions with a slotted spoon and set aside. Let the chestnuts cook covered for 10 minutes more, or until tender but not falling apart. Return the onions to the skillet and keep the mixture warm.

4.

Preheat the oven to 325 degrees.

5.

Season the pork chops with salt and pepper. Dredge lightly with flour, shaking off the excess.

6.

In a large heavy skillet heat the remaining butter and oil. Add the chops 2 to 3 at a time; do not crowd the pan. Sauté the chops until they are nicely browned on both sides. When the chops are done remove them to a casserole and reserve.

7.

When all the chops have been browned discard all but 2 tablespoons of fat from the skillet.

8.

Add the wine, bring to a boil, and reduce to 1 tablespoon. Add the remaining stock and the garlic. Bring to a boil and pour over the chops. Bury the Bouquet Garni among the chops and cover the casserole.

9.

Place the casserole in the center of the oven and braise for 25 minutes. Turn the chops once during their cooking time and baste them once or twice with the pan juices.

10.

When the chops are done transfer them to a serving platter. Degrease the pan juices carefully. Discard the bouquet. Add the onions and chestnuts as well as their cooking juices to the casserole and simmer on top of the stove for 2 to 3 minutes to heat through.

11.

Whisk in the cornstarch mixture; add just enough to thicken the sauce. Taste and correct the seasoning. Spoon the onion-and-chestnut mixture over the chops. Garnish the platter with sprigs of fresh watercress and serve with a potato purée or braised rice.

Sautéed Pork Chops
Martegal

Serves:	**4**
Preparation time:	**35 minutes, plus 24 to 48 hours to marinate**
Cooking time:	**45 minutes**
Type of recipe:	**elementary**
Cost:	**moderate**

Ingredients

4 pork chops, shoulder or loin, cut ¾ to 1 inch thick
Coarse salt
Freshly ground black pepper
2 Tablespoons butter
1 Tablespoon olive oil
1 large sprig fresh thyme
1 onion, peeled and cut in half
½ cup dry white wine
½ cup Brown Chicken Stock (page 531)

Marinade:
¼ cup lemon juice
½ cup olive oil
2 Tablespoons finely minced fresh thyme, or 1 teaspoon dried
2 bay leaves
2 large cloves garlic, finely minced
1 onion, peeled and thinly sliced

Herb Butter:
6 Tablespoons butter, softened
1 Tablespoon finely minced shallots
2 large cloves garlic, peeled and crushed
2 Tablespoons finely minced fresh parsley
2 Tablespoons lemon juice

Garnish:
Sprigs of fresh parsley
1 lemon, quartered

Preparation

1.
One or 2 days ahead prepare the marinade. In a shallow glass or porcelain bowl combine the ingredients for the marinade. Add the chops in a single layer and spoon the marinade over them. Cover the bowl and refrigerate for 24 to 48 hours, turning the chops 2 to 3 times during their marinating period.

2.
While the chops are marinating prepare the herb butter. In a bowl combine the softened butter, shallots, garlic, parsley, and lemon juice. Blend the mixture thoroughly with a fork and chill.

3.
The next day, remove the chops from the marinade and dry thoroughly on paper towels. Season with coarse salt and ground pepper.

4.
In a large cast-iron skillet heat the butter and oil. Add the chops, thyme, and onion. Do not crowd the pan. Sauté the chops over moderate-to-high heat until they are nicely browned on both sides.

5.
Add ¼ cup of the wine to the skillet. Bring to a boil and cook until the wine is reduced to a glaze.

6.
Add ¼ cup stock to the pan and bring to a boil. Cover tightly and simmer the chops over very low heat for 35 minutes, adding a little more wine and a little more stock to the pan every 10 minutes and turning the chops 2 to 3 times. When the chops are

Ragoût of Pork Indienne

Serves:	**6**
Preparation time:	**30 minutes, plus 2 to 4 hours to drain eggplant**
Cooking time:	**2 hours**
Type of recipe:	**elementary**
Cost:	**inexpensive**

done transfer them to a serving platter and keep warm.

7.
Carefully degrease the pan juices. There should be about 2 to 3 tablespoons of sauce in the pan. Discard the onion and thyme.

8.
Remove the skillet from the heat and whisk in the reserved chilled herb butter. When the butter has melted taste the sauce and correct the seasoning, adding more lemon juice to taste.

9.
Spoon the sauce over the chops. Garnish the platter with sprigs of parsley and lemon quarters. Serve immediately accompanied by buttered and parslied new potatoes.

One of the most interesting aspects of cooking is to combine the techniques and flavors of various cuisines. This ragoût is prepared in the traditional French manner using some Indian spices, which give the dish a particularly interesting character.

Ingredients
1 large eggplant, peeled and cut into 1-inch cubes
Salt
3 pounds pork butt, cut into 1½-inch cubes
Freshly ground black pepper
½ cup peanut oil
2 Tablespoons butter
2 onions, peeled and finely minced
2 large cloves garlic, finely minced
1 Tablespoon fresh gingerroot, finely minced
1 hot chili pepper, crumbled
2 teaspoons medium curry powder
1 teaspoon ground cumin
1 teaspoon ground coriander
1 Tablespoon tomato paste
1 can (35 ounces) Italian plum tomatoes, drained and chopped
1 cup Brown Chicken Stock (page 531), or beef bouillon
1 Tablespoon cornstarch, mixed with a little stock

Garnish:
2 cups yogurt, flavored with
2 cloves garlic, crushed

1.

Place the eggplant cubes on a double layer of paper towels. Sprinkle with salt, cover with another layer of paper towels, and let drain for 2 to 4 hours or overnight.

2.

Preheat the oven to 375 degrees.

3.

Dry the meat thoroughly with paper towels. Season with salt and pepper.

4.

In a heavy 10- to 12-inch skillet heat 2 tablespoons oil and the butter. Add the meat a few pieces at a time; do not crowd the pan. Sauté over medium heat until nicely browned on all sides. Transfer the meat to a large casserole and continue sautéing until all the meat is done.

5.

Discard all but 2 tablespoons of fat from the pan. Add the onions, garlic, and gingerroot and cook the mixture until soft and nicely browned, scraping well the bottom of the skillet.

6.

Add the chili pepper, curry powder, cumin, coriander, and tomato paste and cook for another 2 to 3 minutes.

7.

Add the tomatoes, bring to a boil, and cook the mixture for 3 to 4 minutes. Season with salt and pepper and pour into the casserole. Add the stock or bouillon.

8.

Set the casserole in the center of the oven and braise the ragoût covered for 1 hour, 30 minutes, or until the meat is tender but not falling apart.

9.

While the meat is braising, heat the remaining oil in a large heavy skillet and add the eggplant cubes; do not crowd the pan. Sauté until nicely browned on all sides. You may need more oil.

10.

Drain the eggplant in a colander and reserve. Continue sautéing until all the eggplant is done.

11.

When the meat is done remove the casserole from the oven. Carefully degrease the pan juices and place the casserole over low heat. If the sauce seems too thin whisk in a little of the cornstarch mixture and simmer the ragoût until the sauce heavily coats a spoon.

12.

Add the eggplant cubes and heat through. Taste and correct the seasoning. Serve the ragoût hot accompanied by a well-seasoned green salad and a bowl of garlic-flavored yogurt.

Remarks

The ragoût can be made 2 to 3 days in advance and reheated. It can also be frozen successfully. Other vegetables, such as cubed zucchini and thinly sliced peppers sautéed in olive oil, can be added to the ragoût together with the eggplant. This ragoût is mildly spicy. If you like a spicier flavor use 2 hot chili peppers in cooking the ragoût.

Ragoût of Pork
Ticino

Serves: **5 to 6**
Preparation time: **15 minutes**
Cooking time: **1 hour, 45 minutes**
Type of recipe: **elementary**
Cost: **inexpensive**

Ingredients
**1 ounce imported dried Italian
mushrooms
2 cups Brown Chicken Stock (page 531)
or beef bouillon
3 pounds pork butt, cut in 1½-inch cubes
Salt and freshly ground black pepper
2 Tablespoons butter
3 Tablespoons oil
Large pinch flour
2 large onions, finely minced
1½ teaspoons imported paprika
1 Tablespoon tomato paste
1 Bouquet Garni (page 546)
2 teaspoons potato flour, mixed with a
little stock
1 cup sour cream**

Garnish:
Finely minced fresh parsley

Preparation
1.
Wash the mushrooms thoroughly under cold
running water and combine with the stock
or beef bouillon in a small saucepan. Bring
the stock to a boil, cover, and reduce the
heat. Simmer the mushrooms for 20 to 25
minutes, or until tender.
2.
Drain the mushrooms, reserving the stock.
Dice the mushrooms finely and set aside.
3.
Preheat the oven to 350 degrees.
4.
Dry the meat thoroughly with paper towels.
5.
In a 10-inch cast-iron skillet heat 1
tablespoon each butter and oil. Add the

meat cubes a few at a time; do not crowd
the pan. Sauté the meat over
moderate-to-high heat until nicely browned
on all sides. Season with salt and pepper
and transfer to a side dish.
6.
Add 1 tablespoon butter and 1 teaspoon oil
to the skillet and continue sautéing until all
the meat is done.
7.
Return the meat to the skillet and
sprinkle lightly with flour. Cook for
another 2 minutes, shaking the pan
back and forth until all the meat is well
coated with the flour and nicely glazed.
Transfer the meat to a casserole and
reserve.
8.
Heat a little more oil in the skillet and add
the onions and garlic. Sauté the mixture
until the onions are soft and lightly
browned, scraping well the bottom of the
pan.
9.
Add the paprika and tomato paste and cook
the mixture for another 1 or 2 minutes,
being careful not to burn it.
10.
Add the mushroom stock. Bring to a boil
and pour the onion-and-stock mixture over
the meat. Add the Bouquet Garni and cover
the casserole.
11.
Place the casserole in the center of the
oven and braise the ragoût for 1 hour, 30
minutes, or until just tender. When the
meat is done remove it with a slotted spoon
to a side dish. Remove and discard the
bouquet.

Viennese
Ragoût of Pork

Serves: **6**
Preparation time: **35 minutes**
Cooking time: **2 hours**
Type of recipe: **elementary**
Cost: **inexpensive**

Here is a gutsy country stew from Central Europe that is perfect for a cold winter evening. It is a good-natured dish that can be easily reheated. For variation, add 2 sliced garlic sausages to the stew and/or 2 red potatoes, peeled and cubed. These should be added to the stew 15 minutes before the meat is done.

Ingredients

3 pounds pork butt, cubed
Salt and freshly ground black pepper
3 Tablespoons oil (olive)
1 Tablespoon butter
1 dried hot chili pepper, crumbled
3 cups thinly sliced onions
2 teaspoons imported paprika
1 large green pepper, seeded and thinly sliced 1" squares
1 red pepper, seeded and thinly sliced, or ½ cup Italian roasted peppers, thinly sliced
1 can (35 ounces) Italian plum tomatoes, well drained and chopped
1 bay leaf
1 teaspoon dried thyme
1 teaspoon dried marjoram
1 Tablespoon caraway seeds
1 to 1½ cups Brown Chicken Stock (page 531) or beef bouillon
2 cups sauerkraut, well drained (1 lb. 10 oz can)

12.
Place the casserole on the stove over high heat. Add the diced mushrooms and whisk in a little of the potato flour paste; add just enough to thicken the sauce. It should heavily coat a spoon. Taste the sauce and correct the seasoning.

13.
Return the meat to the casserole and heat through over low heat. Add the sour cream and blend it gently into the sauce. Do not let the sauce return to a boil or the sour cream will curdle.

14.
Garnish the ragoût with parsley and serve accompanied by buttered noodles or Basic Risotto (page 327) and a well-seasoned green salad.

Remarks
This ragoût can be done 2 to 3 days ahead. As a matter of fact it is best when done in advance and reheated since the mushrooms will then impart all of their delicious flavor to the ragoût. The ragoût can also be frozen successfully for 6 to 8 weeks.

Preparation

1.
Dry the meat thoroughly with paper towels. Season with salt and pepper.

2.
Heat 2 tablespoons oil and the butter in a large heavy skillet. Add the meat a few pieces at a time; do not crowd the pan. Sauté over moderate-to-high heat until the cubes are nicely browned on all sides.

3.
Remove the meat with a slotted spoon to a side dish and continue sautéing until all the meat is browned.

4.
Transfer the meat to a heavy casserole. Discard all but 2 tablespoons of fat from the pan. Add the chili pepper and cook for 1 minute, or until it turns dark. Discard the chili pepper and add the onions to the skillet. Cook the onions over low heat until they are soft and nicely browned, scraping well the bottom of the pan.

5.
Add the paprika and cook for 1 minute. Add the green and red peppers, tomatoes, and herbs and bring to a boil. Season the mixture with salt, pepper, and caraway seeds. Transfer the mixture to the casserole and add enough stock or bouillon to cover the meat.

6.
Cover the casserole tightly and place in the oven. Braise the meat for 1 hour, 30 minutes, or until tender.

350° oven

7.
When the meat is tender remove it with a slotted spoon to a side dish and reserve.

8.
Place the casserole over high heat and reduce the pan juices until they heavily coat a spoon. Taste and correct the seasoning.

9.
Add the sauerkraut to the casserole and heat through.

10.
Return the meat to the casserole. Heat through and serve the ragoût accompanied by a purée of potatoes or simply slices of black bread and a cucumber-and-sour cream salad.

Remarks
The entire dish should be made a day or so ahead and reheated, either on top of the stove or in a 250-degree oven. This gives a chance for the ragoût to develop flavor.

Roast Leg of Lamb
Paloise

Serves:	**6 to 8**
Preparation time:	**30 minutes**
Cooking time:	**1 hour, 30 minutes**
Type of recipe:	**elementary**
Cost:	**expensive**

A roast leg of lamb, properly seasoned and cooked, makes without doubt one of the easiest and most delicious meals in every season. Here is my favorite way to prepare lamb in the late spring and all during the summer when fresh mint is available. Mint is one of the easiest herbs to grow and is now available in many specialty markets throughout the country.

Ingredients
1 six- to six-and-one-half-pound leg of lamb (weight after trimming)
Coarse salt
Freshly ground black pepper
2 Tablespoons finely minced fresh thyme, or 1½ teaspoons dried
1 teaspoon dried marjoram
1 Tablespoon Dijon mustard
2 teaspoons imported paprika
3 large cloves garlic, peeled and crushed
2 Tablespoons butter
1 Tablespoon olive oil
2 small onions, peeled and cut in half
1 large sprig fresh thyme
1 large sprig fresh rosemary
1 to 1½ cups hot beef bouillon

Sauce:
3 large egg yolks
1 to 1½ teaspoons white wine vinegar
1 ice cube
¾ cup cold butter, cut into 1-inch pieces
Salt and freshly ground white pepper
2 Tablespoons finely minced fresh mint

Optional:
1 tablespoon finely minced fresh thyme

Garnish:
Sprigs of fresh mint or parsley

Preparation
1.
Preheat the oven to 375 degrees.
2.
Season the lamb with salt, pepper, thyme, and marjoram. Rub the roast with mustard and paprika. Make tiny slits along the bottom of the roast and insert the pieces of garlic.
3.
In a large flameproof baking dish heat the butter and oil. Place the roast in the pan and drizzle a little of the hot oil over it. Scatter the onion pieces in the pan and add the sprigs of thyme and rosemary. Set the dish in the oven and roast the lamb for 1 hour, 20 minutes to 1 hour, 30 minutes (or count 12 minutes per pound). Baste the roast every 10 minutes with a little hot stock.
4.
While the roast is in the oven make the sauce. In a heavy enamel 2-quart saucepan, combine the yolks, vinegar, and ice cube. Whisk the mixture over the lowest possible heat until it just starts to thicken. Immediately add 2 pieces cold butter, whisking until the butter is melted. Continue adding the cold butter in pieces until all the butter has been absorbed and the sauce is thick and smooth. (If at any time the sauce shows signs of curdling immediately remove the saucepan from the heat and whisk in 1 tablespoon ice water.)

Roast Leg of Lamb
in
Garlic Sauce

Serves:	**6**
Preparation time:	**25 minutes, plus 2 hours to rest the meat**
Cooking time:	**1 hour, 30 minutes**
Type of recipe:	**elementary**
Cost:	**expensive**

5.
Season the sauce with salt and pepper and add the mint and optional thyme. Place the saucepan in a pan of warm water, place over the lowest heat, and keep warm, whisking it every 10 minutes.

6.
When the roast is done, transfer it to a serving platter. Set aside and keep warm.

7.
Thoroughly degrease the pan juices. Discard the onions and sprigs of rosemary and thyme and place the baking pan on top of the stove. Add any remaining bouillon and boil the pan juices until they are reduced by half.

8.
Add ¼ cup of the pan juices to the mint sauce, whisk to blend, and transfer the sauce to a serving dish.

9.
Spoon any remaining pan juices over the roast. Garnish with sprigs of fresh mint or parsley and serve the remaining sauce on the side.

Remarks
Any leftover mint sauce can be frozen. To defrost and reheat, set the sauce in a saucepan over a pan of warm water and as it melts whisk in a little ice water, plus 2 to 4 tablespoons additional butter.

Ingredients
1 six- to six-and-one-half-pound leg of lamb (weight after trimming)
Salt and freshly ground black pepper
1 teaspoon dried marjoram
1 teaspoon dried thyme
1 teaspoon dried rosemary
1½ teaspoons imported paprika
1½ teaspoons Dijon mustard
2 large cloves garlic, peeled and crushed
4 anchovy fillets, crushed
3 Tablespoons butter
1 Tablespoon oil olive
1 medium onion, peeled and cut in half
2 cups hot Brown Lamb Stock (page 534) or beef bouillon

Sauce:
16 large cloves garlic, peeled
2 tablespoons butter
1 small onion, finely minced, or 3 large shallots, peeled and finely minced
2 large ripe tomatoes, peeled, seeded, and chopped
Salt and freshly ground black pepper
1 teaspoon dried thyme

Optional:
2 tablespoons finely minced fresh basil
1 tablespoon cornstarch, mixed with a little stock

Garnish:
Sprigs of fresh watercress

Preparation

1.
Two hours before roasting season the lamb with salt, pepper, marjoram, thyme, and rosemary. Rub the roast with paprika and mustard. Make tiny slits along the bottom of the roast and insert bits of the garlic and the anchovy fillets. Set the lamb aside at room temperature for 2 hours.

2.
Preheat the oven to 375 degrees.

3.
In a large heavy flameproof baking dish heat the butter and oil. Place the onion halves in the dish, then place the roast in the baking dish and spoon some of the melted butter over it. Place the lamb in the oven and roast for 1 hour, 20 minutes, or 12 minutes per pound, basting it every 10 minutes with a little of the hot stock.

4.
While the lamb is roasting make the sauce. In a small saucepan bring salted water to boil. Add the garlic and cook for 5 minutes, or until tender. Drain the cloves and mash them to a paste in a mortar or purée them in a blender. Set the garlic paste aside.

5.
In a small heavy skillet heat the butter. Add the onion or shallots and cook for 2 minutes without browning. Add the tomatoes, salt, pepper, thyme, and optional basil. Cook the mixture until it is reduced to a thick purée. Add the garlic paste and reserve.

6.
When the lamb is done transfer it to a serving platter, cover it, and keep warm.

7.
Carefully degrease the pan juices. Place the baking dish over high heat and add any remaining stock to the pan. Bring to a boil and reduce the pan juices to ½ cup. Add the tomato fondue and heat through.

8.
Add a little of the optional cornstarch mixture; use just enough to thicken the sauce if necessary. (This may not be necessary if the pan juices have been well reduced and concentrated.) Taste the sauce and correct the seasoning.

9.
Garnish the lamb roast with sprigs of fresh watercress and serve the garlic sauce on the side.

Remarks
Poaching the garlic cloves renders them quite harmless and they will add an interesting and somewhat sweet taste to the sauce. At 12 minutes per pound the lamb will be cooked to medium rare, which is the correct way of serving lamb. However, if you like the meat done more, roast the lamb for 14 minutes per pound.

Braised Leg of Lamb Arlésienne

Serves: **6**
Preparation time: **15 minutes**
Cooking time: **3 hours, 45 minutes**
Type of recipe: **elementary**
Cost: **expensive**

While Provençale cooking is basically simple and straightforward, it is often ingenious in its use of herbs. Here is an unusual dish from Provence that is both simple and absolutely delicious. The slow, long braising of the lamb, with its 50 cloves of garlic, results in a most tender piece of meat that can be served with a spoon, and a rich and concentrated sauce.

Ingredients

1 six-and-one-half- to seven-pound leg of lamb, boned and rolled
Salt and freshly ground black pepper
1 teaspoon dried marjoram
2 Tablespoons finely minced fresh rosemary, or 1 teaspoon dried
2 Tablespoons finely minced fresh thyme, or 1 teaspoon dried
2 large cloves garlic, peeled and finely mashed
2 Tablespoons fruity olive oil
1 Tablespoon butter
¼ cup Armagnac or cognac
1 cup dry white wine
1¼ cups Brown Chicken Stock (page 531)
2 medium onions, peeled and quartered
50 large cloves garlic, peeled
2 teaspoons cornstarch, mixed with a little stock

Garnish:
Sprigs of fresh parsley

Preparation

1.
Preheat the oven to 350 degrees.

2.
Dry the meat thoroughly with paper towels. Season with salt and pepper, then rub with marjoram, rosemary, and thyme. Make tiny slits in the meat and insert pieces of the mashed garlic. Set aside.

3.
In a heavy oval casserole heat the oil and butter. When the fat is very hot add the roast and brown over medium heat on all sides. Add the Armagnac or cognac, spooning it over the meat, and cook, turning the meat until all the cognac has evaporated.

4.
Add the wine and bring to a boil. Add ½ cup stock, the onions, and the garlic. Cover the casserole with foil and then top with the lid. (The casserole must be tightly covered.) Set in the center of the oven.

5.
Braise the lamb for 3 hours, 30 minutes, basting it every 15 to 20 minutes with the pan juices. When the lamb is done transfer it carefully to a deep serving platter. It will be very tender and can easily fall apart. Remove the strings and set aside.

6.
Carefully degrease the pan juices, leaving the onions and garlic in the casserole.

7.
Place the casserole over medium heat and add the remaining stock. Bring to a boil and whisk in a little of the cornstarch mixture; use just enough to thicken the

Braised Lamb
in
Red Wine

Serves:	**6 to 8**
Preparation time:	**30 minutes, plus overnight to marinate**
Cooking time:	**3 hours, 30 minutes**
Type of recipe:	**elementary**
Cost:	**expensive**

sauce. Taste the sauce and correct the seasoning.

8.
Spoon the sauce over the lamb and garnish with sprigs of parsley. Serve with a side dish of a potato-and-turnip purée or gratin of potatoes and a well-seasoned green salad.

Remarks

The long braising of the garlic cloves with the lamb renders them quite harmless. As a matter of fact they will be very sweet, and they will add a marvelous texture to the sauce. The lamb can be cooked hours in advance and reheated in the pan juices in a low oven or over low heat on top of the stove.

Ingredients

1 six to seven pound leg of lamb, boned and rolled
4 Tablespoons butter
1 Tablespoon oil
4 large ripe tomatoes, peeled, seeded, and chopped
Salt and freshly ground black pepper
2 cups beef bouillon or Brown Chicken Stock (page 531)
12 to 16 small white onions
1 teaspoon granulated sugar
1 Tablespoon cornstarch, mixed with a little stock

Marinade:

2 cups burgundy wine
Salt and freshly ground black pepper
2 large cloves garlic, peeled and crushed
2 bay leaves
2 carrots, scraped and sliced
1 large stalk celery, thinly sliced
2 onions, peeled and thinly sliced
1½ teaspoons dried thyme
¼ cup brandy
3 Tablespoons fruity olive oil

Sauce Garnish:

½ cup finely minced fresh parsley
2 large cloves garlic, peeled and finely minced
½ cup Greek black olives, finely minced

Optional:

6 to 8 anchovy fillets, finely minced
1 to 2 Tablespoons tiny capers, well drained

Garnish:
Sprigs of fresh parsley

Preparation

1.
The day before, place the lamb in an earthenware casserole. Add the marinade ingredients and turn the lamb in the marinade. Cover the dish and marinate the lamb in the refrigerator overnight.

2.
The next day dry the lamb thoroughly with paper towels. Reserve the marinade but discard the bay leaves.

3.
Preheat the oven to 325 degrees.

4.
In a heavy oval casserole heat 2 tablespoons butter and the oil. Add the lamb and sauté over moderate-to-high heat until the meat is nicely browned on all sides. Remove the meat to a side dish and reserve.

5.
Discard all but 1 tablespoon of fat from the casserole. Add the tomatoes and season with salt and pepper. Cook over high heat until all the tomato water has evaporated and the mixture is thick. Return the meat to the casserole and season again with salt and pepper.

6.
Add the marinade together with its vegetables to the casserole and add 1½ cups bouillon or stock. Cover the casserole tightly and place in the center of the oven. Braise the lamb for 3 hours, basting every 15 minutes with the pan juices. When the lamb is done it should be easily pierced with a fork.

7.
While the lamb is braising prepare the onions. In a saucepan bring water to a boil. Add the onions and cook for 2 to 3 minutes. Drain the onions and peel.

8.
In a heavy skillet heat the remaining butter. Add the onions, sprinkle with a little sugar, and sauté, shaking the pan back and forth until the onions are nicely browned. They will not brown evenly. Add the remaining ½ cup stock. Season with salt and pepper. Cover the skillet, reduce the heat, and let the onions simmer for 10 to 15 minutes, or until just tender. Set aside.

9.
When the lamb is done transfer it carefully to a carving board. Slice into serving pieces and place overlapping on a serving platter. Cover the platter and keep warm.

10.
Strain the contents of the casserole into a heavy saucepan, pressing down on the vegetables to extract all their juices. Thoroughly degrease the pan juices and bring to a boil over high heat. Cook the pan juices until they are reduced to 1½ cups.

11.
Add the onions and their cooking liquid. Return to a boil and whisk in a little of the cornstarch mixture; use just enough to thicken the sauce. Keep the sauce warm.

12.
Prepare the sauce garnish. In a small bowl combine the parsley, garlic, optional anchovies, and optional capers. Add the

Lamb Shanks
(in the Pot)

Serves:	**4**
Preparation time:	**30 minutes, plus overnight to rest the meat**
Cooking time:	**2 hours**
Type of recipe:	**elementary**
Cost:	**moderate**

olives and blend. Add the mixture to the sauce, taste, and correct the seasoning.
13.
Spoon the sauce over the lamb and garnish with sprigs of parsley. Serve the lamb accompanied by a purée of potatoes.

Here is a delicious and hearty one-dish meal that is perfect for fall, when fresh herbs are still available. It can be cooked several days ahead and reheated. It is excellent for Sunday suppers and casual entertaining. This makes good use of one of the most delicious yet inexpensive cuts of lamb, the shanks.

Ingredients
4 to 6 meaty lamb shanks
6 carrots, scraped and cut in half
2 stalks celery, scraped
1 large onion, peeled and stuck with a clove
1 parsnip, peeled
1 parsley root, or 1 large sprig fresh parsley
1 ripe tomato
8 to 10 cups beef bouillon
Salt
6 black peppercorns
1 bay leaf

Vegetable Garnish:
8 to 10 small red potatoes, unpeeled
6 turnips, peeled and cut in half
4 carrots, scraped and cut in half
4 to 6 small leeks, well rinsed, with most of the greens removed

Optional:
2 hearts celery

Sauce:
4 Tablespoons finely minced fresh parsley
1 dill gherkin, finely minced

2 Tablespoons well-drained capers
3 Tablespoons finely minced fresh basil,
or 3 Tablespoons finely minced fresh
mint
4 to 6 anchovy fillets, finely minced
3 Tablespoons red wine vinegar
6 to 8 Tablespoons fruity olive oil
Salt and freshly ground black pepper

Soup:
2 cups cooked white or red beans
2 Tablespoons finely minced fresh
parsley

Garnish:
4 to 6 slices of day-old French bread,
cut ½ inch thick and sautéed in olive
oil

Preparation
1.
A day ahead, in a large casserole combine
the lamb shanks with the vegetables. Add
enough bouillon to cover the ingredients by
½ inch. Season with salt and peppercorns.
Add the bay leaf and bring the mixture to a
boil.
2.
Reduce the heat and simmer for 1 hour,
30 minutes to 2 hours, or until the shanks
are tender but not falling apart. Skim
the stock every 10 to 15 minutes,
removing the gray scum that rises to the
top.
3.
When the meat is done, remove the
vegetables with a slotted spoon and
discard. Cool the shanks in the cooking
stock and refrigerate overnight.

4.
The next day degrease the cooking stock
thoroughly and bring to a boil. Transfer the
lamb shanks to a platter, cover and keep
warm.
5.
Prepare the vegetable garnish. Add the
potatoes, turnips, and carrots to the
casserole and simmer over low heat for 15
minutes, or until the vegetables are tender;
do not overcook. If the turnips are done
before the potatoes, transfer them to a
serving platter and reserve. When the
potatoes and carrots are done transfer them
to a side dish and reserve as well.
6.
Add the leeks and optional celery hearts to
the pot and simmer until just tender, or for
about 10 minutes. Transfer the celery hearts
and leeks with a slotted spoon to the
serving platter and set aside.
7.
Prepare the sauce. In a bowl combine the
parsley, gherkin, capers, and basil or mint.
Add the anchovies, vinegar, and oil and
whisk the sauce until well blended. Taste
and correct the seasoning. Transfer the
sauce to a small serving bowl and set
aside.
8.
Surround the shanks with the vegetable
garnish. Recover the platter and keep
warm.
9.
Prepare the soup. Add the white or red
beans and the parsley to the lamb broth.
10.
Serve the lamb broth as an appetizer,
garnished with the sautéed French bread

Sautéed Lamb Chops
in
Sauce Creole

Serves:	**4**
Preparation time:	**30 minutes**
Cooking time:	**40 minutes**
Type of recipe:	**elementary**
Cost:	**expensive**

slices. Follow with the main course of lamb shanks and serve the sauce on the side.

Remarks

Other cooked meats, such as tongue, pigs' feet, or a simply poached chicken, can be served in the same way.

Ingredients

4 to 8 loin lamb chops, cut ¾ inch thick
Coarse salt and freshly ground black pepper
3 Tablespoons fruity olive oil
2 Tablespoons butter
¼ cup dry sherry
1 teaspoon tomato paste
¾ cup Brown Chicken Stock (page 531)

Sauce:

2 large green peppers
¾ cup Roasted Red Peppers (page 545), cubed
2 Tablespoons fruity olive oil
1 dried hot chili pepper, crumbled
2 Tablespoons finely minced shallots
4 large ripe tomatoes, peeled, seeded, and chopped
½ teaspoon dried oregano
1 large sprig of fresh basil, or ¼ teaspoon dried
½ teaspoon dried thyme
Salt and freshly ground black pepper
1 Tablespoon tomato paste
1 large clove garlic, peeled and crushed

Optional:
Cayenne pepper

Preparation

1.

Preheat the broiler.

2.

Start by making the sauce. Prepare the green peppers according to the directions on page 545. When cool enough to handle peel, core, and cube finely. Set aside.

3.

Purée the roasted red peppers in a blender, adding a little olive oil. Set aside.

4.

In a 10-inch cast-iron skillet heat 2 tablespoons oil together with the crumbled chili pepper. Add the shallots and cook, without browning, for 2 minutes.

5.

Add the tomatoes, oregano, basil, and thyme. Season with salt and pepper, then bring the mixture to a boil and cook until the tomato water has evaporated and the mixture is thick.

6.

Add the tomato paste and purée the sauce in the blender.

7.

Return the sauce to the skillet, then add the garlic, red pepper purée, and cubed green peppers. Heat the sauce through, taste and correct the seasoning. The sauce should be quite spicy; if it isn't add a dash of cayenne pepper and set aside.

8.

Season the chops with salt and pepper. Heat 1 tablespoon oil and ½ tablespoon butter in each of 2 cast-iron skillets. When the oil is almost smoking add the chops to each and sauté over high heat for 3 minutes. Turn the chops and sauté for

another 4 to 5 minutes, or until done; do not overcook. The chops should still be a little rare. Transfer the chops to a serving platter and continue to finish the sauce in 1 skillet.

9.

Discard the burned fat from the skillet and add a little more butter and oil. Add the sherry and tomato paste to the skillet. Bring to a boil and reduce the mixture to 2 tablespoons. Add the stock, bring to a boil, and reduce by half. Stir the prepared sauce into the skillet and heat through.

10.

Return the chops to the skillet, together with any accumulated juices. Spoon the sauce over the chops and simmer for another minute. Transfer the chops to a serving platter and serve accompanied by a pilaf of rice.

Ragoût of Lamb
à la Genovese

Serves: **6**
Preparation time: **35 minutes**
Cooking time: **2 hours**
Type of recipe: **elementary**
Cost: **expensive**

Ingredients

2 red peppers
3 pounds boneless shoulder of lamb, cubed (1½ to 2 inches)
Salt and freshly ground black pepper
1 Tablespoon butter
¾ cup olive oil
Large pinch of granulated sugar
Flour
2 medium onions, finely minced
2 large cloves garlic, minced, and 2 medium cloves garlic, left whole
4 large ripe tomatoes, peeled, seeded, and chopped
2 Tablespoons tomato paste
1 Bouquet Garni (page 546)
1 large sprig fresh oregano, or 1 teaspoon dried
2 teaspoons fresh thyme, or ½ teaspoon dried
2 to 3 cups Brown Lamb Stock (page 534) or Brown Chicken Stock (page 531)
2 medium zucchini, cut into 1-inch cubes
2 cups fresh basil leaves
2 Tablespoons freshly grated Parmesan cheese

Optional:

1 Tablespoon cornstarch, mixed with a little stock

Preparation

1.
Preheat the broiler.
2.
Prepare the peppers according to the directions on page 545. Remove from the oven and cool. Peel the peppers under cold running water, core, slice thinly and set aside.
3.
Reduce the oven temperature to 350 degrees.
4.
Season the lamb with salt and pepper.
5.
In a large heavy skillet heat the butter and 2 tablespoons oil. Add the lamb cubes; do not crowd the pan. Sauté until nicely browned on all sides. Transfer the cubes to a side dish and continue sautéing until all the meat is done.
6.
Return the meat to the pan. Sprinkle with sugar and flour and cook over high heat for 2 minutes, shaking the pan back and forth until the meat is well covered with the flour and is slightly glazed. With a slotted spoon remove the meat to a large casserole.
7.
Add 2 more tablespoons oil to the skillet. Add the onions and minced garlic and cook, stirring constantly, until the mixture is nicely browned; scrape well the bottom of the pan.
8.
Add the tomatoes, 1 tablespoon tomato paste, salt, pepper, Bouquet Garni, oregano, and thyme. Bring the mixture to a boil and pour over the lamb.
9.
Add the stock, bring to a boil, cover the casserole, and set in the center of the oven. Braise for 1 hour to 1 hour, 20 minutes, or until the meat is tender but not falling apart.

Ragoût of Lamb
with
Prunes

Serves: **6**
Preparation time: **35 minutes, plus 6 hours to soak prunes**
Cooking time: **2 hours**
Type of recipe: **elementary**
Cost: **expensive**

10.
While the lamb is cooking heat 2 more tablespoons oil in a 10-inch skillet. Add the zucchini and cook until the cubes are nicely browned on all sides. Season with salt and pepper and set aside.

11.
In a blender combine the basil leaves, whole garlic, remaining tomato paste, remaining oil, and Parmesan cheese. Blend at high speed until the mixture is smooth. You may need a little more oil. Reserve.

12.
When the meat is done remove it with a slotted spoon to a side dish. Discard the bouquet. Set the casserole over high heat and reduce the sauce until it coats a spoon.

13.
Add the basil mixture, zucchini, and peppers to the casserole. Return the meat and simmer for 10 minutes.

14.
Taste and correct the seasoning. If the sauce seems a little thin whisk in a little of the optional cornstarch mixture. Serve the ragoût from the casserole accompanied by a saffron-flavored rice or crusty French bread.

Remarks

The ragoût can be made 2 to 3 days in advance and reheated. You may also freeze it. Do not add the basil paste until the ragoût has been reheated, for the herb loses its wonderful aroma when frozen.

Ingredients
1½ cups large dried prunes
¾ cup dry white wine
3½ to 4 pounds boneless shoulder of lamb, cut in 2-inch cubes
Salt and freshly ground black pepper
3 Tablespoons butter
1 Tablespoon oil
16 small white onions, peeled
¼ cup plus 1 teaspoon granulated sugar
½ teaspoon ground cinnamon
½ teaspoon ground ginger
Flour
2 cups Brown Chicken Stock (page 531)
¼ cup red wine vinegar
1 Tablespoon cornstarch, mixed with a little stock

Preparation
1.
Combine the prunes and wine in a bowl and soak for 6 hours or overnight.
2.
Preheat the oven to 375 degrees.
3.
Season the lamb with salt and pepper.
4.
Heat the butter and oil in a large heavy skillet and add the lamb a few pieces at a time; do not crowd the pan. Sauté the meat over medium heat until nicely browned on all sides. When the meat is done remove to a side platter and reserve.
5.
Discard all but 2 tablespoons of fat from the pan. Add the onions, sprinkle with salt, pepper, ½ teaspoon sugar, and sauté over low heat until browned. The onions will not brown evenly.

Ragoût of Lamb
with
Leeks

Serves: **6**
Preparation time: **25 minutes**
Cooking time: **2 hours**
Type of recipe: **elementary**
Cost: **expensive**

6.
Return the meat to the skillet, sprinkle with cinnamon, ginger, a little more sugar, and a light sprinkling of flour. Sauté the meat for another 2 minutes, shaking the pan back and forth until the meat is lightly glazed. Transfer the mixture to a large casserole.

7.
Drain the prunes and set aside. Pour the prune wine into the skillet, bring to a boil and reduce the wine to 3 tablespoons, scraping well the bottom of the pan. Add the stock, bring to a boil, and pour over the meat. Cover the casserole tightly and set in the center of the oven.

8.
Braise the meat for 1 hour, 30 minutes, then add the prunes and braise for another 15 to 20 minutes, or until the meat is tender.

9.
With a slotted spoon transfer the meat, prunes, and onions to a bowl and set aside. Carefully degrease the pan juices.

10.
In a small bowl combine the remaining sugar and the vinegar and whisk until sugar is dissolved. Add the sugar mixture to the pan juices.

11.
Set the casserole over high heat, add a little of the cornstarch mixture, and whisk the sauce until it heavily coats the spoon. Taste and correct the seasoning.

12.
Return the meat and prunes to the casserole and heat through. Transfer to a serving dish and serve accompanied by braised brown rice, a risotto, or sautéed potatoes. Sautéed Apples (page 546) are also an excellent accompaniment to the ragoût.

This is a variation of the classic blanquette recipe, which is usually made with either veal or lamb. It is one of those delicious dishes that demands very little of the cook's time and can easily be prepared in advance. Here the lamb is heavily flavored with braised leeks, which to my mind are one of the great year-round vegetables.

Ingredients
4 to 5 large leeks, well rinsed, and with all but 2 inches of greens removed
3 pounds lamb bones, preferably including 1 to 2 lamb shanks
2 large carrots, scraped
3 to 4 stalks celery with leaves
2 medium onions, unpeeled
1 parsley root, scraped, or several large sprigs fresh parsley
Salt
6 black peppercorns
3 to 4 pounds boneless shoulder of lamb, cut into 1½- to 2-inch cubes
5 Tablespoons butter
Freshly ground black pepper
Pinch of granulated sugar
3 large egg yolks
½ cup heavy cream
1 to 2 Tablespoons lemon juice
3 Tablespoons flour

Preparation

1.
Cut the leeks into thin 2-inch julienne strips and set aside.

2.
In a large casserole combine the lamb bones, carrots, celery stalks, onions, and parsley root or sprigs. Add 8 cups water, season with salt, and add the peppercorns. Bring to a boil, reduce the heat, and simmer the lamb stock for 1 hour, 30 minutes, skimming it several times.

3.
Discard the bones, add the lamb cubes, and braise the lamb for another 1 hour to 1 hour, 30 minutes, or until the meat is just tender. Do not overcook.

4.
While the meat is cooking prepare the leeks. In a 10-inch cast-iron skillet heat 2 tablespoons butter. Add the leeks and 3 tablespoons water. Season with salt and pepper and a pinch of sugar. Cover the skillet and braise the leeks for 5 minutes, or until just tender. Set aside.

5.
When the meat is tender remove it with a slotted spoon to a side dish and reserve. Strain the stock through a fine sieve, then chill for 30 minutes to an hour, or until it can be degreased thoroughly. Remove 2 cups of stock, heat the stock in a saucepan, and reserve.

6.
In a bowl combine the yolks and cream. Season with salt and pepper. Add 1 tablespoon lemon juice. Whisk the mixture until thoroughly blended and set aside.

7.
In a heavy 3-quart casserole heat the remaining 3 tablespoons butter over low heat. Add the flour and cook the mixture, stirring constantly for 2 minutes; do not let it brown. Add the hot stock all at once and whisk until the mixture is well blended and smooth.

8.
Bring the mixture to a boil, reduce the heat, and season the sauce with salt and pepper. Simmer gently for 10 minutes, then whisk the cream-and-yolk mixture into the sauce and reheat without letting it come to a boil.

9.
Add the meat and leeks and reheat the ragoût without letting it come to a boil. Taste and correct the seasoning, adding a large grinding of black pepper and little more lemon juice to taste. Serve the ragoût hot accompanied by Mushroom Risotto Piémontaise (page 328).

Remarks
This dish is excellent when prepared 1 to 2 days ahead and reheated slowly, either on top of the stove or in a low 325-degree oven. You may vary the dish by adding to it 1 to 2 carrots cut into thin julienne strips and braised together with the leeks. In the spring I usually add 1 cup fresh peas cooked separately with a little water, and a dollop of butter. Drain and add to the ragoût just before serving.

Sauté of Lamb
in
Lemon Sauce

Serves: **6**
Preparation time: **30 minutes**
Cooking time: **2 hours**
Type of recipe: **elementary**
Cost: **expensive**

Ingredients

3 pounds boneless shoulder of lamb, cubed (1½ to 2 inches)
Salt and freshly ground black pepper
3 Tablespoons olive oil
2 cups finely minced onions
3 cloves garlic, minced
2 Tablespoons minced fresh parsley
Flour
2 cups Brown Chicken Stock (page 531)
2 Tablespoons minced fresh thyme, or 1 teaspoon dried
3 Tablespoons lemon juice
1 large lemon, unpeeled and cut crosswise into thin slices
1 Tablespoon cornstarch, mixed with a little stock

Garnish:

2 Tablespoons finely minced fresh parsley

Optional:

2 Tablespoons finely minced fresh mint

Preparation

1.
Preheat the oven to 350 degrees.

2.
Dry the lamb cubes thoroughly with paper towels. Season with salt and pepper.

3.
In a large cast-iron skillet heat the oil. Add the lamb a few cubes at a time and sauté over medium heat until nicely browned; do not crowd the pan. Remove the sautéed lamb to a side dish and reserve.

4.
Discard all but 2 tablespoons of fat from the pan. Add the onions, garlic, and parsley and cook the mixture until nicely browned, scraping well the bottom of the pan.

5.
Return the lamb to the skillet, sprinkle with flour, and toss the meat until it is well coated with flour and lightly glazed. Transfer the meat-and-onion mixture to a heavy casserole.

6.
Add the stock, thyme, and lemon juice to the pan. Bring to a boil and pour into the casserole. Cover the casserole tightly and place in the center of the oven and braise for 1 hour, 30 minutes to 1 hour, 45 minutes. When the meat is done, remove it to a side dish with a slotted spoon and reserve.

7.
Carefully degrease the pan juices, then add the lemon slices. Cook the sauce for 2 to 3 minutes, whisking in the cornstarch mixture until the sauce heavily coats the spoon. Taste and correct the seasoning.

8.
Return the meat to the casserole and reheat slowly. Transfer the sauté to a serving dish, garnish with parsley, and sprinkle with the optional mint. Serve hot over braised brown rice.

Remarks
The entire sauté can be made 2 or 3 days ahead. It can also be frozen successfully. The lemon slices should be added to the dish at the last moment.

Braised Lamb
with Peas and Mint
à la Marocaine

Serves: **6**
Preparation time: **35 minutes**
Cooking time: **2 hours, 15 minutes**
Type of recipe: **elementary**
Cost: **expensive**

Ingredients

3 pounds boneless shoulder of lamb, cut into 2-inch cubes
2 carrots, scraped and cut in half
2 stalks celery, cut in half
1 large onion, peeled and stuck with a clove
1 large sprig fresh parsley
1 parsnip, scraped
6 black peppercorns
Salt
3 pounds shelled fresh peas
1 Tablespoon granulated sugar
4 Tablespoons butter
1 cup finely minced onions
3 Tablespoons flour
½ to ¾ cup chopped fresh mint

Preparation

1.
In a large casserole combine the lamb, carrots, celery, onion, parsley, parsnip, and peppercorns. Add cold water to cover. Season with salt, bring to a boil, reduce the heat, and simmer partially covered for 1 hour, 30 minutes, or until the meat is tender but not falling apart.

2.
While the meat is cooking combine the peas with the sugar and a pinch of salt in a saucepan. Cover by 1 inch with cold water. Bring to a boil, reduce the heat, and simmer until tender, or for about 8 minutes. Drain the peas and reserve.

3.
When the meat is done, strain it through a fine sieve, reserving the cooking stock. Set the meat aside and keep warm.

4.
Discard the vegetables, return the stock to a saucepan, and reduce the broth over high heat by one third. Reserve 2½ cups of the stock and keep hot.

5.
In a large heavy casserole heat the butter, add the onions, and cook until soft, or for about 5 to 6 minutes. Add the flour and cook for 2 or 3 minutes, stirring constantly without browning.

6.
Add 2 cups hot stock all at once and whisk the sauce until it is thick and smooth. If the sauce is too thick add a little more stock.

7.
Add the mint and simmer the sauce for 3 to 4 minutes.

8.
Return the lamb and peas to the casserole. Gently fold the meat and vegetables into the sauce and simmer for 15 more minutes. Correct the seasoning and serve hot, accompanied by a pilaf of rice and crusty French bread.

Braised Lamb
in
Sweet-and-Sour Sauce

Serves:	**4 to 5**
Preparation time:	**20 minutes**
Cooking time:	**2 hours**
Type of recipe:	**elementary**
Cost:	**expensive**

Ingredients

3 pounds boneless shoulder of lamb, cubed (1½ to 2 inches)
Salt and freshly ground black pepper
3 Tablespoons olive oil
1 Tablespoon butter
Flour
Large pinch of granulated sugar
2 cups finely minced onions
2 Tablespoons brown sugar
⅓ cup red wine vinegar
4 large ripe tomatoes, peeled, seeded, and chopped, or 1 can (35 ounces) Italian plum tomatoes, well drained and chopped
1 Tablespoon tomato paste
1 bay leaf
1 stalk celery, with greens
2 large sprigs fresh parsley
2 cloves garlic, peeled and crushed
1 teaspoon dried thyme
1 to 2 cups Brown Chicken Stock (page 531)
1 Tablespoon arrowroot, mixed with a little stock

Preparation

1.
Preheat the oven to 350 degrees.

2.
Dry the meat thoroughly with paper towels. Season with salt and pepper.

3.
In a large heavy skillet heat 2 tablespoons oil and the butter. Add the lamb cubes a few at a time; do not crowd the pan. Sauté until all the lamb is done.

4.
Return all the lamb to the skillet, sprinkle lightly with flour and sugar, and toss the lamb in the pan until the cubes are evenly browned and nicely glazed. Remove to a casserole and set aside.

5.
Add the remaining tablespoon oil to the skillet. Add the onions and cook until they are soft and nicely browned, scraping well the bottom of the pan.

6.
Combine the brown sugar and vinegar in a small bowl and whisk until thoroughly blended, then add the sugar-and-vinegar mixture to the skillet. Bring to a boil, scraping well the bottom of the pan.

7.
Add the tomatoes and tomato paste. Season with salt and pepper, bring to a boil, and cook until most of the tomato water has evaporated.

8.
Pour the mixture over the lamb in the casserole. Add the bay leaf, celery, parsley, garlic, and thyme. Add enough stock to cover the lamb. Cover the casserole and place in the center of the oven. Braise for 1

Middle Eastern Vegetable-and-Lamb Casserole

Serves: **6**
Preparation time: **35 minutes**
Cooking time: **1 hour, 55 minutes**
Type of recipe: **elementary**
Cost: **inexpensive**

hour, 30 minutes, or until the meat is tender but not falling apart.

9.

When the meat is done, discard the bay leaf and celery stalk. Transfer the lamb with a slotted spoon to a side dish. Strain the pan juices through a sieve and return to the casserole.

10.

Bring the juices to a boil and whisk in the arrowroot mixture; use just enough until the sauce is thick and heavily coats the spoon. Taste and correct the seasoning. The sauce should have a sweet-and-sour taste. You may want to add a little more vinegar or sugar or both.

10.

Return the meat to the casserole and heat through. Add a large grinding of black pepper and serve hot accompanied by buttered parslied new potatoes.

Remarks

The entire dish can be made 2 to 3 days ahead and reheated in a covered casserole in a 300-degree oven.

Ingredients

1½ pounds ground lamb
3 Tablespoons minced fresh parsley
1 Tablespoon ground cumin
1 Tablespoon minced fresh gingerroot
1 Tablespoon dried thyme
½ teaspoon cayenne pepper
2 large cloves garlic, crushed
Salt and freshly ground black pepper
2 Tablespoons butter
1 onion, finely minced, and 2 large onions, thinly sliced
3 Tablespoons water
½ cup bread crumbs, soaked in milk and drained
Flour for dredging
6 to 8 Tablespoons olive oil
2 dried hot chili peppers
2 green peppers, thinly sliced
2 red peppers, thinly sliced
1 Tablespoon tomato paste
4 large tomatoes, peeled, seeded, and chopped
2 medium zucchini, cubed

Garnish:
2 Tablespoons minced fresh parsley

Preparation

1.
Preheat the oven to 350 degrees.

2.
In a large mixing bowl combine the meat, parsley, cumin, ginger, thyme, cayenne pepper, garlic, salt, and pepper. Work the mixture with your hands until it is well blended, then set aside.

3.
In a small heavy skillet heat the butter. Add the minced onion and cook over medium heat until it is soft but not browned.

4.
Add cooked onion to the meat mixture, together with the water and bread crumbs. Blend the mixture thoroughly, then taste and correct the seasoning. Form into small balls, dredge lightly with flour, and set aside.

5.
In a large casserole heat 2 tablespoons oil and add the meatballs a few at a time; do not crowd. Sauté the meatballs over medium heat until they are well browned on all sides, then carefully transfer to a side dish.

6.
When all the meatballs are done discard all but 2 tablespoons of fat (if the oil is burned, discard it completely and add 2 more tablespoons oil to the pan). Add the sliced onions and cook until they are soft and lightly browned. Add the chili peppers and the green and red peppers, and cook for another 2 to 3 minutes, scraping the bottom of the pan with a wooden spoon.

7.
Add the tomato paste, tomatoes, salt, and pepper to the casserole. Bring to a boil, reduce the heat, and return the meatballs to the casserole in 1 layer. Cover and set in the oven. Braise the meatballs for 1½ hours, basting them several times with the pan juices.

8.
While the meat is braising heat the remaining oil in a heavy skillet. Add the zucchini cubes and sauté until they are nicely browned on all sides. Season with salt and pepper and set aside.

9.
Fifteen minutes before the meat is done, add the zucchini cubes to the casserole and continue braising until they are well heated through.

10.
When the meat is done arrange it in a deep oval serving dish. Spoon the sauce and vegetables around it, garnish with parsley, and serve accompanied by crusty bread.

Sautéed Calves' Liver
in
Port-and-Green Peppercorn
Sauce

Serves:	**4**
Preparation time:	**15 minutes**
Cooking time:	**10 to 12 minutes**
Type of recipe:	**elementary**
Cost:	**moderate**

Ingredients

4 slices calves' liver, cut ½ inch thick
Salt and freshly ground white pepper
Flour for dredging
2 Tablespoons Clarified Butter (page 545)
1 teaspoon oil
⅓ cup white port wine
1 teaspoon meat glaze
¾ to 1 cup Brown Chicken Stock (page 531)
1 teaspoon potato flour or arrowroot, mixed with a little cold stock
1 teaspoon green peppercorns, drained and crushed
2 to 3 Tablespoons cold butter

Garnish:

Tiny new potatoes, cooked in their skins and buttered
Finely minced fresh parsley

Preparation

1.
Season the calves' liver slices with salt and pepper. (If there's any filament surrounding the liver, remove it with a sharp knife.) Dredge the slices lightly with flour, shaking off the excess.

2.
Heat the Clarified Butter and oil in a heavy 12-inch skillet, or use 2 ten-inch skillets. When the butter is very hot add the calves' liver. The slices should be placed at least ½ inch apart so they can brown properly. Sauté the liver for 2 minutes on each side. The liver is done when the juices run a pale pink when pricked with a tip of a sharp knife.

3.
Remove the liver slices to a side plate and reserve.

4.
Add the port to the skillet and cook over high heat, scraping the bottom of the pan with a wooden spoon, until the port is reduced to 1 tablespoon.

5.
Add the meat glaze and ¾ cup stock. Bring to a boil and reduce by half. Whisk in the potato flour or arrowroot mixture and the green peppercorns. Taste the sauce and correct the seasoning. Cook the sauce until it heavily coats the spoon. Remove from the heat.

6.
Add to the skillet any juices that may have accumulated around the calves' liver and whisk in the butter. When the butter has melted return the calves' liver to the skillet. Spoon the sauce over the liver slices and

Sautéed Calves' Liver Lyonnaise

Serves:	**4**
Preparation time:	**15 minutes**
Cooking time:	**50 minutes**
Type of recipe:	**elementary**
Cost:	**moderate**

set over the lowest possible heat for 1 to 2 minutes. If the sauce has reduced too much add the remaining ¼ cup stock. Be sure not to let the liver get overdone.

7.
Transfer the calves' liver to a serving platter. Spoon the sauce over each slice and garnish the platter with new potatoes. Sprinkle with parsley and serve immediately.

Remarks
This is a short (concentrated) sauce. There should be 1 to 2 tablespoons of sauce for each slice. If you would like to have more sauce, use a little more stock and do not reduce the stock as much. Whisk in a little bit of Beurre Manié (page 544) instead of the flour or arrowroot mixture.

Here is one of the simplest yet most delicious ways to prepare calves' liver. The success of this dish depends entirely on the quality of the liver and on your skill not to overcook it. Excellent calves' liver is almost never available at a supermarket and only the best butchers usually carry it. However, the darker, grass-fed veal liver can still give excellent results when prepared this way.

Ingredients
1½ pounds calves' liver, thinly sliced
5 Tablespoons butter
1 Tablespoon oil
4 cups thinly sliced onions
Salt and freshly ground black pepper
¼ cup dry Marsala wine
¾ cup Brown Chicken Stock (page 531)
Pinch of flour
1 Tablespoon finely minced fresh sage, or ½ teaspoon dried

Garnish:
Finely minced fresh parsley

Preparation
1.
Slice the liver crosswise into ½-inch strips and set aside.
2.
In a large heavy skillet heat 2 tablespoons butter and the oil. Add the onions. Season with salt and pepper and cook over medium heat for 10 minutes, then lower the heat. Partially cover the pan and continue cooking the onions for 30 to 40 minutes, or until they are very soft and nicely browned. Watch the onions carefully to make sure

Sautéed Calves' Liver Vaudoise

Serves: **4 to 6**
Preparation time: **25 minutes**
Cooking time: **50 minutes**
Type of recipe: **elementary**
Cost: **moderate**

they do not burn. Scrape the onions into a bowl and set aside.

3.
Season the liver with salt and pepper. Add 2 more tablespoons butter to the skillet. When the butter is very hot add the liver and sauté over high heat for 2 to 3 minutes, tossing the strips in the butter. Remove the liver with a slotted spoon to a side dish and reserve.

4.
Add another tablespoon butter to the pan and heat. Add the wine and cook until it is reduced to a glaze. Add the stock, bring to a boil, and cook until reduced to 3 tablespoons.

5.
Sprinkle the pan with a little flour. Season with salt, pepper, and sage. Return the liver and onions to the pan and cook the mixture for 2 more minutes, or just enough to heat through.

6.
Transfer the liver to a serving platter, sprinkle with parsley, and serve immediately.

Remarks
You may vary the dish by adding 2 tablespoons well-drained capers to the reduced pan juices or a mixture of capers and 1 small finely diced dill gherkin, as well as a tablespoon of finely minced fresh parsley and a clove of finely diced garlic. This mixture will give the dish a more Provençale flavor that is equally delicious.

Ingredients
3 Tablespoons sugar
½ cup red wine vinegar
1½ cups hot Brown Chicken Stock (page 531)
6 Tablespoons butter
2 Tablespoons oil
2 Bermuda onions, peeled and thinly sliced
Salt and freshly ground black pepper
4 to 6 slices calves' liver, cut ¼ inch thick
Flour for dredging
⅓ cup port wine
2 teaspoons cornstarch, mixed with a little stock

Garnish:
Sprigs of fresh parsley or watercress

Preparation
1.
In a heavy 2-quart saucepan combine the sugar and vinegar. Cook the mixture over high heat until it caramelizes; it will turn into a heavy reddish-brown syrup. Immediately add the stock all at once. Bring to a boil and cook the mixture until the stock has reduced to 1 cup. Set aside.

2.
In a large heavy skillet heat 2 tablespoons butter and 1 tablespoon oil. Add the onions and cook over moderate-to-high heat for 10 to 12 minutes.

3.
Season with salt and pepper, then partially cover the skillet. Reduce the heat and continue cooking the onions another 30 to 40 minutes, or until they are very soft and

Braised Sweetbreads Forestière

Serves:	**4 to 6**
Preparation time:	**45 minutes, plus 6 to 7 hours to soak and press sweet-breads**
Cooking time:	**1 hour**
Type of recipe:	**elementary**
Cost:	**expensive**

nicely browned. Scrape the onions into a bowl and reserve.

4.
Season the calves' liver with salt and pepper. (If the slices are bound by a filament remove it.) Dredge the slices lightly with flour, shaking off the excess.

5.
Heat the remaining butter and oil in 2 heavy skillets. When the butter is very hot and starts to brown add the liver slices. Do not crowd the pans; the slices should be at least 1 inch apart. Sauté the liver over moderate-to-high heat for 2 to 3 minutes, then turn the slices and sauté for 2 to 3 minutes on the other side. Regulate the heat so the butter does not burn. Test the liver with a tip of a sharp knife. It is done if the juices run a light pink.

6.
Transfer the liver to a side dish. Cover to keep it warm and reserve.

7.
Use 1 skillet to prepare the sauce. Add the port, bring to a boil, and cook until reduced to a glaze. Add the reserved stock and onions, bring to a boil, and whisk in the cornstarch mixture. Whisk the sauce until it has thickened. If the sauce is too thick add a little more stock. Season the sauce with salt and pepper.

8.
Strain any of the accumulated juices around the liver back into the skillet. Place the liver slices on a warm serving platter and spoon the sauce over them. Garnish with parsley or watercress and serve immediately accompanied by parslied new potatoes.

Ingredients
2 pounds fresh sweetbreads
Salt and freshly ground white pepper
Flour for dredging
5 Tablespoons butter
1 onion, peeled and finely diced
1 large carrot, scraped and finely diced
½ cup dry white wine
1½ cups Brown Chicken Stock (page 531)
10 to 12 medium mushrooms, stems removed and caps quartered
1 cup heavy cream
1 Beurre Manié (page 544)

Garnish:
Sprigs of fresh watercress

Preparation
1.
Several hours ahead place the sweetbreads in a large bowl with ice water and let them stand for 2 to 3 hours, changing the water 3 to 4 times.

2.
Peel as much as possible of the thin filament that surrounds the sweetbreads without tearing them. Again place them in a large bowl with ice water for another hour.

3.
In a large saucepan bring salted water to a bare simmer. Add the sweetbreads and poach for 15 minutes without letting the water come to a boil. Drain the sweetbreads and place on a cutting board. Cover with a linen towel and then another cutting board and weigh them down with several heavy cans. Keep the sweetbreads pressed for 2 to 3 hours.

4.
Preheat the oven to 375 degrees.
5.
Season the sweetbreads with salt and
pepper and dredge lightly with flour,
shaking off the excess. In a large heavy
ovenproof skillet heat 3 tablespoons butter.
Add the sweetbreads and sauté over
medium heat until nicely browned on
all sides. Remove to a side dish and
reserve.
6.
Add the onion and carrot to the skillet and
sauté for 2 to 3 minutes without browning.
Add the wine, bring to a boil, and cook
over high heat until reduced to 2
tablespoons. Add the stock, bring
to a boil, and season with salt and
pepper.
7.
Return the sweetbreads to the skillet, cover,
and place in the oven. Braise for 30
minutes, basting every 10 minutes with the
pan juices.
8.
While the sweetbreads are braising, heat
the remaining butter in a small heavy skillet
and add the mushrooms. Season with salt
and pepper and sauté for 2 to 3 minutes
until nicely browned. Set aside.
9.
When the sweetbreads are done transfer
them to a side dish and reserve.
10.
Strain the pan juices through a fine sieve,
pressing down on the vegetables to extract
all their juices. Return to the skillet and boil
over high heat until the pan juices are
reduced to 3 tablespoons.

11.
Add the cream and bring to a boil. Whisk
in bits of the Beurre Manié and cook the
sauce until it heavily coats a spoon. Add
the sautéed mushrooms to the pan and heat
through. Taste the sauce and correct the
seasoning.
12.
Return the sweetbreads to the pan and
spoon the sauce over them. Simmer over
low heat for 3 to 4 minutes or until heated
through.
13.
Transfer the sweetbreads to a serving
platter and spoon the sauce over them.
Garnish with sprigs of fresh watercress and
serve accompanied by braised rice or
buttered noodles.

Remarks
Sweetbreads can be blanched and
weighted down the day before you are
ready to cook them. The entire dish can be
prepared several hours ahead and reheated,
covered, in a 200-degree oven.

Braised Sweetbreads
à la Normande

Serves:	**6**
Preparation Time:	**45 minutes, plus 4 to 5 hours to soak sweetbreads**
Cooking Time:	**1 hour, 15 minutes**
Type of recipe:	**elementary**
Cost:	**expensive**

Ingredients

2 pounds fresh sweetbreads
Salt and freshly ground white pepper
7 Tablespoons butter
2 small golden delicious apples, peeled and quartered
3 Tablespoons calvados or apple brandy
1 large carrot, scraped and thinly sliced
1 large leek, well rinsed and sliced
1 cup finely diced celery
3 cups hot Chicken Stock (page 530)
2 Tablespoons flour
½ cup heavy cream
2 large egg yolks
Lemon juice to taste

Preparation

1.
Soak and peel the sweetbreads according to the directions on page 212 but do not weigh them down. Season with salt and pepper.

2.
Preheat the oven to 325 degrees.

3.
In a cast-iron skillet heat 2 tablespoons butter. Add the apple quarters and sauté over moderate-to-high heat for 4 to 5 minutes, or until nicely browned on all sides. Be sure not to burn the apples. Add the calvados or brandy, shaking the pan back and forth until it has completely evaporated. Set the apples aside.

4.
In a heavy casserole large enough to hold the sweetbreads in 1 layer melt 2 tablespoons butter. Place the sweetbreads in the hot butter and cook for 2 to 3 minutes on each side without browning. Transfer the sweetbreads to a side dish and reserve.

5.
Add the carrots, leek, and celery to the casserole. Stew the vegetables partially covered for 5 minutes over low heat.

6.
Return the sweetbreads to the casserole and add the stock. Cover the casserole and place it in the oven. Braise the sweetbreads for 40 minutes. When done transfer the sweetbreads to a rectangular flameproof baking dish. Cover with foil and keep warm.

Braised Sweetbreads in Port-and-Green Peppercorn Sauce

Serves:	**2 to 3**
Preparation time:	**15 minutes, plus 6 to 7 hours to soak and press sweetbreads**
Cooking time:	**45 minutes**
Type of recipe:	**elementary**
Cost:	**expensive**

7.

Strain the stock, degrease it thoroughly, and return to the saucepan. Boil the stock, reducing it to 2 cups, and reserve.

8.

In a heavy 3-quart saucepan heat the remaining butter over low heat. Add the flour and cook without browning for 2 to 3 minutes, stirring constantly. Add the reserved stock and bring to a boil, then whisk the mixture until smooth. Cover the saucepan and simmer the sauce over low heat for 20 minutes.

9.

While the sauce is simmering combine the cream and yolks in a small bowl and whisk until well blended. Whisk the cream-and-yolk mixture into the sauce and correct the seasoning, adding a little lemon juice to taste.

10.

Add half the sautéed apples to the sauce and heat through. Spoon the sauce with the apples over the sweetbreads. Cover and simmer on top of the stove over the lowest possible heat until the sweetbreads are just heated through. Do not let them cook or they will get tough.

11.

Garnish the baking dish with the remaining sautéed apples and serve the sweetbreads accompanied by braised rice or crusty French bread.

Ingredients

1 to 1½ pounds fresh sweetbreads
1 Tablespoon white wine vinegar
Salt
Freshly ground white pepper
Flour for dredging
2 Tablespoons rendered chicken fat or
Clarified Butter (page 545)
1 teaspoon oil
1 onion, peeled and cut in half crosswise
½ cup red port wine
½ to ¾ cup Brown Chicken Stock (page 531)
1 Beurre Manié (page 544)
1 teaspoon green peppercorns, crushed

Garnish:
Sprigs of fresh watercress

Preparation

1.

Blanch and peel the sweetbreads as directed on page 212.

2.

Place the sweetbreads in a heavy casserole and cover with cold water. Add the vinegar and season lightly with salt. Bring the water to a simmer on top of the stove and poach the sweetbreads over the lowest possible heat for 10 minutes.

3.

Drain the sweetbreads and dry thoroughly with paper towels. Season with salt and pepper and dredge lightly with flour, shaking off the excess. Do not weigh them down.

4.

In a cast-iron skillet heat the chicken fat or Clarified Butter and the oil. Add the

Sautéed Sweetbreads in Sage-and-Lime Butter

Serves:	**4**
Preparation time:	**15 minutes, plus 6 to 7 hours to soak and press sweet-breads**
Cooking time:	**30 minutes**
Type of recipe:	**elementary**
Cost:	**expensive**

Ingredients
2 pounds fresh sweetbreads
1 Tablespoon white wine vinegar
Salt
Freshly ground black pepper
Flour for dredging
2 to 5 Tablespoons butter
2 teaspoons oil
4 Tablespoons finely minced fresh sage
Juice of 1 lime

Garnish:
Sprigs of fresh parsley

Preparation

1.
Blanch and peel the sweetbreads as directed on page 212. When peeling off the surface membrane do not remove the membrane that holds the sections together.

2.
Place the sweetbreads in a shallow casserole. Add cold water to cover, together with the vinegar, and season lightly with salt. Bring to a simmer and cook over low heat for 10 minutes.

3.
Drain the sweetbreads and plunge them into a bowl of ice water. Drain again and place in 1 layer on a cutting board. Top with a linen towel and then another board. Place several heavy cans on top and weigh the sweetbreads down for 1 to 2 hours.

4.
Dry the sweetbreads thoroughly with paper towels. Season with salt and pepper and dredge lightly with flour, shaking off the excess.

sweetbreads, together with the onion, and sauté over moderate-to-high heat for 2 to 3 minutes on each side, or until the sweetbreads are nicely browned. Regulate the heat so that the butter or fat does not burn.

5.
Reduce the heat, add ¼ cup port wine and cook until the port is reduced to a glaze.

6.
Add ⅓ cup stock to the skillet. Cover and braise the sweetbreads over low heat for 25 to 30 minutes, adding a little port to the skillet every 10 minutes and turning the sweetbreads once or twice during their cooking time. (There should be no more than ⅓ to ½ cup pan juices in the skillet during the braising period.)

7.
When the sweetbreads are done transfer them to a serving platter and keep warm.

8.
Add the remaining stock to the skillet, bring to a boil, and whisk in tiny bits of the Beurre Manié; use just enough to thicken the sauce. Add the peppercorns and simmer the mixture for another 2 to 3 minutes. Taste and correct the seasoning. (The sauce should be highly flavored.)

9.
Spoon the sauce over the sweetbreads. Garnish with sprigs of fresh watercress and serve immediately, accompanied by crusty French bread.

Braised Sweetbreads Valencienne

Serves:	**4**
Preparation time:	**30 minutes, plus 4 to 5 hours to soak sweetbreads**
Cooking time:	**45 minutes**
Type of recipe:	**elementary**
Cost:	**expensive**

5.
In a large cast-iron skillet heat 2 tablespoons butter and the oil. Add the sweetbreads, but do not crowd the pan. Sauté over medium heat for 3 to 4 minutes on each side. Adjust the heat and continue cooking the sweetbreads partially covered for another 5 minutes. Regulate the heat so as not to burn the fat. The sweetbreads should be nicely browned. Transfer the sweetbreads to a serving platter and keep warm.

6.
If the butter has burned, discard it. If not, add the remaining butter to the skillet and heat until it turns a hazelnut brown. Remove from the heat.

7.
Add the sage and lime juice to the skillet and stir for 1 to 2 minutes; do not let the sage burn.

8.
Immediately spoon the sage-and-lime butter over the sweetbreads and serve garnished with sprigs of parsley. Serve the sweetbreads accompanied by crusty French bread and a bowl of sweet butter and a side dish of Sweet-and-Sour Braised Onions (page 431).

Remarks
Sweetbreads are quite perishable and should be used as soon as possible. However, you may blanch and weigh the sweetbreads a day ahead and keep them covered in the refrigerator. The sweetbreads may also be sliced before sautéing, in which case they will only take about 3 minutes of cooking.

Ingredients
1½ to 2 pounds fresh sweetbreads
2 Tablespoons white wine vinegar
Salt
5 Tablespoons butter
2 Tablespoons oil
2 Tablespoons finely minced shallots
3 ripe tomatoes, peeled, seeded, and finely chopped
2 Tablespoons finely minced fresh thyme, or 1 teaspoon dried
¼ teaspoon dried rosemary
Freshly ground white pepper
2 teaspoons tomato paste
1 large clove garlic, peeled and crushed
6 to 8 mushrooms, stems removed and caps finely sliced
Flour for dredging
¼ cup dry white wine
¾ cup Brown Chicken Stock (page 531)
½ cup Crème Fraîche (page 544)

Garnish:
Minced garlic
Sautéed whole mushrooms
Sprigs of fresh parsley

Preparation
1.
Blanch and peel the sweetbreads as directed on page 212. After peeling, again soak the sweetbreads for another hour in ice water, adding 1 tablespoon vinegar and a pinch of salt to the water.

2.
Remove the sweetbreads from the water and dry on a double layer of paper towels. Set aside.

3.
In a large heavy skillet heat 2 tablespoons butter with 1 tablespoon oil. Add the shallots and cook for 2 minutes without browning.

4.
Add the tomatoes, thyme, rosemary, salt, and pepper and cook the tomato mixture until the tomato water has evaporated. Add the tomato paste and garlic and transfer the mixture to a bowl. Set aside.

5.
Add another tablespoon butter and more oil to the skillet. Add the mushrooms and sauté for 2 to 3 minutes, tossing them in the pan until they are nicely browned. Season with salt and pepper and add to the tomato mixture.

6.
Season the sweetbreads with salt and pepper and dredge lightly with flour, shaking off the excess. In a large cast-iron skillet heat the remaining butter and oil. When the butter is very hot and the foam starts to subside add the sweetbreads. Sauté over medium heat until they are nicely browned on all sides.

7.
Add the wine to the skillet, bring to a boil, and cook until reduced to 1 tablespoon.

8.
Add ⅓ cup stock to the skillet. Cover and braise the sweetbreads over low heat for 25 minutes, adding 2 to 3 tablespoons of stock every 10 minutes and turning the sweetbreads once or twice during their cooking time. When the sweetbreads are done (they should be nicely browned and glazed) transfer them to a deep serving dish. Cover and keep warm.

9.
Increase the heat and reduce the pan juices to ¼ cup. Add the Crème Fraîche, bring to a boil, and reduce by half. Season with salt and pepper.

10.
Add the tomato-and-mushroom mixture to the skillet and heat through. (If the sauce seems thin, continue cooking until it is well reduced and concentrated.) Taste the sauce and correct the seasoning.

11.
Spoon the sauce over the sweetbreads. Sprinkle with minced garlic and garnish with sautéed mushrooms and parsley. Serve immediately, accompanied by crusty French bread.

Remarks
The tomato-and-mushroom mixture can be prepared several hours ahead. Sweetbreads are at their best when cooked at the last minute; however the entire dish can be kept warm over a pan of warm water for 40 minutes to an hour before serving.

Sautéed Sweetbreads
in
Vermouth Sauce

Serves: **4**
Preparation time: **10 minutes, plus 4 to 5 hours**
to soak sweetbreads
Cooking time: **1 hour**
Type of recipe: **elementary**
Cost: **expensive**

Ingredients
2 pounds fresh sweetbreads
1 Tablespoon white wine vinegar
Salt and freshly ground white pepper
Flour for dredging
2 Tablespoons butter
1 Tablespoon oil
½ cup dry vermouth
1 cup Brown Chicken Stock (page 531)
2 Tablespoons finely minced shallots
½ cup Crème Fraîche (page 544)
1 Beurre Manié (page 544)
4 Tablespoons cold butter

Optional:
1 Tablespoon finely minced fresh tarragon

Garnish:
2 cups Sautéed Cucumber Balls (page 421)

Preparation
1.
Blanch and peel the sweetbreads as directed on page 212. Add the vinegar to the second soaking.
2.
Dry the sweetbreads carefully and thoroughly with paper towels. Season with salt and pepper and dredge lightly with flour, shaking off the excess. Set aside.
3.
In a large heavy skillet heat the butter and oil. Add the sweetbreads and brown over medium heat for 3 to 4 minutes on each side.

4.
Add ¼ cup vermouth to the skillet and reduce to 1 tablespoon. Add 3 tablespoons stock to the pan, cover, and braise the sweetbreads over low heat for 25 minutes, turning them every 5 minutes and adding a little more stock to the skillet every 10 minutes. When the sweetbreads are done transfer them to a side dish and keep warm.
5.
Add the shallots to the skillet and cook for 2 to 3 minutes without browning. Add the remaining vermouth, bring to a boil, and cook over high heat until reduced to 1 tablespoon.
6.
Add the remaining stock, bring to a boil, and reduce to ⅓ cup.
7.
Add the Crème Fraîche, bring to a boil, and whisk in a little of the Beurre Manié; add just enough to thicken the sauce. (You will need about ½ of the Beurre Manié.)
8.
Remove the skillet from the heat. Whisk in the butter a spoonful at a time, and then add the optional tarragon. Taste the sauce and correct the seasoning.
9.
Return the sweetbreads to the skillet and spoon the sauce over them. Reheat the sweetbreads in the sauce over the lowest possible heat and transfer to a serving platter. Garnish the platter with the Sautéed Cucumber Balls and serve immediately, accompanied by a simple pilaf of rice.

Oxtail
Ragoût
Milanese

Serves: **4 to 6**
Preparation time: **30 minutes**
Cooking time: **2 hours, 30 minutes**
Type of recipe: **elementary**
Cost: **inexpensive**

Oxtails are a delicious and inexpensive cut of meat that lends itself best to braising. Some supermarkets carry only frozen oxtails; these are best used for soups. Many markets, however, have specials on fresh oxtails which you should look for. Oxtails should always be cooked 1 to 2 days ahead. This gives them a chance to develop flavor and allows you to properly degrease the sauce.

Ingredients

4 to 5 pounds meaty oxtails, cut into 2-inch pieces
Salt and freshly ground black pepper
3 Tablespoons butter
3 Tablespoons olive oil
Flour
Pinch of granulated sugar
2 cups finely minced onions
2 large cloves garlic, finely minced
1 Tablespoon tomato paste
1 can (35 ounces) Italian plum tomatoes, peeled, seeded, and chopped, or 4 large ripe tomatoes, peeled, seeded, and chopped
1 cup dry white wine
1 Bouquet Garni, composed of 1 sprig fresh parsley, 1 bay leaf, ½ teaspoon dried thyme, 1 stalk celery with leaves, and ½ teaspoon dried oregano
2 to 3 cups Chicken Stock (page 530) or beef bouillon
1 Tablespoon cornstarch, mixed with a little stock
3 Tablespoons finely minced fresh parsley

2 teaspoons finely grated lemon rind
1 large clove garlic, finely minced

Preparation

1.
Preheat the oven to 350 degrees.
2.
Season the oxtails with salt and pepper.
3.
In a large cast-iron skillet heat 2 tablespoons butter and 2 tablespoons oil and add some of the oxtails. Do not crowd the skillet. Sauté the oxtails over moderate-to-high heat until nicely browned on all sides. Remove the oxtails to a side dish and reserve. Continue sautéing the oxtails until all done.
4.
Return all the oxtails to the skillet. Sprinkle with flour, salt, pepper, and sugar. Sauté the oxtails for another 2 to 3 minutes, tossing them back and forth in the pan. Transfer the oxtails to a heavy casserole and reserve.
5.
Add 1 tablespoon butter and 1 tablespoon oil to the skillet. Add the onions and garlic and cook the mixture until soft and lightly browned, scraping well the bottom of the pan.
6.
Add the tomato paste and tomatoes. Cook over high heat until the tomato water has evaporated, then add the wine, bring to a boil, and cook until the wine is reduced by half.
7.
Pour the mixture into the casserole. Add the bouquet, salt, pepper, and stock or bouillon

Braised Tongue
in
Sorrel Sauce

Serves: **6**
Preparation time: **25 minutes, plus 3 to 4 hours to soak**
Cooking time: **3½ hours, 30 minutes**
Type of recipe: **elementary**
Cost: **inexpensive**

and bring to a boil on top of the stove. Cover the casserole and place in the oven. Braise the oxtails for 2 hours, 30 minutes, or until they are very tender.

8.
Remove the casserole from the oven and carefully degrease the pan juices. Remove and discard the bouquet. With a slotted spoon transfer the oxtails to a side dish and reserve.

9.
Place the casserole over direct heat and reduce the pan juices by ⅓. Whisk in a little of the cornstarch mixture, using just enough to thicken the sauce. Taste the sauce and correct the seasoning. Add the minced parsley, lemon rind, and garlic and return the oxtails to the casserole. Heat through. Serve the oxtails hot accompanied by Catalan Saffron Risotto (page 329).

Remarks
Since the oxtails are at their best when prepared a day or two ahead, cool the entire dish after braising, then refrigerate overnight. Carefully degrease the oxtails the next day and reheat over low heat on top of the stove or in the oven. Add the parsley, lemon rind, and garlic mixture to the sauce just before serving.

Ingredients
1 four-pound fresh beef tongue
2 to 3 meaty beef bones
2 large carrots, scraped and cut in half
2 stalks celery, with leaves
2 onions, unpeeled, and 1 small onion, finely minced
1 parsnip, scraped
1 ripe tomato
1 Bouquet Garni (page 546)
Salt and freshly ground black pepper
3 Tablespoons butter
3 Tablespoons flour
2 cups tightly packed sorrel leaves, finely shredded
1 cup sour cream
Lemon juice to taste

Preparation
1.
Let the tongue soak for 3 to 4 hours in cold water.

2.
In a large oval casserole combine the tongue, bones, carrots, celery, 2 whole onions, parsnip, tomato, and bouquet. Season with salt and pepper and cover with cold water.

3.
Bring to a boil, remove the scum that rises to the surface, reduce the heat, and partially cover the casserole. Simmer for 3 hours to 3 hours, 30 minutes, or until tender. Test by piercing the tongue with the tip of a sharp knife.

4.
Remove the tongue to a side dish, strain the stock, and cool for 30 minutes.

Serves:	**6 to 8**
Preparation time:	**30 minutes**
Cooking time:	**3 hours, 30 minutes to 4 hours**
Type of recipe:	**elementary**
Cost:	**inexpensive**

5.
Degrease the stock carefully and place 3 cups stock in a large saucepan. Boil the stock down to 2½ cups and reserve.

6.
In a heavy 10-inch skillet heat the butter, add the minced onion, and cook over low heat for 3 minutes, or until soft but not browned. Add the flour and stir for 1 or 2 minutes. Add the reserved stock all at once and whisk until the sauce is smooth and thick.

7.
Add the sorrel leaves, sour cream, salt, and pepper. Simmer the sauce for 3 to 4 minutes, add lemon juice to taste, and keep the sauce warm over very low heat.

8.
Peel the skin off the tongue; it will come off easily. Trim off the fatty parts, and pull out the loose bones at the butt end.

9.
Slice the tongue crosswise into thin slices, then transfer the slices to the skillet and heat through.

10.
Pour the sauce around the slices and serve on a platter accompanied by boiled tiny new potatoes.

Remarks
The entire dish can be made 1 or 2 days ahead and reheated. The remaining stock can be used for soups, such as onion or cabbage soup.

Ingredients
1 fresh beef tongue weighing 3½ to 4 pounds
2 large carrots, scraped and cut in half
3 stalks celery
2 onions, peeled and each stuck with a clove
1 parsley root, scraped, or 1 parsnip, peeled
1 large sprig fresh parsley
2 bay leaves
8 black peppercorns
1 Tablespoon salt
Half head garlic, unpeeled

Optional:
2 whole ripe tomatoes

Sauce:
1 cup tightly packed basil leaves
4 anchovy fillets, finely minced
5 Tablespoons red wine vinegar
1 Tablespoon unflavored bread crumbs
2 large cloves garlic, peeled and crushed
¾ cup fruity olive oil
3 Tablespoons finely minced fresh parsley
2 Tablespoons well-drained capers
3 dill gherkins, finely minced

Garnish:
Tiny red potatoes, cooked in their skins and sautéed in butter
Sprigs of fresh parsley

Preparation

1.
Rinse the tongue thoroughly under cold running water.

2.
Place the tongue in a large, preferably oval casserole, adding the carrots, celery, onions, parsley root or parsnip, parsley sprig, bay leaves, peppercorns, optional tomatoes, and garlic. Cover with cold water by 3 inches and season with salt.

3.
Bring to a boil, remove the scum that rises to the surface, then reduce the heat and simmer the tongue partially covered for 3 hours to 3 hours, 30 minutes, or until tender.

4.
While the tongue is cooking make the sauce. In a blender or food processor combine the basil, anchovies, vinegar, bread crumbs, garlic, and olive oil. Blend the mixture until smooth.

5.
Pour the mixture into a bowl and add the parsley, capers, and gherkins. Taste and correct the seasoning. The sauce should be tart and highly seasoned. Set aside.

6.
When the tongue is done transfer it to a carving board. Remove the skin; it will slip off easily. Trim any fatty parts and remove any loose bones.

7.
Slice the tongue into ¼-inch slices, place on a serving platter and garnish with tiny cooked new potatoes and sprigs of parsley. Serve the sauce on the side.

Remarks

If the tongue is not to be served immediately return it to the cooking stock and keep warm. You may leave the tongue in the stock refrigerated overnight. The tongue is equally good served cold with a side dish of the sauce. For variation you can add 1 finely minced hard-boiled egg and 2 tablespoons finely minced red onion to the sauce. (The sauce is equally good served over cold poached chicken or boiled beef.)

Poultry and Game

Chicken

Several years ago my husband and I were traveling by car from Spain to Switzerland when we decided to take a detour through the Bresse region of France. Both of us had memories of the unique, superbly flavored chickens that were the specialty of the region and we were looking forward to enjoying the famous *Poulet à la Creme*—chicken braised in rich cream. We were not disappointed! Stopping at Chez la Mère Blanc in Vonnas, one of the loveliest inns in the area, we feasted on local frogs' legs sautéed in a Provençale butter, followed by the tender chicken braised in cream and perfumed with fresh morilles (wild mushrooms). Deciding to stay the night, we spent the afternoon taking lovely walks through the small village with its gentle stream and driving through the lush green countryside. The famous chickens were everywhere—roaming freely around the farms, in yards next to gas stations, even strolling in the village square. At the next day's lunch we ordered the chicken simply roasted. It arrived at our table beautifully browned and garnished with small mounds of spring vegetables. Here were tiny fresh peas, artichoke bottoms sautéed in butter and filled with a mushroom purée, and little turnip and carrot balls glazed in butter. To this day, we recall with nostaglia the incredible flavor and texture of this simply and magnificently prepared bird. But memories can play tricks. The surroundings and atmosphere of a restaurant can often embellish a less-than-perfect meal. Because of my skepticism, I decided to go back to the province of Burgundy two years later

and spend several weeks working with two of the most creative chefs in the area. Georges Blanc and his uncle, Paul Blanc, both own superb restaurants that specialize in chicken preparations, many of which are really quite special, indeed. As they happily confirmed, the "blue-legged" Bresse chicken is in a class by itself. By far the most expensive chicken in France, each one comes to the market tagged and numbered —part of the strict government control.

After my sojourn in Bresse, I wondered whether I would find it hard to accept the reality that neither our chickens nor any other chicken in Europe could ever match that superbly flavored bird. But despite the obvious superiority of the Bresse bird, I find the versatility of cooking chickens so exciting that, if anything, I am cooking them more and more. There is no other meat or fowl that can adapt itself so beautifully to such a great variety of preparations. For the creative cook, here is a bird that can be poached, roasted, stewed, fried, and sautéed. It can be served hot or cold, with or without a sauce. It goes well with almost any seasonal vegetable, and has an affinity for many aromatic herbs and spices. Every ethnic cuisine I can think of has used chicken with creativity and imagination. The *Arroz con Pollo* from Spain is a delicious combination of chicken stewed with tomatoes and onions and bound with a saffron-flavored rice. It was the most popular one-dish meal at home when I grew up, and I serve it as a simple supper dish almost every week. In Morocco, chicken with preserved lemons is the most famous dish; the chicken is stewed together with lemons, olives, and rich aromatic spices. France's *Coq au Vin*, the chicken curries of India, and Austria's spicy Chicken Paprikash as well as our own Southern Fried Chicken are just a few more of the endless variations. They are all so different in texture and taste that one has to marvel at the ability of this fowl to absorb and accept so good-naturedly so many different presentations. (One must also marvel at the ingenuity of cooks all over the world who have made such use of this versatile, simple, and inexpensive fowl.)

For us the reasons to cook chicken are simple: it is delicious, inexpensive, and very high in protein. For several years now Americans have been consuming large amounts of chicken mainly because it is still the best buy in the supermarket. With its growing popularity it is more important than ever to have an interesting chicken repertoire; the knowledgeable cook can easily prepare a delicious chicken dish in as little as thirty minutes. The American shopper is further spoiled by the fact that, for a price, she can buy only chicken parts. As a friend once asked me, "Where else in the world does a chicken come with fourteen wings, six thighs, and a dozen livers?" I find this a rather foolish and uneconomical way to shop. *Every* part of the chicken is useful and if you compare the price of a whole chicken to the price of separate parts, you will be shocked. Once you know how to cut up a chicken (any good butcher will be happy to show you) you can buy them whole in your

supermarket and use the wings, giblets, and backbones for stock.

As mentioned in the chapter on soup, I consider chicken stock the most basic and important stock of all. It is the base for all cream-of-vegetable soups; it is essential in making risottos and other rice dishes; and it is a must for basting all fowl, whether it be chicken, turkey, or duck. Chicken stocks can be made at any time, simmering away even as you prepare some other dish. They can be frozen for later use, and will keep for two to three weeks refrigerated. If you are pressed for time, simply freeze the giblets every time you buy a chicken and make the stock when you have accumulated enough.

When buying chickens above all look for freshness and buy the right kind of chicken for your recipe—fryer, roaster, or stewing chicken. While I was testing the recipes in this book I bought chickens both from my butcher and from the supermarket. I used white birds as well as yellow ones. I tried several of the highly advertised brands, and compared them with freshly killed chickens that came from a farm in Pennsylvania. In the end I decided that as long as the chickens were really *fresh*, they were good. In some regions chickens are better than others. At a recent workshop in Texas I used some local chickens so flavorful that they could easily compare with the best chickens in Europe. In New York and much of the surrounding area, yellow corn-fed chickens have become extremely popular but I find them fatty and watery. This is because they stay packed in ice for as much as thirty-six hours before they reach the supermarket counter. This causes them to absorb a considerable amount of moisture; I find that no matter how carefully you dry them, they still splatter and don't brown properly. This is the major difference between supermarket and butcher-shop chickens. A good butcher will not keep chickens for more than two days. Thus at the butcher's you are somewhat more assured of freshness, and the chickens will probably be less watery. I have found supermarket managers usually happy to tell you the delivery days for poultry; on those days chickens are usually cheaper and just as good as those from the expensive, often less-convenient butcher shop. When you shop in the supermarket note that the chickens are labeled with the last date of purchase. This *should* be an indication of their freshness; however if a particular market does not have a large turnover, and the butcher thinks the chicken is still fresh, he will rewrap it, putting a new purchasing label on it, and put it back on the counter. This means that the date of purchase you see on the label does not guarantee freshness.

The grading of chickens has little to do with their flavor and is more a matter of appearance. A Grade A chicken is one that has no blemishes or surface cuts; in many ways this is a good indication of quality. However, I often buy chickens near my house in the country and although they are ungraded and sometimes have small blemishes, they are absolutely delicious.

To prepare this marvelous bird one hardly knows where to begin. The simplest yet most misunderstood preparation is surely the "roast chicken." To most people, this means seasoning a bird with salt and pepper and then roasting it with a little butter and oil until it is done. "Done" often means overdone, alas, and basting—if it is done at all—is limited to the juices released by the chicken. This often results in a dry, overcooked chicken with hardly any pan juices. I find that the proper seasoning is extremely important to a roast chicken, and I usually make a paste of coarse salt, freshly ground black or white pepper, 2 tablespoons Dijon mustard, 1 teaspoon thyme, and 1 teaspoon imported paprika. First I rub the chicken with the mixture and place a whole, peeled onion in the cavity, then I truss the bird and place it on its side in a roasting pan with 2 tablespoons of melted butter. The chicken is roasted and basted with a rich chicken stock every 10 minutes. A 3-pound chicken is usually done in 1 hour, 30 to 40 minutes. You can easily tell when the chicken is done by piercing the flesh with the tip of a sharp knife—the juices must run clear. For a crisp chicken remove it to a baking sheet and place it quickly in the boiler. Because of the basting the resulting pan juices will be rich and flavorful. They may be thickened with a little Beurre Manié and a variety of seasonal, sautéed vegetables can be added to them. Sautéed cucumbers, mushrooms, or 2 to 3 tablespoons of Provençale Tomato Fondue (page 542) are just some of my favorite variations. Leftover roast chicken is delicious cold and if I have enough (which

I rarely do), I often dice and toss it with a julienne of romaine lettuce and a mustard vinaigrette. It makes a wonderful and simple luncheon or appetizer salad.

Two of the world's classic chicken dishes—the *Poule au Pot* (Chicken in the Pot) and the Scottish Cock-a-Leekie Soup—call for poached chicken. I find poached chickens rather bland unless accompanied by an interesting sauce. If you are not using a large fowl, you must poach the chicken in an already well-flavored rich stock or else both the chicken and resulting broth will be bland and watery. Cold poached chicken is excellent for salads, particularly when bound with a curry or *fines herbes* mayonnaise. The poached Cold Chicken Breasts Veneziana (page 258) are an inexpensive variation of the classic Vitello Tonnato (a dish usually made with poached veal and served in a tuna-flavored mayonnaise). Accompanied by a well-seasoned potato salad, it makes a lovely summer supper or lunch.

My favorite method of cooking chicken is the "sauté." Here the chicken parts are first browned in butter or rendered chicken fat and then braised, covered, on top of the stove. A little stock and white wine must be added to the skillet every 10 minutes. This results in a richly concentrated "short sauce" that is heavenly. To these simple pan juices you might add various seasonal vegetables such as sautéed zucchini, eggplant cubes, roasted red peppers, or a combination of all three. In the summer I usually add a large sprig of either tarragon

or rosemary to the pan. Both herbs have a wonderful affinity for chicken and really enhance the dish with their special, fragrant flavor.

One of the reasons I like to buy chickens whole and cut them up myself is that for a better price, you can take advantage of both the dark and the more delicate light meat. The dark meat of the thighs and leg lends itself better to heartier dishes such as brown sauces, vinegar sauces, and tomato sauces; the chicken breasts with their delicate flavor and texture are better in preparations such as the Sautéed Chicken Breasts in Lemon Cream (page 257). Most people tend to overcook chicken breasts, which makes them stringy and dry. I will never forget one student who asked why the chicken breasts she had been cooking for 30 minutes were still tough. Chicken breasts require only 6 to 8 minutes of cooking and should be served as soon as possible since they tend to dry out quickly. What makes them so versatile, elegant, and yet basic is that they can also be used beautifully in many recipes that call for veal scaloppine. Placed between 2 pieces of waxed paper the chicken breasts are flattened, seasoned with salt and pepper, dipped in flour, and quickly sautéed in hot butter. The pan juices are deglazed with a little white wine, some stock, and a spoonful of heavy cream, then spooned over the chicken breasts. The entire dish takes about 10 minutes to prepare, and every ingredient in it can be bought inexpensively at any supermarket. I enjoy cooking and eating chickens and will probably never run out of interesting ways to serve them. For every season, there are at least 2 vegetables that are excellent with every kind of chicken concoction, either braised with it, added to the pan juices, or served alongside. Whether I am using the dark meat or the more tender and fine-grained chicken breasts, preparing a classic French recipe or an exotic, spur-of-the-moment invention, chicken is an unpretentious, good-natured bird that allows a fabulous range of creativity, both in the preparation and the year-round seasonal accompaniments.

Turkey

At one time, the word *turkey* was synonymous with Holiday Dinner. For my family, like many others, neither Christmas nor Thanksgiving would be complete without a turkey dinner. But more and more turkeys are becoming a popular year-round food; they are readily available, inexpensive, and offer an easy way to feed a large family. While at one time only frozen birds could be found year-round in most supermarkets, today many markets now feature fresh turkeys as well as turkey parts.

As with frozen ducks, it is hard to judge how long a turkey has been in the freezer. Supposedly it is checked by the meat department once a month and weighed; if there is any weight loss, it is defrosted and sold in parts. Every supermarket manager I talked to claimed that the turnover in frozen turkeys is so large these days that there is never any problem with buying a frozen bird. When defrosting place it in the lower part of the refrigerator and allow three days

for a sixteen-pound bird. Dry it thoroughly with paper towels before roasting. I find frozen turkeys almost invariably dry, no matter how well I treat them, and much prefer buying a fresh one. The reason for this dryness is that the "self-basting" label is misleading. Although the turkey is injected with some vegetable shortening or oil, this is just a bit of gimmickry to lead you to believe you can, without any fuss or care, miraculously produce a juicy, wonderfully brown turkey. The truth is that every turkey, much like every roasting chicken, has to be properly seasoned then thoroughly rubbed with softened butter and basted every 10 minutes with a full-bodied chicken stock.

If you are buying a turkey from your butcher, ask for a hen turkey; these are the juiciest of all. Select a bird that has a whitish or bluish flesh, and look for rounded birds with plump breasts. I prefer the younger hen turkey that weighs between 12 and 16 pounds; the larger birds are usually tom turkeys and I find them somewhat drier. In recent years many butchers have started to carry wild turkeys in the fall, but I think they are gamy and tough.

While the stuffed and roasted turkey is still the most popular, I find that bread stuffings tend to dry out the meat since they absorb much of the natural juices. If you are using a bread stuffing, make it yourself and add a large onion diced and sautéed in rendered chicken or duck fat. Avoid overstuffing the turkey and season it carefully, as you would a roasting chicken (see page 227). The roasting method is the same, except that I like to roast a turkey on a bed of *mirepoix* —a mixture of diced aromatic vegetables consisting of a large carrot, 2 onions, and 2 stalks of celery, diced. I baste the turkey with stock every 15 minutes and cover it loosely with foil for the first 2 hours.

Turkey has the same affinity for fruits as has duck. Many accompaniments based on fall fruits—sautéed apples, spiced pears, or poached prunes—are particularly good when added to the pan juices or served as a garnish. One of my favorite seasonal fruits is quince, which you can now find at some specialty markets or New England farm stands during the fall. Poach the quince in a dessert syrup with cinnamon and vanilla and serve as a garnish. For vegetable garnishes, the best are small braised onions (the Sweet-and Sour Braised Onions on page 431 are wonderful with turkey), braised chestnuts, and red cabbage braised with 3 to 4 pears or apples.

In my kitchen, leftover turkey is always turned into a hearty salad. The Turkey Salad Niçoise in *The Peasant Kitchen* and a turkey-and-potato salad bound with a garlic-and-mustard vinaigrette are two of my favorites. Both are inexpensive and wonderfully flavorful. Depending on the season, you may also add some roasted red peppers, diced bacon, cubed and sautéed, finely sliced raw mushrooms, or cooked broccoli florets.

Like chicken, turkey lends itself to a wide variety of preparations. It can often be used with great results in many of the chicken recipes, from the traditional roast turkey with chestnut stuffing to Braised Turkey à la Bourguignonne (braised in dry red wine). Perenially popular, this easily adaptable bird offers the serious cook many more culinary possibilities than we customarily think of. I am happy to see it no longer limited to its traditional biannual appearance on our holiday tables.

Ducks
Like chickens, ducks are still one of the best buys in the supermarket, although they are usually only available frozen. While a really fresh duck is far superior to a frozen one, I have found that the heavy layer of fat protects the flesh from drying out and therefore using frozen ducks can give excellent results.

When buying a frozen duck, look it over carefully and avoid any that show signs of having been defrosted and refrozen. Although there is no final date of sale on frozen ducks, several supermarket meat managers have assured me that the ducks and turkeys are weighed every month; if there is considerable weight loss, they are defrosted and cut up to be sold as "specials."

If you are buying a fresh duck in a supermarket, look it over carefully and avoid any with torn skin; this results in discolored flesh. Be sure to check the last date of sale. Ducks do not keep well, and if they have been vacuum packed for more than two days, they develop an unpleasant gamy flavor.

The best ducks, frozen or not, are from Long Island. These are available in and around the New York area and are often listed as such on restaurant menus everywhere. Unfortunately there is less and less duck farming on Long Island since real estate prices have skyrocketed and many farmers have sold their land to developers. The best fresh ducks are available at Chinese grocery stores in both New York and San Francisco and probably any other city with a large Chinese population. Since the classic Chinese Peking Duck is made with an uneviscerated fowl, the ducks must be extremely fresh. I use these whenever I have the chance, and they are simply delicious.

A frozen duck should be left to defrost in the refrigerator for anywhere from 12 to 16 hours. Rinse the duck thoroughly under running water, remove the neck and liver from the cavity, and dry thoroughly with lots of paper towels, placing a large ball of them inside the cavity. I never use a rack for roasting a duck (or any other fowl, for that matter), since it prevents the pan juices from forming and causes a great deal of splattering in the oven. After trussing the duck, season it with coarse salt and freshly ground white pepper. Heat a little rendered chicken or duck fat in a heavy baking dish and brown the duck on both sides over moderate-to-high heat. This prevents the duck from sticking to the pan during roasting. Do not prick the duck; it is unnecessary, and will only dry it out. Roast it on its side (this protects the breast) in a 350-degree oven for 2 hours, 30 minutes, removing the accumulated fat from the pan

every 10 minutes and basting with hot chicken stock. When the duck is done, put it on a baking sheet and place it in the broiler if you like it crisp. After thoroughly deglazing the pan juices, add some more chicken or duck stock to the pan and thicken the sauce with a little potato starch or cornstarch.

Ducks have a natural affinity for fruits, and are delicious with prunes, apples, pears, pineapple, peaches, cherries, and oranges. Of all the wonderful fruits that enhance the taste of this versatile fowl, the classic Duck à l'Orange is by far the most popular. Although this is admittedly a great combination, I find the garnish of prunes or spiced pears much more interesting. In France, it has become increasingly popular to serve duck accompanied by exotic fruits such as mangoes and kiwis. These do not have enough "character," but can make for an amusing change in appearance, if not in flavor.

In spite of their natural "marriage" with fruit, ducks are equally wonderful when prepared in a green peppercorn sauce or served with an onion marmalade. The Austrian way of seasoning the duck heavily with caraway seeds, roasting it, and serving it on a bed of braised sweet-and-sour red cabbage makes for a gusty and flavorful meal that is both inexpensive and easy to prepare. Unfortunately the French method of braising duck simply doesn't work with our fatty ducks. The classic braised duck with turnips is usually a greasy mess when made with our Peking duck. (On the other hand, braised turnips added to the degreased pan juices of a roasted duck makes a wonderful combination that is reminiscent of the classic dish.) Like chicken, duck is an extremely good-natured bird that can be prepared both simply and elaborately; these days, because of its availability and low cost, it can also make an economical meal. Once it is roasted, it can be kept warm, wrapped in foil for 2 to 3 hours, and its skin crisped just before serving. This makes it not only good for a family dinner, but also for an elegant and impressive dinner party.

Ballottine of Chicken Paysanne

Serves:	**6**
Preparation time:	**45 minutes, plus 4 to 6 hours to chill**
Cooking time:	**1 hour, 45 minutes**
Type of recipe:	**difficult**
Cost:	**inexpensive**

Ingredients

1 three-pound chicken
Salt and freshly ground black pepper
1 teaspoon imported paprika
1 teaspoon dried thyme
1 clove garlic, peeled and crushed
2 Tablespoons butter
1 Tablespoon oil
1 onion, peeled and cut in half
1 to 1½ cups Chicken Stock (page 530) or bouillon

Stuffing:

2 Tablespoons butter
1 onion, peeled and finely minced
¾ pound ground veal
½ pound ground pork
⅓ cup water
2 Tablespoons bread crumbs
2 Tablespoons finely minced fresh parsley
1 teaspoon dried thyme
Salt and freshly ground black pepper
2 cloves garlic, peeled and crushed
Pinch of allspice
½ cup diced smoked ham

Garnish:

Sprigs of fresh parsley

Preparation

1.
Prepare the stuffing. In a small skillet heat the butter. Add the onion and cook over low heat until soft but not browned.

2.
In a bowl combine the ground veal, pork, water, bread crumbs, parsley, and thyme. Add the sautéed onion. Season the mixture with salt and pepper, and add the garlic. Add a pinch of allspice and work the mixture until it is thoroughly combined. Add the smoked ham. Sauté a small amount, then taste and correct the seasoning. The stuffing should be highly seasoned. Set aside.

3.
Preheat the oven to 350 degrees.

4.
Bone the chicken as follows: the object is to remove the rib cage, excluding the wings and legs, in 1 piece without piercing the skin so as not to lose any of the stuffing during cooking.

5.
Place the chicken, breast-side up, on cutting board. Start at neck end, using a small sharp boning knife. Remove the wishbone by lifting the skin to expose the flesh. With a knife scrape the flesh and follow the shape of the wishbone. Free it from its natural position with your fingers and remove.

6.
Cut off the wings at the elbow joints.

7.
Next start cutting the meat away from the rib cage on all sides, keeping your knife as close to the rib cage as possible, and

without piercing the skin of the chicken. Continue working toward the middle.

8.
At the middle, turn the carcass completely around and follow the same procedure from the tail end.

9.
From the inside, cut the legs at the hip joint and the wings at shoulder joint, thus freeing the rib cage. Remove the rib cage in 1 piece.

10.
Bone the legs and wings by scraping away with a knife all the meat from the shoulder bones, side, and drumstick bones. Remove the bones.

11.
Push the drumstick meat and shoulder meat inside the chicken. Season the cavity of the chicken with salt and freshly ground pepper.

12.
Sew the neck opening and fill the chicken with the stuffing, then sew the tail end closed.

13.
Season the chicken with salt and freshly ground pepper. Rub the chicken with paprika, thyme, and garlic and set aside.

14.
In a heavy baking dish heat the butter and oil. Add the onion, cut-side down, and place the chicken in the dish. Spoon a little melted butter over the chicken and add 2 tablespoons stock. Place the dish in the center of the oven and roast the chicken for 1 hour, 30 minutes to 1 hour, 45 minutes, basting the chicken every 10 minutes with the hot stock.

15.
When the chicken is done, transfer it to a serving dish. Let the chicken cool at room temperature.

16.
About 30 minutes before serving slice the chicken crosswise into ½-inch slices and place overlapping on the serving platter. Garnish the platter with sprigs of parsley and serve the chicken accompanied by crusty French bread and the reheated pan juices on the side.

Remarks
The chicken ballottine is a wonderful buffet dish. It has a similar taste to a country pâté but is somewhat more elegant. It can also be served as an appetizer or cold dinner dish accompanied by a well-seasoned green salad or a ratatouille. It can also be served hot accompanied by its pan juices.

Chicken
in Lemon Sauce
(à la Tourangelle)

Serves: **4**
Preparation time: **15 minutes**
Cooking time: **1 hour, 15 minutes**
Type of recipe: **elementary**
Cost: **inexpensive**

Ingredients

1 three-pound chicken, trussed
Salt and freshly ground black pepper
1 teaspoon dried thyme
½ teaspoon dried marjoram
1 small onion, peeled
2 Tablespoons rendered chicken fat or butter
2 teaspoons oil
10 large shallots, peeled
1¼ cups Brown Chicken Stock (page 531)
Juice of 2 large lemons
3 large cloves garlic, peeled and crushed
1 Bouquet Garni (page 546)
1 small bunch fresh tarragon
1 Beurre Manié (page 544)

Garnish:

Sprigs of fresh parsley
12 cherry tomatoes, sautéed in olive oil and seasoned with salt and pepper

Preparation

1.
Preheat the oven to 350 degrees.

2.
Season the chicken with salt and pepper. Rub with thyme and marjoram and place the onion in the cavity.

3.
In a large cast-iron skillet heat the fat and oil. When the fat is very hot add the chicken and brown on all sides. Regulate the heat so that the fat does not burn.

4.
Transfer the chicken to an oval casserole and set aside. Discard all but 2 tablespoons fat from the skillet.

5.
Add the shallots to the skillet and sauté until lightly browned, tossing them in the fat. Add ¾ cup stock, bring to a boil, and cook until reduced by half. Transfer the shallot-and-stock mixture to the casserole.

6.
Add the lemon juice, garlic, bouquet, and tarragon. Bring slowly to a boil on top of the stove. Cover the casserole tightly and place in the oven.

7.
Braise the chicken for 1 hour to 1 hour, 10 minutes, turning it once or twice during its cooking time and basting it with the pan juices. The chicken is done when the juices run pale yellow. Test by piercing the chicken in the thigh with the tip of a sharp knife. When the chicken is done, transfer it to a baking dish and set aside.

8.
Discard the bouquet and tarragon sprigs. Carefully degrease the pan juices, then add

Poached Chicken
à la Lyonnaise

Serves: **4 to 6**
Preparation time: **45 minutes**
Cooking time: **2 hours, 15 minutes**
Type of recipe: **elementary**
Cost: **inexpensive**

the remaining stock to the casserole. Bring to a boil on top of the stove and whisk in bits of Beurre Manié; use just enough for the sauce to coat the spoon. Taste and correct the seasoning. The sauce should have a distinct lemon flavor. Set the sauce on the side and keep warm.

9.
Preheat the broiler.

10.
Place the chicken 6 inches from the source of heat and brown until it is crisp on all sides.

11.
Quarter the chicken and place on a serving platter. Spoon the sauce over the chicken and garnish with sprigs of parsley and sautéed cherry tomatoes. Serve immediately accompanied by a pilaf of rice or crusty French bread.

Remarks
You may substitute a bouquet of fresh marjoram for the tarragon. Since marjoram has a completely different flavor it will vary the dish entirely. When using dried tarragon, add 1½ teaspoons to the stock and simmer covered for 20 minutes, or until the herb has imparted all its flavor. The entire dish can be prepared ahead and kept warm in the sauce. The browning of the chicken under the broiler is optional. It will taste equally good simply braised and served with its pan juices.

In the French province of Bresse, which is famous for its chickens, this is a typical dish prepared by the country women as well as by most of the great chefs in the region. The stuffing of the chicken varies according to the cook and the garnish according to the seasons. Here is a version that I find lends itself particularly well to American kitchens.

Ingredients
1 three- to three-and-one-half-pound chicken
Salt and freshly ground white pepper
2 quarts well-flavored Chicken Stock (page 530)

Stuffing:
½ cup finely cubed carrots
½ cup finely cubed green beans
¾ cup green peas
1½ cups cooked long-grain rice
4 Tablespoons butter
3 chicken livers, cleaned and cubed
2 Tablespoons finely minced fresh parsley
Salt and freshly ground white pepper
2 Tablespoons flour
1 cup hot Chicken Stock (page 530)

Vegetable Garnish:
8 small new potatoes, peeled
4 to 6 small turnips, peeled and cut in quarters
3 to 4 carrots, scraped and cut into 3-inch pieces
3 to 4 small zucchini, cut into 4-inch pieces
1 small cabbage, cut in eighths

Preparation

1.
Start by making the stuffing. Drop the vegetables into boiling salted water and poach until tender, or for about 5 to 6 minutes. Drain well and place in a mixing bowl with the rice.

2.
In a small heavy skillet heat 2 tablespoons butter. When the butter is very hot add the chicken livers and cook over high heat until nicely browned but still pink. Season the livers with salt and pepper and transfer to a chopping board. Mince the livers and add to the rice mixture together with the parsley. Set aside.

3.
In a small heavy saucepan melt the remaining butter. Add the flour and cook without browning for 2 minutes, stirring constantly.

4.
Remove the pan from the heat. Add 1 cup stock all at once and stir until the mixture is thick and smooth. Return the pan to the heat and continue cooking the mixture until it is very thick. Season with salt and pepper and pour into the rice mixture.

5.
With a wooden spoon blend the rice, vegetable, and chicken liver mixture and correct the seasoning. Stuff the chicken with the filling and sew up the opening. Tie the chicken legs with string. Season the chicken with salt and pepper. Set aside.

6.
In a large casserole bring the chicken stock to a boil. Reduce the heat and add the chicken. Poach the chicken covered over low heat for 1 hour, 20 minutes. Do not overcook.

7.
When the chicken is done remove it to a deep serving platter. Cover with foil and keep warm.

8.
Add the vegetable garnish to the pot starting with the potatoes, turnips, and carrots. When these are almost done add the zucchini and continue poaching for 6 to 8 minutes. Do not overcook the vegetables.

9.
With a slotted spoon remove all the vegetables to the platter making a decorative pattern. Keep warm.

10.
Add the cabbage to the pot and cook until tender, or for about 10 to 12 minutes. Drain the cabbage and add to the platter. Serve the broth separately, followed by the chicken and vegetables.

Poached Chicken
in
Parsley Sauce

Serves:	**3 to 4**
Preparation time:	**30 minutes**
Cooking time:	**2 hours**
Type of recipe:	**elementary**
Cost:	**inexpensive**

Ingredients

1 three-pound chicken
Salt and freshly ground black pepper
1 small bunch fresh parsley
½ lemon
6 cups concentrated Chicken Stock (page 530)
2 small onions, unpeeled

Sauce:

5 Tablespoons butter
1 Tablespoon finely minced shallots
1 two-inch piece lemon rind
2 large ripe tomatoes, seeded and finely cubed
Salt and freshly ground black pepper
1 teaspoon dried thyme
¼ cup dry white wine
1 Tablespoon white wine vinegar
3 Tablespoons flour
2 egg yolks
¾ cup heavy cream
½ to ¾ cup finely minced fresh parsley
2 Tablespoons fresh basil leaves, cut into thin julienne strips

Garnish:
Sprigs of fresh parsley

Optional:
1 pound white onions, peeled and poached in stock

Preparation

1.
Season the chicken cavity with salt and pepper. Place the parsley and lemon half inside the cavity. Truss the chicken and set aside.

2.
In a large casserole bring the stock to a boil. Add the onions, lower the heat, and add the chicken, breast-side down. Poach the chicken gently for 1 hour, 15 minutes to 1 hour, 30 minutes, turning it once or twice; do not overcook. The chicken is done when the juices run a pale yellow. (Test for doneness by piercing it in the sides with the tip of a sharp knife.)

3.
When the chicken is done transfer it carefully to a side dish. Cover and keep warm. Measure 2 cups stock. Degrease thoroughly and reserve.

4.
Prepare the sauce. In a heavy skillet heat 2 tablespoons butter, add the shallots, and cook for 2 minutes without browning. Add the lemon rind and tomatoes, and season with salt, pepper, and thyme. Bring to a boil, then reduce the heat and simmer the mixture until the tomato water has evaporated.

5.
Add the wine and vinegar, bring to a boil, and cook until the liquid has evaporated. Set the mixture aside.

6.
In a heavy 2-quart saucepan melt the remaining butter. Add the flour and cook for 2 to 3 minutes whisking constantly. Do not let the flour brown.

Poulet
à la Lyonnaise

Serves: **4**
Preparation time: **15 minutes**
Cooking time: **1 hour, 35 minutes**
Type of recipe: **elementary**
Cost: **inexpensive**

7.
Add the reserved 2 cups stock. Bring to a boil and whisk the sauce until thick and smooth. Add the tomato mixture, season carefully with salt and pepper, cover the saucepan, and simmer the sauce for 15 minutes.

8.
Combine the yolks and cream in a bowl and whisk until well blended. Set aside.

9.
Strain the sauce through a fine sieve and return to the saucepan. Whisk in ½ cup parsley and the basil, then the yolk-and-cream mixture. Heat the sauce without letting it come to a boil. Taste and correct the seasoning. Keep the sauce warm.

10.
Carve the chicken and place it on a serving platter. Spoon the parsley sauce over it. Sprinkle with the remaining parsley and garnish with sprigs of parsley and the optional cooked white onions.

Remarks
If you have good concentrated chicken stock on hand you can prepare the sauce several hours ahead and reheat it. The poaching stock can also be served as a soup. Add 1 large carrot, scraped, finely sliced, and cooked in the soup until tender. Cook 2 cups fine fresh egg noodles separately in salted water, add to the soup, and serve hot. If you don't have fresh basil use 1½ teaspoons dried. Add the dried herb to the tomato mixture.

Ingredients
1 three-pound chicken
Salt and freshly ground black pepper
1 teaspoon dried thyme
3 Tablespoons butter
1 Tablespoon oil
14 to 16 small white onions, peeled
Large pinch of granulated sugar
⅓ cup dry white wine
1 cup Brown Chicken Stock (page 531)
1 Bouquet Garni (page 546)
1 cup Crème Fraîche (page 544)
1 Beurre Manié (page 544)

Optional:
Sautéed whole button mushrooms
½ cup cooked peas
Finely minced fresh parsley

Preparation
1.
Preheat the oven to 350 degrees.
2.
Season the chicken with salt, pepper, and thyme. Truss the chicken.
3.
In a heavy oval casserole heat the butter and oil over medium heat. Add the chicken and sauté until browned on all sides. Transfer the chicken to a side dish and reserve.
4.
Discard all but 2 tablespoons of fat from the casserole. Add the onions, sprinkle with sugar, and season with salt and pepper. Sauté the onions, rolling them back and forth in the casserole until nicely browned. The onions will not brown evenly. With a slotted spoon remove the onions.

Roast Stuffed Chicken
with
Chicken Mousse
Printanière

Serves:	**4**
Preparation time:	**45 minutes**
Cooking time:	**1 hour, 10 minutes**
Type of recipe:	**difficult**
Cost:	**inexpensive**

5.
Add the wine to the casserole, bring to a boil, and reduce to a glaze. Add ½ cup stock, bring to a boil, and reduce the heat.
6.
Return the chicken to the casserole, together with the onions, and add the bouquet. Cover the casserole and place in the oven. Braise the chicken for 1 hour, 20 minutes. When done, transfer the chicken to a serving platter and keep warm.
7.
Thoroughly degrease the pan juices. With a slotted spoon remove the onions to the serving platter and set the casserole over high heat.
8.
Add the remaining stock to the casserole, together with the Crème Fraîche. Bring to a boil and cook the sauce until reduced by one third.
9.
Whisk in bits of the Beurre Manié; use just enough until the sauce heavily coats a spoon. Taste the sauce and correct the seasoning.
10.
Spoon the sauce over the chicken and onions, then garnish with the optional sautéed mushrooms and cooked peas. Sprinkle with parsley. Serve accompanied by crusty French bread or a pilaf of rice.

Ingredients
1 three-pound chicken, boned according to directions on pages 233–34
Salt and freshly ground black pepper
1½ teaspoons dried thyme
2 Tablespoons butter
1 Tablespoon oil
2 small onions, peeled and quartered
1 to 1½ cups Chicken Stock (page 530)
2 teaspoons potato flour, mixed to a paste with a little stock

Stuffing:
2 cups tightly packed fresh spinach
½ pound chicken breasts, all fat removed, then finely cubed
1 egg white
2 teaspoons finely minced shallots
¾ cup cold heavy cream
Salt and freshly ground black pepper

Garnish:
Sprigs of fresh watercress

Optional:
2 cups cooked fresh peas

Preparation

1.
Prepare the stuffing first. Wash the spinach thoroughly under cold running water and remove the stems. In a saucepan bring salted water to a boil. Add the spinach and cook for 3 minutes. Drain the spinach and when cool enough to handle squeeze all the extra moisture out with your hands. Chop the spinach finely and set aside.

2.
In a food processor combine the cubed chicken, egg white, and shallots. Blend the mixture until smooth and, with the motor still running, add ½ cup cream in a slow stream. (The meat will absorb the cream and have a mousselike consistency.) Add the spinach and blend thoroughly into the mixture. Season with salt and pepper and reserve.

3.
Season the inside of the boned chicken with salt, pepper, and ½ the thyme. Sew the opening closed at the tail end of the chicken, pushing the drumstick meat into the skin and sewing the 2 leg openings closed.

4.
Stuff the chicken with the chicken-and-spinach forcemeat and sew the opening closed. Season with salt and pepper and the remaining thyme and set aside.

5.
Preheat the oven to 375 degrees.

6.
In a heavy flameproof baking dish heat the butter and oil over low heat. Scatter the onions in the dish and add the chicken.

Spoon some of the hot butter over the chicken and add 2 tablespoons stock to the pan.

7.
Place the dish in the oven and roast the chicken for 1 hour, adding a little stock every 10 minutes and basting the chicken with the hot pan juices. When the chicken is done transfer to a cutting board and set aside.

8.
Thoroughly degrease the pan juices. Add the remaining stock to the pan, set over high heat, and cook until the pan juices are reduced.

9.
Whisk in a little of the potato flour mixture; use just enough to thicken the pan juices and set aside.

10.
Slice the chicken crosswise into ½-inch slices. Place the slices overlapping on a serving platter and spoon some of the pan juices over each slice. Garnish the platter with the optional cooked peas and the sprigs of fresh watercress. Serve accompanied by crusty French bread and a bowl of sweet butter.

Remarks
The chicken can be roasted several hours ahead and left in the pan juices. Reheat covered in a low oven. Any leftovers are delicious served cold accompanied by well-seasoned watercress salad and crusty French bread.

Roast Chicken
in
Cucumber Sauce

Serves: **4**
Preparation Time: **15 minutes**
Cooking Time: **1 hour, 40 minutes**
Type of recipe: **elementary**
Cost: **inexpensive**

Cucumbers are rarely used in hot preparations—their use seems to be reserved for the salad bowl. Here is a simple dish to which the hot sautéed cucumbers give an unusual and delicious taste.

Ingredients

1 three- to three-and-one-half-pound chicken
Juice of ½ lemon
Salt and freshly ground white pepper
1 teaspoon dried marjoram
1 to 2 cloves garlic, crushed
1 teaspoon Dijon mustard
1 teaspoon imported paprika
5 Tablespoons butter
1 Tablespoon oil
1 onion, peeled and cut in half
1½ cup chicken bouillon
2 cucumbers
¾ cup heavy cream

Garnish:

2 Tablespoons finely minced fresh parsley, or a mixture of finely minced fresh parsley, chives, and dill

Preparation

1.
Preheat the oven to 375 degrees.

2.
Dry the chicken thoroughly with paper towels. Sprinkle the chicken with the lemon juice. Season with salt, pepper, marjoram, garlic, mustard, and paprika, rubbing the seasoning well into the chicken. Truss the chicken and set aside.

3.
In a large flameproof baking dish heat 2 tablespoons butter and the oil. Add the chicken and brown it over moderate heat on both sides.

4.
Add the onion to the pan, as well as a ¼ cup of chicken bouillon.

5.
Place the dish in the oven and roast the chicken for 1 hour, 30 minutes, or until the juices run pale yellow when tested with the tip of a sharp knife. Baste the chicken with the hot bouillon every 10 minutes. Turn the chicken once during the cooking time.

6.
While the chicken is roasting, peel the cucumbers, then cut them in half lengthwise. Remove the seeds with a grapefruit spoon. Cut the cucumbers crosswise into ½-inch pieces and place in a colander. Sprinkle with salt and let drain for 30 minutes over a bowl.

7.
Heat the remaining butter in a heavy skillet. Add the cucumbers and sauté for 3 to 4 minutes, or until lightly browned. Do not overcook. Set aside.

Roast Chicken
Veronese

Serves: **4**
Preparation time: **45 minutes**
Cooking time: **1 hour, 15 minutes**
Type of recipe: **elementary**
Cost: **inexpensive**

8.
When the chicken is done, transfer it to an ovenproof platter and keep warm. Discard the onion and thoroughly degrease the pan juices.

9.
Set the pan over high heat. Bring the pan juices to a boil and reduce by one third. Add the cucumbers and cream and continue cooking the sauce until it heavily coats a spoon. Taste and correct the seasoning. Set aside.

10.
Carve the chicken into serving pieces. Place on a serving platter and spoon the sauce around it. Sprinkle with parsley or the mixture of parsley, chives, and dill and serve immediately, accompanied by Catalan Saffron Risotto (page 329).

Remarks
The entire dish can be completed 1 hour in advance. The chicken can be wrapped in foil and kept warm in a 200-degree oven. If you like the chicken to be crisp run it under the broiler for 3 to 4 minutes on each side before carving.

Ingredients
1 three-pound chicken, split in half lengthwise
1 package (10 ounces) fresh spinach, well washed and stems removed
4 Tablespoons butter
3 Tablespoons finely minced scallions, both green and white parts
1 cup ricotta cheese
2 eggs
½ cup finely diced salami or prosciutto
2 Tablespoons freshly grated Parmesan cheese
Salt and freshly ground black pepper
½ teaspoon dried oregano
½ teaspoon dried thyme
½ teaspoon dried marjoram
½ teaspoon imported paprika
2 small cloves garlic, peeled and crushed
2 Tablespoons olive oil
1 cup hot Chicken Stock (page 530)
1 Beurre Manié (page 544)

Garnish:
Sprigs of fresh parsley

Preparation

1.
Preheat the oven to 350 degrees.

2.
With your fingers gently loosen the chicken skin all the way to the drumstick without breaking it. Set aside.

3.
In a large saucepan bring salted water to boil. Add the spinach and cook for 3 minutes, or until just wilted. Drain the spinach thoroughly and when cool enough to handle mince it finely.

4.
In a small heavy skillet heat 2 tablespoons butter. Add the scallions and spinach and cook the mixture over low heat for 3 to 4 minutes. Transfer to a mixing bowl and add the ricotta, eggs, salami or prosciutto, and Parmesan. Season the mixture with salt, pepper, and oregano and mash the mixture with a fork until well blended.

5.
Carefully slip the stuffing under the chicken skin all the way into the drumsticks. Flatten the stuffing gently. You must be careful not to tear the skin. Season the chicken with salt, pepper, thyme, marjoram, and paprika. Rub with a little crushed garlic.

6.
In a large flameproof baking dish melt the remaining butter and the oil. Place the chicken skin-side up in the baking dish. Remove from the heat and drizzle a little of the oil and butter over the chicken.

7.
Place the baking dish in the center of the oven and roast the chicken for 1 hour to 1 hour, 10 minutes, basting every 10 minutes with a little stock.

8.
When the chicken is done transfer it to a baking sheet. Preheat the broiler and run the chicken quickly under the broiler, being careful not to burn it.

9.
Transfer the chicken to a serving platter and set aside.

10.
Carefully degrease the pan juices. Place the baking dish over high heat and add any remaining stock. Bring to a boil and whisk in a little bit of the Beurre Manié; use just enough to thicken the pan juices.

11.
Spoon the pan juices over the chicken. Garnish the platter with sprigs of fresh parsley and serve immediately.

Remarks
This dish can be served simply accompanied by French bread and a well-seasoned salad or by sautéed creamed mushrooms. The chicken can also be served cold; roast it several hours ahead or the day before and serve it at room temperature.

Perla Meyers' From Market to Kitchen Cookbook

Barbecued Chicken
in
Lime-and-Onion Sauce

Serves: **6**
Preparation time: **15 minutes, plus 24 hours to marinate**
Cooking time: **1 hour, 30 minutes**
Type of recipe: **elementary**
Cost: **inexpensive**

Ingredients
2 small chickens, quartered
5 medium onions, peeled and thinly sliced
4 cloves garlic, peeled and finely minced
Juice of 5 limes
3 small dried hot chili peppers, crumbled
2 to 3 Tablespoons finely minced fresh thyme, or 1½ teaspoons dried
2 bay leaves, crumbled
Coarse salt
Freshly ground black pepper
6 Tablespoons fruity olive oil
½ to ¾ cup Chicken Stock (page 530)
2 teaspoons cornstarch, mixed with a little stock

Garnish:
Sprigs of fresh parsley

Preparation
1.
The night before serving place the chicken pieces in a large porcelain bowl. Add the onions, garlic, lime juice, chili peppers, thyme, and bay leaf. Season with coarse salt and pepper. Drizzle with 3 tablespoons oil and turn the chickens in the marinade to coat them evenly. Cover and refrigerate for 24 hours, turning the chickens several times in the marinade.
2.
The next day prepare the outdoor grill for barbecuing.
3.
In a heavy 12-inch skillet heat the remaining oil. Discard the bay leaves and add the marinade to the pan. Bring to a boil, reduce the heat, and partially cover the pan. Cook the onions for 40 to 50 minutes, or until soft and nicely browned. Keep warm.
4.
Place the chicken pieces on the outdoor grill and cook for 6 to 7 minutes on each side. The chicken should be nicely browned but not charred.
5.
Transfer the chicken pieces to the skillet and spoon the onion mixture over them. Add 2 to 3 tablespoons stock. Cover the skillet partially and simmer the chicken for another 20 minutes, adding a little stock every 10 minutes. Season the chickens with salt and pepper.
6.
When the chickens are done, transfer to a serving platter. With a slotted spoon remove the onions and top the chicken pieces with the onion mixture. Whisk in a little of the cornstarch mixture to thicken the pan juices. Taste and correct the seasoning; the sauce will be quite spicy.
7.
Spoon the pan juices over the chicken. Garnish the platter with parsley and serve accompanied by broiled tomatoes and a well-seasoned green salad.

Sauté of Chicken
Andalouse

Serves:	**4**
Preparation time:	**20 minutes**
Cooking time:	**35 minutes**
Type of recipe:	**elementary**
Cost:	**inexpensive**

Ingredients

4 Tablespoons olive oil
2 zucchini, cubed
Salt and freshly ground black pepper
1 three-pound chicken, cut in eighths
1 Tablespoon butter
2 large cloves garlic, crushed
3 Tablespoons white wine vinegar
Flour
1 cup Chicken Stock (page 530)
2 Roasted Red Peppers (page 545), thinly sliced
1 teaspoon cornstarch, mixed with a little stock

Optional:
1 hot chili pepper

Garnish:
2 Tablespoons finely minced fresh parsley

Preparation

1.
In a small heavy skillet heat 2 tablespoons oil, add the zucchini, season with salt and pepper, and sauté for 4 minutes, or until nicely browned. Drain and set aside.

2.
Dry the chicken thoroughly with paper towels. Season with salt and pepper and set aside.

3.
In a large heavy skillet heat the remaining oil and the butter. Add the chicken pieces, garlic, and optional chili pepper. Sauté the chicken over medium heat partially covered until the pieces are nicely browned on all sides.

4.
Spoon out all but 2 tablespoons of fat from the pan. If the garlic has burned, discard it. Add the vinegar and bring to a boil, scraping well the bottom of the pan. Sprinkle the chicken with flour and cook for 2 minutes, shaking the pan back and forth to coat the chicken evenly.

5.
Add ⅓ cup stock, partially cover the pan, and continue cooking the chicken for 20 minutes, adding a little more stock every 10 minutes.

6.
Add the peppers and cook until heated through, or for about five minutes. Add the zucchini and heat through.

7.
Transfer the chicken with the vegetables to a hot serving dish. Discard the garlic and chili pepper. Bring the pan juices to a boil and add a little of the cornstarch mixture; use just enough for the sauce to be slightly thickened.

8.
Taste, correct the seasoning, and spoon over the chicken. Sprinkle with parsley and serve hot accompanied by roasted potatoes and a well-flavored green salad.

Chicken
with
Broccoli

Serves: **4**
Preparation time: **15 minutes**
Cooking time: **35 minutes**
Type of recipe: **elementary**
Cost: **inexpensive**

Ingredients

1 three-pound chicken, cut in eighths
Salt and freshly ground black pepper
3 Tablespoons olive oil
1 Tablespoon butter
Flour
⅓ cup dry white wine
3 large cloves garlic, peeled and crushed
1 cup Chicken Stock (page 530)
3 cups broccoli florets
1 teaspoon cornstarch, mixed with a little stock

Garnish:
¼ cup finely minced fresh parsley

Preparation

1.
Season the chicken pieces with salt and pepper.

2.
In a large skillet heat the oil and butter and add the chicken pieces; do not crowd the pan. Sauté over medium heat, partially covered, until nicely browned on all sides.

3.
Sprinkle the chicken with flour and cook for 2 more minutes, turning the pieces in the pan until they are evenly coated.

4.
Add the wine, bring to a boil, and reduce to 2 tablespoons. Add the garlic and ½ cup stock. Cover the pan and cook for 20 minutes.

5.
Add the broccoli and remaining stock to the pan. Simmer for another 15 minutes, or until the broccoli is tender.

6.
Transfer the chicken and broccoli to a serving dish. Discard the garlic and whisk in a little cornstarch mixture, cooking the sauce until it coats a spoon.

7.
Spoon the sauce over the chicken, sprinkle with parsley, and serve accompanied by a risotto flavored with the juice of ½ lemon and a touch of cream.

Sauté of Chicken
in
Garlic-and-Tomato Sauce

Serves:	**4**
Preparation time:	**15 minutes**
Cooking time:	**50 minutes**
Type of recipe:	**elementary**
Cost:	**inexpensive**

This gutsy chicken dish comes from Galicia, in northern Spain, where it is often prepared with fresh tuna steaks. The whole unpeeled garlic cloves give the dish a mellow, rather mild flavor that I find quite delicious.

Ingredients

6 small whole chicken legs
Salt and freshly ground black pepper
3 Tablespoons fruity olive oil
2 small onions, peeled and cut in half
Flour
3 Tablespoons dry white wine
½ cup Chicken Stock (page 530)
3 large ripe tomatoes, peeled, seeded, and chopped
18 whole cloves garlic, unpeeled
1 Bouquet Garni (page 546)
1 teaspoon meat glaze
1 Tablespoon cornstarch, mixed with a little chicken stock

Garnish:
Finely minced fresh parsley

Preparation

1.
Dry the chicken legs thoroughly with paper towels. Season with salt and pepper.

2.
Heat the oil in a heavy 12-inch chicken fryer. Add the chicken legs and onions to the pan and brown on both sides over medium heat. When nicely browned, sprinkle the chicken pieces with flour and cook for another 2 or 3 minutes turning the meat once or twice. Remove the chicken pieces from the pan.

3.
Discard all but 2 tablespoons of fat from the pan. Discard the onions if they have burned. Add the wine to the pan, bring to a boil, and reduce to 1 tablespoon. Add the stock, tomatoes, garlic, and Bouquet Garni. Bring the mixture to a boil and season with salt and pepper. Reduce the heat and return the chicken legs to the pan. Cover and simmer for 40 minutes. When the chicken is done, remove to a serving platter and reserve.

4.
Thoroughly degrease the pan juices and discard the bouquet and onions. Strain the pan juices through a fine sieve into a saucepan, pressing down on the garlic cloves to extract all their juices.

5.
Cook the pan juices over high heat until reduced by one third. Add the meat glaze and whisk in a little of the cornstarch mixture; use just enough until the sauce heavily coats a spoon.

6.
Taste and correct the seasoning. Spoon the sauce over the chicken and sprinkle with parsley. Serve with crusty French bread.

Poulet
aux
Tomates

Serves:	**4**
Preparation time:	**20 minutes**
Cooking time:	**45 minutes**
Type of recipe:	**elementary**
Cost:	**inexpensive**

Ingredients

9 to 12 plum tomatoes, peeled
Salt
1 three-pound chicken, cut in eighths and backbone removed
4 Tablespoons fruity olive oil
1½ teaspoons butter
Freshly ground black pepper
2 Tablespoons finely minced shallots
⅓ cup dry white wine
2 teaspoons tomato paste
½ to ¾ cup Brown Chicken Stock (page 531)
1 Bouquet Garni (page 546)
2 large cloves garlic, peeled and crushed
½ teaspoon dried oregano
1 teaspoon dried thyme
2 to 3 Roasted Red Peppers (page 545), thinly sliced

Optional:

1 sprig fresh basil, or ¼ teaspoon dried
1 Tablespoon cornstarch, mixed to a paste with a little stock

Garnish:

Finely minced fresh parsley

Preparation

1.
With the tip of a sharp knife make 2 tiny slits in each peeled tomato. Place in a colander, sprinkle with salt, and let the tomatoes drain over a bowl for 30 minutes to an hour.

2.
Meanwhile dry the chicken pieces thoroughly with paper towels. In a heavy 12-inch chicken fryer heat 2 tablespoons oil and 1½ teaspoons butter. When the fat is very hot, add the chicken and sauté partially covered until the pieces are nicely browned on all sides. Season with salt and pepper and transfer to a side dish.

3.
Discard all but 2 tablespoons of fat from the skillet. Add the shallots and cook for 2 minutes until lightly browned, scraping well the bottom of the pan.

4.
Add the wine, bring to a boil, and cook until reduced to 1 tablespoon. Add the tomato paste and ½ cup stock. Bring to a boil and reduce the heat.

5.
Return the chicken pieces to the skillet, and bury the Bouquet Garni among the chicken. Cover the skillet and simmer the chicken for 30 minutes, adding 2 to 3 tablespoons of stock every 10 minutes. (There should be very little liquid in the skillet; the chicken must not drown. Be careful however, that the pan juices do not reduce too much or the chicken will not cook properly and may burn.)

6.
While the chicken is braising, heat the remaining oil in a small heavy skillet. Add

Sautéed Chicken
in
Brown Lemon Sauce

Serves:	**4 to 6**
Preparation time:	**10 minutes**
Cooking time:	**50 minutes**
Type of recipe:	**elementary**
Cost:	**inexpensive**

Ingredients

1 cup diced salt pork
12 to 14 small white onions, peeled
2 carrots, scraped and cubed
6 small chicken legs
Salt and freshly ground black pepper
4 Tablespoons butter
1 Tablespoon olive oil
1 large onion, peeled and cut in half
Flour
1 cup Brown Chicken Stock (page 531)
1 large Bouquet Garni (page 546)
Juice of 1 large lemon
2 Tablespoons finely minced fresh parsley
2 large cloves garlic, finely minced

the drained tomatoes, garlic, oregano, thyme, and optional basil sprig. Stew the tomatoes gently over low heat for 10 minutes, or until they have rendered all their juices but are not falling apart.

7.
After 30 minutes add the stewed tomatoes and the sliced peppers to the skillet. Simmer covered for another 10 minutes.

8.
With a slotted spoon transfer the chicken, tomatoes, and peppers to a serving platter. Discard the bouquet. Increase the heat and cook the pan juices until well reduced and heavily coating a spoon. (If you like more sauce do not let the pan juices reduce so much; whisk in a bit of the optional cornstarch mixture, adding just enough until the sauce is thickened.)

9.
Taste the sauce and correct the seasoning, adding a large grinding of black pepper. Spoon it over the chicken and garnish with parsley. Serve accompanied by Lemon-and-Chive Risotto (page 329) or Mushroom Risotto Piémontaise (page 328).

Remarks
The entire dish can be prepared several hours ahead and reheated, covered, in a low oven. You may vary the dish by adding ½ pound thinly sliced mushrooms to the pan juices. These should be sautéed separately in 2 tablespoons olive oil and seasoned with salt and pepper. Other vegetables, such as sautéed zucchini or eggplant, can also be added to the pan juices.

Preparation

1.
In a saucepan bring water to boil. Add the salt pork and cook for 3 to 4 minutes. Drain on a double layer of paper towels and set aside.

2.
In another saucepan bring salted water to a boil. Add the white onions and carrots and cook for 5 minutes, or until barely tender. Drain and set aside.

3.
Dry the chicken thoroughly with paper towels. Season with salt and pepper.

4.
In a heavy 12-inch skillet heat 2 tablespoons butter and the oil. Add the chicken legs and halved onion; do not crowd the pan. Sauté over medium heat partially covered until nicely browned on all sides.

5.
Sprinkle the chicken legs lightly with flour and sauté for 2 to 3 more minutes, turning the chicken pieces in the pan until they are evenly browned and coated with flour.

6.
Add the stock, bring to a boil, and reduce the heat. Bury the Bouquet Garni among the chicken pieces and simmer covered for 35 minutes, or until almost tender.

7.
While the chicken is braising, heat the remaining butter in a 10-inch skillet. Add the salt pork and cook until almost crisp. Remove to a side dish with a slotted spoon and reserve.

8.
Add the onions and carrots to the pan.

Sauté for 3 to 4 minutes, or until nicely browned, shaking the pan back and forth to evenly brown the vegetables. Season with salt and pepper and reserve.

9.
When the chicken is almost tender add the salt pork, carrots, and onions to the pan. Sprinkle with lemon juice and simmer for another 10 minutes.

10.
With a slotted spoon transfer the chicken and vegetables to a serving platter. Discard the bouquet. Raise the heat and reduce the pan juices until they heavily coat a spoon. Taste and correct the seasoning; you may need a little more lemon juice.

11.
Add the parsley and garlic and cook for another 2 to 3 minutes. Spoon the sauce over the chicken and vegetables and serve accompanied by braised rice and a well-seasoned green salad.

Remarks
The entire dish can be prepared several hours ahead and reheated. This dish is equally good served cold.

Sautéed Chicken à l'Espagnole

Serves: **4**
Preparation time: **20 minutes**
Cooking time: **35 minutes**
Type of recipe: **elementary**
Cost: **inexpensive**

Ingredients
4 to 5 chicken legs, cut in half
Salt and freshly ground black pepper
4 Tablespoons butter
6 Tablespoons oil
½ to ¾ cup Chicken Stock (page 530)
1 large baking potato, cut into 1-inch cubes
½ pound fresh mushrooms, stems removed and caps cubed
1 cup cooked peas
¼ cup minced fresh parsley
2 large cloves garlic, minced

Preparation
1.
Season the chicken pieces with salt and pepper.
2.
In a large 12-inch chicken fryer heat 2 tablespoons butter and 1 tablespoon oil. Add the chicken pieces and sauté partially covered over medium heat until nicely browned on all sides.
3.
Add 2 tablespoons stock. Cover the pan and simmer the chicken for 25 minutes, adding a little stock every 10 minutes.
4.
While the chicken is cooking, heat the remaining oil in another skillet, add the potato cubes, season with salt and pepper, and sauté over medium heat until the potato cubes are nicely browned and cooked through. Drain and reserve.
5.
Add the remaining butter to the skillet, then add the mushrooms. Season with salt and pepper and sauté for 2 minutes, or until nicely browned. Add to the potatoes and set aside.
6.
When the chicken is cooked, add the potato-and-mushroom mixture to the skillet together with the peas, parsley, and garlic. Simmer for another 2 minutes and transfer to a serving dish. Serve accompanied by French bread and a well-seasoned salad.

Remarks
The entire dish can be prepared 2 to 3 hours ahead and reheated slowly. You can use frozen or canned peas for this dish. For a variation you can add the potato, mushroom, and peas to the pan juices of a roast chicken.

Chicken
in
Tarragon Madeira
Sauce

Serves: **4**
Preparation time: **30 minutes**
Cooking time: **45 minutes**
Type of recipe: **elementary**
Cost: **inexpensive**

Ingredients

6 small chicken legs
3 Tablespoons butter
1 Tablespoon oil
Salt and freshly ground black pepper
Flour
2 medium onions, thinly sliced
Large pinch of granulated sugar
2 Tablespoons finely minced fresh tarragon
¼ cup Madeira wine
1 cup Brown Chicken Stock (page 530)
1 cup heavy cream
1 Beurre Manié (page 544)

Garnish:

2 Tablespoons finely minced fresh parsley
1 Tablespoon finely minced fresh tarragon

Preparation

1.
Dry the chicken thoroughly with paper towels.

2.
In a large heavy skillet heat the butter and oil. Add the chicken legs and cook until they are nicely browned on all sides. Season with salt and pepper and sprinkle lightly with flour. Cook for 2 to 3 more minutes, turning the chicken to coat it evenly with the flour. Transfer to a side dish and reserve.

3.
Add the onions to the pan, sprinkle with sugar, lower the heat, and cook the onions for 5 to 6 minutes, scraping well the bottom of the pan. Allow the onions to brown evenly but do not let them burn.

4.
Add the tarragon to the pan together with the Madeira. Bring to a boil and reduce the Madeira to 1 tablespoon. Add the stock to the pan, bring to a boil, and reduce by half. Return the chicken to the pan, cover, and simmer over low heat for 25 to 30 minutes.

5.
Uncover the skillet. Add the cream and cook over high heat until the cream is reduced by half.

6.
Whisk bits of Beurre Manié into the sauce and continue cooking until the sauce heavily coats a spoon.

7.
Taste and correct the seasoning. Arrange the chicken in a serving dish and spoon the sauce over it. Sprinkle with parsley and tarragon. Serve the chicken accompanied by braised rice.

Remarks
This chicken dish can be made a day in advance and reheated slowly, either on top of the stove or in a 250-degree oven.

Sauté of Chicken Breasts Genevoise

Serves **4**
Preparation time: **15 minutes**
Cooking time: **45 minutes**
Type of recipe: **elementary**
Cost: **inexpensive**

Ingredients

12 to 14 small white onions
5 tablespoons butter
1 Tablespoon oil
1 teaspoon granulated sugar
1½ cups Brown Chicken Stock (page 531)
4 whole chicken breasts, boned, skinned, cut in half, and trimmed of all fat
Salt and freshly ground white pepper
Flour for dredging
½ cup finely diced smoked ham
1 cup heavy cream
1 Beurre Manié (page 544)
1 cup cooked fresh peas

Garnish:

Sprigs of fresh watercress

Preparation

1.
In a saucepan bring salted water to boil. Add the onions and cook for 2 minutes. Drain the onions and peel.

2.
In a cast-iron skillet heat 2 tablespoons butter with 1 teaspoon oil. Add the onions and sugar and sauté the onions, shaking the pan back and forth until nicely browned on all sides.

3.
Add ½ cup stock, cover the pan, lower the heat, and simmer the onions for 15 minutes, or until they are done and the pan juices are reduced to a glaze. Watch the onions carefully for they must not burn. Set aside.

4.
Season the chicken breasts with salt and pepper. Dredge lightly with flour, shaking off the excess.

5.
In a large heavy skillet heat the remaining butter and oil. Add the ham and sauté over medium heat for 2 to 3 minutes. With a slotted spoon transfer the ham to a side dish and reserve.

6.
Add the chicken breasts to the skillet. (You may need a little more butter.) Sauté over moderate-to-high heat until the chicken breasts are nicely browned on all sides. Do not crowd the pan; the chicken must brown quickly without drying out.

7.
Remove the breasts to a side dish and reserve. Discard all but 1 tablespoon of fat from the skillet and add the remaining

Sautéed Chicken Breasts Jardinière

Serves:	**4 to 5**
Preparation time:	**25 minutes**
Cooking time:	**30 minutes**
Type of recipe:	**elementary**
Cost:	**inexpensive**

stock. Bring to a boil and cook until the stock is reduced to ½ cup.

8.
Add the cream, bring back to a boil, and continue cooking until the cream is reduced by one third. Start whisking in bits of Beurre Manié until the sauce coats a spoon. (You will only need about a third.) Taste the sauce and correct the seasoning.

9.
Return the chicken breasts to the skillet, together with the cooked peas, the onions and their pan juices, and the ham. Spoon the sauce over the chicken breasts. Cover the pan and simmer for another 2 or 3 minutes, or until the vegetables and the chicken breasts are just heated through.

10.
Transfer the chicken breasts and vegetables to a serving platter. Garnish the platter with sprigs of watercress and serve immediately, accompanied by a purée of potatoes and turnips.

Remarks

The chicken breasts can be sautéed well in advance and returned to the sauce. They can be re-heated over very low heat just before serving.

Ingredients

5 Tablespoons butter
6 to 8 mushrooms, stems removed and caps quartered
Salt and freshly ground black pepper
1 cup shelled fresh peas
1 carrot, scraped and cubed
1 teaspoon granulated sugar
4 whole chicken breasts, boned, skinned, and cut in half
Flour for dredging
1 Tablespoon oil
1 cup Chicken Stock (page 530)
1 cup heavy cream
1 Beurre Manié (page 544)

Optional:
2 Tablespoons finely minced fresh herbs (chives, dill, parsley)

Preparation

1.
In a small skillet heat 2 tablespoons butter. Add the mushrooms, season with salt and pepper, and sauté over high heat for 2 or 3 minutes, or until nicely browned. Set aside.

2.
In a small heavy saucepan combine the peas and carrots. Add the sugar, a pinch of salt, and cover with water by 1 inch. Bring to a boil, reduce the heat, and simmer until tender, or for about 5 to 6 minutes. Drain and set aside.

3.
Season the chicken breasts with salt and pepper. Dip them into flour, shaking off the excess.

Sauté of Chicken Breasts
with
Sausages à la Romana

Serves: **4**
Preparation time: **10 minutes**
Cooking time: **20 minutes**
Type of recipe: **elementary**
Cost: **inexpensive**

4.
In a large heavy skillet heat the remaining butter and the oil. Add the chicken breasts and sauté over medium heat until nicely browned on both sides. Remove the chicken breasts from the pan.

5.
Add the stock, bring to a boil, and reduce to 3 tablespoons.

6.
Add the cream and bring to a boil; season with salt and pepper and reduce by half.

7.
Return the chicken breasts to the pan. Cover and simmer for 3 to 4 minutes, then add the mushrooms, peas, and carrots and heat through.

8.
Add the optional fresh herbs and cook the sauce for another 2 to 3 minutes. If the sauce seems too thin, whisk in bits of Beurre Manié until the sauce heavily coats a spoon.

9.
Transfer the chicken breasts to a serving platter. Spoon the sauce over the chicken breasts and serve accompanied by sautéed new potatoes.

Remarks
Although this chicken dish requires last-minute preparation, the vegetables can be cooked in advance and reserved. The garnish can include tiny turnip balls or 1 to 2 cups fresh asparagus, cut into 2-inch julienne strips and sautéed in 2 tablespoons butter.

Most chicken breast dishes are delicate in flavor so as not to conflict with the taste of the chicken breasts. For a change I particularly like this version, which has a great deal of character and taste, from the south of Italy.

Ingredients
2 large whole chicken breasts, skinned, boned, and split
Salt and freshly ground black pepper
2 Tablespoons olive oil
4 to 6 sweet Italian link sausages (½ pound)
2 Tablespoons butter
2 cloves garlic, peeled and crushed
1 large sprig fresh rosemary, or 1 teaspoon dried
Flour
⅓ cup dry white wine
½ to ¾ cup Chicken Stock (page 530)

Garnish:
2 Tablespoons minced fresh parsley

Sautéed Chicken Breasts
in
Lemon Cream

Serves:	**5 to 6**
Preparation Time:	**15 minutes, plus 2 hours to prepare the cream**
Cooking time:	**15 minutes**
Type of recipe:	**elementary**
Cost:	**inexpensive**

Preparation

1.
Cut the chicken breasts into 1-inch cubes. Season with salt and pepper and set aside.

2.
In a large heavy skillet heat the oil, add the sausages, and sauté partially covered over low heat until they are nicely browned on both sides, turning them once or twice. Remove the sausages to a cutting board, cut into ½-inch slices and set aside.

3.
Remove all but 1 tablespoon of fat from the pan. Add the butter and, when the butter is hot, add the garlic, rosemary, and chicken pieces.

4.
Sauté the chicken over moderate-to-high heat for 2 to 3 minutes on each side. Sprinkle lightly with flour and cook for another 2 minutes, shaking the pan back and forth to evenly coat the chicken pieces.

5.
Add the wine, bring to a boil, and cook uncovered until reduced to 1 tablespoon. Return the sausage slices to the skillet together with ¼ cup stock. Reduce the heat and simmer for 5 minutes.

6.
Transfer the chicken pieces and sausages to a serving dish. Discard the garlic and rosemary sprig. Add the remaining stock to the pan. Bring to a boil and cook until the pan juices are reduced and syrupy.

7.
Spoon the pan juices over the chicken, sprinkle with parsley, and serve hot accompanied by crusty bread and a well-seasoned salad.

Ingredients

1 cup heavy cream
Juice of 1 large lemon
3 whole chicken breasts, cut in half, skin removed, and flattened
Salt and freshly ground white pepper
Flour for dredging
3 Tablespoons butter
1 Tablespoon oil
1 onion, peeled and cut in half
¾ to 1 cup Chicken Stock (page 530)
1 Beurre Manié (page 544)

Garnish:

8 to 10 small mushrooms, sautéed in a little butter

Optional:

2 Tablespoons finely minced fresh chives or dill

Preparation

1.
A few hours ahead combine the cream and lemon juice in a small stainless steel bowl and let the mixture stand at room temperature for 2 hours.

2.
Season the chicken breasts with salt and pepper. Dredge lightly with flour, shaking off the excess. Set aside.

3.
In a large cast-iron skillet heat the butter and oil. Add the onion, cut-side down, and the chicken breasts. Cook over moderate-to-high heat until the chicken breasts are nicely browned on both sides. Remove the chicken breasts to a side dish and reserve.

Cold Chicken Breasts Veneziana

Serves:	**4 to 6**
Preparation time:	**20 minutes**
Cooking time:	**1 hour, 45 minutes**
Type of recipe:	**elementary**
Cost:	**inexpensive**

4.
Discard all but 1 tablespoon of fat from the pan and add the stock. Bring to a boil and reduce the stock over high heat to ¼ cup.

5.
Discard the onions and lower the heat. Add the lemon cream, season with salt and pepper, and cook the cream mixture until it is slightly reduced. Whisk in bits of Beurre Manié, whisking constantly until the sauce heavily coats a spoon. Do not use too much Beurre Manie or the sauce will have a floury taste.

6.
Return the chicken breasts to the pan. Spoon the sauce over them and simmer them in the sauce for another 3 to 4 minutes. Taste the sauce and correct the seasoning. (The sauce should have a strong lemony taste; if it doesn't you may want to add additional drops of lemon juice.)

7.
Transfer the chicken breasts to a serving platter. Spoon the sauce over them and garnish with optional tiny sautéed mushrooms and a sprinkling of chives or dill.

Remarks
This dish is at its best when prepared at the last minute. You can, however, place the finished dish over a pan of hot water, cover it, and keep it warm for 40 minutes.

Ingredients
1 pound chicken giblets (necks, wings)
2 carrots, scraped
2 stalks celery
1 large onion, peeled
1 sprig fresh parsley
4 cups canned chicken bouillon
salt
4 black peppercorns
3 whole chicken breasts, boned and cut in half

Sauce
2 cups Mayonnaise (page 540)
1 can (3½ ounces) tuna, preferably in olive oil
4 anchovy fillets, finely minced
2 Tablespoons lemon juice

Garnish:
2 to 3 Tablespoons well-drained tiny capers
Quartered lemons
Sprigs of fresh parsley

Chicken Breasts
in
Vinegar-and-Caper Sauce

Serves:	**6**
Preparation time:	**15 minutes**
Cooking time:	**25 minutes**
Type of recipe:	**elementary**
Cost:	**inexpensive**

Preparation

1.
In a large casserole combine the chicken giblets, carrots, celery, onion, parsley, and bouillon. Add 6 cups water, season with salt and add peppercorns. Bring to a boil and simmer for 1 hour. Strain the stock and return it to the casserole. Discard the vegetables.

2.
Add the chicken breasts and simmer in the stock for 8 to 10 minutes; do not overcook. Remove the casserole from the heat and let the chicken breasts cool in the liquid.

3.
Transfer 1 cup stock to a small saucepan. Reduce over high heat to ⅓ cup, then reserve.

4.
Prepare the sauce. In a blender or food processor combine the Mayonnaise, tuna, anchovies, lemon juice, and reduced stock from cooking the chicken and vegetables. Blend the mixture at high speed until smooth. Taste and correct the seasoning.

5.
Two to 4 hours before serving, transfer the chicken breasts to a serving platter. Remove any moisture with paper towels. Spoon the sauce over the chicken breasts, covering them completely. Garnish with capers, lemon wedges, and parsley. Serve chilled but not cold.

Ingredients

4 whole chicken breasts, skin removed, boned, and cut in half
Salt and freshly ground black pepper
Flour for dredging
5 Tablespoons butter
1 Tablespoon olive oil
2 large cloves garlic, crushed
¼ cup red wine vinegar
1½ cups Chicken Stock (page 530)
1 teaspoon meat glaze or 1 cup Brown Chicken Stock (page 531)
1 teaspoon potato starch, mixed with a little stock
2 Tablespoons well-drained tiny capers

Garnish:
Finely minced fresh parsley

Chicken Mousse
with
Watercress Hollandaise

Serves:	**6 to 8**
Preparation time:	**20 minutes**
Cooking time:	**45 minutes**
Type of recipe:	**elementary**
Cost:	**inexpensive**

Preparation

1.
Season the chicken breasts with salt and pepper. Dredge lightly with flour, shaking off the excess.

2.
Melt 3 tablespoons butter and the oil in a large heavy skillet. Add the chicken breasts and garlic and brown the breasts over high heat for 2 to 3 minutes on each side. Remove the chicken breasts to a side dish. If the garlic has burned, discard it.

3.
Add the vinegar to the pan, bring to a boil over high heat, and cook until the vinegar is completely evaporated.

4.
Add 1 cup stock, bring to a boil, and reduce by ⅓. Return the chicken breasts to the pan, lower the heat, and cover the skillet. Simmer for 6 to 7 minutes.

5.
Remove the chicken breasts to a side dish. Add the remaining stock to the skillet, together with the meat glaze, and whisk until well blended. Bring the mixture to a boil and whisk in a little of the potato starch mixture. Add the remaining butter and the capers. Taste and correct the seasoning.

6.
Return the chicken breasts to the pan. Spoon the sauce over them and simmer for 2 to 3 minutes, or until heated through. Transfer the chicken breasts to a serving platter.

6.
Garnish with minced parsley and serve accompanied by Lemon-and-Chive Risotto (page 329).

Ingredients

1 pound chicken breasts, completely trimmed of fat and gristle and cut into small pieces
3 egg whites
1½ cups heavy cream
Salt and freshly ground white pepper

Watercress Hollandaise:

1 bunch fresh watercress, all stems removed
3 large egg yolks
1 Tablespoon lemon juice
3 Tablespoons cold heavy cream
Salt and freshly ground white pepper
1 cup hot melted butter
2 Tablespoons finely minced fresh dill or chives

Garnish:

Sprigs of fresh watercress

Optional:

Sautéed Cucumber Balls (page 421)

Preparation

1.
Preheat the oven to 350 degrees.

2.
Butter a 6-cup loaf pan and set aside.

3.
Place the chicken pieces together with the egg whites in a food processor and grind to a fine purée. (If you do not have a food processor use a blender.)

4.
Start adding the cream to the chicken mixture in a slow stream. The mixture will turn to a fine light mousse. When all the cream has been incorporated season the mixture with salt and pepper.

5.
Pour the mixture into the loaf pan. Bang the pan sharply on the table so that the mousse settles evenly.

6.
Cover the pan with a sheet of well-buttered waxed paper and place in a large pan filled with hot water. The water must come halfway up the sides of the loaf pan. Bake the mousse for 25 minutes, or until it is firm to the touch.

7.
While the mousse is in the oven make the sauce. In a small saucepan bring salted water to a boil. Add the watercress and cook for 2 to 3 minutes. Drain the watercress under cold water and mince finely.

8.
In a blender combine the yolks, lemon juice, and 1 tablespoon cream. Season with salt and pepper. Blend at high speed and add the hot butter in a very slow stream until the sauce is smooth and thick. Add the watercress and blend the sauce until smooth.

9.
Transfer the sauce to a small saucepan and whisk in the remaining cream and the dill. Taste the sauce and correct the seasoning. If not used immediately keep the sauce warm over a pan of warm water, whisking it every 10 minutes to prevent it from curdling. If the sauce shows any signs of curdling add a small ice cube to it and whisk until it is smooth.

10.
Remove the mouse from the oven and let it sit for about 5 minutes before unmolding. Unmold the mousse onto a rectangular serving platter. Wipe the platter of any accumulated juices. Cover loosely with foil and set over a pan of warm water.

11.
When ready to serve spoon the watercress sauce over the mousse and garnish it with optional Sautéed Cucumber Balls and sprigs of watercress.

Remarks
Finely minced dill, mint, or parsley can be added to the cucumbers as well as ½ cup cream or Crème Fraîche. Gourmet cucumbers are sold in many good supermarkets and specialty stores. They come wrapped in cellophane and are less seedy than the garden cucumbers. They remain crisper either in salads or when used in this preparation.

Sautéed Chicken Livers
Lyonnaise

Serves: **4**
Preparation time: **10 minutes**
Cooking time: **15 minutes**
Type of recipe: **elementary**
Cost: **inexpensive**

Ingredients

1 pound fresh chicken livers
Salt and freshly ground black pepper
3 Tablespoons butter
1 Tablespoon oil
2 Tablespoons finely minced shallots
½ cup dry vermouth
1 teaspoon meat glaze
½ cup Brown Chicken Stock (page 531)
1 cup Crème Fraîche (page 544)
1 Tablespoon finely minced fresh tarragon
1 Tablespoon finely minced fresh thyme
1 Beurre Manié (page 544)
1 clove garlic, peeled and crushed

Garnish

Finely minced fresh parsley

Preparation

1.
Clean the chicken livers. Remove any green spots and cut the livers in half. Dry them gently on a layer of paper towels and season with salt and pepper.

2.
Heat 2 tablespoons butter and the oil in a 10-inch cast-iron skillet. Add the chicken livers and sauté over moderate-to-high heat until nicely browned on both sides. Do not crowd the pan. The chicken livers must sauté quickly and remain somewhat rare inside. When the livers are brown, remove with a slotted spoon to a side dish and reserve.

3.
Add the remaining butter to the pan and when hot add the shallots. Cook the shallots for 1 to 2 minutes without browning, scraping well the bottom of the pan.

4.
Add the vermouth, bring to a boil, and cook until reduced to 1 tablespoon.

5.
Add the meat glaze and stock, bring to a boil, and cook over moderate-to-high heat until reduced to 2 tablespoons.

6.
Add the Crème Fraîche and herbs and season with salt and pepper. Bring to a boil and cook until reduced by one third.

7.
Whisk in bits of Beurre Manié; you will need very little. Continue whisking the sauce until it is thick and smooth.

Chicken Livers
in
Mustard-and-Green
Peppercorn Sauce

Serves:	**4**
Preparation time:	**20 minutes, plus 30 minutes for mustard**
Cooking time:	**12 minutes**
Type of recipe:	**elementary**
Cost:	**inexpensive**

8.
Remove the pan from the heat and reduce the heat. Add the garlic to the sauce, then taste and correct the seasoning.

9.
Return the chicken livers together with any accumulated juices to the skillet. Place the skillet over low heat, spooning the sauce over the chicken livers. Heat the chicken livers without letting the sauce come to a boil. Serve immediately on a bed of braised rice, sprinkled with parsley.

Remarks

If you don't have fresh herbs, heat the stock in a small saucepan and add ½ teaspoon dried thyme and ½ teaspoon dried tarragon. Steep the herbs in the hot stock for 30 minutes. The chicken livers make a delicious appetizer. Serve them accompanied by slices of French bread that have been rubbed with the cut side of a garlic clove and sautéed in a mixture of butter and oil until crisp. For variation add 2 artichoke hearts that have been cooked (page 408), cubed, and sautéed in a little butter to the skillet, together with the livers, and heat through.

Ingredients
½ teaspoon dry mustard
1 pound fresh chicken livers
3 Tablespoons butter
1 Tablespoons oil
Salt and freshly ground pepper
2 Tablespoons finely minced shallots
¼ cup dry white wine
1 cup Brown Chicken Stock (page 531)
2 teaspoons Dijon mustard
1 to 2 teaspoons crushed green peppercorns
1 Beurre Manié (page 544)

Sautéed Chicken Livers in an Onion-and-Green Peppercorn Sauce

Serves: **4**
Preparation time: **10 minutes**
Cooking time: **15 minutes**
Type of recipe: **elementary**
Cost: **inexpensive**

Preparation

1.
In a small bowl combine the dry mustard with 1 tablespoon water and set aside for 30 minutes.

2.
Carefully clean the chicken livers, removing any black or green spots. Dry the livers thoroughly with papers towels and reserve.

3.
Heat 2 tablespoons butter and the oil in a large heavy skillet. Add the chicken livers and sauté over high heat for 2 or 3 minutes on each side, or until nicely browned but still rare. Season the livers with salt and pepper and transfer to a bowl.

4.
Add the remaining butter to the pan, then add the shallots and cook for 2 minutes, scraping well the bottom of the pan. Add the wine, bring to a boil, and reduce to 1 tablespoon.

5.
Add the stock to the skillet, bring to a boil, and reduce to a simmer. Whisk in the dry mustard mixture and the Dijon mustard as well as the crushed peppercorns. Whisk in bits of Beurre Manié and cook the sauce until it heavily coats a spoon. Taste and correct the seasoning.

6.
Return the chicken livers to the pan and heat through. Transfer to a serving platter and spoon sauce over the livers. Serve as an appetizer accompanied by sautéed bread triangles or as a main course over a pilaf of rice.

Ingredients

1 pound fresh chicken livers
2 Tablespoons rendered chicken fat, or 3 Tablespoons butter
1½ teaspoons oil
Salt and freshly ground black pepper
2 large onions, peeled and thinly sliced
Pinch of granulated sugar
1 cup Crème Fraîche (page 544)
1 teaspoon green peppercorns, drained and crushed

Optional:
1 Beurre Manié (page 544)

Garnish:
Finely minced fresh parsley

Preparation

1.
Clean the chicken livers carefully, removing any dark green spots. Dry the livers on a double layer of paper towels and set aside.

2.
In a 10- to 12-inch cast-iron skillet melt the fat or butter. Add 1 teaspoon oil and heat until the fat starts to brown. Add the livers; do not crowd the pan. The livers must not touch one another.

3.
Sauté the chicken livers on both sides over high heat until nicely browned. Season with salt and freshly ground black pepper and shake the pan back and forth to cook the livers evenly. Do not overcook. The livers should still be slightly pink.

Roast Turkey
in
Lingonberry Sauce

Serves:	**6 to 8**
Preparation time:	**30 minutes**
Cooking time:	**3 hours**
Type of recipe:	**elementary**
Cost:	**inexpensive**

4.
Remove the skillet from the heat. With a slotted spoon transfer the chicken livers to a sieve. Place over a bowl and drain.

5.
Add the remaining fat or butter and oil to the pan. Add the onions and sugar and cook until the onions are soft and nicely brown, scraping well the bottom of the pan. Do not let the onions burn.

6.
Add the Crème Fraîche and peppercorns to the pan. Bring to a boil and cook over high heat until the cream is somewhat reduced and starts to thicken. Season with salt and pepper. Whisk in bits of optional Beurre Manié; use just enough for the sauce to heavily coat the spoon.

7.
Return the chicken livers to the pan, together with any juice that may have accumulated in the bowl. Heat the livers gently over the lowest possible heat.

8.
Spoon the chicken livers into a serving dish sprinkle with parsley. Serve immediately accompanied by slices of French bread that have been sautéed in a mixture of butter and oil.

Butternut squash is a vegetable that has little individual taste but will give an interesting texture to the sauce. Lingonberries are available in jars in gourmet departments of good supermarkets and specialty stores. They are usually imported from Sweden.

Ingredients
1 seven-to-eight-pound fresh turkey
Salt and freshly ground black pepper
1 teaspoon dried thyme
1 teaspoon dried marjoram
1 teaspoon imported paprika
1 to 1½ teaspoons Dijon mustard
1 whole onion, peeled, plus 2 onions, peeled and cut in eighths
3 Tablespoons butter
1 Tablespoon oil
2 to 2½ cups hot Chicken Stock (page 530)
2 cups butternut squash, cut into ¾-inch cubes
2 heaping Tablespoons brown sugar
2 Tablespoons lingonberries
Juice of half a lemon

Optional:
1 tablespoon cornstarch, mixed with a little stock

Garnish:
Sprigs of fresh watercress

Preparation

1.
Preheat the oven to 350 degrees.

2.
Season the turkey with salt, pepper, thyme, and marjoram. Rub with paprika and mustard. Place the whole peeled onion in the cavity and truss the turkey. Set aside.

3.
Heat 3 tablespoons butter and the oil in a large heavy flameproof baking dish. Scatter the onions in the dish and add the turkey, preferably on its side. Set the dish in the center of the oven and roast the turkey for 2 hours, 30 minutes to 3 hours, basting every 10 to 15 minutes with the stock. Be careful not to burn the onions in the pan. (Don't let the pan juices run dry and be sure to scrape the onions every 10 to 15 minutes.) Turn the turkey once or twice during the cooking time. The bird is done when the juices run pale yellow when pierced with the tip of a sharp knife.

4.
While the turkey is roasting prepare the squash. In a saucepan bring salted water to boil. Add the squash and cook for 2 to 3 minutes, or until the cubes are barely tender. Drain the squash and reserve.

5.
When the turkey is done, transfer it to a serving platter and reserve. Thoroughly degrease the pan juices, leaving the onions in the pan if they have not burned.

6.
Set the baking dish over low heat and add any remaining stock. Add the brown sugar and cook for 2 or 3 minutes scraping well the bottom of the pan.

7.
Add the squash and reheat for 1 to 2 minutes. Add the lingonberries and lemon juice. Taste the sauce and correct the seasoning. It should have a sweet yet somewhat tart flavor. If the sauce is too thin, whisk in a little of the cornstarch and stock mixture, whisking just until the sauce coats a spoon.

8.
Transfer the sauce to a serving bowl. Serve the turkey separately, garnished with sprigs of fresh watercress and with the lingonberry-and-squash sauce on the side.

Remarks
This sauce is equally delicious when made with the pan juices of a roast pork or a roast duck.

Braised
Rock Cornish Game Hens
à la Paysanne

Serves: **4**
Preparation time: **30 minutes**
Cooking time: **1 hour**
Type of recipe: **elementary**
Cost: **moderate**

Ingredients

2 fresh Rock Cornish game hens
Salt and freshly ground black pepper
1 teaspoon dried thyme
3 large cloves garlic, peeled and crushed
2 Tablespoons butter
1 Tablespoon oil
12 to 14 small white onions, peeled
2 medium carrots, scraped and cut in cubes
8 to 10 small new potatoes, peeled
4 to 6 small turnips, peeled and quartered
1 Bouquet Garni, composed of 1 large sprig fresh parsley, 1 teaspoon dried thyme, and 1 bay leaf, tied in cheesecloth
1 cup Brown Chicken Stock (page 531)
1 Beurre Manié (page 544)

Garnish:

2 Tablespoons finely minced fresh parsley

Preparation

1.
Preheat the oven to 350 degrees.

2.
Season the hens with salt, pepper, and thyme and rub with 1 clove garlic. Truss the hens.

3.
In a large heavy skillet heat the butter and oil. Add the hens and brown them lightly on all sides over moderate-to-high heat.

4.
Transfer the hens to a casserole large enough for the hens to fit with the vegetables.

5.
In the fat remaining in the pan add the remaining garlic, onions, carrots, potatoes, and turnips. Season with salt and pepper, then sauté the vegetables over moderate-to-high heat, shaking the pan to brown them evenly. When the vegetables are nicely browned, transfer them with a slotted spoon to the casserole.

6.
Add the bouquet to the casserole, cover tightly, and place in the center of the oven. Braise the hens for 45 minutes. When done, remove the casserole from the oven, place the hens on a baking sheet, and set aside.

7.
Carefully degrease the pan juices in the casserole and discard the bouquet. Place the casserole over moderate heat and add the stock. Bring to a boil and slowly whisk in bits of Beurre Manié; use just enough for the sauce to thicken and to heavily coat a spoon. Keep the sauce and vegetables warm.

Alsatian
Roast Duck

Serves:	**6 to 8**
Preparation time:	**30 minutes**
Cooking time:	**2 hours, 45 minutes**
Type of recipe:	**intermediate**
Cost:	**moderate**

8.
Preheat the broiler.
9.
Place the hens 6 inches from the source of the heat and broil for 2 to 3 minutes on each side, or until crisp.
10.
Remove the hens from the broiler, place them on a serving platter, and spoon the vegetables and sauce around them. Garnish with parsley and serve accompanied by a well-seasoned salad.

Remarks
The vegetables should all be the same size. You can add ½ cup freshly cooked peas to the vegetable mixture before adding the Beurre Manié.

The Alsatian choucroute, a wonderful sauerkraut dish made with sausages and pork, has established Alsace as the region for gutsy, hearty food. However, choucroute is not the only way to use sauerkraut. Here is an interesting version that compliments roast duck.

Ingredients
2 ducks each weighing 4 to 4½ pounds
Salt and freshly ground black pepper
1 Tablespoon butter
2 Tablespoons vegetable oil
2 stalks celery, chopped
1 carrot, scraped and coarsely chopped
2 onions, peeled and coarsely chopped
1½ cups hot Chicken Stock (page 530) or Brown Duck Stock (page 535)
½ cup dry white wine
1 Tablespoon cornstarch, mixed with a little stock

Sauerkraut:
2 Tablespoons butter
1 Tablespoon vegetable oil
1 cup finely minced onions
3 Tablespoons brown sugar
1 cup peeled and chopped tomatoes (3 ripe tomatoes)
2 pounds sauerkraut
Salt
5 peppercorns
2 teaspoons caraway seeds
1 Bouquet Garni (page 546)
2 cups Chicken Stock (page 530)

Optional:
1 to 2 teaspoons granulated sugar
Sprinkling of flour

Garnish:
Cooked tiny new potatoes

Preparation
1.
Start by making the sauerkraut. In a large
heavy casserole heat the butter and oil.
Add the onion and cook over low heat until
lightly browned. Add the brown sugar and
cook for 1 to 2 minutes.
2.
Add the tomatoes, sauerkraut, salt,
peppercorns, caraway seeds, Bouquet
Garni, and stock. Bring to a boil, reduce
the heat, and simmer the sauerkraut for 2
hours. Stir the sauerkraut every 20 minutes
to prevent it from sticking to the casserole.
3.
While the sauerkraut is braising, preheat
the oven to 350 degrees.
4.
Dry the ducks thoroughly with paper towels.
Prick the ducks in their fatty parts (under
the breast) and truss. Season with salt and
pepper and set aside.
5.
In a large oval flameproof baking dish heat
the butter and oil. Add the chopped
vegetables and cook over low heat for 3 to
4 minutes.
6.
Place the ducks on their sides in the baking
dish and place the dish in the oven. Roast
the ducks for 2 hours, 30 minutes, removing
the accumulated fat in the pan every 20

minutes, and basting the ducks with some of
the stock. (You will need about ¾ cup.)
7.
When ducks are done, remove and set
aside. Carefully degrease the pan juices.
8.
Place the pan over direct heat and bring
the pan juices to a boil. Add the wine and
cook until reduced to 2 tablespoons,
scraping well the bottom of the pan. Add
the remaining stock, bring to a boil, and
whisk in the cornstarch mixture. Cook until
the sauce coats the spoon. Strain the sauce
into a small saucepan and keep warm.
9.
Taste the sauerkraut and discard the
bouquet. Correct the seasoning. Add a little
sugar if necessary. If the sauerkraut seems a
little watery bring it to a boil and sprinkle it
with a little flour, stirring until the
sauerkraut juices have evaporated. Place
the sauerkraut on the bottom of a serving
dish.
10.
Carve the ducks. Place them on top of the
sauerkraut and spoon the pan juices over
them. Garnish with tiny new potatoes.

Roast Duck
in
Fresh Grape Sauce

Serves: **4**
Preparation time: **30 minutes**
Cooking time: **2 hours, 45 minutes**
Type of recipe: **intermediate**
Cost: **moderate**

Ingredients

2 ducks, each 4½ to 5 pounds
Salt and freshly ground black pepper
2 Tablespoons butter
1 Tablespoon oil
1 large carrot, scraped and cubed
1 large stalk celery, scraped and cubed
2 onions, peeled and coarsely chopped
1½ cups hot chicken bouillon
1 teaspoon meat glaze
½ cup white port wine
1½ cups Brown Chicken Stock (page 531)
1 Tablespoon cornstarch, mixed with a little stock
3 Tablespoons apricot preserves
1 to 1½ cups seedless thompson green grapes

Garnish:
Tiny bunches of fresh green grapes

Preparation

1.
Preheat the oven to 425 degrees.

2.
Dry the ducks thoroughly with paper towels. Season them with salt and pepper, truss the ducks, and set aside.

3.
In a large flameproof baking dish heat the butter and oil. Add the carrots, celery, and onions and place the pan over low heat. Cook the vegetable mixture for 3 to 4 minutes without browning.

4.
Place the ducks on their side in the baking dish and add ¼ cup chicken bouillon. Place the dish in the oven and roast the ducks for 15 minutes on each side.

5.
Reduce the oven heat to 350 degrees and continue roasting the ducks for 2 hours, 30 minutes, basting every 10 to 15 minutes with the bouillon. Remove the fat from the pan several times during the roasting time. Turn the ducks once. When the ducks are done transfer to a baking dish and keep warm in a very low oven.

6.
Carefully degrease the pan juices. Set the pan over high heat, add the meat glaze and port, and bring to a boil. Cook the port until reduced by half.

7.
Add the stock to the pan and bring to a boil, reducing the stock by half. Strain the pan juices through a fine sieve into a heavy saucepan, pressing down on the vegetables to extract all their juices.

Roast Duck
Landaise

Serves: **4**
Preparation time: **45 minutes**
Cooking time: **2 hours, 30 minutes**
Type of recipe: **intermediate**
Cost: **moderate**

8.

Place the saucepan over low heat and whisk in a little of the cornstarch mixture; use just enough until the sauce is thickened and coats a spoon.

9.

Whisk in the apricot preserves, taste the sauce, and correct the seasoning. You may need a large grinding of black pepper. Set the sauce aside.

10.

When ready to serve, carve the ducks and place on a serving platter. Reheat the sauce slowly over low heat, add the grapes, and heat through. Do not let the sauce come to a boil or the grapes will fall apart. Spoon the sauce over the ducks. Garnish the platter with additional grapes and serve immediately.

Remarks

For an elegant service the grapes actually should be peeled. If you want to peel the grapes drop them into rapidly boiling water for 30 seconds and then peel each grape; the skin will slip off easily. Personally I find the texture of an unpeeled grape to be slightly crunchier and more interesting. The ducks can be roasted several hours ahead and kept warm in a very low oven. They can also be crisped under the broiler 6 inches from the heat for a few minutes before serving. You may also serve the sauce on the side.

Ingredients

2 ducks, each weighing 4½ to 5 pounds
Salt and freshly ground black pepper
2 Tablespoons butter
2 Tablespoons oil
1 small carrot, scraped and cubed
1 stalk celery, diced
2 onions, peeled and chopped
2 cups hot Chicken Stock (page 530)
1 pound sweet Italian link sausages
⅓ cup dry white wine
1 Beurre Manié (page 544)

Beans:

2 cups dried Great Northern beans
1½ cups salt pork, finely cubed
1 large onion, unpeeled
3 whole cloves garlic, unpeeled
1 Bouquet Garni (page 546)
Salt
6 peppercorns
2 Tablespoons butter
3 Tablespoons finely minced shallots
1 cup peeled and finely chopped tomatoes
1 cup heavy cream

Preparation

1.
Prepare the beans. In a large casserole combine the beans with water to cover by 2 inches. Bring to a boil and cook for exactly 1 minute. Set the casserole aside for 1 hour.

2.
Preheat the oven to 375 degrees.

3.
In a small saucepan bring water to boil. Add the salt pork cubes and simmer for 5 minutes. Drain and dry thoroughly on paper towels. Set aside.

4.
Dry the ducks thoroughly with paper towels. Prick them several times in the fatty areas (under the breast). Season with salt and pepper and truss. Set aside.

5.
In a large flameproof baking dish heat the butter and 1 tablespoon oil. Add the carrot, celery, and onion. Cook the mixture over low heat for 2 to 3 minutes without browning.

6.
Put the ducks on their sides in the baking dish. Place in the oven and roast the ducks for 2 hours, 30 minutes, basting every 15 minutes with stock and spooning off the accumulated fat from the dish.

7.
While the ducks are roasting, cook the beans. Add the onion, garlic, and bouquet to the bean water. Season with salt and add the peppercorns. Bring to a boil, cover the saucepan, and simmer over the lowest possible heat for 45 minutes to 1 hour, or until the beans are tender but not falling apart.

8.
Drain the beans and discard the bouquet and onion. The bean water can be reserved for soup. Set the beans aside.

9.
In a large heavy skillet heat the butter. Add the salt pork and sauté until nicely browned on all sides. With a slotted spoon remove to a side dish and reserve.

10.
Add the shallots to the pan and cook for 2 minutes. Add the tomatoes and cook the mixture for another 2 to 3 minutes, scraping well the bottom of the pan. Add the reserved beans and salt pork, cream, salt, and pepper and simmer the beans for 10 minutes, or until the cream has been absorbed completely by the beans. Taste and correct the seasoning. Keep warm.

11.
In a large skillet heat the remaining tablespoon oil. Add the sausages and cook for 2 to 3 minutes on each side, or until nicely browned.

12.
Add the wine to the pan, bring to a boil, and cook until reduced to a glaze. Remove the sausages and reserve.

13.
When the ducks are done quarter them, discard the strings, and keep warm. Degrease the pan juices carefully.

14.
Place the dish over moderate heat and add any remaining stock. Bring to a boil, scraping well the bottom of the pan, and strain the juices into a small saucepan. Whisk in bits of Beurre Manié and cook the sauce until it heavily coats a spoon.

Roast Duck
in
Lemon Sauce
(au Citron)

Serves:	**6 to 8**
Preparation time:	**35 minutes**
Cooking time:	**3 hours**
Type of recipe:	**elementary**
Cost:	**moderate**

15.
Pour ½ cup of the pan juices into the beans. Reheat the beans and taste and correct the seasonings.

16.
Place the beans in a deep serving platter. Top with the quartered ducks, garnish with the sausages, and spoon the remaining sauce over the ducks. Serve hot accompanied by a well-seasoned green salad.

Remarks
The beans can be quick-cooked 1 to 2 days ahead and refrigerated in their cooking liquid. You can then simmer the beans using the slow cooking method (page 99), which results in a more evenly cooked, tender bean.

Ingredients
2 fresh ducks, each weighing 4½ to 5 pounds
Salt and freshly ground white pepper
2 Tablespoons butter
1 Tablespoon peanut oil
2 onions, peeled and coarsely chopped
½ cup cubed celery
1 cup chicken bouillon, canned or homemade
¼ cup granulated sugar
¼ cup red wine vinegar
1½ cups hot Brown Chicken Stock (page 531)
¼ cup white port wine
½ cup currant jelly
1 Tablespoon cornstarch, mixed with a little stock
1 lemon, thinly sliced

Garnish:
Sprigs of fresh watercress
Quartered lemons

Preparation

1.
Preheat the oven to 450 degrees.

2.
Dry the ducks thoroughly with paper towels and season with salt and pepper. Prick the ducks in their fatty parts, and then truss them.

3.
Heat the butter and oil in a large flameproof baking dish. Place the ducks on their sides in the hot fat and add the onions and celery to the pan.

4.
Place the ducks in the oven and add 2 tablespoons chicken bouillon to the pan. Roast the ducks for 15 minutes, then reduce the heat to 375 degrees. Continue roasting the ducks for 2 hours, 45 minutes, removing the accumulated fat from the pan every 10 minutes and basting them with a little bouillon every 10 to 15 minutes. Be careful not to burn the onions. Turn the ducks over to rest on their other side once during the cooking period.

5.
While the ducks are roasting make the caramel. In a heavy 2-quart saucepan heat the sugar and vinegar. Cook the mixture stirring constantly until it caramelizes and turns to a dark brown, very heavy syrup.

6.
Add the stock all at once. Bring to a boil and remove the saucepan from the heat. Set aside.

7.
When the ducks are done place them on a baking sheet and keep warm in a 200-degree oven.

8.
Discard the fat from the pan. Place the pan over high heat and add the port. Reduce the port to 1 tablespoon, scraping well the bottom of the pan.

9.
Add the caramelized stock and bring to a boil. Reduce the mixture by half.

10.
Whisk in the currant jelly and the cornstarch mixture, cooking just enough until the sauce heavily coats a spoon. Taste the sauce and correct the seasoning.

11.
Strain the sauce through a fine sieve into a saucepan and add the lemon slices. Heat through but do not let the sauce cook any more.

12.
If you like the ducks to be crisp, turn on the broiler and broil the ducks 6 to 8 inches from the source of the heat for 2 to 3 minutes on each side, being careful not to burn them.

13.
Remove the ducks from the broiler and carve. Place the quartered ducks on a serving platter and set aside.

14.
Reheat the sauce if necessary over the lowest possible heat and spoon it over the ducks.

15.
Garnish the platter with sprigs of watercress and additional lemon wedges. Serve accompanied by Curried Pilaf of Rice (page 336).

Roast Duck
à la Normande

Serves: **6 to 8**
Preparation time: **45 minutes**
Cooking time: **3 hours**
Type of recipe: **elementary**
Cost: **moderate**

Ingredients

2 fresh ducks, each weighing 4½ to 5 pounds
3 Tablespoons butter
2 Tablespoons oil
3 cups onions, peeled and coarsely chopped
1 carrot, scraped and chopped
1 stalk celery, diced
1 leek, well rinsed and thinly sliced
2 cups hard cider
1 pound mcintosh apples, cored and roughly chopped
3 cups Chicken Stock (page 530)
1 Bouquet Garni (page 546)
Salt and freshly ground white pepper
1 Tablespoon arrowroot, mixed with a little stock

Garnish:
Sautéed Apples (page 546)
Sprigs of fresh watercress

Preparation

1.
Remove the wing tips from the ducks. Cut the necks in 2-inch pieces and the gizzards in half. Set aside.

2.
In a large heavy saucepan heat 1 tablespoon butter and 1 tablespoon oil.

3.
Add the duck trimmings and sauté over moderate-to-high heat until nicely browned. Transfer to a side dish and reserve.

4.
In the fat remaining in the saucepan add 1 cup onions, the carrot, the celery, and the leek. Cook the vegetable mixture for 3 to 5 minutes, or until nicely browned. Do not let the vegetables burn.

5.
Add 1 cup cider, the chopped apples, and the browned trimmings together with 2 cups stock and the Bouquet Garni. Season with salt and pepper, bring to a boil, reduce the heat, and simmer the mixture covered for 1 hour, 45 minutes. Meanwhile prepare the ducks.

6.
Preheat the oven to 350 degrees.

7.
Dry the ducks thoroughly with paper towels, then truss them. Season with salt and pepper and prick them in their fatty parts.

8.
In a large flameproof baking dish heat the remaining butter and oil. Add the ducks, placing them on their sides, and scatter the remaining onions around them. Add a little stock to the pan and set the pan in the oven. Roast the ducks for 2 hours, 45

Roast Duck
in
Port Sauce

Serves:	**3 to 4**
Preparation time:	**20 minutes**
Cooking time:	**2 hours, 45 minutes**
Type of recipe:	**elementary**
Cost:	**moderate**

minutes, basting them every 15 minutes with the hot stock and removing the accumulated fat from the pan.

9.
When the duck stock is finished, discard the bouquet and strain the stock, pressing down on the apples and vegetables to extract all their juices. Let the stock settle and carefully degrease it. Set aside.

10.
When the ducks are done transfer them to a baking sheet. Cover loosely with foil and set in a 200-degree oven.

11.
Carefully degrease the pan juices. Place the pan over high heat and add the remaining cider. Cook the cider until it is reduced to ¼ cup.

12.
Add 1½ cups reserved duck stock and cook until reduced by one third.

13.
Whisk in the arrowroot mixture and cook the sauce until it thickens and heavily coats a spoon. Taste and correct the seasoning. Strain the sauce through a fine sieve into a saucepan and reserve.

14.
Turn on the broiler and place the ducks 6 inches from the source of the heat. Broil the ducks for 2 to 3 minutes on each side until nicely crisp.

15.
Remove the ducks from the broiler. Carve the ducks and place on a serving platter. Garnish with the optional Sautéed Apples and watercress and serve the sauce on the side.

Ingredients

1 four-and-one-half to five pound fresh duck
Salt and freshly ground white pepper
2 Tablespoons butter
1 teaspoon oil
2 medium onions, peeled and quartered
1½ cups Brown Duck Stock (page 535) or Brown Chicken Stock (page 531)
1 orange
1 lemon
⅓ cup red port wine
Juice of 1 orange
½ cup currant jelly
2 teaspoons cornstarch, mixed with a little port
Juice of ½ lemon

Garnish:

Sprigs of fresh watercress
4 to 6 orange slices

Preparation

1.
Preheat the oven to 400 degrees.

2.
Dry the duck thoroughly with paper towels. Season with salt and freshly ground white pepper and truss.

3.
Heat the butter and oil in a heavy flameproof baking dish. Place the duck on its side in the hot fat and sauté over moderate-to-high heat until lightly browned. Turn the duck and sauté on the other side until it is lightly browned. Add the onions to the pan and place the pan in the oven.

4.
Roast the duck for 15 minutes. Reduce the heat to 350 degrees, add ⅓ cup stock to the pan, and roast the duck on its side for 2 hours, 30 minutes. Baste every 15 minutes with ¼ cup stock, while removing the accumulated fat from the pan. Be careful not to let the onions burn.

5.
While the duck is roasting remove the peels of the orange and the lemon with a vegetable peeler, being careful not to include the white membrane. Cut the peels into julienne strips so as to have 2 tablespoons orange rind and 1 tablespoon lemon. Drop the julienne strips into rapidly boiling water for 2 minutes. Drain and set aside.

6.
When the duck is done transfer it to a baking sheet and return it to a warm oven.

7.
Thoroughly degrease the pan juices. With a slotted spoon remove the onions and

discard. Bring the pan juices to a boil on top of the stove and reduce to ½ cup.

8.
Add any remaining stock to the pan, together with the port and orange juice, and bring to a boil cooking the pan juices until they are reduced by half. (You should have about 1 cup of pan juices.)

9.
Whisk in the currant jelly and the reserved orange and lemon strips. When the jelly is completely melted whisk in a little of the cornstarch mixture; use just enough to thicken the sauce. Taste the sauce and correct the seasoning, adding drops of lemon juice to taste. The sauce should have a sweet-tart flavor. Keep the sauce warm.

10.
If you wish, crisp the duck under the broiler, placing it 6 inches from the source of heat. Transfer the duck to a carving board and carve by removing the back bone and quartering the duck.

11.
Place the duck on a serving platter and spoon the port sauce over each piece. Garnish the platter with sprigs of fresh watercress and orange slices. Serve accompanied by a pilaf of rice.

Remarks
The entire dish can be prepared 2 to 3 hours ahead. Wrap the duck in foil and keep it warm in a very low oven, then crisp it under the broiler just before serving. Transfer the port sauce to a small saucepan and reheat just before serving.

Roast Duck
with
Spiced Pears

Serves: **6**
Preparation time: **30 minutes**
Cooking time: **4 hours**
Type of recipe: **elementary**
Cost: **moderate**

Ingredients

2 fresh ducks, each weighing 4 to 4½ pounds
3 Tablespoons duck fat or butter
1½ cups Brown Chicken Stock (page 531)
1 cup chicken bouillon or water
4 to 6 small anjou or bosc pears, partially ripened
1½ cups tawny port wine
1 three-inch stick cinnamon
2 cloves
1 three-inch piece lemon rind
2 to 3 crushed allspice
Salt and freshly ground black pepper
3 medium onions, peeled and cut in half
1 Tablespoon arrowroot, mixed with a little stock

Preparation

1.
Remove the ducks' necks and cut in half. Remove the wing tips.

2.
In a heavy saucepan heat 1 tablespoon duck fat and brown the necks and wing tips until they are nicely browned on all sides.

3.
Add the stock and bouillon or water and bring to a boil. Reduce the heat, and simmer the stock covered for 1 hour to 1 hour, 30 minutes. Set the duck stock aside.

4.
While the stock is simmering prepare the pears. Peel the pears, cut them in half, and core them carefully.

5.
Place the pears in an enamel saucepan. Add the port, cinnamon, cloves, lemon rind, and allspice. Bring to a boil, reduce the heat, and simmer the pear halves covered for 20 to 30 minutes, or until just tender. Do not overcook; the pears should still retain some crispness. When the pears are done set them aside in their poaching liquid.

6.
Preheat the oven to 350 degrees.

7.
Thoroughly dry the ducks with paper towels. Season with salt and pepper and truss.

8.
In a large flameproof baking dish heat the remaining duck fat over medium heat. Place the ducks on their sides in the baking dish and sauté until lightly browned on both sides.

Roast Duck
in
Tarragon Sauce

Serves:	**6 to 8**
Preparation time:	**40 minutes**
Cooking time:	**4½ hours**
Type of recipe:	**elementary**
Cost:	**moderate**

Ingredients

2 fresh ducks, each weighing 4½ to 5 pounds
3 Tablespoons butter
2 Tablespoons oil
1 large carrot, scraped and cubed
1 stalk celery, diced
3 medium onions, coarsely chopped
Salt and freshly ground white pepper
1 Bouquet Garni (page 546)
8 cloves garlic, peeled and crushed
4 cups Chicken Stock (page 530)
¾ cup white wine
1 cup heavy cream
1 Beurre Manié (page 544)
2 Tablespoons finely minced fresh tarragon

Garnish:
Sprigs of fresh watercress

9.
Add the onions to the pan, together with a little reserved stock from the saucepan. Place the dish in the oven and roast the ducks for 2 hours, 30 minutes, removing the accumulated fat from the pan every 10 minutes and then basting the ducks with a ¼ cup duck stock. (Be sure to remove the fat from the pan before adding the stock.) Be careful not to burn the onions. Turn the ducks once during their cooking time.

10.
When the ducks are done transfer them to a baking sheet and return to a warm oven.

11.
Thoroughly degrease the pan juices and discard the onions. Place the baking dish over high heat and add 1 cup of the pear poaching liquid. Bring to a boil, scraping well the bottom of the pan. Cook until the pan juices are reduced by ½.

12.
Add the remaining duck stock, together with the pear halves, and simmer until the pears are well heated through.

13.
Whisk in a little of the arrowroot mixture; use just enough to thicken the sauce. Taste and correct the seasoning. Keep the sauce warm.

14.
Run the ducks under the broiler for 2 to 3 minutes, or until they are nicely crisp and browned.

15.
Carve the ducks and place on a serving platter. Spoon the sauce over the ducks and garnish the platter with the pear halves. Serve immediately accompanied by a pilaf of rice.

Preparation

1.

Remove the wing tips from the ducks. Cut the necks into 2-inch pieces and cut the gizzards in half.

2.

In a large heavy saucepan heat 1 tablespoon butter and 1 tablespoon oil. Add the duck trimmings and sauté until nicely browned. With a slotted spoon remove the trimmings to a side dish and reserve.

3.

To the fat remaining in the pan add the carrot, celery, and 1 onion. Brown the vegetables over moderate-to-high heat for 3 to 5 minutes scraping well the bottom of the pan. Do not let the onions burn.

4.

Season the vegetables with salt and pepper. Add the bouquet, garlic, and 3 cups stock. Return the browned duck trimmings to the saucepan. Cover and simmer for 1 hour, 30 minutes. (This can be done a day or so ahead.) Discard the bouquet, carefully degrease the duck stock, and reserve.

5.

Preheat the oven to 375 degrees.

6.

Dry the ducks thoroughly with paper towels. Season with salt and pepper and truss. Prick the ducks in their fatty parts and set aside.

7.

In a large flameproof baking dish heat the remaining butter and oil over medium heat. Add the remaining onions and place the ducks on their sides in the baking dish. Add ¼ cup stock, set the dish in the oven, and roast the ducks for 2 hours, 45 minutes,

basting every 10 to 15 minutes with a little stock. Remove the accumulated fat from the pan every 10 minutes and be careful not to burn the onions. Turn the ducks once during their roasting time.

8.

When the ducks are done transfer them to a baking sheet and set in a warm oven. Carefully degrease the pan juices, removing every bit of fat.

9.

Place the baking dish over moderate heat. Add the wine and bring to a boil, scraping well the bottom of the pan. Cook the wine until it is reduced to 2 tablespoons.

10.

Add 1½ cups reserved duck stock and cook until it is reduced to ½ cup.

11.

Add the cream. Bring to a boil and whisk in bits of Beurre Manié, cooking the sauce until it heavily coats a spoon. Taste and correct the seasoning. Strain the sauce into a saucepan. Add the tarragon and keep warm.

12.

Carve the ducks and place them on a serving platter. Garnish with watercress and serve the sauce on the side.

Remarks

The ducks can be roasted 2 to 3 hours ahead then wrapped in foil and kept warm in a 200-degree oven. For a crisp duck, open the foil, set the ducks 6 inches from the source of heat, and broil the ducks on both sides for 2 to 3 minutes. Be careful not to burn them. A potato-and-turnip purée is a wonderful accompaniment to this dish.

Roast Squabs
with
Turnips

Serves: **4**
Preparation time: **30 minutes**
Cooking time: **1 hour**
Type of recipe: **elementary**
Cost: **expensive**

Ingredients

4 fresh squabs, each weighing 1 to 1½ pounds
Salt and freshly ground white pepper
1 teaspoon imported paprika
2 teaspoons Dijon mustard
2 cloves garlic, peeled and crushed
4 two-inch-long pieces thinly sliced salt pork, or small squares of pork sheets
4 Tablespoons butter
1 Tablespoon vegetable oil
2 small onions, peeled and cut in half
1 to 1½ cups Brown Chicken Stock (page 531)
1½ pounds small turnips, peeled and quartered
¾ cup heavy cream
1 Beurre Manié (page 544)

Garnish:
Sprigs of fresh watercress

Preparation

1.
Preheat the oven to 375 degrees.

2.
Season the squabs with salt and pepper. Rub with paprika, mustard, and garlic.

3.
Cut the salt pork into 2 by 3-inch rectangles and place them over the breasts of the squabs. Truss the squabs, tying the salt pork securely to the breasts. Set the squabs aside.

4.
In a heavy oval casserole, just large enough to hold the squabs, heat 2 tablespoons butter and the oil. When the butter is very hot add the squabs and brown them over medium heat on both sides.

5.
Spoon out all but 2 tablespoons of fat from the casserole. Add the onions cut-side down, then remove the casserole from the heat. Cover tightly and place in the oven. Roast the squabs for 45 minutes, turning them once during the roasting time and adding 2 to 3 tablespoons stock to the casserole every 10 minutes.

6.
While the squabs are roasting bring salted water to boil. Add the turnips and cook for 5 minutes, or until just tender. Drain the turnips.

7.
In a medium skillet heat the remaining butter. Add the turnips and sauté over medium heat until lightly browned. Shake the pan back and forth to make sure the turnips are browning evenly. Add the cream and cook until completely absorbed

Ragoût of Rabbit
in
Onion-and-Raisin Sauce

Serves:	**3 to 4**
Preparation time:	**20 minutes**
Cooking time:	**1 hour, 45 minutes**
Type of recipe:	**elementary**
Cost:	**moderate**

by the turnips. Season the turnips with salt and pepper. Set aside.

8.
When the squabs are done remove and discard the salt pork pieces, place the birds on a baking sheet, and keep warm.

9.
Carefully degrease the pan juices; there will be quite a lot of fat. Discard the onions. Place the casserole over high heat and bring the pan juices to a boil. If you have not used up all the stock, add it to the casserole at this point.

10.
Whisk in bits of Beurre Manié; use just enough to thicken the sauce. Add the sautéed turnips and heat through. Keep the sauce warm.

11.
Preheat the broiler. Set the squabs 6 inches from the source of the heat and broil for 2 minutes on each side, or until the squabs are crisp. Do not broil for too long a time, since squabs have a tendency to dry out very quickly.

12.
Remove the trussing strings, place the squabs on a serving platter, and spoon the turnips and sauce around them. Garnish with watercress and serve immediately.

Ingredients
⅓ cup golden raisins
½ cup dark raisins
¾ cup dry white wine
1 large rabbit, cut in eighths
Salt and freshly ground black pepper
2 Tablespoons chicken fat, or 2 Tablespoons butter
1 Tablespoon oil
12 to 16 small white pearl onions
3 Tablespoons plus ½ teaspoon granulated sugar
¼ cup cognac or brandy
Flour
1 to 1½ cups Brown Chicken Stock (page 531)
1 Bouquet Garni (page 546)
3 Tablespoons red wine vinegar

Optional:
1 Beurre Manié (page 544)

Preparation

1.
In a small saucepan combine the raisins and wine. Heat the mixture without letting it come to a boil and set aside.

2.
Dry the meat thoroughly with paper towels. Season the rabbit pieces with salt and pepper.

3.
In a 12-inch cast-iron chicken fryer heat the chicken fat or butter with the oil. Add the rabbit pieces; do not crowd the pan. Sauté until nicely browned on all sides.

4.
When the meat is browned transfer to a side plate and reserve. If the fat has burned discard it and substitute with 2 tablespoons butter or chicken fat.

5.
Add the onions to the skillet and sauté, tossing them back and forth in the pan until nicely browned on all sides. Sprinkle with ½ teaspoon sugar, salt, and pepper and shake the pan to coat the onions evenly with the sugar.

6.
Add the cognac. Bring to a boil, scraping well the bottom of the pan, and cook until the cognac is reduced to a glaze.

7.
Return the rabbit to the skillet, sprinkle lightly with flour, and toss the meat pieces in the fat until they are well coated with the flour and lightly glazed.

8.
Add the wine-and-raisin mixture, bring to a boil, and reduce by half.

9.
Add ½ cup stock. Bury the Bouquet Garni among the pieces of meat, cover the skillet tightly, and simmer over low heat for 1 hour, or until the meat is tender. Add a little more stock to the pan every 10 to 15 minutes.

10.
When the meat is done, transfer it with a slotted spoon to a side dish and reserve. Discard the bouquet.

11.
Add the remaining stock to the casserole and simmer over low heat.

12.
Meanwhile, in a small saucepan, combine the remaining sugar and the vinegar. Cook the mixture over high heat until it turns a nutty brown and is caramelized. Spoon a ladle of the hot pan juices into the caramel and stir constantly until the mixture is smooth and well blended.

13.
Pour the caramel mixture into the pan juices, then return the meat to the skillet. Cover and simmer for another 10 to 15 minutes. If the pan juices seem too thin remove the rabbit pieces to a serving platter and whisk bits of Beurre Manié into the sauce until it heavily coats a spoon.

14.
Taste the sauce and correct the seasoning. Spoon the raisin-and-onion sauce over the rabbit pieces and serve accompanied by braised rice.

Remarks
The entire dish may be braised in the oven. It can be prepared several hours ahead and reheated in a low oven.

Fish

I might be standing in the middle of the colorful open markets of Barcelona, Genoa, Nice, or Lisbon looking at the displays of wonderful fish and shellfish, or watching a trawler making its way toward the Aegean coast. I may be exploring New York's Fulton Fish Market at 4 A.M., when the day's deliveries are arriving from the northeastern coast, or I might simply be visiting my local fish market to choose from among the various fish and shellfish beautifully displayed on beds of crushed ice. Whichever place I happen to find myself, the endlessly diverse world of seafood has always been one of the most exhilarating and delicious food experiences I know. And yet, I often wonder why it seems so hard for people in this country to accept fish as part of their meals. Every sensible, sane diet concerned with health and nutrition includes fish. Now more than ever there are many interesting fish dishes offered in restaurants. But while more people today will order fish in a restaurant, they are still unwilling to risk preparing it at home. The simple reason for this is a lack of familiarity with the kinds of fish available, and people's basic fear of asking the fish dealer what to choose, where the various fish come from, and how they ought to be prepared. Rather than be adventurous and make the extra effort, they opt for something else, usually the more familiar poultry or beef.

Taking that initial step into the realm of seafood cookery requires nothing more than a little boldness. Once the decision has been made, the world of fish and its infinite preparations can quickly become more exciting than the world of meat (and in particular beef, which unfortunately seems to dominate our meals!) A treasure of ethnic recipes is available to us from the world over, especially from the Mediterranean countries. It is only natural that the countries bordering the sea have made greater use of the fish varieties that fill their water, often combining them in spectacular and delicious dishes as well as serving them simply and allowing the freshness of the fish to speak for itself. The Scandinavians have developed countless ways to serve herring; the Scotch have contributed the wonderful smoked salmon and finnan haddie, that smoked haddock delicacy; the Japanese have given the world *sashimi*—beautifully carved slices of raw fishes served with soy sauce and a fresh vegetable garnish. In countries such as Yugoslavia or Greece fish is usually grilled whole with just a touch of herbs and olive oil. Southern France, northern Spain, and all of Italy boast many unusual and wonderful-tasting preparations. Sadly, over the past ten years fish has become increasingly expensive, even in these Mediterranean countries. The once-plentiful Mediterranean is often called the "Dead Sea" today because of the scarcity of fish in its waters. Similarly, on a recent trip to Greece I was dismayed to find all the fish dishes more expensive than other dishes on every restaurant menu. And as for the Spanish country cook, for whom cooking without fish would be unheard of, I have often watched these housewives going from stand to stand trying to find fish at a reasonable price, and then settling for a smaller quantity than desired. The culinary wisdom and frugality of the Mediterranean is exemplary and something all of us can learn from. Only taste a few perfectly cooked scallops and a small salmon cutlet, poached and seasoned with sage in a lovely sauce; it can be soulfully satisfying.

How unfortunate that when Americans think of fish they automatically think of deep-fried or broiled fish. While a properly broiled swordfish steak is a great delicacy, there is not one fish restaurant in the country, including those in New York, that can really prepare fish the way the French or the Italians or the Spanish do. This is not because we lack quality or varieties of fish. On the contrary, we have marvelous variety and can command great quality in many regions as well. We are simply not creative when it comes to fish preparation at home and are too afraid to experiment. One of the major reasons for this lack of creativity is that no matter how we look at it, high-quality fish is only available in coastline states. This is difficult to comprehend, since it seems so easy to ship perishable fruits and vegetables to cities across the United States. Fish is highly perishable but we are quite adept now at shipping such foods. Wherever the motivation exists, there is a way. Shrimp, that most loved of all seafoods in the United States, is found almost everywhere. Other kinds of fish get short shrift and the reason is simple. There is not enough demand and the small markets cannot survive, particularly since the price of fish has skyrocketed. However, with the increasing interest in cooking and especially healthy cooking, interest in fish is also growing.

It is exciting to be able to duplicate in your own kitchen a great seafood dish you've had on a trip or have discovered at a good restaurant. With all the fanfare concerning the nouvelle cuisine in recent years (much of which is gimmickry), the one area where genuine creativity has been shown by such chefs as the Troisgros brothers, Michel Guérard, and particularly Freddie Girardet in Switzerland is in the new and startling fish preparations. After several days in the kitchen of Girardet, I realized that fish cookery is far more creative and exciting than meat cookery. Watching this superb chef as he invented and created was an experience I shall never forget! What impressed me most was that this creativity was taking place in Switzerland, hundreds of miles from any sea, in a restaurant run by a self-taught chef whose knowledge of fish came from his interest rather than his background. Everyday his fish are flown in from Brittany, and he is in daily communication with various fishermen. What I realized with great surprise and frustration was that the fish he gets are far fresher than the fish I can buy in New York, even though I live near the sea. Whether it be salmon cutlets in sorrel sauce (now the "chic" dish in many restaurants), or a delicate fish mousse (one of the simplest dishes to prepare), I strongly believe that the recreation of these exciting fish dishes can be achieved easily by the serious, interested cook.

In this country, we have wonderful seafood available to us on both the Atlantic and Pacific coasts, as well as from freshwater sources throughout the country. What could be more delicious than a freshwater trout, straight from a Rocky Mountain stream, fried on an open fire? Or red snapper from Florida or the Gulf of Mexico? Soft-shell crabs from the Chesapeake Bay? Or the marvelous New Orleans shrimp that have inspired the delicious Creole gumbos of the South? Small fish such as butterfish, smelts, Boston mackerel, herring, and whiting are just some of the varieties available from the East. The Pacific is rich in steelhead salmon, salmon trout, abalone, rock cod, and many crustaceans.

The Seattle Pike market is one of the great thrills of seafood shopping. It has a wealth of seafood at such reasonable prices that when I was there several years ago, I wished I had access to a kitchen just to be able to take advantage of all that great fresh seafood. What astonished me was that not a single supermarket in the area carried fish. Visits to these supermarkets clearly revealed that there was not a trace of the richness of the nearby sea. It is an unfortunate reality that the supermarket is not the place to look for fish. Whenever I discussed the availability and freshness of seafood with supermarket executives, I learned that even the best stores received deliveries only twice a week. There is no way that present methods of packing and shipping and the basic lack of knowledge or motivation of supermarket managers can

offer hope for real freshness or variety in the supermarket. This is tragic!

Understanding, buying, and cooking fish is a labor of love. You must find it a challenge and be willing to spend the extra time (and sometimes money) to shop for it; you must also be willing to be creative in your cooking. It is well worth the extra effort. I do not know of any other single food that can be so gratifying or so memorable as a well-prepared piece of fresh fish.

There are four basic methods of cooking fish: poaching, braising, sautéing, and deep-frying. I find grilled fish good only if done over a wooden fire; grilling over charcoal overwhelms the delicate flavor.

It is essential for any serious cook to have fish stock on hand and to make it frequently. It is one of the simplest stocks to make. When you are buying fish be sure to ask the dealer for trimmings, since these are necessary for the stock. (Bottled clam broth is no substitute for fish stock.)

When buying fish in your local market, freshness is the most important consideration. A number of signs will indicate the freshness: the fish should have no odor at all; the gills should have a high sheen; the eyes should be bright; and the flesh should be firm (if you press it with your finger, it should not bear the mark, but rather spring right back). It is also better to buy fish on the bone rather than filleted, since the filleted fish will have lost much of its natural juices.

It is of great importance to know where the fish comes from and when it is in season. Many fish are in season practically year-round but are at their best during one specific period. Swordfish, which is now plentiful in the East in midwinter, is really at its best in June, July, and August. Eastern halibut is at its best in the spring; salmon and halibut are fish that come from both the Atlantic and the Pacific, but Pacific salmon is far superior to the Atlantic variety, while spring eastern halibut is far better than the Pacific fish. Bay scallops are caught all along the Eastern Seaboard, but for those who have had Long Island bay scallops, or the summer bay scallops caught near Cape Cod, there can be no question as to which are superior.

In certain dishes many types of fish are interchangeable. As long as you know some of the characteristics of each fish, you can take advantage of that when you choose a substitution. A red snapper, for example, can be prepared in the same manner as can fillets of sole or striped bass. Both salmon and halibut steaks lend themselves to many similar preparations. When you plan your fish dishes also try varieties of inexpensive fish. These are usually bought by people whose ethnic backgrounds provide them with traditional ways to prepare these less expensive fish. The Chinese love sea bass, and while striped bass is considered a more "elegant" fish, sea bass has a better flavor and a firmer flesh. It can be used

interchangeably with striped bass, which in recent years often has a strong gasoline flavor. Fish such as porgies, grouper, tilefish, and freshwater catfish from the Arkansas-Mississippi-Missouri region are usually inexpensive and very good.

For the average cook, the knowledge of what to look for in fish will not develop overnight. Establish a good rapport with your fish market and feel free to ask questions about the kinds of fish the market carries. Try to get them to bring in more of the varieties you would like to try. Don't be afraid to tap—or to challenge—your fish dealer's knowledge (and ultimately to praise the quality of his fish). This is the only way you will be able to gain the knowledge and expertise so important in appreciating fish.

Baked Bass
à la Catalane

Serves: **4**
Preparation time: **30 minutes, plus 2 to 4 hours to marinate**
Cooking time: **45 minutes**
Type of recipe: **elementary**
Cost: **moderate**

Ingredients

1 three- to three and one-half-pound fresh striped bass, cleaned, but with head and tail left on
¼ cup dry white wine
24 mussels, well scrubbed
3 Tablespoons olive oil
12 to 14 medium fresh shrimp, peeled
2 Tablespoons finely minced shallots
1 Tablespoon minced fresh parsley
1 large clove garlic, minced
1 can (35 ounces) Italian plum tomatoes, drained and chopped
1 teaspoon dried thyme
Salt and freshly ground white pepper

Marinade:

2 Tablespoons olive oil
Juice of 1 lemon
1 teaspoon coriander seeds
Coarse salt

Filling:

3 Tablespoons bread crumbs
3 Tablespoons finely minced fresh parsley
3 cloves garlic, minced
2 Tablespoons olive oil
Salt and freshly ground white pepper

Garnish:

1 lemon, thinly sliced
Optional: 1 Beurre Manié (page 544)

Preparation

1.
Marinate the fish. Place the fish in a large baking dish, sprinkle with olive oil, lemon juice, coriander seeds, and coarse salt. Marinate the fish in the refrigerator for 2 to 4 hours, loosely covered with foil. (This is particularly important if you have bought the fish a day in advance.)

2.
When ready, prepare the filling. In a small bowl combine bread crumbs, parsley, garlic, and olive oil. Season the mixture with salt and pepper and mix well.

3.
Drain the fish and fill with the bread-crumb mixture. Sew up the opening or fasten with toothpicks. Season the fish with a little more salt and pepper. Place in the baking dish.

4.
Preheat the oven to 350 degrees.

5.
In an enamel saucepan, combine the wine with the mussels. Bring to a boil and cook the mussels partially covered until they open. With a slotted spoon remove the mussels and shell all but 8 of them. Discard the shells and any mussels that did not open. Strain the stock and reserve as well.

6.
In a large heavy skillet, heat the olive oil. Add the shrimp and cook over moderate-to-high heat until they turn a bright pink. Remove with a slotted spoon to a side dish and reserve. Add the shallots, parsley, and garlic to the skillet and cook for 1 minute. Then add the tomatoes, thyme, salt, and pepper. Cook the mixture until most of the tomato water has evaporated

Sautéed Mackerel Fillets in Shallot-and-Mustard Sauce

Serves: **4**
Preparation time: **15 minutes**
Cooking time: **20 minutes**
Type of recipe: **elementary**
Cost: **inexpensive**

and then add 1 cup of the reserved mussel stock. Pour the mixture into the baking dish.

7.
Place the lemon slices over the fish. Cover the fish with buttered parchment paper and set in the oven. Bake the fish for 30 minutes.

8.
Add the reserved shrimp and shelled mussels to the pan and continue baking the fish for another 10 minutes.

9.
Increase the heat to broil and uncover the fish. Place the whole unshelled mussels in the baking dish and broil the fish for 2 to 3 minutes. Serve directly from the baking dish accompanied by French bread or parslied new potatoes.

Remarks
The pan juices of the fish will be quite thin. If you want a heavier sauce, remove the fish with the mussels to a serving platter. Place the baking dish with its pan juices over medium heat and whisk in bits of Beurre Manié, until the sauce reaches the desired consistency, then spoon the sauce around the fish.

Ingredients
3 to 4 pounds fresh mackerel fillets
Salt and freshly ground black pepper
Flour for dredging
2 Tablespoons butter
3 Tablespoons fruity olive oil
Juice of 1 large lemon
Finely minced fresh parsley

The Sauce:
¼ teaspoon hot dry English mustard
8 to 12 Tablespoons hot melted butter
2 Tablespoons finely minced shallots
¼ cup white wine vinegar
3 large egg yolks
1 Tablespoon Dijon mustard
1 Tablespoon well-drained capers
Salt and freshly ground white pepper

Garnish:
2 lemons, quartered

Preparation

1.

Prepare the sauce. Combine the dry mustard and 1 tablespoon butter in a small bowl. Blend the mixture until smooth and set aside for 30 minutes.

2.

In a heavy 2-quart saucepan combine the shallots and vinegar and cook the mixture until the vinegar is completely evaporated.

3.

Remove the saucepan from the heat and add the egg yolks. Whisk the yolks until smooth and well blended. Return the saucepan to the lowest possible heat and whisk the egg yolks for 1 or 2 minutes or until a faint steam rises.

4.

Start adding the remaining hot melted butter in a slow stream, whisking the sauce constantly. When all the butter has been added to the sauce it should be thick and smooth. (If at any time the sauce shows signs of curdling, immediately remove the saucepan from the heat and whisk in 1 small ice cube.) When the sauce is done, remove the saucepan from the heat.

5.

Whisk in the mustard mixture together with the Dijon mustard and the capers. Season the sauce with salt and pepper and set in a pan of warm water. Whisk the sauce every 10 minutes to make sure it is not curdling.

6.

Prepare the fish. Dry the fillets thoroughly with paper towels. Season with salt and pepper, and dredge lightly with flour, shaking off the excess.

7.

In a heavy 12-inch skillet heat the butter and 1 tablespoon oil. When the butter is very hot and the foam starts to subside add the mackerel a few fillets at a time; do not crowd the pan. Sauté the fillets over moderate-to-high heat for 2 to 3 minutes on each side. Turn them over once. When the fillets are done transfer them to a serving platter and reserve.

8.

Add a little more olive oil to the pan and when hot add the remaining fillets and again sauté 2 to 3 minutes on each side, or until they are nicely browned. Transfer the remaining fillets to the serving platter.

9.

Sprinkle the mackerel fillets with lemon juice and parsley. Garnish the platter with quartered lemons and serve the mustard-and-shallot sauce on the side.

Remarks

Other fish can be served in the same manner but it should be fish that has a distinctive flavor such as fillet of porgy or red snapper. The sauce is equally delicious when served with poached or braised fish such as salmon or bass.

Braised Porgies
Martegal

Serves: **4**
Preparation time: **25 minutes**
Cooking time: **1 hour**
Type of recipe: **elementary**
Cost: **inexpensive**

Ingredients

3 Tablespoons butter
3 Tablespoons fruity olive oil
3 cups thinly sliced onions
Salt and freshly ground black pepper
2 large ripe tomatoes, peeled, seeded, and cubed
1 teaspoon dried thyme
1 teaspoon dried oregano
½ pound fresh mushrooms, stems removed and caps thinly sliced
2 fresh porgies, each weighing 1½ to 1¾ pound, cleaned but tail and head left on
Coarse salt
2 large sprigs fresh parsley
½ cup heavy cream
¼ teaspoon saffron powder

Optional:
Beurre Manié (page 544)

Garnish:
Finely minced fresh parsley

Preparation

1.
Preheat the oven to 350 degrees.
2.
In a large cast-iron skillet heat 2 tablespoons butter and 1 tablespoon oil. Add the onions, season with salt and pepper, and cook for 10 minutes, or until the onions are soft and start to brown.
3.
Partially cover the skillet and continue cooking the onions until nicely browned, or for about 30 to 35 minutes.
4.
Add the tomatoes, thyme, oregano, salt, and pepper. Bring to a boil and cook the mixture until the tomato water has evaporated. Set the mixture aside.
5.
In a small heavy skillet heat the remaining butter and oil. Add the mushrooms and sauté over high heat until nicely browned. Season with salt and pepper and add to the onion-and-tomato mixture. Reserve.
6.
Oil a large flameproof baking dish.
7.
Season the fish with coarse salt and a large grinding of pepper. Place a large sprig of parsley in the cavity of each fish. Put the fish in the baking dish and spoon the onion-and-mushroom mixture over the fish. Set aside.
8.
Heat the cream and saffron in a small saucepan. Season with salt and pepper and spoon the cream over the fish. Place the dish in the oven and bake for 20 minutes.

Braised Salmon Steaks in Lemon Cream

Serves:	**4**
Preparation time:	**10 minutes**
Cooking time:	**25 minutes**
Type of recipe:	**elementary**
Cost:	**expensive**

9.
Turn on the broiler.
10.
When the fish is baked, place the dish 4 inches from the source of the heat and broil for 3 minutes, or until the top of the fish is nicely browned. Remove from the oven, sprinkle with parsley, and serve directly from the baking dish.

Remarks
If the pan juices seem too thin, you can transfer the fish carefully to a serving platter. Place the baking dish over medium heat and whisk in bits of Beurre Manié until the sauce is thickened. Taste and correct the seasoning. Spoon the sauce over the fish and serve accompanied by parslied new potatoes.

Ingredients
Juice of 1 large lemon
1½ cups Crème Fraîche (page 544)
Salt and freshly ground white pepper
2 Tablespoons finely minced shallots
½ cup dry vermouth
6–8 Tablespoons butter
4 salmon steaks, cut ¾ to 1 inch thick

Garnish:
Finely minced fresh parsley or chives

Preparation
1.
In a small bowl combine the lemon juice and Crème Fraîche. Season lightly with salt and pepper. Whisk the mixture until well blended and set aside.
2.
Preheat the oven to 350 degrees.
3.
In a small enamel saucepan combine the shallots and vermouth and cook the mixture until the vermouth is completely evaporated.
4.
In a large flameproof baking dish melt 2 tablespoons butter over low heat and add the shallots. Season the salmon steaks with salt and pepper and place in 1 layer in the baking dish.
5.
Spoon the lemon cream mixture over the steaks. Cover the dish with buttered foil and bake for 15 to 20 minutes, or until the steaks flake easily when tested with a tip of a sharp knife. Do not overcook the fish or it will be dry.

Serves: **4**
Preparation time: **30 minutes**
Cooking time: **1 hour, 10 minutes**
Type of recipe: **elementary**
Cost: **expensive**

6.
With a spatula transfer the steaks carefully to a serving platter and keep warm.

7.
Strain the pan juices into a saucepan. Cook the liquid over medium heat, reducing if necessary, until it coats the spoon.

8.
Remove the saucepan from the heat and whisk in the remaining butter. Taste the sauce and correct the seasoning. Set aside.

9.
Wipe away any accumulated juices with paper towels and spoon the sauce over each salmon steak. Garnish the platter with parsley or chives and serve accompanied by Sautéed Cucumber Balls (page 421).

Ingredients
2 Tablespoons butter
2 Tablespoons finely minced shallots
4 salmon steaks, cut ¾ inch thick
Salt and freshly ground black pepper

Vinaigrette:
8 Tablespoons fruity virgin olive oil
Juice of 1 large lemon or lime
2 Tablespoons finely minced fresh parsley
1½ Tablespoons finely minced shallots
1 ripe tomato, seeded and finely diced (not peeled)
Salt and freshly ground black pepper
1½ teaspoons coriander seeds

Bouillon:
2 to 3 pounds fish trimmings, preferably cod necks or another whitefish
2 Tablespoons butter
1 large carrot, scraped and diced
2 stalks celery, diced
1 large onion, peeled and diced
1 large Bouquet Garni (page 546)
1 teaspoon salt
6 black peppercorns
3 Tablespoons white wine vinegar
4 cups water

Garnish:
Sprigs of fresh parsley
1 lemon, quartered

Preparation

1.
Start by making the vinaigrette. In a small jar combine the olive oil, lemon or lime juice, parsley, shallots, and fresh tomato cubes. Season the dressing with salt and freshly ground black pepper and set aside.

2.
Put the coriander seeds in a small skillet. Place the skillet over moderate-to-high heat and toast the seeds, shaking the pan back and forth until they start to darken. Place the seeds in a mortar and crush them with a pestle. Add the crushed coriander seeds to the dressing and set aside.

3.
Prepare the bouillon. Wash the fish trimmings thoroughly under cold water until all traces of blood have disappeared. Set aside.

4.
In a large heavy casserole heat the butter. Add the vegetables and cook covered over low heat for 15 minutes, or until tender.

5.
Add the trimmings, Bouquet Garni, salt, peppercorns, vinegar, and water. Bring to a boil, reduce the heat, and simmer the bouillon partially covered for 40 minutes. Strain the bouillon into a bowl and reserve.

6.
Preheat the oven to 350 degrees.

7.
In a large baking dish heat the butter, then add the shallots and 2 cups of hot bouillon.

8.
Season the salmon steaks with salt and pepper and place them in the baking dish.

Cover them with a large piece of buttered waxed paper.

9.
Set the dish in the oven and braise the steaks for 8 to 10 minutes, or until the fish flakes easily when tested with the tip of a sharp knife. Do not overcook or the fish will be dry.

10.
Remove the dish from the oven and with a large spatula, transfer the salmon steaks to a serving platter. Wipe any accumulated juices with paper towels.

11.
Spoon the dressing over the salmon steaks. Garnish with sprigs of parsley and lemon quarters and serve warm. Serve with hot, buttered, parslied new potatoes.

Poached Salmon Steaks
in
Tarragon Sauce

Serves: **4**
Preparation time: **15 minutes**
Cooking time: **25 minutes**
Type of recipe: **elementary**
Cost: **expensive**

Ingredients
3 egg yolks
1 teaspoon cornstarch
¾ to 1 cup heavy cream
Salt and freshly ground white pepper
3 Tablespoons finely minced shallots
½ cup dry vermouth
1½ cups concentrated Court-Bouillon (page 538)
8 Tablespoons cold butter
1 to 2 Tablespoons finely minced fresh tarragon
4 salmon steaks, cut ¾ inch thick

Garnish:
Sprigs of fresh parsley

Preparation

1.
In a bowl combine the yolks, cornstarch, and ¾ cup cream. Season with salt and pepper and whisk the mixture until smooth. Set aside.

2.
In a heavy 2-quart saucepan combine 1½ tablespoons shallots and the vermouth. Cook the mixture over high heat until reduced to 1 tablespoon. Add ½ cup Court-Bouillon and continue cooking the mixture until reduced to 2 tablespoons.

3.
Reduce the heat. Remove the saucepan from the heat and whisk in the egg yolk-and-cream mixture.

4.
Place the saucepan over very low heat and whisk the sauce constantly until it starts to thicken. Add 6 tablespoons butter a little at a time and continue cooking the sauce over the lowest possible heat until the butter is just melted. Add 1 tablespoon tarragon. Taste the sauce and correct the seasoning. Keep it over a saucepan of warm water, whisking it every 10 minutes.

5.
Preheat the oven to 350 degrees.

6.
In a large flameproof baking dish melt 2 tablespoons butter. Add the remaining shallots and remaining Court-Bouillon. Season the salmon steaks with salt and pepper and place in the baking dish.

7.
Butter a large piece of waxed paper, then cover the baking dish with it and place the dish in the center of the oven. Braise the salmon steaks for 10 to 12 minutes, or until they just turn a pale pink. You can turn them over once carefully during their cooking time.

8.
Remove the salmon steaks to a serving platter. With paper towels remove any juices that may have accumulated around the steaks. Spoon a little of the sauce over each steak and sprinkle with a little more tarragon. Garnish the platter with sprigs of parsley and serve with tiny buttered new potatoes.

Remarks
Although the sauce is actually easy to prepare, it has to be watched carefully. If at any time the sauce shows signs of curdling add 1 tablespoon cold heavy cream and whisk vigorously until smooth again and well blended. This is a delicious sauce to be served with other fish as well, such as poached bass or red snapper.

Salmon Steaks
Villefranche

Serves: **4 to 6**
Preparation time: **30 minutes**
Cooking time: **20 minutes**
Type of recipe: **elementary**
Cost: **expensive**

Ingredients

4 to 6 small salmon steaks
Salt

Court-Bouillon:

1 onion, sliced
1 carrot, scraped and sliced
1 stalk celery, sliced
6 black peppercorns
Large sprig fresh parsley
1 bay leaf
3 Tablespoons white wine vinegar

Sauce:

1 tablespoon olive oil
2 large shallots, finely minced
2 large tomatoes, peeled, seeded, and chopped
Salt and freshly ground black pepper
½ cup finely minced green pepper
1 cup prepared zucchini (cubed and poached for 3 to 5 minutes, then drained)
2 cups Mayonnaise (page 540)
2 to 4 Tablespoons finely minced pimientos
Finely minced chives
2 teaspoon curry powder
1 to 2 cloves garlic, crushed

Optional:

1 to 2 finely minced hard-boiled eggs

Garnish:

Sprigs of fresh dill or parsley

Preparation

1.
In a large baking dish combine all the ingredients for the court-bouillon. Bring it to a boil and simmer for 10 minutes.

2.
Add the salmon steaks seasoned with salt, bring to a boil, and cook for exactly 1 minute. Remove the pan from the heat and let the steaks cool covered. When completely cool transfer to a serving platter and set aside.

3.
Prepare the sauce. In a small heavy skillet heat the oil. Add the shallots and tomatoes, season with salt and pepper, and cook until the tomato juices have evaporated. Add the green pepper and cook until slightly tender. Remove and cool.

4.
Poach the zucchini in salted water until barely tender. Remove and cool.

5.
Combine the vegetables and mayonnaise in a mixing bowl, add the pimientos, chives, curry powder, garlic, salt, pepper, and optional minced egg. Taste the mixture and correct the seasoning.

6.
Spoon the sauce over the salmon steaks and garnish with sprigs of parsley and dill. Serve at room temperature accompanied by boiled new potatoes.

Remarks
The poaching stock should be strained and frozen for future use. Any leftover sauce can be served with grilled fillets of sole or boiled scallops or shrimps.

Poached Salmon
in
Watercress Sauce

Serves:	**4**
Preparation time:	**35 minutes**
Cooking time:	**30 minutes**
Type of recipe:	**elementary**
Cost:	**expensive**

Ingredients

1 large bunch fresh watercress
¼ cup heavy cream
4 salmon steaks, cut ¾ inch thick
Salt and freshly ground white pepper
3 Tablespoons butter
2 Tablespoons finely minced shallots, or
3 Tablespoons finely minced scallions
1½ to 2 cups Fish Stock (page 536)
1 cup Crème Fraîche (page 544)
1 Beurre Manié (page 544)

Garnish:

1 cup carrots, scraped and cut into julienne matchsticks
1½ cups green beans, cut into thin julienne matchsticks
Sprigs of fresh watercress

Preparation

1.
Prepare the garnish first. In a large saucepan bring salted water to boil, add the beans and carrots, and cook until barely tender. Strain, run under cold water, and set aside.

2.
Remove the stems from the watercress, reserving only the leaves.

3.
In a small saucepan bring salted water to a boil. Add the watercress leaves and cook for 3 minutes. Drain and transfer to a blender or food processor. Add the heavy cream and purée the mixture until smooth. Set aside.

4.
Season the salmon steaks with salt and pepper.

5.
Preheat the oven to 350 degrees.

6.
In a large enamel flameproof baking dish heat the butter. Add the shallots or scallions and cook for 2 to 3 minutes. Add the salmon steaks in 1 layer, then add the fish stock. Bring to a boil, cover with buttered waxed paper, and set the dish in the oven. Bake the salmon steaks for 12 minutes.

7.
Remove the dish from the oven and carefully transfer the steaks to a serving platter. Cover and keep warm over a pan of hot water.

8.
Strain the pan juices into a heavy enamel saucepan. Bring to a boil and reduce by half. Add the Crème Fraîche and reduce again by half.

9.
Add the watercress purée to the saucepan and whisk in bits of the Beurre Manié, cooking the sauce until it heavily coats a spoon. Taste and correct the seasoning. Set aside.

10.
With paper towels remove any accumulated juices around the salmon steaks. Spoon the sauce over the steaks, then add the carrot-and-green bean garnish. Sprinkle the platter with sprigs of watercress. Serve hot accompanied by buttered and dilled tiny new potatoes.

Cold Salmon Steaks
in
Sorrel Mayonnaise

Serves: **4**
Preparation time: **25 minutes**
Cooking time: **15 minutes**
Type of recipe: **elementary**
Cost: **expensive**

Ingredients

4 salmon steaks, cut ¾ inch thick
Salt and freshly ground black pepper
2 Tablespoons butter
2 Tablespoons finely minced shallots or scallions
2 cups Vegetable Stock (page 539)

Sauce:

3 cups tightly packed fresh sorrel leaves
1 bunch fresh watercress, stems removed
2 large eggs
1½ teaspoons white wine vinegar
¼ teaspoon granulated sugar
2 teaspoons Dijon mustard
¾ to 1 cup oil
2 Tablespoons finely minced scallions (both white and green)
2 Tablespoons finely minced fresh parsley
Salt and freshly ground white pepper
Drops of lemon juice

Garnish:

Sprigs of fresh parsley

Optional:

Slices of avocado, sprinkled with salt and lemon juice

Preparation

1.
Start by making the sauce. In a small saucepan bring 2 cups salted water to a boil. Add the sorrel leaves and watercress and cook for 2 to 3 minutes. Drain immediately, pressing down on the greens to extract all the moisture. Set aside.

2.
In a blender combine the eggs, vinegar, sugar, and mustard. Blend the mixture at high speed and slowly add the oil by droplets, blending constantly until the sauce is thick and smooth.

3.
Add the scallions, parsley, sorrel, and watercress and blend until smooth. Season with salt and pepper and add lemon juice to taste. The sauce should be quite tart. Chill the sauce until serving.

4.
Preheat the oven to 325 degrees.

5.
Season the salmon steaks with salt and pepper.

6.
In a large flameproof baking dish melt the butter. Add the shallots or scallions and cook over low heat for 2 minutes without browning.

7.
Add the stock and place the salmon steaks in the dish. Heat the stock on top of the stove until it almost comes to a boil.

8.
Immediately remove from the heat and cover the baking dish with buttered wax paper. Set the dish in the center of the oven and braise the steaks for 8 to 10 minutes.

Fillets of Sole
in
Basil Cream

Serves: **4**
Preparation time: **15 minutes**
Cooking time: **1 hour**
Type of recipe: **elementary**
Cost: **moderate**

They are done if the fish flakes easily when tested with the tip of a sharp knife. Do not overcook or the fish will be dry.

9.
Let the salmon steaks cool in their poaching liquid. When ready, remove the fish steaks to a serving platter with a spatula.

10.
With paper towels wipe away any liquid that may have accumulated around the fish steaks. Spoon the sauce over the steaks, covering them completely. Garnish the platter with sprigs of parsley and the optional slices of avocado. Serve the salmon steaks accompanied by tiny parslied new potatoes.

Remarks
The sauce can be prepared 1 to 2 days ahead and refrigerated. The salmon steaks can be cooked several hours ahead and left in their poaching liquid until serving. The sorrel mayonnaise is equally good with any hot poached fish, such as bass or salmon.

Ingredients
4 Tablespoons fruity olive oil
3 Tablespoons finely minced shallots
3 ripe tomatoes, peeled, seeded, and chopped, or 1 can (8 ounces) Italian baby tomatoes, well drained and sliced
1 teaspoon dried thyme
½ teaspoon dried oregano
Salt and freshly ground white pepper
1 large sprig fresh basil and 2 tablespoons julienne of basil leaves
2 large cloves garlic, peeled and crushed
4 fresh medium fillets of sole, about 3 pounds
Flour for dredging
2 tablespoons butter
½ cup dry vermouth
1 cup Crème Fraîche (page 544)
1 Beurre Manié (page 544)

Garnish:
Sprigs of fresh basil

Preparation

1.

In a 2-quart saucepan heat 2 tablespoons oil. Add 1 tablespoon shallots, the well-drained tomatoes, thyme, oregano, salt, and pepper. Add the sprig of basil. Cover the saucepan and stew the tomatoes over low heat for 40 to 50 minutes. Check every 10 minutes to make sure the tomatoes are not scorching the bottom of the pan. Add 1 clove garlic and set the tomato mixture aside.

2.

Season the fillets with salt and pepper. Dredge lightly with flour, shaking off the excess.

3.

In a large heavy skillet heat the remaining oil. Add 1 tablespoon butter and heat the mixture until it starts to smoke.

4.

Add the fillets; do not crowd the pan. (You may have to saute the fillets in 2 batches.) Sauté the fillets over moderate-to-high heat for 2 to 3 minutes. Carefully turn the fillets and sauté on the other side until nicely browned. Make sure the oil is not burning in the pan. You may need a little more olive oil.

5.

When done, transfer the fillets to a serving platter, cover loosely with foil, and keep warm.

6.

Add the remaining butter to the pan. When the butter is melted add the remaining shallots and cook for 1 to 2 minutes, or until soft and lightly browned.

7.

Add the vermouth and cook the mixture until reduced to 1 tablespoon.

8.

Add the Crème Fraîche. Bring to a boil and continue cooking until reduced by one third. Add the tomato mixture, then whisk in a little Beurre Manié. You will only need a very little bit; use just enough to thicken the sauce. It should heavily coat a spoon.

9.

Remove the pan from the heat and add the julienne strips of basil and the remaining garlic. Taste the sauce and correct the seasoning.

10.

Spoon the sauce over the fillets of sole and garnish with sprigs of fresh basil. Serve immediately.

Braised Swordfish
in
Garlic Cream

Serves:	**4**
Preparation time:	**10 minutes**
Cooking time:	**10 minutes**
Type of recipe:	**elementary**
Cost:	**expensive**

Ingredients

1½ cups heavy cream
10 to 12 large cloves garlic, peeled
Juice of 1 lemon
Salt and freshly ground black pepper
1½ to 2 pounds fresh swordfish steaks, cut into ½-inch scallops
Flour for dredging
2 to 3 Tablespoons butter
2 teaspoons olive oil
1 large sprig of fresh thyme, or ½ teaspoon dried

Garnish:
Finely minced fresh parsley

Preparation

1.
In a saucepan combine heavy cream and garlic. Simmer the cream partially covered for 15 minutes, or until the cloves are very soft and easy to mash and the cream has reduced by ½. Mash the garlic cloves into a fine paste, add lemon juice to taste, and season the garlic cream lightly with salt and pepper. Set aside.

2.
Season the swordfish scallops with salt and pepper. Dredge lightly with flour, shaking off the excess.

3.
In a large cast-iron skillet heat 2 tablespoons butter with a teaspoon of oil. Add the swordfish scallops in 1 layer, together with the sprig of thyme (If you do not have fresh thyme sprinkle each swordfish with a little dried thyme.) Sauté the scallops over moderate-to-high heat until nicely browned on both sides, turning them carefully. Do not burn the butter. If the butter has burned discard it and add 2 more tablespoons butter to the skillet.

4.
Lower the heat. Add the garlic-and-lemon cream. Partially cover the skillet and braise the scallops for another 3 to 4 minutes, basting them with the cream.

5.
Carefully transfer the fish to a serving platter. Taste the sauce and correct the seasoning. Spoon the sauce over the scallops, sprinkle with parsley, and serve accompanied by Potatoes Arlésienne (page 433) or simply crusty French bread and a cold green bean salad.

Remarks

This dish is equally delicious when made with halibut or salmon steaks. If the steaks are ½ to ¾ inches thick finish their cooking by braising them covered in a low (325-degree) oven to be sure they cook evenly.

Mussels
in
Mustard Sauce

Serves: **6**
Preparation Time: **30 minutes, plus 1 hour to prepare mustard paste**
Cooking Time: **20 minutes**
Type of recipe: **elementary**
Cost: **inexpensive**

Ingredients

1 teaspoon dried mustard, mixed to a paste with 1 Tablespoon water
5 to 6 pounds fresh mussels, well scrubbed
1 cup dry white wine
2 Tablespoons finely minced shallots
1 bay leaf
½ teaspoon dried thyme
1 sprig of fresh parsley
4 Tablespoons butter
3 Tablespoons flour
¾ cup Crème Fraîche (page 544)
2 Tablespoons Dijon mustard
Salt and freshly ground black pepper

Preparation

1.
Make the mustard paste an hour ahead (to let it develop flavor) in a little bowl and set aside.

2.
Clean the mussels thoroughly with a stiff brush under cold water. Place the mussels in a large bowl. Cover with ice cubes until ready to use.

3.
In a large casserole combine ½ cup wine with 1 tablespoon shallots, bay leaf, thyme, and parsley. Add the mussels, partially cover the casserole, and bring to a boil on top of the stove. Cook the mussels until they open, or for about 4 to 5 minutes. Shake the pot back and forth or stir the mussels with a large spoon so they can all open evenly.

4.
Remove from the heat and cool. Shell the mussels and reserve, but discard any that do not open.

5.
Strain the mussel liquid through a double layer of cheesecloth into a saucepan and reduce the liquid over high heat to 1½ cups. Set aside.

6.
In a heavy 2-quart enamel saucepan combine the remaining shallots and wine. Bring the mixture to a boil and reduce over high heat to 1 tablespoon.

7.
Add the butter and, when melted, add the flour and whisk until well blended. Remove the saucepan from the heat and add the

---

Serves: **4**
Preparation time: **30 minutes**
Cooking time: **30 minutes**
Type of recipe: **elementary**
Cost: **inexpensive**

mussel stock all at once. Whisk the mixture until smooth.

8.
Return the saucepan to the heat and simmer the sauce until thick and smooth. Strain the sauce and return to the saucepan.

9.
Add the Crème Fraîche, bring to a boil, and reduce the sauce by one third.

10.
Add the mustard and reserved mustard paste. Taste the sauce and correct the seasoning, adding a large grinding of black pepper.

11.
Drain the mussels of any accumulated juices and add them to the sauce. Heat through over low heat and serve on a bed of braised rice or on individual plates, accompanied by crusty French bread.

Remarks
This dish can be prepared several hours ahead and reheated in the top of a double boiler. You may also serve the mussels on a bed of braised spinach or as an appetizer on individual bread croûtons that have been sautéed in a mixture of butter and oil.

Ingredients
4 to 5 pounds fresh mussels, well scrubbed
2 Tablespoons finely minced shallots
½ cup dry vermouth
1 cup concentrated Fish Stock (page 536)
1 cup heavy cream
1 to 1½ Beurre Manié (page 544)
Salt and freshly ground white pepper
6 Tablespoons butter

Optional:
1 pound fresh fettucine

Garnish:
Finely minced fresh parsley

Preparation

1.
Place the mussels in a large kettle. Cover and steam them over medium heat until all the mussels have opened. Shake the kettle back and forth to cook the mussels evenly. Discard any that have not opened.

2.
Let the mussels cool and, when cool enough to handle, shell them and discard the shells. Spoon a little of the mussel liquid over them and set aside.

3.
Strain the remaining poaching liquid through a fine cheesecloth into a bowl and reserve 1 cup.

4.
In a heavy 2-quart saucepan combine the shallots and vermouth. Cook the mixture over high heat until reduced to 1 tablespoon. Add the stock and reserved mussel liquid. Bring the mixture to a boil and reduce by half.

5.
Add the cream. Bring to a boil and again cook the mixture until reduced by ½.

6.
Start adding bits of Beurre Manié, whisking the sauce constantly until it heavily coats the spoon.

7.
Season carefully with salt and pepper. (The mussel juices are quite salty and you may not need any salt.) Return the mussels to the saucepan and heat through over very low heat. Set aside.

8.
Ten minutes before serving bring salted water to a boil in a large casserole, add the optional fettucine, and cook until barely tender. Drain and return to the casserole.

9.
Add 3 tablespoons butter to the fettucine and season with salt and freshly ground black pepper. Toss the fettucine in the butter. Place servings of fettucine on individual serving plates.

10.
Reheat the mussels in the sauce and whisk in the remaining 3 tablespoons butter. Spoon some of the mussel ragoût onto each plate. Sprinkle with parsley and serve accompanied by plenty of crusty bread.

Remarks
If you do not want to serve the mussels over the fettucine you may serve them either by themselves in small serving dishes or accompanied by a pilaf of rice. The mussel ragoût can be prepared several hours ahead and kept warm in the top of a double boiler and then reheated slowly just before serving. For variation, poach ½ pound small fresh shrimp in a little fish stock. Peel the shrimp and add to the mussel ragoût. Serve the ragoût of mussels and shrimp either over rice or over fresh fettucine.

Sautéed Scallops
à la Basquaise

Serves: **4 to 5**
Preparation time: **45 minutes**
Cooking time: **10 minutes**
Type of recipe: **elementary**
Cost: **expensive**

Ingredients

2 large red peppers
6 to 8 Italian plum tomatoes, peeled (see note)
1½ pounds fresh small sea scallops
Salt and freshly ground black pepper
Flour for dredging
4 Tablespoons butter
1 Tablespoon olive oil
2 Tablespoons finely minced shallots
4 Tablespoons finely minced fresh parsley
3 large cloves garlic, finely minced

Preparation

1.
Preheat the broiler.

2.
Prepare the peppers according to the directions on page 545 and slice thinly. Reserve.

3.
Slice the peeled tomatoes into ½-inch slices and place in a colander to drain.

4.
Season the scallops with salt and pepper. Dredge lightly with flour, shaking off the excess.

5.
In a 12-inch cast-iron skillet heat 2 tablespoons butter and the oil. Add the scallops and sauté over high heat until they are nicely browned on both sides. Transfer the scallops to a side dish and reserve.

6.
Lower the heat and add the remaining butter to the skillet. When the butter is hot add the shallots and cook for 2 minutes, or until lightly browned, scraping well the bottom of the pan.

7.
Add the tomatoes, peppers, 2 tablespoons parsley, and garlic. Season the mixture with salt and pepper and cook for 2 to 3 minutes over low heat.

8.
Return the scallops to the pan and cover. Simmer for 3 minutes.

9.
Transfer the scallops to a deep serving dish. Sprinkle with the remaining parsley and serve accompanied by crusty French bread or sautéed cubed potatoes.

Remarks

Although the peppers can be grilled and sliced a day in advance the scallops have to be prepared at the last minute or they will get hard and rubbery.

Note

You can use canned sliced baby tomatoes instead of the Italian plum tomatoes. Drain the tomatoes thoroughly and stew them, with a pinch of dried thyme and oregano, in 3 tablespoons fruity olive oil over low heat for 30 to 40 minutes.

Sautéed Scallops
à la Bayonnaise

Serves: **4**
Preparation time: **10 minutes**
Cooking time: **10 minutes**
Type of recipe: **elementary**
Cost: **expensive**

Scallop dishes are both easy and quickly prepared. They must, however, be made at the last minute and the scallops should never be overcooked. One of the most delicate of shellfish, scallops are often combined with creamy sauces. Here is a more gutsy version from the Basque region of France.

Ingredients

1 pound fresh bay or small sea scallops
Salt and freshly ground black pepper
3 Tablespoons butter
1 teaspoon oil
2 Tablespoons minced shallots
1 large clove garlic, minced
½ cup finely diced smoked ham
3 to 4 Tablespoons Chicken Stock (page 530) or Fish Stock (page 536)
¾ cup cooked fresh peas
Flour
Lemon juice

Garnish:
2 Tablespoons minced fresh parsley

Preparation

1.
Dry the scallops thoroughly with paper towels. Season with salt and pepper.

2.
In a large heavy skillet heat the butter and oil. Add the scallops; do not crowd the pan. Sauté over high heat until nicely browned on both sides, then remove the scallops with a slotted spoon to a side dish and reserve.

3.
To the fat remaining in the pan add the shallots, garlic, and ham. Sauté for 2 minutes.

4.
Add the stock and bring to a boil, scraping well the bottom of the pan.

5.
Add the peas and a fine sprinkling of flour. Cook for another minute.

6.
Return the scallops to the pan and simmer for another 2 to 3 minutes.

7.
Transfer the mixture to a serving dish and sprinkle with lemon juice. Garnish with parsley and serve accompanied by crusty French bread.

Feuilleté of Scallops Lyonnaise

Serves: **6**
Preparation Time: **45 minutes, plus time to prepare pastry**
Cooking Time: **40 minutes**
Type of recipe: **difficult**
Cost: **expensive**

Ingredients

6 three-inch squares puff pastry (Feuilletés, page 548)
1 egg, beaten with a little water
2 cups Fish Stock (page 536)
1 large sprig fresh parsley
1 bay leaf
1 pound fresh bay scallops or small sea scallops
Salt
4 black peppercorns
½ cup dry white wine
2 tablespoons finely minced shallots
1 cup Crème Fraîche (page 544)
1 Beurre Manié (page 544)
2 Tablespoons minced fresh parsley
2 Tablespoons minced fresh chives or chervil

Preparation

1.
Preheat the oven to 400 degrees.

2.
Place the chilled Feuilletés on a moistened cookie sheet and bake for 20 minutes. Brush with egg wash and bake for another 10 minutes, or until nicely browned. Keep warm in a turned-off oven.

3.
While the Feuilletés are baking, combine the stock, parsley, and bay leaf in an enamel saucepan. Bring the stock to a boil, reduce the heat, and add the scallops. Season with salt and add peppercorns. Poach the scallops over low heat for 5 minutes, or until they turn an opaque white. Do not overcook.

4.
Transfer the scallops with some of the poaching liquid to another saucepan and keep warm. (This is best done by placing the saucepan in a pan of hot water) Bring the remaining stock to a boil and cook over high heat until reduced to 1 cup. Set aside.

5.
In another heavy-bottomed enamel saucepan combine the wine and shallots. Cook the mixture over high heat until reduced to 2 tablespoons.

6.
Add the reserved stock and the Crème Fraîche. Bring to a boil and cook the mixture until reduced by ⅓.

7.
Whisk in bits of Beurre Manié until the sauce heavily coats a spoon.

8.
Drain the scallops and add to the sauce, warm through over low heat, then add the parsley and chives.

9.
Remove the Feuilletés from the oven. Cut each in half horizontally and remove any unbaked dough.

10.
Place the bottom half of each on individual serving plates, fill with the scallop mixture, and top with the other pastry half. Spoon any remaining sauce around the Feuilletés and serve immediately.

Remarks

The Feuilletés can be baked a day ahead and reheated in a slow oven. The scallops can be prepared several hours ahead and reheated in the top of a double boiler over simmering water. For variation you might serve the scallops over a bed of braised white rice.

Sautéed Scallops
Nîmoise

Serves: **4**
Preparation Time: **25 minutes**
Cooking Time: **15 minutes**
Type of recipe: **elementary**
Cost: **expensive**

Ingredients
5 Tablespoons butter
½ pound fresh mushrooms, stems removed and caps quartered
Salt and freshly ground black pepper
1 pound fresh bay scallops
Flour
1 Tablespoon olive oil
¼ cup minced shallots
2 large ripe tomatoes, peeled, seeded, and chopped
1 cup Crème Fraîche (page 544)
1 Beurre Manié (page 544)

Garnish:
2 Tablespoons finely minced fresh parsley

Preparation
1.
In a small heavy skillet heat 2 tablespoons butter. Add the mushrooms and sauté for 3 to 4 minutes, or until nicely browned. Season with salt and pepper and set aside.
2.
Dry the scallops thoroughly with paper towels. Season with salt and pepper and sprinkle lightly with flour.
3.
In a heavy 10- to 12-inch skillet heat 2 tablespoons butter and the oil. When the butter starts to brown add the scallops; do not crowd the pan. Cook the scallops over high heat shaking the pan back and forth until they are nicely browned on all sides. Transfer to a side dish and reserve.
4.
Add the remaining butter to the pan. Add the shallots and cook for 2 minutes, scraping well the bottom of the pan. Add

the tomatoes and cook until the tomato water has evaporated and the mixture is thick. Season with salt and pepper.
5.
Add the mushrooms and Crème Fraîche. Bring to a boil and reduce the sauce by one third.
6.
Whisk in bits of Beurre Manié and continue cooking the sauce until it heavily coats the spoon.
7.
Return the scallops to the skillet and spoon the sauce over them. Simmer for another 2 to 3 minutes, or until the scallops are heated through.
8.
Transfer to a serving dish, sprinkle wish parsley, and serve as an appetizer accompanied by crusty French bread or as a main course over a pilaf of rice.

Scallop Pâté
Parisienne

Serves: **6 to 8**
Preparation time: **45 minutes**
Cooking time: **1 hour, 15 minutes**
Type of recipe: **intermediate**
Cost: **expensive**

Here is an elegant scallop pâté in the tradition of the best French haute cuisine. For years this kind of dish was reserved for the kitchens of fine restaurants but now, thanks to the food processor, every cook can bring a touch of 3-star cooking into his or her kitchen.

Ingredients

1¼ pounds fresh small sea scallops
1 cup Fish Stock (page 536)
1 Bouquet Garni (page 546)
Salt and freshly ground black pepper
3 large egg whites
1½ cups heavy cream
½ teaspoon grated onion
Pinch of cayenne pepper

Sauce:

3 Tablespoons butter
2 Tablespoons flour
3 large egg yolks
½ cup heavy cream
Juice of ½ lemon
Salt and freshly ground white pepper

Optional:

2 Tablespoons finely minced fresh tarragon

Garnish:

Sprigs of fresh watercress

Preparation

1.
Preheat the oven to 350 degrees.

2.
In a small enamel saucepan combine 8 scallops with the stock and bouquet. Season with salt and pepper, then simmer the scallops for 3 minutes, or until they turn an opaque white. Strain the scallops and reserve the stock. Finely cube the scallops and set aside.

2.
In a food processor combine the remaining scallops and the egg whites. Purée the mixture until smooth.

3.
Slowly start adding the cream and blend until all the cream has been incorporated and the mixture is smooth. Season with grated onion, salt, pepper, and cayenne.

4.
Transfer the mixture to a bowl. Fold the cubed scallops into the mixture and then transfer to a well-buttered loaf pan.

5.
Set the loaf pan inside a baking dish and pour enough water into the baking dish so that the water level reaches ⅔ up the sides of the loaf pan.

6.
Cover the pan with a buttered sheet of waxed paper and bake for 1 hour, or until a tip of a knife comes out clean.

7.
While the pâté is baking make the sauce. In a 2-quart enamel saucepan heat the butter, add the flour, and cook stirring constantly for 2 minutes without browning.

Poached Scallops
in
Chive Sauce

Serves:	**4**
Preparation time:	**30 minutes**
Cooking time:	**45 minutes**
Type of recipe:	**elementary**
Cost:	**expensive**

8.
Add the reserved stock all at once and bring the sauce to a boil, whisking constantly until it is smooth and thick. Remove from the heat and set aside.

9.
In a small bowl combine the yolks and cream. Add the lemon juice and whisk the mixture until smooth. Add this to the sauce and reheat but do not let it come to a boil. Taste and correct the seasoning. Add the optional tarragon. Keep warm.

10.
When the pâté is done, run a sharp knife around the edges and unmold it onto a rectangular serving platter. Dry the platter with paper towels and then spoon the sauce over the entire pâté. Garnish with sprigs of watercress and serve hot.

Remarks
The scallop pâté can be made several hours ahead and kept warm in a pan of hot but not boiling water. The sauce can also be made well in advance and kept warm in the top of a double boiler. The pâté could also be served cold accompanied by a mustard-and-herb mayonnaise.

Ingredients
2 Tablespoons finely minced shallots
½ cup dry vermouth
1½ cups hot strong Fish Stock (page 536)
1 pound fresh small sea scallops
1 cup heavy cream
1 Beurre Manié (page 544)
Salt and freshly ground white pepper
4 Tablespoons cold butter
2 Tablespoons finely minced fresh chives
1 Tablespoons finely minced fresh parsley

Scallops
à la Méridionale

Serves:	**4 to 6**
Preparation time:	**35 minutes**
Cooking time:	**15 minutes**
Type of recipe:	**elementary**
Cost:	**expensive**

Preparation

1.

In a heavy-bottomed saucepan combine the shallots and vermouth. Bring the mixture to a boil and reduce to a glaze; there should be no more than 1 teaspoon of liquid left in the saucepan. Set aside.

2.

In an enamel casserole combine the stock and the scallops and simmer for about 3 to 4 minutes until the scallops turn an opaque white; do not let it come to a boil. With a slotted spoon remove the scallops to a bowl, place the bowl over a pan of warm water, cover the scallops, and set aside.

3.

Pour the poaching stock into the saucepan in which you have reduced the shallots. Bring to a boil and reduce the liquid over high heat by half. Add the cream. Bring to a boil and reduce again by half.

4.

Whisk in bits of the Beurre Manié and season the sauce with salt and pepper. If the sauce seems too thin you may need a bit more of the Beurre Manié. The sauce, however, should not be thick.

5.

Remove the saucepan from the heat, and whisk in the cold butter and add the scallops.

6.

Return the saucepan to a very low heat to warm the scallops through; they must not cook any more.

7.

Add the chives and parsley. Taste the sauce and correct the seasoning. Serve the scallops accompanied by crusty bread.

What makes scallops such a wonderful seafood is their versatility. They are delicious when simply sautéed in parsley and garlic butter and equally good when prepared in this delicate wine sauce. Here they are combined with a tomato-flavored fondue with garnish of poached mushrooms.

Ingredients

6 Tablespoons butter
3 Tablespoons finely minced shallots
2 large ripe tomatoes, peeled, seeded, and chopped
1 teaspoon tomato paste
18 small mushrooms, stems removed
Juice of ½ lemon
Salt and freshly ground black pepper
¾ cup heavy cream
3 large egg yolks
2 cups Fish Stock (page 536)
1½ pounds fresh small sea scallops
3 Tablespoons flour
Dash of Tabasco sauce

Preparation

1.
In a small heavy skillet heat 2 tablespoons butter. Add 1 tablespoon shallots and cook for 2 minutes without browning.

2.
Add the tomatoes, season with salt and pepper, and cook over high heat until the tomato water has evaporated. Add the tomato paste and cook for 2 more minutes, or until the mixture is thick. Set aside.

3.
In a small saucepan combine the mushroom caps with 1 cup water. Add the lemon juice, season with salt, and bring to a boil, then reduce the heat and simmer for 3 to 4 minutes. Drain the mushrooms and add to the tomato mixture.

4.
In a bowl combine the heavy cream and yolks. Whisk until well blended and set aside.

5.
In a large enamel saucepan combine the remaining shallots and stock. Add the scallops, season with salt and pepper, and bring to a simmer. Cover and poach the scallops for 3 minutes, or until they turn an opaque white.

6.
Drain the scallops. Add a little of the cooking liquid and keep warm over a pan of warm water. Reserve 1¾ cups of the cooking stock.

7.
In a heavy 3-quart saucepan heat the remaining butter. Add the flour and stir the mixture over low heat for 3 to 4 minutes. Do not let it brown.

8.
Add the reserved stock all at once and increase the heat. Bring to a boil and whisk the sauce until thick and smooth.

9.
Fold the tomato-and-mushroom mixture into the sauce. Add the yolk-and-cream mixture. Season with salt and pepper and a dash of Tabasco sauce. Whisk the sauce and heat through without letting it come to a boil.

10.
Drain the scallops. Add them to the sauce and heat through over low heat; the sauce must not come to a boil. Taste and correct the seasoning. Transfer the scallops to a serving bowl and serve accompanied by crusty French bread or buttered rice.

Remarks
The dish can be prepared 40 minutes ahead and reheated in a double boiler.

Sautéed Scallops
Montélimar

Serves: **4**
Preparation time: **10 minutes**
Cooking time: **15 minutes**
Type of recipe: **elementary**
Cost: **expensive**

Ingredients

1 pound fresh small sea scallops
Salt and freshly ground black pepper
Flour for dredging
3 to 4 Tablespoons butter
1 Tablespoon olive oil
2 Tablespoons finely minced shallots
2 large cloves garlic, peeled and finely minced
2 Tablespoons finely minced fresh parsley
½ cup concentrated Fish Stock (page 536), or dry white wine
1 cup heavy cream
1 Beurre Manié (page 544)

Garnish:
Sprigs of fresh parsley

Preparation

1.
Dry the scallops thoroughly with paper towels. Season with salt and pepper. Dredge lightly with flour, shaking off the excess.

2.
Heat the butter and oil in a large heavy skillet. Add the scallops; do not crowd the pan. Sauté over high heat until the scallops are golden brown on all sides.

3.
Remove the skillet from the heat. With a spatula remove the scallops to a side dish and reserve.

4.
Add the shallots, garlic, and parsley to the pan. You may need an additional tablespoon butter.

5.
Return the pan to the heat and cook the mixture for 2 minutes, scraping well the bottom of the pan.

6.
Add the stock, bring to a boil, and reduce to 2 tablespoons.

7.
Add the cream, bring to a boil, and reduce by one third.

8.
Whisk in bits of Beurre Manié until the sauce heavily coats a spoon.

9.
Return the scallops to the pan and cook for 2 to 3 minutes, or until heated through. Taste and correct the seasoning.

10.
Transfer the scallops to a serving dish. Sprinkle with parsley, and serve hot accompanied by crusty French bread.

Sautéed Scallops
La Napoule

Serves: **4**
Preparation time: **15 minutes**
Cooking time: **15 minutes**
Type of recipe: **elementary**
Cost: **expensive**

Ingredients

1 pound fresh bay scallops or small sea scallops
Salt and freshly ground white pepper
Flour for dredging
3 to 4 Tablespoons butter
1 Tablespoon oil
½ pound fresh small mushrooms, stems removed and caps quartered
1 cup Cream of Fish Stock (page 537)

Optional:
1 Beurre Manié (page 544)

Garnish:
Finely minced fresh parsley, or a mixture of finely minced fresh parsley and tarragon

Preparation

1.
Season the scallops with salt and pepper. Dredge lightly with flour, shaking off the excess.

2.
In a cast-iron skillet heat 2 tablespoons butter and the oil. When the butter starts to brown add the scallops and cook over high heat for 2 to 3 minutes, or until nicely browned on all sides. Shake the pan back and forth to sauté the scallops evenly. Remove the scallops to a side dish and reserve.

3.
Add another tablespoon butter to the pan. Add the mushrooms and sauté for 2 or 3 minutes, or until nicely browned. Season with salt and pepper.

4.
Add the stock to the skillet, bring to a boil, and reduce the sauce over high heat by one third.

5.
Whisk in bits of optional Beurre Manié; use just enough until the sauce heavily coats a spoon.

6.
Reduce the heat to a simmer, return the scallops to the pan, and heat through. Cook for another 2 minutes. Taste and correct the seasoning.

7.
Transfer the scallops to a deep serving platter. Sprinkle with parsley and serve accompanied by crusty French bread.

Sauté of Shrimp
Provençale

Serves: **4**
Preparation Time: **20 minutes**
Cooking Time: **35 minutes, plus additional time for canned tomatoes**
Type of recipe: **elementary**
Cost: **expensive**

The wonderful essence of Provençale cooking is found in this simple dish, in which the shrimp are simply sautéed in fruity olive oil and combined with plenty of garlic, parsley, and stewed tomatoes. Characteristic of the Mediterranean cuisine, this is a delicious dish that can be served as an appetizer or as a main course accompanied by saffron-flavored braised rice.

Ingredients

8 Tablespoons fruity olive oil
3 Tablespoons finely minced shallots
½ cup finely minced fresh parsley
8 Italian plum tomatoes, peeled and seeded, or 1 can (12 ounces) drained sliced plum tomatoes
Salt and freshly ground black pepper
1 bay leaf
1 teaspoon dried thyme
½ teaspoon dried oregano
1 medium zucchini, finely cubed
1 pound fresh medium shrimp
1 dried hot chili pepper
4 large cloves garlic, finely minced

Preparation

1.
In a small heavy saucepan heat 3 tablespoons oil. Add 1 tablespoon shallots, 1 tablespoon parsley, and the tomatoes. Season the mixture with a pinch of salt, a grinding of pepper, bay leaf, thyme, and oregano. Cover the saucepan tightly and simmer the tomatoes for 30 minutes, stirring several times to make sure they are not scorching the bottom of the saucepan. (When using canned tomatoes stew them for 1 hour to 1 hour, 15 minutes, or until they completely lose the acidic canned flavor.) Set aside.

2.
In a small heavy skillet heat 2 tablespoons oil. Add the zucchini cubes and sauté over moderate-to-high heat until they are nicely browned. Season with salt and pepper and reserve.

3.
Peel the shrimp and set aside.

4.
In a 12-inch cast-iron skillet heat 3 more tablespoons oil. Add the chili pepper and cook until it turns black. Discard the pepper.

5.
Add the shrimp; do not crowd the pan. Sauté the shrimp over high heat until they turn a bright pink. Season with salt and pepper and remove to a side dish with a slotted spoon. Reserve.

6.
Add the remaining shallots to the skillet. (You may need a little more oil.) Add all but 1 tablespoon of remaining parsley and all but ½ teaspoon garlic to the skillet.

Macaronade
of
Seafood

Serves:	**4**
Preparation time:	**35 minutes**
Cooking time:	**30 minutes**
Type of recipe:	**elementary**
Cost:	**moderate**

Cook for 1 minute; do not let the mixture brown.

7.
Add the tomato fondue and the sautéed zucchini cubes to the pan and cook the mixture over low heat for 2 minutes.

8.
Return the shrimp to the pan. Cook for 2 to 3 minutes over the lowest possible heat. Sprinkle with the remaining garlic and parsley. Taste and correct the seasoning, adding a large grinding of black pepper.

9.
Remove the shrimp from the heat and serve directly from the skillet, accompanied by crusty French bread or Catalan Saffron Risotto (page 329).

Ingredients
1 pound fresh mussels, well scrubbed
¼ cup dry white wine
4 Tablespoons butter
2 Tablespoons finely minced shallots
1 cup Cream of Fish Stock (page 537)
½ pound small shrimp, peeled
½ pound fresh bay scallops
Salt and freshly ground black pepper
1 cup Crème Fraîche (page 544)
1 Beurre Manié (page 544)
1 pound fettucine

Preparation
1.
In a large saucepan combine the mussels and wine. Bring to a boil and cook covered until the mussels have opened. Shell the mussels and reserve. Discard any mussels that have not opened. Discard all but ½ cup poaching liquid and set aside.

2.
In a heavy saucepan, melt 2 tablespoons butter and add the shallots. Cook for 2 or 3 minutes without browning.

3.
Add the fish stock and bring to a boil. Add the shrimp and scallops. Season the stock with salt and pepper and simmer the mixture for 2 to 3 minutes. After the stock has returned to a boil the scallops should turn an opaque white. Drain the shrimps and scallops, reserving the stock.

4.
Return the stock to the saucepan, together with the reserved mussel stock. Add the Crème Fraîche, bring to a boil, and reduce the mixture by one third, whisking in enough of the Beurre Manié to just thicken

the sauce. The sauce should be of medium thickness.

5.

Return the shrimps, scallops, and mussels to the sauce. Taste and correct the seasoning. Keep warm.

6.

In a large casserole bring salted water to boil. Add the fettucine and cook for 7 to 8 minutes, or until barely tender. Add 2 cups cold water to the pot to stop the fettucine from cooking further.

7.

In a large heavy skillet melt the remaining butter. Drain the fettucine and add to the skillet. Add the seafood sauce and toss lightly with 2 forks. Add a large grinding of pepper and serve directly from the skillet.

Rice and Pasta

When I think back on our family meals in Barcelona, I recall that the single most exciting rice dish I knew was the paella. Although it was considered a peasant dish, making the paella was not an everyday event but rather one reserved for special occasions. I remember our Sunday outings into the mountains, especially in the fall or early spring, when we would make paella on an open fire. We brought along the many ingredients for this classic preparation and would start by sautéing the seafoods and meats. By two or three in the afternoon, the paella would be ready. I never thought rice could taste better, or that it could possibly be prepared any other way. Here was this wonderful grain combined with shellfish or chicken, vegetables, and sausages, and flavored with the exquisite saffron that gave the rice a golden glow.

Today I still consider rice the number one staple of my shopping list. While I remember with special fondness that paella of my childhood Sundays, over the years I have come to learn and appreciate the magnificent, international range of dishes made possible by rice. One of its greatest virtues is its ability to combine beautifully with innumerable inexpensive supermarket basics—chicken livers, parsley, onions, and many seasonal vegetables. I know that I can always come up with an easy, highly satisfying meal planned around a base of rice. Good-natured and friendly, this nutritional grain is simply one of the greatest and most versatile foods available to us.

While some people take rice for granted as nothing more than a basic starch alternative to potatoes, to me rice conjures up images of exotic preparations representing very different ethnic cuisines. Rice is Chinese, Middle Eastern, Spanish, Indian, South American, and African. Each part of the world grows its own special grain according to its soil and climate, and each country has its own distinctive dish. The Iranians have given us "chelo" and "polo." Chelo is cooked-and-buttered rice topped with a variety of sauces and meats; polo somewhat resembles Italian risotto and Indian pilaf, in that the accompaniments are mixed and cooked with the rice. The dishes are always heavily influenced by the seasons, and the ingredients are always available at local markets. The Indians prepare rice flavored with lime, cooked with coconut or nuts and fruits, or flavored with whole or powdered spices. Indian cooks have over twenty different kinds of rice recipes in their repertoire, and this does not even include the sweet rice preparations. Japan has its pearly smooth pressed "sushi" rice. In addition to the basic bowl of rice served in China at every meal, there is of course the great variety of classic fried rice dishes.

While the Spanish are only familiar with their method of cooking rice, and the Northern Italians only with theirs, we have a great advantage in this country because we are exposed to all the cuisines. We can sample and choose from among the many rice dishes, incorporating the techniques and inspirations of different cuisines into one spectacular dish.

If you are as fond of country and regional cooking as I am, you no doubt find rice indispensable. I serve it once or twice a week and never seem to tire of it. We eat rice so often that my ten-year-old son frequently asks in jest if I'm sure I wasn't raised in India or China. It is in fact the ethnic cuisines of the world to which I owe my great appreciation. I may serve a creamy Italian risotto one day and a fluffy pilaf flavored with zucchini and red peppers the next—yet each dish is unique in texture and taste, and I sometimes wonder whether I am actually cooking with the same grain.

Rice is to northern Italy what pasta is to southern Italy. The great risotto originated in the region of the rich and fertile Po valley. While risotto is considered in many parts of Italy to be a cuisine in itself, it has never gained the popularity of pasta in Europe or the United States. The reason for that, as far as our country is concerned, is that most Italian-Americans come from the southern part of Italy and are not familiar with the technique of cooking rice. Risottos are also rarely served in restaurants (both here and in Italy) because the unique cooking method is somewhat more difficult and time-consuming than cooking pasta.

Traditionally risotto is served as a starter rather than as an accompaniment to a main course. The Risotto alla Milanese, served with the classic braised veal knuckles—

Osso Bucco—is the only exception. Today in Italy, where people have become as diet-conscious as they are here, risotto is now generally served by itself as a luncheon dish, followed by a simple green salad and a light dessert like fruit and cheese. Risotto makes a perfect one-dish meal, and is both inexpensive and delicious. It also provides a great way to make use of leftover meats, stews, chicken livers, or tomato sauce.

When cooking a risotto, the object is for the rice to absorb, a little at a time, enough hot broth to swell and form a creamy mixture of tender kernels that are still slightly chewy. The risotto can then be flavored with innumerable ingredients—shellfish, sausages, vegetables, herbs, cheeses, even fruits. Whatever flavoring you choose, the risotto is basically prepared as for A Basic Risotto on page 327.

While much has been written and said in praise of pasta in recent years, little has been said about the versatile character of rice. One of the best things about cooking with rice is its great adaptability to the seasonal kitchen. In spring or summer I use it cold in a salad or as a stuffing. Placed in a ripe tomato, cucumber boats, avocado halves, or green peppers, it makes a truly tantalizing appetizer. Often I add olives, onions, gherkins, anchovies, and green peppers to improvise a delicious picnic lunch. In fall and winter rice becomes even more important. I often use it in combination with meats and vegetables for a good, nourishing one-dish meal like a Spanish paella or *Arroz con Pollo.* One of my family's favorite dinners is Rice à la Florentine—braised rice topped with cooked spinach and fried eggs. Or I might braise the rice with sautéed chicken, pork, or sausages in a tomato-and-onion "sofrito." Leftover rice can be used in a fried rice dish similar to the Chinese with the addition of Mediterranean vegetables. Rice simply braised in butter and flavored with a large handful of finely minced parsley is equally delicious. When it comes to desserts, rice can also play an important role. One of the loveliest desserts I can think of is Lemon Caramel Rice Pudding (page 521), or one flavored with fresh poached apples, poached pears, stewed blueberries, or poached peaches.

Most supermarkets usually carry three types of rice which are explained earlier in the book. These can be prepared in a variety of ways: steamed, boiled, braised, fried, or baked. The success of a rice dish really depends on the cook's knowledge and understanding of which rice to use for each specific dish. There is no mystique involved in cooking rice—the secret lies simply in that the different types require different methods of preparation. Once you have learned what the basic varieties are and how each should be treated, you will find that rice dishes can be as memorable as any other part of a meal. And when you turn your imagination loose, you'll find there really are innumerable ways to serve this humble grain.

If I had to pick the single most popular foreign food in this country, I would probably choose spaghetti. One reason for this is that it is one of the easiest and most inexpensive ways to feed family and friends. Many people don't even think of spaghetti as an Italian dish, but rather as something to throw together with a bottled sauce for a spur-of-the-moment dinner. I am always sad to see this because pasta, with its many variations, is a most wonderful and versatile food and it deserves to be treated with care. Almost no other food besides rice can carry so many sauces, vegetables, meats, or seafood in so many interesting combinations.

Unfortunately pasta is one of the most misused and misunderstood of all Italian foods. A wonderful supermarket staple, it is nourishing, inexpensive, and available in many shapes and sizes. And yet, together with rice, it has fared poorly in this country. This is because the key to using and cooking pasta well lies in knowing the difference between fresh and dried pasta, how to cook it, and how to sauce it with care.

All supermarket pasta is dried. It ranges from the thinnest spaghettini to the thick, tubular macaroni. Good pasta should be made of semolina flour, which is ground durum wheat. Although many domestic brands indicate that they are made of semolina flour, they still differ in taste and texture from the various brands imported from Italy. So far the Italian brands are not available in the supermarkets and have to be purchased at specialty stores. For anyone living in New York, these are easy to find. I find it worthwhile to go out of my way to get the imported Italian dried pasta, but I always keep some domestic pasta on hand, particularly for soups such as minestrone or a dried bean and pasta soup.

Basic pasta dough is always the same. Only the shapes, and sometimes the names, are different. Even in Italy, the names for practically identical shapes of pasta vary from region to region. When choosing spaghetti or other pasta, the main criterion is the kind of sauce you are going to serve. Regular spaghetti is better suited to butter and cream sauces or tomato sauces; thick, tubular pasta (macaroni and rigatoni) are best with the meat sauces.

While the imported dried pasta may be more flavorful and have better texture, it is naturally easier and yet possible to make a good pasta dish with the domestic brands. Of all the pasta consumed in this country, 80 percent is eaten on the East Coast, where there is the heaviest concentration of Italians. Ronzoni, a regional brand now also available in California, is by far the best domestic supermarket pasta available. But even within a given brand, quality can vary from period to period, depending upon the quality of flour used. (I never recommend supermarket "house" brands of pasta, as their lower cost means a sacrifice of quality somewhere along the line.) If you start with a good supermarket pasta, the addition of market staples can actually give you a wonderful variety of seasonal dishes. Each

Italian region has several "classic" ways of preparing certain pasta dishes, and many of them are easily duplicated in the everyday kitchen. However I find that I also enjoy using my imagination when it comes to cooking pasta, and I often incorporate ideas from other ethnic cuisines into the making of a pasta dish.

Some American pasta is impossible to cook properly. This is because it is made to cook quickly, eliminating a lot of the taste and making it nearly impossible to cook *al dente* (which means slightly firm to the teeth.) A good pasta should not overcook easily, and if tasted often during its cooking time, should tell you easily when it is *al dente.* You should be able to feel the texture of the pasta; it should never be soft and gummy. Some American brands, get too soft before ever becoming *al dente.* It is best to experiment with various brands and be on the lookout for a specialty shop that may carry the imported ones.

In recent years making homemade pasta has become increasingly popular. This is in part because people seem to be eating more Italian food in general, particularly northern Italian cuisine, which features lighter pasta dishes. (There is even a frozen fettucine available, with a cream sauce sold in a jar.) But part of the reason homemade pasta is on the rise is that its terrific taste and texture is impossible to find in readymade brands. With the help of either the hand-cranked pasta machine or the more expensive electric one, you can make a batch of homemade noodles in a matter of twenty to thirty minutes. Furthermore, you are in control of the dough, so you can roll it out to the exact thickness you need for the dish you are going to make. Homemade pasta can be used for such great dishes as lasagna and for stuffed pasta such as tortellini and ravioli. These preparations are impossible to buy commercially unless there is an Italian specialty shop nearby that makes them. Even with the luxury of living in New York, where specialty shops do offer fresh pasta, I find that I still prefer making my own. I enjoy it, and find it as easy as making a batch of crêpes. You can also dry homemade pasta and keep it in a cool, dry place for several weeks. It will still cook in less than five minutes.

Almost all fresh pasta is made by combining eggs with flour in the proportion of 2 large eggs to 1 cup flour. It is then kneaded to a smooth dough and run through the machine to the desired degree of thickness. Then it is cut.

Basically there is no difference between the Italian fettucine and the European egg noodle. The Swiss serve buttered noodles with every ragoût, while in Austria noodles are often served as a dessert or as a simple main course with cottage cheese, ground walnuts, and cinnamon sugar. Italy, however, has set the egg noodle apart, giving it the importance it deserves. Fresh fettucine combines beautifully with many vegetables, particularly fresh asparagus, peas, zucchini, and broccoli. Add some good fresh butter, a touch of heavy cream, freshly grated Parmesan cheese, and a

good grinding of freshly grated black pepper, and the dish is complete. In Italy, where pasta is the daily food of both rich and poor, there are so many lovely preparations made with fettucine you cannot help but marvel at the ingenuity.

I have always been fascinated by the fact that the French, with their brilliant sense of food in general, have not done much with pasta. On a recent trip through the southwest of France, I spent several days working in the kitchen of one of the most creative young chefs in the region. I was surprised and pleased to see that he made fresh pasta every day. One of the ways he served it was with sautéed fresh foie gras; the other was with tiny steamed scallops accompanied by a light cream sauce made from a reduction of shallots, vermouth, and crème fraîche. Both dishes were imaginative and original, but unfortunately the noodles were precooked every day and left in the cooking liquid until an order came from the dining room. At that point they would be drained and tossed in hot butter and then sauced. This "technique" would be looked upon with horror by any Italian, and rightly so. Here were two exquisite preparations—both served, sadly, on a bed of bland and soggy pasta.

Many people think that pasta is fattening. But in Italy this is not the case. One reason is that the Italians generally consume wine along with their pasta, and it has been suggested that the acid content of the wine affects the carbohydrates in the pasta. A second, and to me more important reason, is the structure of the Italian meal. In Italy pasta is served as an appetizer, usually in small portions and then followed by the main course. This main course—meat, chicken, or fish—may be accompanied by a vegetable but it is rarely served with potatoes or any other starchy vegetable. In addition it is simply accompanied by crusty bread and followed by a salad.

While it is somewhat presumptuous to expect Americans to change their way of eating, I still believe that when serving pasta, it should be served either as an appetizer followed by a simple main course, or as a light meal following a soup and accompanied by a salad. With the soaring price of food, and the growing concern for healthy, simple, often meatless meals, pasta can fill a very real need for the American cook. It is a wonderful, basic food, easily made or bought in local markets, and it deserves to be an essential part of every cook's repertoire. It can be as memorable and outstanding as any "three-star" dish of the *haute cuisine.*

A
Basic
Risotto

Serves: **4 to 6**
Preparation time: **10 minutes**
Cooking time: **35 minutes**
Type of recipe: **elementary**
Cost: **inexpensive**

The Italian dish risotto is an ingenious way of cooking rice, unique to Northern Italy. While pasta has consistently grown in popularity in this country risotto, although as versatile as pasta, has not. Perhaps this is because preparing a good risotto is time-consuming and demands the cook's undivided attention for about 30 minutes. It cannot be made in advance (therefore it is rarely available on a restaurant menu), but it can be placed over warm water and kept warm for about 20 to 30 minutes. A creamy and properly seasoned risotto is, in my opinion, one of the great dishes of the world. Not only can it be served as an appetizer or light supper dish but it is also a lovely accompaniment to roasts and sautéed chicken and veal dishes. Here is a basic risotto with three of the variations mentioned at the end of some of the recipes in this book. You should, however, use your own creativity and flavor your risotto to your liking with seasonal vegetables, shellfish, herbs, spices, or a mixture of some of the above.

Ingredients
2 Tablespoons butter
1 small onion, peeled and finely minced
1½ cups Italian rice, well rinsed
⅓ cup dry white wine
4 to 5 cups hot Light Chicken Stock (page 531), Beef Stock (page 533), or chicken bouillon
Salt and freshly ground black pepper

Optional:
½ cup heavy cream
2 Tablespoons butter
3 to 4 Tablespoons freshly grated Parmesan cheese

Garnish:
2 Tablespoons finely minced fresh parsley

Preparation
1.
In a heavy 3-quart enamel saucepan melt the butter. Add the onion and sauté over low heat for 3 to 4 minutes, or until very soft but not browned.
2.
Add the rice and stir well until it is blended with the onion mixture. Add the wine and cook over moderate-to-high heat until the wine is completely evaporated.
3.
Start adding the broth ½ cup at a time, stirring constantly. Keep the heat moderately high so that the rice absorbs the liquid but does not dry out too quickly. Continue to add the broth ½ cup a time as liquid is absorbed.
4.
After about 20 minutes start adding the broth ¼ cup at a time. If the rice is still very chewy partially cover the saucepan and let the rice cook a little more slowly, letting it absorb the liquid and stirring it every minute or so. Keep an eye on the risotto at all times; the result must be a creamy mass with a kernel that is soft but still slightly chewy.

5.

When the rice is done season it carefully with salt and pepper. Add the optional cream and butter and stir well. Cook for another 2 to 3 minutes, or until the cream is well absorbed into the rice.

6.

Add the Parmesan cheese and stir until well blended. Transfer the rice to a hot serving dish. Sprinkle with parsley and serve immediately. See variations that follow.

Remarks

The rice may not need the entire amount of stock indicated. This depends upon the degree of heat at which you are cooking the risotto. Risottos that are partially covered half way during cooking time will absorb much less stock—sometimes no more than 2 to 3 cups.

Ingredients

1 ounce dried imported mushrooms, preferably Italian
2 cups beef bouillon, or 2 cups Beef Stock (page 533)
Basic Risotto (page 327)

Preparation

1.

Rinse the dried mushrooms in a colander under cold running water. Place in a saucepan and add the bouillon or stock. Bring to a boil. Reduce the heat and simmer the mushrooms covered for 45 minutes.

2.

Strain the cooking liquid and reserve. Dice the mushrooms and set aside.

3.

Combine the cooking liquid with the stock used in the Basic Risotto. (You will need a total of 4 to 5 cups bouillon.)

4.

When the rice is almost done add the diced mushrooms and continue cooking the rice as directed in the basic recipe.

Lemon-and-Chive Risotto

Catalan Saffron Risotto

Lemon-and-Chive Risotto

Ingredients
2 Tablespoons lemon juice
2 large egg yolks
½ cup heavy cream
Basic Risotto (page 327)

Optional:
2 to 3 tablespoons finely minced fresh chives or dill, or a mixture of both

Preparation
1.
In a bowl combine the lemon juice, egg yolks, and cream. Whisk the mixture until well blended and set aside.
2.
Make the risotto according to the basic method.
3.
Five minutes before the risotto is done whisk in the lemon cream. (Omit the cream mentioned in the basic recipe.)
4.
Add the chives, dill, or the herb mixture and finish cooking the risotto. Taste and correct the seasoning, adding a large grinding of black pepper.

Catalan Saffron Risotto

Ingredients
4 cups Chicken Stock (page 530)
½ teaspoon saffron threads
2 Tablespoons fruity olive oil
1 small zucchini, diced
½ cup diced Roasted Peppers (page 545)
½ cup finely minced fresh parsley
Salt and freshly ground black pepper
Basic Risotto (page 327)

Preparation
1.
Combine the stock and saffron in a saucepan and bring to a boil. Reduce the heat and simmer covered for 20 minutes. Set aside.
2.
In a small cast-iron skillet heat the oil. Add the zucchini and cook until nicely browned. Add the roasted peppers and parsley. Season with salt and pepper and set the mixture aside.
3.
Make the risotto according to the basic method, using the saffron-flavored stock instead. Just before the rice is done add the zucchini mixture and fold it gently into the rice. Serve as an appetizer or as an accompaniment to roast or sautéed or grilled meats.

Risotto
with
Anchovies and Walnuts

Serves: **4 to 6**
Preparation time: **15 minutes**
Cooking time: **35 minutes**
Type of recipe: **elementary**
Cost: **inexpensive**

Ingredients
4 Tablespoons butter
1 teaspoon oil
½ pound fresh mushrooms, stems removed and caps cubed
Salt and freshly ground black pepper
3 Tablespoons finely minced fresh parsley
2 large cloves garlic, peeled and finely minced
4 to 6 finely minced anchovy fillets
1 onion, peeled and finely minced
1½ cups Italian rice
4 to 5 cups chicken bouillon or Chicken Stock (page 530)
½ to ¾ cup heavy cream
½ cup finely diced walnuts

Preparation
1.
In a small heavy skillet heat 2 tablespoons butter and the oil. Add the mushrooms and sauté over high heat for 2 minutes, or until nicely browned. Shake the pan back and forth to cook the mushrooms evenly. Season with salt and pepper and remove from the heat.
2.
Add the parsley, garlic, and anchovies to the skillet and toss the mixture without cooking it any further. Set aside.
3.
In a heavy 3-quart casserole heat the remaining butter. Add the onion and sauté for 2 to 3 minutes without browning.
4.
Add the rice and cook for 1 minute, stirring to coat it well with the butter. Add 1 cup bouillon or stock and bring to a boil.

Reduce the heat and simmer partially covered for 3 to 5 minutes, stirring several times until all the stock has been absorbed.
5.
Add another cup stock and continue simmering the rice, stirring frequently and adding 1 cup stock at a time until the rice is tender but still slightly chewy. The rice should be done in 25 to 30 minutes; by that time it should have absorbed 4 to 5 cups stock.
6.
Add ½ cup cream to the rice and continue cooking for another 5 minutes. If all the cream has been absorbed add the remaining ¼ cup cream.
7.
Add the reserved mushroom mixture to the rice, together with the walnuts, and toss well. Season with salt and a large grinding of black pepper.
8.
Taste the rice and correct the seasoning. Serve the risotto hot as an appetizer or as an accompaniment to roast or grilled meats.

Remarks
The risotto can be kept warm for 40 minutes in a pan of warm water. You may need to add additional cream to the risotto or whip in 2 to 4 tablespoons butter before serving.

Risotto
Florentine

Serves: **4 to 6**
Preparation time: **25 minutes**
Cooking time: **45 minutes**
Type of recipe: **elementary**
Cost: **inexpensive**

Ingredients

**4 cups Chicken Stock (page 530) or
bouillon**
1 teaspoon saffron threads
4 Tablespoons butter
**3 Tablespoons finely minced scallions
(white part only)**
**½ pound fresh spinach, cooked, well
drained, and finely chopped**
1 clove garlic, peeled and crushed
¾ cup heavy cream
Salt and freshly ground black pepper
1½ cups Italian rice
½ cup freshly grated Parmesan cheese

Preparation

1.
In a large saucepan combine the chicken
stock with the saffron and bring to a boil.
Reduce the heat and simmer for 10 minutes.
Keep warm.

2.
In a heavy saucepan heat 2 tablespoons
butter. Add the scallions and cook for 2 to
3 minutes, or until soft but not browned.
Add the spinach and garlic and cook for 2
more minutes. Add the cream and bring to
a boil. Reduce the heat, season with salt
and pepper, and simmer the mixture
covered for 5 minutes. Set aside.

3.
In a large 3-quart saucepan heat the
remaining butter. Add the rice and toss well
in the butter.

4.
Add ½ cup stock and cook uncovered,
stirring constantly until all the stock has
been absorbed. Continue adding stock ½
cup at a time stirring constantly and waiting

until the stock has been absorbed before
adding more.

5.
After 20 minutes taste the rice. It should be
slightly soft but still somewhat chewy. Add
the spinach-and-cream mixture and fold it
gently into the rice. Cover the pan and
continue simmering the rice until it absorbs
the cream. If the rice is still too hard add a
little more stock.

6.
When done add the Parmesan cheese and
fold it into the rice. Taste and correct the
seasoning, adding a large grinding of black
pepper. Serve the rice hot as an appetizer
or as an accompaniment to roast or grilled
meats.

Sausage
Risotto

Serves:	**4 to 6**
Preparation time:	**15 minute**
Cooking time:	**45 minutes**
Type of recipe:	**elementary**
Cost:	**moderate**

A sausage risotto is a gutsy rice dish that should be served as a 1-dish meal accompanied by a well-seasoned salad. It can also be served as an appetizer to be followed by sautéed scallops or grilled fish.

Ingredients

4 Tablespoons butter
1 Tablespoon oil
½ pound sweet Italian link sausages
½ cup dry white wine
1 small onion, finely minced
2 cloves garlic, peeled and finely minced
1½ cup Italian rice
Salt and freshly ground black pepper
4 to 5 cups Chicken Stock (page 530) or chicken bouillon
½ cup heavy cream
½ cup finely minced fresh parsley
2 to 3 Tablespoons freshly grated Parmesan cheese

Preparation

1.
In a 3-quart heavy-bottomed casserole melt 1 tablespoon butter and the oil. Add the sausages and sauté over medium heat nicely browned on all sides. Add 2 tablespoons wine, partially cover the casserole, and continue cooking the sausages until the wine has evaporated. Remove the sausages from the casserole and set aside.

2.
Add a little more butter to the casserole and when hot add the onion and garlic. Cook the mixture until the onions are soft and nicely browned, scraping well the bottom of the pan.

3.
Add the remaining wine, bring to a boil, and reduce to 1 tablespoon.

4.
Add the rice and stir well into the onion mixture. Season with salt and pepper and add 1 cup stock. Bring to a boil and cook over moderate-to-high heat, stirring constantly until the stock has been absorbed.

5.
Continue adding stock ½ cup at a time, stirring the rice constantly until all the stock has been absorbed and the rice is creamy. The rice will be done in about 25 minutes; it should still be slightly chewy.

6.
Add the cream and continue cooking until the rice has absorbed the cream.

7.
Thinly slice the sausages and fold them into the rice, together with the parsley, Parmesan cheese, and remaining butter. Add a large grinding of black pepper.

8.
Taste the rice and correct the seasoning. Serve immediately.

Remarks
Although risottos are at their best when served immediately they can be kept warm in the top of a double boiler over hot but not boiling water for about an hour.

Roquefort
Risotto

Serves: **4 to 6**
Preparation time: **10 minutes**
Cooking time: **30 minutes**
Type of recipe: **elementary**
Cost: **inexpensive**

Ingredients
½ cup heavy cream
3 Tablespoons mild Roquefort cheese, or other mild blue cheese
4 Tablespoons butter
1 onion, peeled and finely minced
1½ cups Italian rice
4 to 5 cups chicken bouillon
2 Tablespoons freshly grated Parmesan cheese
Salt and freshly ground white pepper
5 Tablespoons finely minced fresh parsley, preferably Italian parsley

Preparation
1.
In a blender combine the cream and Roquefort cheese and blend the mixture until smooth. Set aside.
2.
In a heavy 3-quart enamel saucepan melt 3 tablespoons butter. Add the onion and cook over low heat for 3 to 4 minutes without browning. Add the rice and stir until well coated with the butter.
3.
Add 1 cup bouillon and bring to a boil. Reduce the heat and cook the rice uncovered, stirring constantly, until the stock has been absorbed.
4.
Continue adding stock ½ cup at a time and cook the rice, stirring constantly, until it is creamy and tender. The grains should still be somewhat chewy. The rice will take about 25 to 30 minutes to cook.
.
Add the Roquefort-and-cream mixture and blend it gently into the rice. Add the

Parmesan cheese together with the remaining tablespoon butter and season the rice with salt and a large grinding of pepper.
6.
Taste the risotto and correct the seasoning. Just before serving blend the parsley gently into the rice. Serve the rice hot as a accompaniment to roast or sautéed chicken or roast or sautéed veal.

Remarks
The rice should have a distinct yet subtle taste of cheese. Since commercial Roquefort is often quite salty you may need a little more cream to give the rice the right flavor. While you can use long-grain rice it does not compare to Italian rice, which gets creamy yet retains a somewhat chewy grain. For long-grain rice you will only need about 3 cups chicken bouillon.

Risotto
with
Sweetbreads
and Mushrooms

Serves: **6**
Preparation time: **30 minutes, plus 5–6 hours to soak and press**
Cooking time: **1 hour, 30 minutes**
Type of recipe: **elementary**
Cost: **expensive**

Ingredients
1 pound fresh sweetbreads
1 Tablespoon white wine vinegar
4 to 5 cups chicken bouillon
1 ounce dried imported mushrooms
Flour for dredging
2 Tablespoons butter
1 Tablespoon oil
Salt and freshly ground black pepper
1 sprig fresh rosemary, or ¼ teaspoon dried
1 onion, peeled and cut in half
½ cup dry Marsala wine
1 cup Brown Chicken Stock (page 531)

Risotto:
4 Tablespoons butter
1 onion, peeled and finely minced
⅓ cup dry white wine
1½ cups Italian rice
Salt and freshly ground black pepper
½ cup freshly grated Parmesan cheese

Garnish:
Finely minced fresh parsley

Preparation
1.
Soak the sweetbreads for 2 to 3 hours in several changes of ice water. Remove and place in another bowl with ice water. Add the vinegar and soak for another hour.
2.
Drain the sweetbreads and carefully remove as much as possible of the filament surrounding them without breaking them. Place the sweetbreads on a cutting board, cover with a linen towel, and place another board over them. Weigh them down with 2 to 3 heavy cans for 1 to 2 hours.
3.
In the meantime combine 2 cups chicken bouillon and the dried mushrooms in a heavy saucepan. Bring to a boil, reduce the heat, and simmer covered for 20 minutes. Strain the mushrooms and combine the mushroom liquid with the rest of the bouillon. Dice the mushrooms and set aside.
5.
In a 10-inch cast-iron skillet heat the butter and a teaspoon oil and add the sweetbreads. Season with salt and pepper, then add the rosemary and the onion halves. Sauté the sweetbreads over medium heat for 2 to 3 minutes on each side. They should be nicely browned.
6.
Add the Marsala to the skillet, bring to a boil, and cook until reduced to 1 tablespoon.
7.
Add a little stock to the skillet. Cover and simmer for 25 to 30 minutes, adding a little stock every 10 minutes and turning the sweetbreads once or twice. Ten minutes before the sweetbreads are done add the diced mushrooms to the pan and heat through.
8.
When the sweetbreads are done remove them to a cutting board. Cube them and return to the skillet and keep warm.
9.
Make the risotto. In a 3-quart heavy casserole heat 2 tablespoons butter. Add the onion and cook covered over low heat for 3 to 5 minutes, or until the onion is soft

Basic
Rice Pilaf

Serves: **6**
Preparation time: **10 minutes**
Cooking time: **35 minutes**
Type of recipe: **elementary**
Cost: **inexpensive**

but not browned. Uncover the casserole and add the wine. Bring to a boil and cook until the wine is reduced to 1 tablespoon.

10.

Add the rice and blend it well with the onions. Cook for 1 minute, then season with salt and pepper. Add ½ cup reserved broth to the saucepan and cook the rice over medium heat until the liquid has been absorbed, stirring constantly. Continue adding the broth ½ cup at a time and stir the rice constantly until all the stock has been absorbed and the rice is creamy and tender but still slightly chewy. The rice should be done in about 25 to 30 minutes. (The rice must be stirred all the time, adding the broth ½ cup at a time. Be sure not to drown the rice.)

11.

When done, taste and correct the seasoning. Add the remaining butter and Parmesan cheese and fold gently into the rice. Keep warm.

12.

Reheat the sweetbread-and-mushroom mixture over low heat. Fold gently into the risotto and transfer to a deep serving bowl. Sprinkle with parsley and serve as an appetizer or as a simple main course accompanied by a well-seasoned salad.

Remarks

The risotto can be kept warm in the top of a double boiler for 40 minutes. The sweetbreads can be braised several hours ahead and reheated over the lowest possible heat.

A basic pilaf is a simple dish to make and an excellent accompaniment to many roasts and sautéed meat dishes. It can be flavored with spices such as curry, cumin or ground coriander, or combined with fresh minced herbs, such as parsley, dill, chives, and mint.

Ingredients

2 Tablespoons butter
1 small onion, peeled and finely minced
1 ½ cups long-grain rice or converted rice
Salt and freshly ground white pepper
3 cups chicken bouillon or Chicken Stock (page 530)

Optional:
2 to 4 Tablespoons butter

Preparation

1.

In a heavy-bottomed saucepan melt the butter. Add the onion and cook over low heat until soft but not browned. Add the rice and stir until thoroughly coated with the butter. Season with salt and pepper.

2.

Add the bouillon or stock and bring to a boil. Reduce the heat and simmer the rice covered for 25 to 30 minutes. Add the optional butter and fold it gently into the rice. Serve the rice hot. See the variations that follow.

Remarks

The rice can also be braised in a 325 degree oven for 25 to 30 minutes. It can be kept warm over a pan of warm water for 40 minutes to an hour.

Parslied Pilaf

Ingredients
Basic Rice Pilaf (page 335)
1 cup finely minced fresh parsley
Black pepper

Optional:
2 cloves garlic, finely minced

Preparation
1.
Cook the rice as in the basic recipe.
2.
Add the parsley and optional garlic to the finished rice and toss lightly with 2 forks. Add a large grinding of pepper and serve hot.

Remarks
Once the parsley is added to the rice it is best to serve it immediately. In the summer you may also add 2 tablespoons of other herbs such as mint or chervil.

Curried Pilaf of Rice

Ingredients
Basic Rice Pilaf (page 335)
1 Tablespoon curry powder
½ teaspoon ground cumin
1 Tablespoon tomato paste

Optional:
¼ teaspoon hot pepper flakes

Preparation
1.
Melt the butter and add the onion as directed in the basic method for pilaf of rice. Add the curry powder, cumin, and tomato paste as well as the optional hot pepper flakes. Cook the mixture for 1 minute. Do not let it burn.
2.
Add the rice and blend thoroughly into the curry mixture. Add the hot bouillon or stock and continue cooking the rice as directed in the basic recipe.

Remarks
You may garnish the rice with 2 tablespoons white raisins, blanched for 3 minutes in hot water and drained, and 1 cup diced apricots or prunes (cooked according to package directions). Blend the mixture into the curried rice. Serve as an accompaniment to roast duck or pork, or as a garnish to a roast leg of lamb.

You can also sauté 1 cup diced fresh carrots in 2 tablespoons of butter, then add to the raisins together with 2 tablespoons water. Add a pinch of cinnamon and nutmeg. Fold the raisin and carrot mixture into the finished pilaf.

Pilaf of Rice
Provençale

Serves: **4 to 5**
Preparation Time: **25 minutes**
Cooking Time: **1 hour**
Type of recipe: **elementary**
Cost **moderate**

Ingredients

3 Tablespoons fruity olive oil
1 Tablespoon butter
1 small onion, finely minced
½ cup finely minced fresh parsley
**2 cloves garlic, finely minced, plus 1
clove garlic, peeled and crushed**
**1 can (12 ounces) sliced plum tomatoes,
well drained and chopped**
1 teaspoon dried thyme
1 teaspoon dried oregano
1 bay leaf
Salt and freshly ground black pepper
**2 Roasted Red Peppers (page 545),
diced**
1½ cup long-grain rice
2 cups chicken bouillon
1 teaspoon saffron threads
1 dried hot chili pepper
½ pound small fresh shrimp, shelled
1 lemon, quartered

Preparation

1.
In a heavy 3-quart saucepan heat 1
tablespoon oil and the butter over low heat.
Add the onion and 1 tablespoon parsley
and cook the mixture for 1 to 2 minutes
without browning.

2.
Add the crushed clove of garlic, the
tomatoes, thyme, oregano, bay leaf, salt,
and pepper, and peppers and bring to a
boil. Reduce the heat, cover the saucepan,
and simmer the mixture for 30 minutes.

3.
Uncover the saucepan and add the rice.
Stir the rice into the tomato mixture until
well blended. Add the chicken bouillon

and saffron, bring to a boil, and season with
salt and pepper. Reduce the heat and
simmer the rice covered for 25 minutes.

4.
While the rice is cooking prepare the
shrimp. In a cast-iron skillet heat the
remaining oil. Add the chili pepper and
sauté until it turns dark. Discard the chili
pepper.

5.
Add the shrimp, season with salt and
pepper, and cook over high heat for 2 to 3
minutes, or until they turn pink. Add the
remaining parsley and the minced garlic
and cook for another minute. Remove the
skillet from the heat and set aside.

6.
When the rice is done fold the shrimp
mixture into it reserving a few shrimp for
garnish. Toss the rice with 2 forks and taste
and correct the seasoning. Transfer to a
serving bowl. Garnish the rice with the
remaining shrimp and lemons and serve
immediately as an appetizer or as a light
supper dish.

Summer
Pilaf

Serves: **6**
Preparation time: **25 minutes**
Cooking time: **45 minutes**
Type of recipe: **elementary**
Cost: **inexpensive**

Ingredients

2 cups cubed eggplant, unpeeled
Coarse salt
Basic Rice Pilaf (page 335)
4 to 6 Tablespoons olive oil
1 small zucchini, cubed
1 Tablespoon finely minced shallots
2 Tablespoons finely minced fresh parsley
1 large clove garlic, peeled and crushed
1 large tomato, peeled and finely cubed
2 teaspoons tomato paste
1 cup cubed green pepper
2 Tablespoons finely minced fresh basil
¼ teaspoon dried oregano
2 Tablespoons finely diced pimientos
Freshly ground black pepper

Preparation

1.
Sprinkle the eggplant cubes with coarse salt and let them drain in an colander for 30 to 40 minutes.

2.
Prepare the rice following the directions for the basic recipe.

3.
Meanwhile, heat 3 tablespoons olive oil in a cast-iron skillet. Add the eggplant cubes and sauté over moderate-to-high heat until nicely browned in all sides. With a slotted spoon remove to a colander and reserve.

4.
Add a little more oil to the skillet and when hot add the zucchini and sauté until nicely browned. With a slotted spoon transfer the zucchini to the colander and reserve.

5.
Add a little more oil if necessary to the skillet. Add the shallots, parsley, and garlic and sauté for 1 minutes, or until soft but not browned.

6.
Add the tomato, tomato paste, and green pepper to the skillet and bring to a boil. Lower the heat and cover the skillet. Simmer gently for 10 minutes.

7.
Increase the heat and add the basil and oregano, then return the eggplant and zucchini, along with the pimiento, to the skillet and heat through. Cook until the mixture is fairly thick. Season with salt and pepper.

8.
When the rice is done add the vegetable mixture and fold in gently with 2 forks. Serve as an accompaniment to grilled or barbecued meats or sautéed fish steaks.

Persian Lamb
(and Dried Fruit)
Pilaf

Serves: **4**
Preparation time: **15 minutes**
Cooking time: **2 hours, 30 minutes**
Type of recipe: **elementary**
Cost: **moderate**

The Persian method of steaming the rice with butter after it has been cooked, then combining with vegetables, fruit or meat is a wonderful way to use rice. The result is a fluffy light rice dish that allows plenty of room for individual creativity.

Ingredients

1 pound ground lamb
1 Tablespoon grated onion, plus 2 cups finely minced onions
2 cloves garlic, peeled and crushed
1 teaspoon ground cumin
¼ cup water
Salt and freshly ground black pepper
Large pinch cayenne pepper
Flour for dredging
2 Tablespoons oil
7 Tablespoons butter
1 teaspoon granulated sugar
1 cup dried apricots, boiled for 5 minutes and drained
½ cup dark raisins
2 cups beef bouillon or water
½ cup pine nuts
1 cup long-grain rice

Preparation

1.
In a mixing bowl combine the lamb, grated onion, garlic, cumin, and water. Work the mixture with your hands until well blended. Season with salt and pepper and cayenne. Taste the mixture; it should be highly seasoned.

2.
Shape the meat into 1-inch meatballs. Dredge lightly with flour and shake off the excess.

3.
In a 10-inch cast-iron skillet heat 1 tablespoon oil and 1 tablespoon butter and add the meatballs; do not crowd the pan. Sauté until they are nicely browned on all sides, then transfer to a side dish and reserve.

4.
When all the meat is done discard the fat and add the remaining oil to the skillet. Add the minced onions and sugar. Season with salt and a large grinding of black pepper and cook the onions, scraping well the bottom of the pan, until they are nicely browned and glazed, or for about 5 minutes. Do not burn the onions.

5.
Add the apricots, raisins, and meatballs to the skillet. Add 1 cup bouillon and bring to a boil. Cover the skillet tightly and simmer over low heat for 1 hour, 30 minutes, adding a little more bouillon every 15 to 20 minutes.

6.
When cooked, the sauce should be rich and well reduced. Set the pan aside.

Serves:	**4 to 6**
Preparation time:	**20 minutes**
Cooking time:	**45 minutes**
type of recipe-	**elementary**
Cost-	**moderate**

7.
In a small heavy skillet heat 2 tablespoons butter. Add the pine nuts and sauté over medium heat, or until nicely browned. Set aside.

8.
In a large saucepan bring 3 cups salted water to boil. Add the rice and cook for 15 minutes, then drain.

9.
Fold the sautéed pine nuts into the rice and season with salt and pepper.

10.
In a heavy 3-quart casserole melt 2 tablespoons butter over low heat. Add half the rice-and-nut mixture to the casserole, then follow with the lamb-and-fruit mixture. Repeat with the remaining rice-and-nut mixture, then top the rice with the remaining butter.

11.
Place the casserole over the lowest possible heat. Cover with a kitchen towel and then the lid. Drape the kitchen towel back up over the lid and steam the rice for 30 minutes.

12.
Serve as a supper dish accompanied by a cucumber-and-yogurt salad.

Remarks
The lamb-and-fruit mixture can be prepared a day ahead and reheated. The rice can be steamed in a 300-degree oven and kept warm in a 200-degree oven for 1 hour to 1 hour, 30 minutes. You may substitute ground beef for the lamb.

Ingredients
5 Tablespoons fruity olive oil
1 dried hot chili pepper
½ pound fresh small shrimp, shelled
Salt and freshly ground black pepper
2 shallots, peeled and finely minced
3 cloves garlic, finely minced
2 Tablespoons tomato paste
1 cup finely diced green pepper
1½ cups long-grain rice
3 cups hot Fish Stock (page 536) or Chicken Stock (page 530)
¼ teaspoon saffron threads
½ cup cooked fresh peas

Garnish:
Rounds of pimientos
Finely minced fresh parsley
1 large lemon, quartered

Preparation
1.
Preheat the oven to 350 degrees.

2.
In a large heavy casserole heat 3 tablespoons oil. Break the chili pepper into the oil and when the chili pepper turns dark remove it with a slotted spoon and discard.

3.
Add the shrimp to the hot oil and cook over high heat until they turn bright pink. Season with salt and pepper and remove to a side dish.

4.
Add remaining olive oil to the pan. Add the shallots and garlic and cook for 2 minutes without browning.

Braised Onion
Pilaf

Serves: **6**
Preparation time: **10 minutes**
Cooking time: **1 hour, 15 minutes**
Type of recipe: **elementary**
Cost: **inexpensive**

5.
Add the tomato paste and green pepper and cook the mixture for 1 to 2 minutes being careful not to burn the tomato paste.
6.
Add the rice and stir into the tomato paste mixture for 1 minute.
7.
Add the stock, bring to a boil, add the saffron, and season with salt and pepper. Reduce the heat, cover the casserole, and place in the center of the oven.
8.
While the rice is baking, finely dice the shrimp and set aside.
9.
After 25 minutes uncover the rice and add the peas and shrimp. Toss them into the rice with 2 forks. Cover the casserole again and return to the oven. Bake the rice for another 10 minutes or until tender.
10.
Remove the rice from the oven and transfer to a serving dish. Garnish with rounds of pimientos and parsley. Place the quartered lemons around the rice and serve hot, accompanied by a well-seasoned green salad.

Remarks
You can add 1 cup cooked and shelled mussels to the rice together with the shrimp and/or 4 to 6 small fresh sea scallops that have been poached in a little fish or vegetable stock. In Spanish cooking all rice dishes are accompanied by quartered lemons, since lemon juice adds a particularly good taste to rice.

Ingredients
3 tablespoons butter
1 Tablespoon oil
2 large onions, peeled, cut in half, and thinly sliced
Salt and freshly ground black pepper
½ teaspoon granulated sugar
1½ cups long-grain rice
3 cups beef bouillon
1 Bouquet Garni (page 546)
4 Tablespoons freshly grated Parmesan cheese

Optional:
½ pound fresh mushrooms, stems removed and caps thinly sliced and sautéed in butter and oil

Garnish:
Finely minced fresh parsley

Ragoût
of Rice and Pork
Indienne

Serves:	**4 to 6**
Preparation time:	**15 minutes**
Cooking time:	**1 hour, 45 minutes**
Type of recipe:	**elementary**
Cost:	**moderate**

Preparation

1.
In a large heavy saucepan heat 2 tablespoons butter and the oil. Add the onions and season with salt, pepper, and sugar. Cook the onions over medium heat for 10 to 15 minutes, or until soft and starting to brown. Partially cover the saucepan and continue cooking the onions for another 25 to 30 minutes, or until very soft and nicely browned.

2.
Add the rice and stir to blend it well with the onion mixture. Add the bouillon and bring to a boil. Reduce the heat, season with salt and pepper, and add the bouquet. Reduce the heat and simmer the rice covered for 25 to 30 minutes, or until tender.

3.
Uncover the saucepan and discard the bouquet. Add the Parmesan cheese and the remaining butter and fold it gently into the rice.

4.
Transfer the rice to a deep serving bowl. Top with the optional mushrooms and garnish with parsley. Serve as an accompaniment to roast or grilled meats.

Ingredients

2 tablespoons butter
2 to 3 tablespoons olive oil
1 pound pork butt, cut into 1-inch cubes
Salt and freshly ground black pepper
1 dried hot chili pepper, crumbled
1 large onion, peeled and finely minced
2 cloves garlic, peeled and finely minced
1 teaspoon finely minced fresh ginger
1 Tablespoon tomato paste
1½ teaspoons curry powder
1 teaspoon ground cumin
pinch of freshly grated nutmeg
¼ teaspoon ground cardamom
1 teaspoon ground coriander
1 two-inch piece cinnamon stick
2 ripe tomatoes, peeled, finely cubed
1 green pepper, cored and finely cubed
1½ cups long-grain rice
2½ cups Chicken Stock (page 530) or bouillon
2 Tablespoons dark raisins

Optional:
¼ cup pine nuts sautéed in 1 tablespoon oil

Garnish:
Sautéed zucchini slices
Rings of pimientos

Preparation

1.
In a 10-inch cast-iron skillet heat the butter and 1 tablespoon oil. Add the pork cubes and sauté until the meat is nicely browned on all sides. Transfer to a side dish, season with salt and pepper, and reserve.

2.
Add a little more oil to the skillet. When hot add the chili pepper, onion, garlic, and ginger and cook the mixture until soft and lightly browned. Add the tomato paste, curry powder, cumin, nutmeg, cardamom, coriander, and cinnamon stick. Stir the mixture until it is well blended with the onions.

3.
Add the tomatoes and bring to a boil. Reduce the heat, season with salt and pepper, and return the pork to the skillet together with the diced green pepper. Cover the skillet tightly and braise the pork for 1 hour, or until tender.

4.
Add the rice. Stir to blend it well with the pork mixture. Add stock, bring to a boil, and season with salt and pepper. Reduce the heat, cover the skillet, and braise over low heat for 30 minutes without stirring.

5.
Ten minutes before the rice is done add the optional pine nuts together with the raisins. Toss lightly and continue braising the rice until done.

6.
Transfer the rice to a serving dish. Garnish with slices of sautéed zucchini and make a decorative design of the pimiento rounds. Serve the rice hot as a simple supper dish accompanied by a well-seasoned salad.

Remarks
Pork butt is available in specialty stores and all Chinese markets. It is usually not available in supermarkets. You may substitute for the pork butt 2 boned and skinned chicken breasts cut into 1-inch cubes. The entire rice dish can be prepared a day in advance and reheated in a covered baking dish. Place the dish in a pan of hot water in a 350-degree oven and reheat for 1 hour to 1 hour, 30 minutes or until hot.

Spring
Vegetable
Paella

Serves: **6**
Preparation time: **30 minutes**
Cooking time: **45 minutes**
Type of recipe: **elementary**
Cost: **inexpensive**

The traditional paella is a combination of various meats or seafood baked in a saffron-flavored rice with the addition of various vegetables, usually peas, white beans, and pimientos. On a recent visit to Barcelona, my hometown, I had a wonderful paella; to my surprise it was made entirely with vegetables and served as a bed for fried eggs. I have since made this dish in every season simply by using whatever was fresh at the market.

Ingredients

12 thin asparagus spears, scraped
3 cups fresh broccoli florets
5 Tablespoons olive oil
2 small zucchini, cubed
Salt and freshly ground black pepper
2 Tablespoons butter
1 large onion, finely minced
2 large ripe tomatoes, peeled, seeded, and chopped
1 Tablespoon tomato paste
1 Roasted Pepper (page 545), diced, or ½ cup pimientos
1½ cups long-grain rice
3 cups Chicken Stock (page 530), or chicken boullion
½ teaspoon saffron threads
1 cup fresh peas, cooked and drained

Optional:
6 fried eggs

Preparation

1.
Preheat the oven to 350 degrees.

2.
Dice the ends of the asparagus stalks, leaving the spears 3 inches long.

3.
Dice the broccoli stalks, reserving the florets. Set aside.

4.
In a small heavy skillet heat 3 tablespoons olive oil. Add the zucchini and sauté over moderate-to-high heat until nicely browned, or for about 3 to 4 minutes. Season with salt and pepper and set aside.

5.
In a medium saucepan bring salted water to boil. Add the diced asparagus stems and broccoli stalks. Cook for 4 to 5 minutes, or until barely tender. Drain and reserve.

6.
In a medium casserole heat the butter and 1 tablespoon oil. Add the onion and cook over high heat for 10 minutes, or until lightly browned. Reduce the heat, partially cover the saucepan, and continue cooking the onion for another 10 minutes, or until soft and lightly browned. Do not let it burn.

7.
Add the tomato, tomato paste, and Roasted Pepper or pimientos and cook the mixture for 2 to 3 minutes. Season with salt and pepper.

8.
Add the sautéed zucchini and cooked asparagus and broccoli stalks and combine well with the tomato mixture.

Serves:	**3 to 4**
Preparation time:	**15 minutes**
Cooking time:	**none**
Type of recipe:	**elementary**
Cost:	**inexpensive**

9.
Add the rice, stir gently, and add the stock. Bring to a boil, add the saffron, and season with salt and pepper.

10.
Cover the casserole and place in the center of the oven. Bake the rice for 30 to 35 minutes, or until tender and all the liquid has been absorbed.

11.
While the rice is braising, bring salted water to boil in a large saucepan. Add the asparagus spears and broccoli florets and cook for 5 minutes or until barely tender. Drain and keep warm.

12.
Ten minutes before the rice is done add the peas and stir gently into the rice with 2 forks.

13.
When the rice is done transfer it to a serving dish. Garnish with the asparagus spears and broccoli florets and serve hot. Topped with the fried eggs, if desired.

Remarks
The rice can be prepared several hours ahead and kept warm in a pan of hot water in a 200-degree oven. The rice is equally delicious served cold the next day. You may add to the cold rice a garlic vinaigrette made from 2 tablespoons red wine vinegar, 6 tablespoons fruity olive oil, and 1 finely crushed clove of garlic. Blend the vinaigrette thoroughly before tossing it into the rice.

Here is a basic recipe for homemade pasta. The amount of ingredients given will produce 2 sheets of pasta when rolled out by machine. It is easier for the beginner to make the dough in small batches, particularly when using a machine in which the sheets come out about 4 to 5 inches wide. The thickness of the noodles is ultimately a matter of preference and experience. Remember that the noodles should be able to carry a sauce without "collapsing." Very thin pasta cut into narrow noodles is usually best served in chicken broth as in Zucchini and Pasta Soup Milanaise (page 124).

Ingredients
1½ cups flour, preferably semolina flour
2 large eggs
Pinch of salt
1 teaspoon peanut or corn oil

Preparation
1.
Place the flour in a shallow stainless steel bowl. Make a well in the center of the mound and break the eggs into it. Add the salt and oil. Work the mixture with a fork, incorporating more and more flour into the egg mixture. When the mixture seems to get lumpy start working it with your hands, kneading the dough until all the flour has been absorbed.

2.
Dust a wooden surface with flour and transfer the dough to it. Continue kneading for 3 to 4 minutes, or until you have a perfectly smooth ball.

Fettucine in Cream, Tomato, and Basil Sauce

Serves:	**4 to 6**
Preparation time:	**10 minutes**
Cooking time:	**10 minutes**
Type of recipe:	**elementary**
Cost:	**inexpensive**

3.

Attach the pasta machine securely to a working surface. Place the kneading attachment in the machine and turn the knob until the rollers are at their largest opening. Run the dough several times through the opening, dusting it lightly with flour if it seems sticky.

4.

When the dough seems very smooth, turn the knob to the next notch and run the dough through the machine. Keep turning the knob, closing the opening a little more each time you have run the dough sheet through the machine. When the pasta is at the right thickness for your purpose (for fettucine the dough should not be too thick; for stuffed pasta, as thin as possible) place the pasta sheet on a well-floured linen towel and let it dry for 15 minutes.

5.

Place the cutting attachment in the machine (the cutting attachment will only cut 2 shapes of noodles—broad and narrow). The broad one is right for fettucine and noodles. Run the sheet of pasta through the machine and spread the noodles on the towel to dry for 5 minutes before cooking them.

Remarks

Fresh noodles will keep for several weeks. Keep them in a large bowl in a cool, dry place. When dry, the noodles will need 2 to 3 more minutes of cooking.

Ingredients

2 large ripe tomatoes
Salt
3 Tablespoons butter
Pinch of flour
1½ cups heavy cream
Freshly ground black pepper
2 cloves garlic, peeled and crushed
1 cup finely shredded fresh basil leaves
1 pound fresh Fettucine (page 346)
2 Tablespoons finely minced fresh parsley

Garnish:
Bowl of freshly grated Parmesan cheese

Preparation

1.

Cut each of the tomatoes into 6 slices. Do not peel. Remove the seeds and dice the tomatoes finely. Place in a sieve over a bowl, sprinkle with salt, and let the tomato cubes drain for 30 minutes.

2.

In a large cast-iron skillet heat the butter and sprinkle with flour. Add the cream, bring to a boil, and reduce by ⅓, or until it thickens and coats a spoon. Season the cream with salt and a large grinding of black pepper. Add the garlic and basil and set aside.

3.

In a large casserole bring salted water to boil. Add the fettucine and cook for 5 minutes, or until just tender. Drain and add to the skillet.

Fettucine
Balduini

Serves: **4 to 5**
Preparation time: **20 minutes**
Cooking time: **30 minutes**
Type of recipe: **elementary**
Cost: **inexpensive**

4.
Place the skillet over low heat and heat the fettucine in the sauce without letting the sauce come to a boil. Add the diced tomatoes and parsley. Toss the fettucine but do not let the tomatoes cook. Serve immediately from the skillet with a side bowl of freshly grated Parmesan cheese.

Remarks
You can add 1 small zucchini to the sauce. Dice and sauté it in a mixture of 2 tablespoons butter and a little oil until it's nicely browned. You can also add 1 cup finely cubed mozzarella to the fettucine, together with the tomatoes. The mozzarella will just start to melt and will give an additional interesting texture to the sauce. This dish is at its best when done with fresh fettucine. If you can't get any or are unwilling to make it, you can substitute a good commercial brand of flat spaghetti. A commercial brand, however, will need 7 to 9 minutes of cooking.

Ingredients
3 Tablespoons butter
2 Tablespoons finely minced shallots
2 large ripe tomatoes, peeled, seeded and finely diced
Salt and freshly ground black pepper
Pinch of flour
1½ cups heavy cream
1 large clove garlic, crushed
1 large Roasted Red Pepper (page 545) finely cubed
1 pound fresh Fettucine (page 346)

Zucchini:
½ cup flour
1 teaspoon olive oil
Salt and freshly ground black pepper
Peanut oil for frying
2 small zucchini, sliced ⅛ inch thick

Garnish:
2 Tablespoons finely minced fresh parsley
Bowl of freshly grated Parmesan cheese

Preparation
1.
In a 10-inch cast-iron skillet heat the butter, add the shallots, and cook until soft but not browned. Add the tomatoes, season with salt and pepper, and cook until the tomato water has evaporated.
2.
Sprinkle with a pinch of flour and add the cream. Bring to a boil, season with salt and pepper, and cook until the cream is reduced by one third and the sauce coats a spoon.

Fettucine
with Asparagus and Peas
(Primavera)

Serves:	**4 to 5**
Preparation time:	**10 minutes**
Cooking time:	**15 minutes**
Type of recipe:	**elementary**
Cost:	**inexpensive**

3.
Add the garlic and the red pepper and keep the sauce warm.

4.
Prepare the zucchini. In a bowl combine the flour and enough water to make a batter of medium thickness. Add the olive oil and season with salt and pepper.

5.
In a deep, heavy skillet pour the peanut oil to a depth of ¾ inch and heat. When the oil is very hot, dip the zucchini slices in the batter; they should be well coated.

6.
Slide the zucchini into the hot oil and fry until they are golden brown and crisp on both sides. Transfer to a double layer of paper towels and set aside.

7.
In a large casserole bring salted water to a boil. Add the fettucine and cook for 3 to 5 minutes, or until just tender; do not overcook.

8.
Drain the fettucine and transfer it to the skillet in which you have cooked the sauce. Toss the fettucine with 2 forks until it is well coated with the sauce.

9.
Transfer the pasta to a serving bowl, then sprinkle with parsley and the fried zucchini slices. Serve the Parmesan cheese on the side.

Ingredients

½ pound thin fresh asparagus
3 large eggs
Salt and freshly ground black pepper
6 Tablespoons freshly grated Parmesan cheese
¾ to 1 pound fresh Fettucine (page 346)
1 cup shelled fresh peas
3 Tablespoons butter
½ cup diced smoked ham

Green Fettucine Primavera

Serves:	**4 to 5**
Preparation time:	**10 minutes**
Cooking time:	**20 minutes**
Type of recipe:	**elementary**
Cost:	**inexpensive**

Preparation

1.
Scrape the asparagus stalks. Tie them into even bundles and set aside.

2.
Beat the eggs until smooth and season with salt and pepper. Add 2 tablespoons Parmesan cheese and set aside.

3.
In a casserole bring salted water to a boil, add the asparagus and cook for 5 minutes, or until just tender. Do not overcook. Drain the asparagus under cold running water and cut into 1-inch pieces. Set aside.

4.
In a saucepan again bring salted water to a boil. Add the peas and cook until just tender, or for about 5 minutes. Drain and set aside.

5.
In a cast-iron skillet melt the butter over low heat. Add the ham and simmer until just heated through. Add the asparagus and peas and simmer the mixture gently for 2 to 3 minutes. Keep warm.

6.
In a large casserole bring plenty of salted water to a boil. Add the fettucine and cook for 5 minutes, or until just tender; do not overcook. Drain and add to the skillet.

7.
Remove the skillet from the heat. Pour the egg mixture over the fettucine and toss with 2 forks. Add the remaining Parmesan cheese. Add a large grinding of pepper and serve immediately right from the skillet.

Ingredients

2 fresh ripe tomatoes, cubed
Salt
5 Tablespoons butter
1 teaspoon olive oil
2 cups thinly sliced zucchini
Freshly ground black pepper
½ pound fresh mushrooms, stems removed and caps sliced
Sprinkling of flour
1¼ cups heavy cream
½ cup finely minced fresh parsley
1 large clove garlic, peeled and crushed
1 pound green fettucine (long flat green noodles)
4 Tablespoons freshly grated Parmesan cheese

Preparation

1.
Place the tomatoes in a colander, sprinkle with salt, and set over a bowl. Drain the tomatoes for 30 minutes.

2.
In an 8-inch cast-iron skillet heat 2 tablespoons butter and the oil. Add the zucchini, season with salt and pepper, and sauté over moderate-to-high heat until just tender but still somewhat crunchy. Set aside.

3.
In a large 10-inch cast-iron skillet melt the remaining butter over low heat. Add the mushrooms, increase the heat, and sauté over moderate-to-high heat for 2 to 3 minutes, or until lightly browned. Season with salt and pepper, sprinkle with flour, and toss the mushrooms for 1 minute, or until well covered with the flour.

Serves: **4 to 6**
Preparation time: **20 minutes**
Cooking time: **20 minutes**
Type of recipe: **elementary**
Cost: **inexpensive**

4.
Add the cream and bring to a boil. Reduce the heat and simmer until slightly reduced and thickened.

5.
Add the zucchini and tomatoes and sprinkle with ¼ cup parsley. Season with salt and pepper, and add the garlic. Keep the sauce warm over the lowest possible heat. The tomato cubes should still retain their shape.

6.
In a large casserole bring salted water to a boil. Add the fettucine and cook for 9 minutes, or until just tender.

7.
Add 1 cup cold water to the pot to prevent the fettucine from cooking further. Drain in a colander and add to the sauce.

8.
Sprinkle the pasta with Parmesan cheese and the remaining parsley. Toss the fettucine in the skillet, covering them well with the cream sauce. Add a large grinding of black pepper and serve immediately from the skillet.

Ingredients
½ pound fresh spinach, well rinsed
4 Tablespoons butter
½ teaspoon flour
1½ cups heavy cream
2 to 3 Tablespoons finely minced fresh chives
Salt
Freshly ground black pepper
1 pound fresh Fettucine (page 346)
½ cup coarsely grated Parmesan cheese

Garnish:
Bowl of freshly grated Parmesan cheese

Fettucine
à la Tropezienne

Serves:	**5 to 6**
Preparation time:	**15 minutes**
Cooking time:	**15 minutes**
Type of recipe:	**elementary**
Cost:	**inexpensive**

Preparation

1.
In a large saucepan bring salted water to a boil. Add the spinach and cook for 3 minutes. Drain and when cool enough to handle squeeze out all the moisture with your hands. Mince the spinach finely.

2.
In a heavy 1-quart saucepan heat the butter, add the spinach, and cook stirring for 2 minutes. Add the flour and stir until well incorporated.

3.
Add the cream and heat the mixture over low heat until it comes to a boil. Whisk the sauce and cook until it lightly coats a spoon. Add the chives, then season with salt and pepper. Keep warm.

4.
In a large casserole bring salted water to a boil. Add the fettucini and cook for 5 to 7 minutes, or until barely tender. Drain and run under hot water.

5.
Transfer the pasta to a heated serving bowl. Add the sauce and the cheese. Toss the fettucini, adding a large grinding of black pepper. Serve immediately with a side dish of grated Parmesan cheese.

Ingredients
1 cup tightly packed fresh basil leaves, plus 2 Tablespoons fresh basil leaves cut into thin julienne strips
2 large cloves garlic, peeled and coarsely chopped
2 Tablespoons fresh parsley
4 to 6 Tablespoons fruity olive oil
Salt and freshly ground black pepper
1 Tablespoon freshly grated Parmesan cheese
1 cup Tomato Sauce (page 543)
¾ to 1 cup Crème Fraîche (page 544)
1 pound fettucine (long flat noodles)

Garnish:
Bowl of freshly grated Parmesan cheese

Spinach
Gnocchi

Serves: **6**
Preparation time: **30 minutes**
Cooking time: **30 minutes**
Type of recipe: **elementary**
Cost: **inexpensive**

Preparation

1.
In a blender combine the cup of basil leaves, garlic, and parsley. Add just enough olive oil to blend the mixture until smooth. Season with salt and pepper and add the Parmesan cheese. Set the basil paste aside.

2.
In a saucepan heat the tomato sauce over low heat. Add the basil paste and ¾ cup Crème Fraîche. Slowly heat the sauce but do not let it come to a boil. Season with salt and pepper and keep warm.

3.
In a large casserole bring salted water to a boil. Add the fettucine and cook over high heat for 9 minutes, or until just tender. (If fresh fettucine are available to you through a specialty store or if you are making your own the cooking time will be reduced to about 5 minutes.) Do not overcook the pasta. When done add 2 cups water to the pot to stop the pasta from cooking further.

4.
Drain the fettucine and place in a large bowl. Add the sauce and toss lightly. You may want to add a little more Crème Fraîche if the sauce has become too thick.

5.
Add the remaining basil leaves and a large grinding of black pepper. Serve the fettucine immediately with a side bowl of freshly grated Parmesan cheese.

Ingredients

1 package (10 ounces) fresh spinach, well rinsed and stemmed
3 Tablespoons butter, plus ¼ cup butter, softened
1 cup mashed potatoes (about 2 medium potatoes)
⅓ cup all-purpose flour, plus flour for dredging
¾ cup fresh fine bread crumbs
3 large eggs
3 Tablespoons freshly grated Parmesan cheese
Salt and freshly ground white pepper

Topping:

6 Tablespoons melted sweet butter
3 Tablespoons freshly grated Parmesan cheese

Preparation

1.
In a large saucepan bring 1 cup salted water to a boil. Add the spinach and cook for 3 to 4 minutes, or until wilted. Drain and, when cool enough to handle, squeeze the moisture out of the spinach with your hands. Place on a cutting board and chop the spinach roughly.

2.
In a cast-iron skillet melt 3 tablespoons butter over moderate-to-high heat. Add the spinach and sauté for about 2 minutes.

3.
Place the spinach in a food processor or blender and purée.

4.
Transfer the puréed spinach to a large mixing bowl. Add the mashed potatoes, ⅓ cup flour, bread crumbs, eggs, Parmesan cheese, and softened butter. Season the mixture with salt and pepper and blend thoroughly until it forms a smooth dough.

5.
Using a quarter of the dough at a time, roll the dough with your hands on a well-floured surface, shaping it into long cylinders ½ inch thick and approximately 12 inches long. With a sharp knife cut the cylinders into 1 inch pieces and roll them lightly in flour. Repeat with the remaining dough and set the gnocchi aside.

6.
Butter a rectangular baking dish.

7.
Preheat the oven to 325 degrees.

8.
In a large saucepan bring salted water to a boil, then reduce to a simmer. Drop the gnocchi, a few at a time, into the simmering water. When the gnocchi float to the top of the water, cook for 2 to 3 minutes. With a slotted spoon transfer the gnocchi to the buttered baking dish.

9.
Drizzle the gnocchi with the melted butter and sprinkle with the Parmesan cheese. Bake for 25 minutes.

10.
Remove from the oven and serve directly from the baking dish.

Remarks

For variation omit the topping of butter and cheese and instead use the mushroom sauce used in Spinach Ramekins à la Bernoise (page 000). Cover and reheat in the oven for 15 minutes. Serve directly from the baking dish.

Spaghettini
in
Anchovy-and-Mint Sauce

Serves: **4 to 6**
Preparation time: **10 minutes**
Cooking time: **20 minutes**
Type of recipe: **elementary**
Cost: **inexpensive**

Ingredients

3 Tablespoons butter
1 can (2 ounces) flat anchovy fillets, finely minced
1 teaspoon finely minced garlic
½ cup finely minced fresh parsley
3 to 4 Tablespoons finely minced fresh mint
½ cup fruity olive oil
Salt and freshly ground black pepper
1 pound spaghettini (thin spaghetti)

Optional:

8 to 10 thinly sliced Greek black olives
8 to 10 cherry tomatoes, stewed in 2 Tablespoons olive oil for 2 to 3 minutes

Preparation

1.
In a small heavy saucepan heat the butter over low heat. Add the anchovies and cook until they are reduced to a paste.

2.
Add the garlic, parsley, mint, and oil and heat the mixture without letting it come to a boil. Season with a large grinding of black pepper and keep warm.

3.
In a casserole bring 3 to 4 quarts salted water to boil. Add the spaghettini and cook for 7 to 9 minutes, or until barely tender.

4.
Add 2 cups cold water to the casserole to stop the spaghettini from cooking further.

5.
Drain the spaghettini and transfer to a warm serving bowl and spoon the anchovy sauce over the pasta. Add the optional black olives and tomatoes, then toss with 2 forks. Taste the spaghettini, adding a large grinding of black pepper, and serve immediately.

Remarks

Other fresh herbs, such as basil and oregano, can be added to the sauce. An excellent fruity olive oil is a must for this simple dish. You may even like a little more oil or a little more garlic, or both.

Spaghettini
in
Sauce Basquaise

Serves:	**4 to 5**
Preparation time:	**15 minutes**
Cooking time:	**20 minutes**
Type of recipe:	**elementary**
Cost:	**inexpensive**

Ingredients

4 Tablespoons olive oil
1 dried hot chili pepper, or ½ teaspoon pepper flakes
4 to 6 hot Italian link sausages
4 Tablespoons finely minced fresh parsley
3 cloves garlic, finely minced
2 Roasted Green Peppers (page 545), thinly sliced
1 Roasted Red Pepper (page 545), thinly sliced, or ½ cup thinly sliced pimientos
6 large ripe tomatoes, peeled, seeded, and chopped, or 1 can (35 ounces) Italian plum tomatoes, drained and chopped
Salt and freshly ground black pepper
1 teaspoon dried oregano
2 Tablespoons finely minced fresh basil, or 1 teaspoon dried
1 pound spaghettini (thin spaghetti)

Preparation

1.
In a large heavy skillet heat the oil. Add the chili pepper and sausages. Partially cover the pan and sauté the sausages over low heat until nicely browned on all sides and cooked through. Discard the pepper. Transfer the sausages to a cutting board and slice thinly. Set aside.

2.
To the oil remaining in the pan add 2 tablespoons parsley, 2 cloves garlic, and the green and red peppers. Sauté the mixture for 2 or 3 minutes. Add the tomatoes, then season with salt, pepper, oregano, and basil. Bring to a boil, reduce the heat, and simmer for 10 minutes. Return the sausages to the skillet and keep warm.

3.
In a large casserole bring 3 to 4 quarts salted water to boil. Add the spaghettini and cook over high heat for 7 to 8 minutes, or until barely tender. Drain the pasta and add it to the skillet.

4.
Toss the spaghettini in the sauce, then season with salt and a large grinding of black pepper. Sprinkle with the remaining parsley and garlic and serve right from the skillet.

Remarks:
Here is an excellent light supper or Sunday lunch. It is lightly spicy, which makes it interesting. You can add a zucchini finely cubed to the skillet together with the peppers.

Spaghettini
in Blue Cheese
and Cream Sauce

Serves: **6**
Preparation time: **15 minutes**
Cooking time: **20 minutes**
Type of recipe: **elementary**
Cost: **inexpensive**

Ingredients

3 Tablespoons butter
1 teaspoon flour
1½ cups light cream
2 ounces minced Gorgonzola or other mild blue cheese
Salt and freshly ground black pepper
½ cup finely grated Parmesan cheese
1 pound spaghettini or fettucine (thin spaghetti or noodles)

Preparation

1.
In a small heavy saucepan melt the butter over low heat. Add the flour and cook for 1 or 2 minutes stirring constantly; do not let the flour brown.

2.
Add the cream and Gorgonzola and simmer the mixture until thickened. The cream should lightly coat a spoon. Season with salt and pepper, add ¼ cup Parmesan cheese and set aside.

3.
In a large casserole bring 3 to 4 quarts salted water to boil. Add the spaghettini and cook for 7 to 8 minutes, or until barely tender.

4.
Drain the spaghettini, return it to the casserole and pour the sauce over the pasta. Toss lightly with 2 spoons, then add the remaining Parmesan and a large grinding of black pepper. Serve immediately.

Remarks

Mild blue cheese can be used instead of the Gorgonzola, or you may use more cheese depending on your own personal taste. A few fresh mushrooms thinly sliced and sautéed in 2 tablespoons butter can be added to the sauce.

Spaghettini
with
Broccoli

Serves: **4 to 5**
Preparation time: **15 minutes**
Cooking time: **45 minutes**
Type of recipe: **elementary**
Cost: **inexpensive**

Ingredients
1½ pounds fresh broccoli
8 Tablespoons fruity olive oil
½ cup finely minced fresh parsley
3 large cloves garlic, finely minced
1 can (35 ounces) Italian plum tomatoes,
well drained and finely chopped
Salt and freshly ground black pepper
1 teaspoon dried oregano
1 teaspoon dried thyme
1 bay leaf
⅓ cup pine nuts
1 pound spaghettini (thin spaghetti)

Garnish:
Bowl of freshly grated Parmesan cheese

Preparation
1.
Peel the broccoli stalks with a vegetable peeler and remove all the leaves. Slice the stalks crosswise into ¾-inch slices and break the florets into even pieces. Set aside.
2.
In a 10-inch cast-iron skillet heat 4 tablespoons oil. Add ¼ cup parsley and the garlic and cook for 1 to 2 minutes without browning.
3.
Add the tomatoes, season with salt, pepper, oregano, and thyme and add the bay leaf. Reduce the heat and simmer the sauce for 30 minutes partially covered.
4.
While the sauce is simmering heat 2 tablespoons oil in a small skillet. Add the pine nuts and sauté until nicely browned. Set aside.

5.
In a large saucepan bring salted water to boil. Add the broccoli stalks and florets and cook for 5 minutes, or until barely tender. Drain. Add the sliced broccoli stalks to the tomato sauce and keep the florets warm in a colander over a pan of warm water.
6.
In a large casserole bring 4 quarts salted water to a boil. Add the remaining olive oil and the spaghettini. Stir the strands to prevent them from sticking to the bottom of the casserole. Cook for 7 to 8 minutes, or until the spaghettini is just tender; do not overcook.
7.
Drain the spaghettini thoroughly and return it to the casserole. Add the tomato sauce together with the sautéed pine nuts. Toss the spaghettini thoroughly in the sauce adding a large grinding of black pepper.
8.
Transfer the pasta and sauce to a deep serving bowl, top with the broccoli florets, and sprinkle with the remaining parsley. Serve immediately accompanied by a bowl of freshly grated Parmesan cheese.

Spaghettini
in
Green Sauce

Serves:	**4 to 5**
Preparation time:	**15 minutes**
Cooking time:	**20 minutes**
Type of recipe:	**elementary**
Cost:	**inexpensive**

Ingredients

2 cups tightly packed fresh basil leaves
2 Tablespoons red wine vinegar
¾ cup fruity olive oil
1 can (2 ounces) flat anchovy fillets, chopped
½ cup finely minced fresh parsley
4 large cloves garlic, peeled and finely minced
2 Tablespoons well-drained tiny capers
Salt and freshly ground black pepper
1 pound spaghettini (thin spaghetti)

Garnish:
Bowl of freshly grated Parmesan cheese

Preparation

1.
In a blender or food processor combine the basil and vinegar. Add ½ the oil and blend the mixture until smooth. Set aside.

2.
In a large heavy skillet heat the remaining oil. Add the anchovies, parsley, and garlic. Cook the mixture over low heat for 3 to 4 minutes.

3.
Add the basil purée and the capers and heat through. Season with salt and pepper and keep warm over the lowest possible heat.

4.
In a large casserole bring 3 to 4 quarts salted water to boil. Add the spaghettini and cook for 7 to 8 minutes, or until just tender. Drain the spaghettini and add it to the skillet.

5.
Toss the pasta in the warm sauce adding a large grinding of black pepper and a little more olive oil if necessary. Serve right from the skillet accompanied by a side dish of grated Parmesan cheese.

Remarks
The sauce can be made several hours ahead and reheated. A 3½-ounce can of flaked tuna in olive oil can be added to the sauce.

Spaghettini
Niçoise

Serves:	**4 to 6**
Preparation time:	**25 minutes**
Cooking time:	**15 minutes**
Type of recipe:	**elementary**
Cost:	**inexpensive**

Ingredients

8 to 10 fresh Italian plum tomatoes
Salt
3 Tablespoons fruity olive oil
3 Tablespoons finely minced fresh parsley
3 large cloves garlic, finely minced
12 black Niçoise olives, pitted and cut in half (oil-cured olives)
6 anchovy fillets, finely minced
Freshly ground black pepper
1 pound spaghettini (thin spaghetti)

Basil Paste (Pesto):

2 cups tightly packed fresh basil leaves
2 cloves garlic, peeled and chopped
2 Tablespoons pine nuts or walnuts
2 Tablespoons freshly grated Parmesan cheese
6 to 8 Tablespoons fruity olive oil
Salt and freshly ground black pepper

Preparation

1.
Slice the tomatoes into ½-inch slices. Sprinkle with salt and let drain in a colander for 30 minutes.

2.
Make the basil paste. Rinse the basil leaves thoroughly under cold water and drain. Dry with paper towels and combine leaves, garlic, nuts, Parmesan cheese, and olive oil in a blender or food processor and blend until smooth. Season with salt and pepper. Set aside.

3.
Heat the oil in a large heavy skillet. Add the parsley and garlic and cook for 2 or 3 minutes without browning. Add the drained tomatoes, olives, and anchovies and cook until just heated through. Season with salt and pepper and set aside.

4.
In a large casserole bring 3 to 4 quarts salted water to a boil. Add the spaghettini and cook for 7 to 8 minutes, or until just tender. Drain and add to the skillet.

5.
Add the basil paste and toss the spaghettini and the tomato-and-basil mixture over low heat. Add a large grinding of black pepper and serve hot.

Spaghettini Rinaldi with Tomato, Basil, and Clam Sauce

Serves: **4 to 6**
Preparation time: **25 minutes**
Cooking time: **20 minutes**
Type of recipe: **elementary**
Cost: **moderate**

I often wonder whether that small restaurant on the Genoa coast, which used to serve marvelous seafood, still exists. I hope so, for they made the most delicious spaghettini sauce, heavily flavored with basil, tomatoes, and clams.

Ingredients

2 cups tightly packed fresh basil leaves
3 cloves garlic, minced
1 Tablespoon tomato paste
4 Tablespoons freshly grated Parmesan cheese
¾ cup fruity olive oil
Salt and freshly ground black pepper
12 to 16 small clams, well scrubbed
3 Tablespoons finely minced fresh parsley
4 to 6 large ripe tomatoes, peeled and chopped, or 1 can (2 pounds) Italian plum tomatoes, drained and chopped
2 Tablespoons finely minced fresh oregano, or 1 teaspoon dried
Sprinkling of flour
1 pound spaghettini (thin spaghetti)

Preparation

1.
In a blender or food processor combine the basil, two cloves garlic, tomato paste, and Parmesan cheese. Add ½ cup olive oil and blend the mixture until smooth. Season with salt and pepper and set aside.

2.
In a large casserole combine the clams with ½ cup water. Cover and cook over medium heat until the clams open. Remove the clams from the shells and discard any that did not open. Chop the clams finely and set aside. Reserve 1 cup clam broth and combine the diced clams with the reserved broth and keep warm.

3.
In a large heavy skillet heat the remaining oil. Add the parsley and remaining garlic and cook for 1 to 2 minutes without browning. Add the tomatoes and cook the mixture until most of the tomato water has evaporated. Season with salt, pepper and oregano.

4.
Add the basil paste, clams, and clam broth. Cook for 3 to 4 minutes. Sprinkle the sauce with a little flour to thicken it slightly. Set aside.

5.
In a large casserole bring 3 to 4 quarts salted water to a boil. Add the spaghettini and cook for 7 to 8 minutes, or until barely tender. Drain and add to the skillet.

6.
Toss the pasta in the sauce, adding a large grinding of black pepper. Serve immediately.

Spaghettini
in
Seafood Sauce

Serves:	**4 to 5**
Preparation time:	**15 minutes**
Cooking time:	**50 minutes**
Type of recipe:	**elementary**
Cost:	**moderate**

Fresh calamari, or squid, are available in many fish markets catering to Italian customers. I have also seen them in good seafood markets.

Ingredients

1 pound tiny fresh calamari
4 Tablespoons fruity olive oil
1 small dried hot chili pepper, crushed
2 large cloves garlic, minced
2 Tablespoons fresh parsley, finely minced
4 to 6 large ripe tomatoes, peeled, seeded, and chopped
Salt and freshly ground black pepper
1 teaspoon dried oregano
12 littleneck clams, well scrubbed
1 Beurre Manié, made from 2 teaspoons butter blended with 1 teaspoon flour
1 pound spaghettini (thin spaghetti)

Garnish:
Finely minced fresh parsley

Preparation

1.
Clean the calamari thoroughly under cold running water, removing the outer skin (it will slip right off) as well as the inside sack. Slice the calamari thinly crosswise, into rounds.

2.
In a large heavy enamel saucepan heat the oil and add the chili pepper and calamari. Cook over high heat until the calamari turn an opaque white.

3.
Add the garlic, parsley, tomatoes, salt, pepper, and oregano. Bring to a boil,

reduce the heat, and simmer the calamari mixture covered for 30 minutes, or until very tender.

4.
While the calamari is cooking combine the clams with ½ cup cold water in a large saucepan. Bring to a boil and cook covered until the clams open. Remove the clams to a side dish and reserve. Discard any clams that did not open.

5.
Strain the clam juice through a double layer of cheese cloth into the calamari and whisk in bits of the Beurre Manié until the sauce is slightly thickened. Keep the sauce hot.

6.
In a large casserole bring 3 to 4 quart salted water to boil. Add the spaghettini and cook for 7 to 8 minutes, or until barely tender. Add 2 cups cold water to the pot to stop the spaghettini from cooking.

7.
Drain the spaghettini and return to the pot. Add the calamari sauce and toss lightly.

8.
Transfer the pasta and sauce to a serving dish. Garnish with the clams and sprinkle with parsley and a generous grinding of black pepper.

Spaghettini
with
Shrimp Tasca

Serves: **5 to 6**
Preparation time: **20 minutes**
Cooking time: **40 minutes**
Type of recipe: **elementary**
Cost: **moderate**

Ingredients

2 Tablespoons fruity olive oil
1 dried hot chili pepper
½ pound fresh small shrimp, shelled and diced
Salt and freshly ground black pepper
3 cloves garlic, finely minced
3 Tablespoons finely minced fresh parsley
1 cup finely diced green pepper
½ cup cooked green peas
1 pound spaghettini (thin spaghetti)

Tomato Sauce:

3 Tablespoons fruity olive oil
2 Tablespoons finely minced shallots
2 Tablespoons finely minced fresh parsley
1 teaspoon finely minced garlic
1 teaspoon tomato paste
5 to 6 large ripe tomatoes, peeled, seeded, and chopped, or 1 can (35 ounces) Italian plum tomatoes
Salt and freshly ground black pepper
2 Tablespoons finely minced fresh basil, or 1 teaspoon dried
2 Tablespoons finely minced fresh oregano, or 1 teaspoon dried
1 bay leaf

Preparation

1.
Start by making the sauce. In a 10-inch heavy cast-iron skillet heat the olive oil over low heat. Add the shallots, parsley, and garlic and cook the mixture for 1 to 2 minutes without browning. Add the tomato paste and tomatoes. Season with salt and pepper, basil and oregano, and add the bay leaf. Bring to a boil, reduce the heat, and simmer the tomato sauce partially covered for 25 to 30 minutes. When the tomato sauce is done set it aside.

2.
In another 10-inch cast-iron skillet heat the olive oil, add the chili pepper, and cook until the pepper turns dark. Discard the chili pepper.

3.
Add the shrimp and sauté over high heat until they turn bright pink. Season with salt and pepper, reduce the heat, and add the garlic, parsley, green pepper, and peas. Toss the mixture and cook for 2 minutes without letting the parsley or garlic burn.

4.
Immediately add the tomato sauce to the skillet and heat. Taste and correct the seasoning, then keep warm.

5.
In a large heavy casserole bring 3 to 4 quarts salted water to a boil. Add the spaghettini and cook stirring with a wooden spoon to prevent the spaghettini from sticking to the bottom of the casserole. Cook for 7 to 8 minutes, or until the spaghettini is barely tender. Drain and return to the casserole.

6.
Add the shrimp-and-tomato sauce to the casserole and toss with 2 forks. Add a large grinding of black pepper and serve hot.

Remarks

For variation you can garnish this spaghettini with 1 to 2 pounds cooked mussels. To cook the mussels place them in a casserole, cover, and cook for 3 to 5 minutes, or until the mussels open. Discard any unopened mussels.

Spaghettini in Tomato, Anchovy, and Mozzarella Sauce

Serves: **4 to 6**
Preparation time: **15 minutes**
Cooking time: **25 minutes**
Type of recipe: **elementary**
Cost: **inexpensive**

Ingredients

6 Tablespoons olive oil
½ cup finely minced onions
4 large cloves garlic, minced
½ cup finely minced fresh parsley
6 to 8 ripe tomatoes, peeled, seeded, and chopped, or 1 can (35 ounces) Italian plum tomatoes, drained and chopped
½ cup finely minced fresh basil, or 2 teaspoons dried
2 Tablespoons finely minced fresh oregano, or 1 teaspoon dried
Salt and freshly ground black pepper
1 can (2 ounces) flat anchovy fillets, drained and minced
2 Tablespoons well-drained tiny capers
1 pound spaghettini (thin spaghetti)
6 ounces mozzarella cheese, finely cubed

Preparation

1.
In a large heavy skillet heat the oil, then add the onion, 2 cloves garlic, and ¼ cup parsley. Cook the mixture over low heat for 2 or 3 minutes.

2.
Add the tomatoes, basil, oregano, salt, and pepper and cook the mixture partially covered until the sauce is slightly reduced and most of the tomato water has evaporated.

3.
Add the anchovies and capers and keep the sauce warm.

4.
In a large casserole bring 3 to 4 quarts salted water to a boil. Add the spaghettini and cook over high heat for 7 to 8 minutes, or until barely tender.

5.
Drain the spaghettini and add to the skillet. Toss in the sauce and add the mozzarella; the cheese should be barely melted and still retain its texture. Add the remaining parsley and garlic, then taste and correct the seasoning, adding a large grinding of black pepper. Serve immediately, right from the skillet.

Remarks

The sauce can be prepared several hours ahead and reheated. A few finely cubed cooked shrimp are a delicious addition to the dish.

Eggs, Quiches, and Crêpes

Of all the foods available to us, the egg is probably the one most taken for granted. No shopper's cart would be complete without it; it is such an automatic part of our daily eating habit that every refrigerator comes equipped with special shelves just to house it. Yet for some reason, the egg in this country has been pretty much confined to the breakfast table or the baking of cakes. We have yet to explore its wonderful versatility. It is only when you start to think about it, and to enumerate the endless forms and shapes the simple, basic egg can take, and the culinary functions it can serve, that you realize what a truly marvelous and indispensable food it is.

To appreciate the great number of egg dishes, and the other dishes made possible because of eggs, we must turn to Europe. There both the peasant cooks and the chefs of *haute cuisine* have been ingenious over the centuries. With the help of the egg, they have given us mousses, crêpes, pasta, buttercreams, quiches, and soufflés. The French (who hardly ever serve or think of eggs as breakfast fare) have come up with countless ways of garnishing and serving every kind of basic egg preparation you can think of, from Oeufs Durs à la Cressionière (whole hard-boiled eggs on a bed of watercress purée covered with cream sauce) to Oeufs Pochées aux Écrevisses (poached eggs served on tartlet shells filled with shrimp and shrimp sauce), to the classic omelets. Eggs are good hot, cold, scrambled, poached, hard-boiled, coddled, baked, stuffed, shirred, or in omelets. They can work well with

everything from shellfish to chicken livers to steak tartare, and there is not a single vegetable I can think of that doesn't work beautifully with some kind of egg preparation.

When I shop for eggs I always go to a supermarket that has a large turnover, and I always watch for the date marked on the carton. This tells me the last day of sale. I try to buy local eggs, since they are usually fresher and have gone through less shipping and handling. Do not buy eggs at the so-called farmer's stand or a specialty market unless you are sure that there is really a farm nearby where the stand has gotten its eggs or that the shop has a large turnover. Often I find that these stands or shops carry eggs that are of mediocre quality. Since they aren't dated, you have no way of knowing how fresh they are.

I used to buy large eggs and found them quite satisfactory. But in recent years the large eggs seem not to be as large as they once were. I find that now I have to buy eggs labeled extra large in order to get the size I want. However size does vary, and when I buy my eggs at my *real* local farmstand, I find the large eggs to be just that. Look into the carton and decide for yourself. Brown eggs are usually a little more expensive than white. I prefer them, since the shell is a little harder and they don't seem to break as easily in cooking; however there is no difference in taste whatsoever. Freshness is really the key to the flavor of an egg, and that—not color— should always be your criterion.

Eggs will last for two months in the refrigerator, but if I have been away for two or three weeks, I generally use leftover eggs for baking or hard-boiling rather than for fresh preparations such as scrambled or poached eggs. When hard-boiling, I find that a not-quite-so-fresh egg will peel better. The reason that fresher eggs don't peel properly remains one of the cooking mysteries I have yet to solve.

Of all egg preparations, the omelet has really come into vogue in recent years. Many of our great cooks have carefully illustrated and taught the technique of omelet making. With French cooking becoming more and more a part of the everyday kitchen, many cooks have learned the art of making an omelet. The description in Julia Child's first book, *Mastering the Art of French Cooking,* is the best and most detailed explanation. Today omelets are on every restaurant lunch menu, but few cooks use them as starters to meals, the way they are used all over Europe. I find that the omelet makes a wonderful and inexpensive appetizer. Sometimes I serve it simply flavored with finely minced fresh dill or chives, or a julienne of a few sorrel leaves. At other times I fill it with a few sautéed chicken livers, some leftover ratatouille, or a few sautéed mushrooms. On a recent trip to Corsica, I had for the first time an omelet made with bits of fresh goat cheese and finely minced fresh mint, a recipe for which I include in this chapter. I consider it to be a really wonderful find.

When it comes to making the omelet, I feel that no matter how detailed and complete a written description you have, it is still best if you have occasion to observe someone who really knows how to make one. There are two techniques: one where the omelet is made to roll onto itself in the pan (this technique is harder to master); and the other, where the omelet is pushed toward the far end of the skillet and rolled onto the plate. This is the Mediterranean way and is quite easy to do.

Properly made scrambled eggs are another great way to use eggs as an appetizer. The French technique of scrambling the eggs gently in a heavy saucepan produces a moist and creamy, lightly curdled mixture that can be combined with diced cooked asparagus, a few poached bay scallops, or smoked cooked bits of haddock or other smoked fish. Served on a slice of sautéed white bread, they are a delicate and inexpensive appetizer, or even a light supper dish.

A perfectly poached egg is another elegant and creative way to present the egg. Interestingly, many Americans are familiar with and love Eggs Benedict. Brennans, a restaurant in New Orleans, has made its reputation on this marvelous combination of poached eggs, sautéed ham, and English muffin topped with Hollandaise sauce. But there are innumerable ways to feature the poached egg—placed on a bed of braised spinach or warm ratatouille, on a purée of broccoli or peas, or topped with a mustard or tomato sauce and placed on a slice of sautéed ham or eggplant. Although I personally like poaching an egg in an egg poacher, these do not seem to be available everywhere and poaching an egg in a skillet is equally easy to do.

To poach, fill the skillet with water about 2 inches deep and add 1 teaspoon white wine vinegar. This will keep the egg from disintegrating during cooking. Bring the water to a boil and keep it fairly bubbling. In another saucepan bring water to a boil and add the whole, unshelled eggs for exactly 30 seconds but no more. Then break the eggs into the skillet and spoon the hot water over each egg until the whites are set. Using a slotted spoon, remove the egg to a double layer of paper towels and drain. Serve sprinkled with salt, a touch of pepper, and a little salted melted butter. Warming the eggs in hot water first gives them a rounded shape rather than the ragged shape so many poached eggs usually seem to have.

I was once told by a chef I worked with, "There is an egg for every season and a season for every egg." He was so right! Eggs can be made into robust hearty dishes perfect for winter cooking, but they can reflect the mood of other seasons as well. Summer cooking would be incomplete without hard-boiled eggs, but they need not be restricted to that time of year. I particularly like to serve them as part of an hors d'oeuvre table in the summer. I love them filled with a butter-and-fresh herb stuffing, or topped with either a green

mayonnaise or a dill-and-vinegar mayonnaise. It is unfortunate that many cooks have never mastered the art of cooking a hard-boiled egg and too often they cook it at a fast boil. Instead it should be simmered for 8 minutes and rolled back and forth several times to center the yolk, then plunged into cold water to stop any further cooking. There is really nothing simpler or less expensive to serve than a bowl of hard-boiled eggs, some fresh radishes, a bowl of olives, and possibly a good garlic sausage as a light hors d'oeuvre. Together with drinks or wine, this simple array of hors d'oeuvre is so much better than the now ubiquitous crackers and cheese.

In addition to standing up beautifully on their own, eggs also perform other indispensable functions in cooking— blending, leavening, enriching. In serving as a binder to many dishes (in combination with cream), they also make possible some of the most popular dishes. The best example is the classic French quiche or tart, one of the most versatile foods which has now become as familiar at brunches or on restaurant menus as the omelet. I love quiches of all kinds, and never tire of trying out new combinations of vegetables, fish, sausages, and cheese. The Zucchini and Basil Quiche on page 382 is my favorite summer quiche, while the Bacon and Cabbage Quiche (page 337) is a favorite for Sunday suppers and simple family dinners, often accompanied by a soup or peasant salad.

For many people, the most "difficult" aspect of the quiche is making the shell. Working with the dough takes some experience, mainly in achieving the right flakiness and evenness of the crust. The secret is not to overwork it, and a little practice should help you master rolling it out evenly. Again it helps if you have a chance to observe someone who can line a quiche pan properly. I highly recommend the porcelain quiche pan that does not require unmolding the quiche, and which you can serve from directly from the oven. Once mastered, the shell lets you be as creative as you like. If you look around the market, you are sure to come up with many new combinations for fillings. The porcelain pan is also useful for making a "flan," which is basically a quiche but without the pie crust. A flan is usually made from cooked, diced vegetables bound together with a custard and baked in a hot-water bath. It is an interesting way to serve a vegetable such as broccoli, spinach, or cauliflower, and it makes the perfect accompaniment to roasts or grilled meats.

Quiches, like crêpes, are extremely good-natured, and are one of the few dishes that can be frozen successfully. They can also be wonderfully seasonal and inexpensive to make, often calling for supermarket staples and requiring little of the cook's time. If you want to make the shell in advance, you can prepare it, freeze it, and then partially bake it the day you plan to fill it. The filling, whether it be onions, spinach, cabbage, or leeks, takes only minutes to prepare, and the best quiches are still those that are baked no more than one hour before serving.

The invention of the crêpe, like that of the quiche, has been made possible by the existence of the egg. Despite its fancy gourmet-sounding name, the crêpe is nothing more than a pancake made by combining eggs, milk, flour, and some melted butter. It can be used for both savory and sweet fillings and, depending on which one you are making, the batter is either flavored with salt or sugar; in dessert crêpes, a liqueur and some vanilla extract are added. Like the quiche, the crêpe is an important addition to your repertoire because it relies on supermarket ingredients and the staples of every serious cook's pantry. If you cook you are bound to have on hand all of the ingredients necessary to make crêpes. With a little ingenuity you can get many ingredients that will go into interesting and unusual fillings, whether you are serving the crêpes as an appetizer, main course, or for dessert.

As French as it sounds, the crêpe is used in many other countries as well. The Hungarian, or Viennese, palatschinka is a sweet crêpe usually filled either with apricot jam or lingonberries and served simply dusted with confectioner's sugar. The Italian crespelle is often filled with ricotta mixed with sautéed sausage meat, Parmesan cheese, and herbs and topped with either a white sauce or a tomato sauce. A sweet filling of ricotta, grated orange rind, and orange liqueur is also a favorite Italian dessert. Some crêpes, like the Russian blini, have become classics. This is a yeast pancake served almost invariably with either herrings, smoked fish, or on a special occasion caviar. I find this delicious, doughy pancake equally good with a Provençale filling of sautéed eggplant and tomatoes. Or serve it simply with a side bowl of melted garlic-and-anchovy butter.

When it comes to desserts, crêpes are even more versatile. They are the perfect envelopes for such fruits as bananas, apples, pears, strawberries, or raspberries. No food can carry a mixture of liqueurs as well as the crêpe, and you can be as adventurous and innovative as you like when varying the fillings.

To make crepes be sure to get a good pan and to season it carefully. Do not use the crêpe pan for anything else. Make them at your leisure on a day when you have little other cooking to do. If they are to be used within two days, they don't require freezing —they are much better when they have not been frozen. If you do plan to freeze the crêpes, place a sheet of waxed paper between each and then wrap the entire package (usually 12 to 16 crêpes) in thick heavy-duty foil. Freeze, and when ready to use, defrost without unwrapping. Then place in a low, 250-degree oven for 40 minutes, or until the crêpes are well heated through. A crêpe that has been frozen will usually have hard, crackly edges, and it is best used in a sauce or with plenty of melted butter and Parmesan cheese. I never top a crêpe with a cream sauce such as a béchamel, since I find that the combination

contains too much flour and makes the dish too heavy and pasty. Crêpes drizzled with melted butter, sprinkled with Parmesan, and baked covered for 20 minutes make an excellent, much lighter dish.

With today's soaring food prices, the versatile crêpe and quiche should play a major role in every serious cook's repertoire.

Scrambled Eggs
à la Danoise

Serves: **4 to 5**
Preparation time: **10 minutes**
Cooking time: **10 minutes**
Type of recipe: **elementary**
Cost: **moderate**

Egg dishes make wonderful starters to a meal and are often served as such both in France and the Scandinavian countries. Here is a lovely and light appetizer that combines creamy scrambled eggs with poached bay scallops and a sprinkling of fresh dill.

Ingredients
2 to 3 Tablespoons Clarified Butter (page 545)
1 Tablespoon oil
4 to 5 slices white bread, cut into ½ inch slices and crusts removed
2 cups Vegetable Stock (page 539)
1 cup fresh tiny bay scallops
6 large eggs
3 Tablespoons heavy cream
Salt and freshly ground white pepper
5 Tablespoons butter
2 Tablespoons finely minced fresh dill

Garnish:
Sprigs of fresh watercress

Optional:
2 to 3 Tablespoons red caviar

Preparation

1.
Melt the Clarified Butter and the oil in a large heavy skillet. Add the bread slices and sauté over medium heat until lightly browned on both sides. Remove the bread slices to individual serving plates.

2.
In a heavy saucepan heat the Vegetable Stock. Add the scallops and heat for 2 to 3 minutes without letting the stock come back to a boil. Cook just until the scallops turn an opaque white; do not overcook. With a slotted spoon remove the scallops to a side dish.

3.
In a bowl combine the eggs and cream. Season with salt and pepper and whisk the mixture until well blended.

4.
Heat 3 tablespoons butter in a heavy-bottomed 2-quart saucepan. When the butter is very hot, add the egg mixture, immediately reduce the heat, and whisk the eggs constantly until they start to set and form a thick custard with tiny curds.

5.
Immediately remove the pan from the heat and whisk in the remaining butter and the dill. Fold the scallops into the eggs.

6.
Place a large spoonful of the egg-and-scallop mixture onto each slice of fried bread. Garnish each plate with a sprig of fresh watercress and a dollop of the optional red caviar. Serve immediately.

Scrambled Eggs
with
Smoked Haddock

Serves: **4**
Preparation time: **5 minutes**
Cooking time: **5 minutes**
Type of recipe: **elementary**
Cost: **moderate**

Ingredients
8 large eggs
2 Tablespoons cream
Pinch of salt
Large grinding of black pepper
Dash of Tabasco sauce
1 to 1½ cups flaked smoked haddock
3 Tablespoons butter

Garnish:
½ cup cooked fresh peas, or 2
Tablespoons finely minced fresh chives

Optional:
Triangles of white bread, sautéed in butter

Preparation
1.
In a large bowl combine the eggs and cream. Season with salt, pepper and Tabasco sauce. Whip the mixture until well blended and fold in the smoked fish.
2.
Heat the butter in a 10-inch omelet pan or other heavy skillet. When the butter is hot and starts to foam add the egg mixture and cook over moderate-to-high heat for 2 to 3 minutes, scrambling the eggs with a fork to your favorite degree of doneness.
3.
Spoon the eggs onto a serving dish. Sprinkle with the peas or chives and serve accompanied by the sautéed bread. Serve immediately.

Remarks
I use leftover smoked fish for this dish. Be sure that the fish is warm. If it isn't, wrap it in foil and place in simmering water until the fish is heated through. This is a delicious brunch dish but can also be served as a simple supper accompanied by sautéed parslied potatoes.

Omelette
Corse

Serves: **2**
Preparation time: **5 minutes**
Cooking time: **5 minutes**
Type of recipe: **elementary**
Cost: **inexpensive**

Omelet-making is a technique that requires some practice and skill. However, there is a technique used in Spanish cooking which makes omelets even easier for the beginner. When making a omelet it is best to make them individually; that is, 1 omelet per person, each made with 2 or 3 eggs. The following recipe is for 2 individual omelets.

Ingredients

5 to 6 large eggs
4 Tablespoons fresh goat cheese, finely crumbled, or Greek feta cheese, crumbled
2 Tablespoons finely minced fresh mint
Salt and freshly ground black pepper
Dash of Tabasco sauce
2 Tablespoons butter
1 Tablespoon olive oil
½ to ¾ cup hot Tomato Sauce (page 543)

Preparation

1.
In a bowl combine the eggs, cheese, and mint. Mix the mixture until well blended. Season with salt, pepper, and Tabasco sauce.

2.
In a heavy 8-inch omelet pan heat 1 tablespoon butter and 1 teaspoon olive oil. When the butter is very hot and the foams starts to subside add half the egg mixture. Cook the omelet for 2 minutes, letting the eggs settle and lightly brown, then stir with a fork until the eggs start to form a thick mass. Tilt the pan lightly away from you with a spatula and fold the omelet mixture over toward the center. Prod the part closest to you, pushing the omelet toward the far end of the skillet, then jerk the pan roughly so that the omelet folds back onto itself.

3.
Turn the omelet onto a plate and keep warm while you make the second (again buttering the skillet and adding the remaining olive oil).

4.
Place 2 to 3 tablespoons hot Tomato Sauce around each omelet and serve immediately accompanied by crusty French bread and a bowl of sweet butter.

Summer
Frittata

Serves: **6**
Preparation time: **20 minutes**
Cooking time: **25 minutes**
Type of recipe: **elementary**
Cost: **inexpensive**

The frittata is a popular dish in Spain and Italy as well as in southern France. Most cooks in every region have their own favorite versions of this simple egg dish. Since it leaves great room for creativity, you may vary the frittata according to what is fresh at the market or what you have on hand in your pantry or vegetable bin.

Ingredients
8 large eggs
Salt
Freshly ground black pepper
Dash of Tabasco sauce
1 cup finely cubed slab bacon
4 Tablespoons olive oil
1 small onion, thinly sliced
1 clove garlic, crushed
1 small green pepper, cored and cubed
3 Tablespoons diced pimientos
2 small zucchini, finely cubed
2 to 3 medium new potatoes, cooked, peeled, and cubed
2 Tablespoons freshly grated Parmesan cheese

Preparation
1.
Preheat the oven to 350 degrees.
2.
In a large bowl place the eggs, season with salt and pepper, and add a dash of Tabasco. Whisk until thoroughly blended and set aside.
3.
In a 10-inch cast-iron skillet sauté the bacon cubes until almost browned. Remove with a slotted spoon to a side dish and reserve.

4.
Discard all but 1 tablespoon fat from the pan. Add 2 tablespoons olive oil, then add the onion and garlic and cook until the onion is soft and lightly browned.
5.
Add the green pepper, pimientos, and zucchini, season with salt and pepper, then cover the skillet and cook the mixture for 5 to 6 minutes, or until the vegetables are tender.
6.
Add the potatoes and bacon. Cook for another 2 or 3 minutes.
7.
Pour the egg mixture into the pan. Increase the heat and cook for 2 or 3 minutes until the eggs are lightly set.
8.
Sprinkle with Parmesan cheese. Set the pan in the oven and bake for 5 to 7 minutes, or until the eggs are completely set.
9.
Serve the frittata, cutting wedges right from the pan.

Remarks
The frittata is also good served cold as an appetizer.

Tchatchouka
(Rumanian Peppers
and Eggs)

Serves:	**4 to 6**
Preparation time:	**25 minutes**
Cooking time:	**1 hour**
Type of recipe:	**elementary**
Cost:	**inexpensive**

The tchatchouka is a Rumanian dish similar to the Basque pipérade. It is an excellent light supper dish. You may add sautéed link sausages or some thick slices of sautéed bacon. It is equally good cold. Serve with hard-boiled eggs, flaked tuna, and Greek black olives.

Ingredients
6 Tablespoons fruity olive oil
1 dried hot chili pepper
2 large onions, thinly sliced
2 cloves garlic, peeled and crushed
Salt and freshly ground black pepper
1 can (35 ounces) Italian plum tomatoes, well drained and with 1 cup tomato juice reserved
3 Roasted Red Peppers (page 545), thinly sliced
3 large Roasted Green Peppers (page 545), thinly sliced
1 teaspoon dried thyme
1 bay leaf
6 large eggs

Garnish:
Finely minced fresh parsley

Preparation
1.
In a heavy 10-inch skillet heat 3 tablespoons oil. Add the chili pepper, onions, and garlic. Sauté over high heat for 10 minutes, or until the onions are lightly browned. Season with salt and pepper and stir the onions with a wooden spoon. Reduce the heat, partially cover the skillet, and cook the onions for 30 minutes, or until soft and nicely browned. Be careful not to burn them.

2.
Add the tomatoes to the pan together with the peppers. Bring to a boil and season with salt and pepper, thyme, and bay leaf. Cover the skillet and simmer the mixture for 10 or 15 minutes. If the mixture seems to get too dry add some of the reserved tomato juice. Taste and correct the seasoning.

3.
Transfer the vegetable mixture to a rectangular serving dish and keep warm.

4.
In another heavy skillet heat the remaining oil. Break 4 eggs into it carefully, reduce the heat, and fry the eggs until the whites are set. Season with salt and pepper.

5.
With a spatula carefully transfer the eggs to the serving dish, placing them on top of the vegetable mixture. Fry the remaining eggs and add to the dish. Sprinkle with parsley and serve immediately accompanied by crusty French bread.

Remarks
The pepper-and-tomato mixture can be prepared several days ahead and refrigerated. Reheat it in a covered au gratin dish in a 250-degree oven.

Cheese and Asparagus "Pâté"

Serves: **4**
Preparation time: **30 minutes**
Cooking time: **1 hour**
Type of recipe: **elementary**
Cost: **inexpensive**

Ingredients
10 thin fresh asparagus
2 Tablespoon freshly grated Parmesan cheese

Soufflé:
3 Tablespoons butter
3 Tablespoons sifted all-purpose flour
1 cup hot milk
4 large eggs, separated
Salt and freshly ground white pepper
⅓ cup freshly grated Gruyère
3 Tablespoons freshly grated Parmesan cheese
3 Tablespoons freshly grated Danish fontina cheese

Optional:
1 cup Basic Hollandaise (page 545)

Preparation
1.
Remove the asparagus bottoms and scrape the stalks with a vegetable peeler. Tie them in a bundle.
2.
In a large saucepan bring salted water to a boil. Cook the asparagus for 12 to 15 minutes, or until tender. Drain and place on a double layer of paper towels.
3.
Preheat the oven to 375 degrees.
4.
Butter a 1½-quart loaf pan, sprinkle with Parmesan, shake out the excess, and set aside.
5.
Prepare the soufflé. In a heavy saucepan add the butter and melt over low heat. Add

the flour and blend thoroughly with a wooden spoon. Cook the mixture, stirring constantly for 2 or 3 minutes without letting it brown. Add the hot milk all at once and whisk the mixture constantly over medium heat until it is thick and completely smooth.
6.
Remove the saucepan from the heat. Add the egg yolks, 1 at a time, incorporating each yolk completely before adding the next. Season the mixture with salt and pepper and add the Gruyère, the Parmesan and the fontina. Set aside.
7.
In a large stainless steel mixing bowl beat the egg whites with a pinch of salt until they form soft peaks. Fold the soufflé base into the egg whites by hand in order not to break the air pockets.
8.
Place ¾ of the soufflé mixture into the prepared pan, place the asparagus stalks lengthwise on top of the mixture, and spread the remaining soufflé mixture on top of the asparagus. Place the dish in the oven and immediately turn down the heat to 350 degrees. Bake the soufflé for 35 minutes.
9.
Remove the soufflé from the oven and let cool on a wire rack. Once it is cool loosen the sides with a sharp knife and carefully unmold onto a rectangular serving dish.
10.
Slice the "pâté" into ¼-inch slices and serve at room temperature, accompanied by the optional Hollandaise.

Blue Cheese Soufflés
in
Spinach Sauce

Serves: **6 to 8**
Preparation time: **15 minutes**
Cooking time: **25 minutes**
Type of recipe: **elementary**
Cost: **inexpensive**

Ingredients

6 ounces cream cheese
3 large eggs, plus 3 yolks
½ cup heavy cream
4 Tablespoons Gorgonzola cheese, or other good quality blue cheese (mild Roquefort or Pipo Crèm')
4 Tablespoons butter
2 Tablespoons freshly grated Parmesan cheese
Salt and freshly ground white pepper

Sauce:

2 cups tightly packed fresh spinach, well rinsed and stemmed
3 Tablespoons butter
1½ cups heavy cream
3 Tablespoons freshly grated Parmesan cheese
Salt and freshly ground black pepper

Optional:
Bits of Beurre Manié (page 544)

Garnish:
Sprigs of fresh watercress

Preparation

1.
Preheat the oven to 350 degrees.

2.
Butter 6 to 8 four-ounce ramekins. Line the bottoms with buttered waxed paper and set aside.

3.
In a large saucepan bring salted water to boil. Add the spinach and cook for 2 to 3 minutes or until wilted. Drain the spinach and, when cool enough to handle, chop finely and set aside.

4.
In a food processor or blender combine the cream cheese, whole eggs, yolks, and cream and blend well. Blend the Gorgonzola or other blue cheese with the butter into a smooth paste, then add the paste to the processor or blender together with the Parmesan. Season with salt and pepper, then blend well.

5.
Spoon the mixture into the ramekins and place them into a large baking dish. Pour boiling water into the dish until it reaches halfway up the sides of the ramekins. Cover the dish with a sheet of buttered waxed paper and place the pan in the oven. Bake for 20 to 25 minutes, or until the tops of the soufflés are lightly browned and a knife comes out clean when inserted.

6.
While the ramekins are baking, make the sauce. Melt the butter in a heavy skillet over low heat and add the cream. Bring to a boil and cook until the cream is slightly reduced, or for about 3 to 4 minutes. Whisk in a bit of the optional Beurre Manié; you

Bacon and Cabbage
Quiche

Serves:	**6**
Preparation time:	**20 minutes**
Cooking time:	**1 hour**
Type of recipe:	**elementary**
Cost:	**inexpensive**

will need only about ¼ of the butter ball.
Stir the sauce until it heavily coats a spoon,
then add the spinach and the Parmesan
cheese. Season with salt and pepper. Keep
the sauce warm.

7.
When the soufflés are done, unmold them
onto individual serving plates. Spoon a little
of the spinach sauce around each soufflé.
Garnish each with a sprig of fresh
watercress and serve hot as an appetizer
accompanied by crusty French bread and a
bowl of sweet butter.

Remarks
The cheese soufflés can be prepared
several hours in advance, unmolded, and
reheated in an ovenproof serving dish in a
250-degree oven. Cover the soufflés,
placing them in the center of the oven, and
put a pan of hot water on the lower rack so
as to prevent the soufflés from sticking to
the serving dish. The spinach sauce can be
prepared the day before and reheated.

Ingredients
1 small head cabbage, approximately
1½ to 2 pounds
2 Tablespoons butter
½ pound slab bacon, cut into small
cubes
1 onion, peeled and finely minced
Salt and freshly ground black
pepper
3 large eggs
1 cup heavy cream
¾ cup coarsely shredded Gruyère or
imported Swiss cheese
1 nine-inch partially baked Basic Tart
Shell (page 483), in a deep porcelain
quiche pan
¼ cup freshly grated Parmesan
cheese

Preparation
1.
Discard the outer leaves of the cabbage
and quarter the head.
2.
In a large saucepan bring salted water to a
boil. Add the cabbage and cook for 8 to 10
minutes. Drain and, when cool enough to
handle, squeeze out all the excess moisture
from the cabbage.
3.
Slice crosswise into ½-inch slices. Reserve
3 cups of the shredded cabbage and set
aside.
4.
In a large cast-iron skillet melt the butter.
Add the bacon cubes and sauté until lightly
browned but not crisp. With a slotted spoon
remove the bacon cubes to a side dish and
reserve.

Eggplant Quiche Nîmoise

Serves:	**6**
Preparation time:	**30 minutes, plus 2–4 hours to drain eggplant**
Cooking time:	**1 hour**
Type of recipe:	**elementary**
Cost:	**inexpensive**

5.
Remove all but 2 tablespoons fat from the pan. Add the onion and sauté from 2 to 3 minutes, or until lightly browned.

6.
Add the shredded cabbage and bacon cubes. Season with salt and pepper, reduce the heat, and simmer the mixture for 5 to 6 minutes. Set aside.

7.
Preheat the oven to 350 degrees.

8.
In a large bowl combine the eggs with the cream and blend thoroughly. Add the bacon and cabbage mixture together with the Gruyère or Swiss cheese and blend the mixture thoroughly. Taste and correct the seasoning, adding a large grinding of black pepper. Be careful not to salt too much since the bacon adds saltiness to the mixture.

9.
Pour the cabbage and custard into the quiche pan. Sprinkle with the Parmesan cheese and place in the center of the oven. Bake for 30 to 40 minutes, or until the custard has set and the top is nicely browned.

10.
Let the quiche cool for 10 minutes before serving. Serve directly from the porcelain quiche pan accompanied by a well-seasoned green salad.

Ingredients
1 medium eggplant, peeled and cut into 1-inch cubes
Salt
½ to ¾ cup olive oil
3 medium onions, peeled and thinly sliced
Freshly ground black pepper
4 large ripe tomatoes, peeled, seeded, and finely chopped
1 Tablespoon tomato paste
½ teaspoon dried oregano
½ teaspoon dried thyme
2 Tablespoons finely minced fresh basil
3 large eggs
2 Tablespoons coarsely grated Parmesan cheese
Dash of Tabasco sauce
1 nine-inch partially baked Basic Tart Shell (page 483)

Garnish:
6 to 8 flat anchovy fillets
Strips of pimientos
Greek black olives

Preparation

1.
Sprinkle the eggplant cubes with salt and let them drain in a colander for 2 to 4 hours. Dry thoroughly with paper towels.

2.
Preheat the oven to 375 degrees.

3.
In a large heavy skillet heat 4 tablespoons oil. Add the eggplant cubes and sauté over medium heat until nicely browned on all sides. You may need a little more oil. With a slotted spoon remove the eggplant cubes to a colander and reserve.

4.
Add 2 more tablespoons oil to the pan. Add the onions. Season with salt and pepper, partially cover the skillet, and cook over low heat for 30 minutes, stirring them several times to ensure even browning. The onions should be very soft and nicely browned.

5.
Add the tomatoes, tomato paste, oregano, thyme, and basil. Bring to a boil, season with salt and pepper, and cook over high heat until the tomato water has evaporated and the mixture is thick.

6.
Return the eggplant to the skillet. Taste and correct the seasoning. Remove the skillet from the heat and set aside.

7.
In a bowl whisk the eggs until well blended. Add the cheese, salt, pepper, and Tabasco. Fold the egg mixture into the eggplant mixture.

8.
Spoon the eggplant filling into the tart shell. Place the quiche on a baking sheet and bake for 30 minutes or until set and nicely browned.

9.
Remove the quiche from the oven and slide onto a serving platter. Garnish with anchovy fillets and pimientos, placing a black olive on each round. Serve the quiche at room temperature as an appetizer or as a luncheon or light supper dish.

Remarks
The filling can be prepared a day or so in advance. The eggs, however, should not be added to the filling until just before baking. For variation you can add 1 grilled red or green pepper, peeled and diced, to the filling.

Quiche of Sole
Parisienne

Serves:	**6**
Preparation time:	**45 minutes**
Cooking time:	**1 hour**
Type of recipe:	**elementary**
Cost:	**moderate**

Here is an excellent supper dish that combines the technique of a simple tart with a somewhat more elaborate filling. A deep porcelain quiche pan should be used. You may substitute fresh salmon or red snapper fillets for the sole.

Ingredients

5 Tablespoons butter
1 Tablespoon finely minced shallots
1½ cups Fish Stock (page 536)
1 Bouquet Garni (page 546)
2 small fillets of sole, about ¾ pound
Salt and freshly ground white pepper
4½ Tablespoons flour
3 egg yolks, plus 2 egg whites
½ cup heavy cream
1 nine-inch partially baked Basic Tart Shell, in a deep porcelain quiche pan (page 483)

Preparation

1.
Preheat the oven to 350 degrees.

2.
Heat 2 tablespoons butter in a medium flameproof baking dish. Add the shallots and cook over low heat for 2 to 3 minutes without browning. Add the stock and bouquet.

3.
Season the fillets with salt and pepper. Place in the baking dish, cover with buttered foil, and return the baking dish to low heat. Simmer the fillets for 5 to 6 minutes, or until they turn an opaque white. Carefully remove the fillets to a double layer of paper towels and reserve.

4.
Strain the stock into a saucepan. Place the saucepan over high heat and reduce the stock to 1 cup.

5.
In a heavy-bottomed saucepan heat the remaining butter and add the flour. Cook over low heat without browning, stirring constantly for 2 minutes. Add the reserved hot stock all at once and whisk until the sauce is smooth and thick.

6.
Add egg yolks and heavy cream and whisk the sauce until thoroughly blended. Season with salt and pepper and simmer for another 2 to 3 minutes without letting the sauce come to a boil. Remove from the heat.

7.
Beat the egg whites with a pinch of salt until stiff but not dry. Fold the beaten egg whites lightly into the sauce and set aside.

Sorrel Quiche

Serves: **6**
Preparation time: **25 minutes**
Cooking time: **1 hour**
Type of recipe: **elementary**
Cost: **inexpensive**

8.
Break the fillets into small pieces and place in 1 layer in the tart shell. Top with the prepared sauce and place the tart on a baking dish. Bake for 50 minutes, or until the top is nicely browned and the tip of a sharp knife comes out clean.

9.
Remove from the oven and serve the quiche hot as an appetizer or as light supper dish.

Remarks
The quiche can be prepared entirely in advance and reheated in a 250-degree oven for 30 to 45 minutes. It cannot be frozen. You might also try a combination of fish or finely minced, cooked shellfish such as shrimp and mussels. These should be incorporated into the sauce before spooning it into the tart shell.

Sorrel has become the "chic" vegetable of French cooking in recent years. It is almost always combined with fish and eggs. It is, however, a vegetable that has been around for many years and has been used in many interesting ways, such as in this unusual quiche.

Ingredients

1 pound fresh sorrel
3 Tablespoons butter
3 Tablespoons finely minced scallions (both white and green)
Salt and freshly ground white pepper
3 large eggs
1¼ cup heavy cream
½ cup finely grated Gruyère, or a mixture of Gruyère and Parmesan
1 nine-inch partially baked Basic Tart Shell (page 483)

Preparation
1.
Preheat the oven to 350 degrees.

2.
Stem the sorrel and wash thoroughly in cold water. Place the sorrel leaves in a saucepan, bring to a boil, and cook the sorrel for 3 to 4 minutes, or until it is reduced to a purée. Drain in a colander and mince finely. Set aside.

3.
In a small heavy skillet heat the butter, add the scallions, and cook over low heat until soft but not browned. Add the sorrel, season with salt and pepper, and cook the mixture for 3 to 4 minutes, or until the moisture has evaporated. Transfer to a mixing bowl.

Zucchini and Basil
Quiche

Serves:	**6**
Preparation time:	**30 minutes**
Cooking time:	**1 hour**
Type of recipe:	**elementary**
Cost:	**inexpensive**

4.
In a bowl combine the eggs and cream.
Season with salt and pepper, add the grated
cheese, and whisk the mixture until well
blended. Combine with the sorrel mixture
and blend thoroughly.

5.
Pour the mixture into the tart shell and set
in the center of the oven. Bake for 40
minutes, or until the top is nicely browned
and the tip of the knife comes out clean.

6.
Remove from the oven and serve the quiche
warm as an appetizer or as a luncheon dish.

Remarks
You can prepare the quiche several hours
in advance up to the point of baking. It is
best to bake the quiche no more than 30
minutes before serving. The sorrel purée
can be cooked several days ahead and
refrigerated. Sorrel can also be frozen for 2
to 3 months.

Ingredients
1 medium zucchini, grated
Salt
**1 nine-inch partially baked Basic Tart
Shell (page 483)**
2 Tablespoons butter
**½ cup finely minced scallions, greens
included**
1¼ cups heavy cream
3 large eggs
**4 Tablespoons freshly grated Parmesan
cheese**
Freshly ground black pepper
**2 Tablespoons basil leaves, cut into fine
julienne strips**

Papanas aux Fines Herbes

Serves:	**4 to 6**
Preparation time:	**10 minutes, plus 1 hour to rest batter**
Cooking time:	**10 minutes**
Type of recipe:	**elementary**
Cost:	**inexpensive**

Papanas are Rumanian pancakes similar to the Russian blini but much lighter in texture and less filling. Serve these delicious pancakes as an appetizer or light supper dish.

Ingredients
8 ounces cream cheese
1 cup light cream
4 large eggs, separated
1 cup flour
Salt and freshly ground black pepper
2 to 3 Tablespoons finely minced fresh chives
1 Tablespoon finely minced fresh parsley
3 to 4 Tablespoons butter, plus 3 Tablespoons melted butter
1 Tablespoon oil

Garnish:
1½ cups Crème Fraîche (page 544)
2 Tablespoons minced fresh chives

Optional:
4 ounces finely minced smoked salmon, or 3 ounces red caviar

Preparation
1.
In a blender or food processor combine the cream cheese and cream. Blend the mixture at high speed until smooth.
2.
Add the yolks and flour and blend again until smooth.
3.
Pour the mixture into a bowl. Season with salt, pepper, and herbs. Whisk in the melted butter and reserve.

Preparation
1.
Preheat the oven to 350 degrees.
2.
Place the grated zucchini in a colander, sprinkle with salt, and let it drain in a bowl for 25 minutes.
3.
In a small skillet heat the butter. Add the scallions and zucchini and cook the mixture for 2 to 3 minutes. Remove from the heat and reserve.
4.
In a bowl combine the cream and eggs and whisk the mixture until smooth. Add 2 tablespoons Parmesan cheese, salt, and pepper. Add the basil and the zucchini mixture and blend well. Taste and correct the seasoning.
5.
Transfer the mixture to the tart shell. Sprinkle with the remaining Parmesan and set in the center of the oven. Bake for 40 to 50 minutes, or until the quiche is set and nicely browned.
6.
Serve the quiche warm or at room temperature accompanied by thinly sliced tomatoes seasoned with olive oil and vinegar and sprinkled with finely minced basil.

Prune and Bacon
Flan

Serves: **6 to 8**
Preparation time: **10 minutes**
Cooking time: **1 hour, 15 minutes**
Type of recipe: **elementary**
Cost: **inexpensive**

4.
In a stainless steel bowl beat the whites with a pinch of salt until they form stiff peaks.

5.
With a wooden spoon fold the whites into the batter. Do not overmix. Set aside for 1 hour.

6.
Preheat the oven to 200 degrees.

7.
In a large heavy skillet heat 2 tablespoons butter with a little oil. With a small ladle spoon enough of the batter into the pan to make a 4- to 5-inch pancake. Do not crowd the pan. You may only be able to make 2 pancakes at a time.

8.
Cook the pancakes until nicely browned on both sides. Remove to an ovenproof platter and keep warm while continuing to cook the remaining pancakes. You will need more butter and oil.

9.
In a bowl combine the Crème Fraîche, chives, and optional smoked salmon or caviar and blend well. Season the mixture with salt and pepper and set aside.

10.
Serve the pancakes warm with a side dish of the Crème Fraîche mixture.

Ever since I came across this unusual dish in a small restaurant in the southwest region of France it has been one of my favorite accompaniments to roast pork, duck, or turkey. This flan can be made a day in advance and it is excellent reheated the next day.

Ingredients
1 cup finely cubed slab bacon
1 package (1 pound) pitted prunes
4 large eggs
¼ cup flour
¾ cups milk
¾ cup heavy cream
Salt and freshly ground white pepper
Large grinding of nutmeg
2 Tablespoons butter or duck fat

Spinach and Bacon Tart

Serves:	**6 to 8**
Preparation time:	**35 minutes**
Cooking time:	**1 hour, 30 minutes**
Type of recipe:	**intermediate**
Cost:	**inexpensive**

Preparation

1.
Preheat the oven to 350 degrees.

2.
In a saucepan bring water to a boil. Add the bacon cubes and cook for 2 to 3 minutes. Drain and dry on paper towels and set aside.

3.
In a saucepan combine the prunes with hot water to cover. Bring to a boil, reduce the heat, and simmer the prunes for 10 minutes. Drain and set aside.

4.
In a bowl combine the eggs and flour and whisk the mixture until smooth. Add the milk and cream and blend thoroughly. Season with salt, pepper, and nutmeg and set aside.

5.
In a large heavy skillet heat the butter or duck fat. Add the bacon and sauté over medium heat until almost crisp.

6.
Discard all but 2 tablespoons fat from the skillet. Add the drained prunes and blend with the bacon. Simmer the mixture for 2 to 4 minutes over low heat.

7.
Transfer the prunes and bacon to a rectangular baking dish. Pour the mixture into the dish and spread to 1 thin layer. Pour the egg-cream mixture on top. Place in the center part of the oven and bake 35 to 40 minutes, or until the tip of a knife comes out clean and the top is lightly browned.

8.
Remove the dish from the oven and let cool slightly before serving. Serve the flan right from the baking dish.

Ingredients

1 batch of dough for Basic Tart Shell (page 483)
2 packages (10 ounces) fresh spinach, well rinsed
Salt
2 large eggs
½ cup heavy cream
1 teaspoon Dijon mustard
Freshly ground black pepper
Large grinding of nutmeg
½ pound slab bacon, finely diced
4 Tablespoons butter
½ cup finely minced scallions (both green and white parts)
2 cloves garlic, finely minced
Egg wash made with 1 egg beaten with 1 Tablespoon water

Preparation

1.
Preheat the oven to 350 degrees.

2.
Cut the dough in half and roll out 2 circles. One circle should be 10 inches in diameter, the other should be 9 inches.

3.
Line a 9-inch quiche pan with the larger circle of dough. Place a sheet of waxed paper over the dough and fill with dried beans. Bake for 15 minutes or until the dough is set. Remove the paper and return the dough to the oven. Bake for 5 more minutes. Remove from the oven and cool.

4.
In a large heavy casserole combine the spinach with ½ cup water. Season with salt, bring to a boil, reduce the heat, and cook the spinach until completely wilted. Drain the spinach in a colander, pressing down to extract all the water. Transfer the spinach to a cutting board, let it cool, and then mince finely. Set aside.

5.
In a small bowl combine the eggs, cream, and mustard. Whisk the mixture until well blended, then season with salt, pepper, and nutmeg and set aside.

6.
In a small saucepan bring water to boil. Add the bacon and cook for 2 or 3 minutes. Drain and dry thoroughly on paper towels. Set aside.

7.
In a large skillet heat the butter. Add all but 2 tablespoons bacon and sauté until almost crisp. With a slotted spoon remove the bacon to a side dish.

8.
Add the scallions and garlic to the skillet and cook over low heat until soft but not browned. Add the spinach and cook over low heat for 3 to 4 minutes, or until thoroughly heated through. Season with salt and pepper.

9.
Place the mixture in a mixing bowl and add the sautéed bacon and the egg-and-cream mixture. Stir the spinach mixture thoroughly. Taste and correct the seasoning.

10.
Pour the mixture into the tart shell and let it cool completely. Top the tart with the remaining circle of pastry and seal the edges with the back of a knife. Make a small hole in the crust to allow steam to escape. Inser t the remaining bacon bits into the dough.

11.
Brush the dough with the egg wash and place the tart in the oven. Bake for 60 minutes. If the top gets too brown cover with a sheet of foil. Serve the tart warm or at room temperature, as an appetizer or luncheon dish.

Sausage, Ricotta, and Spinach Pie

Serves: **6**
Preparation time: **30 minutes**
Cooking time: **1 hour, 30 minutes**
Type of recipe: **elementary**
Cost: **moderate**

Ingredients

1 pound fresh spinach, well rinsed and stemmed
2 Tablespoons olive oil
2 Tablespoons butter
½ pound Italian sausage, casings removed (preferably spicy or hot)
1 onion, peeled and finely minced
1 large clove garlic, finely minced
1½ cups ricotta cheese
2 large eggs
½ cup freshly grated Parmesan cheese
¼ cup finely minced fresh parsley
¼ cup heavy cream
Salt and freshly ground black pepper
1 batch dough for Basic Tart Shell (page 483)
Egg wash made with 1 egg beaten with 2 Tablespoons water

Preparation

1.
Preheat the oven to 350 degrees.

2.
In a large saucepan bring salted water to a boil. Add the spinach and cook for 2 to 3 minutes, or until just wilted. Drain thoroughly and, when cool enough to handle, chop finely and set aside.

3.
In a large cast-iron skillet heat the oil and 1 tablespoon butter. Add the sausage meat and break it up with a fork. Sauté the meat until nicely browned. With a slotted spoon remove from the pan to a mixing bowl.

4.
Reduce the heat and add the onion and garlic. Sauté for 2 minutes without browning. Add the spinach and remaining butter and continue sautéing over low heat for 2 to 3 minutes, or until the spinach is well heated through.

5.
Transfer the mixture to a bowl. Add the ricotta cheese, eggs, Parmesan cheese, parsley, and cream and blend thoroughly. Season with salt and pepper.

6.
Roll out the pastry dough into 2 ten-inch circles. Line a deep 9-inch porcelain quiche pan. Prick the dough in several places with a fork and spoon the filling into the pan, smoothing it with a spatula.

7.
Top with the second circle of dough. Pinch together around the rim, removing any excess dough, and make a small hole in the center to allow steam to escape. Brush the dough with the egg wash.

8.
Place the dish on a baking sheet and set in the center of the oven. Bake for 50 to 60 minutes, then let the pie rest for 10 minutes before serving.

9.
Serve the pie warm as a light supper dish accompanied simply by a well-seasoned salad.

Entrée
Crêpes

Yields:	**16 to 18 crêpes**
Preparation time:	**10 minutes, plus 30 minutes**
	to 1 hour to rest batter
Cooking time:	**35 to 40 minutes**
Type of recipe:	**elementary**
Cost:	**inexpensive**

There are few foods as ingenious as a crêpe. Not only is it easy and inexpensive to make but it can be used at any part of the meal. A warm spinach crêpe filled with a mixture of cream cheese and sour cream, fresh herbs, and a spoonful of caviar is one of my favorite starters to a meal. The gutsy ricotta-and-sausage-filled crêpe on page 395 is perfect for a simple dinner, and the light Dessert Crêpes (see page 494) lend themselves to endless fillings. Many poached and sautéed fruits, such as apples, pears and bananas are wonderful with crêpes.

The consistency and thickness of a crêpe varies greatly according to what you plan to use it for. Entrée crêpes should be somewhat thicker in order to hold their filling. A dessert crêpe that is not to be filled should be made of a very light batter and be as thin as possible.

Ingredients

1¾ cups sifted all-purpose flour
4 large eggs
1 cup milk
1 cup water
Large pinch of salt
Freshly ground white pepper
¼ cup butter

Preparation

1.
Starting with the flour and eggs, then adding the milk, water, and seasoning, combine all the ingredients except the butter in a blender or food processor. Blend the mixture at high speed, scraping down the sides of the container any flour that may have stuck to it.

2.
In a small saucepan melt the butter. Let the butter cool slightly and then whisk it into the batter. Transfer the batter to a bowl and let it relax for 30 minutes to 1 hour.

3.
Brush the surface of a well-seasoned crêpe pan with a little melted butter. Place the pan over moderate-to-high heat and when the pan is very hot add a spoonful of batter; add just enough to coat the bottom of the pan. Tilt the pan back and forth to cover the surface evenly. Pour any surplus batter back into the bowl. Cook for 1 to 2 minutes, then loosen it with the tip of a sharp knife.

4.
When lightly browned turn the crêpe over with your fingers or spatula and lightly brown the other side. Slide the finished crêpe onto a plate and continue making the crêpes brushing the crêpe pan with a little butter after every 3 to 4 crêpes.

Remarks

Before using a crêpe pan for the first time season it as follows: sprinkle the pan with a thick layer of salt, then cover the salt with 1 inch of vegetable oil. Set the pan over high heat and heat the oil until it is almost smoky. Pour the very hot oil, together with the salt, out of the pan into a clean dry bowl. Wipe the crêpe pan with a large wad of paper towels, using enough paper towels so as not to burn your hand. Wipe the pan thoroughly until the surface is smooth and

Crêpes Fines Herbes
(Herb Crêpes)

Yields:	**20 to 24 crêpes**
Preparation time:	**10 minutes, plus 1 hour to rest batter**
Cooking time:	**35 to 40 minutes**
Type of recipe:	**elementary**
Cost:	**inexpensive**

not a grain of salt remains. The first crêpe is often not successful and may probably have to be discarded. This, however, is a good way to test your batter. If the test crêpe is too thick you may want to add a little more milk or water to your batter. After making 2 to 3 crêpes be sure to brush the pan with a little butter, wiping it again so it is quite smooth. Be sure to regulate your heat so that your crêpes do not burn. If the heat is properly regulated you will have no trouble turning the crêpes with your fingers. You can freeze these crêpes successfully (since they are heavier than dessert crêpes and will not dry out as much). Place a sheet of waxed paper between each and then wrap the entire package of crêpes in heavy-duty foil, making batches of 12 to 14 crêpes each. When needed, place the frozen crêpes in their foil wrapping in a 250-degree oven for 1 hour, 30 minutes to 2 hours, or until they are well heated through.

Ingredients

2 cups milk
1½ cups sifted all-purpose flour
4 large eggs
Large pinch of salt
Pinch of freshly ground white pepper
2 to 3 Tablespoons finely minced fresh herbs (parsley, chives, dill, or chervil or a mixture of parsley and chives or chives and dill)
5 Tablespoons cooled melted butter

Preparation

1.
Combine the milk, flour, eggs, salt, and pepper in a blender or food processor. Blend the mixture at high speed scraping down any flour that may stick to the sides of the container.

2.
Pour the batter into a bowl. Add the herbs and butter and whisk the mixture until well blended. Let the batter rest for an hour or 2 before making the crêpes.

Remarks
These crêpes freeze well and I usually make a large batch of herb-flavored crêpes at the end of the summer for winter use.

Spinach Crêpes

Yields:	**20 to 24 crepes**
Preparation time:	**15 minutes, plus 1 hour to rest batter**
Cooking time:	**45 minutes**
Type of recipe:	**elementary**
Cost:	**inexpensive**

Ingredients

2 cups tightly packed fresh spinach, well rinsed and stemmed
2 cups milk
1½ cups sifted all-purpose flour
3 large eggs
Pinch of salt
Large pinch of freshly ground white pepper
Pinch of freshly grated nutmeg
4 to 5 Tablespoons cooled melted butter

Preparation

1.
Place the spinach in a saucepan and cook over medium heat until completely wilted. Drain the spinach and, when cool enough to handle, squeeze into a ball between your hands to extract all the liquid.

2.
Transfer the spinach to a blender or food processor. Add 1 cup milk and blend the mixture until completely smooth.

3.
Add the remaining ingredients except the butter and blend at high speed until smooth.

4.
Transfer the mixture to a bowl, whisk in the butter and let the batter rest for 1 hour to 1 hour, 30 minutes before making the crêpes.

Remarks

A spinach crêpe freezes well and can be used in many dishes that call for basic crêpes.

Yeast Pancakes (Russian Blini)

Serves:	**4 to 5**
Preparation:	**10 minutes**
Cooking Time:	**10 minutes**
Type of recipe:	**elementary**
Cost:	**inexpensive**

Here is an easy version of the yeast pancake that is a classic in Russian cooking. They make a wonderful first course but can also be served for Sunday brunch or for dessert. Serve them as an appetizer accompanied by a bowl of sour cream flavored with finely minced fresh dill and chives and a dollop of either red or black caviar. You can also serve them with marinated herring, smoked salmon, or smoked whitefish. Personally I also like to serve these pancakes with a side dish of lingonberries and sugared Crème Fraîche.

Ingredients

1 package yeast
2 cups warm milk
2 cups sifted all-purpose flour
4 large eggs, separated
Pinch of granulated sugar
Pinch of salt
4 Tablespoons melted butter
2 Tablespoons butter, for sautéing

Omelette Crépes Forestière (Omelets with Mushroom and Dill Filling)

Serves:	**6**
Preparation time:	**10 minutes**
Cooking time:	**35 minutes**
Type of recipe:	**elementary**
Cost:	**inexpensive**

Preparation

1.
A couple of hours ahead combine the yeast with ⅓ cup warm but not hot water in a bowl and stir until dissolved. When the yeast starts to proof and bubble combine it with the warm milk, flour, egg yolks, sugar, and salt in a blender and blend until smooth.

2.
Transfer the mixture to a bowl. Cover it with a towel and put in a warm draft-free place until the batter doubles in volume, or for about 1 to 1½ hours.

3.
Beat the whites until they form unwavering peaks.

4.
Whisk the melted butter into the batter and then gently fold the egg whites into it. Cover the bowl again and let the batter rest for another 30 minutes.

5.
Heat a 10- to 12-inch cast-iron skillet. Brush it with butter. Add 2 to 3 tablespoons of the batter, making 2 to 3 small pancakes (each pancake should be about 2½ to 3 inches in diameter). Cook the pancakes over medium heat until they are lightly browned on one side and flip them over with a spatula. Cook for another 2 to 3 minutes on the other side and transfer to a serving platter and keep warm. Continue making the remaining pancakes buttering the skillet everytime before adding a spoonful of batter.

Remarks

Yeast pancakes have to be eaten fresh. They cannot be reheated or frozen.

Ingredients

4 large eggs
2 Tablespoons sifted all-purpose flour
2 Tablespoons heavy cream
¼ teaspoon salt
Freshly ground white pepper
1 to 2 Tablespoons butter

Filling:
2 Tablespoons butter
3 Tablespoons finely minced scallions (some greens included)
½ pound fresh mushrooms, stems removed, wiped, and cubed
Salt and freshly ground black pepper
1 cup sour cream
8 ounces cream cheese, softened
2 Tablespoons finely minced fresh dill
2 to 3 Tablespoons freshly grated Parmesan cheese
5 Tablespoons melted butter

Preparation

1.
Preheat the oven to 325 degrees.

2.
Start by making the filling. In a heavy skillet heat the butter over low heat. Add the scallions and cook for 2 minutes, or until just soft and not browned.

3.
Increase the heat, add the mushrooms, and sauté until lightly browned and the mushroom water has evaporated. Season with salt and pepper.

4.
In a bowl combine the sour cream and cream cheese and blend the mixture thoroughly with a fork. Add the mushrooms and dill and mix well. Taste the filling and correct the seasoning. Set aside.

5.
Prepare the omelets. In a bowl whisk the eggs together with the flour and cream until smooth and well blended. Season the mixture with salt and pepper.

6.
Heat a 6-inch crêpe pan. Butter it lightly and add a ladle of the egg mixture. Cook over medium heat until the omelet is set, tilting the pan back and forth while loosening the omelet with the tip of a sharp knife, and lifting it to let any extra batter seep underneath. The omelet should be quite thick. When the underneath is lightly browned, carefully turn the omelet with a spatula and cook for 1 to 2 minutes on the other side, or until lightly browned.

7.
Slip the omelet onto a plate and continue making the remaining 5 omelets, always brushing the pan with butter before adding the batter.

8.
When all the omelets are done, place a heaping tablespoon of the mushroom-and-dill mixture on each. Roll each up and place seam-side down in 1 layer in a well-buttered baking dish. Sprinkle with Parmesan and spoon the melted butter over them. Cover the dish with foil.

9.
Place the dish in the oven and bake for 25 minutes, or until the filling is just heated through. Serve immediately from the dish, as an appetizer or as a light supper dish.

Remarks
The entire dish can be prepared 2 to 3 hours ahead and set aside covered. Heat in a 300-degree oven for 30 to 40 minutes, or until the filling is just heated through.

Crêpes
aux
Fruits de Mer

Serves: **6**
Preparation time: **45 minutes**
Cooking time: **1 hour**
Type of recipe: **elementary**
Cost: **moderate**

Ingredients
12 Entrée Crêpes (page 388)
½ cup heavy cream
2 egg yolks

Filling:
3 pounds fresh mussels
2 cups concentrated Fish Stock (page 536)
3 Tablespoons finely minced shallots
1 Bouquet Garni (page 546)
½ pound medium fresh shrimp
4½ Tablespoons butter
2 Tablespoons shallots
2 tomatoes, peeled, seeded, and finely minced
1 teaspoon tomato paste
Salt and freshly ground black pepper
Pinch of dried thyme
Dash of cayenne pepper
3 Tablespoons flour

Preparation
1.
Preheat the oven to 350 degrees.
2.
Scrub the mussels thoroughly under cold running water. Remove their beards.
3.
In a large enamel saucepan combine the stock, shallots, bouquet, and mussels. Cover the saucepan and cook the mussels over moderate-to-high heat until they open. Discard those that have not opened. Drain the mussels and reserve the stock.
4.
Transfer the stock to a saucepan and add the shrimp. Bring to a boil and cook for 1 minute, or until the shrimp turn a bright pink. Remove the shrimp with a slotted spoon to a side dish and reserve. Cook the mussel stock until it is reduced to 2½ cups and reserve.
5.
In a small heavy skillet heat 1½ tablespoons butter. Add the shallots and cook for 1 to 2 minutes without browning. Add the tomatoes, bring to a boil, and cook the mixture until the tomato water has evaporated and the mixture is reduced to a thick purée. Add the tomato paste, season with salt, pepper, and thyme and add a small dash of cayenne pepper. Set aside.
6.
In a heavy 2-quart saucepan melt the remaining butter. Add the flour and cook without browning, stirring constantly for 2 to 3 minutes. Add the reserved mussel stock and bring to a boil, whisking the sauce until it is thick and smooth.

Omelette Crêpes
à l'Italienne

Serves:	**4 to 6**
Preparation time:	**15 minutes**
Cooking time:	**1 hour**
Type of recipe:	**elementary**
Cost:	**inexpensive**

7.
Spoon half the sauce into a bowl and add the tomato mixture.

8.
Shell the mussels and shrimp and remove the black rims around the mussels. Dice the shrimp and add both shellfish to the bowl. Blend the mixture carefully. Taste and correct the seasoning.

9.
Fill each crêpe with a little of the shellfish mixture. Place them seam-side down in a buttered baking dish and set aside.

10.
In a small bowl combine the cream and yolks and whisk the mixture until well blended. Add to the remaining sauce in the saucepan and blend thoroughly. Reheat the sauce over low heat whisking constantly. Do not let it come to a boil.

11.
Spoon the sauce over the crêpes and cover with foil.

12.
Place the crêpes in the center of the oven and bake for 20 minutes. Uncover and bake for another 10 minutes.

13.
If you wish, place the dish quickly under the broiler to brown the top. Serve directly from the baking dish.

Remarks
The entire dish can be assembled several hours ahead and baked 30 minutes before serving.

Ingredients
4 large eggs
2 Tablespoons sifted all-purpose flour
2 Tablespoons heavy cream
¼ teaspoon salt
Freshly ground white pepper
1 to 2 Tablespoons butter
3 Tablespoons freshly grated Parmesan cheese
1½ cups Tomato Sauce (page 543)

Filling:
1½ cups ricotta cheese
3 Tablespoons freshly grated Parmesan cheese
3 Tablespoons finely minced fresh parsley
2 Tablespoons finely minced fresh chives
3 Tablespoons heavy cream
Salt and freshly ground white pepper

Optional:
1 clove garlic, peeled and crushed

Preparation
1.
Preheat the oven to 325 degrees.

2.
Prepare the filling. In a bowl combine the ricotta and Parmesan cheese, parsley, chives, and cream. Blend the mixture with a fork and season carefully with salt and pepper. Add the optional garlic and set aside.

3.
In a bowl whisk the eggs together with the flour and cream until smooth and well blended. Season with salt and pepper.

Sausage Crêpes
With
Tomato Sauce (Ricca)

Serves:	**6**
Preparation time:	**15 minutes**
Cooking time:	**2 hours**
Type of recipe:	**elementary**
Cost:	**moderate**

4.
Heat a 6-inch crêpe pan or Teflon skillet. Brush lightly with butter and, when the butter is very hot, add a ladle of the egg-cream mixture. Cook over high heat until the omelet is set, tilting the pan back and forth. Loosen the omelet with the tip of a sharp knife and lift it to let any extra batter seep underneath. Cook the omelet until lightly browned. It should be quite thin. Carefully turn the omelet with a spatula and cook for 1 to 2 minutes on the other side, or until lightly browned.

5.
Slip the omelet onto a plate and continue making the remaining 5 omelets, always brushing the pan with a little butter before adding the batter.

6.
When all the omelets are done place a heaping tablespoon of the ricotta mixture on each. Roll each and place the omelets seam-down in 1 layer in a buttered baking dish.

7.
Sprinkle the dish with the Parmesan cheese and spoon the tomato sauce around them. Cover the dish.

8.
Place the baking dish in the oven and bake for 25 minutes, or until the filling is well heated through. Serve immediately directly from the dish.

Here is a dish somewhat similar in taste to the Italian canneloni. The lightness of the crêpes, however, gives the dish a more subtle and refined taste. Serve it as an appetizer, luncheon, or light supper dish.

Ingredients
12 to 14 Entrée Crêpes (page 388)
½ cup freshly grated Parmesan cheese

Sauce:
3 Tablespoons fruity olive oil
1 onion, peeled and finely minced
½ cup dry white wine
2 cloves garlic, finely minced
¼ cup finely minced fresh parsley
1 can (35 ounces) Italian plum tomatoes, chopped, plus packing juice
Salt and freshly ground black pepper
1 large sprig fresh oregano or 1 teaspoon dried
1 teaspoon dried thyme
1 bay leaf

Filling:
2 Tablespoons fruity olive oil
1 pound fresh hot sausage meat, casing removed
¼ cup finely minced onion
2 cloves garlic, finely minced
1¼ cups ricotta cheese
½ cup freshly grated Parmesan cheese
¼ cup finely minced fresh parsley
Salt and freshly ground black pepper

1.
Start by making the sauce. In a heavy
3-quart saucepan heat the oil. Add the
onion and sauté over low heat until soft but
not browned. Add the wine, bring to a boil,
and reduce to 2 tablespoons.

2.
Add the garlic, parsley, and tomatoes as
well as the tomato juice. Season with salt,
pepper, oregano, thyme, and bay leaf.
Partially cover the saucepan and simmer
the sauce until most of the tomato juices
have evaporated, or for about 1½ hours.
When the sauce is done transfer it to a food
processor or blender and purée until
smooth. Put the sauce in a saucepan and
keep warm.

3.
Preheat the oven to 350 degrees.

4.
Meanwhile prepare the filling. In a cast-iron
skillet heat the oil. Add the sausage meat
and break it up with a fork. Sauté over
high heat until the sausage is nicely
browned on all sides. With a slotted spoon
remove the sausage meat to a bowl and
reserve.

5.
Remove all but 2 tablespoons fat from the
pan and add the onion. Sauté over medium
heat until soft, scraping well the bottom of
the pan. Add the garlic and cook for
another minute. Remove the pan from the
heat and scrap the onion-and-garlic mixture
into the bowl with the sausage.

6.
Add the ricotta and Parmesan cheese and
the parsley and blend the mixture

thoroughly with a fork. Taste and correct
the seasoning.

7.
Place 2 tablespoons of the
sausage-and-ricotta mixture on each crêpe.
Roll the crêpes and place them side by
side, seam-side down in a well-buttered
rectangular baking dish. Spoon the tomato
sauce over the crêpes. Sprinkle with
additional Parmesan and bake covered for
25 minutes. Cool the crêpes slightly and
serve directly from the baking dish.

Remarks
The entire dish can be prepared several
hours ahead and reheated in the oven. If
the dish has been refrigerated you may
need 10 to 15 minutes more baking time.
The tomato sauce can be made several
weeks ahead and frozen. For variation you
can add 1 diced Roasted Red Pepper (page
545) to the sauce. You can also top each
crêpe with a thin slice of mozzarella cheese
and bake the crêpes until the cheese is just
melted. Serve the crêpes immediately.

Basil Crêpes
in
Tomato-and-Cream Sauce

Serves: **6**
Preparation time: **15 minutes**
Cooking time: **25 minutes**
Type of recipe: **elementary**
Cost: **inexpensive**

Ingredients
12 to 14 Entrée Crêpes (page 388)
½ cup melted butter
2 Tablespoons freshly grated
Parmesan cheese

Filling:
1 cup tightly packed fresh basil
leaves, all stems removed
2 cloves garlic, peeled and crushed
1 to 2 Tablespoons olive oil
1½ cups ricotta cheese
2 Tablespoons freshly grated
Parmesan cheese
1 large egg, plus 1 large yolk
Salt and freshly ground black
pepper
½ teaspoon dried oregano

Sauce:
1 cup Tomato Sauce (page 543)
½ cup heavy cream
3 to 4 fresh basil leaves, cut into thin
julienne strips
2 Tablespoons finely minced fresh
parsley

Preparation
1.
In a blender combine the basil leaves, garlic, and olive oil. Blend the mixture until smooth.

2.
In a mixing bowl combine the ricotta, Parmesan cheese, whole egg, and egg yolk. Mash the mixture until it is well blended and add the basil paste. Season with salt, pepper, and oregano, and set aside.

3.
Preheat the oven to 350 degrees.
4.
Place a spoonful of the filling on each crêpe. Roll them up and place them seam-side down in a well-buttered rectangular baking dish.
5.
Dribble the crêpes with the melted butter, then sprinkle with the Parmesan cheese. Cover the baking dish and set in the center of the oven. Bake the crêpes for 25 minutes.
6.
While the crêpes are in the oven, prepare the sauce. In a heavy saucepan heat the tomato sauce. Add the cream and heat through, then taste and correct the seasoning. Add the basil leaves and the parsley and transfer the sauce to a small serving bowl.
7.
When the crêpes are done uncover the dish and place quickly under the broiler to brown the top. Serve accompanied by the tomato-and-cream sauce.

Remarks
The entire dish can be prepared several hours ahead and baked just before serving.

Chicken
Pannequets

Serves: **6**
Preparation time: **25 minutes**
Cooking time: **1 hour**
Type of recipe: **elementary**
Cost: **moderate**

Ingredients
12 to 14 Herb Crêpes (page 389)
2 large eggs, plus 1 yolk
½ cup heavy cream
3 Tablespoons finely grated Swiss or Parmesan cheese

Filling:
1 small zucchini, grated
Salt
3 cups full-bodied Chicken Stock (page 530)
1 whole chicken breast, skinned, and cut in half
6 Tablespoons butter
3 Tablespoons flour
Freshly ground white pepper
2 Tablespoons finely minced fresh chives

Preparation
1.
Preheat the oven to 350 degrees.
2.
Place the grated zucchini in a colander, sprinkle with salt, and let drain over a bowl for 30 minutes to 1 hour.
3.
In a saucepan combine the chicken stock and breast. Bring slowly to a boil, reduce the heat, and simmer for 7 to 8 minutes.
4.
Remove the meat from the bone and dice into ½-inch cubes. Dice again into smaller cubes and set aside. Discard the bones and keep the stock hot.
5.
In a heavy-bottomed 2-quart saucepan melt 3 tablespoons butter. Add the flour and cook stirring constantly for 2 minutes.

6.
Add 2 cups reserved chicken stock and bring to a boil whisking constantly until the sauce is thick and heavily coats a spoon. Season carefully with salt and pepper and set aside.
7.
In a small heavy skillet heat the remaining butter. Add the zucchini and sauté for 2 to 3 minutes.
8.
Add the zucchini, together with the chives, to the diced chicken. Add ½ to ¾ cup reserved sauce; add just enough to bind the mixture. Taste and correct the seasoning.
9.
Fill each crêpe with some of the chicken mixture, tucking in the ends. Place in a well-buttered baking dish and set aside.
10.
In a bowl combine the eggs, extra yolk, and cream and blend thoroughly. Add the mixture to the remaining sauce and correct the seasoning.
11.
Spoon the sauce over the crêpes, covering them completely. Sprinkle with the cheese and place in the oven. Bake for 30 to 40 minutes, or until the custard is set and the top is lightly browned.
12.
Serve the crêpes right from the baking dish accompanied by Sautéed Cucumber Balls (page 421) or a watercress salad.

Salmon
Pannequets

Serves: **6**
Preparation time: **45 minutes**
Cooking time: **45 minutes**
Type of recipe **elementary**
Cost: **expensive**

Ingredients

12 to 14 Entrée Crêpes (page 388)
½ cup heavy cream
3 large egg yolks
2 Tablespoon butter
2 Tablespoons finely grated Swiss or
Parmesan cheese

Filling:

5 Tablespoons butter
2 Tablespoons finely minced shallots
2 cups Fish Stock (page 533)
1 pound salmon steak
Salt and freshly ground white pepper
2 Tablespoons finely minced fresh dill
3 Tablespoons flour

Preparation

1.
Preheat the oven to 350 degrees.

2.
Melt 2 tablespoons butter over low heat in a medium flameproof baking dish. Add the shallots and stock. Season the salmon steak with salt and pepper, then place in the baking dish. Cover with buttered waxed paper and set the dish in the center of the oven. Poach the fish for 8 minutes.

3.
Remove the fish from the oven. Strain the fish stock into a saucepan, reserving 2 cups, and keep hot. Flake the fish, discarding the bones and skin, and place in a bowl. Add the dill and set aside.

4.
In a heavy saucepan melt the remaining butter. Add the flour and cook stirring constantly for 2 minutes without browning.

5.
Remove the saucepan from the heat. Add the reserved fish stock all at once and set the saucepan over medium heat. Bring the sauce to a boil, whisking constantly until it is thick and smooth.

6.
Season carefully with salt and pepper, then add ½ to ¾ cup sauce to the salmon mixture; use just enough to bind the filling.

7.
Fill each crêpe with a little of the salmon mixture, using about 1 tablespoon for each crêpe and tucking in the sides of the crêpe to make small envelopes. Place the crêpes in 1 layer in a well-buttered baking dish and set aside.

8.
Prepare the sauce. In a bowl combine the cream and egg yolks and whisk the mixture until smooth. Whisk the cream-and-yolk mixture into the sauce remaining from step 5 above. Taste and correct the seasoning.

9.
Spoon the sauce over the crêpes and top with bits of butter and the grated cheese. Place the dish in the center of the oven and bake for 20 minutes, or until the crêpe filling is set and the tip of a knife comes out clean.

10.
Place the dish in the broiler to brown it lightly and then serve the crêpes from the baking dish.

Remarks
These salmon pannequets can also be made using the Spinach Crêpes or Herb Crêpes on pages 389–90. For variation you can add 1 cup cooked and finely chopped spinach to the salmon-and-dill mixture.

Vegetables

Standing on the checkout line in the supermarket and looking at the produce in other shoppers' carts can be one of the most frustrating and disheartening experiences I know. More than any other food, the fresh fruits and vegetables are dependent on the buyer's ability to determine and judge quality. All too often, the choices that I see around me reflect the common lack of produce-buying expertise and understanding.

One of the things that used to make marketing for vegetables so exciting when I was in Europe was the sense that every season brought something new. But today, with modern methods of transportation and refrigeration, just about every kind of fruit and vegetable—even the most perishable ones—are available throughout the country. We have lost the intensity and individuality that used to mark each season. The year-round profusion of produce of all kinds has minimized our awareness of the seasons, and we rarely stop to ask ourselves, "Is this fruit or vegetable really in season now?" And, if not, "Where does it come from?" Can a cucumber or tomato that has been shipped from 3,000 miles away have the flavor and texture of that local vegetable in its proper season? It is possible—and also very tempting—to buy asparagus in February, strawberries in January, and broccoli in July. Does this mean that the seasons have become absolute? Or that nature has no control over ripeness and quality? Unfortunately the answer is yes—unless you stop to consider how these seemingly "aseasonal" vegetables will

actually *taste*. If you splurge on asparagus in January or broccoli in July, how good will they really be once they are cooked? No matter how tempted I may be to feature some "out of season" vegetable on my menu, I always first ask myself what its natural peak season is. I usually prefer to wait a month or two rather than spend the money and time on a vegetable that will not give me the taste I want.

For me, fresh vegetables have always been a way of life. Growing up I never knew a frozen fruit or vegetable. Freshly prepared vegetables were a basic, important part of our everyday meals because they were inexpensive and could be turned into appetizers or combined in soups, egg dishes, or with rice and little bits of meat. Nowadays so much has been said and written in praise of freshness that many people are discovering the world of vegetables and cannot stop extolling their nutritional value or low calories. While I don't dispute their wonderful health value, fresh vegetables are simply the most wonderful gift of nature to the kitchen and the table. There are so many more vegetables to choose from than there are cuts of meat, and so many more creative ways to prepare them.

I cannot help but look back with a sense of nostalgia to the fabulous markets of my childhood days. It was simple to know what was in season because the minute you entered the market, there it was before you —and plenty of it! Mountains of cabbage, turnips, and carrots in winter; artichokes, peas, and asparagus in the spring. And in summer, a bonanza of many-shaped tomatoes, shiny zucchini, crisp lettuce, and mounds of peppers—yellow, red, and green. It was all there, stand after stand, color upon color. I never remember eating a tomato from October to May, an eggplant in winter, or a mushroom in summer. My mother would never buy a vegetable or fruit until many market stands carried it, so she could compare the quality and price.

At the entrance to the market there were four stands that always had the most beautiful displays, and boasted many seasonal specialties. Here was where you could find the then-exotic avocados, tiny melons in January, elegantly boxed Belgian endive, and pure white asparagus stalks gorgeously arranged in handwoven baskets. Everything seemed so perfect, so untouchable, and so expensive I used to wonder who actually shopped at these stands. One of my secret wishes was that one day I would be able to buy all that glorious produce! And yet today, when I market in Barcelona and pass these stands again, I always stop to look in admiration but I still don't buy my produce there. I prefer to stroll through the market looking and touching the mountains of peas, tasting one here and there, smelling a ripe tomato, crunching on a tender young green bean. These to me are *real,* while the elegant stands seem showplaces too beautifully arranged for anyone to ever reach out and touch.

This is also the way I feel about the magnificent produce at the Farmers' Market in Los Angeles, or some of New York's specialty stores. It is just too decorative, too perfect. I have learned that size and appearance have nothing to do with quality, and that the true beauty of a vegetable comes from its freshness and taste. I can find beauty in small new potatoes or a bin of fresh turnips. A tiny, sun-ripened tomato can have the most wonderful taste, while a large, perfectly formed one is often mealy and tasteless.

Buying vegetables in a supermarket can be an especially frustrating experience. Here you are often forced to deal with cellophane-packaged produce that is untouchable and "packed for your convenience." Rarely do you feel that marvelous sensation of picking and choosing your own. Yet to me, the supermarket is a challenge. I look for the one that displays its produce openly and has a manager I can rely on. I have found that the manager who takes pride in his area is usually willing to go into the stockroom for a bunch of parsley or a fresh package of spinach. As for the all-season, all-purpose vegetables, there is no question but that these should be bought in the supermarket. They are an essential part of the kitchen and with a little knowledge, you can develop wonderful meals using these staples.

Unfortunately, in spite of all the vegetable cookery books and the many magazine articles written in praise of seasonal fruits and vegetables, they are still too little used in the American kitchen. In talking to many produce managers in recent months, I got the same answer over and over again: "No, frozen foods and, in particular, frozen vegetables, are *not* losing their appeal." On the contrary, the new ethnic vegetable concoctions are extremely popular. I can somehow sympathize with the cook who lives in the Midwest, where the long winters limit the choice of fresh vegetables considerably. But frozen vegetables are used for convenience even in regions where there is an abundance of fresh produce, and even during seasons when local farmstands are brimming with freshness. Yet with gardening becoming so popular, I believe that homegrown vegetables have introduced many people to the taste of good, fresh produce. Serious cooks, particularly if they are among the increasing numbers of vegetable gardeners, would never consider cooking the frozen variety. Using fresh produce you can come up with a variety of delicious and inexpensive meals. Combine them with rice as in a vegetable paella; add a seasonal vegetable to the risotto, or combine it with fresh pasta, and you have an instant, excellent meal. No frozen vegetable can ever match the taste or texture of the fresh. Unless I need out-of-season vegetables such as peas or spinach for color and eye appeal (as in a ragoût of lamb or a spinach crêpe), I never bother with the frozen. I feel that it takes more time to eliminate their watery taste and doctor them up than it does to start with fresh.

One of the main reasons vegetable cookery has fared so poorly in this country is that vegetables are mainly served as an accompaniment to the main course along with rice or potatoes and a salad. They come to the table only as the "reflected glory" of the meat or fowl. Because of the basic arrangement of the all-American meal, there is little time left for the cook to devote to each individual preparation. With all three elements required at once, the vegetable is never given the attention it deserves. Often the American cook will end up minimizing the vegetables, frequently with sad results. More often than not the vegetable is overcooked, the salad is quickly tossed with bottled salad dressing, the wonderful and versatile potato is served simply baked—all because it is impossible for the cook to devote enough time and care to each separate food.

If you look at the peasant kitchens of Europe, you will find that the meal is simplified, separating the vegetable from the main course. It is set apart and served as an appetizer, or as an accompaniment to an omelet. These courses are followed by a salad that is carefully prepared and tossed at the last minute. This more leisurely, more appreciative pacing of the meal affords the opportunity of enjoying unusual vegetables that are truly at their best when served by themselves—braised fennel, a ragoût of Brussels sprouts, or a curried ragoût of vegetables are just some of my favorites.

I love every vegetable and have included many unusual preparations in both *The*

Seasonal Kitchen and *The Peasant Kitchen*. For this book I have selected new dishes that I have discovered in recent years and consider to be unusual and exciting. As for the simpler vegetable preparations, I take it for granted that by now these are a part of every serious cook's repertoire. I do not mean to minimize the importance of simply yet perfectly cooked green beans, asparagus, or broccoli. These, together with carrots or turnips, are an essential part of the everyday kitchen. Furthermore they are available practically year-round in good supermarkets. Some of the less common vegetables, such as fennel, leeks, Belgian endive, or sorrel, are items that are usually available only in good specialty shops. They are well worth looking for as their unique flavors can give a whole new dimension to a menu.

In recent years there has been a great deal of publicity given to chefs like Paul Bocuse, Michel Guérard, and the Troigros brothers, mostly because they are considered the "architects" of the voguish nouvelle cuisine. Suddenly there is so much said in favor of beautifully arranged vegetable garnishes that look a little like still-lifes. I spent several weeks in the kitchen of the Troigros brothers. One of the great experiences was to go to market with these great chefs. Theirs is a restaurant that can have the best of everything brought to its doorstep, yet these chefs enjoy the sensation of looking at and touching the fresh produce as if they had never seen it before. I still remember a cold, damp day early in March when Pierre and I arrived at the market and a farmer

handed him a bunch of tiny pink radishes, the first sign of spring! It was as lovely as seeing a bouquet of flowers. The essence of freshness and the love of simple, good things were all captured in that moment.

Pierre Troigros always says, "However you plan to cook a vegetable, treat it with the respect it deserves." When cooking a green vegetable, it is best to cook it in plenty of salted boiling water until it is just tender. Remember that undercooked vegetables are not much better than overcooked ones. Once cooked, drain green vegetables immediately under cold running water and return them to the casserole or saucepan with a lump of fresh butter. Toss lightly, add a large grinding of freshly ground pepper, and serve immediately. You should never let a vegetable "sit" in its cooking liquid, because it will get soggy and lose its taste and texture. I often cook carrots, turnips, or fresh peas with a minimum amount of water, adding a good lump of butter, a pinch of sugar, salt, and pepper to the water. The vegetable is then braised in a little liquid and thus retains more flavor than when cooked in a great deal of water. Vegetables such as zucchini or tomatoes are delicious when braised in a skillet with either butter or a fruity olive oil. Many vegetables such as cauliflower or Brussels sprouts are better when they are first blanched and then braised in the oven with either butter or lemon cream. For sautéing vegetables, I only use olive oil, since the wonderful flavor of this oil has a great affinity for all vegetables, particularly eggplant, tomatoes, peppers, zucchini, and onions. I am also extremely fond of creamed vegetables, especially with the addition of fresh herbs. Cooked beets, cubed and braised in butter and heavy cream with a touch of fresh dill, are simply wonderful. Braised Belgian endive finished with cream and a sprinkling of fresh chives and parsley is both unusual and delicious.

Of all the basic foods available to us, vegetables allow you to be as creative as you wish, since they are much less expensive than meats and will add a wonderfully fresh, seasonal touch to all your meals.

Artichoke
Bottoms

Serves: **2 to 4**
Preparation time: **10 minutes**
Cooking time: **20 minutes**
Type of recipe: **elementary**
Cost: **moderate**

The bottom, or base, of the artichoke is a vegetable delicacy and a favorite among French chefs. The subtle nutty flavor and cuplike shape of this delicious morsel deserves its fame since it lends itself to so many wonderful fillings, both hot and cold. In Italy and Spain the artichoke bottom is often used in ragoûts and as a flavoring for risottos and other rice dishes. It has a wonderful affinity for both veal and chicken, as well as for eggs. Unfortunately artichokes are much more expensive here than in Europe and using only the heart of the artichoke is somewhat extravagant. However you can use the leaves for flavoring an artichoke soup and, when in season, you can often buy artichokes at more reasonable prices. You should, however, know how to prepare the artichoke bottom and use it whenever you can.

Ingredients
4 to 8 large artichokes
Juice of 1 large lemon
2 Tablespoons flour
Salt

Preparation

1.
In a large bowl combine cold water with the juice of ½ lemon. Cut the stems off the artichokes at the base of the bulb. Start breaking off the outer leaves until the leaves start appearing a pale green and form a cone shape. With a sharp stainless-steel knife cut the entire cone off at the base and immediately drop the artichokes into the lemon water.

2.
In a large saucepan combine additional cold water with the flour and the remaining lemon juice. Season with salt and add the drained artichoke bottoms. Bring to a boil and cook for 20 minutes, or until tender.

3.
Drain the artichoke bottoms and with a grapefruit spoon scoop out the entire choke (the fuzzy center of the artichoke). Trim the remaining leaf ends around each artichoke bottom.

4.
Refrigerate the artichokes with some of their cooking liquid. The artichokes will keep well for 3 to 4 days. They maybe served cold marinated in a vinaigrette or, if they are to be used hot, they should be sautéed gently in butter for a few minutes before being filled.

Artichoke Bottoms
in
Lemon Cream

Serves:	**4 to 5**
Preparation time:	**10 minutes**
Cooking time:	**25 minutes**
Type of recipe:	**elementary**
Cost:	**moderate**

In late spring when artichokes are less expensive, it is an affordable luxury to use the bottoms only. Here they are prepared in a light lemon-flavored cream sauce. Reserve the leaves for an artichoke soup.

Ingredients
1 cup heavy cream
1 lemon cut in half, plus juice of 1 large lemon
6 to 8 large artichokes
2 cups Chicken Stock (page 530), or chicken boullion
1 small onion, peeled and cut in half
Salt and freshly ground black pepper
2 Tablespoons butter

Garnish:
Finely minced fresh parsley

Preparation
1.
In a bowl combine the cream and lemon juice. Whisk until well blended, then set aside.
2.
Remove the outer leaves from the artichokes until they are pale green and turning inward to a cone shape. Cut the cones off with a sharp knife, trim the edges, and remove the fuzzy center with a grapefruit spoon. Drop the artichokes into a large bowl of cold water. Add the lemon half and set aside.
3.
In a shallow saucepan combine the artichoke bottoms with the stock and onion. Season with salt and pepper, then bring to a boil and simmer partially covered for 15 to 20 minutes, or until the artichokes are tender. Cool and quarter.
4.
In a heavy skillet heat the butter. Add the artichokes and toss well. Add the lemon cream, bring to a boil, and cook until the cream is well reduced and heavily coats a spoon.
5.
Taste and correct the seasoning. Sprinkle with parsley. Serve as an appetizer or as an accompaniment to grilled or poached fish.

Balkan
Braised
Green Beans

Serves: **4**
Preparation time: **20 minutes**
Cooking time: **40 minutes**
Type of recipe: **elementary**
Cost: **inexpensive**

Ingredients
1 pound fresh green beans
4 Tablespoons fruity olive oil
1 dried hot chili pepper, cut in half
2 cloves garlic, finely minced
¼ cup fresh parsley, finely minced
5 to 6 ripe tomatoes, peeled, seeded, and chopped
1 sprig fresh oregano, or 1 teaspoon dried
1 large sprig fresh thyme, or 1 teaspoon dried
3 large basil leaves, cut into thin julienne strips
Salt and freshly ground black pepper

Garnish:
Finely minced fresh parsley
Bowl of freshly grated Parmesan cheese

Preparation
1.
If possible use very young small green beans. Snap off the tips and leave whole. Rinse under cold running water.
2.
In a large saucepan bring salted water to a boil. Drop the beans a few at a time into the boiling water and cook for 7 to 8 minutes, or until tender but still somewhat crisp.
3.
When done drain the beans and immediately rinse with cold water to stop further cooking and to retain the fresh green color. Set aside.
4.
In a 10-inch cast-iron skillet heat the olive oil over high heat and add the chili pepper.

When the chili pepper has darkened discard it.
5.
Add the garlic, parsley, tomatoes, and herbs. Season the mixture with salt and pepper. Bring to a boil, reduce the heat, partially cover the skillet, and simmer the sauce for 20 to 25 minutes, or until the tomato water has evaporated and the sauce is thickened.
6.
Add the green beans to the skillet and stir thoroughly into the sauce. Cover and simmer for another 10 minutes. Taste the beans and correct the seasoning.
7.
Garnish the bean-and-tomato mixture with parsley and serve directly from the skillet accompanied by a bowl of Parmesan cheese and crusty French bread.

Remarks
This dish is extremely popular in the Basque region of northern Spain. It is often served with the addition of 2 cups cooked white beans and some diced smoked ham or prosciutto. Add the beans and prosciutto to the tomato sauce together with the green beans and simmer for 15 minutes. The dish should be quite spicy; it is traditionally served as an accompaniment to fried eggs and sautéed country sausages.

Green Beans
à la Crème

Serves: **4 to 6**
Preparation time: **10 minutes**
Cooking time: **15 minutes**
Type of recipe: **elementary**
Cost: **inexpensive**

Ingredients
1½ pounds fresh young green beans
3 Tablespoons butter
1 cup heavy cream
Juice of 1 lemon
Salt and freshly ground black pepper
Sprinkling of flour
2 Tablespoons finely minced fresh chives

Preparation
1.
Snap the beans.
2.
In a large casserole bring salted water to a boil. Add the beans and cook for 7 to 8 minutes, or until barely tender. Drain the beans and rinse with cold water to stop further cooking.
3.
In a 10-inch skillet heat the butter. Add the cream, lemon juice, salt, and pepper and bring to a boil. Add the flour and cook the cream until it is reduced and heavily coats a spoon.
4.
Add the beans, toss in the lemon cream, and cook for 2 minutes Sprinkle with chives, then taste and correct the seasoning.
5.
Transfer the beans to a serving dish and serve hot as an accompaniment to roast or sautéed chicken and poached or grilled fish.

Beans
à la Tourangelle

Serves: **6**
Preparation time: **15 minutes, plus overnight to soak beans**
Cooking time: **1 hour, 10 minutes**
Type of recipe: **elementary**
Cost: **inexpensive**

Here is an interesting dish that combines fresh green beans and dried white beans. It is one of my favorite accompaniments to roast lamb, but it is equally good served as a simple supper dish with grilled Italian sausages or hamburgers.

Ingredients
1 cup dried white beans (preferably Great Northern)
1 onion, peeled and stuck with a clove
1 large Bouquet Garni (page 546)
Salt
½ pound fresh young green beans
3 Tablespoons butter
2 Tablespoons finely minced shallots
1 large clove garlic, peeled and crushed
1 cup heavy cream
freshly ground black pepper

Garnish:
2 Tablespoons minced fresh parsley

Preparation
1.
Cover the white beans by 2 inches with cold water in a large saucepan and let them soak overnight.
2.
The next day preheat the oven to 325 degrees.
3.
Drain the beans and cover again with 2 inches of water in a casserole. Add the onion and bouquet, season lightly with salt, and bring the beans to a boil on top of the stove. Immediately remove from the heat and place the casserole, covered, in the center of the oven. Cook for 1 hour, or

Balkan Purée
of
White Beans

Serves:	**6 to 8**
Preparation time:	**35 minutes, plus time to prepare beans in advance**
Cooking time:	**20 minutes**
Type of recipe:	**elementary**
Cost:	**inexpensive**

until tender. Remove from the oven and let the beans cool in their cooking liquid. Set aside.

4.
Snap the green beans and cut into 1-inch pieces.

5.
In a large saucepan bring salted water to a boil. Add the green beans and cook for 5 minutes.

6.
Drain the white beans, discard the onion and the bouquet, and set aside.

7.
In a heavy 10-inch skillet melt the butter. Add the shallots and garlic and cook the mixture until soft but not browned.

8.
Add the white beans and green beans and cook stirring gently for 2 to 3 minutes. Add the cream, bring to a boil, and cook over moderate heat until the cream is reduced and heavily coats the vegetables.

9.
Taste and correct the seasoning. Sprinkle with minced parsley and serve hot.

Remarks
The whole dish can be prepared in advance and slowly reheated on top of the stove. You can add 1 cup cubed bacon, blanched and sautéed in 2 tablespoons butter, to the beans.

Ingredients
2 Tablespoons chicken or duck fat or oil
2 medium onions, peeled and finely minced
2 cloves garlic, peeled and crushed
2 teaspoons imported paprika
1 Tablespoon tomato paste
3 large ripe tomatoes, peeled, seeded, and chopped
Salt and freshly ground black pepper
1 teaspoon dried marjoram
½ teaspoon dried oregano
Large pinch cayenne pepper
4 to 5 cups white beans (Great Northern), cooked according to directions on page 99
2 Tablespoons butter
¾ to 1 cup sour cream

Garnish:
Finely minced fresh parsley

Preparation
1.
In a cast-iron skillet melt the fat or oil. Add the onions and cook over low heat until soft and lightly browned. Do not let the onions burn.

2.
Add the garlic, paprika, and tomato paste and stir the mixture into the onions. Cook for 1 minute, then add the tomatoes. Season with salt and pepper, then add the marjoram, oregano, and cayenne pepper and cook the mixture until the tomato water has evaporated and the mixture is reduced to a thick purée.

Beets and Cucumbers
à la Crème

Serves:	**4 to 6**
Preparation time:	**15 minutes**
Cooking time:	**1 hour, 30 minutes**
Type of recipe:	**elementary**
Cost:	**inexpensive**

3.
Add the previously cooked beans and stir them well into the tomato mixture. Cover the skillet and simmer for 15 minutes. Cool the beans, then purée them in a food processor or blender. You may have to do this in 2 or 3 batches.

4.
Transfer the bean purée to a bowl and whisk in the butter and ¾ cup sour cream. If the purée is very thick add the additional sour cream.

5.
Taste and correct the seasoning, then transfer to a serving bowl. Sprinkle with parsley and serve hot as an accompaniment to roast pork, sautéed pork chops, or roast leg of lamb.

Remarks
The purée can be prepared well in advance and kept warm in the top of a double boiler over hot but not boiling water. The beans may be cooked 3 to 4 days ahead and kept in their cooking water in the refrigerator.

While creamed beets are a delicious accompaniment to veal and chicken dishes, they can also be served as a light appetizer or simple supper dish accompanied by sliced cold smoked ham, a bowl of sweet butter, and thinly sliced black bread.

Ingredients
4 to 5 medium fresh beets
Salt
2 large cucumbers, peeled
1 Tablespoon white wine vinegar
4 Tablespoons butter
Freshly ground white pepper
1 cup heavy cream
2 to 3 Tablespoons finely minced fresh chives
2 Tablespoons sour cream
Lemon juice

Garnish:
2 to 4 Tablespoons finely minced fresh dill

Preparation
1.
Place the beets in a large casserole and cover with cold water. Season with salt, bring to a boil, reduce the heat, and simmer the beets covered for 1 hour, or until tender.

2.
Meanwhile cut the cucumbers in half lengthwise, then remove the seeds with a melon ball cutter. Slice the cucumbers crosswise into ½-inch slices. Place in a colander over a bowl, sprinkle with salt and white wine vinegar, and let drain for 30 minutes to 1 hour.

Gratin
of
Broccoli

Serves: **4 to 6**
Preparation time: **15 minutes**
Cooking time: **45 minutes**
Type of recipe: **elementary**
Cost: **inexpensive**

3.
Drain the beets and, when cool enough to handle, peel. (The skin will come right off.) Cube the beets and set aside.

4.
In a large heavy skillet heat 2 tablespoons butter. Add the cucumbers and sauté over high heat for 3 to 4 minutes, tossing the cucumbers until they are lightly browned. With a slotted spoon transfer to a side dish and reserve.

5.
Add a little more butter to the skillet to the skillet. Add the beets and sauté over low heat for 3 to 4 minutes. Season with salt and pepper.

6.
Add the cream, bring to a boil, and cook until the cream is well reduced and heavily coats the beets. Be careful not to burn the pan juices.

7.
Add the sautéed cucumbers, chives, and sour cream. Fold the mixture gently and simmer the vegetables over the lowest possible heat for another 3 to 4 minutes. Taste and correct the seasoning.

8.
Add a little lemon juice to taste and a large grinding of pepper. Transfer the vegetables to a serving bowl. Garnish with dill and serve hot.

Ingredients
2 pounds of fresh broccoli
¾ cup heavy cream
3 large eggs
1 cup whole milk ricotta
Salt and freshly ground white pepper
½ cup grated Parmesan cheese
3 Tablespoons butter
4 Tablespoons bread crumbs

Preparation
1.
Preheat the oven to 375 degrees.
2.
Remove the tough outer leaves of the broccoli and cut 1 inch off the base, then quarter the branches lengthwise. Peel the stalks with a vegetable peeler and cut them into 2-inch pieces.
3.
In a large saucepan bring salted water to a boil. Add the broccoli, both stems and florets, and cook for 7 to 8 minutes, or until very tender. Drain and rinse with cold water.
4.
Transfer the broccoli to a blender or food processor. Add the cream and purée the mixture until almost smooth. Transfer to a bowl and add the eggs and ricotta. Season with salt, pepper, and ¼ cup Parmesan cheese. Blend well.
5.
Butter a baking dish, then transfer the broccoli mixture to the dish and set aside.
6.
In a small heavy skillet heat the butter, add the bread crumbs, and brown lightly. Sprinkle the top of the broccoli mixture

Broccoli
in
Yogurt Sauce

Serves:	**4**
Preparation time:	**15 minutes**
Cooking time:	**10 minutes**
Type of recipe:	**elementary**
Cost:	**inexpensive**

with the sautéed bread crumbs and the remaining Parmesan cheese.

7.

Place the dish in the center of the oven and bake for 35 minutes, or until set. Test with the tip of a sharp knife; it should come out clean.

8.

Serve hot directly from the baking dish.

Remarks

This dish can be made a day ahead and reheated in a slow oven. Other vegetables, such as escarole or spinach, can be prepared in the same manner.

Ingredients

2 pounds fresh broccoli

Sauce:

3 egg yolks
½ teaspoon cornstarch
1½ cups plain yogurt
2 teaspoons Dijon mustard
1 large clove garlic, crushed
Salt and freshly ground black pepper
Lemon juice

Fricassée of Brussels Sprouts à la Campagnarde

Serves: **4 to 6**
Preparation time: **20 minutes**
Cooking time: **35 to 40 minutes**
Type of recipe: **elementary**
Cost: **inexpensive**

Vegetables ragoûts, or fricassées, are often served in Mediterranean Europe as appetizers, simple lunches, or supper dishes. Here is a robust country vegetable ragoût that I often serve as an accompaniment to sautéed pork chops or roast chicken.

Ingredients

1 cup diced salt pork or bacon
3 Tablespoons rendered chicken or duck fat
12 to 16 small white onions, peeled
Large pinch of granulated sugar
Salt and freshly ground black pepper
1 cup Chicken Stock or Brown Chicken Stock (pages 530–31)
3 to 4 carrots, scraped and cut into 1-inch sticks
2 pints small Brussels sprouts, well trimmed and rinsed

Garnish:
Finely minced fresh parsley

Preparation

1.
Preheat the oven to 350 degrees.

2.
Place the salt pork or bacon in boiling water, cook for 2 minutes and drain. Dry on a double layer of paper towels.

3.
In a small heavy skillet heat 2 tablespoons fat and sauté the bacon cubes until almost crisp. Drain on a double layer of paper towels and reserve.

4.
Add the onions to the skillet, sprinkle with sugar, salt, and pepper and roll the onions

---

Preparation

1.
Remove the tough outer leaves of the broccoli and cut 1 inch off the base. Quarter the branches lengthwise. Peel the broccoli stalks with a vegetable peeler all the way to the flower buds and set aside.

2.
Prepare the sauce. In the top of a double boiler combine the yolks and cornstarch and whisk until well blended. Add the yogurt, mustard, and garlic and place the pan over simmering water.

3.
Whisk the mixture until it thickens and heavily coats a spoon. Do not let it come to a boil. Season with salt, pepper, and a large dash of lemon juice. Keep covered over warm but not boiling water.

4.
In a large casserole bring salted water to a boil. Add the broccoli and cook for 5 to 6 minutes, or until just tender. Drain and immediately rinse under cold water to stop further cooking.

5.
Place the broccoli in 1 layer on a warmed serving platter. Spoon the sauce over the stalks leaving the florets exposed. Serve immediately as an accompaniment to roast or sautéed meats or as an appetizer.

Remarks

For variation you can add 1 teaspoon curry powder and a large pinch of ground cumin to the sauce. The sauce is equally delicious when served with Brussels sprouts or cauliflower.

Carrots
in
Dilled Sour Cream

Serves:	**4 to 5**
Preparation time:	**15 minutes**
Cooking time:	**15 to 20 minutes**
Type of recipe:	**elementary**
Cost:	**inexpensive**

in the fat until they are nicely browned.
Add ⅓ cup stock, lower the heat, and
simmer the onions for 5 minutes, or until
almost tender.

5.
Add the carrots and another ⅓ cup stock.
Cover and continue braising until the
carrots are done.

6.
In a large saucepan bring salted water to a
boil. Add the Brussels sprouts and cook for
8 minutes, then drain.

7.
Heat the remaining fat in a flameproof
baking dish. Add the sprouts in 1 layer and
cover with buttered foil.

8.
Place the dish in the oven and bake the
Brussels sprouts for 20 minutes.

9.
Remove the dish from the oven and add the
onion-and-carrot mixture together with the
reserved stock and bacon or salt pork.
Simmer the mixture for 5 to 7 minutes.
Cook and correct the seasonings. The
vegetable mixture should have absorbed all
but 2 to 3 tablespoons of stock. Spoon the
vegetable ragoût into a serving dish.
Sprinkle with parsley and serve hot.

Remarks
The dish can be prepared 1 or 2 hours
ahead and reheated.

*Carrots are one of the most delicious
year-round vegetables. Look for fresh carrots
with their greens attached; these are much
more delicate than the packaged ones and
will only need 8 to 10 minutes of cooking.*

Ingredients
1 cup Crème Fraîche (page 544)
1 teaspoon flour
**2 to 3 Tablespoons finely minced fresh
dill**
**1½ pounds fresh carrots, peeled and cut
into ¼-inch slices**
¼ cup water
4 Tablespoons butter
1 teaspoon granulated sugar
Salt and freshly ground white pepper

Carrot and Onion Ragoût

Serves:	**4 to 5**
Preparation time:	**15 minutes**
Cooking time:	**30 minutes**
Type of recipe:	**elementary**
Cost:	**inexpensive**

Preparation

1.
In a small bowl mix the Crème Fraîche with the flour and dill and stir until well blended. Set aside.

2.
Combine the carrots with water, butter, and sugar in a heavy-bottomed saucepan. Season with salt and pepper. Bring to a boil, reduce the heat, and simmer the carrots covered for 8 to 10 minutes, or until barely tender.

3.
Uncover the saucepan and spoon off all but 2 tablespoons of the cooking liquid. Increase the heat and add the Crème Fraîche mixture. Bring to a boil, reduce the heat, and simmer the carrots until tender and the sauce is thickened.

4.
Season with salt and pepper and serve hot as an accompaniment to roast chicken or sautéed fish fillets.

Remarks

For variation, flavor the carrots with a combination of dill and freshly minced chives. You can also add 2 to 3 turnips, peeled and cubed.

Ingredients

4 to 6 fresh carrots, scraped
12 small white onions
1 cup diced meaty salt pork
2 Tablespoons butter
1½ teaspoon granulated sugar
Salt and freshly ground black pepper
Pinch of dried thyme
1 bay leaf
½ to ¾ cup Brown Chicken Stock (page 531) or beef bouillon

Garnish:
Finely minced fresh parsley

Preparation

1.
Cut the carrots into ¾-inch cubes and set aside.

2.
Place the onions in rapidly boiling salted water and cook for 5 minutes. Drain and, when cool enough to handle, peel and set aside.

3.
Place the salt pork in rapidly boiling water and blanch for 3 minutes. Drain and dry thoroughly with paper towels.

4.
In a heavy 3- to 4-quart saucepan melt the butter. Add the salt pork and sauté over medium heat until almost crisp. With a slotted spoon remove to a side dish and reserve.

5.
Add the onions to the saucepan and sauté for 3 minutes, tossing them in the fat until lightly browned. The onions will not brown evenly. Be sure to regulate the heat so as

Gratin
of
Cauliflower

Serves:	**6**
Preparation time:	**25 minutes**
Cooking time:	**40 minutes**
Type of recipe:	**elementary**
Cost:	**inexpensive**

not to burn the fat. Sprinkle with half the sugar and continue sautéing partially covered until the onions are lightly caramelized.

6.
Add the carrots and salt pork to the saucepan. Season with salt, pepper, and thyme. Add the remaining sugar and the stock or beef bouillon to the saucepan and bury the bay leaf. Cover tightly and simmer for 20 minutes, or until the vegetables are tender.

7.
Uncover the saucepan, increase the heat, and cook until the bouillon has evaporated. Taste the carrots and correct the seasoning. Discard the bay leaf.

8.
When ready to serve, transfer the vegetables to a serving bowl. Sprinkle with parsley and serve hot.

Remarks:
The dish can be prepared 1 to 3 days ahead and reheated on top of the stove. Six to 8 cubed mushrooms sautéed separately in 2 tablespoons butter can be added to the ragoût.

Ingredients
1 large head cauliflower, stems trimmed and broken into florets
3 Tablespoons butter
Salt and freshly ground white pepper
1½ cups freshly grated Parmesan cheese
Large pinch freshly grated nutmeg
2 large eggs, plus 2 yolks
1 cup heavy cream
⅓ cup fresh white bread crumbs
1 carrot, scraped and cut into 1½-inch julienne strips
8 to 10 fresh green beans, cut into 1½-inch julienne strips

Preparation
1.
Preheat the oven to 375 degrees.

2.
In a large casserole bring salted water to a boil. Add the cauliflower florets and cook for 10 to 15 minutes, or until very tender.

3.
Drain the cauliflower and, when completely cool, purée in a food processor. (If you do not have a food processor purée in small batches in a blender adding a little cream.)

4.
Transfer the purée to a bowl. Whisk in 2 tablespoons butter and season with salt and a large grinding of pepper. Add the grated cheese and nutmeg, then taste the mixture and correct the seasoning.

5.
In a bowl whisk the eggs, yolks, and cream until well blended. Add the bread crumbs and fold the mixture into the cauliflower purée.

Cauliflower and Ham
Tart

Serves:	**6**
Preparation time:	**40 minutes, plus 1 hour, 25 minutes to prepare tart shell**
Cooking time:	**1 hour**
Type of recipe:	**elementary**
Cost:	**inexpensive**

6.
Butter an oval *au gratin* dish and transfer the cauliflower mixture to it. Set aside.

7.
In a small heavy saucepan bring salted water to a boil. Add the carrots and beans and cook until barely tender, or for 3 to 4 minutes. Drain and place atop the cauliflower purée in a decorative design. Cover with buttered waxed paper.

8.
Place the dish inside a larger pan and pour boiling water around it. Set in the oven and bake for 30 to 40 minutes, or until the top is set and slightly browned. Serve the gratin right from the baking dish.

Remarks:
A young cauliflower would actually not take more than 5 to 8 minutes to cook. When preparing cauliflower other than for the gratin the best way to cook it is to steam it and then sauté the still-crisp florets in a mixture of butter and olive oil. Sprinkle with minced fresh parsley, a dash of lemon juice, and possibly a sprinkling of fresh chives. Hot cauliflower is also delicious when tossed in a garlic vinaigrette flavored with finely minced shallots and served as an accompaniment to grilled steaks or roast leg of lamb.

Ingredients
2 large eggs, plus 2 yolks
2 cups heavy cream
½ cup freshly grated Parmesan cheese
Salt and freshly ground white pepper
1 large head cauliflower, broken into small florets (about 2 cups)
2 Tablespoons butter
½ cup finely cubed smoked ham
1 nine-inch prebaked Basic Tart Shell (page 483), in a porcelain quiche pan

Sautéed
Cucumber Balls

Serves:	**4 to 6**
Preparation time:	**10 minutes, plus 30 minutes to drain cucumbers**
Cooking time:	**5 minutes**
Type of recipe:	**elementary**
Cost:	**inexpensive**

Preparation

1.
Prepare the filling. In a large mixing bowl combine the whole eggs, egg yolks, cream, and Parmesan cheese. Add salt and pepper to taste and blend thoroughly. Set aside.

2.
In a 3-quart saucepan bring salted water to a boil. Add the cauliflower florets and cook uncovered over medium heat until very tender. Drain immediately and rinse with cold water to stop further cooking. Set aside.

3.
In a large heavy skillet, heat the butter over medium heat. When hot, add the ham cubes and sauté until lightly browned. When done, transfer the ham to a side dish and reserve.

4.
Remove all but 2 tablespoons of fat from the skillet. Increase the heat to high, add the florets, and sauté until lightly browned on all sides.

5.
When done, remove the cauliflower from the skillet and add together with the reserved ham to the cream-and-egg mixture. Fold gently and pour the mixture into the prebaked tart shell. Bake for 40 to 45 minutes or until a knife when inserted comes out clean.

Sautéed cucumbers are a wonderful accompaniment to roast or sautéed chicken and poached or sautéed fish. They can be combined with the pan juices of a roast or served separately as a vegetable. Since cucumbers have a natural affinity for dill, mint, and parsley you may use any of these herbs as a flavoring. For variation you could add ½ cup Crème Fraîche and a large clove of crushed garlic to the skillet, then sauté the cucumbers until they've absorbed the cream completely.

Ingredients

2 to 4 large cucumbers, preferably gourmet or English cucumbers
Coarse salt
1 Tablespoon white wine vinegar
2 Tablespoons butter
Freshly ground white pepper

Garnish:
Sprinkling of fresh chives, parsley, or dill

Cucumbers
in
Lemon Cream

Serves:	**4 to 6**
Preparation time:	**15 minutes, plus 2 hours to drain cucumbers**
Cooking time:	**20 minutes**
Type of recipe:	**elementary**
Cost:	**inexpensive**

Preparation

1.

Peel the cucumbers. Cut in half lengthwise and scoop out the seeds with a melon ball cutter or a grapefruit spoon. Use the melon cutter to form the cucumber flesh into balls, or cut the cucumbers crosswise into ½-inch slices. Place in a colander, sprinkle with coarse salt and vinegar, and put the colander over a bowl. Let the cucumbers drain for 30 minutes to 1 hour.

2.

In a large cast-iron skillet heat the butter. Add the cucumbers and sauté over moderate-to-high heat for 3 to 4 minutes, or until lightly browned. Season with a large grinding of pepper and sprinkle with parsley, chives, or dill or a mixture of all 3. Serve the cucumbers hot.

Remarks:

The gourmet or English cucumbers are now available in most specialty stores throughout the country. These have fewer seeds and can be formed easily into balls with a melon ball cutter. They also retain a much better crispness when cooked than the all-purpose cucumbers.

Although I find that there are actually few vegetable dishes that are good accompaniments to fish, the mild but subtle taste of these hot cucumbers in a tart lemon sauce go wonderfully well with grilled or poached fish steaks, such as salmon or bass.

Ingredients

4 to 5 large cucumbers
Salt
3 Tablespoons butter
Freshly ground white pepper
1 large lemon, thinly sliced
1 cup heavy cream
½ Beurre Manié (page 544)
3 Tablespoons finely minced fresh chives

Eggplants
à la Bohémienne

Serves: **6 to 8**
Preparation time: **20 minutes, plus 2 to 4 hours
ahead to drain eggplants**
Cooking time: **45 to 50 minutes**
Type of recipe: **elementary**
Cost: **inexpensive**

Preparation

1.
Peel the cucumbers. Cut in half lengthwise
and remove the seeds with a grapefruit
spoon. Cut the cucumbers crosswise into
¾-inch slices. Place in a colander, sprinkle
with salt and let the cucumbers drain for 1
to 2 hours over a bowl.

2.
In a large enamel skillet heat the butter.
Add the cucumbers and sauté over high
heat until lightly browned, shaking the pan
to cover the cucumbers evenly with the
butter. Season with salt and pepper.

3.
Add the lemon slices and cream. Bring to a
boil and cook over high heat whisking in
bits of the Beurre Manié until the sauce
heavily coats a spoon.

4.
Add the chives and cook for another 2
minutes. Taste and correct the seasoning.

5.
Transfer the cucumbers to a serving dish
and serve hot.

Remarks:
You can remove the lemon slices just before
serving. The cucumbers can be prepared 2
to 3 hours ahead and reheated slowly on
top of the stove.

*Eggplants à la Bohémienne is a version of
the ratatouille which is a specialty of the
area around Nice in France. It is usually
prepared simply by stewing equal amounts
of eggplants and ripe tomatoes and
flavoring it with herbs and anchovies. Here
is an interesting version that includes both
onions and olives.*

Ingredients
2 medium eggplants
Salt
½ to ¾ cup olive oil
2 onions, peeled and thinly sliced
**2 cans (35 ounces) Italian plum
tomatoes, well drained and chopped**
**2 Tablespoons finely minced fresh
thyme, or 1 teaspoon dried**
1 teaspoon dried oregano
Fresh ground black pepper
2 Tablespoons well-drained capers
6 to 8 flat anchovy fillets, finely minced
1 cup sliced Greek black olives

Garnish
**2 to 3 Tablespoons finely minced fresh
parsley**

Preparation
1.
A few hours ahead, peel the eggplants and
cut into 1-inch cubes.

2.
Place the cubes on a double layer of paper
towels. Sprinkle with salt, cover with
another double layer of paper towels, and
weight the eggplants down with some cans.
Drain for 2 to 4 hours. Dry thoroughly with
paper towels.

Baked Eggplant Gavina

Serves:	**6**
Preparation time:	**15 minutes, plus 2 to 4 hours to drain eggplants**
Cooking time:	**1 hour**
Type of recipe:	**elementary**
Cost:	**inexpensive**

3.
In a large heavy skillet heat 3 tablespoons oil and add the eggplant cubes; do not crowd the pan. Sauté the eggplant until nicely browned on all sides. Remove to a strainer and reserve. Continue sautéing the remaining eggplant; you will need more oil.

4.
When all the eggplant is done add 3 more tablespoons oil to the pan. Add the onions and cook for 15 to 20 minutes over low heat, or until soft and nicely browned. Do not let them burn.

5.
Add the tomatoes, thyme, oregano, salt, and pepper. Bring to a boil, reduce the heat, and cook until the tomato water has evaporated and the mixture is thick.

6.
Return the eggplant to the pan. Add the capers and anchovies and cook the mixture for another 10 minutes.

7.
Add the olives and heat through, then taste and correct the seasoning. Spoon the mixture into a serving dish and cool to room temperature.

8.
Sprinkle the dish with parsley and serve at room temperature or slightly chilled.

Remarks:
The entire dish can be made 2 to 3 days ahead. It can be served both hot and cold.

I remember once standing in the Barcelona market looking at a basket full of beautifully glossy eggplants and wondering how to prepare this great vegetable. The lady next to me asked, "Have you ever baked eggplants in cream?" It sounded strange but interesting. Her recipe has since become one of my favorite dishes.

Ingredients

3 medium eggplants, peeled
Salt
Flour for dredging
½ to ¾ cup olive oil
2 Tablespoons butter
⅔ cup unflavored bread crumbs, preferably homemade
3 Tablespoons minced fresh parsley
2 large cloves garlic, peeled and finely minced
Freshly ground black pepper
1 cup light cream
2 to 3 Tablespoons freshly grated Parmesan cheese

Preparation

1.
A few hours ahead cut the eggplants crosswise into ½-inch slices.

2.
Place the eggplants on a double layer of paper towels, sprinkle with salt, cover with another layer of paper towels, and weight the eggplant slices down with some cans for 2 to 4 hours.

3.
When drained, dry the eggplant slices thoroughly with paper towels and dredge lightly in flour.

4.
In a large heavy skillet heat 4 tablespoons oil. Add the eggplant slices and sauté a few at a time until nicely browned on both sides. You will have to add more oil to the pan since the eggplant absorbs a great deal.

5.
Remove the eggplant slices to a double layer of paper towels, season with salt and pepper, and set aside.

6.
Preheat the oven to 350 degrees.

7.
In a small heavy skillet heat 2 tablespoons butter and 1 tablespoon oil. Add the bread crumbs, parsley, and garlic and cook the mixture over low heat for 2 to 3 minutes, or until the bread crumbs are nicely browned. Set aside.

8.
Place a layer of eggplant slices in the bottom of a rectangular baking dish, overlapping them slightly. Sprinkle with some of the bread-crumb mixture and season with salt and pepper. Place the remaining eggplant slices in the dish. Sprinkle the remaining bread-crumb mixture and season with salt and pepper.

9.
Pour the cream over the eggplants, sprinkle with the grated cheese, and place the dish in the center of the oven. Bake for 45 minutes, or until the cream has been completely absorbed by the eggplants.

10.
Place the dish under the broiler for 2 minutes, or until the top is nicely browned, and serve right from the dish.

Remarks:
The dish can be completed 2 to 3 hours ahead and kept warm in a 200-degree oven.

Middle Eastern Stuffed Eggplant

Serves: **4**

Preparation time: **25 minutes, plus 2 hours to drain eggplants**

Cooking time: **2 hours**

Type of recipe: **elementary**

Cost: **inexpensive**

Ingredients

2 to 3 medium eggplants
Salt
6 Tablespoons olive oil
2 cups onions, finely minced
2 large cloves garlic, crushed
Freshly ground black pepper
1 Tablespoon granulated sugar
6 large ripe tomatoes, peeled, seeded, and chopped, or 1 can (35 ounces) Italian plum tomatoes

Preparation

1.
Wash the eggplants; do not peel. Cut 4 lengthwise incisions into each eggplant. Sprinkle salt into each cut and let drain in a colander for 2 hours.

2.
In a 10-inch cast-iron skillet heat 3 tablespoons oil. Add the onion and garlic. Season with salt, pepper, and sugar. Cook the mixture over low heat partially covered for 40 to 50 minutes, stirring several times until the onions are soft and nicely browned.

3.
Add the tomatoes and continue simmering the mixture for another 15 minutes.

4.
Preheat the oven to 350 degrees.

5.
While the sauce is cooking dry the eggplant thoroughly with paper towels.

6.
Heat the remaining oil in a large skillet. Add the whole eggplants and sauté them over low heat for 10 minutes, turning them several times. Remove the eggplants and cool. (The eggplants will now be soft and easy to stuff!)

7.
Put some of the tomato mixture into the incisions. Place the eggplants in a baking dish and spoon any remaining tomato mixture into the dish. Drizzle with the oil remaining in the skillet, cover the baking dish, and set in the center of the oven. Bake for 1 hour, 30 minutes, or until the eggplants are soft when pierced with the tip of a sharp knife.

8.
Cool and serve at room temperature right from the baking dish.

Remarks

The eggplants can be made 2 or 3 days ahead and refrigerated. Bring back to room temperature before serving. You may also reheat the dish in a slow oven and serve as an accompaniment to a roast leg of lamb or grilled hamburgers.

Braised Belgian Endive
in
Cream

Serves:	**6**
Preparation time:	**15 minutes, plus 2 to 3 hours to prepare cream**
Cooking time:	**15 minutes**
Type of recipe:	**elementary**
Cost:	**moderate**

Ingredients

Juice of 1 lemon
1 cup heavy cream
12 small heads Belgian endive
3 Tablespoons butter
Salt and freshly ground white pepper
Large pinch granulated sugar
1 cup Chicken Stock or Brown Chicken Stock (page 350–51)
1 Beurre Manié (page 544)

Garnish:

2 Tablespoons finely minced fresh parsley or dill

Preparation

1.
A few hours ahead combine the lemon juice and cream in a bowl. Whisk until well blended and set aside at room temperature for 2 to 3 hours.

2.
When ready, trim the endive of any wilted outer leaves. Trim the base and rinse quickly under cold water. Dry thoroughly with paper towels.

3.
Melt the butter in a large heavy skillet, then add the endive. Season with salt, pepper, and sugar. Over medium heat roll the endive back and forth in the butter until nicely browned on all sides.

4.
Add ½ cup stock, partially cover the skillet, and simmer the endive for 10 to 12 minutes. Add the remaining stock and continue braising the endive, turning them several times, for another 10 minutes or until just tender.

5.
With a slotted spoon remove the endive to a serving dish. Increase the heat, add the lemon cream, and bring to a boil. Season with salt and pepper.

6.
Whisk in bits of the Beurre Manié; use just enough until the sauce heavily coats a spoon. Taste the sauce and correct the seasoning.

7.
Spoon the sauce over the endive. Sprinkle with parsley or dill and serve hot as an accompaniment to roast or grilled fish, veal, or chicken.

Remarks

To prepare the endive in advance finish the sauce, then return the endive to the skillet. Cover and set aside. Reheat the endive in the sauce over low heat just before serving.

Lentils
à la Crème

Serves: **6**
Preparation time: **25 minutes**
Cooking time: **1 hour, 15 minutes**
Type of recipe: **elementary**
Cost: **inexpensive**

Ingredients
1½ cups lentils
1 large onion, peeled and stuck with a clove
1 large Bouquet Garni (page 546)
Salt and freshly ground black pepper
1½ cups diced slab bacon
2 Tablespoons butter
2 Tablespoons finely minced shallots
¾ cup heavy cream
1 large clove garlic, crushed
Sprinkling of flour

Garnish:
Finely minced fresh parsley

Preparation

1.
Rinse the lentils carefully under cold running water. Place in a large saucepan and add enough water to cover the beans with 2 inches of water. Add the onion and bouquet and season with salt and pepper. Bring to a boil, reduce the heat, and simmer the lentils for 45 minutes, or until barely tender. Drain, discard onion and bouquet, and reserve the lentils.

2.
In a small saucepan bring water to boil. Add the bacon cubes and cook for 5 minutes. Drain the bacon and dry with paper towels.

3.
Heat the butter in a large heavy skillet. Add the bacon and sauté until almost crisp. Transfer to a side dish with a slotted spoon and reserve. Discard all but 2 tablespoons of fat from the pan.

4.
Add the shallots and cook for 2 to 3 minutes, or until lightly browned.

5.
Add the cream and garlic and bring to a boil. Season with salt and pepper, sprinkle lightly with flour, and cook the cream until it is reduced and heavily coats a spoon.

6.
Add the reserved bacon and lentils and stir gently with a wooden spoon until the mixture is well blended. Taste and correct the seasoning. Serve the lentils hot as an accompaniment to roast or grilled meats.

Lentils
à la Toulonnaise

Serves: **6**
Preparation time: **25 minutes**
Cooking time: **1 hour, 30 minutes**
Type of recipe: **elementary**
Cost: **inexpensive**

Ingredients
1½ cups lentils
Salt
1 large onion, peeled and stuck with a clove
1 large Bouquet Garni (page 546)
2 Tablespoons olive oil
2 Tablespoons finely minced shallots
2 large cloves garlic, peeled and finely minced
2 large ripe tomatoes, peeled, seeded, and finely chopped
Freshly ground black pepper
½ teaspoon dried thyme
¼ teaspoon dried oregano
1 cup Crème Fraîche (page 544)
Sprinkling of flour

Optional:
½ cup coarsely grated Parmesan cheese

Preparation
1.
Rinse the lentils carefully under cold running water. Place in a casserole and add enough cold water to cover beans with 2 inches of water. Season lightly with salt and add the onion and bouquet. Bring to a boil on top of the stove, lower the heat, and simmer the lentils covered for 45 minutes, or until tender but not falling apart.

2.
While the lentils are cooking, heat the oil in a heavy 10-inch skillet. Add the shallots, garlic, and tomatoes. Season with salt, pepper, thyme, and oregano and cook the mixture until the tomato water has evaporated and the mixture is thick.

3.
Add the Crème Fraîche and bring to a boil. Sprinkle lightly with flour and cook the mixture stirring constantly until it is reduced and heavily coats a spoon. Taste and correct the seasoning.

4.
Drain the lentils. Discard the onion and bouquet.

5.
Add the lentils to the skillet, set over medium heat, and reheat the lentils in the tomato mixture. Stir gently with a wooden spoon until well blended.

6.
Add the optional Parmesan cheese. Taste and correct the seasoning. Serve hot as an accompaniment to roast pork, pork chops, or sautéed pork sausages.

Remarks
The entire dish can be prepared well in advance and reheated slowly on top of the stove. You can add ½ cup diced blanched and sautéed bacon to the lentils.

Sautéed Mushrooms
in
Anchovy-and-Herb Butter

Serves: **6**
Preparation time: **10 minutes**
Cooking time: **4 to 5 minutes**
Type of recipe: **elementary**
Cost: **inexpensive**

Ingredients

1½ pounds fresh mushrooms
5 Tablespoons butter, softened
2 to 3 anchovy fillets, finely minced
1 Tablespoon finely minced shallots
1 large clove garlic, peeled and crushed
2 Tablespoons finely minced fresh parsley
2 Tablespoons fruity olive oil
Salt and freshly ground black pepper

Preparation

1.
Remove the mushroom stems. Wipe the mushrooms with a damp paper towel; do not wash. Quarter the mushrooms and set aside.

2.
In a small bowl combine 4 tablespoons butter, the anchovies, shallots, garlic, and 1 tablespoon parsley. Blend the mixture to a paste with a fork until thoroughly blended and set aside.

3.
In a large heavy skillet heat the remaining tablespoon butter and the oil almost to smoking. Add the mushrooms and sauté over high heat, tossing the mushrooms in the pan for 2 minutes. Do not crowd the pan or the mushrooms will steam and release their juices. If your pan is not large enough to hold the mushrooms in 1 layer sauté in 2 to 3 batches.

4.
Remove the sautéed mushrooms to a flameproof serving dish. Season with salt and pepper, then add the herb butter to the dish and toss the mushrooms in the butter until it is just melted. Sprinkle with the remaining parsley and serve immediately as an accompaniment to roast or grilled meats.

Remarks

This dish is at its best when prepared at the last minute. The butter must not cook; it must just melt into the mushrooms. You may sauté the mushrooms ahead and reheat them on top of the stove, adding the herb butter at the last minute.

Sweet-and-Sour
Braised Onions

Serves:	**4 to 6**
Preparation time:	**15 minutes**
Cooking time:	**1 hour**
Type of recipe:	**elementary**
Cost:	**inexpensive**

Ingredients

2 pounds small white onions
1 cup cubed bacon
2 Tablespoons olive oil
Salt and freshly ground black pepper
2 Tablespoons brown sugar
1 Tablespoon granulated sugar
4 Tablespoons red wine vinegar
½ teaspoon dried thyme
1 bay leaf
¾ cup beef bouillon

Preparation

1.
In a saucepan bring water to a boil. Add the onions and cook for 5 minutes. Drain and, when cool enough to handle, peel the onions and set aside.

2.
Drop the bacon cubes in rapidly boiling water and cook for 3 minutes. Drain and dry thoroughly on paper towels.

3.
In a 10-inch cast-iron skillet heat the oil. Add the bacon cubes and sauté for 2 to 3 minutes, or until crisp. With a slotted spoon remove the bacon cubes to a side dish.

4.
Add the onions to the skillet and sauté over moderate-to-high heat until nicely browned. Roll them back and forth in the fat; the onions will not brown evenly. Season with salt and pepper and add the brown sugar and granulated sugar. Roll the onions in the sugar until browned and caramelized.

5.
Add the vinegar, thyme, and bay leaf. Bring to a boil, reduce the heat, and add ¾ cup bouillon to the skillet. Return the bacon to the skillet. Cover tightly, and braise the onions for 40 to 50 minutes, or until very tender but not falling apart.

6.
Discard the bay leaf. Increase the heat and cook until most of the pan juices have evaporated. Taste the onions and correct the seasoning.

7.
Serve the onions as an accompaniment to roast duck, roast pork, or braised sweetbreads. The onions can also be served chilled as an accompaniment to a country pâté.

Braised Peas Printanière
(with
Mushrooms and Carrots)

Serves: **6**
Preparation time: **30 minutes**
Cooking time: **20 minutes**
Type of recipe: **elementary**
Cost: **inexpensive**

Ingredients
2 teaspoons granulated sugar
3 pounds fresh young peas, shelled
1 cup carrots, scraped and cubed
4 Tablespoons sweet butter
½ pound fresh mushrooms, stems removed and caps cubed
Salt and freshly ground white pepper
1 cup heavy cream
2 Tablespoons finely minced fresh chives

Garnish:
Finely minced fresh parsley

Preparation
1.
In a large saucepan bring 4 cups salted water to a boil. Add 1 teaspoon sugar and peas and simmer uncovered for 5 to 7 minutes, or until the peas are tender. (For mature peas you will need about 1 tablespoon sugar.)
2.
Drain the peas and rinse with cold running water to stop further cooking and to retain their bright green color. Set aside.
3.
In a small saucepan again bring salted water to a boil. Add the remaining sugar and the carrots and simmer uncovered until barely tender. Drain the carrots, rinse with cold water and set aside.
4.
In a large heavy skillet heat 2 tablespoons butter over moderate-to-high heat. Add the mushrooms and sauté for 2 to 3 minutes, or until the mushrooms are nicely browned. Season with salt and pepper and set aside.

5.
Add the remaining butter to the skillet and when melted add the cream. Bring to a boil and reduce by one third.
6.
Lower the heat and return the mushrooms, carrots, and peas to the skillet. Season with salt and pepper and simmer the mixture for 2 to 3 minutes.
7.
Add the chives. Taste and correct the seasoning, then sprinkle with parsley and serve directly from the skillet.

Remarks
Three pounds fresh peas will yield about 3½ cups shelled peas.

Potatoes Arlésienne

Serves: **6**
Preparation time: **15 minutes**
Cooking time: **30 minutes**
Type of recipe: **elementary**
Cost: **inexpensive**

I remember traveling through a village in the south of France on market day, where a peasant woman was cooking her lunch over a small burner. I must have looked hungry for she offered me a taste of deliciously crisp, lemon-flavored fried potatoes. Here is her recipe.

Ingredients

**8 to 10 medium red potatoes
3 Tablespoons finely minced fresh parsley
2 cloves garlic, finely minced
1½ teaspoons lemon rind
4 to 6 anchovy fillets, finely minced
Juice of 1 large lemon
4 to 6 Tablespoons olive oil
1 Tablespoon butter
Salt and freshly ground black pepper**

Preparation

1.
In a large saucepan bring salted water to a boil. Add the potatoes and cook over medium heat until almost tender. Drain the potatoes and cool.

2.
In a small bowl, combine the parsley, garlic, lemon rind, anchovies, and lemon juice. Blend the mixture thoroughly and set aside.

3.
Peel the potatoes and cut into thick slices. Reserve.

4.
Heat 2 tablespoons oil and the butter in a heavy 10-inch skillet. Add the potatoes in 1 layer; do not crowd the pan. You will have to sauté the potatoes in 2 to 3 batches. Cook the potatoes until crisp and nicely browned, turning them carefully so as not to break them. Season with salt and pepper.

5.
When the potatoes are done, remove from the skillet and add a little more oil to the pan. Add the parsley-anchovy-lemon mixture. Cook for 1 to 2 minutes, then return the potatoes to the pan and toss them in the parsley mixture until well coated. Add another sprinkling of lemon juice and serve hot right from the pan.

Remarks
The potatoes can be sautéed well ahead and kept in a 200-degree oven. Do not fold them into the parsley mixture until just before serving.

Peasant
Potato Pie

Serves: **6**
Preparation time: **25 minutes**
Cooking time: **1 hour, 15 minutes**
Type of recipe: **elementary**
Cost: **inexpensive**

Ingredients

2½ pounds all-purpose potatoes, peeled and quartered
½ cup freshly grated Parmesan cheese
2 large eggs
Salt and freshly ground black pepper
2 to 3 Tablespoons olive oil
½ pound hot Italian sausage links, casings removed
⅓ pound prosciutto, sliced into thin julienne strips
1 large Roasted Red Pepper (page 545), finely cubed
1 onion, peeled and finely minced
1 teaspoon minced garlic
½ cup Brown Chicken Stock (page 531) or beef bouillon
¼ cup finely minced fresh parsley
1 can (35 ounces) Italian plum tomatoes, well drained and chopped
½ teaspoon dried oregano
1 Tablespoon Basil Paste (page 359), or ½ teaspoon dried
1 Tablespoon tomato paste
½ cup bread crumbs, plus 2 Tablespoons
⅓ pound mozzarella cheese, diced
2 Tablespoons butter, cut into tiny pieces

Preparation

1.
Preheat the oven to 350 degrees.

2.
In a large saucepan bring salted water to a boil. Add the potatoes and cook uncovered until tender when pierced with the tip of a sharp knife.

3.
Drain the potatoes and, when cool enough to handle, mash them in a mixing bowl until smooth.

4.
Return the mashed potatoes to the saucepan. Cook over low heat, stirring constantly with a wooden spoon, until a thin film forms on the bottom of the pan. (This will dry out the potatoes.) Be careful not to burn them. Remove the potatoes from the heat and transfer to a mixing bowl. Add 3 tablespoons Parmesan cheese and the eggs and season the mixture with salt and pepper. Mix thoroughly and set aside.

5.
In a heavy skillet heat the olive oil over medium heat. Add the sausage meat, breaking it up with a fork into tiny pieces. When the sausage is done transfer it to a bowl. Add the prosciutto and roasted peppers to the bowl and set aside.

6.
Add a little more oil to the skillet. Add the onion and sauté until nicely browned. Add the garlic and cook for a minute or so without browning.

7.
Add the stock or bouillon, increase the heat, and cook until the liquid is reduced to a glaze, scraping well the bottom of the pan.

8.
Add the parsley, tomatoes, oregano, Basil Paste, and salt and pepper to taste. Reduce the heat, cover the skillet, and simmer the mixture for 15 minutes.

Potato and Bacon Gratin

Serves: **6**
Preparation time: **20 minutes**
Cooking time: **1 hour, 45 minutes**
Type of recipe: **elementary**
Cost: **inexpensive**

9.
When the sauce is done transfer it to a food processor and purée. (If you are using a blender make sure to cool the sauce before puréeing.) Add the tomato paste and stir the tomato sauce into the sausage mixture thoroughly. Set aside.

10.
Butter a heavy 2½-quart casserole and sprinkle generously with ½ cup bread crumbs. Line the sides and bottom with ⅔ of the potato mixture. Layer with the sausage-and-tomato mixture and add a layer of the mozzarella cheese. Sprinkle with grated Parmesan cheese and top with the remaining mashed-potato mixture. Sprinkle with the remaining 2 tablespoons bread crumbs and the remaining Parmesan. Dot with 2 tablespoons butter.

11.
Place the casserole in the center of the oven and bake uncovered for 30 minutes, or until the top is nicely browned.

12.
When the pie is done remove from the oven and let it sit for 10 minutes. Serve right from the casserole accompanied by a well-seasoned green salad.

Remarks
The entire dish can be prepared several hours ahead and baked for 30 to 40 minutes. This potato-and-sausage casserole should be served as a 1-dish meal for a family supper or Sunday dinner.

Ingredients
3 large baking potatoes, peeled
8 to 10 slices bacon, cut in half
Salt and freshly ground black pepper
1 cup finely grated Swiss cheese or a mixture of Swiss and Parmesan
4 to 6 Tablespoons butter
¾ cup heavy cream

Preparation
1.
Preheat the oven to 350 degrees.

2.
Thinly slice the potatoes in a food processor or a mandoline. Drop the potato slices into a bowl of cold water to prevent them from turning brown.

3.
Butter a rectangular or oval baking dish. Place a layer of bacon slices in the bottom of the dish.

4.
Drain and dry the potato slices thoroughly with paper towels. Add a layer of the potatoes to the baking dish, slightly overlapping. Season with salt and pepper, sprinkle with cheese, and dot with bits of butter.

5.
Repeat the layers of bacon and potatoes, finishing with a layer of potatoes. Season the potatoes with salt and pepper and sprinkle with the remaining cheese and butter.

6.
Top the dish with the cream. Cover and place the dish in the center of the oven. Bake for 1 hour, 15 minutes.

Gratin of Potatoes and Gorgonzola

Serves:	**6 to 8**
Preparation time:	**20 minutes**
Cooking time:	**35 to 40 minutes**
Type of recipe:	**elementary**
Cost:	**inexpensive**

7.
Uncover the dish and bake for another 30 minutes, or until the potatoes are very tender and the top is nicely browned. Serve directly from the baking dish as an accompaniment to roast or grilled meat.

Remarks
The gratin can be made several hours ahead and reheated in a 200-degree oven. For variation you can add a layer of sautéed thinly sliced onion between each potato layer.

Ingredients
2 cups water
4 cups milk
2 pounds baking potatoes, peeled and thinly sliced
6 Tablespoons butter
3 Tablespoons flour
¼ cup Gorgonzola cheese or other mild blue cheese
4 Tablespoons freshly grated Parmesan cheese
Salt and freshly ground black pepper
Large pinch freshly grated nutmeg

Preparation
1.
Preheat the oven to 375 degrees.
2.
In a large saucepan combine water with 2 cups milk and add the potatoes. Bring to a boil, reduce the heat, and simmer the potato slices for 5 minutes, or until barely tender. Do not overcook. Drain the potato slices and set aside.
3.
In a heavy 2-quart saucepan heat 3 tablespoons butter over low heat. Add the flour and cook, stirring constantly, for 1 to 2 minutes without browning.
4.
Remove the saucepan from the heat and add the remaining 2 cups milk, whisking the mixture until well blended. Return the saucepan to the heat and whisk until the sauce comes to a boil and is completely smooth and thick. Remove from the heat and set aside.
5.
Mash the Gorgonzola in a small bowl with

Gratin of Potatoes and Onions Martegal

Serves:	**4 to 6**
Preparation time:	**15 minutes**
Cooking time:	**1 hour, 50 minutes**
Type of recipe:	**elementary**
Cost:	**inexpensive**

2 tablespoons butter until competely smooth.

6.
Whisk the Gorgonzola and 2 tablespoons Parmesan cheese into the sauce. Season with salt, pepper, and nutmeg and set aside.

7.
Butter a rectangular baking dish. Place an overlapping layer of potatoes in the dish and season with salt and pepper. Sprinkle with a little Parmesan, then make another layer of potatoes. Season again with salt and pepper and spoon the sauce over the potatoes, covering them completely. Sprinkle with the remaining Parmesan and bits of butter.

8.
Set the dish in the upper part of the oven and bake for 25 minutes or until the top is nicely browned. Serve the gratin hot, right from the baking dish.

Remarks
The entire dish can be assembled several hours ahead and refrigerated until baking. You may use other blue cheese, such as Roquefort or a delicious mild French blue cheese called Pipo Crèm'.

Ingredients
4 Tablespoons butter
2 Tablespoons oil
2 Bermuda onions, peeled and thinly sliced
Salt and freshly ground black pepper
¼ teaspoon dried thyme
4 large baking potatoes
1½ cups concentrated Chicken Stock (page 530)

Potato, Onion, and Zucchini Pancake

Serves:	**4 to 6**
Preparation time:	**30 minutes**
Cooking time:	**10 minutes**
Type of recipe:	**elementary**
Cost:	**inexpensive**

Ingredients

1 medium zucchini, unpeeled and finely grated
Salt
4 to 5 large red potatoes
3 Tablespoons butter
2 Tablespoons oil
2 medium onions, peeled and thinly sliced
Freshly ground black pepper

Preparation

1.
Place the grated zucchini in a colander. Season with salt and set over a bowl. Let it drain for 30 minutes.

2.
Meanwhile bring salted water to a boil in a large saucepan. Add the potatoes and cook over medium heat until barely tender. Do not overcook. Drain the potatoes and, when cool enough to handle, peel and grate them coarsely into a bowl. Set aside.

3.
In a small heavy skillet heat 2 tablespoons butter and 1 tablespoon oil. Add the onions, season with salt and pepper, and cook partially covered for 20 minutes until the onions are very soft, but not burned.

4.
Add the onions to the potato.

5.
Squeeze the zucchini with your hands to remove all moisture. Add it to the potato-and-onion mixture. Season with salt and pepper.

6.
In an 8- to 10-inch deep cast-iron skillet heat the remaining butter and oil. When the

Preparation

1.
Preheat the oven to 350 degrees.

2.
In a heavy 10-inch skillet heat 2 tablespoons butter and 1 tablespoon oil. Add the onions, then season with salt, pepper, and thyme. Cook the onions over low heat for 40 minutes partially covered or until they are nicely browned and very soft. Do not let the onions burn; you may need another tablespoon of oil.

3.
Peel the potatoes; do not wash. Clean with damp paper towels and slice thinly. Add the potatoes and the remaining butter to the onions in the skillet and toss the mixture well.

4.
Spoon the potato-and-onion mixture into a well-buttered oval baking dish, arranging the potatoes in an even layer. Season with salt and pepper.

5.
Add the stock; it should cover the potatoes. Cover the dish and place in the oven. Bake for 50 minutes to 1 hour, or until the potatoes are tender and all the stock has been absorbed.

6.
Serve the gratin hot right from the dish as an accompaniment to roast or grilled meat and fish.

Remarks

The entire dish can be assembled several hours ahead and baked 1 hour before serving.

Potato and Turnip Purée

Serves: **4 to 6**
Preparation time: **10 minutes**
Cooking time: **25 minutes**
Type of recipe: **elementary**
Cost: **inexpensive**

butter is very hot and the foam starts to subside add the potato mixture. Flatten it out with a spatula and cook for 3 to 4 minutes over medium heat without stirring.
7.
When the potato pancake is nicely brown underneath invert it quickly onto a plate and slide it back into the skillet. Cook for another 4 to 5 minutes, or until the bottom is nicely browned.
8.
Slide the pancake onto a round serving platter and serve hot.

Ingredients
4 medium all-purpose potatoes, peeled and quartered
4 to 6 medium turnips, peeled and quartered
3 to 4 Tablespoons butter
¾ cup sour cream
Salt and freshly ground black pepper

Preparation
1.
Combine the potatoes and turnips in a large saucepan and cover with 2 inches of salted water. Bring to a boil and cook until both turnips and potatoes are very tender.
2.
Drain the vegetables and mash with a potato masher. (If you use a food processor pour the mixture into the bowl using quick on-and-off movements to avoid the purée becoming too liquid.)
3.
Return the purée to the saucepan and place over low heat. Beat in the butter and sour cream, then season with salt and pepper. Heat through, stirring constantly. Keep the purée warm in the top of a double boiler until ready to serve. When ready to serve transfer to a deep dish and serve hot as an accompaniment to roast or grilled meats.

Potato and Leek Purée

Serves: **4**
Preparation time: **15 minutes**
Cooking time: **35 minutes**
Type of recipe: **elementary**
Cost: **inexpensive**

Ingredients
4 Tablespoons butter
4 large leeks, well rinsed and thinly sliced
Salt and freshly ground black pepper
4 to 6 medium all-purpose potatoes, peeled and quartered
¾ to 1 cup sour cream

Optional:
2 Tablespoons finely minced fresh chives

Preparation

1.
In a large heavy skillet melt 2 tablespoons of butter and add the leeks. Season with salt and pepper and then add ¼ cup water. Cover and simmer the leeks for 5 minutes, or until very tender. Uncover the leeks and cook until all the moisture is evaporated. Set aside.

2.
In a large saucepan combine the potatoes with salted water to cover. Bring to a boil and cook over medium heat until very tender.

3.
Drain the potatoes and combine in a food processor with the braised leeks. Add the remaining butter and the sour cream. Purée the mixture with quick on-and-off movements so as not to liquefy the purée.

4.
Transfer the purée to a double boiler. Season carefully with salt and pepper and keep warm until serving.

5.
Just before serving taste and correct the seasoning, then fold in the chives.

Grilled Tomatoes Antiboise

Serves: **4 to 6**
Preparation time: **10 minutes**
Cooking time: **25 minutes**
Type of recipe: **elementary**
Cost: **inexpensive**

Ingredients
¾ cup fruity olive oil
3 Tablespoons red wine vinegar
Juice of ½ lemon
4 Tablespoons minced fresh herbs (thyme, marjoram), or 1 teaspoon each dried thyme and marjoram
2 crumbled bay leaves
2 cloves garlic, peeled and crushed
Salt and freshly ground black pepper
4 to 5 ripe tomatoes, cut in half crosswise

Garnish:
2 Tablespoons finely minced fresh parsley mixed with
3 Tablespoons bread crumbs

Curried Cold Vegetable Ragoût

Serves:	**6 to 8**
Preparation time:	**25 minutes, plus 1 to 2 hours to drain eggplant**
Cooking time:	**1 hour**
Type of recipe:	**elementary**
Cost:	**inexpensive**

Preparation

1.
In a small saucepan combine ½ cup olive oil, vinegar, lemon juice, herbs, and garlic. Season with salt and pepper. Bring the mixture to a boil, reduce the heat, and simmer for 10 minutes. Keep warm.

2.
Preheat the broiler.

3.
Place the tomatoes in a baking dish and season with salt and pepper. Sprinkle on a little of the parsley and bread-crumb garnish. Drizzle with the remaining olive oil.

4.
Place the tomatoes 6 inches from the source of the heat and broil for 6 to 8 minutes, or until barely tender. Do not let the bread crumbs burn.

5.
Remove the dish from the broiler. Strain the herb dressing over the tomatoes and serve warm.

Remarks

The dressing is at its best when made a day ahead and reheated. This gives the herbs a chance to release all their aroma. The dressing is equally good on other broiled vegetables such like grilled peppers or eggplant.

Ingredients

1 large eggplant, cut into ¾-inch cubes
Salt
⅓ cup olive oil
3 small zucchini, cubed
Freshly ground black pepper
2 cups thinly sliced onions
2 large cloves garlic, peeled and crushed
1 dried hot chili pepper
2 green peppers, cored and thinly sliced
½ cup Roasted Red Peppers (page 545), thinly sliced
2 teaspoons curry powder
1 Tablespoon tomato paste
1 can (35 ounces) Italian plum tomatoes, well drained and chopped, or 4 to 6 large ripe tomatoes peeled, seeded, and chopped
½ cup long-grain rice
1 cup chicken bouillon

Garnish:

2 Tablespoons finely minced fresh parsley

Preparation

1.
A few hours ahead place the cubed eggplant on a double layer of paper towels. Sprinkle with salt and let drain for 1 to 2 hours.

2.
Dry the eggplant cubes with paper towels. In a large heavy skillet heat 4 tablespoons oil. Add the eggplant to the pan and cook until nicely browned on all sides.

3.
Transfer the eggplant to a colander with a slotted spoon and set aside.

4.
Add a little more oil to the pan. Add the zucchini and cook until evenly browned. Season with salt and pepper, transfer to a side dish, and reserve.

5.
To the oil remaining in the pan add the onions, garlic, and chili pepper. Cook the mixture over medium heat partially covered for 20 minutes, or until soft and lightly browned.

6.
Add the peppers and roasted peppers and continue cooking for another 5 minutes. Add the curry powder, tomato paste, and tomatoes. Season with salt and pepper and cook the mixture over high heat for 3 to 4 minutes, or until most of the tomato water has evaporated.

7.
Return the zucchini and eggplant to the pan. Add the rice and bouillon. Cover the pan tightly and simmer for 15 to 20 minutes, or until the rice is tender.

8.
Uncover the pan. Taste and correct the seasoning. Transfer the vegetable ragoût to a serving bowl and cool to room temperature. Sprinkle with parsley and serve as part of a hors d'oeuvre table or as an accompaniment to roast or grilled lamb.

Remarks
This kind of vegetable ragoût is at its best when prepared a day or so ahead to give the vegetables a chance to develop flavor. You may also serve it slightly chilled, sprinkled with lemon juice and a little fruity olive oil and garnished with black olives and quartered tomatoes.

Sauté of Vegetables

Serves: **4 to 5**
Preparation time: **15 minutes**
Cooking time: **20 minutes**
Type of recipe: **elementary**
Cost: **inexpensive**

Ingredients
4 Tablespoons butter
3 large carrots, scraped and cubed
1 celery heart, cubed
4 turnips, peeled and cut into eighths
1 cup Chicken Stock (page 530)
Salt and freshly ground white pepper
Large pinch of granulated sugar
½ cup heavy cream

Garnish
Finely minced fresh parsley

Preparation
1.
Melt the butter in a heavy saucepan. Add the vegetables and ¾ cup stock. Season with salt, pepper, and sugar. Cover the pan and cook over low heat, adding a little more stock if necessary. The vegetables must not brown.
2.
After 10 to 15 minutes check the vegetables. If they are tender uncover the pan and bring the broth to a boil.
3.
Add the cream and cook until it is reduced and heavily coats the vegetables. Taste and correct the seasoning.
4.
Sprinkle with parsley and serve as an accompaniment to roast meats and poached or grilled fish.

Remarks
You can add 1 cup fresh peas to the saucepan and/or 1 cup green beans cut into 1-inch pieces.

Gratin of Zucchini à la Bordelaise

Serves: **4 to 5**
Preparation time: **15 minutes, plus 30 minutes to drain zucchini**
Cooking time: **35 minutes**
Type of recipe: **elementary**
Cost: **inexpensive**

Ingredients
4 medium zucchini
Salt
2 Tablespoons butter
1 cup light cream
3 large eggs
½ cup freshly grated Parmesan cheese
Freshly ground black pepper
1 Tablespoon olive oil
2 Tablespoons bread crumbs
2 Tablespoons finely minced fresh parsley
2 cloves garlic, finely minced
1 Tablespoon finely minced shallots

Preparation
1.
Half an hour ahead cut the zucchini in half lengthwise and then crosswise into ½-inch slices. Place in a colander. Sprinkle with salt and let drain for 30 minutes.
2.
Preheat the oven to 350 degrees.
3.
In a cast-iron skillet melt 2 tablespoons butter. Add the zucchini and sauté over moderate-to-high heat for 3 to 5 minutes, or until lightly browned. Transfer the zucchini to a bowl and set aside.
4.
In a small bowl combine the cream, eggs, and ¼ cup Parmesan cheese. Season the mixture with salt and pepper and whisk until well blended. Pour the mixture over the zucchini and blend thoroughly.
5.
Transfer the zucchini-and-custard mixture to a shallow baking dish or *au gratin* dish and place in the center of the oven. Bake for 25

Serves:	**4 to 5**
Preparation time:	**10 minutes**
Cooking time:	**10 to 12 minutes**
Type of recipe:	**elementary**
Cost:	**inexpensive**

minutes, or until the custard is almost set.

6.
While the zucchini dish is in the oven, heat the oil in a small skillet. Add the bread crumbs, parsley, garlic, and shallots and sauté the mixture over low heat for 1 to 2 minutes.

7.
Sprinkle the mixture on top of the zucchini and return the baking dish to the oven. Continue baking for another 5 to 10 minutes, or until the custard is completely set.

8.
Sprinkle the zucchini with the remaining Parmesan and place the dish in the broiler for 1 minute, or until the bread-crumb mixture is nicely browned.

9.
Remove the dish from the oven and let the gratin cool for about 5 minutes. Serve right from the baking dish as an accompaniment to roast, grilled, or sautéed meats or fish.

Remarks
The zucchini can be sautéed in advance and combined with the custard. The gratin should be baked no more than 30 to 40 minutes before serving. It can be left covered in a warm oven for 10 to 20 minutes.

This simple zucchini dish is an excellent accompaniment to sautéed or baked fish. For variation you can flavor the parsley butter with 2 minced anchovy fillets and you can also add some small white onions to the zucchini while they are stewing.

Ingredients
6 Tablespoons butter
1 Tablespoon olive oil
4 to 6 small zucchini, rinsed and cut into ½-inch rounds
Salt and freshly ground black pepper
⅓ cup Chicken Stock (page 530) or bouillon
2 Tablespoons finely minced fresh parsley
1 large clove garlic, finely minced

Preparation

1.

In a heavy 10-inch skillet heat 2 tablespoons butter and the oil. Add the zucchini, season with salt and pepper, and cook for 2 or 3 minutes until lightly browned.

2.

Add the stock and reduce the heat. Cover the pan and let the zucchini simmer for another 10 minutes, or until tender.

3.

While the squash is cooking combine the remaining butter, parsley, and garlic in a small bowl. Mash the mixture with a fork until thoroughly blended. Season with salt and pepper.

4.

When the zucchini are done remove the pan from the heat. Fold the parsley butter into the zucchini mixture.

5.

Transfer the zucchini to a deep serving bowl. Serve hot as an accompaniment to roast or grilled meats.

Salads and Salad Dressings

Americans eat more salads than any other nation. We associate salads with health, nutrition, low calorie foods, and freshness. In contrast with the French, Italian, or Spaniards we like our salads at every part of the meal—sometimes at the beginning, most often with our meal, and frequently after the main course. But no matter how much stress is put on freshness, on quality of ingredients, or what should or should not go into the salad bowl, many a serious cook unfortunately still reaches for the bottled dressing. I personally believe that it is in small touches such as these that a good cook can elevate the quality of a meal. A well-prepared, properly seasoned salad is as important as a well-seasoned sauce.

Three main ingredients go into most salad dressings and these should be of excellent quality: olive oil, wine vinegar, and mustard. The proportions may vary according to the greens. Sometimes lemon juice is more suitable to a certain green than vinegar. Often the addition of a clove of garlic or a sprinkling of a fresh herb will give the dressing its particular character. It is essential, however, to understand the fundamentals of salad dressings. The proportion of olive oil to vinegar depends largely on the types of greens used. Acidic greens, such as spinach, watercress, curly endive, and escarole will need more vinegar in proportion to olive oil while buttery greens such as Boston, bibb, and field (loose leaf) lettuce should be dressed with a milder proportion. Cooked vegetables such as green beans, beets, and carrots are often more interesting when seasoned with a lemon dressing. Whatever dressing you choose remember that the proportion of dressing to greens is of great importance. You must never drown your salad. The dressing must be placed in the bottom of the bowl with the salad greens on top and not tossed until just before serving. You can chill the salad this way for several hours and then toss at the dinner table before serving.

In the perfect salad there should be no dressing left in the bottom of the bowl. Each leaf should have its share of dressing and absorb it in perfect proportion. When choosing the olive oil, vinegar, and mustard for your dressing select the best quality you can afford. A French wine vinegar such as Dessaux Fils is now available in many supermarkets and in every gourmet shop; the nonfruit but pure olive oils such as Berio and Bertolli are equally available in most supermarkets. The Grey Poupon mustard made after the Dijon formula is my favorite mustard for simple salad dressings. In fact, with these 3 good yet simple ingredients you should be able to make the perfect salad every time.

Green Beans in Walnut-and-Roquefort Sauce

Serves: **4 to 6**
Preparation time: **10 minutes, plus 2 to 4 hours to chill**
Cooking time: **10 minutes**
Type of recipe: **elementary**
Cost: **inexpensive**

Ingredients
⅓ cup Crème Fraîche (page 544)
3 Tablespoons Roquefort cheese
2 Tablespoons white wine vinegar
2 teaspoons Dijon mustard
4 Tablespoons walnut or olive oil
Salt and freshly ground black pepper
1½ pounds young green beans
½ cup finely diced walnuts

Garnish:
2 Tablespoons finely minced fresh parsley

Preparation
1.
In a bowl combine the Crème Fraîche with 2 tablespoons Roquefort. Mash the mixture into a fine paste. Add the vinegar, Dijon mustard, and walnut oil. Season the dressing with salt and pepper and whisk until thoroughly blended. Taste and correct the seasoning. Set the dressing aside.
2.
Snap the beans. In a large saucepan bring salted water to a boil, then add the beans and cook for 7 to 8 minutes, or until just tender. Drain the beans under cold water and transfer to a serving bowl.
3.
When the beans are completely cool, add the dressing and toss lightly. Taste the salad and correct the seasoning.
4.
Sprinkle with the remaining cheese, add the walnuts, and garnish with parsley. Chill the salad for 2 to 4 hours before serving. Serve the salad as an appetizer or as an accompaniment to roast or grilled meats.

Green Bean and Mushroom Salad

Serves: **6**
Preparation time: **20 minutes, plus 2 to 4 hours to marinate and chill**
Cooking time: **10 minutes**
Type of recipe: **elementary**
Cost: **inexpensive**

Ingredients
1 pound fresh green beans, trimmed and washed
Juice of 1 large lime
4 Tablespoons olive oil
1 large clove garlic, crushed
Salt and freshly ground black pepper
¾ pound fresh mushrooms, stems removed and caps thinly sliced
2 to 3 finely minced fresh chives
½ to ¾ cup Crème Fraîche (page 544)

Garnish:
Finely minced fresh parsley

Catalan White Bean Salad

Serves: **6 to 8**
Preparation time: **25 minutes, plus overnight to soak beans and 2 to 4 hours to chill**
Cooking time: **1 hour, 45 minutes**
Type of recipe: **elementary**
Cost: **inexpensive**

Preparation

1.
Drop the beans into rapidly boiling salted water and cook for 7 to 8 minutes, or until tender. Do not overcook. Drain and run under cold water to stop further cooking then transfer to a bowl and set aside.

2.
In a small bowl combine the lime juice, olive oil, garlic, salt, and pepper. Whisk the dressing until well blended. Set aside.

3.
Place the sliced mushrooms in a serving bowl. Add the chives and the dressing. Toss and let the mixture marinate at room temperature for 2 hours.

4.
Cut the beans into 2-inch matchsticks. Add to the mushroom mixture and toss lightly.

5.
Fold in enough Crème Fraîche to coat the vegetables evenly. Taste and correct the seasoning. Serve lightly chilled, but not cold, garnished with minced parsley and accompanied by crusty French bread.

Remarks

Serve this salad as an appetizer; it is both light and refreshing. It can also be served as an accompaniment to grilled or sautéed chicken or fish dishes.

Ingredients

1½ cups dried beans, preferably Great Northern
1 large onion, stuck with a clove
1 bay leaf
Salt
2 cups cubed slab bacon (cut into ½-inch cubes)
2 large Roasted Green Peppers (page 545), thinly sliced
2 large Roasted Red Peppers (page 545), thinly sliced
1 small red onion, thinly sliced

Optional:

5 to 8 fresh mushrooms, thinly sliced

Dressing:

3 Tablespoons red wine vinegar
2 teaspoons Dijon mustard
2 small cloves garlic, crushed
8 Tablespoons olive oil
Salt and freshly ground black pepper

Garnish:

2 Tablespoons finely minced fresh parsley

Serves:	**4**
Preparation time:	**15 minutes, plus 1 to 2 hours to marinate and 30 minutes to chill**
Cooking time:	**10 minutes**
Type of recipe:	**elementary**
Cost:	**inexpensive**

Preparation

1.
Cover the beans with cold water and soak overnight.

2.
Preheat the oven to 325 degrees.

3.
Drain the beans. Place them in a casserole with enough cold water to cover them with 2 inches of water. Add the onion, bay leaf, and salt and cover the casserole. Bring to a boil on top of the stove. As soon as the water comes to a boil, transfer the casserole to the oven. Cook the beans for 45 minutes, or until the beans are tender but not falling apart. Let the beans cool in their cooking water. Discard the onion and bay leaf. Drain and set aside.

4.
In a large heavy skillet sauté the bacon until almost crisp, then remove to a double layer of paper towels and set aside.

5.
Prepare the dressing. In a large salad bowl combine the vinegar, mustard, garlic, and olive oil. Whisk the dressing until it is well blended. Season with salt and pepper.

6.
Add the beans, bacon, peppers, and optional mushrooms. Add the sliced onion and toss the salad. Taste and correct the seasoning, then sprinkle with parsley. Let the salad marinate at room temperature for 2 to 4 hours before serving. Serve the salad at room temperature or lightly chilled.

Remarks
The beans can be cooked 2 to 3 days ahead. They should be left refrigerated in their cooking liquid.

Ingredients
1½ to 2 pounds fresh broccoli
½ cup diced Italian roasted peppers (red) or ½ cups diced pimientos
1 can (7½ ounces) tuna, packed in olive oil
8 to 10 sliced Greek black olives
½ cup thinly sliced red onions
Salt and freshly ground black pepper

Dressing:
2 Tablespoons red wine vinegar
1 large clove garlic, peeled and crushed
1 Tablespoon finely minced fresh parsley
1 teaspoon anchovy paste
6 Tablespoons olive oil

Garnish:
6 to 8 cherry tomatoes
4 to 8 slices hard salami
2 hard-boiled eggs, peeled and cut in half

Optional:
Juice of ½ lemon
4 to 8 rolled anchovy fillets

Preparation

1.
Scrape the broccoli stalks with a vegetable peeler. Remove all the leaves and cut the broccoli lengthwise into even pieces. Slice 1 inch off the bottom of each stalk.

2.
In a large casserole bring salted water to a boil. Add the broccoli and cook for 5 to 7 minutes, or until barely tender. Do not overcook.

Endive and Apple Salad

Serves:	**4**
Preparation Time:	**10 minutes, plus 1 to 2 hours to marinate**
Cooking time:	**none**
Type of Recipe:	**elementary**
Cost:	**moderate**

3.
Drain the broccoli immediately and rinse with cold water to stop any further cooking. Spread the broccoli stalks on a double layer of paper towels.

4.
In a serving bowl combine the broccoli, roasted peppers or pimientos, tuna, olives, and onion. Season with salt and pepper and set aside.

5.
Prepare the dressing. In a blender combine the vinegar, garlic, parsley, and anchovy paste. Add the olive oil and blend the dressing until smooth. Season with salt and pepper.

6.
Pour the dressing over the broccoli salad. Toss lightly and let the salad marinate from 1 to 2 hours at room temperature.

7.
Taste the salad and correct the seasoning. Add a dash of the optional lemon juice and garnish the salad with the cherry tomatoes, salami, hard-boiled eggs, and optional rolled anchovy fillets.

8.
Chill the salad for 30 minutes before serving. Serve the broccoli salad accompanied by crusty French bread and a bowl of sweet butter or as part of an hors d'oeuvre table.

Ingredients
6 large heads Belgian endive
1 large red delicious apple, cored, peeled, and cubed
½ cup diced walnuts
2 Tablespoons golden raisins

Dressing:
Juice of 1 lemon
1½ teaspoons granulated sugar
2 teaspoons Dijon mustard
4 Tablespoons walnut or peanut oil
Freshly ground white pepper
Pinch of freshly grated nutmeg

Tunisian Pepper Salad

Serves: **4 to 5**
Preparation time: **10 minutes**
Cooking time: **10 minutes**
Type of recipe: **elementary**
Cost: **inexpensive**

Preparation

1.
Remove any wilted outer leaves from the endive. With the tip of a sharp knife remove the hard round base. Cut the endive crosswise into ¾-inch slices and set aside.

2.
In a large glass serving bowl combine the lemon juice, sugar, mustard, and oil. Whisk the dressing until smooth and well blended. Season with a large grinding of pepper and a grating of fresh nutmeg.

3.
Add the endive, apples, walnuts, and raisins to the bowl. Toss the salad lightly and marinate for 1 to 2 hours before serving.

4.
Serve the salad lightly chilled as an appetizer accompanied by thinly sliced, buttered black bread.

Remarks

For variation omit the raisins and add 2 tablespoons finely minced fresh dill and 1 cup diced marinated herring to the bowl. Toss and serve the salad as an appetizer.

This simple salad should be quite spicy. It is at its best when the peppers are still warm but is equally delicious at room temperature. Serve it as an appetizer accompanied by crusty French bread.

Ingredients

2 to 3 large Roasted Red Peppers (page 545)
2 large Roasted Green Peppers (page 545)
3 ripe tomatoes
Salt
½ cup finely minced red onions
1 to 2 small hot green chili peppers, finely diced

Dressing:

2 Tablespoons red wine vinegar
4 Tablespoons fruity olive oil
1 large clove garlic, peeled and crushed
Salt and freshly ground black pepper

Garnish:

1 can (3 to 4 ounces) tuna in olive oil, flaked
3 Tablespoons finely minced fresh parsley, preferably Italian
2 hard-boiled eggs, peeled and cut in half

Optional:

½ cup black olives

Danish
Potato Salad

Serves:	**6**
Preparation time:	**30 minutes, plus 2 to 4 hours to chill**
Cooking time:	**25 to 30 minutes**
Type of recipe:	**elementary**
Cost:	**inexpensive**

Preparation

1.
Dice the Roasted Red and Green Peppers and place in a bowl. Set aside.

2.
Cut the tomatoes in half but do not peel. Carefully discard the seeds. Dice the tomatoes and place in a sieve over a bowl. Sprinkle lightly with salt and let the tomatoes drain for 10 to 15 minutes.

3.
Add the tomatoes and the onions and chili peppers to the pepper mixture. Toss lightly and set aside.

4.
In a small bowl combine the vinegar, oil, and garlic and season with salt and pepper. Whisk the dressing lightly and pour over the pepper-and-tomato mixture.

5.
Toss the salad and transfer to a shallow serving bowl. Garnish the salad with the tuna, parsley, hard-boiled eggs, and optional olives and serve immediately.

Remarks

Canned green chili peppers are available in the Mexican food section of most supermarkets. The dressing should not be added to the salad until 30 minutes to 1 hour before serving time or else the tomatoes will lose their crispness.

Ingredients

12 to 14 medium red potatoes
Salt
1 small green pepper, seeded, quartered, and finely cubed
1 cucumber, peeled, seeded, and cubed
2 small dill gherkins, finely diced
¼ cup finely minced fresh dill

Mayonnaise:

2 large eggs
1 Tablespoon Dijon mustard
1 Tablespoon white wine vinegar
Salt and freshly ground black pepper
¾ to 1 cup peanut oil
½ cup finely minced fresh parsley
½ cup minced scallions (white and green parts)
¼ cup finely minced fresh dill

Garnish:

Thin slices of unpeeled cucumber
Whole radishes

Preparation

1.
Start by making the mayonnaise. In a blender combine the eggs, mustard, and vinegar. Season with salt and a large grinding of pepper.

2.
Blend at high speed until the mixture is smooth. With the blender still at high speed add the oil by droplets, adding enough oil until the mixture becomes quite thick.

3.
Add the parsley, scallions, and dill to the mayonnaise. Blend until completely smooth, then taste and correct the seasoning.

Greek
Potato Salad

Serves: **4 to 5**
Preparation time: **20 minutes, plus 4 to 6 hours to chill**
Cooking time: **30 to 40 minutes**
Type of recipe: **elementary**
Cost: **inexpensive**

4.
In a large saucepan combine the potatoes with cold water to cover. Season with salt, bring to a boil, reduce the heat, and simmer the potatoes until just tender. Do not overcook.

5.
Drain the potatoes and cool. (If possible refrigerate for 1 to 2 hours, which will firm the potatoes and make them easier to slice.)

6.
Peel and cube the potatoes. Combine with the green pepper, cucumber, and diced gherkins in a serving bowl.

7.
Add the mayonnaise; use just enough to bind the potatoes and vegetables. If you have any left over you can reserve it and serve with grilled fish or cooked vegetables such as asparagus or artichokes. Taste the salad and correct the seasoning. Cover and chill for 2 to 4 hours before serving.

8.
Thirty minutes before serving bring the salad back to room temperature. Sprinkle with the remaining dill and garnish with additional cucumber slices and whole radishes. Serve as an accompaniment to cold roast chicken or cold poached fish. It is also delicious as an accompaniment to sautéed hamburgers or grilled steaks.

Ingredients
6 to 8 medium red new potatoes
1 small red onion, peeled and thinly sliced
1 cup diced green pepper
2 dill gherkins, finely minced
½ cup sliced green olives
Salt and freshly ground black pepper
1 cup plain yogurt
½ teaspoon ground cumin

Optional:
Dash of Tabasco sauce

Dressing:
1½ Tablespoons red wine vinegar
1 teaspoon Dijon mustard
4 Tablespoons olive oil
1 clove garlic, peeled and crushed
Salt and freshly ground black pepper

Garnish:
Finely minced fresh parsley
6 to 8 Greek black olives

Turkey and Potato Salad Provençale

Serves:	**6 to 8**
Preparation time:	**25 minutes, plus 30 minutes to flavor mustard**
Cooking time:	**20 minutes**
Type of recipe:	**elementary**
Cost:	**inexpensive**

Preparation

1.
In a small bowl combine the vinegar, mustard, olive oil, and garlic. Whisk the mixture until well blended. Season with salt and pepper and set aside.

2.
In a large casserole bring salted water to a boil. Add the potatoes and reduce the heat. Simmer the potatoes partially covered for 30 or 40 minutes, or until tender when pierced with the tip of a sharp knife. Do not overcook.

3.
Peel the potatoes and cool, then cube and place in a serving bowl. Sprinkle with the dressing and toss lightly.

4.
Add the onion, pepper, gherkins, and olives, then season with salt and pepper. Set aside.

5.
In a small bowl combine the yogurt with the cumin and optional Tabasco sauce.

6.
Add the yogurt to the potato-and-vegetable mixture. Toss the salad and chill for 4 to 6 hours or overnight.

7.
Bring the salad back to room temperature and garnish with parsley and olives. Serve as an accompaniment to roast lamb, shish kebabs, or barbecued chicken.

Everyone is always searching for a good way to serve leftover roast turkey. Since I have never liked cold turkey sandwiches I prefer to make this gutsy and simple salad and serve it as a luncheon or light supper dish accompanied by crusty French bread and a bowl of sweet butter.

Ingredients

6 to 8 small red potatoes
4 cups cubed cooked turkey (cut into ¾-inch cubes)
1 green pepper, seeded and finely cubed
¾ cup thinly sliced pimientos
½ cup thinly sliced green olives
2 Tablespoons well-drained small capers
1 small red onion, peeled and thinly sliced
3 small dill gherkins, finely minced
1 cup cooked peas
Salt and freshly ground black pepper

Dressing:

¼ teaspoon dry mustard
3 Tablespoons red wine vinegar
6 to 8 Tablespoons fruity olive oil
1 Tablespoon Dijon mustard
2 cloves garlic, peeled and crushed
Salt and freshly ground black pepper

Garnish:

Finely minced fresh parsley
2 to 3 hard-boiled eggs, peeled and cut in half

Salad Boulonnaise

Serves:	**4 to 6**
Preparation time:	**15 minutes, plus 4 to 6 hours to chill**
Cooking time:	**15 minutes**
Type of recipe:	**elementary**
Cost:	**inexpensive**

Peppers are one of the most important ingredients in the best cooking and they seem to find their way into both hot and cold dishes. This is one of my favorite salads of the region of France near Boulogne. Serve it as an hors d'oeuvre or as an accompaniment to a country pâté.

Ingredients
¾ cup fruity olive oil
3 Tablespoons finely minced fresh parsley
2 cloves garlic, crushed and finely minced
1 dried hot chili pepper
3 Tablespoons mixed fresh herbs (thyme, summer savory, marjoram), or 1 teaspoon dried thyme and ½ teaspoon dried marjoram
1 bay leaf
3 to 4 carrots, scraped and sliced
1 celery heart, or 4 stalks celery, sliced
1 cup small white onions, peeled
3 red peppers, cut into 1-inch cubes
3 green peppers, cut into 1-inch cubes
Salt and freshly ground black pepper
Juice of 2 large lemons

Preparation

1.
In a bowl combine the dry mustard with 1 tablespoon water and let the paste stand for 30 minutes to develop flavor.

2.
In a small jar combine the vinegar, olive oil, mustard, and mustard paste. Add the garlic and season with salt and pepper. Cover the jar and shake until the dressing is smooth and well blended. Set aside.

3.
In a large saucepan bring salted water to a boil. Add the potatoes and cook for 15 to 20 minutes, or until they are tender; do not overcook. Drain the potatoes. When cool enough to handle peel and cube. Set aside.

4.
In a serving bowl combine the turkey, green pepper, pimientos, olives, capers, onion, gherkins, and peas.

5.
Add the potatoes to the salad bowl, then add the dressing and toss the salad lightly, being carefully not to break the potato cubes. Season with salt and pepper. Sprinkle with parsley and garnish with hard-boiled eggs. Serve the salad lightly chilled or at room temperature.

Remarks
Leftover cooked vegetables such as green beans, white beans, or cauliflower can be added to the salad.

Tuscan
Spring Vegetable
Salad

Serves:	**4 to 6**
Preparation time:	**15 minutes, plus 2 to 3 hours to chill**
Cooking time:	**25 minutes**
Type of recipe:	**elementary**
Cost:	**inexpensive**

Preparation

1.
In a heavy enamel saucepan heat the oil over low heat. Add the parsley, garlic, chili pepper, and herbs and cook the mixture for 2 minutes. Do not brown.

2.
Add the carrots, celery, onions, and cubed peppers. Season with salt and pepper. Cover and simmer the vegetables over low heat for 10 to 12 minutes, or until just tender. Do not overcook. The vegetables should still be crisp.

3.
Add the lemon juice and taste and correct the seasoning. Pour the mixture into a serving bowl and chill for 4 to 6 hours before serving.

Remarks
You can substitute 3 tablespoons good red wine vinegar for the lemon juice. You can also add ¾ pound small fresh mushrooms to the saucepan and cook together with the vegetables. The salad will keep for 1 week to 10 days, refrigerated in a covered glass jar.

Ingredients
6 small new potatoes
1 pound fresh green beans
2 young carrots, scraped and thinly sliced
1 teaspoon granulated sugar
Freshly ground black pepper

Dressing:
1 Tablespoon minced fresh parsley
3 Tablespoons finely minced fresh basil leaves
6 Tablespoons fruity olive oil
2 to 3 Tablespoons red wine vinegar
1 clove garlic, crushed
Salt and freshly ground black pepper
1 Tablespoon finely minced shallots

Garnish:
1 Tablespoon minced fresh parsley

Cold Zucchini Salad
in
Green Sauce

Serves:	**6**
Preparation time:	**15 minutes, plus 2 to 4 hours to chill**
Cooking time:	**15 minutes**
Type of recipe:	**elementary**
Cost:	**inexpensive**

Preparation

1.
A couple of hours ahead bring salted water to a boil in a large saucepan. Add the potatoes and cook for 15 to 20 minutes or until tender; do not overcook. Drain and peel the potatoes. Chill for 1 or 2 hours and then slice. Place in a salad bowl and set aside.

2.
Snap the beans. Bring more salted water to a boil in a large saucepan. Add the beans and cook for 7 to 8 minutes, or until barely tender. Drain the beans and run under cold water to stop them from cooking further. Set aside.

3.
In another saucepan combine the carrots with salted water to cover. Add sugar, bring to a boil, and cook for 5 minutes, or until just tender. Do not overcook. Drain the carrots and add together with the beans to the sliced potatoes in the bowl.

4.
In a blender combine the parsley, basil, oil, 2 tablespoons vinegar, and the garlic. Blend the mixture at high speed until smooth. Season with salt and pepper.

5.
Add the shallots and mix well. Pour the dressing over the vegetables and toss lightly. Taste and correct the seasoning, adding a large grinding of black pepper. You may like a little more vinegar. Let the salad marinate for an hour before serving.

6.
Sprinkle with the parsley and serve as an appetizer or accompaniment to roasts or sautéed meats.

Ingredients

1 cup fresh spinach, well rinsed and stemmed
2 large eggs
1 Tablespoon white wine vinegar
2 teaspoons Dijon mustard
¾ to 1 cup peanut oil
3 Tablespoons finely minced fresh parsley
2 Tablespoons finely minced scallions (both green and white part)
Salt and freshly ground black pepper
6 to 8 small zucchini

Optional:
2 Tablespoons finely minced chives

Garnish:
6 to 8 whole radishes
6 black olives

Preparation

1.
In a saucepan bring salted water to a boil. Add the spinach and cook for 2 minutes. Drain the spinach leaves in a colander and, when cool enough to handle, squeeze any remaining moisture out of the leaves with your hands. Chop the spinach finely and set aside.

2.
In a blender combine the eggs, vinegar, and mustard. Blend for 30 seconds at high speed.

3.
Start adding the oil while the blender is still at high speed, adding the oil in droplets. Blend the sauce until it is thick and smooth.

Basic Vinaigrette

4.
Add the spinach, parsley, and scallions and continue blending the sauce until smooth. Season the sauce with salt and pepper and set aside.

5.
In a large saucepan bring salted water to a boil. Add the zucchini and cook for 5 to 6 minutes, or until barely tender. Drain the zucchini on a double layer of paper towels and cool.

6.
Slice the zucchini crosswise into ¼-inch slices. Combine the slices in a serving bowl with enough of the sauce to bind them. (You may have some sauce left over which can be served as a topping for hard-boiled eggs or as an accompaniment to poached fish.) Toss the salad lightly, being careful not to break the zucchini slices. Chill the salad for 2 to 4 hours before serving.

7.
Thirty minutes before serving remove the salad from the refrigerator and bring back to room temperature. Taste and correct the seasoning. Sprinkle with optional chives and garnish with radishes and black olives. Serve the salad as part of an hors d'oeuvre table or as an accompaniment to sautéed or grilled fish.

Remarks
This salad is equally good when served as a luncheon dish. Garnish the bowl with 2 or 3 hard-boiled eggs, peeled and quartered, and a side dish of tuna that has been drained and sprinkled with fruity olive oil and lemon juice. Serve the salad with crusty French bread and a bowl of sweet butter.

Ingredients
1½ Tablespoons good quality red wine vinegar
3 Tablespoons pure olive oil
1 to 2 teaspoon Dijon mustard
Salt and freshly ground black pepper

Preparation
1.
In a small screw-top jar combine the vinegar, olive oil, and mustard.
2.
Cover the jar and shake until the dressing is well blended and smooth.
3.
Season with salt and pepper and reserve.

Remarks
If you are making the dressing in quantity, chill and bring back to room temperature 30 to 40 minutes before serving.

Vinaigrette Lyonnaise

Yields: **enough for a salad serving 4 to 6**

Ingredients

2 to 3 Tablespoons good quality white wine vinegar
4 Tablespoons walnut oil (preferably), or olive oil
4 Tablespoons Crème Fraîche (page 544)
1 Tablespoon Dijon mustard
Salt and freshly ground black pepper
2 Tablespoons finely minced fresh chives or finely minced scallions (greens only)

Optional:

1 to 2 Tablespoons finely minced fresh tarragon, plus 1 to 2 Tablespoons finely minced fresh chervil

Preparation

1.
In the bottom of a glass salad bowl combine the vinegar, oil, Crème Fraîche, and mustard. Season with salt and pepper and whisk the dressing until smooth and well blended.

2.
Add the chives or scallions and optional tarragon and chervil. Serve the dressing with bibb lettuce, Boston lettuce, or Belgian endive or a mixture of all 3.

Remarks

This salad dressing is best when prepared no more than 3 to 4 hours before serving. It is also excellent when used with thinly sliced raw mushrooms or cooked beets.

Vinaigrette Niçoise

Yields: **enough for a salad serving 4**

Ingredients

3 Tablespoons red wine vinegar
8 Tablespoons fruity olive oil
2 Tablespoons finely minced Roasted Red Peppers (page 545)
3 to 4 anchovy fillets, finely minced
1 large clove garlic, peeled and crushed
2 to 3 Tablespoons thinly sliced red onions
Freshly ground black pepper

Optional:

2 Tablespoons freshly grated Parmesan cheese

Preparation

1.
Combine all the ingredients in a blender and blend until smooth.

2.
Season with a large grinding of pepper and transfer to a jar. Chill and bring back to room temperature 30 to 40 minutes before using.

Remarks

This dressing is particularly good with raw spinach, escarole, romaine, and Belgian endive or a combination salad including spinach, romaine, endive, and fresh mushrooms.

Vinaigrette Andalouse

Vinaigrette Provençale

Yields: **enough for a salad serving 4**

Yields: **enough for a salad serving 6 to 8**

Ingredients
2 to 2½ Tablespoons Spanish sherry wine vinegar
6 Tablespoons fruity olive oil
2 Tablespoons finely minced fresh herbs (marjarom, thyme, or oregano), or 2 Tablespoons finely minced fresh parsley
2 Tablespoons finely minced scallions (both green and white parts) or fresh chives
1 large clove garlic, peeled and crushed
Salt and freshly ground black pepper

Preparation
1.
In a small jar combine all the ingredients.
2.
Cover the jar and shake until the dressing is well blended. (For a smoother dressing you can blend the dressing in a blender.)
3.
Season the dressing again with salt and freshly ground black pepper and chill. Bring the dressing back to room temperature 30 to 40 minutes before serving.

Ingredients
3 Tablespoons top quality red wine vinegar
8 Tablespoons pure olive oil, or an excellent fruity olive oil such as Plagniol
1 Tablespoon Dijon mustard
1 to 2 cloves garlic, peeled and crushed
Salt and freshly ground black pepper

Preparation
1.
In a small jar combine all the ingredients.
2.
Cover the jar and shake until the dressing is well blended and smooth.
3.
Season with salt and pepper and chill. Bring the dressing back to room temperature 30 to 40 minutes before making the salad.

Remarks
The Provençale Vinaigrette is particularly good with cooked white beans, lentils, and chick peas. If you are making the dressing more than 4 hours ahead do not crush and add the garlic to the dressing. Instead cut the cloves in half and add to the dressing. Remove just before serving.

Claude's
Lemon Vinaigrette

Yields: **enough for a salad serving 4
to 6**

*My 10-year-old son Claude has made his
own salad dressing for several years. In fact,
he has been reminding me at every possible
occasion that his dressing is by far the most
delicious one he knows. I tend to agree.*

Ingredients
**Juice of 1 large lemon
6 Tablespoons mild olive oil (Berio,
Bertolli, or Sasso)
1 Tablespoon Dijon mustard
2 teaspoons granulated sugar
Salt and freshly ground white pepper
3 Tablespoons finely minced scallions
(white part only) or green onions**

Preparation
1.
In a small jar combine the lemon juice,
olive oil, mustard, and sugar. Cover the jar
and shake until the dressing is smooth and
well blended.
2.
Uncover the dressing and season with salt
and freshly ground pepper. Add the
scallions, then taste and correct the
seasoning. The dressing should have a
definite sweet-sour taste.

Remarks
Use the dressing for buttery greens such as
bibb, romaine, leaf lettuce, or Boston. It is
also delicious when used with a mixture of
greens such as romaine, Belgian endive,
and thinly sliced fresh mushrooms.

Desserts

I cannot imagine any meal, simple or elegant, without the final touch of a delicious dessert. When you walk into a good restaurant one of the first things to catch your eye is often the tantalizing dessert cart. Displayed there are the cakes, tarts, and—to me the most attractive sight of all—a large crystal bowl of beautiful seasonal fruit: plump red or black raspberries or bright cherries. Just as you might choose a dessert with great care when you are eating in a restaurant, it is equally important to plan a dessert that will be in balance with the menu and the season. A choucroûte or a rich cassoulet should be followed by a light, refreshing fruit dessert, while an elegant roast or a grilled meat can set the stage for a rich chocolate delicacy. I find that desserts offer two great opportunities: the chance to create wonderful effects with a minimum of skill, and the opportunity to learn some interesting techniques that can be applied easily to innumerable great desserts.

Nature has a wonderful way of providing us with almost instant desserts at every time of the year. There is little that can equal a perfectly ripe pear, a bowl of fragrant and delicious strawberries, or a cooling slice of melon. In Europe the serving of fresh fruit following a meal—the graceful, meticulous peeling of an orange in Italy or the "carving" of a pear in England—is a ritual unmatched by any other aspect of a meal. Nowadays the sad reality is that more often then not, we are faced with strawberries that lack flavor, the melon does not turn out to be as sweet as we thought, and achieving

the perfect pear means that we have to think about it three or four days ahead to let it ripen in a corner of the kitchen. But I am a great believer in sauces and accents to even the simplest of fruits. A Cointreau or Grand Marnier sabayon, a rum-flavored custard or sugared crème fraîche can bring out and enhance the flavor of many less-than-perfect fruits. Furthermore they can turn the simplest fruit salad into a truly elegant dessert. Fruit compotes or fruits cooked in wine—pears in red wine, peaches in sauterne, or plums in white wine—can also play a major dessert role, as they do in Europe.

I am always fascinated to note that many Mediterranean countries are surprisingly poor in intricate or elaborate desserts. (There is only one popular dessert in Spain —the Crema Catalan, which is essentially a version of Crème Caramel.) The reason for this is that fresh, beautifully ripe fruit is plentiful year-round, and thus it plays a major role as a finishing touch to a meal. A bowl of cherries or some other fruit, depending on the season, is practically the standard dessert in the peasant kitchen. It is countries such as France and Austria that have developed the wealths of rich and elegant desserts that have become synonymous with Grande Cuisine.

Desserts do not necessarily mean cakes and cake decoration. I would rather spend my time creating a wonderful sauce and working out an interesting menu than intricately decorating a cake. Homemade fruit tarts, or flan, or a simple cake, however, can be made easily and with a minimum of technique. A custard of various flavors, a good butter cream, a sabayon sauce, and a simple chocolate sauce—these are a few of the fundamentals that make possible a range of fabulous desserts. Every serious cook should understand the texture and technique of rolling out pastry dough, which allows you to make a delicious fresh fruit tart in every season. Of course nothing can compare to a buttery homemade puff pastry, and a sponge roll filled with a rich butter cream is surely as spectacular as any dessert you can buy in the store.

I am always amused by the fact that the French housewife takes pride in buying a cake from a good pastry shop (of course, in France good pastry shops can be found everywhere). However as I have learned, there are exceptions to every rule. I will never forget one day while I was working at Fauchon, the fabulous gourmet shop in Paris. The chef brought out a number of cakes that did not look as perfect as the usual Fauchon pastry displays. Surprised to see this, I asked him what had happened. "Oh," he explained, "these are for the Comtesse Blanchard. She's giving a dinner party tonight and she doesn't want her guests to know that she has lost her cook and that these are from a store." In *this* country, the serious cook is always proud of giving a homemade touch to desserts, since they are anticipated with such pleasure. Like the American cook, the Comtesse too preferred the "homemade touch."

When planning your meal, it is important to consider the time required for the preparation of each course. If a dessert needs four hours for example, rather than spending so much time on that at the expense of the rest of the meal, I prefer to substitute something simpler and less time-consuming. Or—as I often do—I would serve something that can be made a day in advance. Most of the desserts in this book can be made ahead of time and are even better the next day. One of these is the classic French crêpe; to my mind, it is the most versatile dessert of all. The technique of making crêpes is probably one of the simplest to master, yet it allows you to be creative and experimental, since you can choose from among an enormous variety of delicious fillings. Flour, eggs, and milk are the basis of the crêpe and, with the addition of gelatin and heavy cream, you can also make many elegant mousses and Bavarian creams. While the end results may seem elaborate and complex, all of these start with the basics available at your local supermarket. You can have them on hand at all times—as I do—so you are never at a loss for a dessert, even at the last minute. The realization of how accessible these basics really are, plus the knowledge of a few fundamental, easily mastered techniques will open up a whole new world of desserts.

Ice cream, which is extremely popular here, should also be a source of inspiration to Americans, who are always on the lookout for new desserts. The Swiss "coupe" is a particularly beautiful dessert combining

scoops of ice cream with various fruit
sauces and toppings. Adding a blueberry
sauce or some other seasonal fruit to ice
cream is both an easy and innovative way
to give interest to a familiar favorite.

But whichever cuisine inspires you or seems
the most appropriate to your meal, I have
always found that there is never any course
more welcome than dessert—whether you
opt for the "instant gratification" of a fresh
fruit or choose a more elaborate and
advanced confection.

Chocolate
Almond
Pavé

Serves: **8 to 10**
Preparation time: **35 minutes, plus 24 hours to chill**
Cooking time: **20 minutes**
Type of recipe: **elementary**
Cost: **expensive**

Ingredients

¾ cup softened butter
⅓ cup granulated sugar
2 large eggs, separated
8 ounces semisweet chocolate
2 Tablespoons strong prepared coffee
¼ cup plus 2 Tablespoons dark rum
¾ cup finely ground almonds
Pinch of salt

Sponge Roll:

5 large eggs, separated
Pinch of salt
½ cup granulated sugar
1 teaspoon vanilla extract
1 teaspoon finely grated lemon rind
3 Tablespoons all-purpose flour

Preparation

1.
Prepare the sponge roll first. Preheat the oven to 375 degrees.

2.
Butter a jelly roll pan. Line with a sheet of waxed paper, then butter the paper and sprinkle lightly with flour, shaking off the excess. Set aside.

3.
In a large stainless steel mixing bowl combine the egg whites with a pinch of salt. Beat the whites with a small electric hand beater, gradually adding ½ cup sugar. Beat the whites until they are stiff and form soft peaks. Set aside.

4.
In another stainless steel bowl combine the yolks and remaining sugar and beat until fluffy and pale yellow. Add the vanilla and lemon rind and fold the egg-yolk mixture

gently but thoroughly into the whites. Sprinkle lightly with the flour and again fold gently. Do not over mix or you will deflate the whites.

5.
Spoon the mixture into the prepared jelly roll pan, smoothing it evenly with a spatula. Place in the center of the oven and bake for 12 to 15 minutes, or until the cake is lightly browned.

6.
Unmold the cake onto a damp kitchen towel. Remove the waxed paper and cover with a damp towel. Set aside to cool.

7.
In a stainless steel bowl combine the softened butter and the sugar and beat the mixture with a small electric hand beater until smooth and creamy, or for about 3 to 4 minutes. Add the egg yolks and beat the mixture for another 2 to 3 minutes. Set aside.

8.
In the top of a double boiler combine the chocolate and coffee. Melt the chocolate over medium heat and stir until smooth. Add the rum to the chocolate mixture and mix well. Cool the chocolate completely and then add to the butter-and-yolk mixture, beating with a hand beater until well blended. Fold the ground nuts into the mixture and set aside.

9.
Beat the whites in a stainless steel bowl, adding a pinch of salt, until they are stiff but not dry. Fold the beaten whites into the butter-and-chocolate mixture and set aside.

Demel's
Chocolate Torte

Serves:	**6 to 8**
Preparation time:	**20 minutes**
Cooking time:	**50 minutes**
Type of recipe:	**elementary**
Cost:	**moderate**

10.
Cut the sponge cake into 4 long strips. Lightly oil a 5-cup loaf pan and line it with waxed paper. Butter the paper lightly and then line it on all sides with the sponge cake, reserving one strip for the top. Cut 2 small squares that will fit on each end of the pan.

11.
Sprinkle the sponge cake with a little rum and spoon the chocolate mixture into the pan. Smooth the mixture with a spatula and then cover with the remaining piece of sponge cake. Cover the dish with foil and chill for 24 hours before serving.

12.
About 15 minutes before serving dip the loaf into hot water, and unmold from the pan. Remove the waxed paper and return the loaf to the refrigerator. Serve the pavé chilled, sliced into ½-inch slices.

Remarks
The entire dish can be made 2 to 3 days ahead. Unmold and then wrap it in foil and refrigerate until ready to serve. It will keep for at least a week. You can substitute an orange-flavored liqueur for the rum.

Ingredients
5 ounces semisweet chocolate
¾ cup strong espresso coffee
5 ounces granulated sugar
5 ounces ground blanched almonds
6 large eggs, separated
2 Tablespoons dark rum
2 Tablespoons unflavored bread crumbs

Walnut
Chocolate Torte

Serves: **6 to 8**
Preparation time: **15 minutes**
Cooking time: **1 hour**
Type of recipe: **elementary**
Cost: **moderate**

Preparation

1.
Preheat the oven to 375 degrees.

2.
Butter a 9-inch springform cake mold, then sprinkle with flour, shaking out the excess.

3.
In a small heavy saucepan combine the chocolate and coffee and heat until the chocolate is melted. Add the sugar and almonds and whisk the mixture until well blended. Remove from the heat and chill the mixture until it is thick.

4.
In a bowl combine the egg yolks, rum, and bread crumbs and whisk until well blended. Fold it carefully into the chocolate mixture.

5.
Beat the egg whites until stiff. Fold them carefully into the chocolate mixture.

6.
Pour the cake mixture into the pan and bake for 45 minutes, or until a toothpick comes out clean.

7.
Cool and unmold. Serve the cake with sugared whipped cream flavored with 2 tablespoons cognac.

Remarks

The chocolate cake can be kept for 2 or 3 days. It can also be frozen successfully for 4 to 6 weeks.

Ingredients

6 ounces walnuts, finely ground
¾ cup butter
1 large egg, lightly beaten
⅓ cup granulated sugar
1 heaping cup sifted all-purpose flour
1 teaspoon ground cinnamon
¼ teaspoon baking powder
1 jar (12 ounces) seedless raspberry preserves

Chocolate Glaze:

4 ounces semisweet chocolate
2 Tablespoons prepared coffee
2 Tablespoons confectioners' sugar
3 Tablespoons butter

Lemon
Bavarian Roll

Serves:	**6 to 8**
Preparation time:	**15 minutes, plus 2 hours to chill cream**
Cooking time:	**30 minutes**
Type of recipe:	**elementary**
Cost:	**moderate**

Preparation

1.
Preheat the oven to 350 degrees.

2.
Butter a 9-inch springform and sprinkle with flour, shaking out the excess.

3.
In a large bowl combine the walnuts, butter, egg, sugar, flour, cinnamon, and baking powder. Work the mixture with your hands until it forms a soft ball. Cut or pull apart the dough into 2 equal pieces.

4.
With half the mixture make a flat circle inside the cake pan, spreading it evenly. Spread the jam over the dough. Form another layer of dough by breaking the remaining dough into small flat pieces and shaping them into an even layer.

5.
Place the cake pan in the center of the oven and bake for 50 to 60 minutes, or until nicely browned.

6.
While the cake is baking, prepare the glaze. In the top of a double boiler combine the chocolate and coffee. Melt the chocolate over medium heat, stirring it until it is completely smooth. Add the sugar and stir until dissolved.

7.
Remove the pan from the heat and add the butter. Stir the mixture until the butter is melted, then cool to a spreading consistency.

8.
When ready, remove the cake from the oven and unmold onto a serving platter. Cool the cake and glaze it. Serve at room temperature.

Ingredients

Bavarian Cream:
4 large eggs, separated
6 Tablespoons superfine sugar
1¼ cups hot light cream or milk
1 Tablespoon unflavored gelatin
½ cup freshly squeezed lemon juice
1 teaspoon vanilla extract
Grated rind of 2 lemons

Sponge Roll:
5 large eggs, separated
Pinch of salt
¾ cup granulated sugar
1 teaspoon vanilla extract
1 teaspoon finely grated lemon rind
3 Tablespoons sifted all-purpose flour

Garnish:
Whole fresh strawberries
Small bunches of seedless grapes
Confectioners' sugar

Preparation

1.
Preheat the oven to 375 degrees.

2.
Butter a jelly roll pan and line with a sheet of waxed paper. Butter the paper and sprinkle lightly with flour, shaking off the excess. Set aside.

3.
Make the Bavarian cream. In the top of a double boiler combine the egg yolks and sugar and whisk the mixture until it is fluffy and pale yellow. Add the cream or milk and whisk the mixture until well blended. Set aside.

4.
In a small saucepan combine the gelatin and lemon juice. Whisk until dissolved and place the saucepan over low heat. Simmer until the gelatin is dissolved, then whisk it into the cream-and-yolk mixture.

5.
Set the cream-and-yolk mixture over simmering water and whisk constantly until it thickens and coats a spoon. Remove from the heat and immediately transfer to a mixing bowl. Add the vanilla and lemon rind and chill until the mixture starts to set, whisking it every few minutes.

6.
Beat the egg whites until stiff. When the custard is almost set fold in the beaten whites and chill for 2 hours, or until completely set. Meanwhile prepare the batter for the sponge roll.

7.
In a large stainless steel mixing bowl combine the egg whites with a pinch of salt. Beat the whites with a small electric hand beater, gradually adding ½ cup sugar. Beat the whites until they are stiff and form soft peaks. Set aside.

8.
In another stainless steel bowl combine the egg yolks and the remaining sugar and beat until fluffy and pale yellow. Add the vanilla and lemon rind and then fold the egg-yolk mixture gently but thoroughly into the whites. Sprinkle lightly with the flour and again fold gently. Do not overmix or you will deflate the whites.

9.
Spoon the batter into the prepared jelly roll pan, smoothing it evenly with a spatula. Place in the center of the oven and bake for 12 to 15 minutes, or until the cake is lightly browned.

10.
Unmold the cake onto a damp kitchen towel. Remove the waxed paper and roll the sponge lengthwise into the towel. Set aside to cool.

11.
When the cake has completely cooled carefully unroll it and spoon the Bavarian cream in a heavy layer over the cake, smoothing it with a spatula.

12.
Roll the cake lengthwise and transfer it carefully to a serving platter. Sprinkle heavily with confectioners' sugar and chill.

13.
Twenty minutes before serving remove the cake from the refrigerator and serve garnished with strawberries and seedless grapes.

Fresh Chestnut Mousse
with
Chocolate Sauce

Serves:	**8 to 10**
Preparation time:	**40 minutes, plus 4 to 6 hours**
	to chill
Cooking time:	**1 hour**
Type of recipe:	**elementary**
Cost:	**moderate**

Here is one of my favorite fall desserts. Chestnuts are synonymous with that season and should be used as often as possible. When braised they are a delicious garnish to many meats and can also be used in a variety of desserts.

Ingredients

4 large eggs, separated
1¼ cups hot milk
¾ cup granulated sugar
1 teaspoon vanilla extract
¼ cup cognac or rum (dark)
1 Tablespoon unflavored gelatin
1 cup heavy cream, whipped

Chestnut Purée:

1 pound fresh chestnuts, shelled
¾ cup granulated sugar
1 two-inch vanilla bean
2 cups milk
2 cups water

Chocolate Sauce:

8 ounces semisweet chocolate
1 cup strong espresso coffee
4 Tablespoons butter
1 to 2 Tablespoons cognac

Optional:

1 to 2 Tablespoons granulated sugar

Preparation

1.
Prepare the chestnut purée. In a heavy saucepan combine the chestnuts, sugar, vanilla bean, milk, and water. Bring to a boil, reduce the heat, and simmer for 30 to 40 minutes, or until the chestnuts are very tender. Remove the chestnuts from their poaching liquid and purée in a blender adding a little of the poaching liquid if necessary. Reserve 1 cup of the chestnut purée and set the remainder aside for another purpose.

2.
In the top of a double boiler combine the egg yolks, milk, and ½ cup sugar. Whisk the mixture until smooth, place over simmering water, and whisk until it is thick and lightly coats a spoon. Add the vanilla and cognac or rum.

3.
Dissolve the gelatin in a small saucepan with ¼ cup water. Place the saucepan over low heat and melt the gelatin.

4.
Whisk the hot gelatin into the egg mixture and pour into a bowl. Chill, whisking every 5 minutes until it starts to set.

5.
While the mixture is setting beat the egg whites with the remaining sugar until they form stiff peaks.

6.
Fold 1 cup chestnut purée into the chilled egg mixture and then very gently fold in the whites.

7.
Whip the cream and fold it into the chestnut mixture and transfer the mousse to

Charlotte à l'Arlequin (Vanilla and Chocolate Mousse Charlotte)

Serves:	**6 to 8**
Preparation time:	**1 hour, plus several hours to chill**
Cooking time:	**25 minutes**
Type of recipe:	**moderate**
Cost:	**expensive**

a glass bowl. Chill for 4 to 6 hours or until ready to serve.

8.

When ready to serve, prepare the chocolate sauce. In the top of a double boiler combine the chocolate and coffee and cook over simmering water until the chocolate has melted. Whisk in the butter and, when the butter has just melted, add the cognac. Taste the sauce; you may want to add a little more cognac. If you like the sauce sweeter, add 1 to 2 tablespoons sugar. Serve the sauce hot as an accompaniment to the Chestnut Mousse.

A charlotte is an effective and delicious dessert that is somewhat elaborate but since it can be assembled a day ahead it is well worth the effort.

Ingredients
20 to 24 ladyfingers, commercial or homemade (page 525)
1 cup strong prepared espresso coffee
⅓ to ½ cup dark rum

Chocolate Mousse:
8 ounces semisweet chocolate
2 to 3 Tablespoons prepared strong coffee
¼ cup granulated sugar
2 large egg yolks
7 Tablespoons cold butter
3 large egg whites, beaten until stiff

Vanilla Custard:
3 large egg yolks
⅓ cup granulated sugar
1 cup warm milk
2 teaspoons unflavored gelatin
1 teaspoon vanilla extract
1 cup heavy cream, whipped

Garnish
1 cup whipped cream
Chocolate shavings

Preparation
1.
Start by making the chocolate mousse. In the top of a double boiler combine the chocolate with the coffee. Melt the chocolate, then add the sugar and stir with a wooden spoon until well blended and

completely melted. The mixture should be quite smooth.

2.
Remove the chocolate from the heat and add the yolks, blending thoroughly. Cool the chocolate mixture slightly, then add the cold butter 1 tablespoon at a time, beating the mixture until each piece of butter is well blended with the chocolate.

3.
Stir half the beaten whites into the chocolate mixture, then fold the remainder in gently. Do not overmix. Transfer the mousse to a bowl and chill for 2 to 3 hours, or until set. (This can be done 1 or 2 days in advance.)

4.
Make the vanilla custard. Combine the yolks and sugar in the top of a double boiler. Whisk until thoroughly blended and then add the warm milk. Whisk the mixture until smooth and add the gelatin. Set the pan over simmering water and whisk until the mixture starts to thicken and heavily coats a spoon. Do not let it come to a boil or the yolks will curdle.

5.
Transfer the custard to a stainless steel bowl. Add the vanilla and chill for 20 to 30 minutes, whisking every 10 minutes.

6.
When the custard starts to set fold the whipped cream into the custard, blending thoroughly, and chill for another 20 to 30 minutes, or until the mousse is almost set.

7.
Butter a 6-cup charlotte mold.

8.
Trim 8 to 10 ladyfingers and cut them into triangular wedges. (They should look like thin pie slices.) Dip all but 3 or 4 ladyfingers in the coffee and line the sides of the mold. Drizzle a little rum over each ladyfinger.

9.
Fill half the mold with the chocolate mousse. Tap lightly on the counter to make sure the mousse is evenly distributed on the bottom of the mold.

10.
Top the mousse with the remaining ladyfingers and drizzle with the remaining rum. Add the vanilla custard and again tap the charlotte mold on the counter to make sure the cream is settling into the mold. If the edges of the ladyfingers show above the mold, trim them. Chill the charlotte for 4 to 6 hours before unmolding.

11.
Just before serving unmold the charlotte onto a round serving platter. Fit a pastry bag with a small star nozzle. Garnish the top of the charlotte with rosettes of whipped cream and then sprinkle with chocolate shavings. Serve the charlotte well chilled.

Remarks
Both the chocolate mousse and the ladyfingers can be made several days ahead and refrigerated. It is best to make the vanilla custard just before assembling the dish since it should not be too firm in order to fit properly into the charlotte mold.

Chocolate Soufflé
with
Almond Cream

Serves:	**4 to 6**
Preparation time:	**25 minutes**
Cooking time:	**1 hour, 15 minutes**
Type of recipe:	**elementary**
Cost:	**expensive**

Ingredients

1 cup milk
4 ounces semisweet chocolate
½ cup granulated sugar
1 teaspoon instant coffee
3 Tablespoons butter
4 Tablespoons sifted all-purpose flour
3 large egg yolks
2 Tablespoons almond liqueur
1 teaspoon vanilla extract
¼ teaspoon almond extract
5 large egg whites
Salt

Custard Sauce:

4 large egg yolks
1 teaspoon cornstarch
⅓ cup granulated sugar
1¾ cups hot milk
1 teaspoon vanilla extract
¼ cup almond liqueur

Preparation

1.
Start by making the custard sauce. Beat the yolks, cornstarch, and sugar in the top of a double boiler. Add the milk and vanilla and whisk the mixture until smooth and well blended. Place over simmering water and cook the mixture, whisking constantly until it is thick and heavily coats a spoon. Do not let the custard come to a boil or the yolks will curdle.

2.
Immediately transfer the custard to a bowl. Add the liqueur and place the bowl over crushed ice. Chill the sauce until ready to serve.

3.
Preheat the oven to 325 degrees.

4.
Heat the milk with the chocolate, sugar, and instant coffee in a small saucepan. Whisk until the chocolate is melted and the mixture is smooth. Do not let the milk come to a boil. Set aside.

5.
In a heavy 2-quart saucepan heat the butter over low heat. Add the flour and cook without browning, stirring constantly for 2 minutes. Whisk in the hot chocolate milk and continue cooking until the mixture is very thick.

6.
Add the yolks 1 at a time and stir until each is well blended into the chocolate mixture. Add the liqueur and the extracts and heat through. Set the saucepan aside.

7.
In a stainless steel bowl beat the whites, adding a pinch of salt, until they form very

Chocolate Mousse Roulade

Serves: **6 to 8**
Preparation time: **45 minutes, plus chilling time**
Cooking time: **25 to 30 minutes**
Type of recipe **intermediate**
Cost: **expensive**

stiff peaks. (It is best to beat the whites with a large balloon whisk.)

8.
Fold the chocolate mixture gently into the whites and set aside.

9.
Butter a 6-cup soufflé dish and line it with waxed paper. Butter the paper and then sprinkle with sugar, shaking out the excess. Make a 2-inch foil collar. Butter and sugar the foil, then tie it around the soufflé dish.

10.
Pour the soufflé mixture into the dish, smoothing it with a spatula.

11.
Place the soufflé dish inside a large baking dish, and pour boiling water into the dish to a depth of 1 inch. Bake for 1 hour, 15 minutes.

12.
Remove from the oven and let the soufflé cool. (It will fall back by 1 to 2 inches.) Remove the collar and when the soufflé is cool enough to handle invert it carefully into the palm of your hand and then invert back onto a serving platter.

13.
Spoon the chilled sauce around the soufflé and serve at room temperature.

Remarks
The soufflé can be prepared 2 to 4 hours ahead. Spoon the sauce around it just before serving.

Ingredients
2 ounces semisweet chocolate
1 to 2 Tablespoons espresso or strong coffee
6 large eggs, separated
¾ cup granulated sugar
¼ cup unsweetened cocoa (generous)
Pinch of salt

Mousse:
4 ounces sweet chocolate, preferably Maillard
2 Tablespoons espresso or strong coffee
⅓ cup butter, broken into pieces
2 large egg yolks, plus 4 egg whites
1½ Tablespoons granulated sugar

Optional:
Confectioners' sugar for sprinkling

Preparation

1.
Preheat the oven to 375 degrees. Butter a jelly roll pan 10 by 15 inches. Line the bottom and sides with 1 long piece of waxed paper. Butter and flour the paper. Set aside.

2.
In the top of a double boiler melt the chocolate with the coffee. Set aside to cool slightly.

3.
In a bowl beat the yolks for 4 to 5 minutes until lightly lemon colored. Add half the sugar and continue to beat at high speed for an additional 5 minutes until very thick. On lowest speed add the melted chocolate and then the cocoa, beating only until smooth.

4.
In a large bowl beat the whites with the salt until they begin to thicken. Add the remaining sugar and continue beating until the whites hold their shape and are stiff but not dry. Fold the whites into the chocolate, then turn into the prepared pan, handling the batter lightly. Spread level and place in the oven. Bake for about 25 to 30 minutes.

5.
While the cake is baking, prepare the mousse. In the top of a double boiler melt the chocolate and coffee. Remove from the heat and set aside to cool slightly, then whisk in the butter in bits, making sure the mixture is not too hot to melt the butter. Let it cool completely until it is the texture of thick cream.

6.
Wet and wring out a smooth kitchen towel. Lay flat on a table. When the top of the cake springs back when lightly touched, remove it from the oven. Working quickly cut around the sides of the cake if it is sticking to the pan and turn out onto the prepared towel. Carefully peel off the waxed paper. Starting at the long side, roll the cake and towel together. Place on a rack to cool. It must be completely cool to fill.

7.
When the chocolate mousse mixture has cooled stir in the yolks, one at a time, until thoroughly blended.

8.
Beat the whites until they are thick and foamy. Add the sugar and continue beating until they hold their shape and are stiff but not dry. Fold the whites and chocolate mixture together and chill in the refrigerator until the mousse is quite thick yet spreadable.

9.
Unroll the cake. Spread it generously with the mousse and roll up again. The roulade may be refrigerated at this time for a short while to solidify or for several hours.

10.
Remove from the refrigerator at least 30 minutes before serving, sprinkle with optional confectioners' sugar and slice on an angle for serving.

Chocolate and Chestnut Pudding

Serves:	**6 to 8**
Preparation time:	**35 minutes, plus 4 to 6 hours to chill**
Cooking time:	**15 minutes**
Type of recipe:	**intermediate**
Cost:	**moderate**

Ingredients

¼ cup golden raisins
¾ cup minced chestnuts in brandy (see Remarks)
½ cup cognac or brandy
5 egg yolks
¾ cup granulated sugar
1½ cups hot milk
4 ounces semisweet chocolate
1 teaspoon instant coffee
1 teaspoon vanilla extract
1 envelope unflavored gelatin
1 cup heavy cream
2 packages ladyfingers or 24 homemade (page 525)

Garnish:

Coarsely grated chocolate

Preparation

1.
In a small saucepan bring water to a boil. Add the raisins and let them steep for 5 to 10 minutes. Drain.

2.
In a small bowl combine the chestnuts, raisins, and ¼ cup cognac. Set aside.

3.
In the top of a double boiler combine the egg yolks, sugar, and milk. Whisk the mixture until well blended.

4.
Add the chocolate, instant coffee, vanilla, and gelatin. Set over simmering water and cook the mixture, whisking constantly until the chocolate melts and the sauce heavily coats a spoon. Do not overcook or the custard will curdle.

5.
Transfer the chocolate custard to a bowl and chill until almost set, or for about 30 minutes.

6.
Whip the cream and fold into the custard together with the raisins-and-chestnut mixture. Chill but don't let it set.

7.
Line a 2-quart glass bowl with ladyfingers. Drizzle with a little cognac. Spoon half the chocolate chestnut cream into the bowl, top with a layer of ladyfingers, drizzle with a little more cognac, and top with the remaining chocolate chestnut cream.

8.
Chill for 4 to 6 hours or overnight. Just before serving garnish with coarsely grated chocolate and serve chilled.

Remarks
Brandied chestnuts are available in the gourmet section of most supermarkets.

Mousse
au
Cointreau

Serves:	**6 to 8**
Preparation time:	**25 minutes, plus 2 to 4 hours to chill**
Cooking time:	**20 minutes**
Type of recipe:	**elementary**
Cost:	**moderate**

Ingredients

1 cup milk
5 large eggs, separated
¾ cup granulated sugar
⅓ cup Cointreau plus 3 tablespoons cognac
1 Tablespoon unflavored gelatin
¼ cup orange juice
1 Tablespoon finely grated orange rind
1 teaspoon vanilla extract
1 cup heavy cream, whipped

Garnish:

2 cups fresh raspberries
2 Tablespoons granulated sugar

Preparation

1.
In an enamel saucepan heat the milk.

2.
In the top of a double boiler combine the egg yolks together with all but 2 tablespoons sugar and whisk the mixture until pale yellow. Add the hot milk and the liqueurs and blend thoroughly into the yolk-and-sugar mixture. Place the pan over simmering water and cook, whisking constantly until the mixture lightly coats a spoon. Remove from the heat.

3.
Combine the gelatin and the orange juice in a small bowl and add to the custard. Return the custard to the heat and cook for another 3 to 4 minutes, whisking constantly until steam rises from the custard. Do not bring the custard to a boil or the yolks will curdle. The custard must however be very hot for the gelatin to melt.

4.
Transfer the custard to a stainless steel bowl. Add the orange rind and vanilla and chill the mixture, whisking every 10 minutes until it starts to set.

5.
In the meantime beat the egg whites, adding the remaining 2 tablespoons sugar, until they form stiff peaks.

6.
When the custard has started to set, fold the whites into it and carefully add the whipped cream. Do not overmix; the mousse should not lose its fluffiness. Transfer the mousse to a glass serving dish and chill for 2 to 4 hours, or until ready to serve.

7.
Thirty minutes before serving sprinkle the raspberries with 2 tablespoons sugar and shake the bowl back and forth to coat the berries evenly with the sugar.

8.
Ten minutes before serving top the mousse with the berries and serve chilled.

Remarks

The mousse can be made 1 or 2 days ahead; keep it covered and chilled until serving. You can top the mousse with sugared blueberries instead of the raspberries. For variation you can also serve the mousse in individual glass dessert dishes or porcelain ramekins. Place 1 ladyfinger in each dish, sprinkle it with Cointreau, and top with the mousse. Garnish each dish with a thin orange slice and a sprig of fresh mint.

Souffléed Ricotta and Orange Pudding

Serves: **4**
Preparation time: **20 minutes**
Cooking time: **1 hour**
Type of recipe: **elementary**
Cost: **inexpensive**

Ingredients
1¼ cups water
3 Tablespoons white cornmeal
1 pound whole milk ricotta
½ cup granulated sugar
3 large eggs, separated
1 Tablespoon candied orange peel, finely minced
Grated rind of 1 orange
2 Tablespoons seedless golden raisins
⅓ cup light rum
1 teaspoon vanilla extract

Garnish:
Confectioners' sugar

Optional:
Grand Marnier

Preparation

1.
Preheat the oven to 375 degrees.

2.
In a 1-quart saucepan bring water to a boil. Add the cornmeal, stirring slowly and constantly, and cook the mixture until thick or for about 4 minutes. Remove from the heat and set aside.

3.
In a large mixing bowl combine the ricotta, sugar, egg yolks, orange peel and rind, raisins, rum, and vanilla. Stir in the cornmeal mixture, then beat with an electric mixer until very smooth.

4.
In another bowl beat the whites until they form stiff peaks. Fold the whites into the ricotta mixture.

5.
Butter and sugar a 1½-quart soufflé dish. Spoon the ricotta mixture into the mold and bake for 1 hour.

6.
Remove the soufflé from the oven. Sprinkle with confectioners' sugar and serve warm, sprinkling each serving with a little optional Grand Marnier.

Strawberry
Pots de Crème

Serves:	**6**
Preparation time:	**15 minutes, plus 2 to 4 hours to chill**
Cooking time:	**15 minutes**
Type of recipe:	**elementary**
Cost:	**inexpensive**

Here is one of the simplest and most refreshing spring and early summer desserts. Other berries such as blueberries, raspberries, or blackberries can be substituted for the strawberries. In winter use half a poached pear and red wine on each ramekin.

Ingredients

¾ cup milk
½ cup heavy cream
2 large egg yolks
2 large eggs
⅓ cup granulated sugar
1 teaspoon vanilla extract

Garnish:

24 small ripe strawberries
1 cup red currant jelly
2 Tablespoons Grand Marnier, or other orange-flavored liqueur

Preparation

1.
Preheat the oven to 350 degrees.

2.
In an enamel saucepan combine the milk and cream. Heat the mixture without letting it come to a boil.

3.
Pour the milk-and-cream mixture into a bowl. Add the yolks, whole eggs, sugar, and vanilla and whisk the mixture until well blended. Pour the mixture into 6 six-ounce ramekins.

4.
Set the ramekins in a rectangular baking dish and pour boiling water into the dish. The water should come halfway up the ramekins.

5.
Set the baking dish in the oven and bake the custard for 15 minutes, or until the tip of a knife comes out clean. Remove the ramekins from the oven and cool.

6.
When completely cooled, garnish each ramekin with 4 to 5 whole strawberries. If the strawberries are large cut them in half lengthwise and mound them on each ramekin. Set aside.

7.
In a small saucepan, melt the currant jelly over low heat, add the Grand Marnier, and heat through.

8.
Cool the mixture a little and then spoon it over each strawberry mound, covering completely with the jelly.

9.
Chill the ramekins for 2 to 4 hours before serving.

Basic
Tart Shell

Yields:	**1 nine- or ten-inch tart shell**
Preparation time:	**10 minutes, plus 1 hour to chill**
Cooking time:	**25 minutes**
Type of recipe:	**elementary**
Cost:	**inexpensive**

The pie dough pâté brisée is the most versatile and useful dough in the everyday kitchen. While it does take some practice to achieve the right consistency and to know how to roll it out properly it is well worth the effort. A good pie crust can be used for a variety of quiches, meat pies, and dessert tarts. The key to a successful pie dough is to not knead the dough too much, which hardens it. It should be buttery and flaky but not crumbly. Most cooks who have a food processor delight in making dough in the machine rather than by hand. Unfortunately the food processor overworks the dough in seconds, leaving it elastic and hard. It is best to remove the dough from the food processor bowl before it is shaped into a ball. Gather the pieces gently into 1 mass on a floured service. Wrap the dough in waxed paper and refrigerate for 30 minutes to 1 hour before rolling.

Ingredients

12 Tablespoons cold butter
2 cups sifted all-purpose flour
Pinch of salt
4 to 6 Tablespoons ice water

Optional:

For sweet tart shells add 1 Tablespoon granulated sugar

Preparation

1.
To make the dough by hand cut the butter into ½-inch pieces and combine with the flour in a large stainless steel bowl. Add a pinch of salt and mix the ingredients with your fingers just long enough until the butter pieces are covered with flour and the mixture resembles oatmeal.

2.
Add the ice water, starting with 4 tablespoons only, and sprinkle it evenly over the butter-and-flour mixture. Gently gather the mixture into a ball, working it as little as possible. If the ball seems to crumble add the remaining 2 tablespoons ice water. Do not worry if a little butter shows through the dough. This will only give the pastry a flakier texture.

3.
Place the dough on a floured surface and roll around in the flour. Wrap the ball in waxed paper and chill for 30 minutes or longer.

4.
When the dough is ready place the ball on a lightly floured surface. Flour the rolling pin and roll out the dough, always rolling away from you and turning the dough ¼ turn so as to form a nice even circle. The dough should be about ⅛ inch thick.

5.
Roll the dough onto the pin and unroll again onto a quiche or tart pan. Do not stretch the dough. With your fingers push the dough into the corners or edges of the pan and form a ½-inch lip with your fingers all around.

6.
Roll the pin over the tart pan to remove excess dough. Prick the dough in 3 to 4

Serves:	**6**
Preparation time:	**15 minutes**
Cooking time:	**40 minutes**
Type of recipe:	**elementary**
Cost:	**inexpensive**

places with a fork and make a decorative edge with the blunt edge of a knife.

7.
Refrigerate the dough for 30 minutes before baking or freeze the crust well covered for 2 to 3 hours.

8.
Preheat the oven to 350 degrees. When ready to bake place a sheet of waxed paper in the tart shell and fill with dried beans. This will prevent the crust from shrinking and puffing up. Place the pan on a cookie sheet in the center of the oven and bake for 10 minutes. Remove the waxed paper and dried beans and bake for another 10 minutes. The tart shell is now ready to be filled.

Remarks
This is a partially baked tart shell. For a fully baked tart shell bake for another 10 to 15 minutes, or until the shell is lightly browned. When making a dessert tart shell add the optional sugar to the flour-and-butter mixture. You can also add ¼ teaspoon cinnamon when making dessert tart shells that are to be filled with either apples or pears.

For quiches and meat pies it is best to use a porcelain quiche pan. These are deeper than the removable bottom tart pans and are particularly good for the beginner since they can be served without being unmolded. The ingredients for all quiche recipes in this book have been measured for a 9-inch porcelain pan.

Ingredients
5 Tablespoons butter
6 apples (preferably mcintosh or cortlands), peeled, cored, and cubed
3 to 4 Tablespoons granulated sugar
¼ cup apricot preserves
1 teaspoon lemon rind
Large pinch of freshly grated nutmeg
2 large eggs, plus 1 yolk
½ Tablespoon sifted all-purpose flour
3 Tablespoons dark rum
⅓ cup heavy cream
1 nine-inch completely baked Basic Tart Shell (page 483)
Confectioners' sugar

Garnish:
Bowl of sugared Crème Fraîche (page 544)

Preparation
1.
Preheat the oven to 375 degrees.

2.
In a 10-inch cast-iron skillet melt 2 tablespoons butter and add the apples. Sprinkle with 3 tablespoons sugar and the apricot preserves and cook the mixture over medium heat until the apples are reduced to a thick purée. Be sure to stir the mixture several times with a wooden spoon to prevent the apples from scorching the bottom of the pan.

3.
Remove the apple purée from the heat. Add the lemon rind and nutmeg and transfer the apple mixture to a bowl.

4.
Add the remaining butter to the apple

Chocolate Mousse Tart

Serves:	**6 to 8**
Preparation time:	**45 minutes, plus 5 to 7 hours to chill**
Cooking time:	**30 minutes**
Type of recipe:	**elementary**
Cost:	**moderate**

purée and stir the mixture with a wooden spoon until the butter is incorporated into the apple purée. Set aside.

5.
In a bowl combine the eggs and additional yolk. Add the flour and blend the mixture thoroughly. Add the rum and cream and whisk the mixture until smooth.

6.
Combine the cream mixture with the apple purée. Taste and if not sweet enough add additional sugar to taste.

7.
Spoon the apple custard mixture into the baked tart shell. Place on a cookie sheet and place in the center of the oven. Bake for 30 minutes, or until the tip of a sharp knife comes out clean. Remove the tart from the oven and set aside.

8.
Preheat the broiler. Sprinkle the tart heavily with confectioners' sugar and place the tart in the broiler just long enough to melt the sugar and caramelize it. Remove the tart and cool to room temperature.

9.
Serve at room temperature accompanied by a bowl of sugared Crème Fraîche.

Remarks
The tart can be prepared a day ahead and reheated in a 200-degree oven. The tart may also be served with a Cointreau sabayon instead of the cream.

Ingredients

Tart Shell:
1 cup sifted all-purpose flour
¼ cup granulated sugar
Pinch of salt
4 Tablespoons cold butter
1 large egg yolk
1 Tablespoon ice water
1 Tablespoon vinegar

Filling:
3 large egg yolks
4 Tablespoons granulated sugar
¼ cup Grand Marnier, Crème de Cacao, brandy, or light rum
8 ounces semisweet chocolate
3 Tablespoons prepared coffee
4 Tablespoons butter, softened
1 cup heavy cream

Garnish:
Rosettes of whipped cream
Shaved chocolate

Preparation

1.
Preheat the oven to 350 degrees.

2.
Prepare the shell. In a bowl combine the flour, sugar, and a pinch of salt. Add the butter and work the mixture quickly with your hands until it resembles coarse oatmeal. Add the yolk, water, and vinegar and work the mixture until it becomes a smooth dough. Do not overwork the dough.

3.
Make a ball and wrap the dough in waxed paper. Chill for 30 minutes.

4.
Flatten the ball of dough and place between sheets of waxed paper. Roll it out to a 9-inch circle. Line an 8-inch, removable bottom tart pan with the dough and trim the edges. Prick the bottom of the shell in several places. Set the pan on a cookie sheet and bake for 8 to 10 minutes, or until the dough is just set. Remove from the oven and allow to cool.

5.
Prepare the filling. In the top of a double boiler combine the yolks, sugar, and liqueur. Whisk the mixture until well blended, then set over a pan of simmering water and whisk the mixture until it is thick and smooth. Be very careful not to curdle the eggs. The mixture will thicken very quickly. Remove the pan from the heat and set over a bowl of crushed ice. Whisk the mixture until it is completely cool and thick.

6.
Combine the chocolate with the coffee in a small heavy saucepan. Set in the oven and melt the chocolate. When the chocolate has melted, stir it with a wooden spoon until it is almost completely cool and then stir in the softened butter. When the butter is incorporated add the yolk-and-liqueur mixture and stir well. Chill the mixture for 30 minutes, or until it starts to set.

7.
Whip the cream and fold it into the chocolate mixture. Spoon the mousse into the baked tart shell and smooth it carefully with a large chef's knife. Chill for 4 to 6 hours before serving.

8.
Just before serving garnish the tart with rosettes of whipped cream and chocolate shavings. Serve chilled.

Remarks
The tart will keep for 2 to 3 days. If refrigerated make sure to cover it tightly with foil.

Lemon
Tart

Serves: **6**
Preparation time: **10 minutes**
Cooking time: **40 minutes**
Type of recipe: **elementary**
Cost: **inexpensive**

Lemons are the best of the all-season fruits since the deliciously tart flavor adds a refreshing touch to an elaborate winter menu as well as a light summer meal. This tart should be made in a deep porcelain quiche pan.

Ingredients
7 large eggs
Pinch of salt
¾ cup granulated sugar
½ cup lemon juice
Grated rind of 1 large lemon
1 teaspoon vanilla extract
1 8- to nine-inch partially baked Basic Tart Shell (page 483)

Garnish:
Confectioners' sugar

Preparation
1.
Preheat the oven to 350 degrees.
2.
Separate 4 of the eggs. Set the remaining 3 aside. In a stainless steel bowl beat the whites with a pinch of salt until fluffy. Add ¼ cup sugar, beating constantly until the whites are stiff and glossy. Set aside.
3.
In another bowl combine the yolks, whole eggs, remaining sugar, lemon juice, rind, and vanilla. Whisk the mixture until well blended and pale yellow.
4.
Fold the whites gently into the egg-and-lemon mixture. Do not use a beater.
5.
Pour the mixture into the prebaked shell and set on a baking sheet. Bake for 40 minutes, or until the tip of a knife comes out clean.
6.
Remove the tart from the oven and let it cool. If you have used a removable bottom pan, unmold the tart. Place it on a serving platter and sprinkle with confectioners' sugar. Serve at room temperature.

Remarks
This tart is particularly delicious when accompanied by sugared blueberries, raspberries, strawberries, or blackberries.

Pear Tart
with
Hot Chocolate Sauce

Serves: **6**
Preparation time: **30 minutes**
Cooking time: **40 to 45 minutes**
Type of recipe: **elementary**
Cost: **moderate**

Ingredients

1 nine-inch partially baked Basic Tart Shell (page 483)

Pastry Cream:
3 large egg yolks
2 Tablespoons cornstarch
⅓ cup granulated sugar
1 cup warm milk
1 teaspoon vanilla extract
3 Tablespoons almond liqueur

Pears:
4 to 5 small fresh pears
Juice of ½ lemon
4 cups water
1¾ cups granulated sugar
1 two-inch piece vanilla bean
1 three-inch stick cinnamon
1 two-inch piece lemon peel

Chocolate Sauce:
8 ounce semisweet chocolate
1 cup prepared coffee
2 to 3 Tablespoons granulated sugar
4 Tablespoons butter, softened

Optional:
1 Tablespoon almond liqueur

Preparation

1.
Start by making the pastry cream. In a bowl combine the egg yolks, cornstarch, and sugar and whisk the mixture until thoroughly blended and smooth. Add the milk and blend thoroughly.

2.
Transfer the mixture to a heavy-bottomed saucepan and cook over low heat, whisking constantly until it is very thick. Be careful not to scorch the bottom of the pan. Immediately transfer the pastry cream to a bowl. Add the vanilla and liqueur and chill until ready to use.

3.
Preheat the oven to 350 degrees.

4.
Peel the pears, cut in half lengthwise, and core them. Drop the pears into a bowl of cold water, adding the lemon juice. This will prevent the pears from turning dark.

5.
In a large saucepan combine the water, sugar, vanilla bean, cinnamon, and lemon peel. Bring to a boil, reduce the heat, and simmer for 15 minutes. Drain the pears and add them to the sugar syrup. Poach the pears until tender and then let them cool completely in the sugar syrup.

6.
Bake the tart shell according to the directions on page 484, and then cool. When the tart shell is completely cooled, spoon the pastry cream into the shell, smoothing it with a spatula. Drain the pears and dry gently with paper towels. Place the pears in a decorative pattern on top of the pastry cream. Set aside.

Walnut Caramel Tart

Serves: **6**
Preparation time: **30 minutes**
Cooking time: **1 hour, 15 minutes**
Type of recipe: **elementary**
Cost: **inexpensive**

7.
Prepare the sauce. In a saucepan combine the chocolate and coffee and heat over low heat until the chocolate has melted. Stir the mixture until it is smooth, then add the sugar and optional liqueur and keep warm over a pan of hot water. Just before serving whisk in the softened butter and serve the tart with the sauce on the side.

Remarks
The tart can be assembled 4 to 6 hours ahead. If you prefer to serve the tart without the chocolate sauce, it should be topped with an apricot glaze. To make the glaze, heat ¾ cup apricot preserves in a small saucepan and add a little lemon juice to taste. Strain the preserves over the pears and garnish with toasted slivered almonds.

Ingredients
1¼ cups heavy cream
½ cup granulated sugar
2 Tablespoons water
2 large eggs, plus 3 yolks
½ cup honey
2 Tablespoons dark rum
1 cup finely minced walnuts
1 nine-inch partially baked Basic Tart Shell (page 483)

Preparation
1.
Preheat the oven to 350 degrees.
2.
Heat the cream in the saucepan without letting it come to a boil. Set aside.
3.
In a small heavy saucepan, combine the sugar and water and cook until it turns a nutty brown. Do not stir until the sugar starts to caramelize. Remove the saucepan from the heat and immediately add all the cream, whisking constantly.
4.
Return the saucepan to the heat and cook for 2 minutes until the cream and caramel are well blended. Set aside.
5.
In a bowl combine the eggs, yolks, honey, and rum. Whisk the mixture until well blended. Add the cream mixture and then the walnuts and whisk again until thoroughly blended.
6.
Pour the mixture into the tart shell. Put it on a baking sheet and place the tart in the center of the oven. Bake for 50 minutes to 1 hour, or until a knife tip comes out clean. Serve warm or at room temperature.

Plum
Tart

Serves: **6**
Preparation time: **20 minutes**
Cooking time: **1 hour, 10 minutes**
Type of recipe: **elementary**
Cost: **inexpensive**

Ingredients

¾ **cup blanched almonds**
⅓ **cup granulated sugar**
1 large egg
2 Tablespoons butter, softened
¼ **teaspoon almond extract**
1 teaspoon vanilla extract
1 teaspoon lemon rind
1 unbaked 8-inch Basic Tart Shell (page 483)
1 can (2 pounds) whole plums, well drained and cut in half, or 24 fresh Italian prune plums, pitted and quartered
1 cup currant jelly
2 Tablespoons port wine

Preparation

1.
Preheat the oven to 350 degrees.
2.
In a food processor combine the almonds and sugar. Blend the mixture for 30 seconds, or until smooth. Do not grind to a paste.
3.
Add the egg, butter, almond and vanilla extracts, and lemon rind and blend for another 20 seconds. Transfer the mixture to the unbaked tart shell and spread it evenly with a rubber spatula.
4.
If using canned plums, cut then in half, remove the pits, and place them in 1 layer over the almond mixture (or arrange the fresh plums in a decorative pattern).
5.
Place the tart on a baking sheet and put in the center part of the oven. Bake the tart for 1 hour.
6.
When the tart is done remove from the oven and let it cool.
7.
Heat the currant jelly and port wine until melted and smooth. Spoon the currant jelly mixture over the entire tart and let it cool to room temperature. Serve the tart warm or at room temperature.

Remarks

A bowl of sweetened Crème Fraîche (page 544), flavored with 2 tablespoons Crème de Cassis, is an excellent accompaniment to this delicious tart.

Strawberry Custard Tart au Caramel

Serves: **6**
Preparation time: **15 minutes**
Cooking time: **20 minutes**
Type of recipe: **elementary**
Cost: **inexpensive**

Ingredients

3 large eggs
4 Tablespoons granulated sugar
1 Tablespoon sifted all-purpose flour
1 teaspoon vanilla extract
1 teaspoon orange extract
1¼ cups heavy cream
1 nine-inch partially baked Basic Tart Shell (page 483)

Optional:

1 to 2 teaspoons finely grated orange rind

Garnish:

1½ to 2 Tablespoons granulated sugar
2 cups small whole strawberries, stemmed
Caramel Syrup (page 507)

Preparation

1.
Preheat the oven to 350 degrees.

2.
In a bowl combine the eggs and sugar and beat the mixture until smooth and creamy. Add the flour and whisk until well blended. Add the vanilla, orange extract, and optional orange rind and cream and whisk until the mixture is completely smooth.

3.
Place the tart shell on a cookie sheet. Pour the custard mixture into the shell and set in the center of the oven. Bake for 20 minutes, or until the mixture is set. Test with a tip of a knife; it should come out clean. Do not however, overbake the custard or it will lose its creaminess.

4.
Remove the tart from the oven and cool to room temperature.

5.
Thirty minutes before serving sprinkle the sugar over the strawberries and toss lightly. You may need more or less sugar depending on the sweetness of the strawberries. Place the strawberries in a decorative design on the custard, covering it completely. Serve with a side bowl of Caramel Syrup.

Souffléed Cheese Tart

Serves:	**6 to 8**
Preparation time:	**20 minutes**
Cooking time:	**55 minutes**
Type of recipe:	**elementary**
Cost:	**inexpensive**

Ingredients

Tart Shell:
1 cup sifted all-purpose flour
¼ cup granulated sugar
1 large egg yolk
1 Tablespoon milk
2 teaspoons vanilla extract
Pinch of salt
¼ cup butter, cut into small pieces

Optional:
Large pinch of ground cinnamon

Topping:
1½ pounds ricotta
4 eggs, separated
½ cup golden raisins
Rind of 1 large lemon
1 Tablespoon orange liqueur
1 cup granulated sugar
1½ teaspoons vanilla extract

Preparation

1.
Preheat the oven to 375 degrees.

2.
Prepare the shell. In a mixing bowl combine the flour, sugar, egg yolk, milk, vanilla, salt, and optional cinnamon. Add the butter, and work the mixture with your hands until smooth and well blended; do not overmix.

3.
Flatten the dough with your hands, fitting it in an even layer into a 9-inch cake pan. Shape the dough to come up ½ inch around the sides. Prick the dough and bake for 10 minutes, or until nicely browned. Remove from the oven and set aside.

4.
In a large bowl combine the ricotta, egg yolks, raisins, lemon rind, orange liqueur, sugar, and vanilla. Beat the mixture with a small electric hand beater until thoroughly blended.

5.
In another bowl beat the whites until they form stiff peaks. Fold the whites gently into the cheese mixture.

6.
Pour the mixture into the prebaked tart shell. Set in the center of the oven and bake for 45 minutes, or until firm and nicely browned.

7.
Unmold the tart and serve the same day.

Viennese
Apple Tart

Serves: **6 to 8**
Preparation time: **20 minutes**
Cooking time: **40 minutes**
Type of recipe: **elementary**
Cost: **inexpensive**

While French fruit tarts are usually open faced, Viennese fruit tarts are usually covered with a sugar crust. Here is one of my favorite apple tarts with a sugar crust. Serve it accompanied by sugared Crème Fraîche (page 544).

Ingredients

Tart Shell:
2 cups sifted all-purpose flour
½ cup granulated sugar
10 Tablespoons butter, softened
1 large egg yolk
1½ Tablespoons milk
1½ Tablespoons distilled white vinegar
1 large egg, mixed with 1 Tablespoon water

Filling:
2 Tablespoons butter
2 pounds golden delicious apples, peeled, cored, and cut in thirds
⅓ cup granulated sugar
3 ounces dark raisins
1 teaspoon ground cinnamon
large pinch of nutmeg
1 teaspoon vanilla extract
1 to 2 teaspoons lemon juice

Optional:
2 Tablespoons raspberry jam

Preparation

1.
Preheat the oven to 375 degrees. Have ready a 9-inch springform pan.

2.
Prepare the tart shell. In a mixing bowl combine the flour, sugar, butter, egg yolk, milk, and vinegar. Work the mixture with your hands until it forms a soft ball. Divide in two.

3.
Use half the dough and flatten it, shaping it into the 9-inch springform, bringing the dough up ½ inch along the sides of the pan. Bake the dough for 10 minutes, or until golden brown. Remove from the oven and set aside, in the pan, while you prepare the filling.

4.
In a large heavy skillet heat the butter. Add the apples, sugar, raisins, cinnamon, nutmeg, and vanilla and cook the mixture until the water has evaporated. Taste the apples and add lemon juice to taste. Cool.

5.
When the apple mixture has cooled down sufficiently, spread the optional raspberry jam on the baked crust, then top with the apple mixture.

6.
Cover the apple mixture with the remaining dough by rolling out small flat disks and piecing them together until they cover the entire apple mixture. Prick the crust in several places.

7.
Brush the crust with an egg wash made from the egg and water. Bake the tart in the

Dessert Crêpes

Yield	**14 to 16 crêpes**
Preparation time:	**10 minutes**
Cooking time:	**30 minutes**
Type of recipe:	**elementary**
Cost:	**inexpensive**

preheated oven for 25 minutes, then remove from the oven and let it cool on a rack, in the pan.

8.
When cool remove the tart from the pan. Serve at room temperature.

Remarks
This tart will keep for 2 or 3 days. Cover well with foil and keep in a cool place. It does not have to be refrigerated.

Ingredients
1 cup sifted all-purpose flour
1½ cups milk
3 large eggs
2 teaspoons granulated sugar
1 teaspoon vanilla extract
3 Tablespoons butter, melted and cooled

Optional:
2 to 3 Tablespoons Cointreau or cognac

Preparation
1.
In the container of a blender or a food processor combine the flour, milk, eggs, sugar, vanilla, and optional liqueur. Blend the mixture at top speed for 30 seconds, scraping down the sides of the bowl with a rubber spatula and blending the mixture again for 30 seconds. Whisk in the cooled melted butter and transfer the mixture to a bowl. Let stand at room temperature for an hour.

2.
Heat a 6-inch crêpe pan and brush it very lightly with butter. When the pan is very hot, remove it from the heat and add 2 tablespoons of the batter. Quickly turn the pan in all directions to coat its entire surface; immediately pour any excess batter back into the bowl. Place the pan over moderate heat and cook the crêpe until it is lightly browned. Loosen it with the tip of a sharp knife, lift the edge, and then, quickly, with the tips of your fingers, turn the crêpe. Brown the crepe lightly on the other side and slide it onto a plate. Brush the pan again with butter after every 3 crêpes.

Apple Crêpes Bretonne

Serves:	**6**
Preparation time:	**35 minutes**
Cooking time:	**20 minutes**
Type of recipe:	**elementary**
Cost:	**inexpensive**

Remarks

If the crêpes are to be used within a day or two, they can simply be stacked on a plate, covered, and refrigerated. Bring the crêpes back to room temperature before filling. If they are to be frozen, place a sheet of waxed paper between each crêpe and wrap them in heavy-duty foil. Although crêpes freeze well, they are never as good as when made fresh, but they are still good to have on hand for an elegant last-minute dessert. Frozen crêpes can be defrosted at room temperature before using or placed in a 250-degree oven until they are defrosted and lightly heated through.

Ingredients

1 batch Dessert Crepes (page 494)

Filling:

2 Tablespoons butter
4 golden delicious apples, peeled and cut into eighths
2 Tablespoons granulated sugar
2 Tablespoons finely minced crystallized ginger
2 Tablespoons calvados or cognac
½ to ¾ cup apricot preserves
Large pinch of freshly grated nutmeg

Topping:

¼ cup dark rum
3 Tablespoons calvados or apple brandy

Preparation

1.
In a large heavy skillet heat the butter. Add the apples and sugar and cook the apples over moderate-to-high heat, shaking the pan back and forth until the apples are nicely browned and sugar is caramelized. Watch carefully; the sugar must not burn.

2.
Add the ginger, cognac, and apricot preserves. Cook the mixture for another 3 to 4 minutes, then add a large pinch of nutmeg and set aside.

3.
Fill each crêpe with a little of the apple mixture. Roll them up and place in a well-buttered rectangular baking dish. Cover and set aside.

4.
Thirty minutes before serving preheat the oven to 300 degrees.

Serves: **6**
Preparation time: **35 minutes**
Cooking time: **1 hour**
Type of recipe: **elementary**
Cost: **inexpensive**

5.
Place the crêpes in the oven and heat for 15 to 20 minutes, or until just heated through.
6.
In a small saucepan heat the rum and calvados or brandy but do not bring to a boil.
7.
Remove the baking dish from the oven. Pour the hot liquor mixture over the crêpes and ignite. Serve immediately right from the dish.

Remarks
You can assemble the dessert several hours ahead and reheat it just before serving. You can serve a side dish of softened rum raisin ice cream mixed with 1 cup whipped cream as a garnish to the apple crêpes.

Ingredients
12 Dessert Crêpes (page 494)

Filling:
2½ pound apples, preferably mcintosh or cortland
3 Tablespoons butter
⅓ cup granulated sugar
½ cup dark raisins
½ cup water
Grated rind of 1 orange
1 teaspoon ground cinnamon
Large pinch of freshly grated nutmeg
¼ cup Grand Marnier

Sauce:
6 Tablespoons butter
⅓ cup granulated sugar
Juice of 1 large orange
Juice of ½ lemon
⅓ cup dark rum
¼ teaspoon ground ginger

Garnish:
Rind of 1 large orange, cut into fine julienne strips, then parboiled for 3 minutes and drained
Bowl of sugared Crème Fraîche (page 544)

Preparation
1.
Peel the apples, then core and cube them.
2.
In a 10-inch cast-iron skillet melt the butter, add the apples, then add the sugar and raisins. Sauté the apples over medium heat until they are soft and start to caramelize; be careful not to scorch the pan. Add the

Banana Crêpes and Rum Sauce

Serves: **6**
Preparation time: **15 minutes**
Cooking time: **15 minutes**
Type of recipe: **elementary**
Cost: **inexpensive**

water, orange rind, cinnamon, and nutmeg. Bring to a boil, reduce the heat, and simmer the apples partially covered for 10 minutes, or until the apples are reduced to a thick purée. Add the Grand Marnier and set aside.

3.
Preheat the oven to 325 degrees.

4.
Fill each crêpe with a tablespoon of the apple filling and place seam-side down in a well-buttered *au gratin* dish. Set aside.

5.
Make the sauce. In a heavy-bottomed saucepan melt the butter over low heat. Add the sugar and cook the mixture until it turns a light brown. Add the orange juice, lemon juice, and rum. Bring to a boil, reduce the heat, and simmer the sauce for 3 minutes.

6.
Add the ginger, taste the sauce, add more sugar or lemon juice to taste. The sauce should have a sweet yet somewhat tangy flavor.

7.
Spoon the sauce over the crêpes. Cover the dish and set in the oven. Bake the crêpes for 25 to 30 minutes.

8.
Uncover and sprinkle the crêpes with the orange julienne. Serve directly from the baking dish accompanied by a side dish of sugared Crème Fraîche.

A batch of dessert crêpes is good to have on hand at any time. While crêpes freeze well, they're really better when prepared a day or two in advance, covered and refrigerated. Here the crêpes are filled with sliced bananas that have been sautéed in butter and brown sugar. You may vary the filling by using peeled and quartered golden delicious apples or peeled and quartered bartlett pears instead of the bananas. However, I have found bananas to be one of the simplest and most delicious last-minute fillings for crêpes.

Ingredients
12 Dessert Crêpes (page 494)

Filling:
3 Tablespoons butter
4 Tablespoons brown sugar
4 slightly firm bananas, peeled and sliced
1 teaspoon finely grated orange rind
¼ teaspoon ground ginger
Large pinch of freshly grated nutmeg

Sauce:
6 Tablespoons butter
8 Tablespoons granulated sugar
½ cup freshly squeezed orange juice
1 teaspoon finely grated orange rind
⅓ cup dark rum

Garnish:
Bowl of vanilla ice cream mixed with ½ cup heavy cream, whipped and flavored with a little rum

Chestnut Crêpe Torte

Serves:
Preparation time: **30 minutes, plus 8 to 12 hours to chill**
Cooking time: **20 minutes**
Type of recipe: **elementary**
Cost: **moderate**

Preparation

1.
Preheat the oven to 325 degrees.

2.
Start by making the sauce. In a heavy saucepan heat the butter and sugar and cook the mixture until the butter turns a light brown and the sugar starts to caramelize. Immediately add the orange juice and bring to a boil. Whisk until the sugar is melted and the sauce is smooth. Add the orange rind and rum. If the sauce is not sweet enough add more sugar to taste. Keep the sauce warm.

3.
In a large heavy skillet heat the butter and sugar over low heat. Add the sliced bananas and cook until the bananas are well heated through and covered with the sugar-and-butter mixture. Add the orange rind, ginger and nutmeg and keep warm.

4.
Fill each crêpe with a little of the banana mixture. Roll it up and place it seam-side down in a buttered *au gratin* dish. Spoon the sauce over the crêpes. Cover with foil and set in the oven. Bake for 25 to 30 minutes, or until the crêpes are well heated through. Serve the crêpes warm with a side dish of vanilla ice cream mixed with rum-flavored whipped cream.

Ingredients

Crêpe Batter:
1½ cups milk
3 Tablespoons cognac or brandy
3 large eggs, separated
1 teaspoon vanilla extract
1½ cups sifted all-purpose flour
1½ Tablespoons granulated sugar
5 Tablespoons butter, melted

Mousse and Meringue:
2 large eggs, separated
8 Tablespoons granulated sugar
¼ cup cognac or brandy
8 ounces semisweet chocolate
2 Tablespoons prepared coffee
4 Tablespoons cold butter
1 cup canned chestnut purée, preferably imported
1 cup heavy cream

Preparation

1.

Preheat the oven to 300 degrees.

2.

Start by making the crêpe batter. In a blender or food processor combine the milk, cognac, egg yolks, and vanilla. Blend thoroughly. Add the flour and sugar and again blend thoroughly. Transfer the mixture to a bowl and whisk in the melted butter. Let the batter rest for 1 hour to 1 hour, 30 minutes.

3.

While the batter is resting make the mousse. In a stainless steel mixing bowl combine the yolks and 4 tablespoons sugar. Beat the mixture until it is pale yellow and forms a ribbon. Add the cognac and set aside.

4.

In a small heavy saucepan combine the chocolate and coffee. Place the saucepan in the oven and when the chocolate is melted remove the pan from the oven and stir the chocolate until completely smooth.

5.

Add the yolk mixture to the chocolate and blend thoroughly. Let the mixture cool completely. Add the butter 1 tablespoon at a time and whisk until completely incorporated.

6.

Fold the chocolate mixture into the chestnut purée and chill the mixture for 30 minutes to 1 hour, or until it is almost set.

7.

Whip the cream and fold it gently into the mousse. Chill the mousse for another 2 hours.

8.

While the mousse is setting, beat the 3 egg whites and fold them gently into the crêpe batter. Make the crepes in an 8-inch cast-iron skillet following the procedure on page 000. (The crêpes should be slightly thicker than usual.)

9.

When the mousse is set place a crêpe on a round serving platter. Cover with a thick layer of the mousse and continue making layers using 12 to 14 crêpes in all. Cover and chill the torte for 4 to 6 hours or overnight.

10.

Preheat the broiler.

11.

In a large stainless steel bowl beat the remaining 2 whites adding 4 tablespoons of sugar, 1 tablespoon at a time, and beating the whites until they form a stiff meringue. Spoon the meringue over the torte in a decorative swirl and place the torte quickly in the broiler until it is just browned. Remove from the oven and serve immediately.

Remarks

The entire dessert can be prepared 2 to 3 days ahead and chilled, but the meringue should be made no more than 1 to 2 hours ahead. You can also substitute a chocolate sauce for the meringue and simply spoon the sauce over the torte and serve.

Lemon Crêpes

Serves:	**6**
Preparation time:	**45 minutes, plus 2 to 4 hours to chill**
Cooking time:	**25 minutes**
Type of recipe:	**elementary**
Cost:	**inexpensive**

Ingredients

12 to 18 Dessert Crêpes (page 494)
Confectioners' sugar

Filling:
6 large egg yolks
⅔ cup granulated sugar
4 Tablespoons cornstarch
2 cups milk
1 teaspoon vanilla extract
1 Tablespoon grated lemon rind

Sauce:
6 Tablespoons butter
¾ cup granulated sugar
⅔ cup freshly squeezed lemon juice
1 Tablespoon lemon rind

Preparation

1.
Start by making the lemon filling. (This can be done 1 to 2 days ahead of time.) In a bowl combine the yolks and sugar. Whisk the mixture until it is pale yellow and forms a ribbon. Gently stir in the cornstarch and continue whisking until the mixture is smooth and the cornstarch is completely dissolved.

2.
Heat the milk in a saucepan and then whisk it into the yolk-and-cornstarch mixture.

3.
Transfer the mixture to a heavy-bottomed saucepan. Place over medium heat and whisk constantly until the sauce is very thick. Be careful not to scorch the bottom of the pan. As soon as the cream is done transfer it to a bowl. Add the vanilla and lemon rind and chill covered for 2 to 4 hours or overnight.

4.
Preheat the oven to 325 degrees.

5.
Place a tablespoon of the lemon cream on each crêpe and fold it in thirds, pressing down lightly on each crêpe to flatten it. Place the crêpes overlapping in an ovenproof baking dish and set aside.

6.
Prepare the sauce. In a saucepan combine the butter and sugar. Melt the butter over low heat and add the lemon juice and rind, whisking the mixture until the sugar is dissolved. Simmer for 2 to 3 minutes. Taste and, if the sauce is too tart, add more sugar and cook for another 2 to 3 minutes, or until the sugar is dissolved.

7.
Spoon the sauce over the crêpes. Cover tightly with foil and place in the center of the oven. Bake for 20 to 25 minutes, or until the crêpes are well heated through.

8.
Uncover the crêpes. Sprinkle heavily with confectioners' sugar and place in the broiler until the sugar is melted and caramelized. Serve immediately right from the baking dish.

Remarks

It is best to make the crêpes a day or so ahead and keep them covered in the refrigerator. If you do, heat the crêpes in a 200-degree oven until well heated through before filling. The entire dish can be prepared several hours ahead and kept covered at room temperature in a cool place. Bake in a 300-degree oven for 30 minutes, or until heated through.

Crêpes
in
Orange Caramel Butter

Serves: **6**
Preparation time: **15 minutes**
Cooking time: **15 to 20 minutes**
Type of recipe: **elementary**
Cost: **inexpensive**

Here is a take-off on the famous Crêpes Suzettes. I have never quite understood why this classic dessert is considered so difficult. As it happens, all crêpe preparations are easy once you have mastered the making of crêpes, which, although time consuming, is also pretty simple. Crêpes can be made well in advance and reheated in a slow oven. They are best when made the same day or a day in advance. The butter mixture can be made several days ahead and reheated in a large skillet; it can also be frozen successfully. The sauce itself can be served over ice cream or poached fruit such as peaches or pears.

Ingredients
¾ cup butter
¾ cup granulated sugar
¾ cup freshly squeezed orange juice
Grated rind of 1 orange
1 teaspoon lemon rind
Lemon juice to taste
12 to 14 Dessert Crêpes (page 494)
½ cup orange-flavored liqueur, such as Grand Marnier, Cointreau, or Triple Sec
2 Tablespoons cognac or brandy

Preparation
1.
In a heavy 2-quart saucepan melt the butter. Add the sugar and cook the mixture until it turns hazelnut brown. Immediately add the orange juice, bring to a boil, and reduce the heat. Add the orange and lemon rind as well as the lemon juice and transfer the sauce to a heavy 10-inch skillet.
2.
Fold the crêpes in half and then in half again. Place them in the orange sauce.
3.
Ten minutes before serving reheat the crêpes and the sauce over very low heat. Add the orange liqueur and cognac and spoon the sauce over the crêpes.
4.
Transfer the crêpes to a serving platter and serve immediately.

Remarks
The crêpes can be placed in the warm sauce 1 to 2 hours ahead. Cover the skillet and keep warm in a very low oven.

Orange
Custard
Crêpes

Serves: **6**
Preparation time: **25 minutes**
Cooking time: **35 minutes**
Type of recipe: **elementary**
Cost: **moderate**

Ingredients
12 Dessert Crêpes (page 494)

Filling:
1 cup ricotta cheese
4 Tablespoons granulated sugar
2 large eggs, separated
1 teaspoon orange extract
2 Tablespoons orange liqueur (Grand Marnier or Cointreau)
1 teaspoon vanilla extract
2 Tablespoons grated orange rind
2 Tablespoons butter, softened
½ cup golden raisins, plumped in hot water and well drained
Pinch of salt

Custard:
1 cup milk
1 cup light cream
½ cup granulated sugar
4 large eggs
1 teaspoon vanilla extract
¼ cup orange liqueur

Garnish:
1 medium navel orange
½ cup granulated sugar
2 to 3 Tablespoons water

Preparation
1.
Start by making the cheese and orange filling. In a mixing bowl combine the ricotta, sugar, egg yolks, orange extract, liqueur, vanilla, and orange rind. Beat the mixture until well blended and then add the softened butter and raisins. Blend the mixture thoroughly.
2.
Beat the egg whites, adding a pinch of salt, until they form stiff peaks. Fold the beaten whites lightly into the cheese-and-orange mixture and taste for sweetness. You may want to add a little more sugar.
3.
Fill each crêpe with some of the filling and place in 1 layer seam-side down in a buttered baking dish. Set aside.
4.
Preheat the oven to 350 degrees.
5.
For the custard, combine the milk, cream, and sugar in a saucepan and heat without letting it come to a boil. Remove from the heat and add the eggs. Whisk the mixture until thoroughly blended and add the vanilla and the orange liqueur. Pour the custard mixture over the crêpes and place the dish in the oven. Bake for 25 minutes.
6.
While the crêpes are baking prepare the orange caramel garnish. Cut the ends off the orange and then slice without peeling.
7.
In a small heavy skillet combine the sugar and water. Cook the mixture until it turns a caramel color; do not let it get too dark. Remove from the heat and immediately dip

Crêpes aux Poires

Serves: **6**
Preparation time: **45 minutes**
Cooking time: **45 minutes**
Type of recipe: **elementary**
Cost: **inexpensive**

each orange slice into the caramel and then transfer it to a well-oiled baking sheet. If the caramel shows signs of getting too thick return it to a low heat adding 1 teaspoon water and reheating until it is melted. Keep the caramelized orange slices on the side until the crêpes are done.

8.
When the crêpes are done and the custard is set, remove from the oven. Arrange the orange slices on top slightly overlapping and serve warm.

Remarks
The entire dish can be prepared several hours ahead and then baked 25 to 30 minutes before serving. The caramelized orange slices are an optional garnish but they add an interesting touch to the dish. If you plan to make the caramelized oranges you will have to prepare them no more than 20 to 30 minutes before they are to be served.

Ingredients
2 large ripe bartlett pears
3 cups water
½ to ¾ cup granulated sugar
1 two-inch piece vanilla bean
12 to 14 Dessert Crêpes (page 494)

Pastry Cream:
3 large egg yolks
⅓ cup granulated sugar
3 Tablespoons cornstarch
1 cup milk
¾ teaspoon vanilla extract
3 Tablespoons Grand Marnier, or other orange-flavored liqueur

Sauce:
6 Tablespoons butter
⅓ cup granulated sugar
⅓ cup freshly squeezed orange juice
⅓ cup apricot liqueur
¼ cup cognac or brandy
2 Tablespoons strained apricot preserves
Lemon juice

Garnish:
Grated rind of 1 lime

1.
Start by poaching the pears. Peel the pears and place them in a saucepan with the water, ½ cup sugar, and the vanilla bean. (If the pears are not ripe you will need the additional ¼ cup sugar.) Bring the mixture to a boil, reduce the heat, and poach the pears partially covered until tender, or for about 20 to 30 minutes. Let the pears cool in their poaching liquid and set aside.

2.
Make the pastry cream. Combine the yolks, sugar, and cornstarch in a mixing bowl and mix until smooth. Add the milk and whisk the mixture until well blended.

3.
Transfer the mixture to a heavy 2-quart saucepan and cook over low heat whisking constantly until the custard becomes very thick. Be careful not to scorch the bottom of the pan. Immediately transfer the pastry cream to a bowl. Add the vanilla and Grand Marnier and chill the sauce for 30 minutes to an hour.

4.
Remove the pears from their poaching liquid, core, and dice finely. Combine the diced pears with the pastry cream.

5.
Fill each crêpe with a heaping tablespoon of the pastry cream-pear mixture. Place the crêpes seam-side down in 1 layer in an *au gratin* dish and set aside.

6.
Preheat the oven to 300 degrees.

7.
Make the sauce. In a heavy saucepan combine the butter and sugar. Bring the mixture to a boil and cook over high heat until the mixture turns hazelnut brown. Immediately add the orange juice and whisk the sauce until smooth. Add the liqueur, cognac, and apricot preserves. Taste the sauce and add lemon juice to taste.

8.
Spoon the sauce over the crêpes. Cover the dish and set in the center of the oven. Bake the crêpes for 10 to 15 minutes. The filling should still be chilled, but the sauce and the crêpes should be well heated through.

9.
Remove the dish from the oven. Uncover and sprinkle with grated lime rind. Serve immediately.

Remarks
The entire dessert can be made in advance. The pears can be poached several days ahead and left in their poaching liquid. Both the pastry cream and the sauce can be made a day or 2 in advance. If you have a batch of crêpes on hand in your freezer this elegant dessert can be assembled in a matter of minutes.

Apple
Meringue
Pudding

Serves: **4 to 6**
Preparation time: **20 minutes**
Cooking time: **40 minutes**
Type of recipe: **elementary**
Cost: **inexpensive**

Ingredients

4 Tablespoons butter
3 pounds mcintosh apples, quartered, peeled, and cored
½ cup apricot jam
Grated rind of 1 large orange
½ cup dark rum
1⅓ cup granulated sugar
1 two-inch piece vanilla bean
2 cups water
3 to 4 medium golden delicious apples, peeled, cored, and sliced
1½ cups Macaroons (page 524), crushed to a coarse crumb
3 egg whites

Preparation

1.
In a heavy casserole melt the butter. Add the quartered apples, apricot jam, and grated orange rind and cook the mixture partially covered over medium heat for 15 to 20 minutes stirring occasionally.

2.
Uncover the casserole and add ¼ cup rum. Increase the heat and cook the apples, stirring several times, until they are reduced to a very thick purée. Taste the purée for sweetness, adding a little more sugar if necessary. Remove the apple purée from the heat and set aside.

3.
In another heavy casserole combine ⅔ cup sugar, the vanilla bean, and water. Bring to a boil, reduce the heat, and simmer covered for 15 to 20 minutes.

4.
Add the apple slices to the casserole, reduce to a simmer, and poach the slices

for 2 to 3 minutes, or until just tender; do not overcook. Drain the apple slices and set aside.

5.
Preheat the broiler.

6.
In a rectangular porcelain baking dish spread the apple purée in an even layer. Cover the entire layer with the macaroon crumbs and sprinkle with the remaining ¼ cup rum. Place the reserved apple slices on top in a decorative pattern and set aside.

7.
In a stainless steel bowl beat the egg whites with an electric hand mixer, adding the remaining ⅔ cups sugar, 1 tablespoon at a time, until the egg whites form a stiff meringue. Spoon the meringue over the apple slices, creating a decorative pattern.

8.
Place the pudding in the broiler until just browned. Remove from the oven and serve at room temperature.

Remarks:
The entire dessert can be prepared a day or 2 ahead but the meringue should not be added to the dish until just before serving. You can sprinkle the meringue with finely sliced slivered almonds before placing it in the broiler.

Apple Pudding Normand

Serves: **6**
Preparation time: **15 minutes**
Cooking time: **1 hour**
Type of recipe: **elementary**
Cost: **inexpensive**

Ingredients
¾ cup golden raisins
¼ cup calvados or brandy
2 Tablespoons butter
6 golden delicious apples, peeled, cored, and cut in eighths
¼ cup granulated sugar
1 teaspoon lemon rind

Batter:
8 Tablespoons butter
½ cup plus 2 Tablespoons granulated sugar
3 large eggs, separated
½ cup sifted all-purpose flour
1 cup milk
1½ teaspoons vanilla extract
Pinch of salt

Garnish:
Bowl of sweetened Crème Fraîche (page 544) or a bowl of vanilla ice cream

Preparation

1.
Preheat the oven to 350 degrees.

2.
In a small bowl combine the raisins and calvados or brandy and let the raisins marinate for 15 to 20 minutes. Drain and reserve both raisins and liquid.

3.
In a large cast-iron skillet melt the butter. Add the apples, sugar, lemon rind, and raisins. Sauté the apples for 5 to 7 minutes, or until they are soft and caramelized. Shake the pan back and forth to prevent the apples from scorching the pan. Set aside.

4.
Prepare the batter. In a bowl cream the butter with ½ cup sugar until the mixture is smooth. Add the yolks and blend well. Add the flour and milk and whisk the mixture until smooth. Add the vanilla and the reserved liquid from the raisins and set aside.

5.
Whisk the whites with a pinch of salt until they form stiff peaks. Fold the whites gently into the batter.

6.
Butter a rectangular pudding dish. Arrange the apples and raisins in the dish and spoon the batter over them. Place the dish in the oven and bake for 1 hour, or until a knife comes out clean.

7.
Remove the dish from the oven and sprinkle with 1 or 2 tablespoons sugar. Turn the oven to broil and place the dish in the broiler until the sugar has melted and is caramelized.

8.
Serve the apple pudding warm or at room temperature with a side dish of vanilla ice cream or a bowl of sweetened Crème Fraîche

Banana Potpourri
in
Caramel Syrup

Serves: **4 to 5**
Preparation time: **10 minutes**
Cooking time: **10 minutes**
Type of recipe: **elementary**
Cost: **inexpensive**

Bananas are a fruit that we often take for granted. It is always available at every market and is somehow limited to the fruit salad bowl. I recently had this refreshing dessert in Morocco and wondered why I had not thought of using bananas in this way before.

Ingredients
¾ cup granulated sugar
2 Tablespoons water, plus ¼ cup hot water
¼ teaspoon ground ginger
Juice of 1 large lime
¼ cup banana liqueur
2 to 3 Tablespoons dark rum
4 large bananas, peeled and cut into ¼-inch slices
1 to 1½ cups seedless thompson green grapes

Garnish
Grated rind of 1 lime

Optional:
A few tiny sprigs of fresh mint

Preparation
1.
In a small heavy saucepan combine the sugar with 2 tablespoons water and blend well. Place the saucepan over high heat and bring to a boil. Cook without stirring until the mixture turns a hazelnut brown. Immediately add the ¼ cup hot water and stir the mixture until the sugar is melted and the mixture is smooth.
2.
Remove the saucepan from the heat and add the ginger, lime juice, banana liqueur, and rum. Transfer the mixture to a bowl and chill.
3.
Place the sliced bananas in a shallow round glass serving dish. Add the grapes and spoon the caramel syrup over the fruit.
4.
Garnish the dish with the grated lime rind and optional mint leaves and serve slightly chilled or at room temperature.

Remarks
The caramel syrup can also be used as a topping for ice cream. It can be made 2 to 3 weeks in advance and kept in a covered jar in the refrigerator. The syrup should not be used to top the bananas until just before serving or the bananas will get too soft.

Cherry Compote
au
Grand Marnier

Serves:	**6**
Preparation time:	**20 minutes, plus 24 hours to marinate**
Cooking time:	**45 minutes**
Type of recipe:	**elementary**
Cost:	**inexpensive**

Ingredients

2 oranges
½ cup Grand Marnier or other orange-flavored liqueur
3 cups red burgundy wine
1 four-inch stick cinnamon
1 cup granulated sugar
3 cloves
2 pounds fresh cherries, stems removed

Garnish:
Thinly sliced oranges

Preparation

1.
With a vegetable peeler remove the orange rind from the oranges without including any of the white membrane. Cut the orange rind into very thin julienne strips and set aside.

2.
In a saucepan bring 1 cup water to boil, add the orange strips, and cook for 3 minutes. Drain and transfer to a bowl.

3.
Add the Grand Marnier to the bowl with the orange peel and marinate the mixture for 24 hours.

4.
In a heavy enamel saucepan combine the wine, cinnamon, sugar, and cloves. Bring to a boil, reduce the heat, and add the cherries. Cook over low heat for 25 minutes.

5.
Remove the saucepan from the heat and transfer the contents to a glass bowl. When completely cool add the marinated orange strips together with the Grand Marnier. Chill the compote until serving.

6.
Just before serving garnish the bowl with orange slices and serve moderately chilled.

Remarks
This compote can be made a week in advance and refrigerated in a covered glass jar. You can add the marinated orange strips to the cherry compote 1 or 2 days ahead of serving.

Fresh Figs in Raspberry Soured Cream

Serves:	**4 to 6**
Preparation time:	**10 minutes**
Cooking time:	**none**
Type of recipe:	**elementary**
Cost:	**moderate**

In the last 2 to 3 years fresh figs have become increasingly available in good produce markets outside the West Coast. Although still far too expensive, figs are a wonderful fruit that can be served in several creative ways.

Ingredients
2 cups Crème Fraîche (page 544)
¼ to ⅓ cup granulated sugar
1 package (10 ounces) frozen raspberries
12 large ripe fresh figs

Optional:
1 cup fresh raspberries

Garnish:
Sprigs of fresh mint

Preparation
1.
In a bowl combine the Crème Fraîche with ¼ cup sugar and blend thoroughly.
2.
Purée the frozen raspberries in the blender. Strain them through a fine sieve and add to the Crème Fraîche. Whisk the mixture until blended. Taste, adding more sugar to taste.
3.
Transfer the raspberry soured cream to a shallow glass serving bowl and set aside.
4.
Place a mound of the optional fresh raspberries in the center of the bowl.
5.
Quarter the figs and place them on the cream in a decorative design. Garnish with the sprigs of mint and serve the dessert chilled.

Baked Pears Framboise

Serves:	**4 to 6**
Preparation time:	**10 minutes**
Cooking time:	**30 minutes**
Type of recipe:	**elementary**
Cost:	**inexpensive**

Ingredients
4 large partially ripe bartlett pears
Lemon juice
2 Tablespoons butter
¾ cup dry white wine
¼ to ⅓ cup granulated sugar
3 Tablespoons raspberry syrup
½ cup finely chopped blanched almonds

Garnish:
1 cup fresh raspberries

Optional:
1½ cups Crème Fraîche (page 544), sweetened with 2 Tablespoons sugar

Preparation
1.
Preheat the oven to 350 degrees.
2.
Peel the pears, cut them in half lengthwise, then carefully core them. Place them cut-side down in a well-buttered baking dish. Sprinkle the pears with lemon juice and place tiny bits of butter on each half. Set the dish aside.
3.
In a saucepan combine the wine, sugar, and 2 tablespoons raspberry syrup. Bring to a boil.
4.
As soon as the sugar is dissolved pour the wine over the pears. Place the baking dish in the oven and bake the pears for 15 to 20 minutes, or until tender when pierced with the tip of a sharp knife.

Fresh Peaches in Sauterne Sauce

Serves:	**6**
Preparation time:	**30 minutes, plus 4 to 6 hours to chill**
Cooking time:	**15 minutes**
Type of recipe:	**elementary**
Cost:	**inexpensive**

5.
Transfer the pears to an ovenproof serving platter, placing them cut-side down in a decorative pattern.

6.
Place a flameproof baking dish over high heat and cook the pan juices until well reduced and syrupy. Add the remaining tablespoon raspberry syrup. (Taste the pan juices; if too sweet add a little more lemon juice.) Spoon the sauce around the pears.

7.
Sprinkle the pears with the almonds.

8.
Preheat the broiler.

9.
Put the pears in the broiler just until the almonds are nicely crisp. Be sure not to burn them.

10.
Remove the dish from the oven and cool to room temperature. Place the fresh raspberries in a small mound in the center of the dish and sprinkle lightly with sugar. Serve the pears at room temperature with an optional side bowl of sweetened Crème Fraîche.

Remarks

If you cannot get fresh raspberries purée ½ cup frozen raspberries and add the purée to the reduced pan juices. Since frozen raspberries are quite sweet you may need additional lemon juice in the sauce. Serve the optional sweetened Crème Fraîche as a side dish.

Ingredients
6 large ripe fresh peaches
Juice of 1 large lemon
½ cup peach brandy
2 Tablespoons superfine sugar

Sauce:
4 large egg yolks
½ cup granulated sugar
¾ cup sauterne wine
½ teaspoon ground cinnamon
Large pinch of freshly grated nutmeg
½ cup heavy cream, whipped

Garnish:
½ cup thinly sliced blanched almonds

Preparation

1.
Drop the peaches into boiling water for 30 seconds. Peel the peaches and place them in a shallow bowl. Sprinkle with lemon juice.

2.
In a small bowl combine the brandy and sugar and mix until the sugar is dissolved. Pour the mixture over the peaches, toss them gently in the brandy, and chill for 4 to 6 hours or overnight.

3.
Prepare the sauce. In the top of a double boiler combine the yolks and sugar and whisk until the mixture is pale yellow and thick. Add the sauterne.

4.
Place the pan over simmering water and whisk the mixture constantly until it is thick and heavily coats a spoon. Be careful not to overcook the sauce or the yolks will curdle.

Fresh Peach
Trifle

Serves:	**6 to 8**
Preparation time:	**25 minutes, plus 24 hours to chill**
Cooking time:	**10 minutes**
Type of recipe:	**elementary**
Cost:	**inexpensive**

5.
Transfer the sauce to a bowl. Add the cinnamon and nutmeg and chill for 30 minutes.

6.
Fold the whipped cream into the sauce and chill again.

7.
Preheat the oven to 325 degrees.

8.
An hour before serving drain the peaches thoroughly. Place them in a shallow glass serving dish and spoon a little of the sauce over each peach.

9.
Place the almonds on a baking sheet and place in the oven for 5 minutes, or until they are toasted and their edges are lightly browned. Remove from the oven, cool, and then sprinkle each peach with toasted almonds. Serve chilled but not cold.

Remarks
The sauce can be prepared 1 or 2 days ahead and refrigerated. The almonds can be toasted several hours ahead and set aside. Do not combine the peaches with the sauterne sauce until an hour before serving since the peach juices may water down the sauce.

Ingredients
6 large ripe fresh peaches
¾ cup granulated sugar
⅓ cup peach or apricot brandy
6 large egg yolks
2 cups hot milk
1 teaspoon vanilla extract
3 layers of sponge cake
⅓ to ½ cup cream sherry
2 Tablespoons toasted thinly sliced almonds

Peaches
à la Fermière

Serves:	**6**
Preparation time:	**20 minutes, plus 2 to 4 hours to chill**
Cooking time:	**5 minutes**
Type of recipe:	**elementary**
Cost:	**inexpensive**

The wonderful fresh, farm cheese has all but disappeared from French markets. But the delicious combination of that cheese with fresh fruits and cream can still be found in some small country restaurants. I adapted this recipe to the American kitchen and it has since been one of my favorite summer desserts.

Ingredients

6 large ripe freestone peaches
2 to 3 Tablespoons granulated sugar
1/3 cup peach brandy
8 ounces cream cheese
1/2 cup confectioners' sugar
1 cup heavy cream
2 cups fresh blueberries

Preparation

1.
Drop the peaches into boiling water for 30 seconds. Peel and cut into 1/4-inch segments. Combine the peaches with 1/4 cup sugar and the peach or apricot brandy. Set aside.

2.
Place the sliced almonds on a cookie sheet and set in a 300-degree oven toast for 5 minutes, or until lightly browned. Set aside.

3.
In the top of the double boiler combine the egg yolks, remaining sugar, and hot milk. Whisk the mixture until smooth, then cook over simmering water, whisking constantly until the mixture heavily coats a spoon. Do not bring to a boil or the sauce will curdle.

4.
Transfer the sauce to a bowl, add the vanilla, and chill for 2 to 4 hours.

5.
Set aside a few peach segments for the garnish, then begin assembling the dessert. In a 2-quart glass bowl place 1 layer of sponge cake. Drizzle with sherry and top with 1/3 of the peach mixture.

6.
Add a thick layer of custard and continue filling the dish in layers, finishing with the custard.

7.
Arrange the remaining peach segments in a decorative design on tap. Sprinkle with toasted almonds and chill for 24 hours before serving.

Poached Peaches
in
Frangipane Cream

Serves:	**6**
Preparation time:	**35 minutes**
Cooking time:	**15 minutes**
Type of recipe:	**elementary**
Cost:	**moderate**

Preparation

1.
Bring water to a boil in a large saucepan. Drop the peaches into the boiling water and cook for 30 seconds. Remove the peaches and peel.

2.
Slice the peaches into eighths. Place the sections in a bowl, sprinkle with sugar and peach brandy, and chill for 2 to 4 hours.

3.
In a bowl combine the cream cheese and confectioners' sugar. Beat the mixture with an electric mixer until smooth. Set aside.

4.
Whip the heavy cream and fold gently into the cheese mixture. Chill until serving.

5.
Thirty minutes before serving drain the peaches reserving the juices. Combine with the blueberries and the cream mixture and fold gently. If the mixture seems too thick add some of the peach juices. Transfer to a glass serving bowl and serve chilled.

Remarks

You can use just peaches or nectarines without adding blueberries for the dessert, or make it with blueberries only.
Raspberries or strawberries cannot be used since they cannot take the heaviness of the cream mixture.

Ingredients

4 large egg yolks
½ cup granulated sugar
3 Tablespoons cornstarch
2½ cups warm milk
2 teaspoons vanilla extract
¼ teaspoon almond extract
½ cup finely ground toasted almonds
1 cup heavy cream, whipped
6 large ripe freestone peaches
1 cup apricot preserves
½ cup peach or apricot brandy
Juice of ½ lemon

Preparation

1.
In a large mixing bowl combine the egg yolks and sugar. Beat the mixture until well blended and pale yellow. Add the cornstarch and ½ cup milk. Whisk until smooth. Add the remaining milk, blend thoroughly, and transfer to a heavy-bottomed saucepan.

2.
Set the saucepan over medium heat and whisk the mixture until very thick and smooth. Transfer to a bowl and add the vanilla and almond extracts and the ground almonds. Blend well and cool.

3.
As soon as the cream is cooled, fold in the whipped cream, cover, and chill.

4.
In a large saucepan bring water to boil. Add the peaches and poach for 30 seconds. Peel the peaches, cut in half, and remove the pits. Place the peach halves in a bowl and set aside.

Pear and Apple Compote in Sauterne

Serves:	**4 to 6**
Preparation time:	**10 minutes**
Cooking time:	**30 minutes**
Type of recipe:	**elementary**
Cost:	**inexpensive**

5.
In a heavy saucepan combine the apricot preserves, brandy, and lemon juice. Heat the mixture and set aside.

6.
Pour the almond cream into a shallow serving dish and smooth it with a spatula. Top with the peaches, cut-side down. Strain the apricot glaze over the peaches, covering them completely. Chill until ready to serve.

Remarks
If the peaches are not very ripe peel and then poach them in a sugar syrup (see below) until tender but not falling apart.

Optional Sugar Syrup:
4 cups water
1½ cups granulated sugar
1 two-inch stick cinnamon
1 three-inch piece vanilla bean

1.
Combine the ingredients in an enamel saucepan. Bring to a boil and simmer covered for 10 minutes.

2.
Add the peaches and poach until tender.

Remarks
Other fruit such as apples, pears, or plums can be poached in the same syrup.

Ingredients
4 cups sauterne wine
1½ cups granulated sugar
1 large piece lemon rind
1 three-inch stick cinnamon
1 three-inch piece vanilla bean
3 cloves
3 partially ripened bartlett pears, peeled, cored, and cut in quarters
2 golden delicious apples, peeled, cored, and cut in eighths
½ cup apricot preserves

Optional:
2 fresh quince, peeled, cored, and cut in eighths
Juice of ½ lemon

Garnish:
Rind of 1 lime, finely grated

Pear Flan
with
Red Wine Sauce

Serves:	**4 to 6**
Preparation time:	**30 minutes**
Cooking time:	**45 minutes**
Type of recipe:	**elementary**
Cost:	**moderate**

Preparation

1.
In a large enamel casserole combine the sauterne, sugar, lemon rind, cinnamon stick, vanilla bean, and cloves. Bring to a boil, reduce the heat, and simmer the mixture for 15 minutes.

2.
Add the pears, apples, and optional quince and poach partially covered until the fruit is tender. You may have to check the various fruits for doneness and transfer the ones that are tender earlier to a serving bowl.

3.
When all the fruit is done, transfer it to the serving bowl. Add the apricot preserves to the syrup and cook for 2 to 3 minutes. Taste the syrup and if it is too sweet add the optional lemon juice.

4.
Strain the syrup through a fine sieve over the fruit and sprinkle with the lime rind. Serve the compote chilled, accompanied by butter cookies.

Remarks

Quince is a marvelous fruit that is slowly regaining popularity in this country. It is particularly good in compotes but can also be served in a custard that is flavored with either rum or any other liqueur of your choice. For variation you can add 1 cup seedless thompson green grapes to the fruit bowl just before serving. The grapes should not be cooked.

Ingredients

6 large fresh bartlett pears, partially ripe
2 Tablespoons butter
½ cup granulated sugar
1¼ cups light cream
1 Tablespoon sifted all-purpose flour
3 large eggs
1 teaspoon vanilla extract
Large pinch of freshly grated nutmeg

Wine Sauce:

1 cup red wine
½ cup granulated sugar
1 one-half-inch stick cinnamon
2 two-inch piece vanilla bean
1 one-half-inch piece lemon peel
½ cup currant jelly
1 teaspoon cornstarch, mixed with a little wine

Preparation

1.
Preheat the oven to 350 degrees.

2.
Peel the pears, then core them and cut in eighths. (If the pears are not to be used immediately, place them in a bowl of cold water and add the juice of ½ lemon. This prevents the pears from darkening.)

3.
Heat the butter in a large enamel skillet, add the pears and 2 tablespoons sugar. Sauté the pears until nicely browned and their juice have evaporated. Taste the pears; if they are not sweet enough add a little more sugar during the cooking. Transfer the cooked pears to a nine-inch round baking dish or porcelain quiche pan.

Poached Pears
à l'Orange

Serves:	**6**
Preparation time:	**15 minutes**
Cooking time:	**30 minutes**
Type of recipe:	**elementary**
Cost:	**inexpensive**

4.
In a bowl combine the cream, flour, eggs, vanilla, nutmeg, and remaining sugar. Whisk the mixture until well blended, then pour over the pears.

5.
Set the dish in the oven and bake for 45 minutes, or until a knife comes out clean.

6.
While the flan is baking, prepare the sauce. Combine the wine, sugar, cinnamon stick, vanilla bean, and lemon peel in an enamel saucepan. Bring to a boil and simmer for 15 minutes.

7.
Add the currant jelly and cornstarch mixture and simmer until the syrup is thick. Discard the vanilla bean, cinnamon stick, and lemon peel and cool the syrup.

8.
When the pear flan is done, cool to room temperature. Cut into wedges and serve right from the dish, with the wine syrup on the side.

Remarks

The wine syrup can be made several days ahead and refrigerated. It can also be served with poached pears or peaches, fresh sliced strawberries, and sliced oranges.

Poached pears are a delicious, almost year-round dessert. They can be topped with a variety of interesting sauces or used as a topping for a custard.

Ingredients

6 large bartlett or bosc pears, partially ripe
Juice of ½ lemon
6 cups water
1½ cups granulated sugar
1 three-inch piece vanilla bean
1 three-inch stick cinnamon

Sauce:
Rind of 2 large oranges, cut into ⅛-inch julienne strips
¾ cup freshly squeezed orange juice
1 cup currant jelly
½ cup Cointreau
2 Tablespoons cognac or brandy
¼ teaspoon ground cinnamon
Large pinch of freshly grated nutmeg

Optional:
1 to 2 tablespoons granulated sugar

Preparation

1.
Prepare the sauce. In a small saucepan bring water to a boil. Add the orange strips and cook for 5 minutes, then drain and reserve.

2.
In a large enamel saucepan combine the orange juice and currant jelly. Heat the mixture over low heat until the jelly has melted and the mixture is completely smooth. Taste and add sugar, if

Poached Pears
in
Ricotta-and-Orange Cream

Serves:	**4 to 5**
Preparation time:	**10 minutes**
Cooking time:	**30 minutes**
Type of recipe:	**elementary**
Cost:	**inexpensive**

necessary. Heat until the sugar is dissolved.

3.
Remove from the heat and add the Cointreau, cognac or brandy, cinnamon, nutmeg, and the reserved orange strips. Chill the sauce until serving.

4.
Peel the pears, then drop them immediately into a large bowl of cold water and add the lemon juice. This will keep the pears from turning brown.

5.
In a large casserole combine the water, sugar, vanilla bean, and cinnamon stick. Bring to a boil, add the pears, reduce the heat, and simmer for 20 to 25 minutes, or until the pears are tender when tested with the tip of a sharp knife. If the pears are of unequal ripeness you may need to test them several times.

6.
When all the pears are done, transfer them to a bowl. Pour the poaching liquid over them and cool.

7.
Just before serving place each pear on an individual serving dish. Spoon some of the orange sauce on each pear and serve chilled but not cold.

Remarks
When peeling orange rind be sure not to include any of the white membrane. I often marinate the orange julienne strips in grenadine after they have been blanched. Grenadine turns the orange strips to a brilliant red, which adds a particularly lovely touch to this dessert.

Ingredients
2 cups water
1 cup granulated sugar
1 three-inch stick cinnamon
1 large piece lemon rind
1 two-inch piece vanilla bean
4 to 5 partially ripe bartlett pears
Juice of ½ lemon

Cream:
2 cups ricotta
¼ to ⅓ cup Grand Marnier, or other orange-flavored liqueur
1 Tablespoon grated orange rind
1 teaspoon orange extract
Large pinch of freshly grated nutmeg

Garnish:
Julienne of orange peel, boiled for 3 minutes, drained, and soaked in a little orange liqueur

Optional:
6 orange slices, cut in half

Preparation
1.
In a saucepan combine the water, sugar, cinnamon stick, lemon rind, and vanilla bean. Bring the mixture to a boil, reduce the heat, and simmer covered for 15 minutes.

2.
Peel the pears. Cut in half and remove the core with a tip of a sharp knife.

3.
Add the pears to the sugar syrup, sprinkling them immediately with a little lemon juice to prevent the pears from turning dark.

Persimmon
Parfait

Serves: **4 to 6**
Preparation time: **15 minutes, plus 2 to 4 hours to chill**
Cooking time: **none**
Type of recipe: **elementary**
Cost: **inexpensive**

Poach the pears over low heat for 10 minutes or until tender. Drain and place them cut-side down on a round shallow glass platter. Discard the vanilla bean and cinnamon stick.

4.
Boil the syrup down to 1 cup then remove from the heat and cool.

5.
Use the reduced syrup to make the cream. Add the ricotta, Grand Marnier, orange rind, orange extract, and nutmeg. Whisk the mixture until smooth and well blended. You can add additional orange rind if you like.

6.
Press the ricotta mixture through a fine sieve over the pears covering them completely. Press down well on the ricotta to extract all the juices.

7.
Garnish the platter with the orange julienne and optional halved orange slices. Serve the pears lightly chilled but not cold.

Remarks
The dessert can be prepared a day ahead and refrigerated. It should be brought back to room temperature and chilled for 10 minutes before serving.

Ingredients
3 to 4 ripe persimmons
1 cup Crème Fraîche (page 544)
3 to 4 Tablespoons granulated sugar
Large pinch of freshly grated nutmeg

Optional:
1 Tablespoon cognac

Preparation
1.
Cube the persimmons; it is not necessary to peel them. Remove any black spots.

2.
Combine the persimmons with the Crème Fraîche and sugar in a serving bowl. Add nutmeg and optional cognac. Chill for 2 to 4 hours. Serve in individual parfait glasses or red wine goblets.

Remarks
The season of persimmon unfortunately is extremely short in most parts of the country. It is often hard to find them ripe. To ripen the persimmon place it in a brown paper bag and leave at room temperature for 2 to 3 days.

Praline Pudding
with
Brandied Custard

Serves: **6**
Preparation time: **30 minutes**
Cooking time: **1 hour, 30 minutes**
Type of recipe: **elementary**
Cost: **moderate**

Ingredients
¾ cup milk
2 teaspoons instant coffee
3 Tablespoons butter
6 Tablespoons sifted all-purpose flour
5 Tablespoons granulated sugar
½ cup walnut Praline Powder (page 547)
1 teaspoon vanilla extract
4 large egg yolks
Pinch of salt
5 large egg whites

Custard:
1¾ cups milk
6 large egg yolks
½ cup granulated sugar
1 teaspoon vanilla extract
2 to 3 Tablespoons brandy or cognac

Preparation
1.
Start by making the custard. Heat the milk in a saucepan without letting it come to a boil.
2.
In the top of a double boiler combine the yolks and sugar. Whisk the mixture until smooth and pale yellow. Add the warm milk and blend thoroughly.
3.
Set the pan over simmering water, whisking constantly until the custard thickens and coats a spoon. Do not overcook or the custard will curdle. Remove from the heat and transfer to a serving bowl. Whisk in the vanilla and brandy or cognac and chill until serving.

4.
Preheat the oven to 350 degrees.
5.
In a small saucepan combine the milk with the instant coffee and heat without letting it come to a boil. Keep warm.
6.
In a heavy 2-quart saucepan heat the butter over low heat. Add the flour and cook stirring constantly for 2 to 3 minutes without browning.
7.
Remove the saucepan from the heat and add the milk all at once. Whisk the mixture until it is well blended and smooth and return to low heat. Stir constantly until the mixture is thick and comes away from the sides of the pan.
8.
Add the sugar, Praline Powder, and vanilla. Whisk the mixture until thoroughly blended, then add the yolks and return the mixture to low heat without letting it come to a boil. Remove from the heat and set aside.
9.
Add a pinch of salt to the whites and start beating with an electric mixer until very frothy, then switch to a large balloon whisk and finish beating the whites until they form unwavering peaks.
10.
Fold a little of the whites into the pudding mixture to loosen it. Then reverse the process and add the pudding to the remaining whites. Fold gently but thoroughly and set aside.
11.
Butter a 6 cup-soufflé dish and sprinkle heavily with sugar, shaking out the excess.

Prunes and Chestnuts
in
Cognac-and-Custard Sauce

Serves:	**4 to 6**
Preparation time:	**30 minutes**
Cooking time:	**15 minutes**
Type of recipe:	**elementary**
Cost:	**inexpensive**

Spoon the pudding mixture into the dish and smooth the top with a rubber spatula. Place the soufflé dish inside a baking pan and add boiling water to measure two-thirds up the side of the soufflé dish. Set in the center of the oven and bake for 60 minutes.
12.
Remove the soufflé dish and let it cool. The pudding will fall back and shrink from the side of the pan. When completely cool unmold the pudding into your hand and invert it back onto a serving platter. Spoon the brandied custard around the pudding and serve lightly chilled.

Remarks
The custard can be prepared several days ahead and refrigerated. The pudding can be prepared the day before serving and chilled. Remove from the refrigerator 30 to 40 minutes before serving, since the pudding should be served lightly chilled but not cold. Spoon the custard around the pudding no more than 5 to 10 minutes before serving or else the pudding will get soggy.

Ingredients
2 cups water
1 cup milk
¾ cup granulated sugar
1 two-inch piece vanilla bean
½ to ¾ pound large chestnuts, peeled (page 547)
1 pound large prunes

Custard:
1½ cups milk
6 large egg yolks
½ cup granulated sugar
1½ teaspoons vanilla extract
¼ cup cognac or brandy
3 Tablespoons orange liqueur

Optional:
1 Tablespoon finely grated orange rind

Preparation
1.
Start by making the custard. In a saucepan heat the milk without letting it come to a boil.
2.
Combine the yolks, sugar, and hot milk in the top of a double boiler. Whisk the mixture until thoroughly blended. Place over simmering water and whisk until the custard thickens and coats a spoon. Do not let it come to a boil or the eggs will curdle. (A custard is usually done when steam rises from the pan. To be sure use a spoon to test if the custard is done.) Remove from the heat and transfer to a bowl.
3.
Add the vanilla, cognac, orange liqueur, and optional orange rind and whisk until

Lemon Caramel
Rice Pudding

Serves:	**6**
Preparation time:	**15 minutes, plus 6 hours to chill**
Cooking time:	**2 hours**
Type of recipe:	**elementary**
Cost:	**moderate**

smooth. Chill the custard for 4 to 6 hours or overnight.

4.
In an enamel saucepan combine the water, milk, sugar, and vanilla bean. Add the chestnuts and simmer covered over low heat for 45 minutes, or until the chestnuts are just tender but not falling apart. Cool the chestnuts in the poaching liquid and set aside.

5.
Place the prunes in a saucepan. Cover with boiling water and simmer for 10 minutes, or until tender but not falling apart. Chill the prunes until serving.

6.
Two to 4 hours before serving thoroughly drain the prunes and chestnuts in 2 separate colanders. Combine the fruit in a serving bowl and fold the custard gently into the fruit so as not to bruise it. Serve lightly chilled but not cold.

Remarks
Both the prunes and chestnuts can be cooked a day or 2 ahead. The custard can be cooked 2 to 3 days in advance and refrigerated in a covered jar. Serve the custard over just the poached prunes or add 1 apple, peeled and poached in a sugar syrup, to the prune-and-custard mixture.

Rice puddings are popular desserts in all Mediterranean countries. The Greeks flavor their rice heavily with cinnamon, the Italians with candied fruit, and the Spanish with lemon and caramel. Here is the Catalan version of this delicious yet simple dessert.

Ingredients
Rind of 1 large lemon
2 cups milk
2 cups light cream
1 cup granulated sugar
½ cup long-grain rice
2 Tablespoons water
6 large egg yolks
1½ teaspoons vanilla extract

Preparation
1.
Cut the lemon rind into thin slivers and reserve.

2.
In a large saucepan heat the milk and cream. Add ½ cup sugar and whisk until dissolved.

3.
Add the rice and lemon rind. Transfer the mixture to the top of a double boiler and place over simmering water. Cook the rice mixture for 1 to 1½ hours, or until very tender and thick.

4.
While the rice is cooking heat the remaining sugar with the water in a small saucepan. Cook the mixture without stirring until it turns a light hazelnut brown. Do not overcook or the caramel will have a burnt flavor.

Catalan
Rice Flan

Serves:	**6**
Preparation time:	**15 minutes, plus overnight to chill**
Cooking time:	**2 hours**
Type of recipe:	**elementary**
Cost:	**inexpensive**

5.
Pour the caramel into a rectangular baking dish. (A porcelain pudding dish is ideal for this dessert.) Rotate the dish back and forth to coat the bottom evenly with the caramel. Set aside.

6.
Preheat the oven to 350 degrees.

7.
Beat the yolks together with the vanilla in a mixing bowl until well blended.

8.
When the rice is done fold the egg-yolk mixture into the rice. Taste and if it lacks tartness add a little more lemon rind.

9.
Pour the mixture into the pudding dish. Place the dish in a larger baking dish and pour boiling water in; it should reach halfway up the sides of the pudding dish. Place the baking dish in the oven and bake the pudding for 30 minutes. Remove from the oven and chill for 6 hours before serving.

Remarks
The pudding may be done 2 to 3 days ahead and chilled. You can vary the pudding by using orange rind and some orange liqueur instead of the lemon rind. This pudding can also be made in a 6-cup ring mold and when unmolded you can fill the center with sugared strawberries, blueberries, or raspberries.

Ingredients
3½ cups milk
1 three-inch piece vanilla bean
½ cup long-grain rice
1 cup granulated sugar
Peel of 1 large lemon
3 egg yolks
Pinch of freshly grated nutmeg
2 Tablespoons water

Garnish:
Sugared blueberries or sugared strawberries

Optional:
1 cup heavy cream, whipped

Preparation
1.
In a enamel saucepan heat the milk together with the vanilla bean.

2.
In the top of a double boiler combine the rice, vanilla bean and milk, ½ cup sugar, and lemon peel. Set the pan over simmering water and cook covered for 1 hour, 30 minutes, or until the rice is very tender.

3.
When the rice is done strain the mixture into a bowl and discard the lemon peel and vanilla bean. Reserve the rice.

4.
Measure and save 1½ cups cooking liquid. (If the rice has absorbed most of the milk add additional cream or milk to measure 1½ cups.) Whisk the milk with the egg yolks, then add the nutmeg and fold the mixture into the rice. Set aside.

French
Bread
Pudding

Serves:	**6 to 8**
Preparation time:	**20 minutes**
Cooking time:	**1 hour**
Type of recipe:	**elementary**
Cost:	**inexpensive**

5.
Preheat the oven to 350 degrees.

6.
In a small heavy saucepan heat the remaining ½ cup sugar and the water. Cook the mixture without stirring until it turns a rich hazelnut brown. Do not let it get too dark or it will burn. Immediately pour the caramel mixture into a 6-cup ring mold and turn the mold back and forth so as to coat it evenly with the caramel.

7.
Spoon the rice mixture into the mold and set the mold in a baking dish. Add boiling water to the dish; the water should come halfway up the sides of the mold. Cover the mold with foil.

8.
Set the mold in the oven and bake for 30 minutes, or until the mixture is set and the tip of a knife comes out clean. Remove the mold from the oven and chill the rice flan overnight.

9.
The next day run a sharp knife around the sides of the mold and unmold the rice onto a serving platter. Fill the center with sugared strawberries or blueberries and serve lightly chilled but not cold with an optional side dish of whipped cream.

Ingredients
⅓ cup dark rum, heated
⅓ cup golden raisins
⅓ cup candied fruit, finely minced
Butter
8 slices good quality white bread, crust removed
3 cups milk
4 large eggs, plus 3 yolks
1½ teaspoons vanilla extract
⅔ cup granulated sugar
Freshly grated nutmeg

Caramel:
½ cup granulated sugar
2 Tablespoons water

Macaroons

Serves: **4 to 6**
Preparation time: **5 minutes**
Cooking time: **15 minutes**
Type of recipe: **elementary**
Cost: **inexpensive**

Preparation

1.
Preheat the oven to 350 degrees.

2.
Make the caramel. In a small heavy saucepan combine the sugar and water and cook the mixture without stirring until it starts turning a nutty brown color. Stir with a stainless steel spoon and cook for 1 more minute until the mixture is evenly brown; do not let it burn.

3.
Pour the hot caramel into a 6-cup rectangular baking dish. Rotate the dish back and forth to coat the bottom evenly with the caramel. Set aside.

4.
Heat the rum with the raisins and the candied fruit in a small saucepan and let the mixture marinate for 15 minutes.

5.
Butter the bread slices on both sides and set aside.

6.
Combine the milk, eggs, yolks, vanilla, and sugar and whisk until thoroughly blended.

7.
Place a layer of buttered bread in the dish. Sprinkle with the fruit mixture, top with buttered bread, and pour the milk mixture into the dish. Place the pudding in a pan of hot water and bake for 40 to 50 minutes.

8.
Sprinkle with freshly grated nutmeg and serve at room temperature.

Ingredients

1 cup blanched whole almonds
1 cup granulated sugar
3 large egg whites
½ teaspoon vanilla extract
½ teaspoon almond extract

Preparation

1.
Preheat the over to 325 degrees.

2.
Place the almonds on a cookie sheet and set in the center of the oven. Toast the almonds for 5 to 10 minutes, or until lightly browned. Remove from the oven and increase the oven temperature to 400 degrees.

3.
Grind together the almonds and ¾ cup sugar in a blender or food processor gradually adding the egg whites. The mixture should be like a soft purée. Add the vanilla and almond extract.

4.
Butter a baking sheet and dust with flour. Spoon little ½- to 2-inch rounds onto the sheet, placing them 2 inches apart. Sprinkle with the remaining sugar and place in the center of the oven. Bake for 15 minutes, or until the macaroons are lightly browned.

5.
Remove from the oven and cool. The macaroons will crisp up as they cool. Store the macaroons in a well-sealed cookie box. They will keep for several weeks.

Basic
Ladyfingers

Yields:	**24 ladyfingers**
Preparation time:	**25 minutes**
Cooking time:	**15 minutes**
Type of recipe:	**elementary**
Cost:	**inexpensive**

Remarks

To make macaroon crumbs place any desired quantity of macaroons in a plastic bag or paper bag and roll them into crumbs with a rolling pin. For macaroon powder (finer than macaroon crumbs) place the macaroons in the top of a blender or in a food processor and grind for 1 minute at top speed. Transfer to a jar and refrigerate. The macaroon powder will keep for 2 to 3 weeks. Macaroon crumbs or powder can be used for toppings to ice cream, poached pears, soufflés, and crêpes. They can sometimes be used as a substitute for praline powder, but they impart a very different flavor.

Ingredients

3 large eggs, separated
Pinch of salt
½ cup superfine sugar
½ teaspoon vanilla extract
⅔ cup sifted all-purpose flour
Confectioners' sugar

Preparation

1.
Preheat the oven to 325 degrees.

2.
Butter a cookie sheet, then sprinkle with flour, shaking off the excess. Set aside.

3.
In a large stainless steel mixing bowl combine the egg whites with a pinch of salt. Beat the whites with an electric hand beater until they form soft peaks. Continue beating, gradually adding the sugar until a stiff meringue is formed—about 1 to 2 minutes. Set aside.

4.
In a small mixing bowl combine the egg yolks and vanilla. Blend thoroughly and beat until smooth. Fold the yolks gently into the meringue.

5.
Sift the flour on top of the meringue mixture and fold it in gently but do not overmix. Set aside.

6.
Fit a pastry bag with a round ¼-inch nozzle Fill the pastry bag with the batter and pipe ladyfingers approximately 4 inches long and 1 inch wide onto the cookie sheet, placing them 2 inches apart.

7.
Sprinkle with confectioners' sugar. Let the ladyfingers absorb the sugar for about 3 to 4 minutes, then sprinkle them again heavily.
8.
Bake the ladyfingers for 12 to 15 minutes, or until they turn a pale beige and are somewhat crisp.
9.
Remove the ladyfingers from the oven and transfer them to a rack. Cool the ladyfingers and store in a airtight cookie jar. The ladyfingers will keep for several days.

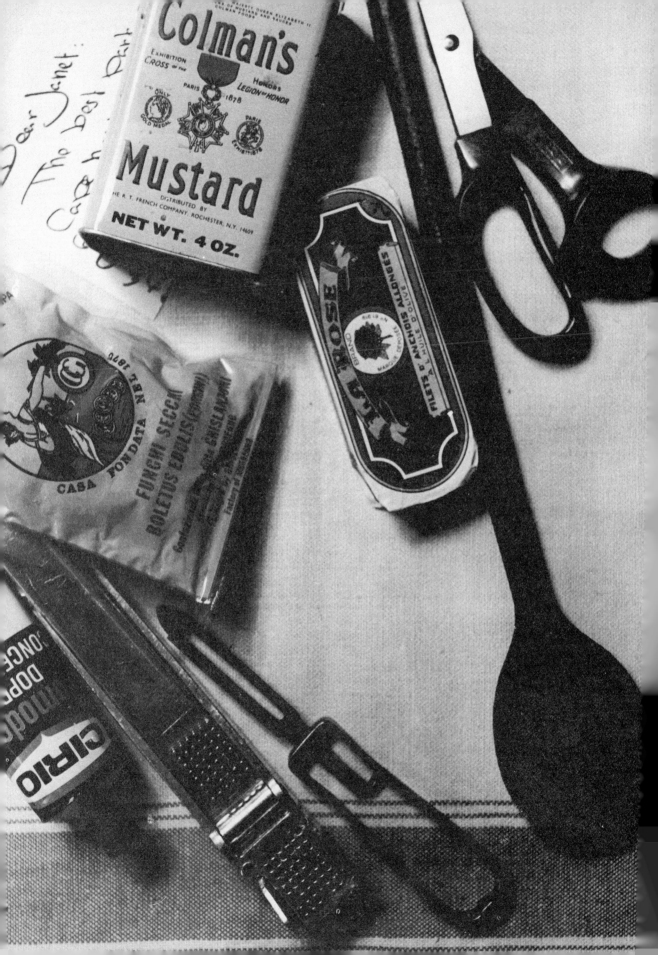

Basics:
Stocks, Sauces, and Basic Preparations

Chicken
Stock

Yields:	**2 to 2½ quarts**
Preparation time:	**10 minutes, plus overnight to chill**
Cooking time:	**1 hour, 30 minutes to 2 hours**
Type of recipe:	**elementary**
Cost:	**inexpensive**

Ingredients

1 three-pound chicken, quartered
10 to 14 chicken wings, or 2 pounds chicken necks and gizzards
2 large carrots, scraped and cut in half
2 large stalks celery, with tops cut in half
1 parsley root, scraped, or 1 small bunch of fresh parsley
1 bay leaf
1 large leek, well rinsed, with 3 inches of greens included, or 1 large onion, peeled and stuck with a clove
Large pinch of salt
6 to 8 black peppercorns

Preparation

1.
A day ahead combine the listed ingredients in a large casserole. Add 12 to 14 cups cold water. (The water should cover the ingredients by 2 inches.) Bring to a boil slowly on top of the stove, carefully skimming the scum that rises to the top.

2.
Partially cover the casserole and simmer the stock for 1 hour, 30 minutes to 2 hours. When done cool the stock uncovered.

3.
Strain the stock and, when completely cool, chill uncovered until the next day.

4.
The following day thoroughly degrease the stock, then transfer to a casserole. Bring to a boil and put the stock in 1-quart containers. Again cool the stock uncovered and when completely cool refrigerate or freeze.

Remarks

All stocks must be cooled uncovered to prevent them from turning sour. If the stock is refrigerated bring it back to a boil every 3 to 4 days. Cook the stock for 3 to 4 minutes. Transfer to a jar and cool again uncovered, then chill. Stock can be frozen successfully for 6 to 8 weeks. When using a chicken stock for chicken soups, such as the Spinach Crêpe Soup Printanier (page 117) or a chicken and liver dumpling soup, use a large 4- to 5-pound fowl and season the stock more heavily with salt. You will have to cook that stock for 3 to 4 hours.

Light Chicken Stock

Yields: **1 quart**
Preparation time: **10 minutes**
Cooking time: **1 hour**
Type of recipe: **elementary**
Cost: **inexpensive**

A light chicken stock can be made by bolstering a canned chicken bouillon. This is good to have on hand for last-minute cooking. It is also practical for vegetable soups when the vegetable itself has great character, such as cabbage and broccoli, or for a soup where a piece of salt pork or bacon is added to the broth during cooking. This stock is good for basting roasts.

Ingredients

2 cans (13¾ ounces) chicken bouillon
6 to 10 chicken wings or necks
1 onion, peeled and stuck with a clove
1 small carrot, scraped
1 stalk celery
1 sprig fresh parsley
Pinch of salt

Preparation

1.
Combine the above ingredients in a medium-sized casserole. Bring to a boil, reduce the heat, and simmer the stock covered for 45 minutes to 1 hour.
2.
Cool the stock uncovered. Strain and use immediately or refrigerate in glass jars.

Remarks
The stock will keep for several days. Bring it back to a boil every 3 to 4 days if it is not to be used immediately.

Brown Chicken Stock

Yields: **about 2 quarts**
Preparation time: **45 minutes, plus overnight to chill**
Cooking time: **3 to 4 hours**
Type of recipe: **elementary**
Cost: **inexpensive**

Brown Chicken Stock is by far the most important stock in the everyday kitchen. While it is somewhat of a chore to make it is worth the effort to create a multitude of wonderful dishes and sauces that would otherwise lack both taste and texture. Brown Chicken Stock is in a sense a simplified brown stock. It should be made mostly with veal bones, usually hard to find in the average supermarket. The chicken wings give the stock a gelatinous quality and the beef adds the richness of color and texture.

Ingredients

14 to 18 chicken wings
2 to 3 pounds chuck steak with bone, or
3 to 4 pounds meaty veal or beef bones, some knuckle bones included
2 large carrots, scraped and coarsely chopped
2 large onions, peeled and coarsely chopped, plus 2 small onions, unpeeled
2 cups celery, coarsely chopped
1 large Bouquet Garni (page 546)
Salt
6 black peppercorns

Optional:
1 parsley root scraped

Preparation

1.
Preheat the broiler.

2.
Cut the chicken wings in half and place the wings in 1 layer in a roasting pan. They should lie quite flat. Place the roasting pan 4 to 6 inches from the source of the heat and broil the chicken wings until well browned, turning them over and browning them on the other side. When the wings are done remove them to a casserole and set aside.

2.
Place the meat or bones in the roasting pan and broil until well browned on both sides, being careful not to burn the bones. When done transfer the meat and bones to the casserole and reserve.

3.
Spoon 2 to 3 tablespoons of the pan drippings into a 10- to 12-inch cast-iron skillet. Heat the drippings and add the chopped carrots, onions, and celery. Sauté until nicely browned. Do not let the onions burn.

4.
Transfer the browned vegetables to the casserole. Add the bouquet, salt, peppercorns, whole onions, and optional parsley root. Add enough water to cover the ingredients by 2 inches. Bring to a boil on top of the stove, reduce the heat, and simmer the stock partially covered for 3 to 4 hours, skimming it several times.

5.
When the stock is done strain it into a large bowl. Let it cool uncovered and then chill overnight.

6.
The next day thoroughly degrease the stock. Return it to a casserole and bring to a boil. Let cool and transfer to containers or jars. Refrigerate the stock covered or freeze it.

Remarks
Brown Chicken Stock will keep for several months in the freezer. If refrigerated it should be brought back to a boil every 2 to 3 days.

Beef Stock
(also called
White Stock)

Yields:	**2 to 2½ quarts**
Preparation time:	**10 minutes, plus overnight to chill**
Cooking time:	**3 to 4 hours**
Type of recipe:	**elementary**
Cost:	**inexpensive**

A good hearty beef stock is a must in certain soups, particularly the classic onion soup, a bean soup, and the gutsy regional soups of Central and Mediterranean Europe such as an Alsatian cabbage soup, a good lentil soup, and all the other soups made with dried legumes. It is also good for basting roasts and deglazing the pan juices of a rib roast.

Ingredients
5 to 6 pounds meaty beef bones, including some knuckle bones
2 large carrots, scraped and cut in half
2 to 3 stalks celery, with tops cut in half
2 large leeks, well rinsed and with 3 inches of greens included
1 onion, unpeeled
1 parsley root, scraped, or 1 small bunch fresh parsley
6 to 8 black peppercorns
1 to 2 large ripe tomatoes
1 head garlic, unpeeled
Salt

Optional:
2 pounds veal knuckle bones

Preparation
1.
A day ahead combine the above ingredients in a large casserole and cover with water. The water should cover the ingredients by 2 inches. Slowly bring to a boil and thoroughly skim off the scum that rises to the top. Partially cover the casserole and simmer over low heat for 3 to 4 hours, skimming several times during the cooking time.
2.
When the stock is done strain it into a large bowl and cool. Chill the stock uncovered overnight.
3.
The next day degrease the stock thoroughly. Transfer to a casserole and bring to a boil. Cook for 3 to 4 minutes.
4.
Again let the stock cool completely before transferring it to 1-quart jars or containers. Cover the jars, refrigerate, or freeze.

Brown
Lamb
Stock

Yields:	**1½ to 2 quarts**
Preparation time:	**10 minutes, plus overnight to chill**
Cooking time:	**3 hours**
Type of recipe:	**elementary**
Cost:	**moderate**

Few recipes call for lamb stock since you can use a well-flavored Beef (white) Stock or a Brown Chicken Stock. However, whenever you are making a ragoût of lamb you will automatically find yourself with lamb bones, since the best ragoût is made from the boned shoulder of lamb. Make sure that the butcher gives you these bones and then use them either for a simple lamb stock (follow directions for Chicken Stock on page 530) or make a Brown Lamb Stock. This is wonderful as a flavoring for a ragoût, for basting a roast leg of lamb, or for a sauce for lamb chops.

Ingredients

4 to 6 pounds lamb bones
1 Tablespoon peanut oil
2 large onions, peeled and finely chopped
2 large stalks celery, minced
2 carrots, scraped and chopped
1 Bouquet Garni (page 546)
½ teaspoon fennel seeds
1 teaspoon peppercorns
Large pinch of salt

Optional:
2 lamb shanks

Preparation

1.
Preheat the broiler.

2.
Place the lamb bones and optional shanks in a roasting pan and place 6 inches from the source of the heat. Broil the bones until nicely browned on all sides. Be sure not to burn them. Turn to broil evenly. Transfer the browned bones to a large casserole and set aside.

3.
Transfer 2 tablespoons of the lamb drippings to a 10-inch cast-iron skillet. Add the oil and heat.

4.
Add the chopped vegetables and sauté until evenly browned. Do not let the onions burn.

5.
Transfer the browned vegetables together with the bouquet, fennel seeds, peppercorns, and salt to the casserole. Add enough water to cover by 2 inches, then bring to a boil, reduce the heat, and cook the stock partially covered for 2 or 3 hours. When the stock is done strain and cool completely. Chill the stock overnight.

6.
The next day degrease the stock thoroughly. Transfer to a casserole, return to a boil, and cool completely before refrigerating or freezing.

Brown
Duck
Stock

Yields: **about 2 cups**
Preparation time: **10 minutes**
Cooking time: **2 hours**
Type of recipe: **elementary**
Cost: **inexpensive**

In most duck recipes you can substitute Brown Chicken Stock for duck stock. If, however, you plan to roast 2 or more ducks you can improve the flavor, color, and texture of the stock by adding the browned necks, gizzards, and wing tips to the stock, which will result in a richer, more flavorful sauce.

Ingredients

2 Tablespoons rendered duck fat (as described in step 1), or 2 Tablespoons oil
Necks, gizzards, and wing tips of 2 or more ducks
2 cups coarsely chopped vegetables (carrots, celery, and onion)
3 cups Brown Chicken Stock (page 531)
1 Bouquet Garni (page 546)

Preparation

1.
Remove some of the duck fat from the cavity of the ducks. Place in a cast-iron skillet and render the fat over low heat for 10 to 15 minutes. Or add the oil to a cast-iron skillet and heat.

2.
Add the duck necks, giblets, and trimmings and sauté over moderate-to-high heat until nicely browned on all sides.

3.
Add the chopped vegetables and continue sautéing until the nicely browned.

4.
Transfer the giblets and vegetable mixture to a saucepan. Add the stock and, if necessary, add a little more water to cover. Add the bouquet, bring to a boil, reduce the heat, and simmer the stock covered for 1 hour to 1 hour, 30 minutes.

5.
Strain the stock and use for basting the duck and in finishing a sauce.

Remarks
Any leftover duck stock can be frozen in a small covered container.

Fish
Stock

Yields: **about 2 quarts**
Preparation time: **10 minutes**
Cooking time: **30 to 40 minutes**
Type of recipe: **elementary**
Cost: **inexpensive**

A Fish Stock is one of the simplest to make. (It can also be one of the least expensive if the fish market gives you the trimmings.) It requires good whitefish trimmings, some vegetables, white wine, water, and seasoning. After a short cooking time of 30 minutes the stock is ready to be used. I rarely make fish stock in great quantity for freezing but rather make it as I need it. However, you can freeze fish stock successfully for several weeks. In the following stock the vegetables are sautéed before being combined with the trimmings. You may simplify the stock by simply combining all the ingredients and poaching them in the liquid for the required time. Personally I feel that the following method results in a somewhat richer stock.

Ingredients

3 Tablespoons butter
1 large onion, peeled and coarsely chopped, plus 1 whole onion, peeled and stuck with a clove
1 cup chopped celery
1 carrot, scraped and chopped
3 pounds whitefish trimmings, such as cod, tilefish, whiting
1 large Bouquet Garni (1 teaspoon thyme, several sprigs parsley, 1 bay leaf, and some celery tops)
1½ cups dry white wine
6 to 8 black peppercorns
Large pinch of salt

Preparation

1.
In a large, heavy enamel casserole heat the butter. Add the chopped vegetables and sauté over low heat without browning for 5 to 6 minutes or until soft.

2.
Add the fish trimmings, bouquet, whole onion, wine, peppercorns and salt. Add enough water to cover (do not use more than 6 cups). Bring the stock to a boil slowly. Reduce the heat and simmer partially covered for 30 to 40 minutes, skimming the stock carefully every 10 minutes.

3.
When the stock is done strain it into a large bowl and cool. If the stock tastes thin return it to the casserole and reduce by ⅓ over moderate-to-high heat. (As it reduces the stock will become more flavorful.) Cool the stock thoroughly before refrigerating.

Remarks

The stock can be frozen in 1-quart plastic containers for 4 to 6 weeks.

Cream of Fish
Stock

Yields:	**about 1½ quarts**
Preparation time:	**10 minutes**
Cooking time:	**1 hour**
Type of recipe:	**elementary**
Cost:	**inexpensive**

A Cream of Fish Stock is in a sense both a stock and a cream sauce. It adds great taste and texture to many fish preparations, particularly steaks such as salmon, swordfish, and halibut. It can also be flavored with herbs and used with various shellfish preparations such as sautéed scallops, poached shrimp, or mussels.

Ingredients

3 to 4 pounds whitefish trimmings, such as cod necks, tilefish
2 Tablespoons butter
1 cup finely minced onions
1 cup dry white wine
4 cups heavy cream
Pinch of salt
6 white peppercorns
1 Bouquet Garni (page 546)

Preparation

1.
Place the fish trimmings in a large bowl and rinse under cold running water for 15 to 20 minutes, or until the trimmings are completely white and all traces of blood have disappeared.

2.
In a large, heavy enamel casserole heat the butter. Add the onions and sauté until soft but not browned. Add the wine, fish trimmings, and cream. Season with salt, then add peppercorns and bouquet. Bring to a boil, reduce the heat, and simmer the stock partially covered for 1 hour.

3.
Cool the stock. Strain into a large bowl and, when completely cool, transfer to 1-quart jars or containers. Refrigerate or freeze.

Remarks
If the stock is refrigerated return it to a boil every 2 to 3 days. Let it cool before covering it and refrigerating it again.

Court-Bouillon

Yields:	**about 2 quarts**
Preparation time:	**10 minutes**
Cooking time:	**45 minutes**
Type of recipe:	**elementary**
Cost:	**inexpensive**

A Court-Bouillon is particularly good for poaching whole fish that are to be served cold such as salmon, trout, or bass. An acidulated fish stock is not as intense as one made with wine, therefore it allows the fish to retain more of its natural flavor. A Court-Bouillon, however, cannot be used for sauces, for it lacks body. If however the court-bouillon is frozen and used over and over again to poach fish it ends up as a rich fish stock that can and should be used for sauces.

Ingredients

2 to 3 pounds whitefish trimmings, such as cod necks, tilefish, whitefish
1 to 2 carrots, scraped and coarsely sliced
2 stalks celery, with greens coarsely sliced
1 onion, peeled and stuck with a clove
3 to 4 cloves garlic, unpeeled and crushed
1 leek, well rinsed and coarsely sliced
1 large Bouquet Garni (page 546)
2 Tablespoons white wine vinegar
Coarse salt
6 to 8 black peppercorns

Preparation

1.
In a large casserole combine the fish trimmings and vegetables. Add enough water to cover by 1 inch, then season with salt and add peppercorns. Bring to a boil, reduce the heat, and simmer the mixture covered for 25 minutes.

2.
Add the vinegar and simmer for another 15 minutes.

3.
Strain the bouillon and chill uncovered until using.

Remarks
If you plan to poach a fish in the bouillon reheat it to boiling before using it.

Vegetable Stock

Yields: **4 to 5 cups**
Preparation time: **5 minutes**
Cooking time: **45 minutes**
Type of recipe: **elementary**
Cost: **inexpensive**

A Vegetable Stock is excellent to have on hand at all times. It is perfect for poaching fish steaks or fillets as well as shellfish such as shrimp or scallops. I particularly like to poach fish of great character such as swordfish or salmon in the Vegetable Stock as the fish retains its own characteristic flavor.

Ingredients

2 stalks celery, diced and greens included
1 large carrot, scraped and cubed
1 large onion, peeled and sliced
1 large leek, well rinsed and coarsely sliced with 2 inches of greens included
Coarse salt
6 black peppercorns
3 to 4 sprigs fresh parsley
1 bay leaf
3 large cloves garlic, unpeeled and crushed
2 Tablespoons white wine vinegar
4 to 6 white peppercorns, slightly crushed

Optional:

1 large sprig fresh tarragon
1 large sprig fresh thyme
1 ripe tomato

Preparation

1.
In an enamel casserole combine all the vegetables. Add 4 to 5 cups water, then season with salt, black peppercorns, parsley, bay leaf, and garlic. Bring to a boil, reduce the heat, and simmer covered for 25 minutes.

2.
Add the vinegar, white peppercorns, and optional herbs and tomato. Simmer the vegetable stock for another 10 to 15 minutes.

3.
Cool the stock and strain. When completely cool refrigerate it in a covered jar.

Remarks
The stock will keep for 2 to 3 weeks. Bring it back to a boil every few days to prevent it from turning sour.

Mayonnaise

Yield: **1½ cups**
Preparation time: **5 minutes**
Type of recipe: **elementary**
Cost: **inexpensive**

Ingredients
2 whole eggs
1 to 1½ teaspoons white wine vinegar
2 teaspoons Dijon mustard
Pinch of salt
¾ to 1 cup peanut oil

Preparation
In the container of a blender combine the eggs, vinegar, mustard, and salt. Blend the mixture at high speed for 30 seconds, then with the blender still at top speed start adding the oil by droplets. As the mayonnaise begins to thicken, add the remaining oil until the mayonnaise is thick and smooth. Taste and correct the seasoning. Transfer to a jar and keep refrigerated.

Remarks
A mayonnaise made in a food processor will require more oil than one made in the blender. You may add another egg yolk if you are making the mayonnaise in the food processor, which will cut down on the amount of oil. You may flavor a mayonnaise with various spices or herbs. Curry, cumin, crushed garlic, chives, and dill are all interesting additions to a homemade mayonnaise.

Basic Hollandaise

Yields: **1½ cups**
Preparation time: **10 minutes**
Cooking Time: **5 minutes**

A Hollandaise can be made easily in a blender or food processor. While this is a foolproof method, the result is a compact, somewhat heavy sauce. To loosen the sauce I prefer to transfer it to a heavy saucepan and over the lowest possible heat whisk in 2 to 4 tablespoons cold Crème Fraîche (page 544). When making a Hollandaise on top of the stove I prefer to use a hot-water bath (placing the saucepan in a heavy skillet filled with hot water) and whisk in cold butter rather than hot melted butter.

Ingredients
4 large egg yolks
1 to 2 Tablespoons lemon juice, or 1½ teaspoons white wine vinegar
2 to 3 teaspoons Dijon mustard
1 cup hot melted butter, or 2 sticks cold butter, cut into ¾-inch pieces
Salt and freshly ground white pepper
2 to 4 Tablespoons Crème Fraîche or 2 Tablespoons cold heavy cream

Preparation
1.
For the foolproof method, place the yolks and lemon juice or vinegar in a blender or food processor. Add the mustard and blend the mixture at high speed.
2.
Slowly pour in the hot melted butter by droplets, continuing to blend the mixture at high speed until the sauce is smooth and thick.
3.
Transfer the Hollandaise to a heavy saucepan, place over the lowest possible

Herb-Flavored
Hollandaise

heat, and whisk in 2 tablespoons Crème Fraîche. Season with salt and pepper and adjust its taste by adding a little more mustard or vinegar or lemon juice to taste.

4.
Keep the sauce warm over a pan of warm but not hot water, whisking it every 10 minutes and adding extra Crème Fraîche if the sauce gets too thick. If the sauce shows any signs of curdling immediately add a small ice cube, whisking the sauce thoroughly until the cube is melted and the sauce is smooth.

5.
To make the sauce by hand combine the yolks, mustard, and vinegar or lemon juice in a heavy-bottomed saucepan. Add 2 tablespoons of cold heavy cream and whisk the mixture until well blended.

6.
Place the saucepan inside a deep frying pan filled with hot water. (The water should come halfway up the side of the saucepan.) Place the skillet over low heat and whisk the yolk mixture until it starts to thicken.

7.
Add the cold butter 1 piece at a time, whisking constantly until each piece has been absorbed by the egg-yolk mixture.

8.
When all the butter has been absorbed taste the sauce. Season it carefully with salt and pepper. You may add additional vinegar or lemon juice or mustard as well as 2 to 3 tablespoons Crème Fraîche. Keep the sauce warm in the pan of warm water whisking it every 10 minutes.

Finely minced fresh herbs such as dill, chives, parsley, and sorrel go extremely well with Hollandaise sauce. For a very smooth-textured herb Hollandaise transfer the sauce with the herbs with your choice to a blender or food processor and blend until smooth. You may also vary the Hollandaise by using lime juice instead of vinegar. Spices such as curry, cumin, coriander, or green peppercorns are also wonderful flavorings for Hollandaise. These herb-flavored sauces are served as an accompaniment to grilled lamb and sautéed or grilled fish steaks.

Provençale Tomato Fondue

Yields:	**about 3 cups**
Preparation Time:	**15 minutes, plus 4 to 6 hours to drain tomatoes**
Cooking Time:	**1 hour**
Type of Recipe:	**elementary**
Cost:	**inexpensive**

This delicious mixture of tomatoes, shallots, and herbs stewed in fruity olive oil is one of my favorite year-round staples. I keep a jar in the refrigerator and use it as a topping or filling for omelets, in a quiche mixture, or as an accompaniment to many vegetable dishes either poached or sautéed. It is equally good with grilled meats or sautéed fish. You can make it successfully with a good brand of canned Italian plum tomatoes.

Ingredients

4 to 5 pounds fresh tomatoes, peeled, or 2 cans (35 ounces) Italian plum tomatoes, well drained
Salt
½ cup fruity olive oil
½ cup finely minced shallots
4 large cloves garlic, finely minced
1 bay leaf
Freshly ground black pepper
1 large sprig fresh thyme, or 1 teaspoon dried
½ teaspoon dried marjoram
1 Tablespoon tomato paste
6 Tablespoons melted butter
1 cup fresh basil leaves, cut into julienne strips

Preparation

1.
Several hours ahead quarter the tomatoes and place them in a large sieve over a bowl. Sprinkle the tomatoes with salt and let them drain for 4 to 6 hours. (If using canned tomatoes drain the tomatoes through a sieve and let the tomatoes stand at room temperature for 4 to 6 hours.)

2.
Heat the oil in a large heavy-bottomed saucepan. Add the shallots, garlic, and bay leaf and cook the mixture over low heat for 2 to 3 minutes, or until soft but not browned.

3.
Add the tomatoes and season with salt, pepper, thyme, marjoram, and tomato paste and cook over high heat for 15 minutes, stirring every few minutes to prevent the mixture from scorching.

4.
Reduce the heat and continue cooking the tomato purée for 45 minutes, or until very thick. Be sure to stir several times to prevent scorching. Season with salt and pepper and set aside.

5.
Combine the melted butter and basil in a blender and blend the mixture at high speed for 30 seconds. Add the basil mixture to the tomato purée, blend thoroughly, and correct the seasoning.

6.
Transfer the fondue to a jar and store in the refrigerator until needed. The tomato fondue will keep for 2 to 3 weeks; it can also be frozen.

Remarks

When making the fondue in the winter substitute 1 teaspoon dried basil for the fresh basil and add 1 teaspoon dried oregano to the sauce. The fresh basil of course gives the fondue its particularly delicious flavor.

Tomato Sauce

Yield: **about 4 to 5 cups**
Preparation time: **15 minutes**
Cooking time: **2 hours**
Type of recipe: **elementary**
Cost: **inexpensive**

A good tomato sauce should be made from fresh ripe tomatoes. It is one of the best summer and early fall sauces. However in some regions this would limit this delicious and versatile sauce to 3 months out of the year. A good brand of canned Italian plum tomatoes can be used in those months when fresh tomatoes are not available.

Ingredients

3 Tablespoons fruity olive oil
1 large onion, peeled and finely minced
1 stalk celery finely minced
1 carrot, scraped and finely diced
3 Tablespoons finely minced fresh parsley
3 large cloves garlic, peeled and finely minced
2 Tablespoons fresh basil, chopped, or 1 teaspoon dried
1 large sprig fresh oregano, or 1 teaspoon dried
1 bay leaf
4 to 5 pounds ripe tomatoes, peeled and coarsely chopped, or 2 cans (35 ounces) Italian plum tomatoes, drained and chopped
2 Tablespoons tomato paste
Salt and freshly ground black pepper

Preparation

1.
In a large heavy enamel casserole heat the oil. Add the onion, celery, carrot, parsley, garlic, and herbs and cook the mixture over low heat partially covered until soft but not browned.

2.
Add the tomatoes and tomato paste and season with salt and pepper. Bring to a boil, reduce the heat, and cook the sauce covered for 1 hour, 30 minutes to 2 hours, stirring several times to prevent the sauce from scorching. Taste the sauce and correct the seasoning.

3.
Strain the sauce through a fine sieve or pass it through a food mill and refrigerate in covered jars.

Remarks

If the sauce is too thin uncover and let it reduce to the desired consistency. You can freeze the tomato sauce for 2 to 3 months. The sauce can also be left unstrained and simply blended in the blender or the food processor. This will make a heartier, heavier sauce.

Crème Fraîche

Yields: **2 cups**
Preparation time: **5 minutes**
Cooking time: **none**
Type of recipe: **elementary**
Cost: **moderate**

Crème Fraîche, or soured heavy cream, can now be bought in some fine specialty stores. It is both easier and much cheaper to make it yourself. Crème Fraîche is used in all French cooking mainly because the French seldom use heavy cream. (It is harder to find heavy cream in France than Crème Fraîche.) You can sometimes substitute heavy cream in recipes calling for Crème Fraîche but do not substitute with sour cream, which curdles in cooking. Personally I find Crème Fraîche to be so versatile (I use it in fish cookery, salad dressings, and sugared as an accompaniment to desserts) that I have some on hand at all times.

Ingredients
2 cups heavy cream (not ultra-pasteurized)
3 Tablespoons buttermilk

Preparation
1.
Combine the cream and buttermilk in a glass jar and whisk until well blended. Cover the jar and set aside in a warm place until the cream sours and thickens.
2.
Chill and use in recipes as indicated.

Remarks
Crème Fraîche can take from 8 to 24 hours to sour and thicken; it depends mainly on the temperature of your kitchen. Be sure to keep it in a warm, draft-free place. Once done stir it thoroughly, cover, and refrigerate. It will keep for 10 days to 2 weeks. It cannot be frozen.

Beurre Manié

Yields: **8 balls**
Preparation time: **5 minutes**
Type of recipe: **elementary**
Cost: **inexpensive**

A Beurre Manié is used in both classic and peasant cooking to thicken sauces. It is a flour-and-butter paste that can be formed into a ball and held successfully for several weeks. It is useful to make several of these butter balls and keep them refrigerated in a covered jar. The Beurre Manié is used mostly in white sauces. For brown sauces or tomato sauces I prefer using a little arrowroot or potato flour mixed with either a little stock or water. I then enrich the sauce off the heat with some cold butter. You will rarely need an entire Beurre Manié in any recipe in this book since it is preferable to reduce the sauce naturally before thickening it so as to intensify the flavor. You can store the remaining portion of Beurre Manié in a covered jar and refrigerate it.

Ingredients
8 Tablespoons slightly softened sweet butter
8 Tablespoons sifted all-purpose flour

Preparation
1.
Cut the butter into small pieces and combine with the flour in a bowl. Work the mixture with a fork until completely smooth and well blended.
2.
Chill for a few minutes—just long enough so you can form the butter balls in your hands. Form the 8 balls and place in a covered jar. Chill until needed.

Clarified Butter

Roasted Red or Green Peppers

Serves: **varies**
Preparation time: **5 minutes**
Cooking time: **5 to 7 minutes**
Type of recipe: **elementary**
Cost: **inexpensive**

Clarified Butter is used for sautéing bread, delicate meats such as chicken or calves' liver, or fish fillets and steaks. It can be made in large quantities and stored covered in the refrigerator.

Clarified Butter should be made with unsalted butter only. In fact all recipes in this book call for unsalted butter, which is available in most large supermarkets. When buying unsalted butter be sure that the label reads specifically "unsalted butter" or "sweet unsalted butter". Many types of butter read "sweet butter" and are in fact salted.

Preparation

To make clarified butter melt any desired quantity butter in a heavy saucepan over low heat. As soon as the butter is melted and very foamy remove the pan from the heat and carefully skim off the foam with a spoon. Strain the clear yellow part of the butter through a fine sieve. Be sure to leave all of the residue on the bottom of the pan and discard. Clarified butter can then be stored in a covered jar in the refrigerator.

Ingredients
Red or green bell peppers

Preparation

1.
Preheat the broiler.

2.
Place the peppers on a baking sheet and broil until the skins of the peppers are blackened and somewhat charred. Turn the peppers to brown them evenly on all sides. Do not let them get too charred or the peppers will be overcooked and impossible to peel.

3.
As soon as the peppers are done remove them from the broiler. Wrap each in a damp paper towel and cool.

4.
When cool enough to handle peel off the charred skin. Core and remove the seeds.

Remarks
Roasted peppers will keep for several days in a covered jar. If you are going to use the peppers for an appetizer or hors d'oeuvre marinate them in a mixture of red wine vinegar and fruity olive oil in a covered jar for 10 days to 2 weeks.

Bouquet Garni

Sautéed Apples

Yields: **1 bouquet**
Preparation time: **5 minutes**
Cooking time: **none**
Type of recipe: **elementary**
Cost: **inexpensive**

Serves: **4 to 6**
Preparation time: **5 minutes**
Cooking time: **10 minutes**

A Bouquet Garni is a seasoning bag composed of 3 aromatic herbs. It is used in French and Mediterranean cooking for flavoring many soups, ragoûts, and stocks. It usually consists of parsley, thyme, and bay leaf plus sometimes a celery stalk with its tops and/or a fennel stalk depending on the dish. Aromatic spices such as peppercorns, either black or white, are also usually added to most dishes calling for a bouquet. For fish cookery I often add 3 to 4 slightly crushed coriander seeds. While the thyme and bay leaf can be used either fresh or dried, parsley and celery must be used fresh.

Ingredients
3 to 4 large sprigs fresh parsley, preferably Italian
1 bay leaf
1 large sprig fresh thyme, or 1 teaspoon dried

Optional:
1 stalk celery, with leaves
1 stalk fennel, with leaves
6 to 8 peppercorns

Preparation
1.
If using fresh herbs tie the herbs together with a small piece of kitchen string.
2.
If using dried thyme, place the entire bouquet in a piece of cheesecloth and tie it with a kitchen string.
3.
Use as directed in the recipes.

Ingredients
4 large, partially ripe golden delicious apples
2 to 3 Tablespoons unsalted butter
1 Tablespoon granulated sugar or 2 Tablespoons brown sugar
Pinch of freshly grated nutmeg

Preparation
1.
Peel and core the apples, then cut into eighths.
2.
Heat the butter over medium heat in a large, heavy iron skillet. Without crowding the pan, add the apples and sprinkle with sugar. Sauté the apples over fairly high heat for 3 to 4 minutes, shaking the pan back and forth until the apples are browned and caramelized. Be careful not to burn them.
3.
Sprinkle with nutmeg and transfer to a serving dish. Serve as an accompaniment to roast pork, duck, or turkey.

Remarks
You may add a sprinkling of cinnamon and ginger, depending what you are serving the apples with. The apples can be sautéed an hour ahead of time and reheated in the skillet in which they were cooked.

Chestnuts

Praline Powder

Yields:	**about 1 cup**
Preparation time:	**10 minutes**
Cooking time:	**10 minutes**
Type of recipe:	**elementary**
Cost:	**moderate**

Dishes requiring chestnuts usually call for fresh chestnuts available in produce markets in the fall. You can also use canned imported whole chestnuts for chestnut purées, soups, and stuffings. Dried chestnuts are available in Chinese and Italian groceries and have to be soaked in water overnight to reconstitute them. They have a somewhat smoky flavor and lend themselves best to stuffings and soups.

For desserts fresh chestnuts are preferable to any type of preserved ones. To peel fresh chestnuts, use the tip of a sharp knife and cut a small incision in the flat side of each nut. Drop the chestnuts into boiling water and cook them for 2 to 3 minutes. Remove 2 to 3 chestnuts at a time and peel off both the outer coat and the inner skin of each. If a chestnut does not peel easily return it to the boiling water for another minute to heat it through and then peel it.

Remarks
Uncooked, peeled chestnuts can be frozen for 2 to 3 months. Chestnuts can also be peeled by the roasting method. If you plan to use this method preheat the oven to 450 degrees and brush the flat side of the chestnut lightly with oil. Place the chestnuts on a baking sheet and put them in the oven for 6 to 8 minutes, or until the shells have loosened. Peel the chestnuts as soon as they are cool enough to handle. You can also bake the chestnuts for 20 to 30 minutes until soft and then peel them. Use these immediately for stuffings or in combination with vegetables such as red cabbage or Brussels sprouts.

Praline Powder is a wonderful basic to have on hand at all times. It can be used as a topping for all poached fruits and ice creams. Walnuts may be substituted for the almonds in some preparations.

Ingredients
1 cup blanched whole almonds
½ cup granulated sugar
2 Tablespoons water

Preparation
1.
Oil a baking sheet and set aside.
2.
In a saucepan combine the almonds, sugar, and water. Cook the mixture over moderate heat until it turns a hazelnut brown, stirring it from time to time to make sure the mixture is cooking evenly.
3.
Pour the caramelized almond mixture onto the baking sheet and let it cool completely. The caramel must be completely hardened.
4.
Break the almond-and-caramel mixture into pieces and grind the pieces in a blender or food processor to the desired consistency.

Remarks
The Praline Powder can be stored in a covered jar in the refrigerator for 2 to 4 weeks. It is a wonderful addition to a soufflé and can be used as a topping for crêpes, sautéed apples, and poached pears.

Feuilletés
(Puff Pastry)

Preparation time: **1 hour, plus 5 hours, 40 minutes chilling time**
Type of recipe: **difficult**
Cost: **moderate**

Ingredients:

3 cups sifted all-purpose flour
Pinch of salt
1¾ cups plus 2 Tablespoons cold butter
1 cup ice water
Flour for dusting

Preparation

1.
In a large mixing bowl combine the flour and the salt. Add 6 tablespoons butter, cut into little bits. With your hands incorporate the butter bits into the flour until the mixture resembles cornflakes. Add the ice water and mix well. Knead the dough just until it is smooth. If the dough is sticky, add a little more flour to produce a smooth ball. Dust the dough with some flour and place in the refrigerator. Let rest for 10 minutes.

2.
While the dough is resting, knead the remaining butter with your hands until it becomes a pliable ball. Set aside.

3.
Remove the dough from the refrigerator. Lightly flour a large working surface and dust a French rolling pin. Roll the dough into a large square ¼ inch thick. Place the ball of kneaded butter in the center and fold the sides of the dough over the butter, as if you were folding an envelope, so as to enclose the butter completely. Flour the dough, wrap in foil, and refrigerate for 30 minutes.

4.
Flour the work surface and rolling pin once more and place the folded dough in front of you so that the line of the last fold is perpendicular and to the right of you. Roll out the dough into a rectangle ¼ inch thick and measuring 18 inches by 8 inches, but do not roll over the ends of the dough. When the rectangle is 18 inches long, roll across the dough to flatten the ends and to achieve uniform thickness.

5.
Brush off the excess flour and fold the dough in thirds, as if you were folding a business letter. Be sure that when you fold the dough the edges of the dough match up perfectly or there will be no evenness in rising once the dough is baked. This completes the first turn.

6.
Give the dough a quarter turn so that the line of the fold is to the right and perpendicular to you. Roll out the dough again into a rectangle as in step 4. Brush off the excess flour and fold into thirds, completing the second turn. Make 2 indentations with your fingertips to signify 2 turns have been completed. Dust the dough lightly with flour, wrap in foil, and let rest in the refrigerator for 1 hour.

7.
Give the dough 2 more turns, making a total of 4, following the same procedure as in steps 4 to 6. Make sure to relax the dough for 1 hour in the refrigerator after each turn. After the fourth turn, chill the dough for 2 hours. The dough is now ready to be used for the desired recipe.

Remarks
After the second turn, the dough can be refrigerated and the final turns can be completed the following day. After the final turn, the puff pastry will keep in the refrigerator for 1 week. If the pastry is not used within 1 week, you can freeze it. When you are ready to use it, defrost the dough in the refrigerator until it becomes manageable and proceed with the desired recipe.

Table of
Metric Equivalents

Weight (in Common Units)

1 ounce	=	28.35 grams
1 pound	=	16 ounces
	=	453.59 grams
	=	0.45 kilograms
1 gram	=	0.035 ounce
1 kilogram	=	2.2 pounds

Volume (in Common Units)

1 tablespoon	=	3 teaspoons
	=	0.5 fluid ounce
	=	14.8 milliliters
1 cup	=	16 tablespoons
	=	0.5 pint
	=	8 fluid ounces
2 cups	=	1 pint
	=	16 fluid ounces
	=	236.6 milliliters
4 cups	=	1 quart
	=	32 fluid ounces
	=	0.9463 liter
1 pint	=	2 cups
	=	0.5 quart
	=	4.73 deciliters
	=	0.4732 liter
1 quart	=	4 cups
	=	2 pints
	=	1.06 liters
1 gallon	=	4 quarts
	=	3.79 liters

Oven Temperatures

Fahrenheit		Celsius (nearest convenient degree)
200°	=	95°
225°	=	105°
250°	=	120°
275°	=	135°
300°	=	150°
325°	=	165°
350°	=	175°
375°	=	190°
400°	=	205°
425°	=	220°
450°	=	230°
475°	=	245°
500°	=	260°
525°	=	275°
550°	=	290°

Index